2/24/87

To Roger and Sharon

Here's a few tortes like you've never seen them! Hope you find lots of great meal here.

Fondly,

Ken

THE GLOBAL KITCHEN

THE
GLOBAL KITCHEN

The Authoritative Reference on Cooking, Seasoning, and Dieting with Ethnic and Natural Foods

Karen Gail Brooks and Gideon Bosker, M.D.

ANDREWS AND McMEEL, INC.
A Universal Press Syndicate Company
KANSAS CITY·NEW YORK

Library of Congress Cataloging in Publication Data

Brooks, Karen.
  The global kitchen.

  Bibliography: p.
  Includes index.
  1. Cookery, International.   2. Cookery (Natural foods).
I. Bosker, Gideon.   II. Title.
TX725.A1B763   641.5′636   81-12803
ISBN 0-8362-2104-4   AACR2

To our mothers, Dorka and Ethel, who taught us the meaning of good food

CONTENTS

Preface xi

Introduction xii

Acknowledgments xviii

PART 1

How to Use this Book
  Culinary Essentials   3
  Seasoning Essentials   5
  Nutritional Essentials   6
  Recipe Analysis Charts   8
  Menu Planning   10
  Recipes   10

Chapter 1
  Africa—Yam Session   13

Chapter 2
  Brazil—The Manioc Connection   39

Chapter 3
  Chile and Peru—Pick a Pack of Peppers   59

Chapter 4
China—Wok Don't Fly 83

Chapter 5
France—Love and Quiches 113

Chapter 6
Greece—Feta Accompli 143

Chapter 7
Hungary—Noodles and Strudels 167

Chapter 8
India—Some Like It Hot 191

Chapter 9
Italy—Favorite Pasta Time 215

Chapter 10
Lebanon—Open Sesame! 239

Chapter 11
Mexico—Tortilla Flats 263

Chapter 12
Poland—From Chopin to Cake Pan 293

Chapter 13
Russia—A Borsch You Can't Beet 315

Chapter 14
Scandinavia—Oat Cuisine 337

Chapter 15
United States—The Melting Pot 361

PART 2

Nutrition and Health 391
Essential Nutrients 394
Calories 394
Fats 396
Protein 403
Carbohydrates 409

Fiber 412
Vitamins 414
Minerals 421

Food 429
Cereals and Grains 429
Starchy Roots 430
Legumes, Nuts, and Seeds 432
Vegetables 433
Sugar, Syrup, and Honey 435
Fruits 436
Meat, Fowl, and Fish 436
Milk and Milk Products 437
Cheese 438
Fats and Oils 438
Herbs and Spices 439

Appendix 441

Index 489

PREFACE

This book is for people who want to improve the quality of their life through eating. The recipes contained in it have been designed for those who have a sophisticated palate and also recognize that dietary factors play an important role in the maintenance of good health.

Most of us do not have the time or money to read and purchase the large number of ethnic cookbooks and guides to nutrition that would be required for following a well-designed diet. This cookbook is our answer to the need for a consolidated source of exciting and varied foreign recipes and practical dietary information. In this single volume we have distilled the nutritional, culinary, and seasoning essentials of fifteen different cuisines, so that you may partake in the best and most healthful eating our planet has to offer.

We are happy to share our gourmet creations from around the world, as well as nutritional information and cooking concepts, so that your eating may become a healthier experience and your cooking a more creative endeavor.

KAREN GAIL BROOKS
GIDEON BOSKER, M.D.

INTRODUCTION

To eat is a necessity, but to eat intelligently is an art.

La Rochefoucauld

Despite the fact that vegetarianism has finally made its way into the mainstream of cooking consciousness, its evolution from culinary infancy has been a long and difficult one. Many people simply accepted this style of eating as the end-all answer to their nutritional cravings, without realizing that it could also blossom into a distinctive and gastronomically appealing cuisine of its own.

Those of us who joined the "better eating" campaign in the 1960s knew that meatless cooking would have to be *stylized* in order for it to develop into an influential culinary and nutritional movement. This meant doing away with a rudimentary diet that relied upon the same ingredients over and over again to ensure palatability. As our tastebuds matured and became more discriminating, we awaited the birth of a new cuisine—one that was as innovating as it was nutritious, and at the same time sophisticated, yet practical.

Perhaps nothing revitalized meatless cooking more than people's growing interest in exotic flavors. Gourmet and novice cooks alike have become enchanted by the adventuresome spirit and aesthetic appeal of international dishes. Ethnic cooking, because it utilizes many different food combinations and because it is also natural-foods oriented, appeared to be the ideal framework for developing recipes that would satisfy both health-conscious cooks and connoisseurs of good food. With this in mind, we have spent the past few years conceiving and perfecting the *ultimate diet*—one that would bring nutrition and taste into the same focus.

Our book is concerned with opening up the creative possibilities that exist within an ethnic diet—one that eschews red meat but includes fish and poultry. Not only will you have access to a large number of recipes, but you will also be turned-on to culinary skills, seasoning secrets, and nutritional concepts that will help you devise healthful and tantalizing dishes. These ideas are intended to give you the confidence and expertise to walk into your kitchen, take inventory of the ingredients on hand, and whip up a wholesome meal worthy of rave reviews.

The fifteen chapters in this book, each examining a different cuisine, have been designed to help you harness the powers of both cooking and nourishing. To obtain these skills, you will be taken, in step-by-step fashion, through the *Culinary, Seasoning,* and *Nutritional Essentials* of what we believe are the world's most exciting foreign kitchens. Without being an exhaustive treatise on individual styles of ethnic cooking, the chapters will familiarize you with all the information required to originate authentic and healthful meals from around the world. Your aptitude for improvisation will take leaps and bounds as you learn the application of the *Essentials* for each cuisine.

An intelligent cook knows that it is just as important to meet nutritional requirements as it is to appeal to gastronomical needs. Too many cooks have been preoccupied with the capacity of a meatless diet to provide an adequate amount of protein. Although protein planning certainly deserves consideration, other dietary factors play an equal, if not more important, role in maintaining good health. For this reason, the *nutritional* concepts are devoted to aspects of recipe and menu planning that are of concern to people who want to follow a healthful diet: learning to moderate consumption of calories, cholesterol, and saturated fat; complementing protein; and ensuring an adequate intake of vitamins and fiber. To help plan your diet, chapters also include *Recipe Analysis Charts* that specify the calorie, protein, carbohydrate, fat, cholesterol, and fiber content of the recipes contained within. In addition, you will find tailor-made menus for well-balanced, high-protein, low-calorie, low-cholesterol, and low-fat meals based on each style of cooking.

The recipes collected in this book are intended to bring you the ultimate experience in international dining. Many of these thoroughly tested dishes are our own culinary creations, while others are hard-won acquisitions from Epicurean friends. The majority of them do not call for meat, although you will encounter a number of preparations that contain fish or poultry.

Everyone will find this book invaluable for different reasons, but it is intended especially for people who realize that cooking is an art to be practiced with skill, originality, and love. Novice cooks will enjoy discovering new ways to put a professional and exotic touch into their meals, while experienced cooks and vegetarian gourmets can use our culinary concepts to further refine their seasoning and cooking techniques. We have included nutritional information that everyone will find not only interesting and relevant, but also easy to incorporate into just about any recipe. Calorie-counters and those on restricted low-fat diets will be happy to find dishes that will take the monotony out of menu planning. To determine how this book may best serve as your cooking companion and reference guide, we recommend that you first read the introductory chapter, *How to Use This Book*.

Eating can play an important role in shaping the quality of your existence. Our hope is that this cooking-resource book will give you control over this facet of your life. If we have succeeded in our endeavor, you will become an accomplished ethnic cook who can readily apply nutritional concepts to any meal. We hope this book will bring you one delicious step closer to the world's healthiest and most exciting food creations.

ACKNOWLEDGMENTS

We are deeply indebted to all our international friends who kindly shared their culinary wisdom, seasoning secrets, and family recipes. Without their assistance, this book could not have been brought to its fruition. Our special thanks to:

Muriel Auerbach, Dr. Lucia Beare, Oscar Kahan, Rita Kosok, Chris Meranze, Amy Mills, Luz Maria Reiter, Señora Maria Aroya de Rouret, Jorge Rubalcava, and Vivian and Edwardo Vellejo for providing insights into the cuisines of Brazil, Chile, Mexico, and Peru;

Rose Abrams, Samuel Berk, Marianne Forsyte, Margie Greene, David Igdaloff, June Lewis, Mary Reynolds, and Winifred Rush for expert advice on the cooking styles of Hungary, Poland, and Russia;

Dorka Raynor, Gerry Lehrberger, Danielle Rubalcava, Maya Rybalka, and Frank Waldman for divulging their knowledge on French cooking;

Master Chef Chi-Siung Chen and Robin Suskind for inspiration in the Chinese cuisine;

Katherine Giannes and Maria Sgouros for skillful guidance in the Greek kitchen;

Patricia Gillespie and Marilee Tillistrom for research assistance on the cooking styles of Scandinavia;

Henriette Bulus for unlimited time and energy devoted to the culinary customs of North Africa and Lebanon;

David Gaitu, Barbara Taurog, and June Taurog for providing invaluable information on the cuisines of West and South Africa;

Vince Bommarito of Tony's, St. Louis, Missouri, Nancy Hoyt, and Michael Reedy for much appreciated assistance in the varied cooking styles of Italy;

and Will Hoyt, Jim Levinson, and Arif Shah of Koh-i-noor's, St. Louis, Missouri, for counsel in the cuisine of India and for the Pakistani recipes which appear in this book.

We also wish to extend our appreciation to the department of dietetics at Emanuel Hospital, Portland, Oregon, for analyzing the recipes.

Finally, the following individuals stand out for contributions above and beyond the call of duty:

Alan Fleishman for unfailing support; Craig Fleishman for sage advice; Nelson and Syd Buhler for unbridled enthusiasm; Lillian Zavadil and Sandi Johnson for Olympian typing skills; Richard Meeker for rapid-fire suggestions; Pearlie Mae Brooks for distinguished tastebuds; and our editor, Donna Martin, for relentless brainstorming.

PART 1

HOW TO USE THIS BOOK

Each of the fifteen cuisines included in this book is considered separately in a chapter of its own. Chapters are subdivided into four sections arranged in the following order: *Culinary Essentials, Seasoning Essentials, Nutritional Essentials*, and *Recipes*. Such a format affords you easy access to the cooking concepts, seasoning skills, and nutritional aspects of each foreign kitchen. Furthermore, these complementary segments can be used to supplement information contained in other international, vegetarian, or nutrition-oriented cookbooks. In order that you may derive the maximum benefits from these culinary and dietary concepts, we highly recommend that you first read the following descriptions of each section.

Culinary Essentials

The *Culinary Essentials* are designed to orient you to the food choices, cooking concepts, and creative possibilities of each cuisine. Because many of the cooking styles may at first be unfamiliar, we have tried to define their personality, or "gastronomic gestalt," at the beginning of each section. This information will give you a handle on the foods and flavors that distinguish each cuisine, as well as what is needed in the way of ingredients and kitchen equipment.

The *Culinary Essentials* will acquaint you with exotic foods so that you will feel comfortable with your first attempts to use them. Our philosophy is that the use of unusual and lesser-known foods must be mastered in order to create exciting and original meals. At the same time, it is important to eliminate the frustration of coming upon an uncommon ingredient in a foreign recipe. To this end, we have tried to define unusual ingredients with respect to taste or texture. Suggestions are also made for incorporating these foods into other recipes and meals.

When necessary, we indicate outlets for foods that are likely to be new additions to your cooking repertoire. Oftentimes, you will have to shop at ethnic markets, specialty food shops, delicatessens, or health-food stores to purchase unusual foods. When a particular ingredient can be found in a supermarket or neighborhood grocery store, we pass this information along for your convenience. Fortunately, most large supermarkets have departments which carry foreign and specialty items, especially those commonly used in Mexican, Italian, Jewish (kosher), and Oriental cooking.

Whenever possible, we attempt to bring global cooking into the realm of natural foods. Certain foreign dishes have more nutritional value when they are prepared with natural, rather than highly processed, ingredients. To make you aware of possible alternatives, tips are given when one item is nutritionally preferable to another: Whole wheat tortillas, for example, are a fine substitute for the popular white flour variety used in Latin American cookery. Pasta made with buckwheat, soy, or artichoke flour may be considered for Italian cooking, as it is richer in protein and has more flavor than its white noodle counterpart. Other nutrition-minded suggestions are made for the selection of dairy products, cooking oils, nuts, seeds, cereals, and grains.

The *Culinary Essentials* will also tell you which kitchen tools are indispensable for each cuisine. Pointers are given for substituting common utensils for ones that are more specialized. Depending upon your preferences, you can decide whether to splurge on an exotic gadget or be thrifty and improvise with something on hand. Our inclination is to be frugal; with a little ingenuity your basic equipment can easily be adapted for more specialized cooking purposes.

Scattered among our practical tips are bits of cooking wisdom that will allow you to put a creative and personal touch into each ethnic cuisine. These culinary "pearls," which have evolved out of our cooking successes (and failures), are intended to help you select ingredients and garnishes that will shower a dish with uniqueness. Ideas are offered for ways to assemble dishes and meals that will titillate the palate with complementary colors and textures.

Finally, this section will acquaint you with ancient food customs that can bring an authentic atmosphere to your table. For instance, you will enjoy practicing the time-honored traditions that determine the order and fashion in which food courses are served. Because many cultures do not rely upon knives and forks, you may be scooping up your dinner with delicate flat breads, chopsticks, or even your fingers! We will also share a traditional ending for most meals; this may include a special brew of tea or a humble offering of fruit and nuts. Surely, everyone will be delighted to participate in these mealtime rituals.

· With each burst of energy, ethnic cooking becomes a more rewarding experience. By the time you have completed the *Culinary Essentials*, you should be prepared to shop for new ingredients, assemble kitchen utensils, select unusual foods, combine dishes that are complementary, and create a colorful ambiance for your meals. At this point, you will be ready to learn one of the most elusive cooking skills—the art of seasoning food.

Seasoning Essentials

Becoming a master of dried leaves and fragrant powders is one of the most important and complex aspects of foreign cooking. If, on a daily basis, you can supply your palate with an exciting array of tastes and textures, you will be able to maintain enthusiasm for cooking. The *Seasoning Essentials* will teach you how to unleash distinctive flavors of both domestic and foreign herbs and spices so that you can create enticing dishes. After learning this precious art, you will have the power to improvise meals and transform humble staples into exotic delicacies.

The *Seasoning Essentials* are composed of two parts: (1) a discussion of the flavors that highlight each cuisine, and (2) a *Seasoning Chart* that consolidates this information. In the former, you will become acquainted with the constellation of seasonings that exemplifies each different cuisine. These ideas will help you devise triumphant dishes that will pique the appetite with an authentic, yet original, amalgamation of ethnic flavors. You can use these spicy secrets to shape the personality of a foreign dish so it will suit your own taste preferences. Your instincts for turning ordinary dishes into exceptional ones will blossom with each new insight.

The *Seasoning Charts* elaborate upon the flavors that are indispensable to a particular style of cooking. This detailed list is not limited to herbs and spices. Any ingredient intrinsic to the mélange of flavors that constitutes the "soul" of a cuisine also receives recognition. For convenience, we indicate when it is possible to substitute one herb or spice for another.

These charts will alleviate your fear of experimenting with unfamiliar flavorings. Cooks who freely add a pinch of this and that already have a notion of what to expect from their leaves and spices. To give you this confidence, you will find a description of the flavor and, when it seems important, the aroma of each seasoning. In general, herbs and spices will be classified as aromatic (fragrant), pungent (sharp and stinging), acrid (sharp and bitter), or piquant (pleasantly biting). You will be warned about flavors which, because of their fiery nature, should be used sparingly.

Because ethnic cuisines employ herbs and spices in different ways, the awareness of special relationships between certain foods and flavorings is a prerequisite to becoming a seasoning expert. A combination may be complementary or inharmonious depending upon the cooking style. In Lebanese cooking, for example, cinnamon is not restricted to the pastry kingdom, but is also vital to entrées prepared with potatoes, lentils, or acorn squash. Mexican cooks employ cayenne pepper to fuel the heat of an enchilada sauce, while Indian cooks use this fiery spice to season cool, tangy yogurt salads. You will discover more of these complementary combinations by referring to the *Seasoning Charts* throughout the book.

Many charts include proportions for homemade seasoning blends, which are invariably fresher and more flavorful than commercially prepared versions. With a little kitchen alchemy, you will be able to concoct your own Italian seasoning, Mexican chili powder, or Greek herb blend. You will also find formulas for exotic preparations like Indian *Garam Masala* and Moroccan *Ras El Hanout*. Many mixtures, such as the Peruvian herb blend and Scandinavian spice blend, are unique to this book. These versatile seasonings provide a perfect harmony of flavors and, what's more, they are wonderful for enlivening dishes at the last minute.

Seasoning blends do not call for fresh herbs, even though they are more potent and fragrant than the dried variety. Unfortunately, fresh herbs are not easy to obtain, but if you do have access to them, we highly recommend their use for general cooking purposes. To substitute fresh herbs for dried ones, use at least three times the amount called for in the recipe. For example, one tablespoon of fresh, chopped dill is roughly equivalent in potency to one teaspoon dried dill weed.

At the end of each chart you will find a list of flavorings less commonly used in the culinary style. Feel free to use these secondary seasonings when you are looking for something to give your creations a touch of the unusual. Many of the herbs and spices which occupy a secondary position in one cuisine will be described in full detail in another chapter.

Upon completion of the *Seasoning Essentials*, you should be able to characterize and utilize the herbs and spices intrinsic to a given cuisine. By highlighting exotic flavorings and offering new ideas for well-known herbs and spices, these sections are guaranteed to expand your cooking horizons. With enough experience, the elusive art of seasoning will become a permanent part of your cooking repertoire.

Nutritional Essentials

Planning satisfying and nutritionally balanced meals is both a challenging endeavor and a prerequisite to good health. In order to sensibly orchestrate your nutrient intake, it is important to gain some familiarity with the calorie, protein, fat, carbohydrate, fiber, cholesterol, and vitamin composition of foods regularly used in meatless cooking. You will find that ethnic vegetarian recipes, in particular, employ a large number of unusual and lesser-known food items. Although learning to cook with a varied and exotic food repertoire is certainly to your advantage, the nutritional planning of such an eclectic diet can be a formidable task. For these reasons, we have oriented our discussions in the *Nutritional Essentials* around those facets of cooking and meal planning that are of greatest concern to most people: balancing protein; reduction of fat, calorie, and cholesterol intake; lowering the consumption of refined sugar; and ensuring an adequate intake of dietary fiber.

There are three parts contained in the *Nutritional Essentials* sections: (1) a discussion of the important nutritional features of each cuisine, (2) *Recipe Analysis Charts*, and (3) a *Menu Planning Section*. These complementary sections emphasize the practical aspects of maintaining a healthful diet. The *Recipe Analysis Charts* are formulated to provide you with all the information you need to follow the *Dietary Goals for the United States*, as set forth by the Senate Select Committee on Nutrition and Human Needs. In general, the *Nutritional Essentials* will be of greatest value if you first familiarize yourself with the concepts presented in Part Two of this book: *Nutrition and Health*.

Creating meatless meals that provide an adequate and balanced amount of essential amino acids can easily be accomplished within the context of foreign cooking. This is because many cultures have empirically evolved food combinations which utilize the concept of protein complementation. Examples of high-protein formulas would include the bean and sesame seed dishes of Lebanese cuisine, the corn and bean combinations of Mexico, the wheat and cheese dishes used in Italian cooking, as well as many others.

By introducing you to ingredients which are rich in essential amino acid content, the *Nutritional Essentials* will teach you how to maximize the protein content of ethnic meals. For instance, you will learn that Parmesan cheese in the Italian cuisine or soybean curd in the Chinese kitchen are excellent sources of the essential amino acids. Such information will help you design high-protein meals and make recipe manipulations that will increase the yield of this important nutrient in your cooking creations. Strategies for complementing amino acids are also emphasized in the *Nutritional Essentials*. Because many of these protein-planning concepts fit neatly and logically into the scheme of ethnic cooking, you will find them easy to apply to your meal planning endeavors.

Although fiber is not an essential nutrient per se, there is considerable evidence that high-fiber diets may prevent cancer of the large bowel, lower the insulin needs for diabetics, and reduce the incidence of diverticulosis of the colon. For these reasons, learning which foods are high in fiber content should be considered an important part of nutrition planning. Fortunately, vegetarian meals supply considerable amounts of this foodstuff because they utilize plenty of fresh vegetables, fruits, and seeds.

The *Nutritional Essentials* will help you enlarge your repertoire of high-fiber foods so that you are not dependent solely upon bran products to meet your dietary fiber needs. In fact, many of the more tasty and satisfying foods commonly used in ethnic dishes are rich in dietary fiber. Examples include *tahini* (sesame seed butter), tamarind, and a chocolatelike flavoring, carob powder.

Because of the association of heart disease with saturated fat and cholesterol intake, many people are trying to reduce their consumption of these nutrients. Even young individuals are seriously attempting to reduce their intake of saturated fat and cholesterol-rich foods, while consuming the majority of their dietary fat in polyunsaturated form. For those who have had a heart attack or even have a strong family history of heart disease, these redirections in dietary behavior are likely to be an important preventative health measure.

You will find suggestions for planning meals and devising dishes that are low in saturated fat and high in polyunsaturates. Many of these recommendations are concerned with making food *choices* and *substitutions*; as a result, they will not hem you into cooking exclusively low-fat meals.

In order to give you the flexibility to plan your dietary fat intake, we have featured vegetable oils, nuts, and seeds, which are low in saturated fat and high in polyunsaturates. When cheeses or other dairy foods are an integral part of a cuisine, we will point out those products which are low in saturated fat so you may use them if desired. More specific information regarding the total fat content and composition of our recipes can be found in the *Recipe Analysis Charts*.

We are also concerned with making you aware of the iron, vitamins B_{12} and D, calcium, and phosphorus content of vegetarian foods. Because the content of these nutrients varies from one cuisine to another, we have called attention to those foods which are especially rich in these dietary essentials. A comprehensive analysis of the vitamin and mineral content of each cooking style would not be particularly useful for planning your diet, but if you do require more specific information of this kind, you may consult the standard food composition charts which can be found in any nutrition textbook.

Recipe Analysis Charts

The *Nutritional Essentials* will help you develop cooking skills and food habits that are in line with good health. As your talents and planning skills mature, your diet will unquestionably begin to take on more of a nutritional personality. Of course, in order to sensibly plan your diet, you will have to know the nutrient make-up of the dishes you prepare.

Unless you are an experienced dietician, this can be a tedious and time-consuming endeavor. However, by developing a "feel" for the calorie and nutrient content of those food combinations that crop up repeatedly in different recipes, you can evolve this nutritional "sixth sense." With enough experience, you will be able to scan a list of ingredients used in *any* recipe, and arrive at an approximation of its nutritive value.

For every cuisine in this book, we have included *Recipe Analysis Charts* that specify the calorie, carbohydrate, protein, fat, cholesterol, and fiber content of an average serving portion for each of our recipes. These charts, which list the dishes in ascending order according to their calorie content, will be an invaluable aid for fine-tuning your intake of major nutrients and food energy. With the help of these analyses, even people who follow restricted diets will be able to make appropriate recipe and food choices.

The nutrient values in the *Recipe Analysis Charts* have been calculated using all the ingredients listed in the recipe, except spices and optional ingredients. When a recipe allows for the use of one item or another (for example, margarine or butter), the nutrient content of the *first* item listed (margarine, in this case) is the figure used for the recipe calculation. The average content *per serving* has then been determined according to the *maximum* number of portions that the recipe will yield. In other words, when a recipe yields four to six servings, the recipe analysis will reflect the calorie, protein, fat, etc., content of a portion size which is one-sixth of the recipe.

As you may know, the Senate Select Committee on Nutrition and Human Needs has developed the *Dietary Goals for the United States.* Those who gave origin to this report believe, as we do, that the *Dietary Goals* may be a major step toward reducing the incidence of our most prevalent and debilitating diseases.

Briefly, the *Dietary Goals* recommend that we: (1) increase our consumption of complex carbohydrates and naturally occurring sugars to account for about one-half of our daily energy intake; (2) reduce saturated fat consumption to account for about 10 percent of our total energy intake—with polyunsaturated and mono-saturated fat accounting for 10 percent of our total calorie intake each; (3) substitute nonfat milk for whole milk; (4) reduce cholesterol consumption to 300 mg. per day; (5) decrease consumption of refined sugar; (6) limit intake of sodium (salt); and (7) consume only as many calories as we expend; if overweight, decrease energy (calorie) intake and increase energy expenditure (exercise).

So that you can follow these recommendations, the *Recipe Analysis Charts* include the *percentage contributions* which the major dietary nutrients make to the total caloric content of each recipe in this book. These percentages are listed in parentheses beneath the *absolute* amount of protein, fat, and carbohydrate (CHO) contained in each recipe.

For example, a typical recipe analysis looks like this:

Name of Recipe	Quantity	Calories	CHO gms.	Protein gms.	Total Fat gms.	Saturated Fat gms.	Choles- terol mg.	Dietary Fiber gms.
Guacamole Enchilada	each	373	33 (35%)	22 (24%)	17 (41%)	2 (5%)	4	1.7

This means that of the 373 calories contained in each serving, 35 percent is derived from carbohydrate, 24 percent from protein, and 41 percent from total fat, which includes mono- and polyunsaturates as well as saturated fat. Because people are particularly concerned with the saturated fat content of their food, a separate calculation has been made for this nutrient. In the above example, 5 percent of the total caloric content is derived from saturated fats. In order to calculate the percentage of calories provided by mono- and polyunsaturates, simply subtract the percentage supplied by saturated fat (i.e., 5 percent) from the percentage of total fat (41 percent), which in this case (41 minus 5) equals 36 percent.

Most of the recipes in this book employ complex carbohydrates that contain natural rather than refined sugar. This is in line with the recommendations of the *Dietary Goals*. Because we rely upon herbs and spices to enhance our recipes, your salt intake will be kept to a minimum. In fact, you will find that many of the cooking strategies in this book closely follow the nutritional guidelines set forth in *Dietary Goals*.

The information in the *Recipe Analysis Charts* is meant to be useful and easy to apply to your meal planning. If you happen to be on a diet that requires a specified or restricted intake of one or more of the major nutrients, these charts will be invaluable to planning interesting and well-balanced meals within these guidelines.

Menu Planning

The *Menu Planning* section of each chapter offers a choice of five different menus: *Well-Balanced Lunch or Dinner Menus, High Protein Meals, Low Calorie Specialties, Low Saturated Fat Selections*, and *Low Cholesterol Menus*. Not only do these meal combinations consolidate nutritional information contained in the *Recipe Analysis Charts*, but they bring together complementary ethnic recipes.

Each menu plan conforms to specific nutritional parameters: The *Low Calorie Specialties* contain a mere 500 to 700 calories per meal, which is suitable for most people who wish to follow a diet of moderate weight reduction. *Low Saturated Fat Selections* contain less than 8 grams of saturated fat per menu; these menus supply less than 10 percent of your total caloric intake of saturated fat, which is acceptable for those watching their fat intake. The *Low Cholesterol Menus* provide no more than 50 mgs. of cholesterol per meal. You are guaranteed at least 30 grams of high-grade protein from our *High Protein Meals*; each of these menus supplies about one-half of your daily protein allowance. The *Well-Balanced Lunch or Dinner Menus* are just that—a healthful mixture of protein, fat, complex carbohydrate, fiber, and other essential nutrients; these menus conform closely to the recommendations of the *Dietary Goals*.

Nutrition and cooking buffs alike will find that the *Nutritional Essentials* contain stimulating discussions and valuable information for planning nutritional foreign meals. You can refer to these selections over and over again to help you make dietary manipulations that are in the best interest of your health.

Recipes

Every chapter concludes with a collection of unusual recipes that captures the flavorful spirit of each kitchen. These dishes are unique because they explore new possibilities for taste and textures without relying upon "convenience foods." Our exotic creations can be counted on to provide versatile and delicious additions to any catalogue of recipes.

We have oriented our selections around lunch and dinner because these meals are the main contributors to dietary and gastronomical needs. Each chapter offers enough appetizers, soups, salads, main courses, side dishes, and desserts to assemble a complete and well-balanced meal. Miscellaneous entries such as breads, beverages, and sauces will vary from cuisine to cuisine.

Breakfast menus, per se, have not been emphasized because they do not require a tremendous amount of variation from day to day. However, if a special breakfast or Sunday brunch is on your agenda, you can use our ethnic dishes to make it an international affair. There are enough egg, cheese, fruit, and bread recipes in this book to help you devise a memorable morning meal.

With a little imagination, you will find innumerable ways to prepare enticing and entertaining meals. Be adventurous: Mix and match recipes from different chapters. For example, an international buffet will imbue your dinners with interesting flavors. For a hot and spicy banquet, select an assortment of African, Indian, and Chinese dishes. A Latin fiesta might include a variety of Brazilian, Peruvian, and Chilean delicacies. To stage a Mediterranean feast, combine savories from France, Greece, Italy, and Lebanon. Or, to entertain Eastern European epicures, go with a Polish and Hungarian menu.

Throughout the selections in each chapter, we have tried to convey the art of improvising meals. You can use our recipes as models for the culinary concepts set forth in each cuisine. Many of our dishes are accompanied by variations that demonstrate how a recipe can lend itself to creativity with simple substitutions.

The most sensational (and sometimes disastrous) meals are oftentimes the culinary brainstorms of daring cooks. You must be willing to take a few risks with new ingredients and seasonings if you want to originate something out of the ordinary. If you have a flop, pass it on to the compost and savor a peanut butter sandwich instead. You are destined to have some failures, but, ultimately, these experiences will be your best teacher. And, remember, the world's the limit.

CHAPTER 1

AFRICA
Yam Session

Culinary Essentials

The African continent encompasses several exciting, but relatively under-explored, culinary styles. Each is characterized by certain spicing inclinations, ingredients, and methods of preparation. The West African kitchen is distinguished by its fiery peanut sauces, lemon-flavored rice, and starchy tubers. South African cooking, which draws upon the influence of the Far East, arouses the palate with pungent curry flavors, while the North African fare embraces salads and anise-scented breads inspired by Middle East cuisine. Despite variations in the choice of foods and flavorings, the tastes and textures of these regional cuisines are complementary. An awesome African feast can be made by mixing and matching selections from different regional styles.

West Africa is the home of original "soul food" cooking. Ingenious ways to prepare okra, sweet potatoes, pumpkins, and peanuts have been devised within this enticing cuisine. Unfortunately, these foods are often overlooked in our own markets because we assume that their gastronomic potential is limited. But extraordinary possibilities with such humble ingredients do exist and West African recipes will teach you how to incorporate them into your eating regime. For example, okra, a seldom used green vegetable pod, provides a colorful contrast to the sweet potatoes and cabbage used in a piquant chicken stew called *Maffe*. Fresh pumpkin, forever doomed to fill up pie shells in American kitchens, adds a unique touch to tomato-rich *Senegalese Fish*. And a feverish peanut sauce is responsible for the vibrant flavor of *Congo Chicken Moambe*, a festive mélange garnished with diced papayas and fried plantains.

While most West African ingredients are readily accessible, a few items—true yams, plantains, and cassava—will require a trip to a Latin American market. The true yam, which is quite different from the dark-orange yam found in your supermarket, is a large, white tuber with a firm texture and distinctive flavor. Do not restrict the use of true yams to our recipes—they may be boiled, baked, or fried like any other tuber with excellent results. If unavailable, either American yams or sweet potatoes may be substituted. Plantains, though starchier and less sweet than cultivated bananas, are a real treat for those who enjoy exotic fruits. These long, thick, tropical bananas are never eaten out of hand, but rather sautéed until golden brown or mashed into soups, stews, or desserts. Cassava, a fibrous root that tastes somewhat like a moist, white potato, merits attention from serious ethnic cooks. This mildly flavored vegetable may be sliced and boiled like squash, seasoned to taste, and served with any African meal. When mashed and shaped into little dumplings called *Fufu*, cassava is integral to *Ghana Light Soup*, a rich broth deeply flavored with smoked herring. One could say that *Fufu* is to *Ghana Light Soup* what matzo balls are to chicken soup. If cassava isn't available, don't despair, *Fufu* may also be made with yams.

The cuisine of South Africa shares many ingredients with her West African neighbors. Pumpkins, sweet potatoes, and peanuts, as well as corn, cabbage, and coconuts are used extensively in both styles. South African cooking, however, was heavily influenced by Malaysian chefs who arrived with their spicy cooking methods in the eighteenth century. Therefore, in addition to the aforementioned ingredients, it is not unusual for a South African recipe to call for the ingredients of a Far Eastern curry dish: chutney, coconut milk, rice, or fresh green chilies.

North Africa, on the other hand, is of an entirely different culinary cast, having little in common with either West or South African cooking. This style, which includes both Moroccan and Tunisian cooking, is more mysterious and elusive. Breads redolent of orange flower water, soups pungent with onion, and tea as sweet as nectar, have given this cuisine the illustrious title of "the most sensuous food on earth."

The offerings of North Africa are exotic but subtle enough to please most neophytes. Recipes generally call for familiar ingredients like dates, carrots, almonds, and sweet red peppers. Orange flower water, which is frequently used in the same way that we employ vanilla extract, may be obtained at Middle East or gourmet food shops.

If you can't face another night of lettuce and tomato with a side of vinaigrette, Moroccan salads will rally your appetite. *Moroccan Carrot Salad*, imbued with orange juice, honey, and orange flower water, exemplifies the North African passion for sweet and clear citrus flavors. Lemon wedges and slivered almonds provide the finishing touch for this delightful mixture, but you can embellish it further with chopped figs or pistachio nuts. If you're looking for something that hints of a faraway land, try the *Minted Tomato Salad with Lemon-Pepper Dressing*. In this composition, green peppers and scarlet tomatoes are juxtaposed with sweet mint leaves and hot chili peppers. The result is a colorful, exhilarating mixture that will complement almost any entrée.

Much of the fun of a North African meal lies in the ritual presentation which begins with a special hand-washing process. Pour warm, perfumed water from an ewer over the hands of each guest and provide each person with a small moist towel to use as a napkin. The head of the household claps his or her hands and the meal begins.

North Africans eat with the first three fingers of their right hands—to eat with five fingers would appear gluttonous. If dining sans silverware seems barbaric to some of your friends, try to convince them otherwise— this seductive food never tastes the same when consumed with a fork. If desired, you may serve *L'Hobz* (Moroccan Bread) or pocket bread to mop up juices. After the main course is consumed, the ceremonial washing of the hands is not only refreshing, but necessary.

Honey-rich *Mint Tea*, which may be sipped for hours on end, signifies the close of the meal. Desserts are simple, oftentimes little more than a bowl of fresh fruit and nuts. However, you can serve crumbly *Moroccan Almond Cookies* and be assured that your guests will not complain about licking their fingers afterward.

Seasoning Essentials

African meals can range from spicy-hot to savory-sweet. By mixing and matching recipes from different regional styles, you can titillate your palate with the entire spectrum of exotic tastes that emanate from this continent. West African recipes, lively with ginger, dried red chili peppers, and garlic, can be called upon when you want something rich and fiery. South African dishes, scented with mace and cinnamon, will provide delicate aromas and pungent-sweet flavors. And North African creations, zesty with cumin, aniseed, and coriander, can be elicited for dramatic contrasts and intriguing alliances.

Fresh ginger, known for its scenting and stinging properties, is invaluable to all styles of African cooking. This gnarled, beige-colored root can be found in the produce section of large supermarkets and oriental grocery stores. For optimum flavor, choose firm, plump pieces with large knobs and avoid those that are old and shriveled—the younger the root, the juicier the ginger will be. To use, slice off a one-inch piece and trim away the peel; mince with a sharp knife or shred on the wide holes of a flat-sided grater. The unused portion may be wrapped in plastic and refrigerated for three weeks.

You can concoct a simple but unique side dish by grating fresh ginger root over cooked vegetables such as yams, carrots, or collard greens; a splash of melted safflower margarine or butter is the finishing touch. A plain peanut or tomato sauce can be elevated into something quite extraordinary with a hint of fresh ginger. Or try mingling this lively spice with your favorite chicken stew, fish preparation, or fresh fruit salad.

When African cooks want their dishes to pack some punch, they fortify them with a combination of ginger and cayenne pepper. You can employ this exuberant twosome whenever a warm, full-bodied taste is desired. For convenience, season your inventions with the *West African Spice Blend*, which utilizes ground ginger, cayenne pepper, and white peppercorns. This well-balanced mixture is great for brightening the flavor of a dish at the last minute. You will also find it to be a marvelous enhancer for steamed okra, peanut soup, sliced avocados, or *Fried Plantains*.

When the mood for creative kitchen alchemy strikes, you will enjoy preparing *Ras El Hanout*, an intricate blend of North African seasonings. This unusual combination sets well-known flavorings such as allspice and cardamom against obscure ones like orrisroot and lavender flowers. The result is a mixture that is unrivaled in its ability to enrapture the palate. Ingredients are flexible to what you have on hand and uncommon ingredients, if unavailable at a spice shop, may be omitted. But remember, the more exotic the seasonings, the more elusive your blends will be. Used in small amounts as background flavoring, *Ras El Hanout* will work wonders with vegetable stews, rice, or couscous, a fine semolina grain available in many large supermarkets and fancy food stores.

AFRICAN SEASONING CHART

ANISEED has a powerful aroma and distinct licoricelike flavor. It is highly prized in North African cooking, especially in breads, cookies, and occasionally, fish, tomato, or egg preparations. For many, aniseed is an acquired taste, so use it sparingly at first, adding ¼ teaspoon to a dish that serves four persons; increase the amount as desired. For bread baking, however, you can use up to one teaspoon of this pungent herb to season two loaves.

CAYENNE PEPPER is popular throughout Africa; it must be used skillfully and with an authoritative hand. This ground red capsicum is so sharp and acrid that it cannot possibly be made to harmonize with certain seasonings; but it is also so indispensable as a contrasting and catalyzing flavor, and so stimulating when properly used, that many dishes are lifeless without it. A good pinch of cayenne will add zest to almost any soup, sauce, stew, or egg dish. It may be sprinkled successfully over sliced yams, fried plantains, peanut soup, or spinach. As a rule, add 1 teaspoon cayenne to a dish for 6 persons and increase the amount as desired. For spicy dishes, this lively seasoning works well in combination with ginger, garlic, cumin, or coriander.

CINNAMON and CASSIA are responsible for the pleasant fragrance and somewhat sweet flavor that characterize many African dishes. The difference between the two is profound and can significantly influence the taste of a dish. Ceylon, or true cinnamon, has a delicate nature that is best suited for baked goods, fruit dishes, yams, couscous, and North African salads. Cassia, more robust and nippy, is preferred for spicy stews and South African curries. Ground cinnamon or cassia should be used for quick-cooking dishes; cinnamon sticks, which impart a richer flavor than the ground variety, are recommended for long-simmered dishes such as boiled rice, stewed sweet potatoes, or custard pies.

CUMIN SEEDS have powerful scenting abilities. The whole seeds have a musty aroma, but when freshly ground, they release a fragrance that is at once stimulating and alluring. When mingled with coriander and cayenne pepper, ground cumin will impart a magnificent pungency to lentil dishes, eggs, or chickpea soup. A piquant dressing for roasted pepper or grated carrot salads can be made with equal proportions of olive oil and lemon juice seasoned to taste with ground cumin, minced fresh garlic, and cayenne pepper.

DRIED RED CHILI PEPPERS are treasured by African cooks, who employ them in ways that epitomize their culinary skills. These small, shriveled, and elongated pods can be stored indefinitely and still retain their fiercely sharp taste. Whole dried chilies should be used when full potency is desired; if a milder flavor is required, slice the tips off the ends and shake out the seeds. Whole ones may be simmered in a tomato or peanut sauce and removed before serving. One crushed pepper will turn ½ cup of oil and lemon juice into a fiery African salad dressing. When combined with freshly grated ginger root, crushed chili pods are also an excellent seasoning for *Fufu* or coconut milk-based dishes.

GINGER has a spicy aroma and pepper-sweet flavor that is cherished in all styles of African cooking. It is invaluable to South African curries, North African *tagines* or stews, as well as West African peanut dishes. The freshly grated root lends distinction to chicken, tomato-based sauces, vegetable casseroles, collard greens, and rice. To feel its full effect, use up to 1 tablespoon in a dish to serve 4 persons. Ground ginger may be sprinkled over sliced avocados, papaya, boiled sweet potatoes, or fried plantains. Jamaican ginger, available on most spice racks, is the best preground variety available. Ground or fresh ginger blends well with most seasonings, especially dried red chilies, cinnamon, cloves, bay leaves, and onions.

MACE is the fragrant husk that surrounds the nutmeg seed. Its flavor is more subtle and refined than nutmeg, and somewhat more aromatic, but the two may be used interchangeably. When dried and pressed into flat "blades," mace is used much like stick cinnamon—simmered in a dish and removed before serving. Ground mace is called upon more frequently than blade mace. Along with cinnamon, nutmeg, and pepper, it is one of the most important South African seasonings. Its spicy fragrance is beneficial to mealie bread, eggs, and vegetables such as string beans, carrots, red cabbage, and cauliflower. Mace blends kindly with most flavorings and, when properly used, is not overpowering.

RAS EL HANOUT is known in Morocco as the "top of the shop" or "head of the house spice mixture." This intricately flavored blend, which contains anywhere from 10 to 25 ingredients, will add a tantalizing and esoteric quality to golden spiced rice, couscous, or vegetable stews. As a rule, add ½ to 1 teaspoon to a dish that serves 4 persons. Proportions and ingredients may change according to your taste preferences. For variation, add any of the following: aniseed, saffron, paprika, cassia, or rose petals. Use whole spices whenever possible. Grind each ingredient separately in a mortar before measuring. Store in an airtight container.

- ½ teaspoon each: white pepper, turmeric, lavender flowers, and orrisroot
- ¾ teaspoon each: mace, allspice, Ceylon cinnamon, black pepper, and ginger
- 1 dried pepper crushed
- 5 green cardamom pods, coriander seeds, and cumin seeds
- ¼ whole nutmeg, grated (or ¾ teaspoon ground)
- 2 whole cloves

WEST AFRICAN SPICE BLEND is a spicy-hot mixture that may be used in small amounts to perk up sliced tomatoes, steamed okra, soups, stews, avocados, papayas, peanut sauce, yams, or fried plantains. It is especially handy for jazzing up a dish at the last minute or revitalizing leftovers. Combine and store in an airtight container:

- 4 tablespoons ground Jamaican ginger
- 2 tablespoons cayenne pepper
- 2 tablespoons ground white peppercorns

Other seasonings found in African cookery: fenugreek, coriander, cardamom, mint, nutmeg, cloves, allspice, peppercorns, curry, saffron, thyme, turmeric, bay leaves, parsley, green chili peppers, sesame seeds, orange flower water, rose water, and garlic.

Nutritional Essentials

African cooking combines a myriad of wholesome ingredients into exotic, nutritious dishes that anyone can enjoy. Among the foreign cuisines represented in this book, the innovative recipes of this kitchen rank highest in average protein content (21 percent of total calories) and dietary fiber (1.4 grams per dish). Additionally, the total and saturated fat content of African recipes are lower than that of any other cuisine except the Lebanese. Only when it comes to calories—284 per average portion—may you need to moderate your consumption of this vigorous food.

What does all this mean for the nutrition-conscious cook? First, you can expect African dishes—especially those with chicken or fish—to provide substantial quantities of high-quality protein; with an average of 15 grams per serving, a three-course meal can meet the entire minimum daily adult requirement of protein. This diet is also ideal for people who need to moderate their fat and cholesterol intake. Finally, because many of the offerings in this cuisine constitute an entire meal in themselves, you can save calories while still meeting your nutritional requirements. In short, African cooking is both delicious and good for your health; much of this has to do with the ingredients which are commonly employed in native recipes.

African dishes are replete with sound, natural sources of carbohydrates and dietary fiber: pumpkins, carrots, cabbage, plantains, yams, sweet potatoes, rice, and okra. In general, the carbohydrate content of these foods is quite high, while the fat content is correspondingly low; consequently, this cuisine is able to offer a number of low calorie specialties: *Pumpkin Puffs* (55 calories), *Moroccan Carrot Salad with Orange* (83 calories), and *Londalozi Cabbage Salad* (131 calories).

Bananas and plantains each contain about 100–150 calories per average-sized fruit. They are excellent sources of potassium and contain appreciable amounts of phosphorus, vitamins A and C, and other essential minerals. Plantains, unlike bananas, are frequently used as a vegetable rather than a fruit; they are never eaten raw, and when prepared as *Fried Plantains* make a superb accompaniment to most entrées.

One of the most popular (and unusual) vegetables you will encounter is the yam, an elongated tuber, which in its *true* form is seldom found in this country except in Latin American markets. As a rule, when you are preparing African dishes which employ yams, you will have to use the moist-meated American yam or the dry-meated sweet potato. The American yam, high in complex carbohydrates, is very nutritious, containing more than twice the daily allowance of vitamin A, one-third of the recommended vitamin C allowance, and a number of other essential vitamins and minerals. Boiled, a 3½-ounce serving contains 114 calories; the same amount yields 141 calories when baked. You will enjoy making yams or plantains into *Fufu*, the traditional accompaniment for smoky-flavored *Ghana Light Soup*. Containing protein, fat, and carbohydrate in equal proportions, *Ghana Light Soup* is representative of a filling, well-balanced and highly nutritious African meal. It should be served as a single course, making the 527 calories per serving much less intimidating.

When it comes to flavor enhancers, many regional styles of African cooking use peanuts, which really are not nuts at all, but legumes related to peas and beans. Three exceptional, protein-rich dishes—*West African Peanut Soup, Senegalese Chicken with Peanut Butter Sauce,* and *Congo Chicken Moambe*—use peanut butter as a main ingredient. Peanuts, like most nuts, are high in protein, and can supply nonmeat-eaters with most of the essential amino acids needed for a balanced diet. In small quantities, nuts also supply potassium, iron, thiamine, phosphorus, and a few vitamins.

Nuts do, however, have a nutritional drawback—their extremely high fat content. For this reason, they should be used in moderation by those on low-calorie regimes. The cholesterol-conscious cook will be happy to know that the fat in peanuts, walnuts, pecans, and almonds is predominantly polyunsaturated, with walnuts the highest of all in polyunsaturated fatty acids. Cashews, on the other hand, contain substantial amounts of saturated fat and should be avoided by those on low-fat, low-cholesterol diets. Coconuts are extraordinarily high in saturated fat and virtually out of bounds for anyone on a low-fat program.

As mentioned earlier, African dishes are rich in protein, largely because they rely on fish and chicken for main courses; vegetables and cheese are scarce in this part of the world. Among the popular meats, chicken is an excellent choice for weight-watchers, as it ranks lowest in calorie count. Poultry is also low in fat, and what it does contain is 64 percent unsaturated, making it desirable for individuals on low-fat, low-cholesterol diets. In addition to high-quality protein, chicken is also a good source of iron, calcium, phosphorus, and some vitamins. Two of our African recipes combine chicken with peanut-butter sauce—a favorable nutritional strategy; the lysine-rich chicken meat complements the lysine-deficient peanut protein, boosting the usable protein content by about 20 percent.

ALMOND COOKIES

YIELD: *Approximately 36 cookies*

½ pound safflower margarine or
   sweet cream butter, softened
1 egg, well beaten
1⅔ cup sifted powdered sugar
½ teaspoon each: vanilla extract,
   almond extract, and orange
   flower water*

½ cup finely ground almonds
½ teaspoon baking powder
2¼ cups unbleached white flour
⅓ cup powdered sugar
36 whole almonds (approximately)

Available at Greek or Middle Eastern grocery stores

1. Preheat oven to 350 degrees.
2. To make dough, in a large bowl, cream together the margarine or butter, egg, and the 1⅔ cups powdered sugar until smooth. Stir in the extracts, orange flower water, ground almonds, baking powder, and flour. Stir well after each addition.
3. Place the ⅓ cup powdered sugar in a flat bowl. Pinch off walnut-size pieces of dough and roll between your palms. Flatten balls slightly and dip one side into the sugar. Place flattened balls, sugar-side-up, 2 inches apart on a lightly greased baking sheet. Press a whole almond in the center of each one. Bake in preheated oven from 10 to 12 minutes or until golden brown. Allow to cool and crisp before storing.

CONGO CHICKEN MOAMBE

YIELD: *6 to 8 servings*

1 fryer chicken, cut up (3 pounds)
6 tablespoons peanut oil, divided
2 medium-sized onions, finely
   diced
3 large tomatoes, puréed
1 6-ounce can tomato paste
2 or 3 cloves garlic, minced
1 tablespoon grated ginger root
3 dry red chili peppers, crushed (or
   substitute 1 teaspoon cayenne
   pepper)

3 green onions, finely chopped
½ cup peanut butter (smooth, not
   chunky)
Cooked rice
1 large papaya, peeled, seeded, and
   diced
Fried Plantains (the following
recipe) or substitute 3 sliced
bananas sautéed until lightly
browned

1. Clean chicken and pat dry. Heat 4 tablespoons of the peanut oil in a heavy soup pot. Brown the chicken pieces on both sides, turning frequently with tongs. Remove and set aside. Heat remaining oil in the pot and sauté the onions until golden. Add the puréed tomatoes, tomato paste, garlic, ginger root, crushed chili peppers or cayenne pepper, and green onions. Return chicken to the pot and submerge in the sauce. Cover and cook over low heat 15 minutes, or until chicken is tender, stirring occasionally. Remove chicken from pot and set aside. Remove 1 cup of sauce

from the pot and place in a blender with the peanut butter. Purée until smooth and stir back into the pot. Return chicken to the pot. Simmer 10 minutes, stirring occasionally. Be sure peanut butter mixture is thoroughly incorporated into the tomato sauce.

2. To serve, place a serving of cooked rice on each plate. Mound a serving of chicken over the rice and cover generously with the sauce. Garnish each portion with diced papaya and fried plantains or bananas. This dish is an entire meal in itself. If desired, as an accompaniment serve something light such as *Roasted Pepper Salad* (p. 30).

FRIED PLANTAINS

YIELD: 4 to 6 servings

---

4 large, very ripe plantains*
¼ cup peanut or safflower oil
*Available at Latin American grocery stores

1 teaspoon grated ginger root
¹⁄₁₆ teaspoon cayenne pepper

Slice plantains into ½-inch rounds. Heat oil in a large heavy skillet. Stir in the seasonings. Add plantains. Fry until golden brown and crisp, turning frequently. Serve hot.

FUFU GAITU

YIELD: Serves 6 to 8

---

1 fresh or 1 package frozen
  cassava* (2 pounds)
*Available at Latin-American grocery stores

3 large green plantains*
1 true yam* (2 pounds)

1. Peel cassava, plantains, and yam. Cut into pieces. Wash well and put into a large kettle or soup pot. Cover with water and boil for 45 minutes or until tender. Drain in a colander.

2. Remove the cassava pieces. Mash to a fine paste in a mortar with a pestle. Form the smooth paste into a ball. Set aside. Repeat process with plantains and then the yam. (It may be necessary to add small amounts of water in the mashing process if the mixture hardens as it cools).

3. Place the ball of cassava and plantain in a large wooden bowl and knead the two together. Divide it into 6 or 8 balls. This is cassava-plantain *fufu*. Divide the mashed yam into 6 balls to make yam *fufu*. Serve as a side dish or with *Ghana Light Soup* (the following recipe).

Note: Mashed yam may be mixed with the mashed cassava to make yam-cassava *fufu*, but the yam and plantain are never mixed together.

GHANA LIGHT SOUP

YIELD: *Serves 6*

6 smoked herring*
6 cups water
1 large onion, coarsely chopped
6 ounces tomato paste
3 fresh ripe tomatoes, peeled and
  cut into segments
1 medium-sized eggplant, peeled
  and cubed

½ pound fresh mushrooms
12 fresh or ½ package frozen okra,
  sliced
1 teaspoon salt
½ to 1 teaspoon cayenne pepper
Fufu Gaitu (preceding recipe)

*Available at Italian grocery stores

1. Break each fish in half. Place in a large soup pot with 3 cups of the water, the onion, and tomato paste. Bring to a boil and cook for 15 minutes on medium-high heat. Add tomatoes, eggplant, whole mushrooms, okra, salt, cayenne pepper, and remaining water. Boil from 20 to 30 minutes more or until liquid is reduced and thickened. Taste and adjust seasonings. Soup should be spicy hot.
2. Place 1 ball of cassava-plantain *fufu* and 1 ball of yam *fufu* in each soup bowl. Ladle fish, vegetables, and soup over *fufu*. Serve as a main course.

GOLDEN SPICED RICE

YIELD: *6 servings*

1 cup uncooked long-grain white
  rice
1 teaspoon salt
1 teaspoon turmeric
2 to 3 tablespoons peanut oil or
  safflower margarine
1 medium-sized onion, sliced into
  rings

3 tablespoons safflower margarine
3 tablespoons honey
2 cloves garlic, pressed
½ cup chopped dates
¼ to ½ cup chopped almonds—
  optional
1 teaspoon ground cinnamon
6 whole dates for garnish

1. In a 2-quart saucepan, combine the rice, salt, and turmeric. Add enough water to cover rice and bring to a rolling boil. Cover, reduce heat to low, and simmer until rice is tender and water absorbed—from 20 to 30 minutes. Do not stir rice while cooking.
2. Meanwhile, heat the oil in a skillet and sauté the onion rings quickly—keep them firm, not limp. Set aside. In a small saucepan, heat over a low flame the 3 tablespoons margarine, honey, and garlic. Remove from heat when margarine has melted and mixture is thoroughly blended.
3. Preheat oven to 350 degrees.
4. Toss cooked rice with dates, almonds, and cinnamon. Transfer to a round baking dish. Pour margarine-honey mixture over the rice. Arrange sautéed onion rings over the top and place whole dates inside the rings. Bake in preheated oven for 20 minutes. Serve immediately.

LABLABI *(Tunisian Chickpea Soup)*   *YIELD: 6 to 8 servings*

---

1 pound (2 cups) chickpeas, soaked
  overnight in enough water to
  cover
2 to 3 tablespoons safflower
  margarine or butter
1 to 2 onions, chopped
3 to 4 garlic cloves, crushed
2 celery ribs, chopped

2½ quarts hot water or *Vegetable
  Stock* (p. 383)
1 teaspoon each: cayenne pepper,
  ground cumin, and ground
  coriander
Salt and freshly ground pepper to
  taste
Juice of 1 lemon
⅓ cup olive oil

1. Drain water off chickpeas. Rub beans with your fingers to remove as many skins as possible.
2. Heat margarine or butter in a large soup pot. Sauté the onions until lightly browned. Add the garlic and celery and sauté briefly. Add the chickpeas and cover with 2½ quarts hot water or hot vegetable stock. Bring to a boil, cover, reduce heat, and simmer gently until beans are tender—about 1½ hours. Add the seasonings, lemon juice and olive oil. Simmer 5 minutes longer. Taste and adjust seasonings.
Variation: Add 2 skinned and chopped tomatoes at the start of cooking.

L'HOBZ *(Moroccan Bread)*   *YIELD: 3 loaves or approximately 24 servings*

---

2 teaspoons sugar
2 cups very warm water
1½ packages active dry yeast
5 cups unbleached white flour
2 cups whole wheat flour
2 teaspoons salt
* Available at Greek or Middle Eastern stores

1 to 2 tablespoons orange flower
  water*—optional
1 tablespoon each: anise seed and
  sesame seed
Cornmeal
Vegetable oil

1. Dissolve the sugar in the warm water. Sprinkle in the yeast and stir to dissolve. Let stand 5 minutes or until foamy. Sift flours and salt together into a large mixing bowl. Make a well in the center and add the yeast mixture, orange flower water, and seeds. Stir gently but thoroughly, adding water, a little at a time, as needed to form a stiff dough. Turn out on a lightly floured board. Knead from 10 to 20 minutes or until smooth and elastic.
2. Divide dough into 3 equal pieces. Shape each piece into a ball. Place balls, one at a time, into a well-greased bowl and work with your hands to form each into a cone shape. Sprinkle 2 large baking sheets with cornmeal and place cones upside down on the sheets. Flatten with your palms to form a circle approximately 8 inches wide and 1 inch thick. Brush the tops

with vegetable oil and let rise in a warm, draft-free spot, covered, until doubled in bulk—about 1½ to 2 hours.
3. Preheat oven to 375 degrees.
4. Pierce loaves with a fork halfway between the center and the edges or make a few shallow half-moon slashes. Bake in preheated oven until the tops are lightly browned and the bottoms sound hollow when tapped— about 1 hour. Cool on wire racks.

LONDOLOZI CABBAGE SALAD

YIELD: 16 servings

---

1 head white cabbage (2 pounds), shredded
4 medium-sized carrots, grated
1 medium-sized fresh pineapple, peeled, cored, and cubed

Juice of 1 orange (approximately ¼ cup juice)
½ cup safflower mayonnaise
3½ ounces peanuts

Combine the cabbage, carrots, and pineapple in a salad bowl. Squeeze the orange juice over the mixture. Add the mayonnaise—just enough to moisten. Sprinkle peanuts over the top and serve immediately.

MAFFE *(Senegalese Chicken with Peanut Butter Sauce)*

YIELD: 6 to 8 servings

---

1 large fryer chicken, cut up (about 3 pounds)
Water to cover
1 teaspoon salt
½ teaspoon black pepper
1 teaspoon each: ground ginger and red (cayenne) pepper
2 medium-sized true yams* or sweet potatoes, cut into eighths
1 large carrot, cut diagonally into thick slices

½ pound okra, stemmed and cut crosswise into 3 pieces
½ head small cabbage, cut into wedges
1 bunch leeks, cleaned and cut into chunks (white part only)
½ to ¾ cup peanut butter (smooth not chunky)
3 cups cooked rice
Crushed peanuts (roasted and unsalted) for garnish—optional

*Available at Latin American grocery stores

1. Clean chicken and place in a soup pot with just enough water to cover. Bring to a boil and skim the surface until clear. Add the seasonings and cook until chicken is tender—about 30 minutes. Remove chicken and set aside.
2. Place the yams or sweet potatoes and carrot in the soup pot. Bring to a slow boil and boil gently until almost tender. Add the okra, cabbage, and leeks. Reduce heat to low and simmer until vegetables are barely tender. Remove all vegetables from the pot and set aside with the chicken.

3. Place 2 cups of the soup stock in a blender with the peanut butter. Purée until smooth. Pour any remaining stock into a container and reserve for another use. Return peanut butter mixture to the pot and cook over medium heat until smooth, stirring constantly. If mixture is too thick, thin it out with some of the reserved stock. Taste and adjust seasonings, adding more cayenne pepper and ginger if spicier flavor is desired. Return chicken and vegetables to the pot and simmer, covered, for 10 minutes.

4. *To serve*: Place ½ cup rice in each bowl. Mound a serving of chicken and vegetables over the rice. Generously cover each serving with the peanut butter sauce, and garnish, if desired, with crushed peanuts. This dish is considered an entire meal in itself and requires no accompaniments, except perhaps a light salad. *Fried Plantains* (p. 22) may be served for dessert.

MEALIE BREAD
(Steamed Corn Pudding)   *YIELD: 8 servings*

---

2 quarts water
5 cups fresh corn kernels, or
   substitute frozen corn kernels
   (thoroughly defrosted)
2 large or 3 medium eggs
2 tablespoons safflower margarine,
   melted

3 teaspoons double-acting baking
   powder
¼ to ½ cup brown sugar
2 tablespoons flour
1 teaspoon salt
¼ teaspoon each: mace and nutmeg

1. Preheat oven to 375 degrees. Adjust rack to the middle of the oven.

2. Place water in a large saucepan and bring to a boil. Meanwhile, place half of the corn kernels in a blender with the eggs. Purée until corn is broken into pieces but not completely smooth. Add the rest of the corn along with the remaining ingredients. Purée until thoroughly combined but not smooth. Pour mixture into a well-greased 9- × 5- × 3-inch loaf pan. Cover with a double thickness of aluminum foil and seal the edges tightly. Place the loaf in a large, shallow pan and fill the pan halfway up the sides with the boiling water. Bake in a preheated oven 1½ hours or until inserted knife comes out clean.

3. Remove loaf pan from both the oven and water-filled pan. Let stand at room temperature, uncovered, 5 to 10 minutes. To unmold, run a knife around the edges of the tin. Turn a plate upside down over the bread and invert the two. Tap the pan firmly on a flat surface and the bread should unmold easily. Cut into slices and serve hot or at room temperature with safflower margarine or butter; honey or maple syrup may also be served as an accompaniment.

MELK TERT
(South African Custard Pie)   YIELD: 6 to 8 servings

Flaky Pastry: *
1½ cups all-purpose flour
  Pinch of salt
 ½ teaspoon double-acting baking
  powder
1½ tablespoons superfine sugar
 6 tablespoons butter, chilled and
  cut into ¼-inch pieces
 1 egg
 1 to 2 tablespoons milk

Filling:
2 cups whole milk
2 cinnamon sticks
1 vanilla bean or 1 teaspoon vanilla
  extract
½ cup evaporated milk
6 tablespoons sugar
4 tablespoons cornstarch
  Pinch of salt
2 tablespoons safflower margarine,
  cut into small pieces
½ teaspoon orange extract
2 teaspoons brandy—optional
2 tablespoons apricot jam—
  optional
2 eggs, lightly beaten
1 tablespoon sugar combined with
  ½ teaspoon cinnamon

1. *To prepare pastry:* Sift the flour, salt, and baking powder into a large mixing bowl. Stir in the sugar. Rub in the butter with your fingertips until the mixture is the consistency of coarse meal. Beat the egg and combine it with 1 tablespoon of milk. Pour egg mixture all at once into the flour mixture and gather into a soft dough; add the remaining tablespoon of milk if dough seems too dry. Return ball to mixing bowl, cover, and refrigerate while preparing filling.

2. *To prepare filling:* Place the milk, cinnamon sticks, and vanilla bean in a saucepan. Heat over moderate flame until bubbles appear around the edges. Remove from heat, cover with a tight-fitting lid, and let steep 15 minutes. Place the evaporated milk, sugar, cornstarch, and salt in a blender and whirl quickly until smooth. Add to saucepan, return to stove, and cook 2 minutes over low heat, stirring constantly with a wooden spoon. Add the margarine, vanilla extract (if you did not use a vanilla bean), orange extract, and brandy. Stir constantly until the margarine melts. Remove from stove and set aside, stirring occasionally to prevent a layer of skin from forming on the surface.

3. Preheat oven to 350 degrees. Adjust rack to the middle of the oven.

4. Remove pie crust from refrigerator. Roll out between two pieces of waxed paper (for complete directions on rolling out a pie crust *see Never-Fail Pie Crust*, p. 380). Line a 9-inch pie plate with the pastry and flute the

---

*Note: This crust may be used in any recipe that requires a flaky pastry crust such as fruit or cream pies. To use for savory pies, such as quiche, eliminate the sugar.

edges. Strain the apricot jam and brush it over the bottom and sides of the pie crust with a pastry brush. Add the beaten eggs to the reserved milk mixture. Pour the entire mixture through a fine sieve into the pie shell. Discard the cinnamon sticks and vanilla bean. Sprinkle the top with cinnamon-sugar mixture. Bake in preheated oven until filling is firm and inserted knife comes out clean—about 35 to 40 minutes. Serve cold or at room temperature.

MINTED TOMATO SALAD WITH LEMON-PEPPER DRESSING

YIELD: 6 servings

Salad:
 1 large green pepper, seeded and chopped
 1 large sweet red pepper, seeded and chopped
 1 bunch green onions, chopped
 4 firm, ripe tomatoes, chopped
12 sprigs parsley, chopped
 6 sprigs fresh mint, chopped, or
 2 teaspoons dried mint leaves

Dressing:
 1 dried red chili pepper
 ⅓ cup peanut oil
 Juice of 1 lemon
 Salt and pepper to taste

1. Mix together the salad ingredients. Place in a salad bowl and set aside.
2. Cut the ends off the red chili pepper and shake out the seeds. Place in a bowl with a little of the oil and let stand until soft. Mix the lemon juice into the remaining oil. Crush the softened pepper and add to the lemon-oil mixture. Season with salt and pepper. Taste and adjust seasonings. Add a little cayenne pepper if dressing is not spicy enough. Toss dressing with salad and serve immediately.

MOROCCAN MINT TEA

YIELD: 6 servings

2 teaspoons green or gunpowder tea
½ cup honey
1 tablespoon rose water*

1 to 1¼ cups firmly packed fresh spearmint
6 cups boiling water

*Available at Greek or Middle Eastern grocery stores

Place the green tea, honey, rose water, and mint leaves in a large teapot. Cover with the boiling water and let steep at least 15 minutes before serving. Taste and adjust sweetness. Moroccan tea should be very sweet. Stir well and pour into teacups that have been rinsed with boiling water to prewarm them.

Note: Spearmint is considered the best mint for Moroccan tea, although other kinds of mint are acceptable. If fresh mint is not available, replace **1 cup fresh leaves with ½ cup dried leaves**. Just be sure your dried leaves are not old and flavorless.

MOROCCAN ORANGE-DATE SALAD

YIELD: 4 servings

---

4 large oranges
12 dates, pitted and halved
Orange flower water*

2 tablespoons lemon juice
¼ cup chopped pistachio nuts
4 fresh or dried figs

Available at Greek and Middle Eastern grocery stores and some supermarkets

Peel oranges, removing all white pith. Cut into slices. Put into a bowl with the dates. Sprinkle with orange flower water and the lemon juice. Marinate for 1 hour. To serve, arrange orange slices and dates on individual salad plates. Sprinkle with chopped pistachio nuts. Top with a fig.
Variation: For a sweeter salad, add 2 teaspoons powdered sugar and ¼ teaspoon allspice to the marinade.

PUMPKIN PUFFS

YIELD: Approximately 40 puffs

---

2 cups cooked pumpkin,* cooled
and mashed
¾ to 1 cup whole wheat or
unbleached white flour
1 teaspoon baking powder
½ cup sugar

½ teaspoon salt
1 egg, slightly beaten
Safflower or vegetable oil for
frying
1 tablespoon sugar combined with
1 teaspoon cinnamon

A 2½-pound pumpkin yields 2 cups cooked pumpkin. Canned pumpkin may also be used.

1. Place pumpkin in a large mixing bowl and stir until smooth and creamy. Combine ¾ cup of the flour with the baking powder, sugar, and salt. Add to pumpkin along with the egg. Add the remaining ¼ cup flour only if needed to make the batter stiff (but not dry).
2. Pour oil 2½ to 3 inches deep into a large, heavy saucepan or deep fryer. Heat to 375 degrees. Drop pumpkin batter by heaping teaspoonfuls, a few at a time, into the hot oil. Fry until golden brown, turning once with tongs. Drain on paper towels. Sprinkle cinnamon-sugar over all the puffs and serve immediately as a side dish or dessert. If desired, puffs may be kept warm in a low oven until ready to serve.
Variations: Replace pumpkin with mashed sweet potatoes. Drizzle honey over the puffs or dust them with powdered sugar in place of the cinnamon-sugar mixture.

ROASTED PEPPER SALAD

YIELD: *4 servings*

---

2 large green peppers
4 small-to-medium-sized sweet red
  bell peppers
3 tablespoons olive oil
2 tablespoons lemon juice

1 teaspoon ground cumin
¼ to ½ teaspoon cayenne pepper
1 clove garlic, pressed
¼ to ⅓ teaspoon salt
Lemon slices for garnish

1. Preheat broiler.
2. Place both green and red peppers close together on a foil-covered baking sheet. Place the rack about 3 inches under the broiler so that the tops of the peppers are about 1 inch below the heat. Leave the oven door partially open so that you can watch closely and prevent peppers from burning. Turn peppers frequently with tongs until they are dark and blistered. Remove from oven and wrap in a damp towel for 5 minutes. Remove towel and rub peppers until the skin flakes off. Remove the seeds and stems and cut peppers into strips.
3. Combine the remaining ingredients and pour over the pepper slices. Transfer to a serving plate and garnish with lemon slices. Serve at room temperature.
Note: To serve 6 or 8 persons, double the amount of green and red peppers. Double the amount of olive oil and lemon juice, but not the cumin, cayenne pepper, garlic and salt. Beat together until well-blended. Taste and add more spices or garlic as needed.

SENEGALESE FISH

YIELD: *6 to 8 servings*

¼ cup peanut oil
2 medium-sized onions, diced
1 6-ounce can tomato paste
1 bay leaf
2 dry red peppers, crushed, or
  cayenne pepper to taste
  Salt and pepper to taste
2 quarts water
3 sweet potatoes, cut into fourths
6 medium-sized white potatoes, cut
  into halves

6 carrots, cut into 2-inch pieces
1 medium wedge pumpkin, cut
  into chunks—optional
1 head of cabbage, cut into 6
  wedges
2½ pounds any ocean fish, cut into
  fillets*
2 cups raw rice
  Lemon wedges for garnish

1. Heat the oil in a large soup pot. Add onions and sauté until golden. Add tomato paste, bay leaf, red peppers or cayenne, salt, pepper, and water. Stir to mix thoroughly. Add sweet potatoes, white potatoes, carrots, and pumpkin chunks if desired. Bring to a boil. Cover and cook 10 minutes. Add cabbage wedges. Simmer until vegetables are almost tender.

2. Place the fish on top of the vegetables. Cover and simmer 8 minutes or until fish is done. Carefully remove fish and vegetables from liquid with a slotted spoon. Put into a baking dish and cover with foil. Set oven to lowest temperature. Place fish and vegetables in oven to keep warm but not cook.

3. Transfer the liquid to a 3-quart saucepan. Measure out and return to the pot 4 cups of liquid. Bring to a boil. Add rice. Cover and simmer until rice is fluffy and liquid is absorbed—about 20 to 30 minutes.

4. Reheat the remaining sauce. Add more crushed red peppers or cayenne if a hotter flavor is desired.

5. To serve: Put rice in the center of a large platter. Arrange fish over rice. Surround with alternate pieces of vegetables. Garnish with lemon wedges. Ladle heated sauce into a warm gravy bowl and spoon a little of the remaining sauce over fish and vegetables.

Note: Whole ocean fish cut into 1-inch steaks may also be used, but allow approximately 15 minutes cooking time. Bass fillets may be substituted for the ocean fish. Do not overcook or fillets will fall apart.

SHELADA GHEZO-MAA ALCHIN
(Moroccan Carrot Salad with Orange)   *YIELD: 4 to 6 servings*

1 pound carrots, washed well and grated
½ cup plus 2 tablespoons orange juice (preferably fresh-squeezed)
1 to 2 tablespoons honey

1 tablespoon orange flower water*
¼ cup chopped blanched almonds, toasted
Lemon wedges for garnish

Available at Greek or Middle Eastern grocery stores

Place grated carrots in a large bowl and chill. Combine the orange juice, honey, and orange flower water. Pour over carrots and toss thoroughly. Turn out onto a serving platter and sprinkle with almonds. Serve cold, surrounded by lemon wedges.

Variation: For a sweeter salad, add 1 cup chopped, pitted dates or figs to the grated carrots. Dust the top with powdered sugar.

SOUTH AFRICAN RICE SALAD   *YIELD: 6 servings*

2 cups cooked rice
2 green peppers, chopped
1 whole pimiento, chopped
4 tomatoes, peeled and cubed
2 tablespoons chopped parsley
2 tablespoons chopped onion
2 fresh peaches, sliced
Salt to taste (about 1 teaspoon)

Pepper to taste (about ½ teaspoon)
1 clove garlic, minced
1 tablespoon curry powder (preferably imported Madras curry powder)
3 tablespoons chutney
¾ cup good quality mayonnaise

Combine the rice, green peppers, pimiento, tomatoes, parsley, onion, peaches, salt, and pepper. Stir the garlic, curry powder, and chutney into the mayonnaise. Combine with the rice so that all the mixture is moistened with the dressing. Chill before serving.

TUNA FROM GABON
YIELD: 6 to 8 servings

½ cup peanut oil, divided
1 yellow onion, finely chopped
1 green onion, finely chopped
3 shallots, finely chopped
1 clove garlic, mashed
1 tomato, finely chopped
1 teaspoon flour
1 cup water

Juice of 2 lemons
1 teaspoon ground ginger or a
2-inch piece of ginger root, grated
Salt and pepper to taste
Dash hot pepper to taste
3 pounds fresh tuna (or any ocean
fish) cut into steaks or fillets
1 cup cornmeal

1. *To prepare sauce*: Heat 2 tablespoons of the oil in a large skillet. Sauté the onions, shallots, garlic, and tomato until tender. Make a paste of the flour and a little water. Mix with the lemon juice and remaining water. Add to the vegetables with the ginger, salt, pepper, and hot pepper. Stir and simmer 10 minutes.
2. Preheat oven to 400 degrees.
3. *To assemble*: Roll the pieces of fish in the cornmeal. Put into an oblong baking dish. Sprinkle with the remaining oil. Bake 15 minutes. Cover with the sauce. Bake 10 to 15 minutes longer. Serve with rice.

WEST AFRICAN LEMON RICE
YIELD: 4 servings

1 cup long-grain brown rice
2 cups hot water
Juice of 2 lemons

1 tablespoon safflower margarine
or butter—optional
1 teaspoon salt

Wash the rice well. Place in a dry 9-inch skillet over medium heat. Stir constantly until rice "pops" or is lightly browned. Remove from heat. Place rice, water, lemon juice, and margarine in a heavy 2-quart saucepan. Bring to a boil for 5 minutes. Reduce heat to low, cover with a tight-fitting lid, and simmer 45 minutes or until all the liquid is absorbed and rice is tender. Do not stir during cooking or rice will become gummy. Remove from heat and let stand 2 minutes to steam-dry. Season with salt and fluff with a fork before serving.

Note: To prepare with long-grain white rice simmer 15 minutes (instead of 45 minutes) or until all the liquid is absorbed.

WEST AFRICAN PEANUT SOUP

YIELD: 4 to 6 servings

2 tablespoons peanut oil
1 medium-sized onion, diced
4 cups vegetable or chicken stock
2 red potatoes, diced with peels
2 carrots, diced

2 leeks, diced (white part only)
Cayenne pepper to taste (about ¼ teaspoon)
Salt and pepper to taste
½ cup smooth peanut butter
Chopped parsley and scallions to garnish

1. Heat the oil in the bottom of a soup pot. Sauté the onion until golden brown—about 10 minutes. Add the broth, bring to a boil, and add the potatoes, carrots, and leeks. Reduce heat to low and simmer until potatoes are tender—about 25 minutes.
2. Pass soup through a sieve or food mill, or purée until thick and smooth in a blender. Return to soup pot and stir in cayenne, salt, and pepper. Add peanut butter and simmer 5 minutes, stirring constantly, until peanut butter is incorporated smoothly into the soup. Taste and adjust seasonings. Serve hot, garnished with chopped parsley and scallions.

AFRICA/RECIPE ANALYSIS CHART

Name of Recipe	Quantity	Calories	CHO gms.	Protein gms.	Total Fat gms.	Saturated Fat gms.	Choles- terol mg.	Dietary Fiber gms.
1. Pumpkin Puffs	per serving	55	6 (44%)	1 (7%)	3 (49%)	—	18	.3
2. *Shelada Ghezo-Maa Alchin* (Carrot Salad with Orange)	per serving	83	12 (58%)	2 (10%)	3 (32%)		—	—
3. Moroccan Mint Tea	per glass	88	22 (100%)	—	—	—	—	—
4. Roasted Pepper Salad	per serving	91	6 (26%)	1 (4%)	7 (70%)	1 (10%)	—	.9
5. Almond Cookies	each	105	14 (53%)	1 (4%)	5 (43%)	1 (9%)	9	.1
6. Moroccan Bread	per average slice	129	26 (81%)	4 (12%)	1 (7%)	—	—	.3
7. Londolozi Cabbage Salad	per serving	131	14 (43%)	3 (9%)	9 (48%)	2 (14%)	—	1.2
8. Minted Tomato Salad with Lemon-Pepper Dressing	per serving	169	10 (24%)	3 (7%)	13 (69%)	2 (11%)	—	1.7
9. West African Lemon Rice	per serving	173	37 (86%)	4 (9%)	1 (5%)	—	—	.4
10. Fried Plantains	per serving	198	26 (53%)	1 (2%)	10 (45%)	2 (9%)	—	.5
11. Mealie Bread	per serving	217	37 (68%)	6 (12%)	5 (20%)	1 (4%)	70	.6
12. West African Peanut Soup	per serving	239	18 (30%)	8 (13%)	15 (57%)	3 (11%)	—	1.3
13. Moroccan Orange-Date Salad	per serving	245	45 (73%)	5 (8%)	5 (19%)	—	—	2.2
14. South African Rice Salad	per serving	255	27 (42%)	3 (5%)	15 (53%)	3 (11%)	—	1.5
15. *Melk Tert* (South African Custard Pie)	per serving	268	33 (49%)	7 (10%)	12 (41%)	3 (10%)	93	—
16. Golden Spiced Rice	per serving	314	53 (68%)	3 (4%)	10 (28%)	2 (6%)	—	.8

Name of Recipe	Quantity	Calories	CHO gms.	Protein gms.	Total Fat gms.	Saturated Fat gms.	Choles- terol mg.	Dietary Fiber gms.
17. *Lablabi* (Tunisian Chickpea Soup)	per serving	335	38 (45%)	12 (14%)	15 (41%)	2 (5%)	—	3.0
18. Ghana Light Soup	per 1½-cup serving	364	14 (15%)	41 (45%)	16 (40%)	—	—	2.0
19. Tuna from Gabon	per serving	419	18 (17%)	44 (42%)	19 (41%)	2 (4%)	1	.4
20. Ghana Light Soup with Cassava-Plantain *Fufu*	per serving	437	29 (27%)	42 (38%)	17 (35%)	—	—	3.6
21. Ghana Light Soup with *Fufu Gaitu*	per serving	527	46 (35%)	43 (33%)	19 (32%)	—	—	5.1
22. Senegalese Fish	per serving	562	84 (60%)	34 (24%)	10 (16%)	1 (2%)	19	3.0
23. Congo Chicken *Moambe*	per serving	608	28 (18%)	43 (28%)	36 (54%)	9 (13%)	184	2.5
24. *Maffe* (Chicken with Peanut Butter Sauce)	per serving	638	47 (29%)	45 (28%)	30 (43%)	8 (11%)	184	2.9

Numbers in parentheses (%) indicate percentage of total calories contributed by nutrient.

MENUS
LOW CALORIE SPECIALTIES
(500 to 700 calories per meal)

WEST AFRICAN PEANUT SOUP
ROASTED PEPPER SALAD
MEALIE BREAD
Sliced Tangerines

TUNA FROM GABON (without rice)
SHELADA GHEZO-MAA ALCHIN
(CARROT SALAD WITH ORANGE)
Baked Apples
Kenyan Coffee

LONDOLOZI CABBAGE SALAD
Steamed Asparagus
GOLDEN SPICED RICE
ALMOND COOKIES
Hot Mint Tea

●

LOW CHOLESTEROL MENUS
(Less than 50 mgs. of cholesterol per meal)

GHANA LIGHT SOUP with
FUFU GAITU
Sliced Tomatoes
Fresh Mangos

LONDOLOZI CABBAGE SALAD
MEALIE BREAD
Curried Green Beans
Baked Pumpkin with Honey and
Ginger

TUNA FROM GABON
WEST AFRICAN LEMON RICE
Steamed Collard Greens
Dates and Papayas

●

LOW SATURATED FAT SELECTIONS
(Less than 8 grams of saturated fat per meal)

SENEGALESE FISH
Corn on the Cob with Safflower
Margarine
Sliced Oranges and Papayas
Hot Tea or Coffee

GHANA LIGHT SOUP with
CASSAVA FUFU
FRIED PLANTAINS

MINTED TOMATO SALAD WITH LEMON-PEPPER DRESSING
LABLABI (TUNISIAN CHICKPEA SOUP)
Pocket Bread
MOROCCAN MINT TEA

●

HIGH PROTEIN MEALS
(30 grams or more of protein per meal)

CONGO CHICKEN MOAMBE
ROASTED PEPPER SALAD
Fresh Pineapple
Hot Tea

LABLABI
(TUNISIAN CHICKPEA SOUP)
MOROCCAN BREAD
MOROCCAN ORANGE-DATE
SALAD
GOLDEN SPICED RICE
MELK TERT

MAFFE (CHICKEN WITH PEANUT BUTTER SAUCE)
Steamed Okra
PUMPKIN PUFFS
Chilled Apple Juice

●

WELL BALANCED LUNCH OR DINNER MENUS
(Selections that conform to recommendations in Dietary Goals for United States*)*

MOROCCAN ORANGE-DATE
SALAD
LABLABI (TUNISIAN CHICKPEA
SOUP)
ROASTED PEPPER SALAD
Apple Juice

MOROCCAN BREAD
SHELADA GHEZO-MAA ALCHIN
(CARROT SALAD WITH ORANGE)
SENEGALESE FISH
ALMOND COOKIES
Anise Tea

Fresh Fruit
WEST AFRICAN LEMON RICE
MAFFE (CHICKEN WITH PEANUT BUTTER SAUCE)
MELK TERT
Orange Spice Tea

CHAPTER 2

BRAZIL
The Manioc Connection

Culinary Essentials

Ethnic food adventurers in search of new gastronomic experiences will find Brazilian food original and full of zest. This diverse cuisine has a distinct West African and Portuguese accent. Unlike most South American kitchens, where tortillas and corn products reign, Brazilian cooking is rich with coconut milk, limes, black beans, hot peppers, and peanuts. Add to these lively ingredients the flavors of tropical fruits—bananas, papayas and avocados—and you have numerous possibilities for exuberant and eclectic creations.

Before tackling a Brazilian menu, take a trip to a Latin American grocery store and stock up on a few uncommon items that will give your dishes a distinct foreign flavor. For example, no Brazilian meal is complete without manioc,* a mealy grain derived from the cassava root. Brazilians sprinkle manioc over everything from soup to vegetables, much like Italians use Parmesan cheese. If unavailable, substitute dry farina or cream of wheat, lightly toasted in a low oven. *Dendê*, a heavy palm oil, provides the strong taste and golden hue that characterizes many Brazilian dishes. Because it is difficult to locate, even in Latin markets, we have substituted peanut or olive oil in our recipes. Although there is no equivalent replacement, you may simulate the intense orange-yellow color of *dendê* by adding a good-size pinch of turmeric and paprika to your cooking oil. When available, be sure to try this unusual taste enhancer in any Brazilian recipe (except desserts or salad dressings).

Manioc is sometimes found under the name gari.

Latin groceries also carry salt cod and dried shrimp, which are favored additions to a piquant seafood stew called *Vatapá*. Other ingredients— black beans, Brazil nuts, cornmeal, fresh coconuts, and papayas—are obtainable not only at the Latin stores, but also at large supermarkets.

The easiest way to give your meals an exotic slant is to use hearts of palm. These tender, pale-white spears, water-packed in cans, are available in most grocery and gourmet food stores. Although they are expensive, their delicate flavor and versatile asparagus-like texture merits a splurge. When drained, chilled, and sliced into thick rounds, hearts of palm make an excellent salad, especially combined with a mustard-accented vinaigrette dressing. Whole, they may be cloaked with cheese sauce or sprinkled with ground Brazil nuts. Whether puréed for soups or chopped into omelets, this intriguing vegetable is worthy of exploration.

Familiarity with Brazilian food products, as well as the technique for preparing coconut milk,* will help you undertake a host of new epicurean recipes with ease. To aid your cooking task, you will want a sieve or food mill for bean soups, a heavy cast-iron skillet for *Frigideira* ("skillet dishes"), a four-cup mold for rice flour or cornmeal puddings, and a springform pan for *Torta de Cebolas* (onion pie). Empadinhas tins, available at gourmet cooking shops under the name "petite or tartlet molds," are nice for savory pastries, but a standard twelve-cup muffin tin will suffice.

Anyone raised on mashed potatoes and frozen vegetables will find the profusion of Brazilian side dishes a fascinating affair. For example, *Farofa*, a light dish of manioc meal, butter, eggs, and chopped prunes is a fine escort for black bean or poultry dishes. Seafood fare can be enhanced by *Pirão de Arroz*, a chilled pudding of coconut milk and rice flour, shaped in a mold. For colorful contrast, you might complement your entrées with a tropical fruit salad, steamed okra or kale, baked pumpkin, or rice that is garnished with fresh tomatoes and fresh coriander leaves.

Cover your table with an old lace or embroidered tablecloth and scatter an assortment of green leaves across the center to simulate a typical Brazilian table setting. An attractive, yet simple hors d'oeuvre platter can be assembled with sardines, black olives, hard-boiled eggs, and Edam cheese. If you wish to serve bread, hard-crusted French bread or homemade cornbread is similar to popular Brazilian varieties. To give your plates a festive appearance, garnish them with grated beets, sliced sweet red peppers, avocado wedges, or pineapple chunks. And please, don't forget the manioc.

Seasoning Essentials

Brazilian foods are richer than they are highly seasoned and more pepper-hot than spicy. Creamy coconut milk, dried shrimp, garlic, fresh chili peppers, and parsley are the backbone of this sumptuously flavored cui-

---

*See Seasoning Chart.

sine. Common household herbs—basil, thyme and oregano—are rarely used in this cooking style, while sweet spices—cinnamon, cloves and ginger—are usually restricted to baked goods.

Coconut milk offers a fertile field for exhibiting your seasoning sense. A humdrum black bean dish can be turned into an esoteric one if you simmer the legumes in coconut milk. For seafood casseroles, try this cloudy, off-white liquid as a cooking stock in place of wine or broth. Brazilian cooks do this with *Vatapá*, a brilliant composition of coconut milk, fresh shrimp, peanuts, and cornmeal. You might also try substituting it for heavy cream in your favorite Latin American cream soup, pudding, cake, or creamed corn recipe. The results will be splendid for their delicacy of taste.

Nothing cools the sting of a hot pepper better than coconut milk, which explains why these two are often coupled together. The extremely hot peppers commonly used in Brazilian recipes are called *malagueta*. They are nearly impossible to find in this country and Tabasco sauce or *jalapeño* peppers (fresh or tinned) must be substituted. Traditionally, a dish of *malagueta* peppers and *dendê* oil* is offered with meals as a hot sauce. You can make a similar preparation by covering *jalapeño* peppers with olive oil. Spoon this lively mixture over cooked vegetables, beans, seafood, or poultry dishes, and you won't have to worry about seasoning the dish beforehand!

Brazilian dishes that do not employ hot peppers are intended to be appreciated for their own natural savor, unmasked by rich sauces, spices, or strong seasonings. You can always depend upon a few cloves of garlic, sautéed onions, chopped parsley, or freshly ground pepper to achieve a distinctive accent. If a little gusto is in order, we recommend a pinch of ground coriander seeds, cayenne pepper, dried red chili pepper, or a splash of *Brazilian Hot Sauce Blend*.

BRAZILIAN SEASONING CHART

BRAZILIAN HOT SAUCE BLEND can be used in any dish in need of a mild piquant addition, such as fish, chicken, beans, or vegetables. Covered and refrigerated, this slightly tangy blend will keep for up to 2 weeks.

Combine in a blender and purée until smooth:

    1 dozen fresh yellow chilies—blanched, rinsed, and seeded
    1 tablespoon fresh lime or lemon juice
    2 to 3 tablespoons *dendê*, peanut, or olive oil
    1 small garlic clove
      Salt to taste

---

*See Culinary Essentials

COCONUT MILK (Thick) is not to be confused with the milky liquid found inside a fresh coconut. This thick, creamy milk is made from the ground meat of fresh coconuts pulverized with water. Homemade coconut milk is the most flavorful, but canned coconut cream, available in large supermarkets, may be substituted for convenience.

To prepare ½ to 1 cup thick coconut milk: Use 1 large (2½-pound) coconut. Pierce the three "eyes" on the upper flat end and let the milk drain into a container. Reserve for another use. Place the coconut in a 350-degree oven for 15 minutes. Remove from oven, crack open with a hammer, and discard the shell. Trim away the brown skin and finely grate the white meat (this can be done in a blender if cut into small pieces). Place in a blender with ½ cup hot water or milk and pulverize at high speed. Strain liquid into a bowl through a large piece of dampened cheesecloth, squeezing as hard as possible to extract the juice. Or place in a fine-mesh strainer, set over a bowl, and press with the back of a spoon to extract liquid. The liquid is called *thick* coconut milk. Reserve grated meat to prepare *thin* coconut milk.

COCONUT MILK (Thin) yields a greater amount than thick coconut milk. First prepare thick coconut milk (above). Place reserved coconut meat in a saucepan with 2 cups hot water or milk. Bring to a quick boil, reduce heat, and cover with a lid. Simmer 30 minutes. Strain again as above. Yield: 1½ to 2 cups.

DRIED RED CHILI PEPPERS give zing to mildly flavored Brazilian dishes. Use ½ to 1 teaspoon of this piquant, coarsely ground capsicum to enliven black or white beans, black-eyed peas, cornmeal dishes, shrimp stews, and vegetables—such as *chayote* (a tropical squash), tomatoes, green peppers, and onions. Substitute equal amounts of Tabasco sauce when necessary.

DRIED SHRIMP have a pleasant, salty flavor and a somewhat fibrous texture. These miniature sea creatures are an important ingredient in *vatapá*, a chicken or seafood stew prepared with coconut milk, ground nuts, and hot peppers. Some recipes require that they first be soaked in warm water for 30 minutes and then pulverized in a blender or with a mortar and pestle. Add ½ to 1 cup of dried shrimp to any *vatapá* or black-eyed pea recipe. Dried shrimp are available at Latin American or oriental markets. To prepare your own, spread deveined shrimp (fresh, canned, or frozen and thawed) on a baking sheet. Place in a preheated 300-degree oven until thoroughly dried. Store in an airtight container.

GARLIC should be used discreetly in this cuisine, accenting other ingredients, but keeping its own identity somewhat anonymous. One minced clove of fresh garlic will add a delightful pungency to stuffed peppers, bean soups, kale, collard greens, okra, eggs, or Brazilian rice. A combination of fresh garlic, ground coriander seed, and pulverized hot peppers will give your Brazilian dishes a snappy disposition.

MALAGUETA **PEPPERS** are extremely hot and aromatic. They are frequently used in Brazilian cooking, but quite difficult to find in this country. When available, try them in any recipe that calls for hot peppers. Otherwise, use Tabasco or *jalapeño* peppers. It is best to pulverize any hot pepper in a blender or with a mortar and pestle before adding to a dish.

PARSLEY is not doomed as a garnish in Brazil. This freshly chopped addition is used liberally to season onion or shrimp pies, potato and egg dishes, *farofa*, hearts of palm, seafood casseroles, and poultry. The taste-enhancing properties of parsley can be improved by soaking it in a marinade of oil and lemon juice or sautéing it with onions and tomatoes. Italian flat-leaf parsley has a more robust personality than the decorative curly variety. Use the leaves and stems too, the latter having infinitely more flavor.

Other seasonings used in Brazilian cooking: nutmeg, cinnamon, coriander, bay leaf, ginger, cloves, orange-flower water, and sesame seeds.

Nutritional Essentials

Nutritionists might tear their hair in despair at the way a meal in Brazil is planned. There is seldom much regard given to what's good for you. Dishes tend to be hefty in calories and excessive in saturated fat. This cuisine does, however, offer many tempting gastronomic opportunities. And if you want to enjoy some of them without feeling that you're doing your body in, you must apply a little nutritional *savoir faire* to get around the dietary pitfalls.

Brazilian cookery, along with French cuisine, on the average, has more calories derived from saturated fat (about 19 percent) than any other cuisine represented in this book. This largely reflects the use of coconut milk in dishes such as *Pirão de Arroz* (Rice Flour Pudding) and *Feijão de Côco* (Black Beans with Coconut Milk). The saturated fat content of these dishes is a whopping 58 percent and 45 percent, respectively. Given this nutritional breakdown, it should be clear that Brazilian food is not for everyone, and certainly not for individuals who are trying to reduce their intake of fat and calories.

One way to avoid the potential excesses of Brazilian fare is to indulge in this cuisine only occasionally. But the selections are so delicious that this may be more difficult than it seems. As a compromise, accompany main courses with simple, low-calorie fruit or vegetable side dishes. *Fresh Fruit Ambrosia* is a mere 142 calories per serving and thanks to the papayas, is rich in vitamins A and C as well. And rather than making two or three rich Brazilian dishes for a single meal, select only one and serve it with a piece of fruit, *Steamed Rice*, or *Brazilian Fruit Salad*.

What about vegetables? While Brazilian cooks eschew the heavy use of this foodstuff, they do occasionally employ three unusual varieties: hearts of palm, kale, and okra. Hearts of palm, the young terminal bud of a tropical palm tree, is a popular vegetable in Brazil. Because it is available fresh in the United States only in Florida, generally only canned hearts of palm are known to North American kitchens. These creamy white cylinders are about 40 percent protein, which is quite substantial for a member of the vegetable group. Sample this tasty food in *Saladas de Palmitos #1* when you want a salad that is quite moderate in the calorie and saturated-fat department.

Kale, a hardy-leafed green that can be cooked like spinach, is a primitive member of the cabbage family. Distinguished by its rich Vitamin A, calcium, and iron content, these curly greens are comparable to broccoli and corn in their protein content. Okra, a pod vegetable, can be steamed and served as a low-calorie side dish with almost any Brazilian meal.

It is worth enjoying the unique flavors of *Fish Moqueca*, which at 340 calories and 40 grams of protein, supplies almost the total daily recommended protein allowance. Cheese-rich dishes such as *Potato and Cheese Frigideira* and the wonderful Brazilian dessert or side dish *Bananas Assadas Com Queijo* also provide plenty of usable protein, the latter at the expense of 450 calories.

Farina, a commonly used substitute for *manioc* meal, is the grain staple for Brazilian cooking as it is practiced in this country. Similar to wheat flour in protein composition, but higher in calcium and phosphorus, farina can be used to complement the protein in bean, nut, and cheese dishes. Sprinkle lightly over *Vatapá* (Shrimp and Coconut Stew) and *Feijão de Côco* to boost the usable protein content.

ARROZ BRASILEIRO
(Brazilian Rice)   *YIELD: 6 servings*

2 tablespoons peanut oil or safflower margarine
1 small onion, minced
1 clove garlic, minced
1½ cups uncooked long-grain rice
2 tomatoes, peeled, seeded, and chopped

3 cups boiling water or vegetable stock
1 teaspoon salt
1 bay leaf
Lemon wedges for garnish
Chopped fresh coriander leaves for garnish—optional

Heat oil in a 2-quart saucepan. Sauté the onion and garlic until transparent, but not browned. Add the rice and stir constantly until rice is hot. Add the tomatoes, boiling water or stock, salt, and bay leaf. Boil 5 minutes, cover, and reduce heat to low. Simmer until rice is tender and water is absorbed. Remove from heat and let stand, covered, several minutes. Remove bay leaf. Fluff with a fork, transfer to a serving dish, and surround with lemon wedges and fresh coriander.

BANANAS ASSADAS COM QUEIJO
(Baked Bananas with Cheese)   *YIELD: 4 servings*

4 large, ripe (but firm) bananas
1 tablespoon melted safflower margarine or butter
½ cup brown sugar
½ cup grated Parmesan or cheddar cheese

1 cup light cream or milk
2 tablespoons brown sugar
2 large well-beaten eggs
1 teaspoon cinnamon
⅓ teaspoon nutmeg

1. Preheat oven to 325 degrees. Peel bananas and slice in half lengthwise. Lay cut-side down in a shallow, oblong baking dish. Pour melted margarine over bananas. Combine ½ cup brown sugar with cheese and sprinkle over bananas. Combine cream with 2 tablespoons brown sugar and beaten eggs. Pour mixture over bananas, making sure bananas are well coated. Sprinkle cinnamon and nutmeg over the top.
2. Place in the oven and bake for 20 minutes. Spoon banana halves into individual serving bowls (allow two halves per person) and serve immediately as a side dish or light dessert.
Variation: For a more festive dish, top bananas with finely ground peanuts, toasted chopped Brazil nuts, or grated coconut. Or, for dessert, top each serving with a scoop of vanilla ice cream.

CREME DE ABACATE
(Avocado Cream Dessert)

2 large ripe avocados, chilled
4 tablespoons fresh lime juice
4 tablespoons confectioners' sugar

1 large scoop vanilla ice cream
Lime wedges for garnish

Peel, seed, and slice avocados. Whip the avocados on low speed in a blender with the lime juice, sugar, and ice cream. Pour into chilled sherbet glasses or dessert dishes. Serve immediately or chill, but do not freeze. Garnish each glass with a lime wedge. Do not prepare too far in advance because the avocados will darken.

Variation: For *Banana Cream*—Substitute 4 large, ripe, mashed bananas for the avocados and replace the lime juice with lemon juice. If desired, add 2 tablespoons rum to either the Banana or Avocado Cream.

EMPADINHAS DE CAMARÃO
(Shrimp Patties)

Pastry:
2½ cups all-purpose flour (may use part whole wheat flour)
½ cup vegetable shortening, melted
½ teaspoon salt
1½ teaspoons water
3 egg yolks, well-beaten
4 to 6 tablespoons cold milk
3 egg whites (set aside)

Filling:
3 tablespoons peanut oil
1 small onion, minced
2 or 3 cloves garlic, minced
½ to ¾ pound baby shrimp
2 tomatoes, diced
Salt and freshly ground pepper to taste
¼ teaspoon cayenne pepper or to taste
3 teaspoons cornstarch
2 or 3 spears hearts of palm or cooked asparagus, diced
2 eggs, well beaten
¼ cup grated Parmesan cheese

1. *To prepare pastry*: Place the flour in a large mixing bowl. Add the melted shortening. Combine the salt, water, and egg yolks, and stir into the flour. Add the milk, a few tablespoons at a time, until the flour is moistened and dough almost cleans the sides of the bowl. Gather into a ball, wrap in plastic, and refrigerate 30 minutes. Meanwhile prepare the filling.

2. *To prepare filling*: Heat oil in a 9-inch skillet and sauté the onion and garlic. Add the shrimp, tomatoes, and seasonings. Cover and simmer 15 minutes. Dissolve cornstarch in a little water and add to shrimp mixture, stirring well. Add hearts of palm or asparagus and remove skillet from stove. Stir in 2 beaten eggs. Taste and adjust seasonings. Let cool before filling pastries.

3. *To assemble empadinhas*: Roll out pastry as thinly as possible on a lightly floured board with a lightly floured rolling pin. With a knife or jar lid, cut out rounds 1 inch larger than the cups of a standard 12-cup muffin tin or imported *empadinhas* tin. If pastry is crumbly you may pat each round in the palm of your hand. Press rounds firmly into the muffin cups leaving a little overhang. Fill ¾-full with shrimp mixture and top each filling with 1 teaspoon grated Parmesan cheese. Cover each with a pastry round, pinching the edges together with your fingers. Flute the edges as you would a pie crust or flatten the rim with the tines of a fork dipped in water.
4. Preheat oven to 375 degrees.
5. Beat the egg whites well and brush lightly over each pastry. Bake in preheated oven 20 minutes or until nicely browned. Let cool slightly before serving.
Variations: Instead of Parmesan cheese, each filling may be topped with a slice of hard-boiled egg and a slice of black olive. Tuna or crabmeat may be substituted for the shrimp. Butter may be substituted for half of the shortening.

FAROFA
(Toasted Manioc Meal)   *YIELD: 6 to 8 servings*

---

1 stick safflower margarine or butter
2 eggs, well beaten

1½ cups *manioc* flour or farina
2 tablespoons chopped, pitted prunes

Melt margarine in a large skillet over medium heat. Add eggs and stir frequently until they are soft scrambled. Add *manioc* or farina, reduce heat to low, and stir frequently until toasted, about 8 minutes. Stir in chopped prunes. Serve hot or at room temperature as a side dish or accompaniment to *Feijão de Côco* (the following recipe) or any black bean dish. *Farofa* can also be used as a stuffing for chicken or turkey.

FEIJÃO DE CÔCO
(Black Beans with Coconut Milk)   *YIELD: Approximately 12 half-cup servings*

---

2 cups (1 pound) black beans, soaked overnight
1 large onion, chopped
2 to 3 cloves garlic, crushed
1 tomato, peeled, seeded, and coarsely chopped
2 tablespoons chopped parsley

¼ cup olive oil, divided
Thick coconut milk*
1 teaspoon Tabasco sauce or 1 small hot pepper, pulverized
Salt and freshly ground pepper to taste

*See Seasoning Chart.

1. Pick over beans for stones and wash well. Add enough cold water to cover and soak overnight.
2. Drain water off beans and place them in a heavy 2½-quart saucepan. Add enough fresh water to cover an inch above the beans. Bring to a boil, reduce heat, and simmer 2 hours or until tender. Add boiling water as needed while cooking to maintain about one quart of liquid.
3. In a large skillet, sauté the onion, garlic, tomato, and parsley in 2 tablespoons of the oil. Remove 1 cup of beans, along with a little liquid, and add to the skillet over medium heat. With the back of a large spoon, mash the beans with the vegetables until thick and smooth. Return skillet mixture to saucepan, stir well, and simmer about 30 minutes.
4. While beans are simmering, prepare thick coconut milk according to the directions given at the beginning of this chapter.
5. Mash and press beans through a coarse sieve or food mill until mixture resembles a thin purée. Any beans that do not press through may be saved for *Frijoles Refritos* (p. 279). Add the remaining 2 tablespoons of olive oil, thick coconut milk, and Tabasco or hot pepper to the purée. Season liberally with salt and freshly ground pepper.
6. *To serve*: Spoon purée into soup bowls and serve hot or cold as a first course accompanied by *Farofa* (preceding recipe) if desired. Leftovers may be refrigerated and reheated.
Note: *Feijão de Côco* may be made a day or two in advance, or follow directions through step 2, refrigerate beans, and continue recipe the day you wish to serve it.

FRESH FRUIT AMBROSIA   *YIELD: 6 servings*

---

2 ripe papayas, peeled, seeded, and sliced
1 fresh pineapple, peeled, cored, and cut into chunks
2 ripe bananas, sliced
2 or 3 plums, sliced

½ to ¾ cup freshly squeezed orange juice
1 tablespoon orange liqueur—optional
Mint leaves for garnish

Combine fruits, orange juice, and liqueur. Place in 6 individual chilled dessert bowls and garnish each with mint leaves.
Variations: Add any of the following: ¼ cup unsweetened coconut, ¼ cup chopped Brazil nuts, ¼ cup chopped pitted prunes, or wheat germ to sprinkle over the top.

MOUSSE DE CASTANHAS-DO-PARÁ E CHOCOLATE
(Brazil Nut Chocolate Mousse) YIELD: 6 servings

6 ounces semisweet chocolate
pieces
2 ounces water
1 ounce Grand Marnier liqueur
4 large egg yolks
½ cup superfine sugar

½ cup heavy cream, whipped
½ cup finely ground Brazil nuts,
toasted
4 large egg whites, at room
temperature
Pinch of salt

1. Place the chocolate pieces, water, and liqueur in the top of a double boiler over hot, not boiling, water. When chocolate is almost melted, remove from heat and stir until smooth. Transfer to a large bowl and set aside to cool.
2. Beat egg yolks in a large mixing bowl, gradually adding sugar in a thin stream. Continue beating until mixture is a thick, pale-lemon color, and ribbons fall back to the surface when mixture is lifted. Combine with melted chocolate, beating well with a wire whisk. Fold in whipped heavy cream and Brazil nuts.
3. In a clean, dry bowl with clean beaters, beat the egg whites on low speed until frothy. Add the pinch of salt and beat on high speed until stiff peaks form. Carefully fold ¼ of the egg whites into the chocolate mixture to lighten it. Spoon remaining whites on top and gently fold into mousse. Divide mixture evenly into 6 dessert bowls or stemmed glasses and chill overnight, or for at least 5 hours before serving.

FISH MOQUECA
(Fish with Lemon-Pepper Sauce) YIELD: Serves 6

6 coriander seeds or 1 teaspoon
ground coriander
1 small onion, chopped
1 small hot pepper such as *jalapeño*
or *serrano*, chopped
1 clove garlic
2 tomatoes, peeled, seeded, and
chopped
1 teaspoon salt

Juice of 1 large lemon
2½ pounds white fish fillets, cut into
1-inch pieces
¼ cup peanut or olive oil
¼ cup water
Paprika
Steamed Rice (p. 52)
1 lemon cut into wedges for
garnish
Fresh parsley sprigs for garnish

1. *To make marinade*: Purée coriander seeds, onion, hot pepper, garlic, tomatoes, salt, and lemon juice in a blender. Lay fish in a shallow 9- by 13-inch dish, cover with marinade, and let stand 1 hour.
2. Place fish in marinade in a deep saucepan or a Dutch oven. Add the oil, water, and paprika. Cook covered over moderately low heat until the fish

flakes easily when tested with a fork—about 5 to 8 minutes. Taste marinade to see if it needs more salt.

3. *To serve*: Transfer to a heated platter and surround with Steamed Rice. Garnish with lemon wedges and fresh parsley.

PIRÃO DE ARROZ
(Rice Flour Pudding)   *YIELD: 4 to 6 servings*

Thick coconut milk*	**½ teaspoon salt**
Thin coconut milk*	**¾ cup rice flour**
*See Seasoning Chart	

1. Prepare thick and thin coconut milk, according to directions given at the beginning of this chapter, and combine the two liquids together. Measure out 2½ cups and save any remaining liquid for another use.

2. Place half the coconut milk (1¼ cups) and the salt in a heavy 2-quart saucepan. Beat remaining coconut milk (1¼ cups) and rice flour together until smooth; set aside. Heat coconut milk and salt over low heat until very hot, but not boiling, stirring frequently. Using a wooden spoon, stir in the coconut milk-rice flour mixture. Cook over low heat, stirring constantly, until mixture comes away from the sides of the pan and holds its shape. Spoon into a well-greased bowl, 4-cup mold, or individual 1-cup molds. Refrigerate until chilled. Unmold and serve cold as an accompaniment to piping-hot *Vatapá* (p. 54) or any seafood stew.

Variations: 1. Replace coconut milk with 2½ cups water. Combine all ingredients in a blender until smooth. Cook as directed above.

2. To prepare *Pirão de Milho* (Corn Pudding): Replace coconut milk with 2½ cups water. Replace rice flour with corn flour. Combine all ingredients in a blender until smooth. Cook as directed above. When corn pudding holds its shape, beat in 1 tablespoon softened safflower margarine or butter before pouring into the molds.

POTATO AND CHEESE FRIGIDEIRA
(Brazilian Skillet Dish)   *YIELD: 8 servings*

---

1 pound red cooking potatoes	**1 cup grated Edam or Muenster**
2 large yellow onions, thinly sliced	**cheese, divided**
4 tablespoons peanut oil, divided	**1 large tomato, sliced**
2 cloves garlic, pressed	**5 large eggs**
1 teaspoon paprika	**¼ to ½ teaspoon dried red chili**
Salt and freshly ground pepper to	**peppers or cayenne pepper**
taste	**Salt to taste**
½ cup chopped fresh parsley	**Sliced black olives for garnish—**
	optional

1. Place potatoes in a large saucepan and add enough water to cover. Bring water to a boil and cook over medium heat until tender—about 20 minutes.
2. Meanwhile, in a large skillet over moderate heat, lightly brown the onions in 1 or 2 tablespoons of the peanut oil. Remove from skillet and set aside. Drain water off potatoes, peel if desired, place in a large bowl, and coarsely chop. Add garlic and paprika.
3. Heat remaining peanut oil in a large skillet over moderate heat and lightly brown potatoes. Season with salt and freshly ground pepper. Remove from skillet, combine with parsley and ½ cup of the grated cheese. Set aside.
4. Preheat oven to 350 degrees.
5. Place potato-cheese mixture in a well-greased 2-quart casserole dish. Cover with browned onions. Place the tomato slices over the onions. Beat together the eggs and dried chili pepper until frothy. Add salt to taste. Pour egg mixture evenly over the tomato slices and top with remaining ½ cup grated cheese.
6. Bake in a preheated oven for 35 minutes or until eggs are set. Let cool five minutes before serving. Garnish with sliced black olives.

SALADA DE BRASILEIRO
(Brazilian Salad)   *YIELD: 4 to 6 servings*

½ cup seedless grapes
½ cup sliced bananas
½ cup diced apple
½ cup diced celery

½ cup chopped walnuts
6 tablespoons safflower
  mayonnaise
2 tablespoons light cream
Juice of ½ lemon

Combine the grapes, bananas, apple, celery, and walnuts. Thin out mayonnaise with the cream and lemon juice. Toss with fruit. Chill before serving.

SALADA DE PALMITO
(Hearts of Palm Salad #1)   *YIELD: 4 small servings*

---

1 14-ounce can hearts of palm,
  chilled
1 tablespoon fresh lime or lemon
  juice

5 teaspoons olive oil
1 tablespoon Dijon mustard
½ teaspoon salt (or to taste)
Freshly ground pepper to taste

Drain hearts of palm thoroughly. Cut each spear diagonally into ½-inch pieces. Combine the lime or lemon juice, olive oil, mustard, salt, and pepper. Beat well with a fork. Toss with hearts of palm and serve immediately.

SALADA DE PALMITO
(Hearts of Palm Salad #2)   YIELD: *6 servings*

---

1 14-ounce can hearts of palm, chilled

1 small green pepper, seeded and sliced into rings

1 small sweet red bell pepper, seeded and sliced into rings

6 thinly sliced red onion rings

2 hard-boiled eggs, quartered

1 tomato, cut into wedges

1 ripe avocado, peeled and sliced—optional

¼ cup olive oil

¼ cup peanut oil

2 tablespoons freshly-squeezed lime or lemon juice

1 tablespoon Dijon mustard

Salt and freshly ground pepper to taste

Thoroughly drain hearts of palm and slice into bite-size pieces. Combine with green and red peppers, red onion, hard-boiled eggs, tomato, and avocado. Place the oils, lime or lemon juice, mustard, salt, and pepper in a screw-top jar. Shake vigorously until well blended. Combine with salad ingredients and serve immediately.

STEAMED RICE   YIELD: *6 servings*

1½ cups raw rice

3 cups cold water

1 teaspoon salt

2 teaspoons safflower margarine or butter—optional

Combine all the ingredients in a 3-quart saucepan. Place over high heat and bring to a boil. Reduce heat to low, stir rice one time, cover with a tight-fitting lid, and simmer until all the liquid is absorbed—from 12 to 15 minutes.

TORTA DE CEBOLAS
(Onion Pie)

YIELD: 10 slices

Pie Dough:
1¼ cups cornstarch
  Pinch of salt
 1 cup whole-wheat or all-purpose
  flour (may use part rice or potato
  flour)
⅔ cup chilled safflower margarine
  or butter
 3 large, well-beaten eggs

Filling:
 3 tablespoons safflower margarine
  or peanut oil
 2 pounds yellow onions, thinly
  sliced
  Salt, freshly ground pepper, and
  nutmeg to taste
 4 large eggs
1½ cups milk or light cream
 1 tablespoon cornstarch
 1 teaspoon dry mustard
½ teaspoon salt
½ cup chopped fresh parsley
  Parmesan cheese for topping
  Fresh parsley sprigs for garnish

1. *To prepare crust*: Sift together the cornstarch, salt, and flour into a large mixing bowl. Using a pastry blender, or two knives, cut in the margarine or butter until the mixture is coarse. Add the beaten eggs, a little at a time, while tossing and mixing with a fork. When all is lightly moistened, gather dough into a smooth ball. Chill about 15 minutes.

2. Tear off two large pieces of waxed paper. Dust one piece with a little flour. Place the dough in the center and flatten it slightly. Dust the top of the dough with flour. Place another piece of waxed paper on top of the dough and roll out with a rolling pin. Line the bottom and sides of a spring form pan with the dough (see *Never-Fail Pie Crust* Step 3, p. 380).

3. *To prepare filling*: Heat the oil or margarine in a large skillet over medium heat. Add half the onions and sauté until transparent. Season liberally with salt, pepper, and nutmeg. Transfer to a plate to cool. Repeat process with remaining onions, adding more oil or margarine if necessary.

4. Preheat oven to 350 degrees.

5. Beat together the eggs, milk or cream, cornstarch, dry mustard, salt, and parsley. Distribute onions evenly over the dough in the bottom of pan. Pour egg mixture over onions. Cover with a fairly thick layer of Parmesan cheese. Bake in oven until knife inserted comes out clean—about 40 minutes.

6. *To serve*: Remove pie from oven and let stand at least 5 minutes before cutting. Serve hot as a main dish or cut into thin wedges and serve as an appetizer. Garnish the inner rim of the pie with fresh parsley sprigs.

VATAPÁ
(Brazilian Shrimp and Coconut Stew) YIELD: *4 to 6 servings*

½ cup grated coconut
1 cup milk
1 tablespoon peanut or olive oil
1 onion, chopped
2 cloves garlic, minced
2 fresh, hot chili peppers, seeded and chopped
2 cups water
1 bay leaf
½ pound boned white fish fillets or salt cod* (See Note)

½ pound fresh shrimp, shelled and deveined
Salt and freshly ground pepper to taste
3 ounces dried shrimp*—optional
1 cup ground peanuts, toasted
¼ cup yellow cornmeal
2 tablespoons safflower margarine or butter
1 tomato, peeled, seeded, and chopped

Available at Latin American markets.

1. *To make coconut milk:* In a small saucepan bring the grated coconut and milk to a boil. Remove from heat and let stand 30 minutes. Strain through a cheesecloth-lined colander or fine-mesh strainer, catching liquid in a bowl. With the back of a large spoon, press coconut shreds against the sides of the colander to extract as much liquid as possible. Discard shreds and set milk aside.

2. In a large pot, heat the oil over medium heat and sauté the chopped onion and garlic. Add chili peppers, water, and bay leaf. Cut fish into 2-inch pieces and add to pot along with fresh shrimp, salt, and pepper. Bring mixture to a boil, reduce heat to low, and simmer, uncovered, for 10 minutes. Remove from heat. Strain stock and reserve liquid. In a separate bowl, set aside the fish mixture.

3. Bring reserved coconut milk to a boil in a 2-quart saucepan. Add the dried shrimp, ground toasted nuts, cornmeal, and reserved fish stock, stirring continuously. Reduce heat to low and cook 10 minutes longer, stirring frequently. Return to soup pot along with reserved fish mixture, margarine, and tomato. Serve hot in deep bowls accompanied by *Pirão de Arroz* (p. 50) or *Steamed Rice* (p. 52).

Note: Salt cod must be soaked in water (to cover) at least 6 to 8 hours or overnight. Change soaking water several times, drain, and rinse well before using.

BRAZIL/RECIPE ANALYSIS CHART

Name of Recipe	Quantity	Calories	CHO gms.	Protein gms.	Total Fat gms.	Saturated Fat gms.	Cholesterol mg.	Dietary Fiber gms.
1. Fresh Fruit Ambrosia	per serving	142	32 (90%)	2 (6%)	1 (4%)	—	—	1.8
2. Steamed Rice	per serving	164	37 (90%)	4 (10%)	—	—	—	.10
3. *Arroz Brasileiro* (Brazilian Rice)	per serving	168	28 (66%)	3 (7%)	5 (27%)	1 (5%)	—	.5
4. *Salada de Palmito* (Hearts of Palm Salad #1)	per serving	177	4 (9%)	2 (5%)	17 (86%)	2 (10%)	—	.9
5. *Salada de Brasileiro*	per serving	202	8 (16%)	2 (4%)	18 (80%)	2 (9%)	2	.7
6. Potato and Cheese *Frigideira*	per serving	227	13 (23%)	10 (18%)	15 (59%)	5 (20%)	209	.9
7. *Farofa*	per serving	233	24 (41%)	5 (9%)	13 (50%)	2 (8%)	78	.2
8. *Creme de Abacate* (Avocado Cream Dessert)	per serving	260	21 (32%)	3 (5%)	18 (63%)	2 (7%)	8	2.1
9. *Pirão de Arroz* (Rice Flour Pudding)	per serving	264	17 (26%)	4 (6%)	20 (68%)	17 (58%)	—	—
10. *Empadinhas de Camarão* (Shrimp Patties)	per serving	276	22 (32%)	11 (16%)	16 (52%)	4 (13%)	15	.3
11. *Salada de Palmito* (Hearts of Palm Salad #2)	per serving	298	11 (15%)	5 (7%)	26 (78%)	3 (9%)	105	1.8
12. Fish *Moqueca*	per serving	300	8 (11%)	40 (53%)	12 (36%)	1 (3%)	25	.5
13. *Vatapá*	per serving	360	15 (17%)	21 (23%)	24 (60%)	8 (20%)	52	.7
14. *Torta de Cebolas* (Onion Pie)	per serving	366	33 (36%)	10 (11%)	22 (53%)	6 (15%)	224	.8

Name of Recipe	Quantity	Calories	CHO gms.	Protein gms.	Total Fat gms.	Saturated Fat gms.	Choles- terol mg.	Dietary Fiber gms.
15. *Feijão de Côco* (Black Beans with Coconut Milk)	per serving	399	32 (32%)	11 (11%)	25 (57%)	20 (45%)	—	4.5
16. *Bananas Assadas com Queijo* (Baked Bananas with Cheese)	per serving	450	60 (53%)	14 (12%)	17 (35%)	8 (16%)	183	1.0
17. *Mousse de Castanhas-do-Pará e Chocolate* (Brazil Nut Chocolate Mousse)	per serving	508	26 (20%)	11 (9%)	40 (71%)	17 (30%)	237	1.2

Numbers in parentheses (%) indicate percentage of total calories contributed by nutrient.

MENUS
LOW CALORIE SPECIALTIES
(500 to 700 calories per meal)

SALADA DE PALMITO
(HEARTS OF PALM SALAD #1)
FISH MOQUECA
STEAMED RICE
Watermelon

SALADA DE BRASILEIRO
EMPADINHAS DE CAMARÃO
(SHRIMP PATTIES)
Steamed Kale with Lemon Wedges
Sliced Bananas with Prunes
Brazilian Coffee

Red and Green Pepper Rings
POTATO AND CHEESE FRIGIDEIRA
Steamed Okra
CREME DE ABACATE (AVOCADO CREAM)
Hot Tea with Lemon

•

LOW CHOLESTEROL MENUS
(Less than 50 mgs. of cholesterol per meal)

Baked Red Snapper Garnished with
Sliced Tangerines
SALADA DE BRASILEIRO
Sliced Papayas
Brazilian Coffee

FEIJÃO DE CÔCO (BLACK BEANS
WITH COCONUT MILK)
French Bread
Sliced Tomatoes Garnished with
Coriander Leaves
Fresh Pineapple

FISH MOQUECA
Sliced Avocados with Lime
Baked Bananas with Rum
Orange Spice Tea

•

LOW SATURATED FAT SELECTIONS
(Less than 8 grams of saturated fat per meal)

TORTA DE CEBOLAS (ONION PIE)
ARROZ BRASILEIRO
(BRAZILIAN RICE)
Baked Pumpkin with Honey and
Ginger
Sliced Mangos with Orange Liqueur
Yerba Maté Tea

FISH MOQUECA
Baked Squash with Cinnamon
STEAMED RICE
CREME DE ABACATE
(AVOCADO CREAM)

FRESH FRUIT AMBROSIA
EMPADINHAS DE CAMARÃO
(SHRIMP PATTIES)
FAROFA
Brazilian Coffee

HIGH PROTEIN MEALS
(30 or more grams of protein per meal)

FAROFA
TORTA DE CEBOLAS (ONION PIE)
FRESH FRUIT AMBROSIA
BANANAS ASSADAS COM
QUEIJO (BAKED BANANAS WITH
CHEESE)

FEIJÃO DE CÔCO (BLACK BEANS
WITH COCONUT MILK)
POTATO AND CHEESE
FRIGIDEIRA
Sliced Oranges
MOUSSE DE CASTANHA DE PARÁ
E CHOCOLATE (BRAZIL NUT
CHOCOLATE MOUSSE)

SALADA DE PALMITO (HEARTS OF PALM SALAD #2)
VATAPÁ
PIRÃO DE ARROZ (RICE FLOUR PUDDING)
Sliced Apples and Plums

•

WELL BALANCED LUNCH OR DINNER MENUS
(Selections that conform to recommendations in Dietary Goals for United States)

FISH MOQUECA
STEAMED RICE
BANANAS ASSADAS COM
QUEIJO (BAKED BANANAS WITH
CHEESE)
Red Wine

ARROZ BRASILEIRO
(BRAZILIAN RICE)
TORTA DE CEBOLAS (ONION PIE)
Sliced Guavas with Neufchâtel
Cheese
Yerba Maté Tea

EMPADINHAS DE CAMARÃO
(SHRIMP PATTIES)
STEAMED RICE
FRESH FRUIT AMBROSIA
Brazilian Coffee

CHAPTER 3

CHILE AND PERU
Pick a Pack of Peppers

Culinary Essentials

Anyone who extols the wonders of Mexican food will surely want to delve into the splendors of Chilean and Peruvian cooking. Like Mexican cuisine, these two culinary styles will lure you into the seductive world of chili peppers and coriander leaves, fiery bean stews and tropical fruit. But the similarity stops there! Don't expect to find enchiladas or refried beans in the kitchens of Chile and Peru.

European-influenced Chilean dishes are stimulating yet refined. Unique sauces made of chili peppers, coriander leaves, or reddish-orange *achiote* seeds* lend distinction to this enticing cuisine. When you cook Chilean-style, expect to find lemony string bean salads, creamy corn custards, and savory pastries filled with chicken, raisins, and onions. The more assertive Peruvian cuisine will flavor your table with spicy walnut sauces, sparkling seafood casseroles, and unique garnishes such as marinated red-onion rings and sliced sweet potatoes. Combine ideas from both of these intriguing styles and you'll be able to prepare unbeatable South American meals.

Despite the fact that a few South American food products are unavailable in the United States, Chilean and Peruvian dishes are easily adaptable to American kitchens. Cooking techniques are familiar ones, and the required utensils fall into the "basics" category—heavy skillets, a blender, soup pot, etc. Staples such as potatoes, corn, avocados, and nuts can be easily obtained at most stores. If perchance there is a Latin American market nearby, you might find imported cheeses such as creamy-soft *Queso*

*See Seasoning Chart.

Blanco or *Quesillo*, a salty table cheese. If these are not available, you will find mozzarella, Muenster, Parmesan, or Gruyère acceptable cooking cheeses for these cuisines.

Fish fanciers in search of innovative ways to prepare their favorite sea creatures need not look any further—the cookery of Chile and Peru is replete with novel seafood recipes that are appropriate for both festive and everyday occasions. Although some of the commonly-used Latin seafoods such as abalone, corbina, and *congrio* are either unavailable or difficult to obtain in the United States, you will find sea bass, scallops, sole, or flounder eminently satisfying for a South American repast.

Soup enthusiasts will enjoy *Caldillo de Congria*, a stewlike potage of considerable elegance. In this easy-to-assemble preparation, fillet of sole (which can be substituted for the native *congrio*) is draped over potatoes and tomatoes and simmered in a fragrant broth laced with wine—a splendid food. *Seviche*, an intriguing salad of raw fish "cooked" in lemon and lime juice, will appeal to those who like stimulating flavors. Accented with chili peppers, red onions and garlic, *Seviche* almost explodes in your mouth, though a nibble of the sweet potato garnish will help dampen the fire.

Excursions into Chilean and Peruvian cooking are bound to please the avid potato eater. As in most South American kitchens, this vegetable is more than something to mash and slather with gravy in the name of leftovers. You will find the white-meated varieties invaluable for salads, soups, and side dishes. The more picturesque sweet potato can be enlisted as a colorful and edible garnish. When you want to transform the humble potato into a pièce de résistance, try *Papas a la Huancaina*—Peru's most famous dish. A luxurious sauce of cheese, chilies, and lemon juice is the hallmark of this culinary showpiece; marinated red-onion rings, black olives, and red bell peppers provide the embellishing touches.

To convey an authentic ambiance for a combined Chilean-Peruvian meal, place a loaf of hard-crusted French bread on your table alongside a bowl of *Pebre*, a coriander-thick hot sauce essential to the overall liveliness of the food. For a colorful centerpiece, arrange straw flowers and an assortment of gourds in a flat wicker basket. A dish of fresh chili peppers (*ají*) is always present along with a bottle of dry red wine.

Commence the meal with *entradas* or appetizers, such as raisin-studded *Chicken Empañadas* (baked turnovers) or *Humitas*, corn-filled corn husks folded and tied like a parcel package and steamed until tender. The next two courses in a full-dress feast are soup and salad. For a simple entrée, you might serve a fluffy *Tortilla de Platanos* (Banana Omelet) or perhaps *Picante de Camarones*, a spicy shrimp stew augmented with green peppers and tomatoes. On more convivial occasions, consider *Ají de Gallina*, a highly unusual chicken stew with a coarse, stringy texture and red-orange color. When tossed with Parmesan cheese and a spicy walnut sauce, this dish takes on a marvelous piquancy that belies its odd appearance.

Dessert can range from a simple platter of fresh fruit to *Mil Hojas*, a hedonistic concoction that boasts sixteen thin layers of pastry spread with apricot preserves and thick cream. On the modest side, there is *Arroz con Leche*, a sweet, creamed rice pudding scented with vanilla and cinnamon. A rich brew of South American coffee beans or a cup of *Yerba Maté* tea is the appropriate beverage to conclude the meal. Instant coffee, to put it kindly, would be heretical to a discerning South American palate.

Seasoning Essentials

The foods of Chile and Peru are spicy, but not so much as to alarm a bashful palate. Chili peppers and fresh coriander provide the key flavors while limes, basil, and oregano add sparkle and zest. Although you can toss these seasonings into a simmering soup or casserole just like any other taste enhancer, you can also employ them in special pastes and condiments unique to these cuisines.

One of the most popular enliveners for Chilean food is *colór*, an orange-tinted oil with a mild but distinctive flavor. *Colór* is not something you purchase, but is rather a mixture you make yourself by simmering *achiote* seeds or paprika in hot oil. (Complete instructions are given in the *Seasoning Chart*.) You might say that *colór* is to the Chilean cook what soy sauce is to the Chinese. Its ability to add taste, eye appeal, and authenticity to bean stews, poultry, and soups is unrivaled.

Some cooks like to have several varieties of *colór* on hand for different dishes. If you're feeling adventurous, you can concoct several batches, each with a distinctive flavor: Simmer a few dried red peppers in one batch to make "hot *colór*" for fiery dishes, or add a clove of garlic to another for a "pungent *colór*."

If you have a passion for incendiary flavors, *Red Chili Paste* will help set your world on fire. This homemade blend (see *Seasoning Chart*) of dried red chili peppers, garlic, oil, and stock can be used in place of fresh chilies in most Chilean or Peruvian recipes. When sauces, shrimp stews, or *empañada* fillings are in need of depth and drama, you can add a small amount of this lively mixture. Or as an alternative, you can place a bowl of *Red Chili Paste* on your dinner table and let everyone season their own dish to taste. Those who want their paste to have more flavor than heat may substitute half the amount of dried red peppers with sweet red bell peppers.

When working with fresh hot chilies, wear rubber gloves to protect your skin from these volatile peppers. With dried chilies, rubber gloves are not a necessity, but you should wash your hands well with soap and water after touching them. With either variety, be sure not to touch your eyes, since the burning sensation that will ensue is quite discomforting.

To prepare fresh chilies, place them under cold running water, pull out the stem, and break them in half. Brush out the seeds and discard. If desired, trim away any fleshy ribs inside. Bear in mind that the seeds are the hottest part and you may want to leave a few in for fiery dishes. Canned green chilies should be rinsed in cold water to remove the brine in which they are packed. Like fresh chilies, they may be seeded and stemmed before they are used. Whole dried red chili peppers should be diced and soaked in boiling water to cover 30 minutes before they are used.

Of course, not all Chilean and Peruvian dishes are seasoned with hot peppers, chili paste, or exotic *achiote* seeds. Many creations take their character from common flavorings such as limes, lemons, oregano, and basil. If showering foods with various herbs is your *tour de force*, you will want to have the *Peruvian Herb Blend* on hand. You can count on this delicately-balanced mixture of oregano, coriander, and cumin to impart a well-defined flavor to vegetables, soups, or egg dishes.

CHILEAN AND PERUVIAN SEASONING CHART

ACHIOTE is also called *Annatto*. These small, reddish-orange, dried seeds are derived from the *Bixa Orellana* plant. When crushed and added to hot oil or liquid, they impart a delicate flavor and deep, rust-colored hue. Use them to season chicken, potatoes, and occasionally, rice. You might say *achiote* is to Latin American cooking what saffron is to French cooking—a powerful coloring agent with a mild but distinctive flavor that cannot be duplicated by other seasonings. Look for *achiote* seeds at Latin American or Indian food shops. There is no substitute.

BASIL is held in high esteem by Chilean cooks who find its lovely fragrance a great asset to their ever-present corn dishes. As a rule, 4 cups of fresh or frozen corn kernels will benefit from 1 tablespoon fresh, or 1 teaspoon dried, basil. A good pinch of basil is also a welcome addition to fresh salads or zucchini squash. Use this herb alone or in combination with cumin, oregano, or thyme to season Chilean foods.

CHILI PEPPERS that are most commonly used in native Chilean and Peruvian cooking are called *ají*, or Andean chilies. *Ají* is not available in the United States, but suitable substitutes are listed below. Be sure to wear rubber gloves when handling fresh chili peppers as their volatile oil can be quite irritating to the skin. Both dried and fresh chilies can be found in Latin American stores and some supermarkets.

Use one of the following in any Chilean or Peruvian recipe calling for dried red peppers:

Cayenne—peppers are long, thin, and extremely hot. Ground cayenne pepper or red pepper flakes (made from the cayenne pepper) are both convenient for cooking purposes.

Hontaka—is a long, thin, and wrinkled Japanese pepper with a potent flavor. One crushed *hontaka* chili can be used in place of 2 or 3 *pequín* chilies. Use in dishes where a well-defined fiery flavor is desired.

Mirasol Colorado—is a large, mild, red chili pepper popularly used in Peruvian dishes. It is more difficult to find than some of the other varieties.
Pequín—chilies are small, round, bright-red peppers, favored in potato and chicken dishes and sauces. Use judiciously—they are extremely hot, and a few go a long way. *Pequín* chilies are sometimes found under the name *tepín*.

Use one of the following in any Chilean or Peruvian recipe calling for fresh green chilies:

Anaheim—is a long, mild pepper best suited to gentle-natured dishes. It is superb in *pebre* (Chilean hot sauce). If unavailable, substitute a mild green Fresno chili or a medium-sized yellow wax chili.
Jalapeño—is a dark-green pepper available fresh or canned. It is hot, juicy, and often pulverized before using. An excellent choice for *seviche* (raw fish salad), cold tomato sauces, and long-simmered stews.
Serrano—is a hot, bright, green pepper about 1 or 2 inches long. It is interchangeable with *jalapeño* peppers and can be used in most sauces.

COLÓR is also called *annatto oil*. This homemade mixture will impart an attractive hue and pleasant flavor to many Chilean dishes. Stir it into a simmering bean or chicken stew in need of color and taste; start with 1 tablespoon to a dish that serves 6 persons and increase the amount to taste. Add *colór* to clear soups, just before serving, as a garnish. When stored in a clean container with a tight-fitting lid, it will keep indefinitely at room temperature.
To prepare: Heat 8 tablespoons peanut oil in a small skillet over a moderate flame. Add 3 to 4 tablespoons *achiote* seeds and stir with a wooden spoon until the oil acquires a deep-red color (the longer you simmer the oil, the darker the color will be). Remove from heat and cool. Strain into a jar and discard seeds. If *achiote* is unavailable, substitute 2 tablespoons paprika. Do not strain, but rather skim off any paprika that rises to the surface.

CORIANDER is used extensively in Chilean and Peruvian cooking. The strongly-flavored fresh herb (called *cilantro*) lends character to potatoes, tomatoes, chicken, seafood, and rice. Try adding a small amount of *cilantro* to your favorite vegetable dish or fish soup, and see how the flavor improves. These aromatic leaves can be used to garnish almost any dish except desserts. Look for fresh coriander at Latin American or oriental markets. When stored in a plastic bag, it will keep one week. Dried coriander leaves, available at spice shops and some supermarkets, may be substituted in recipes that call for fresh coriander in small amounts.

LIMES can be used in place of lemons to give an intriguing personality to your Chilean and Peruvian favorites. Their refreshing tang is especially appealing in marinated vegetable salads or *pebre*, Chile's renowned hot sauce. A good squeeze of lime juice will add new interest to boiled fish, shrimp, or avocados. Limes have a clear citrus perfume that contrasts well with the pungent aroma of a hot pepper. They are also beneficial for heightening the flavor of garlic and red onion.

PERUVIAN HERB BLEND will spruce up potato casseroles, chicken stews, and vegetable soups. It works best with baked or long-simmering dishes and is handy for enlivening sauces.

Combine and store in an airtight container:

1   tablespoon dried oregano
1½ teaspoons dried or ground coriander
1   teaspoon ground cumin seed
¾   teaspoon cayenne pepper or crushed *pequín* chilies

RED CHILI PASTE can be used in almost any recipe that calls for fresh or dried red chilies. If desired, place a bowl of red chili paste on your dinner table as a condiment to be used like Tabasco sauce or *Salsa Cruda* (Mexican table sauce).

To prepare: Measure out ¾ cup *pequín* or *hontaka* chilies. Snip off the ends of each chili pepper, shake out the seeds, and discard. Place the seeded pods in a bowl and cover with boiling water. Let stand 2 hours. Drain and discard water. Place chilies in a blender with 1 large minced garlic clove, 5 tablespoons olive or peanut oil, ⅛ teaspoon salt, and 1½ cups boiling vegetable or chicken stock. Purée until smooth. Transfer to a bowl or clean jar and keep covered in the refrigerator. It will keep several weeks.

Other seasonings found in Chilean and Peruvian cookery: oregano, cumin, paprika, cinnamon, nutmeg, thyme, garlic, and dried mustard.

Nutritional Essentials

The recipes of Chile and Peru should carry a warning for weight watchers: "Eat me on special occasions only." Higher than all other cuisines in average number of calories (326 per serving), Chilean and Peruvian recipes employ substantial amounts of oil and cheese. This reflects the heavy European influence upon Chilean and, to a lesser extent, Peruvian cooking. Cholesterol and saturated fat counters will have to choose offerings from these unusual cuisines carefully, as the average fat content is 50 percent; 17 percent of the total caloric content is derived from saturated fats.

Several dishes, however, will meet the needs of those on restricted calorie regimes. *Seviche*, a highly seasoned fish salad, is rich in protein (63 percent) and low in calories (133 per average portion). Remarkably, a single serving will supply nearly one-half of the recommended adult daily protein allowance. *Pebre* (Chilean Hot Sauce) can be spooned over sliced bread, salads, and cooked vegetables such as carrots, celery, and cauliflower. This zesty blend, containing a mere 43 calories per tablespoon, makes an excellent substitute for high-calorie toppings such as butter and cream or cheese sauces.

Like other Latin American styles, Chilean and Peruvian cooking utilize large amounts of cooking oil; consequently, the fat content of their dishes is considerable. Several dishes, however, do contain less than 40 percent fat: *Cranberry Bean Stew with Corn*, *Chilean Tamales*, *Sweet Creamed Rice*, and *Chicken Empañadas*. To increase the polyunsaturated fat content of your cooking oil, you may substitute one-half of the required amount of peanut or olive oil with safflower oil.

Fish and shrimp are popular in these cuisines, and so there is plenty of protein available there. Complementary protein combinations such as nuts and chicken, fish and cheese, and grains and dairy products are also found in many recipes.

Remember that many Chilean and Peruvian dishes can be accompanied by selections from Mexico. This will allow you more flexibility when it comes to designing Latin meals that are sparing in calories and fat. Finally, many of the high-calorie dishes in this chapter are entire meals in themselves—*Papas a la Huancaina*, *Chicken with Spicy Walnut Sauce*, and *Chilean Seafood Casserole*—so you do not need to add calories in the form of side dishes. Instead, by eating these fancy dishes along with a simple bowl of fruit or a green salad, even calorie-watchers can incorporate them into their menu plans.

AJÍ DE GALLINA
(Chicken with Spicy Walnut Sauce)   *YIELD: 4 to 5 servings*

Chicken:
  1 chicken, cut up (3½ pounds)
    Water to cover
  1 onion, cut into quarters
  1 leek
  1 carrot

Garnish:
  1 pound sweet potatoes, boiled
    until tender—optional
  1 hard-boiled egg, cut into strips
  6 black olives, cut into strips

Sauce:
  2 cups crustless bread cubes (from
    fresh bread)
  1 cup evaporated milk
  ½ cup peanut oil (or use part olive
    oil)
  1 onion, finely chopped
  2 cloves garlic, minced
  ½ to 1 teaspoon ground cumin
  ½ cup ground walnuts
    Salt and pepper to taste
  ¼ cup peanut oil or olive oil
  2 or 3 tablespoons red chili paste*
    or dried red chilies
  2 teaspoons *achiote* seeds*—
    optional
  ½ cup grated Parmesan cheese

*See Seasoning Chart.

1. *To prepare chicken*: Place chicken in a soup pot with enough water to cover. Add onion, leek, and carrot. Bring to a boil and skim surface with a slotted spoon. Reduce heat to low and cook, covered, until meat is tender but not falling off the bones. Remove chicken and cool. Discard skin and bones. Cut chicken into thin strips. Strain and reserve stock for another use.

2. *To prepare sauce*: Soak bread cubes in milk for 5 minutes. Mash with a fork to make a paste. Heat ½ cup oil in a large skillet. Brown the onion and garlic. Add cumin, bread paste, walnuts, salt, and pepper. Place in a blender and whirl until smooth and creamy. Wipe skillet clean. Heat remaining ¼ cup oil in skillet until hot. Add chili paste and *achiote* seeds. Cook, stirring constantly, for 1 minute. Add blender mixture, reduce heat, and simmer 5 minutes, stirring constantly, until thick.

3. *To assemble*: Add Parmesan cheese and chicken to sauce. Simmer 15 minutes or until cheese melts and chicken is heated through, stirring occasionally. Thin with chicken stock if necessary. Transfer to a serving platter and surround, if desired, by sweet potatoes cut into chunks. Arrange strips of hard-boiled eggs and olives in a spokelike pattern on the top. Serve immediately.

ARROZ CON LECHE
(Sweet Creamed Rice)   *YIELD: 6 servings*

4⅓ cups whole milk
  1 cinnamon stick
  1 teaspoon vanilla extract
  ½ cup plus 2 tablespoons long-grain
    rice

1 teaspoon safflower margarine or
  butter
½ cup sugar
Ground cinnamon

1. Place the milk, cinnamon stick, and vanilla in a heavy, 4-quart pot. Bring to a boil and slowly add the rice and margarine. Lower heat to medium and partially cover pot with a lid. Cook at a slow boil for 30 minutes. Rice should be tender and milk should have the consistency of unwhipped heavy cream. Remove cinnamon stick.
2. Slowly stir in the sugar. Stir 2 to 3 minutes until sugar dissolves. Pour into dessert bowls. Dust with ground cinnamon. Let cool and serve at room temperature.

AQUACATES RELLENOS
(Avocados Stuffed with Vegetables)   *YIELD: 6 servings*

¼ cup each: peanut and olive oil
2 tablespoons lemon juice
1 teaspoon salt (or to taste)
½ teaspoon pepper (or to taste)
1 to 3 teaspoons finely chopped
  jalapeño pepper
1 clove garlic, minced
1 cup diced boiled potatoes
½ cup shredded carrots
½ cup cooked green peas
¼ cup finely chopped green onions
  with tops
½ to ¾ cup cubed mozzarella or
  Chihuahua* cheese

3 ripe avocados
  Lemon juice to brush on
  avocados
6 tablespoons safflower
  mayonnaise
6 tablespoons plain low-fat yogurt
  or sour cream
1 tablespoon chopped *cilantro*—
  optional
½ teaspoon ground cumin seed
  Pimiento strips for garnish
  Lettuce leaves

*Available at Latin American grocery stores.

1. Place the peanut oil, olive oil, lemon juice, salt, pepper, *jalapeño* peppers, and garlic in a screw-top jar. Shake vigorously to blend thoroughly. Place potatoes, carrots, and peas in a bowl. Cover with oil-lemon juice mixture. Let stand 30 minutes, stirring occasionally. Add onions and cheese cubes. Stir well.
2. Cut avocados in half. Remove the pits and brush with lemon juice to prevent discoloration. Divide vegetable filling into 6 portions and fill the avocado halves.

3. Combine the mayonnaise, yogurt or sour cream, *cilantro*, and cumin. Spread 2 tablespoons over each avocado half. Garnish with pimiento strips. Place on lettuce leaves and serve immediately as a first course, luncheon entrée, or side dish.

CALDILLO DE CONGRIA
(Chilean Fish, Tomato, and Potato Soup)   YIELD: 6 servings

1 cup peanut oil
2 large onions, thinly sliced
2 carrots, cut into strips
1 green pepper, cut into strips
2 tomatoes, peeled and diced
3 potatoes, sliced
1 garlic clove, minced

Salt to taste
Freshly ground white pepper
1 cup water
2½ pounds fillet of sole (6 portions)
1 cup white wine
Lemon wedges

1. Place oil and onions in a heavy soup pot. Sauté until golden. Add carrots, green pepper, tomatoes, potatoes, garlic, salt, pepper, and water. Simmer until vegetables are tender, stirring frequently.
2. Lay fish fillets on top of vegetables. Cover and cook 20 minutes. Pour in the wine. Season fish with salt and pepper. Simmer 10 more minutes.
3. Carefully spoon one portion of fish into each soup bowl. Cover with broth and vegetables. Serve with lemon wedges.

CHILEAN CHICKEN EMPAÑADAS   YIELD: 16 to 18 empañadas

Dough:
2 cups water
2 teaspoons salt
5 cups unbleached white flour (may substitute part whole-wheat)
⅔ cup vegetable shortening
2 eggs, well beaten
1 egg white to brush on dough before baking

Filling:
4 large chicken breasts, skinned and deboned
2 onions, finely chopped
2 tablespoons safflower margarine or butter
2 tablespoons peanut or safflower oil
½ teaspoon dried oregano
1 teaspoon chili powder
Salt to taste
Freshly ground white pepper to taste
Pinch of cayenne pepper
3 tablespoons chicken stock
¼ cup dark raisins—optional

1. *To prepare dough*: Combine the water and salt. Place in a saucepan and heat until warm. Sift flour onto a large cutting board. Make a well in the center. Put the shortening into the well and work it into the flour by hand until crumbly. Alternately add beaten eggs and salt-water until a soft dough is formed (you may not need to add all of the water). Shape dough into a ball and knead for 5 minutes. Cover with a towel while preparing filling.
2. *To prepare filling*: Dice chicken into small squares. In a large skillet sauté the onions in margarine and oil until tender but not brown. Season with oregano, chili powder, salt, pepper, and cayenne. Add diced chicken and chicken stock. Simmer until mixture is of a consistency that will hold together, but is not dry. Taste and adjust seasonings. Stir in raisins.
3. *To assemble empañadas*: Separate dough into 16 to 18 equal portions about the size of a medium potato. Roll dough thinly into 6- or 7-inch rounds. Place 2 tablespoons of filling below the center of each. Fold in half to form a crescent. Pinch edges together to seal. To shape the edges, start at one end of the crescent and fold the corner edge over to form a triangle shape. Continue forming triangles around the edge so that the folds overlap each other and create a "rope" effect.
4. Preheat oven to 350 degrees. Beat 1 egg white with 1 tablespoon of water. Brush tops of *empañadas* with eggwash. With a fork, prick each *empañada* 4 times to allow steam to escape while baking. Arrange 2 inches apart on an ungreased baking sheet and bake until lightly browned—about 8 minutes. Serve immediately.
Variation: *Shrimp and Scallop Empañadas*: Substitute 1 pound cooked and chopped shrimp and ½ pound cooked and minced scallops for the chicken. Substitute clam juice for the chicken stock.

CHUPE DE LOCOS
(Chilean Seafood Casserole)   YIELD: 8 servings

2 pounds scallops	1 teaspoon each: thyme and
1 cup white wine	tarragon
1 loaf French bread	Salt and freshly ground pepper
½ cup milk	1½ cups grated Gruyère or
1 large onion, finely minced	Emmentaler cheese
1 clove garlic, mashed	⅛ teaspoon cayenne pepper
1 tablespoon peanut oil	½ stick safflower margarine or
2 tablespoons safflower margarine	butter, cut into pieces
2 tablespoons chopped parsley	

1. In a large skillet cook the scallops, in enough wine to barely cover, until tender. Remove and discard crust from bread. Shred enough bread to make 2 cups. Place in a bowl and pour enough milk over it to make a soft mush. Set aside.
2. In a separate skillet sauté the onion and garlic in the peanut oil and margarine until onion is transparent. Add seasonings and salt and pepper to taste. Add cooked scallops and just enough of the wine juice to make a

sauce. Squeeze most of the milk from the bread and mix with the scallops. Add ¾ cup of the cheese and the cayenne pepper. Stir together. Taste and adjust seasonings. Mixture should be spicy. Place in a gratin or 2-quart casserole dish. Cover with remaining cheese and dot with the ½ stick of margarine or butter. If desired, the dish may be refrigerated at this point and baked before serving.

3. Preheat oven to 400 degrees.

4. Bake in preheated oven until cheese is melted. For a browner top, turn oven to broil. Watch carefully as the melted cheese burns easily. Serve immediately accompanied, if desired, by steamed rice.

Variation: Replace 1 pound scallops with 1 pound fresh shrimp.

ENSALADES DE POROTOS VERDE
(Chilean Marinated String Bean Salad)   *YIELD: 8 servings*

---

2 pounds fresh string beans
¼ cup finely chopped green onions
   with tops
1 tablespoon chopped *cilantro** or
   1½ teaspoons dried coriander
   leaves
¼ teaspoon cumin seed

1 teaspoon salt
1 large garlic clove
3 tablespoons peanut oil
   Juice of 1 lemon
2 to 3 tomatoes, peeled, seeded,
   and chopped—optional

*Available at Latin-American grocery stores.

1. Trim ends off beans and remove the strings. With a sharp knife, cut diagonally, into thin lengthwise strips to obtain a French-cut. Place in a vegetable steamer and cook until just tender, but still firm. Let cool and combine in a bowl with the chopped onions and *cilantro*. Set aside.

2. Grind the cumin seed, salt, and garlic to a paste in a mortar with a pestle. With a fork, beat in the oil and lemon juice. Combine with the string beans and refrigerate several hours to let flavors develop, stirring occasionally. Toss with tomatoes and serve cold.

HUMITAS
(Chilean Tamales)   *YIELD: Approximately 48 humitas*

---

12 ears of corn with husks
1 large onion, finely chopped
1 large garlic clove, mashed
½ to 1 teaspoon cayenne pepper

3 tablespoons safflower margarine
2 tablespoons fresh chopped basil
   or 2 teaspoons dried basil
1 teaspoon each: salt and sugar

1. *To prepare corn*: Remove husks and silk from corn. Discard silk but reserve husks. With a sharp knife, remove the kernels from the corn. Reserve the cobs. Put corn into a food processor, food grinder, or blender, and chop to a consistency of mush. In a skillet, sauté the onion, garlic, and cay-

enne in the margarine. When barely golden, add the corn mush, basil, salt, and sugar. Taste and adjust seasonings. Mixture should be spicy.

2. *To assemble and steam humitas*: For each *humita* use 2 large husks, one overlapping the other at the center. Place 2 tablespoons of filling in the center. Fold bottom to overlap center. Fold top to overlap center. Fold sides under making certain they overlap each other to form a sealed packet. Tie neatly with string and knot securely. Cover the bottom of a large pot with a layer of corn cobs. Pour 1 cup boiling water over cobs. Lay *humitas* on top of cobs, cover with a lid, and steam over low heat for 40 minutes.

3. *To serve*: Place *humitas* in a serving dish. Each person cuts open a packet and eats the corn out of the husk. Allow 5 to 8 per person. Open any leftover *humitas* and place the filling in a baking dish. Reheat in a moderate oven and serve plain or covered with tomato sauce.

MIL HOJAS
(Thousand Leaf Pastry)*

YIELD: *16 servings*

---

7 cups all-purpose flour	8 egg yolks
2 sticks safflower margarine or butter, well-chilled and cut into small pieces	12 tablespoons warm milk
	4 cans sweetened condensed milk
	2¼ cups (18 ounces) apricot preserves

1. Sift flour into a mixing bowl. With a pastry cutter or your fingertips, work in the margarine pieces until mixture is the size of peas. Stir in the egg yolks gradually with a fork or wooden spoon. Add the warm milk, mix well, and gather into a ball. Cover with a dry towel and let rest 4 hours.

2. Preheat oven to 350 degrees.

3. Divide dough into 15 equal pieces about the size of golf balls. With a lightly floured rolling pin, roll out the first ball on a wooden board into a very thin 10½-inch circle. Cover with a 10-inch plate and cut around it. Trim off excess dough. Place on an ungreased baking sheet or pizza pan. Prick with a fork in 3 or 4 places. Bake in preheated oven until it begins to brown and small bubbles appear—about 6 to 8 minutes. Remove from oven and lay on a towel to cool. Repeat process until 15 layers are made. Use reserved scraps for the last circle.

4. Submerge the cans of condensed milk, unopened, in a large pot of water. Bring to a boil for 30 minutes. Remove from boiling water with tongs. Open the cans and scrape the solidified contents into a bowl. If mixture is too thick to spread, thin out with 2 tablespoons of regular milk.

5. To assemble, sandwich 3 layers of pastry together by spreading each layer with thickened condensed milk. Add a fourth layer and spread with apricot preserves. Continue layering in this manner—3 layers with milk and the 4th with apricot preserves, until you have 15 layers. Crush the 16th into very fine crumbs with a rolling pin. Sprinkle crumbs over entire top. Spread any remaining condensed milk around the sides like an icing.

*Note: This is best when prepared a day ahead of serving.

PAPAS A LA HUANCAINA
(Huancayo Potatoes with Cheese and Chili Sauce)   YIELD: 6 to 8 servings

1 small onion sliced into rings
  Juice of 1 large lemon
½ teaspoon crushed red chili pepper
  or pequín chili
4 medium-large red potatoes
  Lettuce leaves
1 cup grated mozzarella or
  Muenster cheese
1 teaspoon turmeric
½ to 1 teaspoon crushed chili
  pepper or pequín chili

2 hard-boiled egg yolks (reserve
  the whites for garnish)
  Salt and freshly ground pepper to
  taste
½ cup evaporated milk or light
  cream
¼ cup olive or peanut oil
  Any of the following as
  garnishes: sliced hard-boiled
  eggs, sliced red pepper, sliced
  and seeded fresh hot pepper,
  sliced black olives, or chopped
  scallion greens.

1. Place onion rings in a bowl and cover with lemon juice and ½ teaspoon crushed chili pepper. Let marinate, basting occasionally, while preparing the rest of the dish.
2. Place potatoes in a pot with enough lightly salted water to cover. Boil until tender but not bursting. Drain, cool slightly, and slice into rounds. Line a platter with lettuce leaves and arrange potatoes over them.
3. *To prepare sauce:* Whirl the grated cheese, turmeric, crushed chili pepper, hard-boiled egg yolks, salt, freshly ground pepper, and milk in a blender until creamy. Heat the oil in a heavy skillet and add cheese mixture. Stir with a wooden spoon until the sauce is cooked and firm.
4. *To serve:* Spoon sauce over potatoes and decorate with any of the optional garnishes. The more garnishes, the more attractive the dish will look. Drain lemon juice off of onion rings and place them on top of garnishes.

PASTEL DE CHOCLO
(Spicy Corn Custard)   YIELD: 12 servings

½ cup yellow raisins
1 cup boiling water
1 large green pepper, seeded and
  cut into thin strips
2 large onions, finely chopped
3 tablespoons peanut oil
1 to 2 heaping tablespoons chili
  powder
1 teaspoon each: dried oregano and
  ground cumin seed
½ teaspoon cayenne pepper or to taste

14 pitted black olives—optional
12 ears of corn
1 stick safflower margarine
2 eggs, well beaten
½ cup flour
½ cup light cream
1 teaspoon baking powder
1 tablespoon sugar
1 teaspoon salt
1 teaspoon dried basil or 1
  tablespoon chopped fresh basil

1. Soak raisins in boiling water for 20 minutes. Do not drain.
2. In a large skillet, sauté the green pepper and onions in the peanut oil until tender. Add chili powder, oregano, cumin, and cayenne pepper. Add raisins and water to skillet and stir well. Simmer 10 minutes. Taste and adjust seasonings, adding a little more water if mixture becomes too dry. Place in a 9- by 12- by 2-inch baking dish. Dot with black olives.
3. Preheat oven to 400 degrees.
4. Remove kernels from corn with a sharp knife. Coarsely chop in a food processor, food grinder, or blender. Melt margarine in a large skillet and add corn. Mix to coat corn evenly with margarine. Add beaten eggs and stir constantly until well blended. Dissolve flour with the cream and add baking powder. Add to corn in skillet. Season with sugar, salt and basil. Taste and adjust seasonings. Spread evenly over the top of the raisin mixture. Do not stir.
5. Bake in preheated oven from 30 to 40 minutes or until toothpick or knife inserted in center comes out clean. Brown 1 or 2 minutes under the broiler if a browner top is desired. Cut into squares and serve immediately.
Variation: Replace green pepper and 1 of the onions with 2 whole chicken breasts, halved, skinned, deboned, and finely minced (this may be done in a food grinder or food processor).

PEBRE
(Chilean Hot Sauce)   YIELD: *Approximately 2 cups or 8 servings*

---

2 bunches *cilantro** (fresh coriander)	Juice of 1 lemon
3 to 4 green onions, finely chopped with tops	½ teaspoon salt
	2 tablespoons peanut oil
2 fresh Anaheim chilies, seeded and finely chopped, or red chili paste ** to taste	1½ teaspoons white vinegar
	⅓ cup water
	1 tomato, skinned and finely chopped

Available at Latin American grocery stores and some supermarkets.
**See Seasoning Chart.*

1. Place *cilantro* in a large bowl filled with cold water. Wash well and pick over carefully, discarding any blemished or wilted leaves and stems. Drain in a colander and shake off excess moisture. Place on paper towels to dry. Chop, very finely, enough leaves and stems to measure 1 cup. Save remaining *cilantro* for another use.
2. Place finely chopped *cilantro* in a bowl. Combine with remaining ingredients. If hotter flavor is desired, add a little Tabasco sauce or cayenne pepper. Let stand at room temperature, covered, for several hours or overnight to let the flavors develop. *Pebre* will keep several days, covered. The flavor improves with age.
3. Serve as a sauce for fresh sliced tomatoes, boiled or baked potatoes, or fish. Or use as a spread or dip for French bread. *Pebre* is also a good accompaniment to *Porotos Granados* (p. 74).

PICANTE DE CAMARONES
(Spicy Peruvian Shrimp with Tomatoes)   *YIELD: 4 to 6 servings*

2 cups medium shrimp, cleaned
    and cooked
½ cup safflower oil or peanut oil
1 clove garlic
1 cup sliced onion
1 green pepper, cut into strips
3 cups stewed tomatoes
*See Seasoning Chart.

1 teaspoon red chili paste* or
    crushed dried red chilies
1½ teaspoons brown sugar
1 teaspoon salt
¼ teaspoon pepper
2 tablespoons cornstarch
2 tablespoons water
6 hard-boiled eggs—optional

1. Heat the oil in a large soup pot. Sauté the garlic clove and remove. Add onion and green pepper. Cover and simmer until tender. Add tomatoes, red chili paste or crushed chili pepper, sugar, salt, and pepper. Continue simmering for about 1 hour, stirring occasionally. Dissolve cornstarch in water to make a paste. Stir in and simmer a few minutes longer until thick. Taste and adjust seasonings.
2. Cut hard-boiled eggs in half and place in a serving dish. Cover first with the shrimp and then the sauce. Serve immediately, accompanied by rice.

POROTOS GRANADOS
(Cranberry Bean Stew with Corn)   *YIELD: 8 servings*

3 cups fresh, shelled cranberry
    beans or 1½ cups dried cranberry,
    pinto, or navy beans, soaked
    overnight
2 garlic cloves, minced
6 ears corn
3 tablespoons peanut oil
½ onion, diced
*See Seasoning Chart.

1 green onion, chopped with tops
2 sprigs fresh oregano or ½
    tablespoon dried oregano
Salt to taste
Color (Annatto oil)*—optional
Pebre (p. 73) as an
    accompaniment—optional

1. Place soaked beans in a heavy 5-quart pot with enough water to cover. Bring to a boil, reduce heat to low, and simmer, partially covered, for 1 hour. Add garlic and continue simmering until almost tender—about 30 to 60 minutes (it will take longer for dried beans).
2. Meanwhile, remove the husks and silks from the corn. Run ears back and forth on the fine side of a 4-sided grater, set over a large bowl, to remove as much corn as possible. With a sharp knife, scrape down ears to remove any remaining corn. The mixture will be a thick mush. Set aside.
3. When beans are almost tender, heat the peanut oil in a small skillet. Sauté the diced onion and chopped green onion. Add to beans, along with

oregano, salt, and corn mush. Cook over medium heat, stirring frequently until thick. Remove from heat and stir in *colór*. Serve hot in soup bowls as a main course or side dish. If desired, top each serving with a few spoonfuls of *Pebre*. This is a filling dish—with French bread and fresh fruit it makes a most satisfying meal.

Variation: Add 1 winter squash, peeled, seeded, and cut into bite-size pieces when you add the garlic in step 1. Three to 6 tomatoes, peeled, seeded, and chopped, may also be added.

SALAD SALPICON
YIELD: 6 servings

Salad:
- ½ head white cabbage, shredded
- ¼ head red cabbage, shredded
- 1 medium-sized red onion, thinly sliced
- 3 hard-boiled eggs, sliced
- 2 tablespoons capers—optional
- 2 cups boiled potatoes, diced
- 1 green pepper, thinly sliced

Dressing:
- ½ cup olive oil
- ¼ cup peanut or safflower oil
- ¼ cup wine vinegar
- 1 tablespoon Dijon mustard
- 1 garlic clove, mashed
- 1 teaspoon salt
- ¼ teaspoon pepper
- ¼ teaspoon fine herbes
- Dash of Worcestershire sauce

Garnishes:
- Leafy lettuce such as bibb, Boston, or red leaf, washed
- 3 to 4 firm ripe tomatoes, quartered
- 12 black olives, pitted
- 3 carrots, shredded

1. Combine salad ingredients in a bowl. Place dressing ingredients in a screw-top jar. Shake vigorously to blend thoroughly. Taste and adjust seasonings. Toss the salad with just enough dressing to lightly coat.

2. Line a salad bowl with lettuce leaves. Mound the salad in the bowl and flatten the surface. Alternately arrange the quartered tomatoes and olives around the outer rim. Place the shredded carrots in the center. Serve immediately as a main course or side dish.

Variation: Substitute any of the following for the potatoes: 2 cups cold cooked chicken, shrimp, mussels, salmon, or tuna chunks.

SEVICHE
(Fish Marinated in Lime and Lemon Juice)   *YIELD: 4 servings*

1 pound white, firm-fleshed, fish fillets such as red snapper, sole, or flounder
1 red onion, finely chopped
4 hot green peppers, such as *jalapeño* or *serrano*, seeded and minced
1 teaspoon crushed red chili pepper
1 garlic clove, minced

½ teaspoon salt (or to taste)
Freshly ground pepper to taste
Juice of 3 lemons
Juice of 4 limes
Lettuce leaves
3 cooked sweet potatoes, cut into chunks—optional as a garnish
3 cooked ears of corn, broken into thirds—optional as a garnish

1. *To prepare Seviche*: Cut fish fillets into small pieces. Place in a large strainer and rinse with boiling water. Shake strainer well to remove excess water. Place fish in a flat glass or ceramic dish. Combine with chopped onion, hot pepper, red chili pepper, garlic, salt, and pepper. Combine lemon and lime juices and pour over fish. Stir well to mix thoroughly. Cover and refrigerate 12 hours or overnight. If you are in a hurry, marinate the dish at least 3 to 4 hours or until the fish is "cooked"—milky white and opaque.
2. *To serve*: Line one serving platter (or individual salad plates) with lettuce leaves. Place *Seviche* in the center and garnish with chunks of sweet potatoes and corn. Serve as an appetizer or salad.

TORTILLA DE PLATANOS
(Banana Omelet)   *YIELD: 2 to 4 servings*

4 eggs, separated
Salt and freshly ground pepper to taste
⅛ to ¼ teaspoon cayenne pepper
Generous pinch of brown sugar

2 medium-sized ripe bananas
2 tablespoons safflower margarine
Chopped parsley sprigs for garnish

1. In a mixing bowl, beat the egg yolks, salt, pepper, cayenne pepper, and brown sugar until frothy and lemon-colored. Beat whites in another bowl (preferably a copper one) with a wire whisk until they stand in peaks but are not dry. Carefully fold into the egg mixture.
2. Peel and split bananas in half lengthwise. Cut each half into 4 pieces. Heat the margarine in a 9-inch skillet until sizzling. Add banana chunks and sauté quickly until tender and lightly browned on all sides. Pour egg mixture over bananas and cook over medium heat, lifting the edges to allow uncooked parts to run underneath. When set, but still a bit runny on top, turn off the heat, cover with a lid, and let steam for a minute or two

until puffy and just moist, but not dry. Cut open-faced into 4 wedges or fold in half and serve immediately, garnished with parsley.

ZUCCHINI SQUASH WITH WINE AND SHALLOTS

YIELD: 4 servings

2 medium-sized zucchini squash
3 tablespoons peanut or olive oil
1 tablespoon safflower margarine or butter
6 shallots, peeled and minced, or substitute 2 green onions, chopped

1 clove garlic, finely minced
½ teaspoon each: basil and thyme
¼ cup white wine
¼ cup vegetable or chicken stock
½ cup grated Gruyère or Swiss cheese

Wash and slice zucchini into ½-inch rounds. Set aside. Heat oil and margarine in a saucepan. Sauté the shallots and garlic until transparent but not brown. Add zucchini, basil, thyme, wine, and stock. Cook over medium heat for 15 minutes, stirring occasionally. Place in a serving bowl and sprinkle grated cheese over the top.

CHILE and PERU/RECIPE ANALYSIS CHART

Name of Recipe	Quantity	Calories	CHO gms.	Protein gms.	Total Fat gms.	Saturated Fat gms.	Choles- terol mg.	Dietary Fiber gms.
1. *Humitas* (Chilean Tamales)	per serving	37	6 (65%)	1 (11%)	1 (24%)	—	—	—
2. *Pebre* (Chilean Hot Sauce)	per serving	43	3 (28%)	1 (9%)	3 (63%)	1 (21%)	—	.3
3. *Ensalades de Porotos Verde* (Marinated String Bean Salad)	per serving	93	10 (43%)	2 (9%)	5 (48%)	1 (10%)	—	1.0
4. *Seviche*	per serving	133	10 (30%)	21 (63%)	1.0 (7%)	—	15	1.0
5. *Tortilla de Platanos* (Banana Omelet)	per serving	192	14 (29%)	7 (15%)	12 (56%)	3 (14%)	314	.4
6. Zucchini Squash with Wine and Shallots	per serving	201	6 (12%)	6 (12%)	17 (76%)	5 (24%)	16	1.0
7. *Papas a la Huancaina*	per serving	240	25 (42%)	8 (13%)	12 (45%)	4 (15%)	94	1.2
8. *Pastel de Choclo* (Spicy Corn Custard)	per serving	254	27 (43%)	5 (8%)	14 (49%)	3 (11%)	53	1.5
9. *Arroz con Leche* (Sweet Creamed Rice)	per serving	255	41 (64%)	7 (11%)	7 (25%)	4 (14%)	19	.1
10. *Picante de Ca-marones* (Spicy Peruvian Shrimp with Tomatoes)	per serving	259	13 (20%)	9 (14%)	19 (66%)	2 (7%)	47	1.0
11. *Porotos Gra-nados* (Cranberry Bean Stew with Corn)	per serving	262	41 (63%)	11 (17%)	6 (20%)	1 (3%)	—	1.7
12. Salad Salpicon	per serving	294	18 (24%)	6 (8%)	22 (68%)	3 (9%)	157	2.0
13. Chilean Chicken *Empañadas*	per serving	367	37 (40%)	21 (23%)	15 (37%)	4 (10%)	58	.3

Name of Recipe	Quantity	Calories	CHO gms.	Protein gms.	Total Fat gms.	Saturated Fat gms.	Choles- terol mg.	Dietary Fiber gms.
14. *Chupe de Locos* (Seafood Casserole)	per serving	411	39 (38%)	21 (20%)	19 (42%)	6 (13%)	24	.3
15. *Caldillo de Congria* (Fish, Tomato and Po- tato Soup)	per serving	486	27 (22%)	36 (30%)	26 (48%)	7 (13%)	25	1.8
16. *Aquacates Re- llenos* (Avocados Stuffed with Vegetables)	per serving	526	21 (16%)	7 (5%)	46 (79%)	7 (12%)	8	3
17. *Mil Hojas* (Thousand Leaf Pastry)	per serving	854	137 (64%)	18 (8%)	26 (28%)	11 (12%)	204	.2
18. *Ají de Gallina* (Chicken with Spicy Walnut Sauce)	per serving	978	19 (7%)	59 (24%)	74 (69%)	42 (39%)	145	1.0

Numbers in parentheses (%) indicate percentage of total calories contributed by nutrient.

MENUS
LOW CALORIE SPECIALTIES
(500 to 700 calories per meal)

**POROTOS GRANADOS
(CRANBERRY BEAN STEW
WITH CORN)**
PEBRE (CHILEAN HOT SAUCE)
**ENSALADES DE POROTOS VERDE
(MARINATED STRING BEAN
SALAD)**
**ARROZ CON LECHE
(SWEET CREAMED RICE)**
Coffee

SEVICHE
**PASTEL DE CHOCLO
(SPICY CORN CUSTARD)**
Tomato Wedges and Red Onion Rings
Sliced Bananas
Iced Mint Tea

Carrot Sticks and Sliced Cucumbers
PAPAS A LA HUANCAINA
PICANTE DE CAMARONES (SPICY SHRIMP WITH TOMATOES)
Sliced Peaches
Orange Spice Tea

●

LOW CHOLESTEROL MENUS
(Less than 50 mgs. of cholesterol per meal)

**CHUPE DE LOCOS
(SEAFOOD CASSEROLE)**
Romaine Lettuce with Vinaigrette
Baked Winter Squash
Cantaloupe
Chilled Cider

**AQUACATES RELLENOS
(AVOCADOS STUFFED WITH
VEGETABLES)**
PEBRE (CHILEAN HOT SAUCE)
Corn on the Cob with Safflower
Margarine
Red Grapes and Bananas
White Wine

CALDILLO DE CONGRIA (FISH, POTATO, AND TOMATO SOUP)
Whole Grain Crackers
Sliced Green Peppers
ARROZ CON LECHE (SWEET CREAMED RICE)
Coffee

●

LOW SATURATED FAT SELECTIONS
(Less than 8 grams of saturated fat per meal)

CHILEAN CHICKEN EMPAÑADAS
ENSALADES DE POROTOS VERDE
(MARINATED STRING BEAN
SALAD)
Baked Pumpkin with
Cinnamon and Honey
Fresh Papayas
Hot Tea

SEVICHE
HUMITAS (CHILEAN TAMALES)
Sliced Tomatoes and Avocados
ARROZ CON LECHE
(SWEET CREAMED RICE)
Coffee

TORTILLA DE PLATANOS (BANANA OMELET)
POROTOS GRANADOS (CRANBERRY BEAN STEW WITH CORN)
French Bread
Fresh Cherries
White Wine

●

HIGH PROTEIN MEALS
(30 or more grams of protein per meal)

CALDILLO DE CONGRIA (FISH,
POTATO, AND TOMATO SOUP)
SALAD SALPICON
French Bread
PEBRE (CHILEAN HOT SAUCE)
Sliced Oranges
Red Wine

HUMITAS (CHILEAN TAMALES)
AJÍ DE GALLINA (CHICKEN WITH
SPICY WALNUT SAUCE)
Shredded Lettuce with Vinaigrette
Fresh Pineapple
Coffee

AQUACATES RELLENOS (AVOCADOS STUFFED WITH VEGETABLES)
ZUCCHINI SQUASH WITH WINE AND SHALLOTS
MIL HOJAS (THOUSAND LEAF PASTRY)
Hot Tea

●

WELL BALANCED LUNCH OR DINNER MENUS
(Selections that conform to recommendations in Dietary Goals for United States)

CHILEAN CHICKEN EMPAÑADAS
Fresh Garden Salad
**ARROZ CON LECHE
(SWEET CREAMED RICE)**
Red Wine

**PASTEL DE CHOCLO
(SPICY CORN CUSTARD)**
**CHUPE DE LOCOS
(SEAFOOD CASSEROLE)**
Sliced Tomatoes Garnished with
Parsley
Fresh Strawberries
Hot Mint Tea

ENSALADES DE POROTOS VERDE (MARINATED STRING BEAN SALAD)
POROTOS GRANADOS (CRANBERRY BEAN STEW)
French Bread
MIL HOJAS (THOUSAND LEAF PASTRY)
Coffee

CHAPTER 4

CHINA
Wok Don't Fly

Culinary Essentials

Few cuisines are as exalted as that of China. The proliferation of regional Chinese restaurants, cookbooks, and food products in this country attests to its immense popularity. What makes this culinary style such a desirable and sought-after gastronomic experience? It's low in fat and cholesterol and rich in nutrients for one thing, and it requires a minimum of fuel and cooking time. What's more, Chinese food is extremely palatable, pleasing to look at, and economically feasible for everyone's budget.

There are five major schools of Chinese cooking, but we have concentrated on what we consider the most interesting and diverse regional styles: Szechuan, Hunan, and Peking. Szechuan foods tend to be oily and highly spiced with red chili peppers, garlic, and ginger. Hunan flavors are similar to Szechuan but richer, hotter, and occasionally, sweet and sour. Peking dishes are distinguished by light, mildly-seasoned creations such as wine-cooked seafood, soft-fried vegetables, and savories dipped in plum or *hoisin** sauce.

Most American cities have Chinatowns or Oriental markets where you can find ingredients commonly used in regional Chinese dishes. The majority of these items are relatively inexpensive and go a long way. Once opened, canned products such as plum or oyster sauce will keep indefinitely when transferred to a clean jar, tightly capped, and refrigerated. Water-packed bamboo shoots, water chestnuts, and bean curd will keep one week after opening if you keep them refrigerated and change the water daily.

See Seasoning Chart.

Serious Chinese cooks will want to have two different vinegars on hand—a mildly sweet rice vinegar to use as an all-purpose seasoner, and a Chinese red vinegar to use as a table sauce or flavor-enhancer for hot and sour dishes. White vinegar and red-wine vinegar may be substituted, respectively. Rice wine, made of fermented glutinous rice, is another essential ingredient that is also available at oriental markets. This sharp, clean-tasting liquid tames pungent odors and imparts a heady fragrance to marinades and soups. Dry sherry, cognac, dry white wine, or vermouth are suitable alternatives.

Stock your kitchen with a collection of canned or bottled items that can be enlisted to doctor up a dish, that might be substituted for a missing ingredient, or that can act as a dipping agent: Thick and salty oyster sauce can be used much like soy sauce as a cooking condiment or table sauce; fermented black beans are a marvelous addition to seafood or bean curd; plum sauce, a chutneylike mixture of plums, apricots, and chilies, is a popular sweet and pungent dipping sauce; Szechuan preserved vegetables will give a deep, spicy taste to stir-fried vegetables and soups; and exotic canned fruits such as litchis, kumquats, loquats, or mandarin oranges can be served as a no-fuss dessert.

Dried delicacies, such as cloud ears (tree ears) and tiger lily buds (golden needles), are great for festive dishes. These unusual ingredients will keep indefinitely on your shelf and need to be soaked in hot water to render them edible. Cloud ears, which look like dried wood chips, when placed in hot water expand into clusters of soft, gelatinous petals reminiscent of "clouds" or "ears." They do not have a noticeable flavor or aroma, but their resilient texture and crinkly appearance are unsurpassed. Tiger lily buds will swell into long golden strands which may be bow-tied to make them prettier and easier to manage. You can add these lovely "needles" to almost any soup or stir-fried dish, as their delicate nature appeals to most palates. Dried black mushrooms are also worth trying. They have a meatier texture and more concentrated flavor than fresh ones. Cost-conscious cooks should use the thinly-sliced variety for everyday cooking; thick-capped black mushrooms, which have cracked surfaces and a superior flavor, are more expensive and usually reserved for special occasions.

It is no wonder that *tofu* or soybean curd is celebrated in numerous Chinese dishes. This versatile ingredient has a neutral flavor that readily assumes the character of more decisive ingredients and a custardlike consistency that makes a perfect foil to crisp vegetables and water chestnuts. Look for *tofu* in Oriental markets, health food stores, and large supermarkets where it is sold compressed into one-pound cakes and water-packed in plastic containers. Hard or medium-firm *tofu* is best for general cooking purposes and stir-frying; soft *tofu* is suitable for soups or puddings.

Since there are many gadgets specifically designed for the Oriental cook, your selection of kitchen gear should be determined by how often you plan to prepare Chinese meals. If nothing else, invest in a good wok, an all-purpose concave pan that can be used for quick-stir and deep frying. The best woks are made from cast iron or stainless steel and have long single handles rather than short side handles. A heavy, rectangular-shaped Chinese cleaver or sharp kitchen knife, and a wide, heavy cutting board or chopping block are also essential. For stir-frying, you will need a long wooden spoon or shovel-shaped spatula; a wide, wire-mesh spoon is also helpful for tossing ingredients in hot oil and scooping them out quickly. In time, you may want to add some specialty items like a bamboo basket to rinse vegetables, a special rice cooker, or oil pots for individual cooking liquids. These are luxuries, however, and not necessities.

When it comes to stir-frying and deep-frying, the Chinese preference for using peanut oil is understandable: It has a delicate, unobtrusive flavor and does not burn at high temperatures. However, any vegetable oil, such as safflower, corn, or soybean, can be used with satisfactory results. Margarine, butter, and shortening, all of which burn easily, and olive oil, considered too heavy, are not acceptable substitutes; sesame oil* is used only as a seasoning agent. Avoid raw peanut oil, sold in health food stores, which tends to scorch foods. Most cooking oils can be used repeatedly if they are poured through a cheesecloth-lined strainer into an empty container to remove unwanted particles; if stored tightly-capped at room temperature, they will keep indefinitely.

The art of Chinese cooking lies in a perfect marriage of colors, textures, flavors, and aromas. As chief matchmaker, your job is to create a harmonious alliance between a number of diverse elements. For example, play ingredients off each other by varying them in hue, coarseness, and shape. If two dishes share similar color schemes, don't hesitate to substitute one item for another, bearing in mind that the order in which you stir-fry may have to be changed. Think of cutting techniques—slicing, grating, shredding, and mincing—as a means of altering textures. Juxtapose hot, sweet, and pungent dishes at one meal as an overture to the many taste and olfactory sensations available. Above all, avoid repetition and monotony. With an imaginative, flexible, and to some degree, playful spirit, you will soon realize there are fifty different ways to prepare each dish.

A fine Chinese dinner is a feast for the eyes as well as the stomach. Though it is not a requirement, classical Oriental dishware—chopsticks, rice paddles, shallow soup bowls, individual rice bowls, and porcelain spoons—will naturally enhance your setting. Serving pieces of various shades, shapes, and sizes, filled with artistically arranged food, will whet the appetite and heighten the appreciation of the meal. You can modulate your plates and platters to fit the occasion, just as you would ingredients. Dark-colored foods, for example, look handsome against light-colored plates, while vegetables cut into long, thin strips, are especially attractive on hexagonal-shaped platters.

---

*See Seasoning Chart.

Ordinarily, a family meal includes three or four small-portioned dishes of equal status, rather than an entrée flanked by subordinate side dishes; most meals are served with steamed rice or thin Chinese noodles. Soup is not served beforehand, but rather sipped slowly throughout the meal or offered as a final course. And although it is a popular custom in Westernized Chinese restaurants, tea is not served with dinner. Instead, cold beer is preferred with spicy foods, or soup is relied upon solely as a hot beverage. However, tea may be taken after the meal along with a platter of fresh fruit, which frequently serves as dessert. As far as fortune cookies are concerned—who needs them? Your good fortune is to have been fulfilled by an incredible feast without bread, heavy sauces, or overly sweet confections. Now that's what the Chinese call a wealth of health and happiness.

Seasoning Essentials

The roles of Chinese seasonings are diverse. They accentuate the natural flavor of foods without dominating or overwhelming them, provide contrast and balance to a dish, and neutralize undesirable aromas. To understand this ancient art, you must become familiar with China's basic spices and condiments and learn which ones will exude the desired hot, sour, sweet, salty, or bitter flavors. Once this is accomplished, you will be equipped to offset and harmonize flavors as well as adjust proportions as necessary.

As a rule, hot and sour flavors, as in *Hot and Sour Soup*, are derived from black or Szechuan peppercorns (hot), vinegar (sour), and a little soy sauce. Therefore, if you desire your soup hotter, increase the amount of pepper; if a more sour taste is in order, increase the amount of vinegar. To counterbalance a fiery dish with a sweet flavor, mix a little brown sugar or honey into a marinade or sauce. Garlic, ginger root, or star anise can be called upon to impart a memorable fragrance, while salty tastes can be elicited from soy sauce or plain salt. Scallions and leeks contribute what are considered bitter flavors.

Marinating is one of the most effective means for imbuing your specialties with a deep flavor and rich aroma. Chinese marinades are seasoned mixtures that both enhance and tenderize ingredients prior to stir-frying. Usually, they are made of soy sauce, rice wine, vinegar, salt, and sugar; spicy dishes often include minced garlic, grated ginger root, or hot bean paste in their marinades. For example, you can give bean curd a well-spiced and "meaty" taste by marinating it in a sauce tinged with hot bean paste; while chicken, scallops, and shrimp perk up when soaked in a ginger and garlic-spiked blend.

Pungent seasonings and condiments release their most influential flavors when placed in hot cooking oil, which absorbs their tastes and distributes them to other ingredients. To achieve this effect, heat oil in a wok until hot (a faint wisp of smoke is your signal). Then, add your potent seasonings such as garlic, ginger, red chili peppers, or Szechuan pepper-corns and stir-fry briskly for 15 to 20 seconds—just long enough to flavor the oil. Only then is the bulk of the dish—vegetables, seafood, chicken, etc.—tossed into the highly-seasoned oil, which permeates individual ingredients.

After stir-frying, a group of "light seasonings," which includes soy sauce, sesame oil, and sometimes vegetable or chicken broth, are added to lightly glaze a dish. Often, these mixtures, as well as marinades, include a little cornstarch which serves to bind and thicken the sauce, helping it ad-here to the food. Once a dish is served, there should be no need to add salt and pepper or drown the fare in soy sauce. However, certain dishes, such as *Spring Rolls* and *Pot Stickers*, obtain additional piquancy from table sauces such as *hoisin*, red chili oil, or soy sauce mixed with a little vinegar.

Anyone who enjoys hot and spicy Chinese food should become ac-quainted with hot bean paste and hot chili oil; once you are addicted to their stimulating flavors, it is hard to prepare a Chinese meal without them. A few tablespoons of hot bean paste, which can be added to either the marinade or hot oil, will lend a dark glowing hue and muted hotness to your creations. Hot chili oil, a tongue-tingling blend of peanut oil and red chili peppers, is used more as a table sauce than as a cooking agent. How-ever, it can be added to marinades, bean curd, vegetables, or noodles when you desire a reddish color and oily, pepper-hot taste. After a few encoun-ters with these two dynamic condiments, the fiery nature of Szechuan and Hunan foods will never elude your palate again.

CHINESE SEASONING CHART

CHILI SAUCE* or chili paste is a red, exceedingly hot sauce made from pulverized fresh red chili peppers. Used sparingly, it adds a terrific pi-quancy to shrimp dishes and stir-fried vegetables. This thin, fiery blend also serves as a dipping sauce. Many Chinese groceries carry *Thai Chili Sauce* which has a superb flavor. Look for the one with the brightly colored label or for a Chinese variety called *Chili Paste with Garlic*. For cooking pur-poses, only 1 to 2 teaspoons of either variety is necessary.

GARLIC is used liberally in Szechuan, Hunan, and northern Chinese dishes. It teams especially well with ginger and hot bean paste; this pun-gent trio will please those who enjoy hot food. A simple dipping sauce can be made from a mixture of soy sauce, crushed garlic, and sesame oil; pro-portions vary according to tastes. For cooking purposes, peel a clove and smash it with the side of a cleaver to facilitate slicing or mincing. To flavor

---

* Available at Oriental markets as well as some gourmet food shops or large supermarkets that have an Oriental food section.

1 pound of vegetables, poultry, or seafood, use 1 teaspoon minced garlic (mild), 1 tablespoon minced garlic (moderately hot), or 3 to 5 tablespoons minced garlic (very hot and pungent).

GINGER ROOT is used extensively in Chinese cooking. Fresh ginger, which is light brown, knobby, and fibrous, has a nippy, spicy flavor and aroma. It is treasured for its ability to enhance everything from soups to desserts. Ginger is always used with seafood as it neutralizes "fishy" odors. To flavor 1 pound of vegetables, bean curd, or seafood, use 1 to 2 teaspoons grated ginger root (mild), 1 tablespoon minced ginger root (moderately hot), or 3 tablespoons minced ginger root (hot, spicy, and aromatic). To prepare ginger juice, which can be added to quick-cooked soups or delicate dishes, slice and peel the root and pulverize through a garlic press. Ginger root will keep several weeks wrapped in plastic and refrigerated. Cleaned, sliced, and covered with salted water or sherry, it will keep indefinitely. (Save the ginger-spiked sherry for cooking.)

HOT BEAN PASTE* is responsible for the fiery flavor most often associated with Szechuan cooking. This thick sauce, made of soybeans, salt, and crushed chili peppers, is meant for the heavier, spicier dishes, not the delicate ones. The best variety, which hails from the People's Republic of China, contains salty fermented black beans. Use 1 to 2 tablespoons per pound of vegetables, poultry, bean curd, or seafood to obtain a deep spicy flavor and rich brown color. Because the potency and saltiness of hot bean paste varies from brand to brand, you may have to adjust the amount in each recipe. Those who want flavor but not heat may substitute Japanese *miso* paste. Either variety will keep indefinitely when refrigerated (once opened, canned products should be transferred to clean jars).

HOT CHILI OIL* is also called red oil or pepper oil. This potent seasoning doubles as a dipping sauce and flavor enhancer for stir-fried dishes. Use 1 to 2 teaspoons of this red-hot liquid to flavor bean curd, vegetable, poultry, or seafood dishes. Though it is available in small bottles, you can make your own: Heat 1 cup peanut oil in a small saucepan over low heat until hot and add one of the following—½ cup dried red chili pepper flakes; 12 whole dried red chili peppers; 3 tablespoons red (cayenne) pepper; or ½ cup dried *pequín*** chilies. Heat 1 minute, stirring frequently. Remove from heat and cool. Let stand, covered, several days to let the flavor develop. Strain oil through a cheesecloth into a narrow bottle and it will keep indefinitely. Whether store-bought or homemade, there is no equivalent substitute for hot chili oil.

**Available at Oriental markets as well as some gourmet food shops or large supermarkets that have an Oriental food section.*
***Available at Latin American markets and spice shops.*

HOISIN SAUCE* will appeal to those who like heavy, spicy foods. This thick, brownish-red sauce, made from soybeans, garlic, chili peppers, and other spices, imparts a sharp, but slightly sweet flavor, and a rich dark hue. It should be used sparingly to season bean curd, poultry, or seafood and may also be served as a dipping sauce. Once opened, canned *hoisin* sauce should be transferred to a clean jar and refrigerated. In this manner it will keep indefinitely. There are no substitutes.

RED PEPPERS are frequently employed in Szechuan and Hunan cooking to stimulate the palate and the appetite. They are available fresh or dried at Oriental or Latin American markets and some spice shops. Whole dried red peppers, which are bright red, thin, and about 2 inches long, are sometimes soaked in warm water before using. The seeds, which are the hottest part, can be removed if desired. It is advisable to wear rubber gloves when handling the fresh or dried chilies as their volatile oils may irritate the skin and eyes. For stir-fried dishes, whole peppers are occasionally charred in hot oil before other ingredients are added, giving the oil an intense and rich flavor. Fresh peppers, seeded and shredded, dried whole peppers or red pepper flakes may be added to any dish in need of heat. Cayenne pepper or Tabasco sauce may be substituted if necessary. A moderately hot dish would use 3 or 4 peppers, but you can use up to 10 peppers if you really like your food sweltering hot.

SESAME OIL* is not to be confused with delicate sesame oil found in health food stores. Chinese sesame oil, which has a rich brown color and distinct nutlike flavor derived from toasted sesame seeds, acts as a seasoning agent rather than a cooking oil. This dense oil should be used in small amounts only because its concentrated essence would be overpowering in large quantities. Use up to 2 teaspoons per pound of vegetables, bean curd, seafood, or poultry. As a garnish, sesame oil is poured over food just before it is served. There is no equivalent substitute.

SOY SAUCE* is a salty brown liquid made from fermented soybeans, wheat, and salt. The Chinese do not drown their food in it as Westerners do, but rather, use it in small amounts to enrich sauces and marinades. Both light and dark soy sauce are enlisted by this cuisine. Light soy sauce, a thin-bodied liquid with a mild flavor and beany aroma, works best with delicate foods. Use it in soups, seafood preparations, and other dishes in which a dark color is undesirable. Dark or "black" soy sauce, characterized by a molasseslike tang, is thicker and more robust. This variety is best suited for dishes in need of both a distinctive flavor and dark color; dishes made with hot bean paste or *hoisin* sauce in particular will benefit from this

---

* *Available at Oriental markets as well as some gourmet food shops or large supermarkets that have an Oriental food section.*

pungent seasoning. Use either variety, seasoned to taste with white vinegar, as a dipping sauce for *Spring Rolls* or *Pot Stickers*; proportions are usually 2 parts soy sauce to 1 part vinegar.

SZECHUAN PEPPERCORNS* are also called flower peppercorns. These rough, reddish-brown seeds impart a gentle, but spicy, taste with a cinnamonlike after-kick. Though peppery in nature, they are not related to black peppercorns, which are hotter and less delicate. Whole Szechuan peppercorns are often dry-roasted in a heavy skillet over low heat; this procedure heightens their flavor and facilitates grinding. To crush, place on a wooden board and pulverize with a rolling pin, or grind in a mortar with a pestle. For convenience, store in a pepper mill and grind as needed. This whole or crushed spice is welcome in almost any stir-fried Szechuan dish. In general, 6 to 8 whole or 1 teaspoon crushed peppercorns are sufficient to season a dish for 4 persons.

Other seasonings used in Chinese cooking: dried tangerine peel, cinnamon, star anise, white pepper, coriander (Chinese parsley), dried shrimp, dried scallops, sweet bean paste, five powdered spices, fennel seed, black sesame seeds, cloves, and sesame paste.

Nutritional Essentials

If the health-conscious gourmet wishes to avoid heart disease, obesity, and other diet-related problems, he must savor rich dishes on special occasions only. Within the context of Chinese cooking, however, one can indulge in exotic and fulfilling dishes on a daily basis without suffering the consequences of dietary indiscretions. Although this combination of good eating and health may seem like a paradox, the fact is that the Chinese diet is high in nutrients and fiber, low in calories (a mere 206 calories per average portion in our recipes), and virtually devoid of saturated fat and cholesterol. No wonder this culinary style has been called the diet of the future—eating lightly but still eating well.

The Chinese are not fascinated by great chunks of meat such as roasts or steaks, while butter, cheese, and milk are practically unknown in this Oriental kitchen. These preferences encourage a low-saturated fat, low-calorie intake. Lacking large quantities of beef-derived protein, the Chinese rely upon chicken and seafood in moderate amounts for this important nutrient. Treat yourself to *Kung Pao Shrimp* or *Shredded Chicken with Hot Bean Sauce*, each of which contains about one-half of an adult's minimum daily protein requirement. The usable protein in these highly spiced creations has been enhanced by complementing shrimp with cashews and chicken with peanuts.

If beef is not your meat, you needn't worry. The Chinese, with their nu-

---

Available at Oriental markets as well as some gourmet food shops or large supermarkets that have an Oriental food section.

tritional ingenuity, have created a "meatless cow" from soybeans. When cooked down to a custard-soft consistency and pressed into bricklike cakes, soybeans are transformed into a low-cost, highly nutritious food called tofu—also known in the West as bean curd or soybean cake. Discovered by Chinese royalty in 164 B.C., tofu has been the low-cost protein staple of the East Asian diet for two thousand years and is presently an important food for more than one billion people. Given that one billion people can't be wrong, we have included three delicious recipes which use bean curd as their principal ingredient: Bean Curd with Garlic-Ginger Sauce, Hot and Sour Soup, and Ma-Po Dou-Fu (Szechuan Bean Curd in Hot Sauce).

The virtues of these delicate, but firm, creamy-white soybean cakes can be extolled to no end. They come in several varieties, from soft to medium-firm to hard or as deep-fried puffs. Low in saturated fat and free of cholesterol, this adaptable food is a key to planning delicious meatless meals, not only in the Chinese cuisine, but in American and Japanese vegetarian kitchens as well.

Nutritionally, tofu is perhaps the finest source of low-cost, high-quality protein. An eight-ounce serving can supply almost one-third of your daily protein requirement. Moreover, tofu's unique amino acid composition makes it not only a basic protein source, but also a remarkable protein booster. And by combining tofu with rice (standard practice in most Chinese recipes) you can increase the usable protein content of your dish by about 30 percent.

Tofu does not contain as much protein by weight as meat, fish, or poultry, but it can contribute substantial amounts of this nutrient, especially when it is combined with and complemented by other ingredients in stir-fried dishes and soups. Its calcium content is comparable to that of milk.

The Chinese diet is replete with a variety of unique vegetables, most notably cloud ears, dried black mushrooms, tiger lily buds, bamboo shoots, water chestnuts, and Chinese cabbage. All of these are low in calories; bamboo shoots and water chestnuts are distinguished by their potassium content, and Chinese cabbage is enriched with vitamins A and C. Chinese vegetables should be lightly stir-fried in oil and served crisp.

Nutritionally speaking, nuts—especially peanuts, walnuts, and cashews—make a fine addition to most Chinese wok recipes. Sprinkling nuts over vegetable-oriented dishes, such as Tri-Color Vegetables, Broccoli with Tangy Sauce, or Hot and Sour Vegetables, and serving them over rice, will augment their protein content considerably.

Although 60 percent of the caloric content of our Chinese recipes is derived from fat (the highest of any cuisine in this book), you can take solace in the fact that the overwhelming majority is polyunsaturated. This breakdown reflects the frequent use of peanut oil in stir-frying. The cholesterol content of most dishes is negligible and the calories sufficiently low to make the Chinese diet, on the whole, a rather happy and well-balanced nutritional arrangement.

BROCCOLI WITH TANGY SAUCE

YIELD: 4 servings

---

10 cloud ears*—optional

Tangy Sauce:
  1 tablespoon chopped scallions
  1 to 2 teaspoons grated ginger root
  5 garlic cloves, minced
  2 teaspoons sesame oil**
  1 to 2 tablespoons hot chili oil**
  1 dried red pepper, seeded—
    optional
  1 tablespoon rice vinegar or white
    vinegar
  1 teaspoon sugar
  1 tablespoon soy sauce
  Available at Oriental markets.
**See Seasoning Chart.

Vegetables:
  1 pound fresh broccoli
  8 tablespoons peanut oil
  5 ounces water chestnuts, sliced
  1 teaspoon cornstarch
  1 teaspoon water

1. Place cloud ears in a bowl and cover with boiling water for 30 minutes. Rinse thoroughly. Cut away and discard any tough parts. Set aside.
2. *To prepare sauce:* Place all sauce ingredients in a bowl and stir briskly to combine thoroughly.
3. *To prepare broccoli:* Remove and discard outer leaves. Trim off tough stem ends. Slash stalks lengthwise or cut tops into flowerets and stalks into diagonal slices. Place in 1½ inches boiling, salted water, to which a generous pinch of baking soda has been added, to help broccoli retain its color. Cook until not quite tender—5 to 6 minutes. Remove and rinse with cold water to prevent further cooking.
4. Heat oil in wok until tiny bubbles and a hint of smoke appear. Add broccoli, water chestnuts, and cloud ears. Stir-fry 1 minute until all are coated with oil. Add tangy sauce and stir-fry up to 1 minute. Stir cornstarch into water and add to wok. Stir-fry 30 seconds. Transfer to a heated serving platter. Serve immediately, accompanied by rice.

CHIAO-TZU
(Pot Stickers)

YIELD: 20 pot stickers

Wrappers:
2 cups sifted unbleached white flour
½ teaspoon salt
½ cup plus 1 tablespoon hot water

Frying:
3 tablespoons corn or peanut oil, divided
1 cup water, vegetable stock, or chicken stock

Filling:
5 ounces frozen spinach, partially thawed and broken into small pieces
¼ cup minced water chestnuts or grated carrots
1 cup shredded Chinese cabbage or regular white cabbage
4 large fresh mushrooms, finely minced
2 scallions or green onions, finely minced
1 teaspoon light soy sauce*
1 teaspoon dry sherry or vermouth
1 teaspoon sesame oil*
1½ tablespoons grated ginger root
1 teaspoon garlic powder
1 tablespoon fresh or 1½ teaspoons dried coriander leaves
Pinch of sugar
Salt to taste

*See Seasoning Chart.

1. *To prepare wrappers*: Combine the flour and salt. Add the hot water and stir briskly with a wooden spoon or mix with your hands to form a smooth ball (or place flour and salt in a food processor or blender and add hot water; blend until dough forms a single mass). Knead 10 to 15 minutes or until very smooth and elastic. Cover with a damp kitchen towel and let dough rest from 15 to 30 minutes.
2. *To prepare filling*: Combine all the ingredients. Taste and adjust seasonings and set aside.
3. *To roll out and fill wrappers*: Knead dough again for a few minutes. Divide in half and roll each portion into a cylinder. With a sharp knife, cut each cylinder into 10 equal pieces. Flatten each piece with your palms. Then roll each piece with a rolling pin into a 2-inch circle, turning it an inch or so in a clockwise direction as you roll, to keep it uniform. Keep remaining pieces under a damp towel as you work to prevent dough from drying. Place a scant tablespoon of filling in the center of each circle. Fold dough over filling to form a half circle, and pinch the edges together at the center of the rim. With your fingertips, make 3 or 4 small pleats at each end to gather the dough around the filling; pinch tightly to seal.
4. *To fry*: Heat 2 tablespoons of the oil in a 12-inch skillet over medium-high heat. Add the pot stickers, pleated side up, and cook until golden brown on the bottom. Add the water or stock, cover with a tight-fitting lid, and

cook over medium heat until water has evaporated, about 10 minutes. Add the remaining tablespoon of oil around the sides of the pan and swirl gently to coat the bottom. Let fry uncovered another minute or two. Place a serving plate over the skillet and invert pan quickly or loosen the pot stickers gently with a spatula and transfer to a heated platter. Serve with hot chili oil (see *Seasoning Chart*), or a combination of light soy sauce mixed with Chinese red vinegar to taste.

CHINESE VEGETABLE BROTH

YIELD: Six cups vegetable broth or 1½ quarts

6½ cups water
6 dried mushrooms*
½ head Napa* (Chinese cabbage) or green cabbage, shredded
2 green onions, cut in half lengthwise
1 3-inch piece Szechuan preserved vegetable,* thoroughly washed

1 teaspoon grated ginger root
1½ tablespoons soy sauce
½ teaspoon salt
Pepper to taste
½ teaspoon yeast extract or Marmite**—optional

*Available at Oriental markets.
**Available at specialty food shops.

Place all the ingredients in a 3-quart saucepan. Bring to a boil, reduce heat to low, and simmer 45 minutes. Line a colander with damp cheesecloth and place over a large bowl. Pour broth into colander. Reserve stock and discard all but the mushrooms (destemmed), which can be saved for another use.

CHUNJUAN
(Spring Rolls)

YIELD: 12 to 14 spring rolls

6 to 8 large, dried black mushrooms*
2 tablespoons peanut oil
½ whole chicken breast, skinned, boned, and shredded
8 ounces bamboo shoots, shredded
2 ribs celery, very thinly sliced
Tops of 4 green onions, finely chopped

3 to 4 large leaves of Chinese cabbage, sliced into thin strips
6 ounces baby shrimp
2 tablespoons cornstarch
1 cup rich chicken broth
1 package of egg-roll wrappers or spring roll skins*—thaw if frozen
1 egg, well beaten
2 to 3 cups vegetable oil for deep frying

*Available at Oriental markets.

1. Place black mushrooms in a bowl. Cover with boiling water and let stand 20 to 30 minutes. Drain, rinse thoroughly, and remove tough stems. Cut into thin shreds and set aside.

2. Heat a wok over high heat for 15 seconds. Add the peanut oil and shredded chicken. Stir-fry 1 minute or until chicken has almost turned white. Add the bamboo shoots, mushrooms, and celery. Stir-fry 1 minute or until celery is translucent. Add green onion tops, cabbage, and shrimp. Stir-fry about 20 seconds. Add cornstarch to chicken broth and add to wok. Stir until mixture begins to thicken. Remove from heat and set aside to cool.

3. Separate the egg- or spring-roll wrappers. Lay one in front of you on a clean, dry, flat surface. Place 2 to 3 tablespoons of filling on one end of the wrapper. Roll up tightly, folding the edges in as you roll to form a cylinder with neatly tucked-in ends. Paint the seam with beaten egg to seal. Place on waxed paper for 15 minutes to dry. Repeat process with remaining wrappers.

4. Place vegetable oil in a deep fryer, deep skillet, or wok that can be placed directly on heat. Heat until wisps of smoke appear. Fry from 5 to 7 at a time (depending upon the size of the pan) until lightly browned (they will darken a little after removing), turning occasionally. Place on paper bags for proper draining. Keep warm in a low oven until ready to serve. Serve with any of the following: *hoisin* sauce, Worcestershire sauce, hot mustard, sweet and sour sauce, or a mixture of soy sauce and vinegar.

Note: Uncooked spring rolls can be wrapped in waxed paper and frozen for future use. Thaw before frying.

GANBIAN SIJIDOU
(Dry-Sautéed String Beans)   *YIELD: 4 servings*

---

1 pound string beans	2 teaspoons hot chili oil**
4 to 6 dried black mushrooms	3 tablespoons unsalted peanuts
¼ cup dried shrimp*	1 to 2 teaspoons grated ginger root
3 to 4 tablespoons minced scallions	2 tablespoons Szechuan vegetable*
2 tablespoons soy sauce	1 teaspoon each: sesame oil** and
¼ to 1 cup peanut oil	brown sugar

*Available at Oriental markets.
**See Seasoning Chart.

1. *To prepare vegetables*: Wash string beans, pat dry, and trim ends. Place dried mushrooms and dried shrimp in a bowl and cover with boiling water. Let stand 30 minutes. Drain and rinse well. Cut and discard tough stems from mushrooms. Mince mushrooms and shrimp and combine in a bowl with scallions and soy sauce. Marinate 15 minutes.

2. *To prefry string beans*: Heat peanut oil in a wok or large skillet until very hot. Add a handful of string beans and fry until the skin is wrinkled and the beans are tender. Transfer to paper towels with a slotted spoon to drain. Continue frying remaining beans by handfuls, allowing oil to reheat between batches if necessary.

3. *To complete frying*: Remove all but 2 tablespoons of the oil from wok (strain oil and save for a later use). Heat with the hot chili oil until lightly smoking. Add peanuts and ginger root, stirring vigorously for 30 seconds. Add mushroom mixture, Szechuan vegetable, sesame oil, and sugar. Stir-fry until the scallions begin to brown. Return string beans to wok and stir-fry until heated through. Transfer to a heated serving platter and serve with rice.

HOT AND SOUR MIXED VEGETABLES

YIELD: 4 servings

1 medium-sized zucchini
½ pound string beans
4 dried red peppers

Seasonings:
1 teaspoon cornstarch
1 teaspoon soy sauce
1 tablespoon Chinese red vinegar*
   or rice vinegar
2 teaspoons brown sugar
1 teaspoon sesame oil**
 Available at Oriental markets.
** *See* Seasoning Chart.

4 tablespoons peanut oil
1 teaspoon Szechuan
   peppercorns**
2 teaspoons grated ginger root
2 teaspoons minced scallions
¾ cup shredded carrots
1 cup miniature corn* or substitute
1 cup straw mushrooms*

1. *To prepare vegetables*: Wash zucchini and cut into julienne strips. Place in a colander, sprinkle with salt, and let stand 10 minutes. Rinse, pat dry, and set aside. Trim ends off string beans and cut into bite-size pieces. Parboil string beans for 2 minutes in rapidly boiling water. Drain and rinse in cold water; set aside. Cut ends off dried red peppers and shake out seeds; cut in half and set aside.

2. *To prepare seasonings*: In a small bowl stir the cornstarch into the soy sauce until smooth. Add vinegar, sugar, and sesame oil. Set aside.

3. *To stir-fry vegetables*: Heat peanut oil in a wok until hot (not smoking). Add dried red peppers and Szechuan peppercorns, stir-fry quickly—5 to 10 seconds. Do not let dried peppers burn. Add ginger root, scallions, and remaining vegetables and stir-fry 1 minute. Add seasonings and stir-fry another minute or 2. Serve immediately with rice.

HOT BEAN CURD WITH GINGER-GARLIC SAUCE

YIELD: 4 to 6 servings

1 pound bean curd
1 tablespoon safflower margarine
½ cup minced fresh mushrooms

Seasonings:
2 teaspoons cornstarch dissolved in
1½ tablespoons water
1 tablespoon rice wine or dry
sherry
2 teaspoons soy sauce
½ to 1 teaspoon salt
1 to 2 teaspoons sesame oil*
*See Seasoning Chart.

6 tablespoons peanut or safflower
oil
3 cloves garlic, minced
2 tablespoons grated ginger root
1 to 2 tablespoons hot bean paste*
1 scallion or green onion, chopped

1. Cut bean curd into ¾-inch cubes and set aside. If desired, place cubes in a pot of boiling water until they begin to float; gently remove, and drain before using. (This technique helps firm up bean curd and is especially recommended for the soft Japanese variety.)
2. Heat the margarine in a skillet. Sauté the minced mushrooms and set aside. Combine the seasonings and set aside.
3. Heat the peanut or safflower oil in a wok or large heavy skillet until hot. Add the garlic, ginger root, and hot bean paste. Stir-fry 15 seconds. Add the bean curd, sautéed mushrooms, scallion, and seasonings. Toss gently until mixture has thickened and bean curd is heated through. Transfer to a warm platter and serve immediately. This dish is best served over rice.

KUNG PAO SHRIMP

YIELD: 4 servings

6 dried black mushrooms*
¾ to 1 pound medium shrimp
2 teaspoons water
1 beaten egg white
½ teaspoon grated ginger root
2 garlic cloves, pressed
½ teaspoon salt
1½ tablespoons each: rice wine and
soy sauce
1 teaspoon each: rice vinegar and
cornstarch
*Available at Oriental markets.

⅛ teaspoon dry mustard
¼ cup peanut oil
3 to 6 dried red peppers
3 garlic cloves, minced
1 teaspoon grated ginger root
1 chopped scallion with tops
½ cup sliced water chestnuts
¼ cup whole cashews
¼ cup unsalted peanuts

1. Place dried mushrooms in a bowl and cover with boiling water. Let stand from 20 to 30 minutes. When soft, drain off water; remove and discard tough stems. Slice mushroom caps and set aside.
2. Meanwhile, shell and devein shrimp. In a bowl combine the water, beaten egg white, ½ teaspoon grated ginger root, 2 pressed garlic cloves, and salt. Add shrimp and marinate 15 minutes.
3. In another bowl, combine the rice wine, soy sauce, vinegar, cornstarch and dry mustard. Set aside.
4. Heat peanut oil in a wok over high heat until it bubbles and smokes a little. Add red peppers (the more you add the hotter the dish will be) and stir-fry until slightly charred. Reduce heat and add the minced garlic and 1 teaspoon grated ginger root. Stir-fry 10 seconds.
5. Add shrimp with marinade and stir-fry until barely pink. Add sliced black mushrooms, chopped scallion, sliced water chestnuts, nuts, and reserved cornstarch mixture. Stir quickly, cover, and cook 2 minutes. Serve immediately with cooked rice.

LOVER'S EGGPLANT

YIELD: 4 to 6 servings

Eggplant:
   2 small eggplants
   4 cups safflower or peanut oil for frying
   2 teaspoons minced garlic
   1 tablespoon grated ginger root
   1 tablespoon hot bean paste* or
   1 *serrano* chili pepper, seeded and minced
   1 cup vegetable or chicken stock
   1 teaspoon sesame oil*
**See Seasoning Chart.*

Sauce:
   1 tablespoon soy sauce
   1 teaspoon rice vinegar or white vinegar
   1 teaspoon cornstarch, dissolved in a little water
   Pinch of pepper
   2 tablespoons chopped scallions
   1½ teaspoons grated ginger root

1. Combine all the sauce ingredients and set aside.
2. *To prepare eggplant*: Cut stems off eggplants. Cut each in half, then in quarters, and finally into 2-inch chunks. Heat oil in a wok or 3-quart saucepan to 375 degrees. Add eggplant and fry 4 minutes until tender and lightly browned. Remove with a wire or slotted spoon to paper towels for draining. Remove leftover oil from wok. Strain, reserve 2 tablespoons, and save remainder for another use. Wipe wok clean.
3. Heat the reserved oil (2 tablespoons) in wok until hot. Add garlic, ginger root, and hot bean paste. Stir-fry 15 seconds. Add vegetable or chicken stock and bring to a boil for 2 minutes. Add eggplant and sauce, reduce heat to medium, and stir-fry until eggplant and sauce are warmed through. Transfer to a heated serving platter. Pour the sesame oil over all and serve immediately with rice.

MANDARIN PANCAKES

YIELD: 24 pancakes

1 cup unbleached white flour or
  all-purpose flour
1 cup whole wheat flour or
  all-purpose flour

¾ cup boiling water
1 to 2 tablespoons peanut oil

1. *To prepare dough*: Sift both flours into a large bowl. Make a well in the center and add the boiling water. Stir quickly but gently with a wooden spoon until a soft dough is formed. Turn onto a lightly floured board and knead 10 minutes or until smooth and elastic. Cover with a slightly damp towel and let rest 10 minutes.

2. *To roll out pancakes*: Divide dough in half. Roll each piece into a 12-inch cylinder. Cut each roll into 12 equal pieces. Pat each piece into a 2-inch circle. Brush the top of each circle lightly with oil. Sandwich 2 circles together, oiled sides facing inward. With a rolling pin, roll each sandwich into a 6- or 7-inch circle, rotating an inch or so in a clockwise direction as you roll to keep a uniform shape. Keep rolled circles covered with a slightly damp towel to prevent them from drying out as you work.

3. *To cook pancakes*: Place a heavy ungreased 8-inch skillet over high heat for 30 seconds. Reduce heat to medium and cook pancakes, one at a time, until they puff slightly and little brown specks appear on the surface. Do not brown pancakes—they should be delicately cooked.

4. As each pancake is finished, carefully separate the sandwiches into separate pancakes and stack on a plate. Serve immediately or wrap in foil and refrigerate or freeze for later use. Reheat pancakes in a steamer or low oven until warm. Fill with *Moo Shu Vegetables* (p. 101), *Dry-Sautéed String Beans* (p. 95), or serve plain with *hoisin* sauce.*

*See Seasoning Chart.

MA-PO DOU-FU

(Szechuan Bean Curd in Hot Sauce)

YIELD: 6 to 8 servings

1 pound bean curd, drained
2 tablespoons safflower margarine
¼ pound fresh mushrooms, finely
  minced
2 tablespoons cornstarch
½ cup water or chicken stock
1 to 2 teaspoons hot chili oil*
1 to 2 tablespoons rice wine or dry
  sherry

½ teaspoon each: salt and ground
  Szechuan pepper*
1 to 2 teaspoons brown sugar
4 to 6 tablespoons peanut oil
2 tablespoons minced garlic
1 tablespoon grated ginger root
2 to 3 tablespoons hot bean paste*
2 scallions, chopped
1 cup fresh shelled or frozen peas

*See Seasoning Chart.

1. Cut bean curd into small cubes. Set aside.
2. *To prepare sauce*: Heat margarine in a small skillet. Sauté minced mushrooms until well coated with margarine and slightly cooked. In a bowl, combine the cornstarch, water or chicken stock, hot chili oil, rice wine, salt, Szechuan pepper, and sugar. Taste and adjust seasonings. Add mushrooms and marinate 15 minutes.
3. Heat peanut oil in a wok until very hot. Add garlic and ginger; stir-fry 10 seconds. Add bean paste and scallions; stir-fry 15 seconds. Add mushrooms with sauce and peas, stirring frequently for about 1 minute. Add bean curd and stir-fry until hot. Serve immediately over rice.

MOCK CHINESE MEATBALLS   YIELD: *Approximately 16 mock meatballs*

1 cup boiling water
1 cup soy grits (unflavored)
2 tablespoons soy sauce
2 tablespoons oyster sauce*
⅛ teaspoon ground ginger
¼ teaspoon cinnamon
⅛ teaspoon ground cloves
⅛ to ¼ teaspoon crushed, dried red chili peppers

2 garlic cloves, finely chopped
1 tablespoon brown sugar or honey
1 egg, well beaten
Cornmeal (about ½ cup)
1 quart peanut oil for frying
Shredded lettuce
Chopped scallions and fresh coriander* for garnish

*Available at Oriental markets.

1. Pour boiling water over soy grits and let stand 10 minutes. Add soy sauce, oyster sauce, seasonings, garlic, and sugar. Let stand for 1 to 2 hours at room temperature.
2. Add beaten egg, and enough cornmeal so that mixture can be formed into balls that hold their shape (about ¼ cup). Shape mixture into walnut-size balls and roll each one in remaining cornmeal. Set aside.
3. Place peanut oil in a deep, heavy saucepan. Heat to 375 degrees (if you don't have a thermometer, drop a bread cube into the hot oil for exactly 60 seconds—if it browns, the oil is ready). Deep-fry balls in hot oil, 6 or 8 at a time, until golden-brown and crusty, turning occasionally with tongs. Drain on paper towels.
4. To serve, line a platter with shredded lettuce. Arrange meatballs attractively on the lettuce and garnish with chopped scallions and fresh coriander leaves.
Note: There are many ways to serve mock meatballs. For example, they may be added to soups right before serving, or tossed with sweet and sour sauce as a main course. For an appetizer, dip them in *hoisin* or your favorite sauce. Recipe may be doubled to serve more people.

MOO SHU VEGETABLES

(Stir-fried Eggs and Vegetables with Mandarin Pancakes)   YIELD: 12 Moo Shu *pancakes*

2 tablespoons safflower margarine
¼ pound fresh mushrooms, minced

Marinade:
1 teaspoon hot chili oil*—optional
1 teaspoon rice wine or dry sherry
½ teaspoon cornstarch
2 teaspoons soy sauce or *hoisin* sauce*
½ teaspoon ground Szechuan pepper*

½ cup dried tiger lily buds**
½ cup cloud ears**
1 tablespoon rice wine or dry sherry
½ teaspoon salt
1½ tablespoons soy sauce
½ teaspoon sesame oil*
3 tablespoons peanut oil, divided
3 eggs, well beaten
1 teaspoon grated ginger root
12 Mandarin Pancakes (p. 99), warmed
Plum sauce** or *hoisin* sauce*
3 whole scallions, cut in half lengthwise and shredded

*See Seasoning Chart.
**Available at Oriental markets.

1. Heat margarine in a large skillet until hot. Add mushrooms and sauté. Combine marinade ingredients in a bowl. Add sautéed mushrooms and let stand 20 minutes. Meanwhile, combine lily buds and cloud ears in another bowl. Cover with boiling water and let soak 20 minutes. Drain lily buds and cloud ears and rinse thoroughly. Set aside. Do not drain mushrooms from marinade.

2. Combine rice wine, salt, soy sauce, and sesame oil. Set aside. Heat 1 tablespoon of the peanut oil in a wok until hot. Add eggs and scramble lightly. Remove and set aside. Wipe wok clean and heat remaining oil until hot. Add mushrooms with marinade and stir-fry for 30 seconds. Add lily buds, cloud ears, rice-wine mixture, and ginger root. Stir-fry 1 minute longer. Add eggs and cook until warmed through. Transfer to a heated serving platter.

3. *To serve:* Place *Moo Shu* on the table along with the Mandarin Pancakes, a dish of plum or *hoisin* sauce, and a plate of shredded scallions. Let each person place a pancake on his plate and spread one of the sauces lightly on the surface. Cover sauce with shredded scallions. Place about 2 tablespoons *Moo Shu* in the center and roll up jelly-roll fashion. Eat with your fingers.

NOODLES WITH PEKING SAUCE

YIELD: 4 servings

2 tablespoons safflower margarine
½ pound fresh mushrooms, minced

Marinade:
1 teaspoon Chinese red vinegar* or
   white vinegar
1 teaspoon grated ginger root
½ teaspoon each: sesame oil,**
   brown sugar, and rice wine or
   dry sherry
½ teaspoon ground Szechuan
   pepper**

1 cucumber, peeled
½ to ¾ pound Chinese noodles* or
   thin vermicelli noodles
2 tablespoons peanut oil
4 garlic cloves, minced
2 scallions, chopped with tops
1 tablespoon hot chili oil**
1 or 2 teaspoons hot bean paste**
1 teaspoon peanut oil or safflower
   margarine
2 eggs, well beaten

   *Available at Oriental markets.
**See Seasoning Chart.

1. Heat margarine in a wok or skillet until hot. Sauté mushrooms, remove from heat, and let cool. Combine ingredients for marinade in a bowl. Add mushrooms and let stand 15 minutes. Cut cucumber in half, remove seeds, and cut each half into thin slivers. Set aside.
2. Bring 4 to 6 quarts salted water to a boil in a large pot. Add noodles and cook until tender. Meanwhile, heat oil in a wok until barely smoking. Add garlic, scallions, hot chili oil, and hot bean paste. Stir-fry 10 seconds. Add mushrooms with marinade and stir-fry 1 minute. Reduce heat and let sauce simmer a few minutes. Just before serving, heat the 1 teaspoon of peanut oil in a small skillet and add the eggs. Scramble gently.
3. *To serve*: Drain noodles in a colander and rinse quickly with cold water. Transfer to a serving bowl. Top with warm scrambled eggs, cucumbers, and finally, the sauce. Serve immediately.

PRECIOUS VEGETABLES WITH
SZECHUAN SAUCE

YIELD: 4 servings

12 fresh string beans
1 medium-sized green pepper
¼ pound fresh mushrooms
4 to 6 dried red peppers

Sauce:
¼ cup peanut oil
1 tablespoon hot chili oil*
1 tablespoon rice vinegar or white
   vinegar
½ teaspoon salt
2 teaspoons soy sauce
1 teaspoon honey
1½ teaspoons cornstarch
1½ teaspoons water
*See Seasoning Chart.

1 tablespoon peanut oil
1 tablespoon hot chili oil*
2 tablespoons minced scallions
2 teaspoons grated ginger root
4 garlic cloves, minced
¼ cup sliced water chestnuts
¼ cup unsalted peanuts
1 tablespoon sesame oil*

1. *To prepare vegetables*: Wash and trim ends from string beans; cut into thirds and set aside. Wash and remove seeds from green pepper; cut into strips and set aside. Quickly wash mushrooms and pat dry; slice and set aside. Slice the ends off the red peppers and shake out seeds (the more peppers you use the hotter the dish will be); set aside.
2. *To prepare sauce:* Combine all the sauce ingredients, except the cornstarch and water, in a small bowl. Stir well to blend and set aside. In a separate bowl dissolve the cornstarch in water. Set aside.
3. *To stir-fry vegetables*: Heat the 1 tablespoon peanut oil and the 1 table-spoon of hot chili oil in a wok until hot. Add scallions, ginger root, garlic, and red peppers. Stir-fry about 10 seconds. Add string beans and stir-fry 1 minute. Add green pepper and stir-fry 30 seconds. Add the mushrooms, water chestnuts, and peanuts. Stir-fry less than 1 minute. Add sauce and stir-fry, making sure vegetables are coated. Add cornstarch mixture, stir-ring slowly to slightly thicken sauce. Pour the sesame oil over the entire mixture and serve immediately with rice.
Variation: Add ¼ pound scallops (cut in half) to the wok along with the fresh mushrooms and water chestnuts.

ROBIN'S SHRIMP IN TOMATO-CHILI SAUCE   YIELD: 6 servings

Sauce:
6 tablespoons ketchup
1 tablespoon grated ginger root
1 tablespoon pressed garlic
½ to 1 teaspoon chili sauce*
3 tablespoons dry sherry or rice
   wine, divided
2 teaspoons cornstarch

*See Seasoning Chart.

Shrimp and Vegetables:
1 pound medium-sized raw
   shrimp, shelled and deveined
4 tablespoons peanut oil, divided
1 medium-sized onion, cut into ½-
   inch slices
1 green pepper, seeded and sliced
   into ½-inch pieces
6 fresh mushrooms, quartered
6 ounces bamboo shoots, sliced

1. Combine the ketchup, ginger root, garlic, chili sauce, and 2 tablespoons of the dry sherry. Set aside. In another bowl, combine the remaining tablespoon of sherry with the cornstarch. Add to chili sauce and set aside.
2. Carefully run a sharp knife up the back of each shrimp to make a deep slit lengthwise; then slit each shrimp crosswise. (Do not cut completely through shrimp.) This allows the shrimp to fan and roll up into a wad when cooked.
3. Heat an ungreased wok until moderately hot. Add 2 tablespoons of the peanut oil along with the shrimp. Stir-fry 1 to 2 minutes or until shrimp are barely cooked. Remove and set aside. Wipe wok clean with paper towels, then reheat over a moderate flame. Add remaining oil and onion and stir-fry 30 seconds. Add green pepper, mushrooms, and bamboo shoots, stir-frying for another 30 seconds. Return shrimp to wok and stir-fry another 30 seconds.
4. Push shrimp and vegetables with a wooden spoon away from the center of the wok to form a ring or doughnut shape. Place reserved chili sauce in the center and heat just until it bubbles. Toss with shrimp and vegetables and serve immediately over rice.

SHREDDED CHICKEN WITH HOT BEAN SAUCE *YIELD: 4 servings*

1 pound chicken (may use breasts or a combination of breasts and thighs)

Marinade:
2 teaspoons cornstarch
2 teaspoons rice wine, dry sherry, or water
½ teaspoon sesame oil*
1 egg white
1 tablespoon minced garlic
1 teaspoon brown sugar
2½ teaspoons grated ginger root
1½ to 2 tablespoons hot bean paste*
 *See Seasoning Chart.
** Available at Oriental markets.

¼ cup cloud ears** or straw mushrooms**
3 tablespoons chicken stock or water
1 tablespoon soy sauce
1 teaspoon rice vinegar
1 teaspoon crushed Szechuan pepper*
¼ cup peanut or safflower oil
1 carrot cut into thin, 2-inch strips
2 scallions, chopped
½ cup unsalted peanuts or walnut halves—optional
½ cup water chestnuts, cut into matchstick slivers—optional

1. Skin and bone the chicken. Cut into thin strips. Combine the marinade in a mixing bowl. Taste and adjust seasonings. Add more hot bean sauce for hotter flavor or more ginger root and garlic for pungency. Add chicken, toss well so that all pieces are coated, and let stand 15 minutes.
2. Meanwhile, place the cloud ears in a bowl. Cover with boiling water and let stand 15 minutes. Drain and set aside. If using canned straw mushrooms, drain and measure out ¼ cup (or more if desired).
3. Combine the chicken stock or water, soy sauce, vinegar, and crushed Szechuan pepper in a small bowl. Set aside.
4. Heat the peanut or safflower oil in a wok until hot. Add the carrot and stir-fry 30 seconds. Add the chicken and marinade. Stir-fry until chicken turns almost white in color. Add the cloud ears or straw mushrooms, scallions, peanuts or walnuts, and water chestnuts. Stir-fry 1 minute, briskly flipping and tossing ingredients. Add the reserved chicken stock-soy sauce mixture and heat another minute, stirring constantly. Transfer to a heated platter and serve immediately.

SUANLA TANG
(Hot and Sour Soup)

YIELD: 8 servings

¼ cup dried tiger lily buds*
5 dried black mushrooms*
½ pound bean curd
5 spinach leaves, washed and
  stemmed
½ cup sliced bamboo shoots
5 cups *Chinese Vegetable Broth*
  (p. 94) or rich chicken stock
1 teaspoon hot chili oil**

5 tablespoons Chinese red vinegar*
  or rice vinegar
1 or 2 tablespoons light soy sauce
¾ teaspoon salt
1 teaspoon freshly ground black
  pepper
1 tablespoon cornstarch
2 tablespoons water
1 egg, slightly beaten
2 green onions, chopped with tops

*Available at Oriental markets.
**See Seasoning Chart.

1. Place lily buds and dried mushrooms in a bowl. Cover with boiling water and soak 20 minutes. Drain off water and rinse thoroughly. Cut tough stems from mushrooms and discard. Slice mushrooms into thin slices.
2. Cut bean curd into ¼-inch slices. Cut each slice into thin strips. Cut spinach leaves into strips.
3. Bring broth or stock to a boil and add all the ingredients except the cornstarch, water, egg, and green onions. Boil gently 10 minutes. Taste and adjust seasonings—add more vinegar for a more sour flavor or add more pepper for a hotter flavor. Dissolve cornstarch in water and stir slowly into soup. Boil 1 minute. Pour beaten egg in very slowly, stirring constantly until the egg coagulates into thin shreds. Float green onions on top and serve immediately.

TRI-COLOR VEGETABLES

YIELD: 4 servings

2 medium-sized sweet red bell
  peppers
1 small yellow squash
½ pound snow peas
2 scallions or green onions

4 to 6 tablespoons peanut or
  safflower oil
8 whole Szechuan peppercorns*
1 tablespoon grated ginger root

*See Seasoning Chart.
**Available at Oriental markets.

Seasonings:
1 tablespoon rice wine or dry
  sherry
2 teaspoons soy sauce or oyster
  sauce**
1½ teaspoons brown sugar
1 teaspoon sesame oil*
  Salt to taste

1. Core and seed the red peppers and cut lengthwise into neat, uniform strips. Slice the yellow squash in half lengthwise and then into quarters. Cut each quarter into 1½-inch strips. Trim the ends off the snow peas; remove strings by pulling them along the edge of the pod. Mince the scallions or green onions. Place each of these vegetables in separate piles near the wok.
2. Combine the seasonings in a small bowl and set aside.
3. Heat the oil in a wok or heavy 12-inch skillet until hot. Add the peppercorns and stir-fry for 15 or 20 seconds to season the oil. Remove peppercorns and discard. Toss ginger root into the oil and stir around for 10 seconds. Add the red peppers and squash. Stir-fry 1 minute or until partially tender. Add the snow peas, scallions, and seasonings. Stir-fry briskly from 30 to 60 seconds, tossing and flipping the vegetables until all are coated with the seasonings and snow peas are cooked but not wilted. Transfer to a hot platter and serve immediately.

CHINA/RECIPE ANALYSIS CHART

Name of Recipe	Quantity	Calories	CHO gms.	Protein gms.	Total Fat gms.	Saturated Fat gms.	Cholesterol mg.	Dietary Fiber gms.
1. Chinese Vegetable Broth	—	—	—	—	—	—	—	—
2. Mandarin Pancakes	each	45	8 (71%)	1 (9%)	1 (20%)		—	.1
3. *Chiao-Tzu* (Pot Stickers)	each	52	11 (85%)	2 (15%)	—	—	—	.2
4. Hot Bean Curd with Ginger-Garlic Sauce	per serving	88	6 (27%)	7 (32%)	4 (41%)		—	.2
5. *Suanla Tang* (Hot and Sour Soup)	per serving	103	14 (54%)	5 (19%)	3 (27%)	—	39	1.0
6. Mock Chinese Meatballs	per serving	147	7 (19%)	5 (14%)	11 (67%)	2 (12%)	20	.2
7. Tri-color Vegetables	per serving	158	7 (18%)	1 (3%)	14 (79%)	3 (17%)	—	.6
8. *Ma-Po Dou-Fu* (Bean Curd in Hot Sauce)	per serving	174	9 (21%)	3 (7%)	14 (78%)	3 (16%)	—	.5
9. *Chunjuan* (Spring Rolls)	per serving	178	6 (13%)	7 (16%)	14 (71%)	3 (15%)	38	.3
10. Robin's Shrimp in Tomato-Chili Sauce	per serving	206	13 (25%)	16 (31%)	10 (44%)	2 (9%)	94	.9
11. Lover's Eggplant	per serving	207	7 (14%)	2 (4%)	19 (72%)	2 (9%)	—	1.2
12. *Moo Shu* Vegetables	per serving	209	18 (34%)	6 (11%)	15 (55%)	3 (13%)	157	.4
13. Hot and Sour Mixed Vegetables	per serving	232	19 (33%)	3 (5%)	16 (62%)	3 (12%)	—	2.0
14. Shredded Chicken with Hot Bean Sauce	per serving	280	11 (16%)	23 (33%)	16 (51%)	3 (10%)	38	.8
15. Precious Vegetables with Szechuan Sauce	per serving	362	13 (14%)	8 (9%)	32 (77%)	6 (15%)	—	3.2

Name of Recipe	Quantity	Calories	CHO gms.	Protein gms.	Total Fat gms.	Saturated Fat gms.	Choles- terol mg.	Dietary Fiber gms.
16. Broccoli with Tangy Sauce	per serving	377	15 (16%)	5 (5%)	33 (79%)	5 (12%)	—	2.3
17. *Kung Pao* Shrimp	per serving	390	26 (27%)	22 (23%)	22 (50%)	3 (7%)	106	2.6
18. *Ganbian Sijidou* (Dry- Sautéed String Beans)	per serving	412	15 (15%)	7 (7%)	36 (78%)	7 (15%)	—	1.8
19. Noodles with Peking Sauce	per serving	451	48 (43%)	13 (12%)	23 (45%)	4 (8%)	157	1.1

Numbers in parentheses (%) indicate percentage of total calories contributed by nutrient.

MENUS

LOW CALORIE SPECIALTIES
(500 to 700 calories per meal)

MOO SHU VEGETABLES
MANDARIN PANCAKES
HOT AND SOUR MIXED
VEGETABLES
Cantaloupe
Dragon Well Tea

MA-PO DOU-FU
TRI-COLOR VEGETABLES
Steamed Rice
Sliced Apples and Bananas
Lychee Tea

ROBIN'S SHRIMP IN TOMATO-CHILI SAUCE
LOVER'S EGGPLANT
Steamed Rice
Sliced Oranges and Pears
Jasmine Tea

•

LOW CHOLESTEROL MENUS
(Less than 50 mgs. of cholesterol per meal)

LOVER'S EGGPLANT
GANBIAN SIJIDOU
(DRY-SAUTÉED STRING BEANS)
Steamed Rice
Casaba Melon
Jasmine Tea

CHIAO-TZU
(POT STICKERS)
BROCCOLI WITH TANGY SAUCE
Steamed Rice
Sliced Apples and Dates
Dragon Well Tea

PRECIOUS VEGETABLES WITH SZECHUAN SAUCE
MA-PO DOU-FU
Steamed Rice
Fresh Plums and Apricots
Green Tea

•

LOW SATURATED FAT SELECTIONS
(Less than 8 grams of saturated fat per meal)

**CHIAO-TZU
(POT STICKERS)
HOT BEAN CURD WITH GINGER-
GARLIC SAUCE**
Steamed Rice
Preserved Kumquats
Green Tea

**MOCK CHINESE MEATBALLS
SUANLA TANG
(HOT AND SOUR SOUP)
NOODLES WITH PEKING SAUCE**
Mandarin Oranges
Black Tea

**CHUNJUAN
(SPRING ROLLS)
KUNG PAO SHRIMP**
Steamed Rice
Lychee Nuts
Oolong Tea

•

HIGH PROTEIN MEALS
(30 or more grams of protein per meal)

**CHUNJUAN
(SPRING ROLLS)
NOODLES WITH PEKING SAUCE
BROCCOLI WITH TANGY SAUCE
SUANLA TANG
(HOT AND SOUR SOUP)**
Jasmine Tea

**SHREDDED CHICKEN WITH HOT
BEAN SAUCE**
Steamed Rice
**GANBIAN SIJIDOU
(DRY-SAUTÉED STRING BEANS)**
Honeydew Melon
Oolong Tea

KUNG PAO SHRIMP
Steamed Rice
PRECIOUS VEGETABLES WITH SZECHUAN SAUCE
Mandarin Oranges
Chrysanthemum Tea

•

WELL BALANCED LUNCH OR DINNER MENUS

(Selections that conform to recommendations in Dietary Goals for United States*)*

SUANLA TANG
(HOT AND SOUR SOUP)
NOODLES WITH PEKING SAUCE
Bananas and Dates
Chrysanthemum Tea

CHIAO-TZU
(POT STICKERS)
MOO SHU VEGETABLES
MANDARIN PANCAKES
Jasmine Tea

SHREDDED CHICKEN WITH HOT BEAN SAUCE
HOT AND SOUR MIXED VEGETABLES
Steamed Rice
Preserved Kumquats
Lychee Tea

CHAPTER 5

FRANCE
Love and Quiches

Culinary Essentials

It doesn't take credentials from the *Cordon Bleu* or a battery of copper pots and pans to turn out superb French meals. Anyone with a fairly well-stocked kitchen, an aptitude for following instructions, and a willingness to sacrifice quantity for quality, can evoke the spirit of French provincial cooking. We are not speaking about *haute* (high) *cuisine*, a highly evolved art which, at its finest, requires the skills of a professional chef. Though sophisticated in appearance, *haute cuisine* has its drawbacks: expensive ingredients, elaborate kitchen gear, extensive cooking time, and excessively rich foods. As a result, this prestigious culinary style is becoming a rarity, even in France. The mood today is away from elaborate saucing and more towards the natural flavor of fresh foods. Light, simply prepared meals are in and calorie-laden creations, except on occasion, are out. This new trend makes French cooking more accessible not only to everyday cooks, but also to individuals with dietary restrictions.

French cooking is not a freewheeling style, and careful attention to procedures and timing are integral to the success of most dishes. However, it is a mistake to be intimidated, as many cooks are, by a recipe that looks lengthy or complex. After all, a recipe is merely a set of instructions presented in a step-by-step fashion. And the French, with their respect for classical cooking techniques, often explain each step in great detail. While this makes a recipe appear difficult, exhaustive directions, if precise, can help you avoid cataclysmic errors. Be sure to read a recipe through completely and assemble the necessary ingredients before you begin—many failures occur halfway through the cooking process when a key ingredient or tool is nowhere to be found.

A chef once said that the best utensils for this cuisine are "the mouth and the mind." Of course, a few accessories are necessary to supplement these natural endowments. If your budget allows, a food processor or blender can help you perform innumerable time-consuming chores such as kneading bread and making pastry dough. For sauces and beating egg whites, you should have a large and small wire whisk, preferably one with many loops. An unlined copper bowl is also essential for beating egg whites (they can also be whipped in an electric mixer but the volume will be less). Heavy saucepans and skillets in graduated sizes and a heavy metal 4½-quart Dutch oven or soup pot will equip you to prepare sauces, omelettes, sautéed vegetables, soups, and stews. A small nonstick frying pan is more practical and, in our opinion, better suited for crêpes than a fancy crêpe pan. In time, you may want to add a number of gadgets or serving pieces that will give your meals a French flair: a pastry bag to decorate desserts, ceramic gratin dishes for vegetables and seafood, or a soup tureen, to name a few.

Most French recipes call for familiar ingredients and most items are readily available at large supermarkets. Quality is an important consideration when selecting your groceries if you adhere to the French principle of "eating better but eating less." Inferior products, vegetables, and seasonings will never produce superior dishes. For example, excellent marinades or vinaigrettes depend upon fine virgin olive oil or delicate peanut oil. Dijon mustard, which may be stirred into sauces or brushed over prebaked pie shells to give quiche a piquant accent, puts prepared mustard to shame. And capers, pickled flower buds packed in bottles, lend a unique flavor and classy touch to salads, sauces, and seafood that is unrivaled by any other ingredient. There is one quality-wise concession, however, that is worth considering: While most chefs would probably hang up their aprons rather than give up butter, we feel safflower margarine should be on hand for everyday cooking; it is best to restrict the use of unsalted or sweet cream butter to special occasions, pastry doughs, and desserts.

Imported cheeses can be relied upon to impart character and variety to your meals. Complement an hors d'oeuvre platter with mellow but distinctively flavored cheeses such as Beaumont, Reblochon, St. Paulin, or Port du Salut. Other popular accompaniments include Brie, Camembert, Gourmandise, and Muenster. At the meal's end, when tastebuds are more seasoned, consider something a bit stronger or livelier to escort a fresh fruit course—pungent Chevrotin, tangy St. André, or nut-studded Rambol. Or, be adventurous and present your own *Mock Boursin Cheese*, a creamy, *Neufchâtel*-based blend with a delicate herb flavor.

Soup sets the tone of the meal. If you are having several courses, serve a light broth to whet the palate without spoiling the appetite. For a simple supper, you might serve a hearty potage or *Basque Peasant's Soup* as an entrée and flank it with sourdough bread, fresh fruit, and cheese.

While appetizers and soups are modestly presented, French entrées will give you the opportunity to capture the imagination. Novice cooks should be able to prepare the *Cauliflower and Shallot Tart* or *Asparagus Quiche* without difficulty. You can leave an individual stamp on these versatile vegetable pies by substituting—in whatever proportions please you—sliced mushrooms, shrimp, or broccoli in place of the cauliflower or asparagus. Cheeses can be varied too; nutlike Emmentaler is a nice variation of Swiss cheese, while a sharp cheddar is a pleasant change from Parmesan cheese.

Experienced cooks will want to try their hand at *Soufflé au Fromage*, which is lofty, ethereal, and barely laced with nutmeg and Gruyère cheese. *Crêpes Ratatouille à la Sauce Mornay*, a mélange of eggplant, zucchini, and tomatoes wrapped in crêpes and robed with cheese sauce, will also provide an interesting challenge.

There are many respectable French desserts that do not require advanced pastry skills. An easy but elegant finale can be assembled by topping liqueur-soaked strawberries with *Crème Fraîche*, a tangy-smooth sauce that tastes like a cross between whipped and sour cream. For a more memorable climax, you might prepare *Pavé au Chocolat*, a molded and chilled cake-pudding made with layers of choclate butter cream and lady fingers. Though not at all time-consuming to devise, this handsome dessert has the look of something right out of a fine *patisserie*. But no one will ever guess that yours is the product of someone who graduated not from the *Cordon Bleu*, but from the school of trial and error.

Seasoning Essentials

If there is one word that characterizes the art of French seasoning, it is *subtlety*. While triumphant French dishes are dependent upon an intricate network of flavorings, nevertheless a flood of seasonings, wine, cream, and garnishes is antithetical to the essence of French cookery. Simplicity of flavors should be the ultimate goal of your creations, and this comes with diligence, precision, and an authoritative hand.

Because herbs are the foundation of the French kitchen, basil, thyme, tarragon, bay leaves, and chervil should always be within reach. Though herbs may be used—in varying combinations and proportions—to season numerous dishes, it helps to remember with which foods these essential ingredients have an affinity: basil with tomatoes, eggplant, and seafood; thyme with vegetables, cheese, and fish; bay leaves with rice, fish, and poultry; tarragon with eggs, oil, and vinegar; and chervil with lettuce, eggs, potatoes, and spinach. While these herbs can stand on their own as flavor providers, they also work well in combination with others.

French cooking, perhaps more than any other culinary style, emphasizes the use of *fresh* herbs, especially basil, tarragon, chervil, and parsley. This poses a problem for most city-dwellers who do not have access to fresh aromatic leaves. As mentioned in the *Seasoning Essentials* sections throughout this book, the difference between fresh and dried herbs is one of great magnitude, and those cooks wishing to maintain the integrity of

French dishes should seriously consider growing their own. A sunny window is all you need, or lacking adequate light, a grow lamp will do. If dried herbs are to be substituted for fresh ones, remember to adjust the recipe to use only one-third of what is called for. If possible, buy dried herbs at a spice shop; they are less apt to be stale and may be purchased in small quantities.

Neither fresh nor dried herbs respond well to heat. With the exception of bay leaves or saffron—which may be added at the start of the cooking process—herbs are usually added to soups, sauces, or long-simmering dishes near the final stages of cooking. When using dried herbs to season a sauce with a low moisture content, such as mayonnaise-based *Sauce Basilique*, you can revive them in a small amount of hot water to restore their elasticity. This manipulation makes it easier to incorporate them into a smooth composition.

The flavor of most herbs is well-complemented by members of the onion family—garlic, shallots, leeks, and chives. A pinch of tarragon and hints of minced garlic and shallots will turn a banal salad dressing into a well-integrated vinaigrette. You can make your stocks, soups, and savory pies more lively with touches of chopped leeks and thyme. Or, spruce up your favorite omelet with minced chives and chervil.

Unfortunately, there is no magic blend that can ensure a successful creation. But, if you combine common sense and seasoning restraint with an array of fresh herbs and high-quality ingredients, you will undoubtedly rise above the common rut.

FRENCH SEASONING CHART

BASIL leaves impart an intense aroma and sweet, clove-pepper tang to soups, vinaigrettes, herb butters, eggplant, tomatoes, and seafood. Fresh basil is preferred to dried; its flavor is more defined and its aroma more fragrant. To preserve fresh basil, place a layer of leaves in a clean, dry jar with a tight-fitting lid. Cover with a layer of coarse (kosher) salt; alternate layers of leaves and salt until the jar is full, ending with the salt on top. In this manner, you may keep fresh basil on your shelf indefinitely. You can also devise your own basil oil which makes a fine substitute for expensive olive oil. To prepare, pack a clean jar with basil leaves and cover with peanut, corn, or safflower oil. Store in a cool, dark place for one week; strain and discard the leaves. While dried basil is less satisfying than fresh, it may be added in small amounts to quiches, marinades, vegetables, and rice pilafs with moderate success.

BAY LEAVES are essential to numerous soup, rice, fish, and poultry dishes. These pungent leaves of the bay laurel tree must be used with restraint as their flavor can be quite domineering. European or Turkish bay leaves are the ones most frequently used, but we prefer California bay leaves, which are more aromatic and flavorful; usually, one-half of a California bay leaf will obtain the same results as a whole European leaf. As a rule, use ½ to 1 leaf to season a dish that serves 6 persons. Always remove the leaf before serving.

BOUQUET GARNI is a mixture of herbs, tied with a thread, and placed in a simmering sauce or soup. Classically, it is comprised of 2 or 3 sprigs of parsley, a small bay leaf, and a sprig of thyme; occasionally celery leaves or fennel branches are included. Sometimes the bundle is wrapped in cheesecloth so other herbs—crushed garlic or dried orange peel—may be added. Use bouquet garni to season stocks, stews, fish broths, or sauces such as *velouté* or brown sauce. When sufficient savor has been imparted, the bouquet garni should be removed and discarded.

CHERVIL is highly esteemed in French cooking for its delicate tarragon-like flavor. The fresh herb, which looks like a cross between curly and flat-leaf parsley, is preferred to the dried and may be grown at home. Chervil marries well with other herbs, especially tarragon, chives, and parsley. Use it to give warmth and new interest to your favorite egg, herb butter, salad, or savory crêpe recipe. A small amount of this anise-flavored herb will also do wonders for spinach or potato salad.

FINES HERBES or finely chopped herbs, are a mixture of two or more seasonings used to flavor omelets, grilled fish, potatoes, or poultry. In its simplest form, *fines herbes* are comprised of equal proportions of minced parsley and chives. You may add any of your favorite French herbs such as tarragon, marjoram, chervil, mint, basil, or savory, depending upon the desired taste. Dried *fines herbes* can be found in the spice section of the supermarket, but you will do best to prepare your own.

GARLIC plays a significant role in flavoring the foods of southern France. This pungent member of the onion family makes a superb addition to hearty vegetable potages, seafood dishes, and savory sauces in small amounts. Press a clove of garlic into your favorite vinaigrette and add a dab of Dijon mustard to produce a sharp and delectable dressing for crisp greens. Melted butter or margarine, seasoned with minced garlic, can be brushed over sliced French bread or croutons with interesting results. The French would find garlic powder an unacceptable substitute, to put it kindly, for the fresh cloves.

LIQUEURS account for the triumphant taste of highly celebrated desserts such as Grand Marnier soufflé, crêpes Suzettes, and chocolate mousse. If you shy away from these concentrated spirits because of their cost, you might consider making your own. Once you get the basic process down, and it is indeed a simple one, you can experiment with your own flavor combinations by varying the basic extracts.

To make the *Liqueur Base*, combine in a large saucepan and heat to the boiling point, stirring frequently: the rind (yellow part only) of 1 lemon, 3 cups granulated sugar, and 2 cups water. Reduce heat to low, and simmer 5 minutes uncovered. Strain and let cool before preparing liqueurs.

Amaretto (almond liqueur): Combine 1½ cups *Liqueur Base* with 1½ cups vodka, 1 vanilla bean split in half lengthwise, and 1½ tablespoons almond extract. Place in a clear bottle with a tight-fitting lid, and store in a cool, dark place at least one month.

Crème de Fraises (Strawberry liqueur): Prepare recipe for *Amaretto*, substituting the almond extract with strawberry extract and replacing the vanilla bean with 2 teaspoons vanilla extract.

Crème de Menthe (mint liqueur): Prepare recipe for *Crème de Fraises* substituting 2 tablespoons mint extract for the strawberry extract.

SAFFRON consists of dried orange-red stigmas found in the flowers of the *crocus sativus*, cultivated primarily in Spain. It has an elusive honey-spice fragrance and distinctive pungency that most palates find pleasant and exotic. Saffron is mostly cherished, however, for the beautiful color it imparts to dishes when infused with hot liquid. Fortunately, a small amount of the "world's most expensive spice" goes a long way; an infinitesimal quantity lends a rich golden hue to clear soups, fish stews, bouillabaisse, and rice pilaf. Buy saffron threads rather than the powdered variety to be sure it has not been adulterated. To prepare, dissolve a half dozen threads in a few tablespoons of hot liquid or water from whatever dish you are using; let the mixture stand until it takes on a brilliant orange color before returning it to the preparation. Mexican saffron or *achiote*, available at Latin American markets, can be used as an inexpensive substitute for the *color*, not the *flavor*, of saffron.

TARRAGON is used extensively in French cooking. Its distinctive flavor, reminiscent of licorice, gives character and liveliness to omelets, vinaigrettes, grilled fish, poultry, quiche, and béarnaise sauce. Tarragon butter, which has an affinity with carrots or rice, can be made by stirring 1 tablespoon fresh or 1 teaspoon dried tarragon with ½ cup melted butter or margarine; season to taste with salt and pepper. Be sure to use French tarragon; a variety called Russian tarragon is inferior both in flavor and aroma. To give your salad dressings a distinguished taste and pronounced bittersweet scent, try using tarragon vinegar for a change.

THYME is an essential component of bouquet garni and, therefore, enters into the background flavoring of numerous dishes. It goes into various soups, cheese, and fish dishes, and is favored with vegetables such as eggplant, potatoes, and zucchini. Thyme's rich aroma and gentle pungency are asserted well in combination with wine, leeks, cream, or brandy.

VANILLA BEANS are long, thin, dark-brown pods that produce a flavor far superior to vanilla extract. Aside from their primary function as a taste enhancer for coffee and chocolate dishes, dried vanilla pods intensify the sweetness of dessert sauces or soufflés, homemade ice cream, and custards. In cakes and fruit confections, they have a talent for bringing out unsuspected flavors and smoothing out the raw taste of flour and eggs. An unsplit pod may be used repeatedly; it will retain its bouquet even after heating or steeping in hot liquid, provided it is washed and dried afterwards. Vanilla sugar is one of the best ways to utilize the pods. Place 1 or 2 beans, split lengthwise to increase its flavor, in a sugar canister and let stand several weeks to absorb the aroma; keep the container refilled as the sugar is used up and the pods will release their lovely perfume indefinitely. As a rule, substitute 3 teaspoons vanilla extract for 1 vanilla bean.

Other seasonings found in French cookery: angelica, aniseed, cloves, cinnamon, citrus rinds, caraway seeds, cayenne pepper, coriander, chives, spice Parisienne, fennel, nutmeg, savory, mace, marjoram, white peppercorns, parsley, sorrel, paprika, burnet, oregano, allspice, juniper berries, rosemary, and horseradish.

Nutritional Essentials

From the nutritional point of view, the French cuisine is filled with both good news and bad news. First, the good news: Because of its accent on dairy foods, the French vegetarian kitchen is packed with high quality protein that can be substituted for other foods—meats, poultry, and fish—in the protein group. It is a diet rich in calcium, phosphorus, riboflavin, and vitamin A. What's more, the French infatuation with green salads, vegetable dishes, and fruit desserts assures a repertoire of low-calorie, low-fat options to offset the "heavier" fare of this cuisine. Finally, if you follow the dictum, "small portions of good things," you can trim a substantial number of calories off your French meals.

The bad news is no secret: French cooking—with its myriad rich cheese sauces, egg-based soufflés, and rich desserts—strikes fear (or more accurately, love-hate) in the hearts of weight-watchers and individuals who are trying to cut down their fat and cholesterol intake. Consequently, if there is a key to enjoying the amazing offerings of the French cuisine, it is *moderation.*

Contrary to what you might expect, you will encounter a number of recipes in this chapter that are low in fat, cholesterol, and calories. Despite this fact, among the cuisines presented in this book, French cooking ranks highest in average cholesterol content (74 mg. per average serving). This country also shares "top honors" with Brazil in the saturated fat department (19 percent of total caloric intake is in the form of saturated fat). While this breakdown may deter individuals on a very strict cholesterol and fat diet, there is still some cause for optimism: With an average of 239 calories per dish, French recipes are still within the province of calorie-conscious gourmets.

When you think of meatless French cooking, think "cheese." Fortunately, there are a variety of cheeses from which to choose. Given the selection, you will be able to follow a well-balanced diet desirable for most people, or you can adopt a modified (low-fat or low-calorie) cheese regimen suitable for your particular health needs. As a start, consult Table 7 (on p. 447) to help choose the type of cheese best suited to your dietary requirements.

There are several cheese-based recipes in this chapter: *Potatoes with Cheese*, *Ratatouille à la Sauce Mornay*, *Cauliflower and Shallot Tart*, *Mock Boursin*, and *Cheese Soufflé* to mention just a few. Gruyère, Swiss, Parmesan, and Neufchâtel cheese are the ones most commonly used because, as far as cheeses go, they fall into the low-to-moderate fat and calorie groups.

It should also be emphasized at this point that there is no need to eliminate high calorie dairy dishes from your diet. While cheese dishes are a concentrated source of calories (and protein) when it comes to planning your diet, *moderation*, not exclusion, is what's important. Most soft, creamy cheeses—frequently used as appetizers or dessert items—such as Double or Triple Crèmes should usually not be included in weight-reduction plans. So that your palate can experience the Triple Crème "taste," without the excessive calories, we have included a recipe for *Mock Boursin* cheese, which at 88 calories per ounce, is about 50 percent lower than store-bought *Boursin* (a Triple Crème).

Many types of cheese are available as *processed* cheese, such as processed Swiss made from natural Swiss, processed Gruyère made from natural Gruyère, and processed cheddar made from natural cheddar. The principal difference between natural and processed cheese is the use of a salt-based emulsifier in the latter. This manipulation nearly triples the salt content of processed cheeses; thus, individuals on low-salt diets should use processed cheeses sparingly.

As mentioned earlier, this notable cuisine favors the use of vegetables in a number of side dishes as well as entrées. It is primarily these recipes that will allow you to sample the fine aspects of French cooking, while keeping your fat, calories, and cholesterol intake at an acceptable level. Recipes that fall into this category include *Carottes Bourguignonne*, *Leek and Potato Soup*, and the *Endive and Beet Salad*.

Peas, carrots, and spinach are among the predominant vegetables employed in French cooking. Within the vegetable group, peas are one of the better sources of protein. Their amino acid make-up complements especially well with grain and nut protein, so try combining dishes with these ingredients into a single meal. Carrots are touted for their vitamin A content, which is not lost through cooking. Spinach is a high-fiber, leafy green that is rich in vitamin A and also contains iron, magnesium, and other minerals.

The French diet, despite its excesses, can be adapted to most dietary patterns. A good rule of thumb is to have at least one, perhaps two, vegetable-based dishes along with one cheese, egg, or chicken-based course per meal. The result will be a well-balanced offering that can easily be accommodated by your belt line—no extra notches needed!

BASIC CRÊPE BATTER

YIELD: 18 Crêpes

1 cup milk
½ teaspoon salt
1 teaspoon sugar
½ stick safflower margarine or
sweet butter

2 cups sifted whole wheat or all-
purpose flour
1 tablespoon safflower or vegetable
oil
4 whole eggs
1 cup water

1. Heat milk, salt, sugar, and margarine in a saucepan over low heat until margarine has melted.
2. Put the flour in a large bowl. Make a well in the center. Add the oil, eggs, and water. Beat well with a wire whisk. Pour in the milk mixture and blend well. Strain through a fine sieve. Refrigerate at least 2 hours.
3. Use a crêpe pan, or a skillet with a 7-inch bottom, to make the crêpes. Brush skillet lightly with oil. Heat over a medium flame. Add a scant ¼ cup of batter quickly turning skillet from side to side to coat bottom.
4. Brown crêpe lightly. Turn with a spatula. Fry reverse side for about ½ minute. Place on a clean towel. Continue this process until all the batter is used, brushing skillet each time with oil.
Note: To freeze, place a sheet of waxed paper between each crêpe. Wrap in heavy duty foil. Seal with freezer tape. Thaw before using.

CAROTTES BOURGUIGNONNE
(Simmered Carrots Burgundy)

YIELD: 8 servings

2 pounds carrots (about 12 large
ones), washed and trimmed
½ teaspoon salt
Water to cover
3 tablespoons safflower margarine
or butter

2 medium-sized onions, sliced and
separated into rings
2-3 cloves garlic, minced
1 heaping tablespoon flour
Salt and freshly ground white
pepper
¼ cup chopped parsley

Place whole carrots and the ½ teaspoon of salt in a 3-quart saucepan with enough water to cover. Bring to a boil and partially cover. Lower heat, and boil slowly from 10 to 15 minutes or until carrots are only half-cooked. Drain and reserve 2 cups of the liquid. In a large heavy skillet, heat the margarine or butter. Add the onion rings and garlic and cook until brown. Cut carrots into ½-inch pieces. Return carrots to the 3-quart saucepan with browned onions and garlic. Sprinkle with the flour. Put over high heat and keep turning until carrots are brown. Add reserved liquid, and season to taste with salt and pepper. Simmer from 10 to 15 minutes or just until tender. Spoon into a serving dish. Garnish with chopped parsley.

CAROTTES RÂPÉES
(Shredded Carrot Salad)   *YIELD: 6 servings*

1½ pounds fresh carrots
¼ cup each: olive and peanut oil
  Juice of 1 lemon
2 shallots, minced—optional
1 large garlic clove, pressed

Salt to taste
Freshly ground black pepper to
  taste
Pinch of sugar
Black olives for garnish

Shred carrots and set aside in a bowl. Beat the oils and lemon juice well with a wire whisk. Add the shallots, garlic, salt, pepper, and sugar and beat until thick and smooth. Pour over carrots and mix together well. Place carrots in the center of a serving platter and surround with black olives.

CAULIFLOWER AND SHALLOT TART   *YIELD: 6 to 8 servings*

1 partially baked pie shell (p. 128)
1 small head of cauliflower broken
  into tiny flowerets (about 2½
  cups)
2 shallots or green onions, finely
  chopped
¾ pound Swiss or Gruyère cheese,
  grated
½ cup bread crumbs

1½ cups light cream
3 egg yolks
½ teaspoon salt
¼ to ½ teaspoon each: ground
  pepper, tarragon, and thyme
  Pinch of cayenne pepper
¼ cup slivered almonds or chopped
  filberts—optional

1. Prepare pie shell.
2. Place flowerets in a vegetable steamer with ½ inch of water. Steam 5 minutes or just until barely tender. Drain thoroughly and rinse with cold water to stop cooking process. Set aside.
3. Preheat oven to 350 degrees.
4. Combine the shallots or green onions, cheese, bread crumbs, cream, egg yolks, and seasonings. Distribute cauliflower evenly over the partially baked pie shell. Add the cream-egg yolk mixture. Sprinkle slivered almonds or filberts over the top. Bake in a preheated oven until knife inserted in center comes out clean—about 40 minutes. Cool slightly before cutting.

CHICKEN CRÊPES WITH
BRANDY-CREAM SAUCE

YIELD: 12 Chicken Crêpes

12 crêpes (p. 122)

Filling:
  **3 tablespoons safflower or peanut
  oil**
  **1 medium-sized onion, finely
  chopped**
  1 large garlic clove, pressed
  2 cups fresh mushrooms, sliced
  4 cups diced, cooked chicken

Sauce:
  **3 tablespoons safflower margarine
  or butter**
  3 tablespoons flour
  1 cup chicken stock
  ⅛ teaspoon nutmeg
  **½ teaspoon each: thyme and
  marjoram**
  **Dash Tabasco sauce or cayenne
  pepper**
  Salt and pepper to taste
  2 tablespoons brandy, divided
  3 egg yolks
  1 cup light cream
  Juice of ½ lemon
  Parmesan cheese

1. Heat the oil in a large skillet. Sauté onion and garlic until golden. Add mushrooms and cook 3 minutes. Stir in the chicken. Set aside.
2. *To prepare sauce*: Melt margarine in a small saucepan. Add flour and stir to make a smooth paste. Gradually add chicken stock. Continue stirring until mixture thickens. Stir in the seasonings and 1 tablespoon of the brandy. Beat egg yolks with cream and add slowly. Heat until hot, stirring constantly. Do not boil.
3. Mix ⅔ of the sauce with the chicken filling. Taste and adjust seasonings. Add remaining tablespoon of brandy and lemon juice to the remaining ⅓ sauce. Set aside.
4. *To assemble crêpes*: Fill the lower third of the crêpes with 2 to 3 table-spoons of the chicken filling. Roll each into a cylinder shape. Place closely together in a shallow, buttered baking dish. Spoon remaining sauce over crêpes. Sprinkle with Parmesan cheese. Refrigerate until ready to use.
5. Preheat oven to 400 degrees. Bake from 10 to 15 minutes or until sauce is bubbly and crêpes are lightly browned.

CRÈME FRAÎCHE

YIELD: 1 cup

  1 cup heavy cream
  2 tablespoons buttermilk

1. In small saucepan heat cream to 85 or 90 degrees. Pour into a small glass bowl. Stir in buttermilk. Cover and let stand at room temperature until thickened (from 12 to 36 hours). Do not stir.
2. Store in a covered container in refrigerator. This will keep for one week.

CRÊPES RATATOUILLE À LA SAUCE MORNAY
(Crêpes Stuffed with Eggplant and Zucchini and
Topped with Cheese Sauce)   *YIELD: 12 crêpes*

Ratatouille:
  1 small eggplant
  Salt
  ⅓ cup olive oil for sautéing
  eggplant
  2 garlic cloves, pressed
  6 tablespoons peanut or olive oil
  for sautéing vegetables, divided
  6 garlic cloves, divided
  1 medium-sized zucchini, diced
  1 green pepper, seeded and diced
  2 yellow onions, minced
  3 tomatoes, seeded and cut into
  pieces
  Generous pinch of cayenne
  pepper
  Salt and freshly ground pepper to
  taste
  ½ to 1 teaspoon each: dried
  oregano, basil, and thyme
  ¼ teaspoon ground coriander—
  optional

Sauce Mornay:
  4 tablespoons butter
  4 tablespoons all-purpose flour
  2¾ cups hot whole milk
  ½ teaspoon salt
  ¼ teaspoon dry mustard
  Pinch of pepper
  Pinch of freshly grated or ground
  nutmeg
  1 cup grated Gruyère or Swiss
  cheese

12 Crêpes (p. 122)

1. *To prepare eggplant:* Peel and slice eggplant into ½-inch rounds. Salt each slice liberally and place in a colander to drain for 30 minutes. Rinse well and pat dry with paper towels. Cut into small cubes.

2. *To prepare ratatouille:* Heat the ⅓ cup olive oil and 2 pressed garlic cloves in a 2-quart saucepan. Add eggplant and sauté until browned. Remove to a bowl and set aside. Repeat process, individually sautéing the zucchini, green pepper, and onions, heating 2 tablespoons oil and 2 pressed garlic cloves for each batch. Combine each sautéed vegetable with the eggplant. Add the tomatoes and seasonings. Taste and adjust seasonings and set aside.

3. *To prepare Mornay sauce:* In a heavy 2- to 3-quart saucepan, melt the butter. Add the flour, stirring constantly with a wire whisk over low heat for 3 to 5 minutes, taking care that the roux does not brown. Slowly add the hot milk, beating constantly. Bring to a slow boil and reduce heat immediately to simmer. Add seasonings and grated cheese, stirring until cheese has melted. Remove from heat.

4. Preheat oven to 375 degrees. Adjust rack ⅓ down from the top of the oven.

5. *To assemble crêpes:* Combine 3 tablespoons of sauce with the filling. Place a big spoonful of filling on the lower third of each crêpe and roll into cylinders. Arrange side by side in a shallow pan, seam-side-down. Pour the re-

maining sauce over the crêpes. Brown lightly in preheated oven and serve immediately.

Note: To make *ratatouille* as a side-dish, prepare steps 1 and 2. Place all ingredients in a large pot and simmer 35 minutes uncovered. Serve hot or cold.

FRAISES À LA YAOURT
(Fresh Strawberries with Yogurt)   YIELD: 6 servings

---

1 quart fresh ripe strawberries	½ teaspoon vanilla extract
1 tablespoon superfine sugar or honey	½ cup plain low-fat yogurt

Wash and hull berries. Cut in half and chill. Just before serving, add the sugar or honey and vanilla to the yogurt. Beat until smooth. Spoon berries into sherbet dishes. Decorate tops with a dollop of whipped yogurt.

Variation: *Fraises à la Crème*: Sprinkle halved strawberries with ¼ cup Cointreau or Grand Marnier liqueur before chilling. Replace yogurt with whipped *Crème Fraîche* (p. 124). To whip *Crème Fraîche*, chill the beaters and the small bowl of an electric mixer until very cold. Beat the crème until thick and doubled in volume.

GERRY'S BOUILLABAISSE BISQUE   YIELD: 8 servings

---

2 onions, diced	½ teaspoon each: dried orange peel, black pepper, and white pepper
3 tomatoes, coarsely chopped	½ bay leaf
3 garlic cloves, pressed	3 drops Tabasco sauce
2 tablespoons olive oil	¼ teaspoon cayenne pepper (or to taste)
¼ teaspoon crushed fennel seed or 2 sprigs fennel leaves	1 3¼-ounce tin of oil-packed sardines, undrained
2 generous pinches pulverized saffron—optional	1 6½-ounce can of clams with juice
1½ cups of water	1 7¾-ounce can of salmon or white tuna with juice
2 tablespoons safflower margarine or butter	6 large mushrooms, thickly sliced
1 large carrot, diced	1 pint light cream
1 red potato, diced	4 tablespoons dry white wine—optional
2 green onions or leeks (white part only), diced	Salt to taste
¼ teaspoon each: basil, oregano, and thyme	

Place the onions, tomatoes, garlic, oil, fennel, and saffron in a 4-quart kettle. Add 1½ cups water. Bring to a rapid boil for 5 minutes. Add the margarine or butter, carrot, potato, and green onions or leeks. Cook 10 minutes over medium-high heat. Add seasonings, reduce heat to medium low, and cook 15 minutes. Add the undrained sardines, clams, and salmon or tuna. Add the mushrooms and simmer 15 minutes longer. Stir in the cream, wine, and salt. Taste and adjust seasonings. Heat through, but do not boil. Serve hot in deep bowls as a soup course or as an entrée accompanied, if desired, by rounds of toasted French bread.

GRATIN PARMENTIER
(Potatoes with Cheese)   YIELD: 6 servings

3 garlic cloves, minced
6 tablespoons safflower margarine
   or butter
6 medium-sized potatoes, peeled
   and thinly sliced

Salt and freshly ground white
   pepper
1½ cups grated Gruyère or Parmesan
   cheese
¾ cup light cream

1. Preheat oven to 375 degrees
2. Sauté the garlic in the margarine or butter until golden. Brush the bottom of an 8- by 10-inch glass baking dish with a little of the melted garlic-margarine mixture. Cover with a layer of sliced potatoes. Sprinkle with salt, pepper, and ⅓ cup of the grated cheese. Drizzle over the cheese ⅓ of the melted margarine. Repeat process to make 3 layers. Cover the top heavily with the remaining cheese. Pour the cream evenly over the top.
3. Bake uncovered for 45 minutes to 1 hour or until cheese forms a crust on the top and potatoes are tender.

LEEK AND POTATO SOUP
YIELD: Approximately 3 quarts or
12, 1-cup servings.

2 tablespoons safflower or peanut
   oil
1 large onion, diced
2 garlic cloves, minced
1 large bunch of leeks
2 quarts boiling vegetable or
   chicken stock
2 carrots, diced

4 large potatoes, diced
¼ cup chopped fresh parsley
1 sprig fresh thyme or 1 teaspoon
   dried thyme
Salt and pepper to taste
2 small turnips, thinly sliced
½ small head of cabbage, shredded

Heat the oil in a heavy skillet. Add the onion and garlic and sauté until transparent. Wash the leeks well. Discard the green stems. Cut into chunks and add to the onion. Simmer until tender. Transfer to a large soup pot along with the boiling stock. Add the carrots, potatoes, parsley, and thyme. Season to taste with salt and pepper. Simmer 30 minutes. Add the turnips and cabbage. Cook 15 minutes longer. Taste and adjust seasonings.

LEMON PASTRY

YIELD: 1 8- or 9-inch pastry shell

1½ cups unbleached white flour
1 egg yolk
4 ounces (1 stick) chilled butter, cut
into ½-inch pieces

Pinch of salt
Grated rind of 1 lemon
1½ to 2 tablespoons cold water

1. Sift flour onto a pastry board. Make a well in the center and add the egg yolk, butter, salt, and lemon rind. Work the center ingredients to a paste with your fingertips, then work it quickly into the flour. Add enough cold water to moisten the dough so that it can be gathered into a ball. Wrap dough in waxed paper and chill from 30 to 60 minutes.
2. Place dough on a lightly floured pastry cloth or board and gently flatten. With a lightly floured rolling pin, roll dough from the center out, forming a circle about ⅛-inch thick and approximately 1½ inches larger than an 8- or 9-inch pie pan. Reflour the cloth or board and rolling pin as necessary. Dust the surface of the rolled dough with a veil of flour; fold dough gently into quarters. Place in a pie plate with the point of the wedge at the center and carefully unfold. Pat loosely, then press firmly, but gently, against the sides and bottom of the pan without stretching the dough. With a pair of kitchen scissors, trim the edges so that they are slightly larger than the outside of the rim. Twist the edge of the dough between your thumb and index finger to flute the rim.
3. Bake as directed according to the filling used. For directions on how to prebake a pie shell see *Never-Fail Pie Crust* (p. 380).

MOCK BOURSIN CHEESE

YIELD: four 5-ounce Boursins—approximately 8 servings each

2 cups Homemade Cream Cheese
(p. 378) or 2, 8-ounce packages
Neufchâtel cheese
1 stick safflower margarine
4 garlic cloves, pressed
½ teaspoon each: dried basil and
thyme

¼ teaspoon crushed tarragon leaves
¼ teaspoon ground coriander
⅛ teaspoon each: crushed sage
leaves and marjoram
Pinch of mace and crushed
rosemary
Salt and freshly ground pepper to
taste

Soften cream cheese and margarine to room temperature. Cream together (preferably in an electric mixer which will make the cheese fluffier) and stir in the seasonings. Taste and adjust seasonings. Shape into 4 rounds or press into small crocks for serving. This may be wrapped in waxed paper and aluminum foil and frozen for a later use.

PAVÉ AU CHOCOLAT
(Chocolate Butter Cream Molded in Ladyfingers)   YIELD: 10 to 12 servings

Chocolate Butter Cream*
  6 ounces semisweet chocolate chips
  1 tablespoon instant coffee
  ⅓ cup hot water
  4 egg yolks
  1 tablespoon vanilla extract
  1 stick safflower margarine or
    unsalted butter, slightly softened

Ladyfinger Mold:
  1 pint fresh strawberries**
  4 tablespoons almond, orange, or
    banana liqueur
  4 ounces cold water
  12 ounces ladyfingers

1. Place chocolate chips in a blender. Dissolve coffee in the hot water and pour over the chips. Blend at high speed until smooth. Add the egg yolks, one at a time, at high speed. Add the vanilla. Add the margarine or butter, bit by bit, until smooth and well blended. Set aside.

2. Wash and stem the strawberries and set aside. Combine the liqueur and cold water in a wide, shallow bowl. Split ⅓ of the ladyfingers in half. Quickly dip them, one at a time, in the liquid. Line the bottom of an 8-inch spring form pan with the dipped halves, filling in any holes with pieces of ladyfingers. Cover with half of the chocolate butter cream. Quickly dip the remaining whole ladyfingers in the liquid and arrange over the butter cream. Cover with remaining butter cream, smoothing out the top with a rubber spatula.

3. Cut the berries in half and arrange a circle of them, cut-side-down, along the outer edge of the chocolate butter cream. Working towards the center, arrange another circle with the stem ends pointing the opposite way of the outer circle. Continue making circles, alternating the direction of the stem ends, until all berries are used up. If desired, place a whole berry in the center.

4. Chill for 6 hours or overnight. Butter cream must be firm before unmolding or dessert will fall apart. To serve, remove the sides of the spring form pan, leaving the dessert attached to the bottom of the pan. Serve chilled

*Note: Chocolate Butter Cream may also be used to frost a 9- × 13-inch cake, or 2, 8-inch cakes.

**If strawberries are not in season, line the bottom of the spring form pan with waxed paper before filling with ladyfingers and butter cream. When properly chilled, remove the sides of the spring form pan and invert the dessert on a serving plate. Peel off waxed paper and decorate the top with rosettes of whipped cream, piped through a pastry bag, to serve.

PEAS MARSEILLES

YIELD: 6 servings

4 tablespoons safflower margarine
  or butter, divided
½ cup minced onion
1 cup sliced fresh mushrooms
3 tablespoons water
3 cups of fresh shelled or frozen
  peas, cooked

½ cup shredded lettuce
½ teaspoon Spice Parisienne
½ teaspoon salt
¼ teaspoon pepper
⅛ teaspoon nutmeg

1. Melt 2 tablespoons of the margarine or butter in a 9-inch skillet. Sauté the onion until tender. Remove and set aside.
2. Melt 1 tablespoon of margarine in the same skillet. Add the mushrooms and sauté for 3 minutes. Remove and set aside.
3. Put the water and remaining 1 tablespoon of margarine in the skillet. Add the cooked peas and lettuce. Simmer until the lettuce is wilted. Add the onion, mushrooms, Spice Parisienne, salt, pepper, and nutmeg. Heat and serve immediately.

POISSON AU BEURRE NOIR
(Fish with Dark Butter Sauce)

YIELD: 6 servings

½ pound safflower margarine or
  butter
2½ pounds fish fillets (sole, bass, or
  flounder)
  Salt to taste

Freshly ground black pepper to
taste
Parsley sprigs
Lemon wedges

1. Preheat oven to 450 degrees.
2. Put the margarine or butter in a baking dish. Heat in the oven until foaming and a deep nut-brown in color. Remove from oven. Dip the fillets in the browned margarine. Turn and coat the other side. Season to taste with salt and pepper.
3. Bake for 15 or 20 minutes or until fish flakes easily with a fork. Transfer to a heated platter. Garnish with parsley and lemon wedges.
Variation: Add 1 tablespoon capers to browned butter.

POISSON BASILIQUE DE DORKA RAYNOR
(Poached Fish with Basil Sauce)   *YIELD: Serves 2*

Sauce Basilique:
- 3 tablespoons good quality mayonnaise
- Juice of ½ lemon
- 1 teaspoon Dijon mustard
- 1½ teaspoons fresh chopped or ½ teaspoon dried basil
- 4 tablespoons capers—optional
- Chopped parsley for garnish

Poached Fish:
- 1 teaspoon fresh chopped or ¼ teaspoon dried basil
- 13 ounces clear consommé
- 13 ounces water
- 1 bay leaf
- 1 large carrot, sliced
- 1 rib celery, diced
- 1 small white onion, sliced into rings
- 2 small red potatoes, sliced
- 2 large, lean, fish fillets such as sole, freshwater trout, flounder, or halibut

1. *To prepare sauce*: Place mayonnaise in a bowl. With a fork or whisk, slowly beat in lemon juice until creamy smooth. Add mustard and basil, beating thoroughly. Stir in capers. Place in a small serving bowl. Garnish with parsley and set aside.

2. *To prepare poaching liquid*: Sprinkle the basil over the bottom of a large frying pan. Combine the consommé and water and add to skillet, along with bay leaf. Add carrot, celery, onion rings, and potatoes. Bring to a boil, reduce heat to low, cover with a lid, and simmer 15 minutes.

3. *To poach fish*: With a sharp knife, lightly score the milky side of the fillets, next to the skin, to keep fillets from curling during poaching. Remove lid from skillet and submerge fish in poaching liquid. Simmer 5 to 8 minutes until fish flakes easily with a fork. With a slotted spoon remove fish and poached vegetables to a serving platter. Spoon a little poaching liquid over all and serve immediately with the sauce.

POMMES DE TERRE AUX FINES HERBES
(Potatoes with Fine Herbs)   *YIELD: 4 servings*

- 1½ pounds small new potatoes
- 4 tablespoons peanut oil
- 1 tablespoon safflower margarine or butter
- 2 eggs
- 2 large garlic cloves, finely minced

- 2 tablespoons finely chopped parsley
- 1 teaspoon *fines herbes**
- Salt to taste
- Freshly ground white pepper to taste

*See Seasoning Chart.

1. Peel potatoes if desired. Cut into rounds ⅛-inch thick. Wash in several changes of cold water to remove starch. Dry well with a towel.
2. Preheat oven to 400 degrees. Heat the oil and margarine in a heavy skillet. Add the potatoes and sauté for 5 minutes. Beat eggs with the garlic, parsley, and *fines herbes*.
3. Put potatoes in a casserole. Cover with beaten eggs. Season with salt and pepper. Cover and bake 30 minutes or until tender when pierced with a fork.

POULET AU CITRON
(Lemon Chicken)   YIELD: *6 servings*

---

3 small broilers, split in half
1 teaspoon each: tarragon, parsley, basil, chervil, and sage
6 lemons, divided
2 cups dry white wine
1 tablespoon peanut oil

Salt and freshly ground white pepper to taste
2 tablespoons safflower margarine or butter
2 medium-sized onions, diced
3 carrots, diced
4 tablespoons cream

1. Clean chickens. Wash and pat dry. Sprinkle with the herbs. Make a marinade with the juice from 4 of the lemons, the wine, peanut oil, salt, and freshly ground pepper. Pour over the chickens and refrigerate from 3 to 4 hours, turning occasionally.
2. Preheat oven to 350 degrees.
3. Heat the margarine or butter in a heavy skillet. Sauté the onions until tender. Add the carrots and a pinch of each of the herbs. Sauté 3 minutes to blend the flavors. Transfer to a large baking dish. Remove chickens from the marinade. Reserve marinade and place chickens, skin-side down, on the vegetables. Bake 1½ hours or until browned and cooked.
4. Meanwhile, pour the marinade into an enamel saucepan and cook, uncovered, over medium-high heat until marinade is reduced by one-half of its original volume. When the chickens are done, skim off the fat from the pan juices. Pour the reduced marinade over all. Stir in the cream and bake from 5 to 10 minutes more.
5. *To serve*: Place the chicken halves on a warm serving platter. Spoon the pan gravy over them. Garnish with the 2 remaining lemons, cut into slices.
Variation: Add to the cream either 1 tablespoon Moutarde de Meaux or Moutarde l'Ancienne (available at specialty food stores and some supermarkets).

QUICHE AUX ASPERGES
(Asparagus Quiche)

YIELD: *6 servings as an entrée;*
10 servings as an appetizer

½ pound fresh asparagus
1 partially baked pie shell (p. 128)
Dijon mustard
1 cup grated Swiss or Emmentaler
  cheese
3 large eggs
¾ cup light cream
½ cup plain yogurt (or substitute
  milk or cream)

1 teaspoon grated lemon rind
¼ teaspoon each: tarragon, thyme,
  and basil
½ teaspoon salt
Freshly ground pepper to taste
¼ cup grated Parmesan cheese
1 teaspoon safflower margarine or
  butter—optional

1. *To prepare asparagus*: Break each spear as far down as it easily snaps. Discard tough ends. Place spears in a vegetable steamer with 1½-inches water. Steam until just tender. Do not overcook—soggy asparagus has no redeeming features. Remove from steamer and let cool. Cut each spear into thirds.
2. Preheat oven to 375 degrees. Adjust rack to middle.
3. *To assemble*: Brush the bottom of the prebaked pie shell with Dijon mustard. Distribute grated cheese evenly over the mustard-covered shell. Cover with a layer of asparagus. Beat eggs well with cream, yogurt, lemon rind, and seasonings. Pour over asparagus. Sprinkle Parmesan over the top, along with a generous pinch of each of the herbs used to season the eggs. Top with margarine or butter, cut into bits. Bake in a preheated oven from 25 to 30 minutes or until knife inserted in middle comes out clean.
4. Cut into slices and serve hot, warm, or cold as an entrée or appetizer.
Variations: Any steamed or sautéed vegetable such as broccoli, cauliflower, or mushrooms may be substituted for the asparagus. Adjust seasonings accordingly. Try varying your cheeses too. Gruyère, cheddar, or even cream cheese, alone or in combination, are delicious additions to quiche.

SALADE D'ENDIVES AVEC BETTERAVES
(Endive and Beet Salad)

YIELD: *4 servings*

4 Belgian endive
½ cup shredded cooked beets

½ cup coarsely grated apples
Vinaigrette Bulus (p. 137)

Wash endive. Split in half or cut into fourths. Arrange each on a salad plate. Sprinkle 2 tablespoons shredded beets and 2 tablespoons grated apple over each endive. Coat lightly with *Vinaigrette Bulus*.

SALADE NIÇOISE

YIELD: 8 servings

½ pound string beans
4 medium-sized red potatoes
½ cup olive oil
½ cup peanut oil
⅓ cup red wine vinegar
1 tablespoon each: minced green onion and parsley
1 teaspoon each: salt, tarragon, and basil
½ teaspoon each: dry mustard and thyme

2 garlic cloves, minced
Freshly ground pepper to taste
1 head of leaf or butter lettuce, washed and chilled
2 tomatoes, quartered
2 hard-boiled eggs, quartered
8 thinly-sliced red onion rings
2 tablespoons each: capers and chopped parsley—optional
Anchovy fillets—optional
1 7-ounce can white tuna, packed in water

1. Blanch green beans in boiling water and chill. Place potatoes in a pot with enough water to cover. Bring to a boil and cook just until tender when pierced with a fork. Drain water, and if desired, peel while warm (we prefer to leave the skins on). When cool, cut potatoes into ¼-inch rounds.

2. *To prepare vinaigrette*: Thoroughly combine, in a bowl with a fork or in a screw-top jar, the oil, vinegar, green onion, parsley, salt, tarragon, basil, dry mustard, thyme, garlic, and pepper. Beat or shake vigorously until mixture is creamy and thick.

3. Place string beans and potatoes in separate bowls. Cover each with half of the vinaigrette and chill at least 2 hours before serving, basting occasionally.

4. *To serve*: Drain vinaigrette off string beans and potatoes and reserve. Line a platter with the lettuce leaves. Arrange beans, potatoes, tomatoes, hard-boiled eggs, and onion rings in an attractive design over the greens.

Garnish with capers, fresh parsley, and anchovy fillets. Drain water off tuna, break it into chunks, and arrange around the edge of the platter or in the center. Pour reserved vinaigrette over all and serve immediately.

SAUCE VANILLE

YIELD: Approximately 1½ cups

3 egg yolks
½ teaspoon vanilla
6 tablespoons sugar

½ cup half-and-half
2 tablespoons Grand Marnier Liqueur
½ cup heavy cream, whipped

NOTE: Make one day ahead of serving.

1. Beat egg yolks, vanilla, and sugar together in a mixer. Bring half-and-half to a boil. Slowly add to egg mixture and beat well until thickened. Refrigerate overnight.

2. Fifteen minutes before serving, add the Grand Marnier and whipped cream to ½ cup of the sauce. Save remaining sauce for another use.

SPINACH SALAD WITH HOMEMADE CROUTONS AND VINAIGRETTE

YIELD: 6 to 8 servings

Croutons:
 2 slices French or Italian bread
 1½ tablespoons safflower margarine
  or butter

Salad:
 1 pound fresh spinach
 ½ pound mushrooms, washed and
  sliced
 2 to 4 ounces Roquefort cheese,
  crumbled
 Vinaigrette François (p. 137)

1. *To prepare croutons:* Cut bread into ½- to ¾-inch cubes. Melt margarine in a heavy skillet. Add bread cubes and toss until brown. Cool before adding to salad.
2. Wash spinach well; remove stems and discard. Dry in a salad spinner or with paper towels. Tear into bite-size pieces. Place in a salad bowl along with mushrooms and cheese. Toss with just enough *Vinaigrette François* to lightly coat the ingredients. Sprinkle with croutons to serve.

SOUPE PAYSANNE
(Basque Peasant's Soup)   *YIELD: Approximately 2½ quarts or 10, 1-cup servings*

 2 tablespoons safflower or peanut
  oil
 1 large onion, diced
 2 garlic cloves, minced
 2 quarts boiling vegetable or
  chicken stock

 ¼ cup chopped fresh parsley
 5 medium-sized red potatoes, diced
 1 sprig fresh, or 1 teaspoon, dried
  thyme
 Salt and pepper to taste
 2 bunches watercress

1. Heat oil in a skillet. Sauté onion and garlic until tender. Transfer to a large soup pot that contains the boiling stock. Add the parsley, potatoes, and thyme. Season to taste with salt and pepper. Simmer 30 minutes. Add more stock, if needed, to cover vegetables.
2. Wash the watercress. Remove the stems. Chop the leaves coarsely. Add to the soup and cook 20 minutes longer. Taste and adjust seasonings.
Variation: Substitute one large bunch of sorrel for the watercress. Wash, remove tough stems, and chop coarsely.

SOUFFLÉ AU GRAND MARNIER

YIELD: 6 servings

3 tablespoons flour
1 cup milk
½ cup sugar
2 tablespoons unsalted butter, softened
4 egg yolks

½ cup Grand Marnier Liqueur
6 egg whites, at room temperature
Pinch of cream of tartar
Sauce Vanille—optional (p. 134)

1. *To prepare baking dish*: Butter the sides and bottom of a 1½-quart soufflé dish. Sprinkle granulated sugar (about 2 tablespoons) in the bottom. Turn and tilt to coat the sides; tap and shake out excess. Set aside.
2. *To prepare the base*: Place the flour in a small saucepan and add a little milk, stirring to make a paste. Add remaining milk and the ½ cup sugar. Cook over moderately high heat. Remove from heat. Spread the softened butter over the top. Cool slightly. Scrape mixture into the large bowl of a mixer. Beat in egg yolks. Add Grand Marnier.
3. Preheat oven to 425 degrees. Adjust rack to middle.
4. *To complete soufflé*: In a clean, dry bowl (preferably copper), beat the egg whites with a wire whisk until frothy. Add cream of tartar. Beat until whites stand up in stiff peaks, but are not dry. Fold ¼ of the whites carefully into the soufflé base to lighten it. Add remaining whites, gently folding over with a rubber spatula from bottom to top 12 times. Work quickly and delicately. Carefully spoon into prepared soufflé dish.
5. Place soufflé on middle rack. Immediately lower heat to 375 degrees. Bake 30 minutes without opening oven door. When finished, it should be browned and puffy, and when touched gently, there should be an indication of firmness. Serve immediately, accompanied, if desired, by *Sauce Vanille* (p. 134).

SOUFFLÉ AU FROMAGE
(Cheese Soufflé)

YIELD: 4 servings

3 tablespoons clarified butter (See Note)
3 tablespoons flour
1 cup hot whole milk
½ teaspoon salt
¼ teaspoon pepper
Pinch of nutmeg and cayenne pepper

4 egg yolks (large graded) at room temperature
6 egg whites (large graded) at room temperature
Pinch of cream of tartar
4 ounces Gruyère or Parmesan cheese, grated

1. Butter a 1½-quart soufflé dish. Set aside.
2. Melt the 3 tablespoons of clarified butter in a 1½-quart heavy enamel saucepan. Add the flour and cook the roux, stirring for about 3 minutes,

without browning. Pour in the hot milk gradually, stirring vigorously with a wire whisk. Blend in the seasonings and cook over medium heat, stirring constantly until mixture is thick. Transfer to a large bowl. Cool slightly.

3. Preheat oven to 425 degrees. Adjust rack to middle.

4. Beat in the egg yolks one at a time with a wire whisk. Put the egg whites in a clean, dry, copper bowl and beat with a clean wire whisk until they are stiff, but not dry. (You may do this step with an electric mixer, but the volume will be smaller. Add a pinch of cream of tartar when the whites are frothy). Lightly fold ⅓ of the beaten whites into the yolk mixture to lighten it. Stir in the cheese. Gently fold in the remaining whites.

5. Spoon mixture into the soufflé dish. Place in the oven and immediately lower the temperature to 375 degrees. Bake from 30 to 35 minutes without opening the oven door. Soufflé should be lightly browned on top, firm on the sides and bottom, and a little runny in the center. Serve immediately.

Variation: Substitute ¾ cup chopped, cooked vegetables, such as broccoli or cauliflower, or 1 cup chopped cooked seafood for the cheese.

Note: Melt one stick of sweet butter in a saucepan until it foams. Remove from heat. Pour through a cheesecloth-lined strainer into a bowl to remove impurities. The remaining liquid is the clarified butter. Refrigerate until ready to use.

VINAIGRETTE BULUS

YIELD: ½ cup

2 tablespoons wine vinegar
6 tablespoons olive oil (or part
  peanut oil)
1 teaspoon each: lemon juice and
  Dijon mustard

1 garlic clove, crushed
¼ teaspoon basil
⅛ teaspoon salt
Big pinch of freshly ground
  pepper

Combine all ingredients in a screw-top jar and shake vigorously for a minute or until thick and smooth. Taste and adjust seasonings.

VINAIGRETTE FRANÇOIS

YIELD: 1⅓ cups

½ cup peanut oil
½ cup olive oil
⅓ cup red wine vinegar
2 teaspoons Dijon mustard
¼ teaspoon salt

Pinch of sugar
1 garlic clove, pressed
4 shallots, chopped—optional
⅛ teaspoon freshly ground black
  pepper

Combine all ingredients together in a screw-type jar. Shake vigorously until creamy and thoroughly blended. Taste and adjust seasonings. Serve at room temperature.

FRANCE/RECIPE ANALYSIS CHART

Name of Recipe	Quantity	Calories	CHO gms.	Protein gms.	Total Fat gms.	Saturated Fat gms.	Cholesterol mg.	Dietary Fiber gms.
1. *Sauce Vanille*	per table-spoon	34	3 (35%)	1 (12%)	2 (53%)	1 (27%)	36	—
2. *Fraises à la Yaourt* (Fresh Strawberries with Yogurt)	per serving	65	12 (74%)	2 (12%)	1 (14%)	—	—	1.5
3. Mock *Boursin* Cheese	per 1-oz. serving	88	3 (14%)	1 (5%)	8 (81%)	4 (40%)	16	—
4. Vinaigrette *Bulus*	per table-spoon	94	1 (4%)	—	10 (96%)	1 (0%)	—	—
5. *Carottes Bourguignonne*	per serving	96	13 (54%)	2 (8%)	4 (38%)	1 (9%)	—	1.4
6. *Soupe Paysanne* (Basque Peasant's Soup)	per 1-cup serving	103	17 (66%)	2 (8%)	3 (26%)	—	—	.8
7. Basic Crêpe	each	105	11 (42%)	4 (15%)	5 (43%)	1 (9%)	71	.3
8. *Crème Fraîche*	per table-spoon	107	1 (4%)	1 (4%)	11 (92%)	7 (59%)	42	—
9. Leek and Potato Soup	per 1-cup serving	115	19 (66%)	3 (10%)	3 (24%)	—	—	1.3
10. Vinaigrette *François*	per table-spoon	130	1 (3%)	—	14 (97%)	2 (14%)	—	—
11. Peas Marseilles	per serving	131	12 (37%)	5 (15%)	7 (48%)	1 (7%)	—	1.0
12. Lemon Pastry	per slice	201	18 (36%)	3 (6%)	13 (58%)	7 (31%)	65	.1
13. *Carottes Râpées* (Shredded Carrot Salad)	per serving	202	9 (18%)	1 (2%)	18 (80%)	3 (13%)	—	1.2

Name of Recipe	Quantity	Calories	CHO gms.	Protein gms.	Total Fat gms.	Saturated Fat gms.	Cholesterol mg.	Dietary Fiber gms.
14. Spinach Salad with Homemade Croutons and Vinaigrette	per serving	211	6 (11%)	4 (8%)	19 (81%)	3 (13%)	8	.5
15. *Salade d'endives avec Betteraves* (Endive and Beet Salad)	per serving	220	8 (15%)	2 (4%)	20 (81%)	2 (8%)	—	1.0
16. *Soufflé au Grand Marnier*	per serving	237	32 (54%)	7 (12%)	9 (34%)	5 (19%)	224	—
17. *Poisson au Beurre Noir* (Fish with Dark Butter Sauce)	per serving	245	—	32 (52%)	13 (48%)	3 (11%)	25	—
18. *Gerry's* Bouillabaisse Bisque	per serving	272	17 (26%)	15 (22%)	16 (52%)	5 (17%)	24	1.0
19. *Pavé au Chocolat*	per serving	288	32 (44%)	4 (6%)	16 (50%)	6 (19%)	213	.5
20. *Pommes de Terre aux Fines Herbes* (Potatoes with Fine Herbs)	per serving	315	30 (38%)	6 (8%)	19 (54%)	4 (11%)	138	1.0
21. *Soufflé au Fromage* (Cheese Soufflé)	per serving	333	8 (10%)	19 (23%)	25 (67%)	14 (38%)	375	—
22. *Poulet au Citron* (Lemon Chicken)	per serving	346	12 (14%)	43 (50%)	14 (36%)	4 (10%)	37	1.0
23. Chicken Crêpes with Brandy-Cream Sauce	each	349	16 (18%)	24 (28%)	21 (54%)	7 (18%)	207	.4
24. Crêpes Ratatouille *à la Sauce Mornay*	each	361	23 (25%)	11 (12%)	25 (63%)	8 (21%)	96	1.3
25. *Gratin Parmentier* (Potatoes with Cheese)	per serving	410	31 (30%)	13 (13%)	26 (57%)	7 (15%)	51	1.0

Name of Recipe	Quantity	Calories	CHO gms.	Protein gms.	Total Fat gms.	Saturated Fat gms.	Choles-terol mg.	Dietary Fiber gms.
26. *Salade Niçoise*	per serving	414	17 (16%)	10 (10%)	34 (74%)	6 (13%)	78	1.0
27. *Poisson Basilique de Dorka Raynor* (Poached Fish with Basil Sauce)	per serving	439	25 (23%)	42 (38%)	19 (42%)	3 (6%)	30	1.5
28. *Quiche aux Asperges*(Asparagus Quiche)	per slice	468	27 (23%)	19 (16%)	36 (61%)	15 (29%)	228	.7
29. Cauliflower and Shallot Tart	per serving	526	26 (20%)	20 (15%)	38 (65%)	21 (36%)	262	1.0

Numbers in parentheses (%) indicate percentage of total calories contributed by nutrient.

MENUS

LOW CALORIE SPECIALTIES

(500 to 700 calories per meal)

CHICKEN CRÊPES WITH BRANDY-
CREAM SAUCE
CAROTTES RÂPÉES (SHREDDED
CARROT SALAD)
Red and Green Grapes

SOUPE PAYSANNE (BASQUE
PEASANT'S SOUP)
MOCK BOURSIN CHEESE
Hot French Bread
CRÊPES RATATOUILLE À LA
SAUCE MORNAY

Broiled Tomato Halves with Basil
QUICHE AUX ASPERGES (ASPARAGUS QUICHE)
CAROTTES BOURGUIGNONNE
Fresh Fruit Board

●

LOW CHOLESTEROL MENUS

(Less than 50 mgs. of cholesterol per meal)

GERRY'S BOUILLABAISSE BISQUE
SALADE D'ENDIVES AVEC
BETTERAVES (ENDIVE AND BEET
SALAD)
with
VINAIGRETTE BULUS
Tangerines and Nectarines

POISSON AU BEURRE NOIR (FISH
WITH DARK BUTTER SAUCE)
PEAS MARSEILLES
Artichoke Heart and Raw Mushroom
Salad
Honeyed Grapefruit

LEEK AND POTATO SOUP
MOCK BOURSIN CHEESE
Whole Grain Crackers
CAROTTES BOURGUIGNONNE
Apples and Green Grapes

●

LOW SATURATED FAT SELECTIONS

(Less than 8 grams of saturated fat per meal)

POULET AU CITRON (LEMON
CHICKEN)
Herbed Rice
SPINACH SALAD WITH
HOMEMADE CROUTONS
VINAIGRETTE FRANÇOIS
Blueberries and Peaches

SOUP PAYSANNE (BASQUE
PEASANT'S SOUP)
CRÊPES RATATOUILLE À LA
SAUCE MORNAY
Sliced Cucumbers
Fresh Raspberries

SALADE NIÇOISE
Hot French Bread (without butter)
FRAISES À YAOURT (FRESH STRAWBERRIES WITH YOGURT)

HIGH PROTEIN MEALS
(30 or more grams of protein per meal)

CAULIFLOWER AND SHALLOT
TART
SALADE NIÇOISE
French Bread
Sliced Peaches with
CRÈME FRAÎCHE

SOUFFLÉ AU FROMAGE (CHEESE
SOUFFLÉ)
POMMES DE TERRE AUX FINES
HERBES (POTATOES WITH FINE
HERBS)
SPINACH SALAD WITH
VINAIGRETTE FRANÇOIS
FRAISES À LA YAOURT (FRESH
STRAWBERRIES WITH YOGURT)

POISSON BASILIQUE DE DORKA RAYNOR
(POACHED FISH WITH BASIL SAUCE)
SALADE D'ENDIVES AVEC BETTERAVES (ENDIVE AND BEET SALAD)
with
VINAIGRETTE BULUS
Sliced Oranges with Cointreau

●

WELL BALANCED LUNCH OR DINNER MENUS
(Selections that conform to recommendations in Dietary Goals for United States)

SOUPE PAYSANNE (BASQUE
PEASANT'S SOUP)
CAROTTES BOURGUIGNONNE
POULET AU CITRON (LEMON
CHICKEN)
Fresh Fruit Board

LEEK AND POTATO SOUP
POISSON AU BEURRE NOIR (FISH
WITH DARK BUTTER SAUCE)
SOUFFLÉ AU GRAND MARNIER

POISSON BASILIQUE DE DORKA RAYNOR
(POACHED FISH WITH BASIL SAUCE)
PEAS MARSEILLES
French Bread
Pears and Brie

CHAPTER 6

GREECE
Feta Accompli

Culinary Essentials

Enter the world of Greek cooking and discover how easy it is to turn natural, inexpensive ingredients into imaginative creations. If you are willing to spend a little extra time in the kitchen and shop around for a few imported products, you can delight your family and friends with anise-scented breads, lemon-tangy salads, oil-rich vegetables, and honey-sweet desserts.

The most challenging and rewarding Greek dishes are prepared with filo dough. Simple foods enveloped in these translucent, paper-thin sheets of pastry take on a mysterious and dramatic appearance. Filo pastries can be stuffed and rolled into cylinders, cut into triangles, or whole sheets layered into deep-dish delights. When filled with spinach, cheese, chopped nuts, or sweet custard, they are always fun to make and sensational to eat.

With a little practice, anyone can produce elegant appetizers, entrées, and desserts with filo dough. Although the basic techniques used in our recipes are not difficult, filo does require time, patience, and following directions carefully. As a modern cook, you already have one advantage in your favor: the availability of commercially-made filo dough, which eliminates the laborious task of producing your own.

If there is a Greek bakery in your neighborhood, you can probably find fresh filo; otherwise use frozen filo, available at Greek or Middle Eastern groceries, large supermarkets, or gourmet food shops. At these same outlets, you will also find fresh or frozen *kataifi*, soft white strands of shredded wheatlike pastry that is used in a nut-filled confection of the same name, *Kataifi*. *Tarama*, an inexpensive carp roe pâté available in ten-ounce jars, is another unusual and fine-tasting Greek ingredient. When pounded with bread crumbs, olive oil, and lemon juice, this salmon-colored spread becomes a delicious appetizer called *Taramasalata*.

For convenience, stock your pantry with a few ready-made items that can be used to round out a meal. Greek olives, for example, are indispensable in salads or as an accompaniment to appetizers. Juicy, meaty, *kalamata* olives, considered the most delicious, are superb with feta cheese and Greek wine. Olive fanciers may also want to sample either marinated cracked green olives or salty, shriveled black olives. Jar-packed *tourshi* (spicy pickles), *dolmades* (rice-stuffed grape leaves), or mildly hot *solanika* peppers can serve as refreshing additions to an hors d'oeuvre platter.

The possibilities with imported Greek cheeses are enormous, and experimenting with their flavors and textures can be a rewarding experience. Feta cheese, now carried by many supermarkets, is the most popular and frequently used. This is a good baking cheese—it crumbles easily and has a distinct, salty flavor that blends superbly with vegetables, eggs, and seafood. *Kasseri*, or "Greek provolone," is milder, richer, and firmer than feta. This marvelous table cheese is an ideal companion for crusty bread, fresh fruit, and a well-dressed salad. If a recipe calls for a hard-grating cheese, you can use *Kasseri* or *Kefalotyri*, a Romano-like cheese made from goat's milk. Cheese-lovers should also try *Mizithra*, a mild, "pot" cheese that is excellent with pasta or as a table cheese.

Greek cooking requires more in the way of unusual ingredients than elaborate kitchen equipment; once your shelves are stocked, the preparation of most dishes is relatively easy. For filo recipes, you will need a soft pastry brush, cheesecloth, and a large baking sheet. If Greek salads appear frequently on your table, a salad spinner is unbeatable for quick-drying lettuce. Since lemons are a ubiquitous ingredient, you may want a tool that will extract their juices efficiently—an old-fashioned wooden lemon reamer or a hand citrus juicer.

Appetizers are an important feature of a Greek dinner. Typically, one lingers over wedges of Greek cheese, a variety of olives, raw vegetable sticks, and bits of seafood, several hours before eating. For special occasions, the selection might be enlarged to include *Skordalia* (a thick, garlic-pungent sauce served with fried zucchini or eggplant), *Tyropitta* (miniature cheese pies), and bowls of fruit, figs, or pistachio nuts.

A Greek meal begins with soup, usually a thick bean potage or *Avgolemono* which is a rich, tart chicken broth prepared with a frothy blend of eggs and lemon juice. Sometimes soup is the main course, eaten with chunks of bread and a salad garnished with feta cheese, anchovy fillets, and *kalamata* olives. You can embellish any recipe for Greek salad with artichoke hearts, garbanzo beans, sliced beets, or tangy *Feta Cheese Salad Dressing*.

Fresh fruit or jam-sweetened yogurt is the finale for many a Greek repast. But, on special occasions, more lavish creations, such as honey-drenched pastries, appear on the table. While they may seem extravagant and time-consuming to prepare, these delicacies are well worth the effort. Few desserts can stand up against a pecan-studded *Kataifi* perfumed with oranges and cloves, or *Galatobouryko*, a layered filo pie oozing with custard and dripping with sweet, cinnamon-spiked syrup. If this food is fit for the gods, why settle for anything less?

Seasoning Essentials

Greek dishes are full of seasoning surprises. They are spicy without being hot, and rich but not elaborately sauced. Instead of hot peppers and cream-enriched concoctions, fresh lemons, olive oil, oregano, and dill provide the leading flavors. Though not as evident, cinnamon, mint, thyme, and garlic play strong supporting roles. Once you learn how to manipulate these diverse seasonings, you can give almost any dish a Greek accent.

As a cooking companion for this cuisine, fresh lemons are unrivaled. From the tangy salad that starts the meal, to the honey-sweet pastry that ends it, you can count on a squeeze of lemon juice to improve every course. You might try it as a tasty substitute for vinegar in your favorite Greek salad dressing. The next time you poach fish, add the juice of one lemon to keep it firm. To prevent the discoloration of artichokes, potatoes, cauliflower, or rice, place a piece of lemon in the cooking water. It does not take long to realize that this modest citrus fruit has unlimited talents.

Many Greek recipes call for a combination of lemon juice and olive oil. Just as bottled lemon juice would make a poor substitute for fresh lemons, there is no replacement for high quality olive oil. As a flavor-enhancer, pure olive oil is unsurpassed among cooking oils. The best hail from Italy, but health food stores carry cold-pressed California olive oil which is decent. Fine olive oil is expensive, so use it wisely and sparingly to sauté vegetables, dress salads, season sauces, or flavor marinades. For economical and nutritional purposes, we often use a combination of olive and peanut or safflower oil, the exception being when the distinct flavor of olive oil is crucial to a dish.

Olive oil and lemon juice, in equal proportions, are your ticket to a delectable, no-fuss salad dressing. This tangy mixture will also make baked chicken, boiled shrimp, and freshly-steamed spinach more interesting. Throw in a pinch of thyme, basil, parsley, or dill, and you have a piquant, herbed marinade that may be used in unlimited ways.

Your Greek favorites will also benefit from oregano, king of Greek herbs. Dried oregano leaves can be used liberally to season fresh vegetable salads, vinaigrettes, cheese pies, stuffed tomatoes, or eggplant-based *Moussaka*. Those who find its flavor too forthright may tone it down with a little dill, thyme, or parsley. Oregano lovers can intensify this herb's pungent quality with freshly ground coriander or crushed fennel seeds.

Oregano may be the mainstay of Greek dishes, but it is mint that will provide the exciting, unexpected touches. When steamed string beans or rice pilaf are in need of an elegant garnish, there is nothing more refined than a crown of fresh mint leaves. A few sprigs can be simmered with beans or vegetables to strike a flavorful note. And no one can accuse a salad laced with fresh or dried mint of being dull.

Cinnamon should also be used selectively and creatively. A delicate béchamel sauce touched with cinnamon is exquisite. Tomato or spinach dishes will take on an elusive spiciness when gently tinged with this versatile seasoning. Use cinnamon as a background flavor and it will add, almost imperceptibly, an indefinable zest to your Greek dishes.

It may be easy to keep cinnamon subdued, but there is nothing nonchalant about garlic. Compared to other Mediterranean cuisines, Greek cooking employs garlic less enthusiastically; it is usually added sparingly to soups, cheese pies, chickpeas, and eggplant dishes. The one dish in which this noble herb comes into its own is *Skordalia*, a marvelous, garlic-laden dip made with potatoes and ground nuts. For this famous Greek blend to retain its authenticity, it must be mashed with at least six to eight cloves of garlic. *Skordalia* is not for alliophobics (otherwise known as garlic haters): one batch, if properly prepared, is potent enough to ward off a week's worth of evil spirits.

GREEK SEASONING CHART

CINNAMON has a seductive, bittersweet quality quite unlike any other spice. It is as fragrant as cloves and mace, but more delicate and less cloying. Ground cinnamon blends nicely with savory dishes, especially poultry. A healthy pinch will give snap to *moussaka*, Greek holiday breads, baked fish, pine nut-studded pilafs, and béchamel sauce. Cinnamon's spicy tang can be sharpened with a dash of cayenne pepper or allspice. For pastry syrup and tomato sauce, use high-quality cinnamon sticks—their flavor is more pronounced than the ground variety, and they can be removed when the job is completed.

DILL imparts a heady aroma and delicate pungency to Greek fare. Fresh dill is penetrating, distinctive, and appreciated for its ability to heighten the taste of vegetables and sour foods. To give whole artichokes a superb flavor, add a small bunch of fresh dill to the cooking water. Yogurt sauces and cheese-based salad dressings will benefit from as much as 2 chopped tablespoons per cup. Dried dill weed is suited to baked dishes such as spinach or cheese pies, vegetable casseroles, and stuffed tomatoes. It is compatible, and often interchangeable, with oregano and mint.

GARLIC plays a background role in this cuisine compared to other Mediterranean kitchens. A couple of chopped cloves will give a pleasant pungency to bean soups, boiled chickpeas, baked eggplant, cheese dishes, and savory filo pastries. However, there is no limit to the amount that can be added to *skordalia* sauce. Start with 6 cloves in 2 cups of mashed potatoes, and add as necessary to achieve the desired taste.

GREEK HERB BLEND is especially good with baked or long-simmered dishes—casseroles, soups, stews, and savory filo pastries. Its rich fragrance and well-herbed flavor will help revive interest in leftovers or bland foods. Vegetables and salad dressings are better for its presence as are eggs, rice, and poultry.

Combine and store in an airtight container:

    3   tablespoons dried oregano
    1   tablespoon dill weed
    1   teaspoon sesame seed
    ½   teaspoon each: coriander and thyme
    ¼   teaspoon crushed mint leaves
    ⅛   teaspoon fennel seed
    1   crushed bay leaf

LEMON JUICE is indispensable for its sharp tang and clear citrus perfume. It has enough character to flavor or garnish a dish on its own. As a background seasoner, it has the ability to liberate lesser flavors. The juice of 1 lemon will add liveliness and sophistication to artichokes, zucchini, and string beans. To prepare a piquant salad dressing, combine equal proportions of lemon juice and olive or peanut oil. For a mellower dressing, use 1 part lemon juice to 3 parts oil. The sweet syrups poured over Greek pastries rarely use more than one-half a lemon for sparkle.

MAHLEPI is a unique spice derived from hard, black cherry seeds. It lends an unusual spiciness to cakes, cookies, or sweet yeast breads and must be ground before using. *Mahlepi* is available at Greek or specialty food stores. When unobtainable, substitute 2 teaspoons vanilla extract for ½ to 1 teaspoon *mahlepi*.

MINT is a strongly aromatic and potent herb. Even in small doses, it is emphatic and pervasive; and, though its cool, sweet zest appeals to many, it is strongly disliked by others. Used discreetly, it adds a pleasant and unusual touch to Greek salads, sauces, and rice pilafs. For an offbeat flavor, add a few sprigs of fresh mint to simmering bean soups, chickpeas, or spinach-rice pilaf. With cucumbers, yogurt, tomatoes, eggplant, or string beans, fresh or dried mint can be excellent.

OLIVE OIL is almost synonymous with Greek cooking. The majority of Greek vegetable, poultry, and fish dishes are cooked with, or bathed in, olive oil. The secret to top-notch preparations is to use only pure, un-adulterated, virgin olive oil. It imparts a delicate, warm, and fruity bouquet that cannot be duplicated by other cooking mediums.

OREGANO leaves provide the pungent taste and aroma frequently associated with Greek food. Dried oregano leaves give oomph to most vegetable and poultry dishes. Feta cheese, dusted with oregano and doused with olive oil and lemon juice, makes a superb appetizer. Sprinkle oregano over a casserole just before it goes into the oven to intensify its flavor. To season salad dressings, use as much as 1 tablespoon for ½ to 1 cup oil. Marjoram may be substituted in a pinch, but its nature is much milder. Avoid ground oregano, which is virtually without character.

THYME has a warm, deep, aromatic quality that blends well with other Greek seasonings, especially oregano and dill. A generous sprinkling of this versatile herb brings uncommon interest to cheese or egg dishes, vegetables, and soups. Thyme dries better than most herbs. It retains much of its flavor and develops none of the strawlike taste which plagues many dried herbs. Substitute 1 teaspoon dried thyme for 2 sprigs fresh thyme whenever necessary.

Other seasonings found in Greek cooking are: basil, bay leaf, sesame seed, cumin, parsley, white pepper, mustard seed, tarragon, saffron, marjoram, nutmeg, fennel seed, coriander, rosewater, allspice, sage, anise seed, anise oil, and summer savory.

Nutritional Essentials

Eating Greek food generally qualifies as a Lucullan experience, and as such, makes us prone to dietary excesses. With an average of 303 calories per dish and a 56 percent total fat content, the Greek cuisine ranks second in these categories among the ethnic cooking styles presented in this book. The high-salt content of these foods—olives, anchovies, feta cheese—may also impose limitations for some people, especially those with high blood pressure. In short, Greek cookery requires some degree of planning in order to meet the dietary needs of weight-watchers and fat-conscious cooks.

Despite these drawbacks, all is not lost when it comes to the nutritional aspects of Greek food. This cuisine is renowned for its varied salad combinations, featuring wholesome and healthful ingredients such as lettuce, beets, potatoes, green peppers, and cucumbers. Lettuce, in particular, is an essential part of most Greek salads and has much to offer. Contributing a fair amount of vitamins C and A, calcium, iron, and other minerals, these crisp greens will contribute plenty of fiber with only a minimum number of calories (84 per head) to your diet. If iron intake is a consideration, as it may be in pregnancy, choose Boston or Bibb lettuces, both of which are high in this nutrient. Spinach, another leafy green used extensively in this kind of cooking, is higher in protein than lettuce. Try it in baked dishes such as *Spanakopitta* or the *Spinach and Rice Pilaf*. The *Greek Salad Supreme* combines a number of nutritious ingredients. With 159 calories, 7 grams of protein, and 2.4 grams of fiber per average serving, this is a good alternative for calorie-watchers. The *Villager's Salad* is another low-calorie specialty that nicely complements Greek entrées.

When it comes to the excessive salt content of the Greek diet, cheese is one of the main culprits. Feta, a semisoft, tangy, and salty cheese is employed in many dishes. A one-ounce portion contains only 75 calories (low for cheese), but a considerable amount of sodium (316 mgs). Parmesan, *Kasseri*, and *Kefalotyri* (Greek romano)—frequent additions to the Greek table—are very high in salt content and should not be consumed in large quantities by people who are watching their salt intake.

Because Greek cooking relies heavily on oil for its baked dishes, a high fat intake is almost unavoidable. Peanut and olive oils—the most commonly used—are both high in saturated fat, the former slightly higher than the latter. Olive oil is much lower than peanut oil in polyunsaturates and, for this reason, might be less desirable for those on low-fat, low-cholesterol diets. While it is difficult to avoid the use of peanut or olive oils and still maintain the integrity of Greek cookery, you can always compromise by combining equal parts safflower oil with one or the other. This manipulation will substantially increase the polyunsaturated fat content of your cooking oil.

Unless you jog, sweat a lot (a salt-losing endeavor), or absolutely do not care about the composition of your diet, you will find it difficult to eat rich, heavy Greek foods on a daily basis. Though this diet is generally high in calories, salt, and total fat, most of the recipes can be incorporated into well-balanced meals. One way to do this is to combine the higher calorie entrees with one of the low-calorie Greek salads. Still another is to eat Greek main courses only on special occasions. Of course, if you happen to be thin, and are in the mood to indulge, by all means this cuisine should provide regular offerings for your dinner table.

DOMATES YEMISTES ME RIZI
(Baked Tomatoes Stuffed with Rice)   *YIELD: 8 servings*

8 large firm tomatoes
4 tablespoons olive oil
1 onion, chopped
¾ cup uncooked long-grain rice
6 ounces tomato paste
3 teaspoons finely chopped garlic
  cloves or 1 teaspoon garlic powder

¼ cup fresh chopped parsley
¼ cup fresh chopped dill, or 1
  tablespoon dill weed
½ teaspoon dried oregano
Salt and pepper to taste
4 tablespoons peanut oil
½ cup water

1. Slice tops off tomatoes and reserve. Carefully scoop out and reserve the pulp, leaving a wall about ⅓-inch thick. Discard any tough cores or seeds. Chop the pulp and set aside. Sprinkle salt in the tomato shells and turn upside down on paper towels to drain.

2. Heat the olive oil in a large heavy saucepan. Sauté the onion until transparent but not brown—about 5 minutes. Add the chopped pulp, rice, tomato paste, garlic, herbs, salt, pepper, peanut oil, and water. Simmer, uncovered, 5 minutes or until mixture thickens.

3. Preheat oven to 350 degrees.

4. Place tomatoes in a 9- by 13-inch baking pan. Fill ½ to ¾ full with rice filling. Cover with reserved tops. Pour any remaining rice filling over the tomatoes. Bake in a preheated oven, covered, until rice is tender—about 20 to 30 minutes. Serve lukewarm or cold.

Variation: Add 2 tablespoons currants and pine nuts to rice filling, or top each filled tomato with grated hard cheese before putting the top on.

FAKI YIAHNI
(Lentil Soup)   *YIELD: 6 to 8 servings*

1 pound (2 cups) lentils
2 cups water
½ cup olive oil, divided
1 medium-sized onion, finely
  chopped
2 garlic cloves, peeled and cut into
  slivers

2 bay leaves
½ cup vinegar
2½ quarts hot water
Salt and pepper to taste

Wash lentils well. Place in a soup pot with 2 cups water. Bring to a boil and cook over medium heat until all liquid evaporates—watch carefully so lentils do not burn. Add half of the oil, reduce heat to low, and add the onion, garlic, and bay leaves. Stir constantly for 5 minutes. Add the vinegar and 2½ quarts hot water. Return to a boil, reduce heat, and simmer gently until tender—about 1½ hours. Stir in remaining oil, season to taste, and cook 5 minutes longer, stirring occasionally. Serve immediately.

FETA CHEESE SALAD DRESSING

YIELD: Approximately 2½ cups

1 cup plain, low-fat yogurt or sour cream
½ cup crumbled feta cheese
½ cup creamed cottage cheese
Juice of 3 lemons

2 tablespoons each: peanut oil and olive oil
1 or 2 garlic cloves, minced
Oregano to taste
Salt and pepper to taste

Place all ingredients in a blender and whirl until smooth.

GALATOBOURYKO
(Custard Baked in Filo)

YIELD: 24 pieces

2 quarts milk
½ stick safflower margarine or butter
1 cup semolina* or farina
1 cup sugar
7 large eggs, well beaten

1 tablespoon vanilla
1 pound unsalted butter or safflower margarine
1 pound filo dough* (if frozen let thaw 48 hours in refrigerator)
Kataifi Honey-Orange Syrup (p. 154)

Available at Greek or Middle Eastern grocery stores and some supermarkets.

1. *To prepare filling*: Put the milk and the ½ stick of margarine or butter in a large pot and heat until melted. Do not boil. Slowly add the semolina or farina and sugar. Stir until well mixed. Add the beaten eggs stirring constantly until mixture thickens—about 10 minutes. Remove from heat and stir until filling is cool. Stir in the vanilla and set aside.
2. Melt the pound of butter or margarine.
3. *To assemble Galatobouryko*: Remove filo dough from box and keep covered at all times with a lightly dampened cloth to prevent leaves from drying. Place a sheet of filo in a greased 10- by 14-inch baking pan. With a soft pastry brush, paint on a layer of melted butter and coat well, working as quickly as possible. Repeat until you have covered 6 layers in this manner. Place the next layer so that it overlaps one side by 3 inches. Brush with melted butter. Repeat process so that there is a 3-inch overlap on all 4 sides of the pan. Spread the cooled custard over the filo and fold the extended sheets in toward the center. This will prevent the filling from running down the sides of the pan. Cover with remaining leaves, brushing each as before. Trim excess from sides with a sharp knife to fit into pan.
4. Preheat oven to 350 degrees.
5. Bake 35 minutes or until evenly browned. Remove from oven and cut into 3⅓-inch squares. Cut each square diagonally in half. Let cool completely.
6. Prepare syrup. Pour hot syrup very gradually over the cooled pastry.
Note: *Galatobouryko* may be frozen before baking. Thaw from 3 to 4 hours at room temperature, then bake.

GREEK CHEESE PIE

YIELD: 6 to 8 servings

1 9-inch unbaked pie shell (p. 380)
½ pound feta cheese
1 cup light cream
3 eggs
1 teaspoon thyme
   Dash pepper

1 small garlic clove, crushed
1 teaspoon cornstarch
6 large pitted black Greek olives
6 large pitted green olives
1 pimiento, cut into strips

1. Prick pie crust well with a fork. Place in a freezer for 10 minutes.
2. Preheat oven to 425 degrees. Bake pie shell 10 minutes on middle rack. Let cool before filling.
3. Break feta into small pieces. Put in an electric blender with the cream and eggs. Beat until smooth. Add the thyme, pepper, garlic, and cornstarch. Blend a few seconds longer. Pour into the pie shell.
4. Bake for 10 minutes. Arrange olives over top. Bake 25 minutes longer or until set. Decorate with pimiento strips. Serve warm.
Variation: Substitute half of the feta cheese with pot cheese. Add ½ teaspoon oregano.
Note: May be made earlier in the day and reheated.

SOUPA FAKI
(White Bean Soup)

YIELD: 6 to 8 servings

1 pound Northern or white beans
1 cup chopped celery, including
   some leaves
1 carrot, thinly sliced
1 small onion, chopped
2 garlic cloves, pressed—optional

½ cup olive oil, divided
2½ quarts hot water
1 pound fresh or canned tomatoes,
   peeled, chopped, and drained
Salt and freshly ground pepper to
taste

Soak beans in water to cover overnight. The next day, drain and rinse with cold water. Place in a large pot along with the celery, carrot, onion, garlic, and ¼ cup of the olive oil. Cook over medium heat, stirring constantly for 5 minutes. Add the hot water and tomatoes. Bring to a boil. Lower heat and cook until beans are tender—about 45 minutes to 1 hour. Add remaining olive oil and cook 5 minutes longer. Season to taste with salt and pepper and serve hot.

GREEK HOLIDAY BREAD   YIELD: 3 loaves, approximately 12 servings each

¾ pound lightly salted butter
2 cups whole milk
2½ packages yeast
6 eggs
2 cups sugar
*Available at drugstores

¼ to ½ teaspoon anise oil*
2½ to 3 pounds all-purpose flour
1 egg
½ teaspoon water
½ cup sesame seeds

1. Melt the butter in a small saucepan. Set aside to cool. Scald the milk and cool to lukewarm. Stir in the yeast until dissolved. Add to the cooled butter. Set aside.

2. In a large mixing bowl or pot, beat the eggs well. Beat in the sugar and anise oil. Add the milk and butter mixture and blend thoroughly. Begin adding the flour, 2 cups at a time, beating well after each addition until a dough that can be handled easily is formed. Knead with a dough hook, or by hand, until smooth and elastic, about 10 minutes. Place in a greased bowl. Cover with a towel and set in a warm, draft-free place until doubled in bulk. Punch down and let rise again. Punch down and cut dough into 3 equal portions. Shape into rounds.

3. Prepare one loaf at a time. Cut the first round into 3 pieces. Using your hands, roll each piece into an 18-inch rope. Braid the ropes; shape into a ring and place one end on top of the other. Press ends together gently with fingers. Fit into a greased, round 8-inch aluminum foil pan. Repeat process to form 3 braided loaves. Cover with a towel and set aside to rise again.

4. Preheat oven to 350 degrees.

5. Beat the egg and water together to make a wash. Brush the tops of the loaves with the wash and sprinkle liberally with the sesame seeds. Bake 45 minutes or until an inserted toothpick comes out clean. Serve when thoroughly cooled, or wrap in heavy-duty foil and freeze in the disposable pans.

Note: For Easter bread, insert a red-dyed, hard-boiled egg in the center of the braided loaf after it begins to rise. For the New Year, insert a dime, wrapped in foil, into each loaf before baking. The slice with the dime is supposed to bring good luck during the year to the finder. Traditionally, the first slice is for the house, the second for the master, the third for the mistress, the fourth for the eldest son, and then by age throughout the family.

GREEK SALAD SUPREME

YIELD: 6 to 8 servings

---

1 head romaine or iceberg lettuce, cored
1 medium-sized cucumber, peeled and sliced
3 green onions, chopped with tops, or 4 shallots, minced
½ green pepper, seeded and chopped

1 cup cooked chick-peas or Northern beans
1 rib celery, chopped
1 small red onion, thinly sliced
8 artichoke hearts or anchovy fillets
1 cup sliced beets or tomatoes
Feta Cheese Salad Dressing (p. 151)

Wash lettuce. Dry in a salad spinner or pat dry with paper towels. Tear into bite-size pieces. Combine with remaining ingredients and toss with enough *Feta Cheese Dressing* to coat all ingredients.

KATAIFI
(Shredded Wheat Pastry)

YIELD: 24 squares

Honey-Orange Syrup:
1½ cups sugar
½ cup honey
1 cup water
1 cinnamon stick
4 whole cloves
Juice of ½ lemon
1 thick slice orange with peel

Pastry:
1 pound *kataifi* dough*
½ pound safflower margarine or unsalted butter
1 pound pecans, blanched toasted almonds, or walnuts, coarsely chopped
⅓ cup sugar
1 teaspoon cinnamon

Available at Greek grocery stores. If frozen, let thaw at room temperature for 2 hours.

1. *To prepare syrup*: Place the sugar, honey, water, cinnamon stick, and cloves in a heavy saucepan. Bring to a boil over medium heat, stirring constantly. Add the lemon juice and orange slice. Boil gently 15 to 20 minutes or until syrup spins a fine thread when dropped from a spoon. Remove from heat. Discard cinnamon stick, cloves, and orange slice. Let cool.
2. *To unwrap dough*: Using both hands, gently pull the *kataifi* strands apart so they do not stick together too much. Place in a large bowl. If they seem too dry, sprinkle lightly with a little milk. Cover with a towel.
3. Preheat oven to 350 degrees.
4. *To assemble Kataifi*: Melt the margarine or butter. Brush a little on the bottom of a 9- by 12-inch baking dish. Cover the entire bottom of the dish with half of the dough, gently pressing the mixture with the palm of your hand. Drizzle over half of the melted margarine. Combine the nuts, sugar, and cinnamon. Sprinkle evenly over the layer of dough. Layer remaining dough evenly over the nut mixture, flattening gently with your hands.

Drizzle remaining margarine evenly over the top. Bake 30 minutes in preheated oven or until golden brown.

5. As soon as pastry is removed from oven, pour the cold honey-orange syrup over the top, a little at a time, to give the pastry time to absorb the liquid. Cover baking dish with a linen towel or clean kitchen towel for 2 hours to soften the top of the pastry. Remove towel and cut into squares to serve.

Variation: *Short Cut Kataifi*: Hollow out large shredded wheat biscuits with a knife to form deep pockets. Fill with nut mixture and brush generously with melted butter. Place on a well-greased baking sheet and bake in a preheated 300-degree oven from 25 to 30 minutes. Remove from oven, saturate with cold syrup, and let cool before serving.

Note: If *kataifi* dough is unavailable, substitute regular shredded wheat (cereal) biscuits, slightly crushed.

LAHANIKA PSITA
(Baked Green Vegetable Casserole)   *YIELD: 6 servings*

---

3 medium-sized red or white potatoes, cut into eighths
Water to cover
1 pound tomatoes, fresh or canned
¼ pound string beans, trimmed and sliced
¼ pound fresh okra, sliced, or ¼ pound eggplant, peeled and cubed
1 large zucchini, cut into ½-inch rounds
1 large onion, sliced

6 large mushrooms, cut into halves
Salt and freshly ground pepper to taste
3 to 4 garlic cloves, cut into thin slivers
½ cup chopped parsley
1½ tablespoons chopped fresh dill or 1½ teaspoons dill weed
1 teaspoon each: dried oregano and thyme
⅛ cup each: peanut and olive oil

1. Place potatoes in a pot with enough water to cover. Boil 10 minutes. Drain off water and set aside.

2. Skin tomatoes if fresh (drop into boiling water for 10 seconds and peel off skins) and cut into quarters. If using canned tomatoes, drain off juice and crush them.

3. Preheat oven to 350 degrees.

4. Combine all the vegetables and seasonings and place in an oiled 2-quart casserole. Drizzle peanut and olive oil evenly over the top. Cover and bake in a preheated oven 1 hour or until vegetables are fork-tender. Uncover for the last 15 minutes of baking. Serve hot, cold, or at room temperature as a main course or side dish.

Variation: Any of the following may be substituted for the zucchini, string beans, mushrooms, or okra: fresh peas, carrots, green peppers, or celery. Fresh or dried basil may replace the dill.

MARINATED CHICKEN WITH LEMON-OREGANO SAUCE

YIELD: 4 servings

1 frying chicken, cut up (3 pounds)
½ cup olive oil
Juice of 3 lemons
3 tablespoons dried oregano

4 tablespoons safflower margarine or butter, cut into small pieces
1 cup uncooked long-grain rice
Salt and freshly ground pepper to taste

1. Arrange chicken pieces in a Dutch oven or heavy 3-quart casserole dish with a lid. Combine the oil, lemon juice, and oregano. Pour over chicken and dot with margarine or butter pieces. Marinate, covered, at room temperature for 3 hours.
2. Preheat oven to 350 degrees.
3. Bake chicken, covered, 1 hour in preheated oven. Meanwhile, place rice in 6 cups boiling water. Reduce heat to low, cover, and simmer until tender. Drain, rinse, and set aside. After chicken has baked 1 hour, uncover and bake 10 minutes longer.
4. Remove chicken from Dutch oven with a slotted spoon or tongs. Stir rice into remaining juices. Season to taste with salt and pepper. Transfer rice to a serving platter and arrange chicken over the top. Serve immediately.

MEATLESS MOUSSAKA

YIELD: 12 servings

3 medium-sized eggplants, peeled and cut into ½-inch slices
1 stick safflower margarine or butter, melted
4 medium-sized potatoes, peeled and thinly sliced
4 medium-sized zucchini

Cream Sauce:
6 tablespoons butter
6 tablespoons flour
3 cups whole milk
4 eggs, well beaten
½ teaspoon cinnamon
½ teaspoon nutmeg
Salt and freshly ground pepper

Tomato Sauce:
2 medium-sized onions, finely chopped
2 garlic cloves, pressed
3 tablespoons peanut oil
1 16-ounce can Italian pear-shaped tomatoes
1 16-ounce can tomato sauce
½ cup dry red wine
1 bay leaf, crumbled
½ teaspoon dried oregano
½ teaspoon cinnamon
¼ cup chopped fresh parsley
Salt and freshly ground pepper

1½ cups grated *Kasseri,** *Kefalotyri,** or romano cheese

*Available at Greek or Middle Eastern grocery stores.

1. Salt the eggplant slices. Put in a colander and let stand for 1 hour to remove bitterness. Rinse under cold water and pat dry. Arrange on a baking sheet. Brush each side lightly with half the melted margarine or butter. Broil until brown on both sides, but watch carefully to avoid burning. Remove slices to drain on paper towels.

2. In a large heavy skillet, sauté the potatoes in the remaining margarine until brown. Remove from skillet and drain on paper towels. Wash and slice zucchini into ¼-inch rounds. Set aside.

3. *To prepare tomato sauce*: In a large saucepan, sauté the onions and garlic in hot peanut oil until tender. Add remaining sauce ingredients and simmer 30 minutes. Taste and adjust seasonings. Set aside.

4. *To prepare cream sauce*: Melt the butter in an enamel saucepan. Stir in the flour and cook 3 to 5 minutes, stirring constantly, until well blended to make a roux. Add the milk gradually, stirring constantly, until the sauce is smooth and thick. Mix 2 or 3 tablespoons of the sauce into the beaten eggs. Then slowly add the eggs to the sauce. Heat through and remove immediately from burner. Stir in the cinnamon, nutmeg, salt, and pepper. Taste and adjust seasonings.

5. Preheat oven to 350 degrees.

6. *To assemble Moussaka*: Grease a 10- by 14-inch baking dish. Arrange layers of eggplant, potatoes, zucchini, and tomato sauce, sprinkling each layer with ¼ cup grated cheese. Repeat process until all vegetables are used, beginning and ending with eggplant. Bake for 20 minutes. Pour cream sauce over casserole. Sprinkle top with the remaining ½ cup of grated cheese. Bake 30 minutes more. Remove from oven. Cut into squares and serve hot.

PATATO SALATA
(Greek Hot Potato Salad)   *YIELD: 6 servings*

---

6 medium-sized red potatoes	2 tablespoons dried oregano
1 onion, finely chopped or sliced	1 teaspoon finely minced garlic
Juice of 2 large lemons	cloves
¼ to ½ cup olive oil	Salt and freshly ground pepper to taste

Peel potatoes if desired. Place in a pot with enough water to cover. Boil until tender, but not bursting. Drain off water and cut potatoes into eighths. Place in a bowl and combine with the onion. Combine remaining ingredients and pour over potatoes. Toss lightly and serve warm. Potatoes may be chilled before serving if desired, although the seasonings must be mixed with hot potatoes for maximum flavor.

SKORDALIA
(Garlic Sauce)   YIELD: *Approximately 3½ cups or 8 to 10 servings*

6 to 8 garlic cloves
2 cups slightly mashed, cold
    potatoes (about 1½ pounds boiled
    potatoes)
½ cup vinegar

½ cup peanut or olive oil
½ cup olive oil
Salt and freshly ground pepper to
taste

1. Peel garlic and pound to a paste in a mortar with a pestle (or with the back of a spoon). Place in a blender (or use an electric mixer) along with the potatoes and vinegar. Add the peanut oil and olive oil slowly to obtain as smooth and creamy a consistency as possible. For blender use, if the vortex ceases to form, turn off, stir with a rubber spatula, and turn motor on again. Season to taste with salt and pepper. For stronger flavor, add more mashed garlic.
2. Serve chilled or at room temperature as a dip for raw vegetables, fried zucchini, fried eggplant, fried salt cod, or boiled artichokes. As a sauce, *Skordalia* is delicious poured over cold sliced beets or hard-boiled eggs.
Variation: For a richer sauce add 1 or 2 egg yolks. Or replace half of the potatoes with ground almonds or walnuts.

SPAGHETTI me TSIGARISTO VOOTIRO
(Pasta with Browned Butter Sauce)   YIELD: *6 servings*

6 quarts water
2 teaspoons salt
1 pound whole wheat spaghetti or
    thin vermicelli noodles
12 tablespoons safflower margarine
    or butter

¼ pound *Kefalotyri* (Greek romano)
or Parmesan cheese, freshly
grated
Freshly ground pepper

1. Bring the water and salt to a boil in a large soup pot. Add the pasta and boil until tender, but firm to the bite. Drain in a colander and rinse with cold water. Return to the pot and rewarm over low heat, stirring frequently to avoid sticking.
2. Melt the margarine or butter in a small skillet over medium heat until brown. Stir frequently and watch carefully to prevent burning.
3. Place half of the pasta on a heated serving platter. Top with half of the grated cheese and half of the melted margarine or butter. Repeat another layer with remaining ingredients. Top with freshly ground pepper. Serve at once.
Variation: Replace pasta with 3 cups cooked rice. Or add 1 tablespoon minced garlic to the butter.

SOUPA AVGOLEMONO
(Egg and Lemon Soup)   *YIELD: 6 to 8 servings*

---

2 quarts *Chicken Soup* (p. 301)
½ cup uncooked long- or medium-
  grain rice

4 eggs
Juice of 2 lemons
Salt and pepper to taste

1. Bring soup to a boil and add the rice. Reduce heat to low and simmer, partially covered, until rice is tender—about 15 to 20 minutes.
2. Meanwhile, separate the eggs. Beat the whites with a wire whisk in a clean, dry, copper bowl until soft peaks form. In a separate bowl, beat the yolks with the lemon juice until thick and creamy. Using over and under strokes, carefully fold yolks into whites with a rubber spatula.
3. Add ¼ cup of soup, a little at a time, to the egg mixture, stirring constantly as you add. The temperature of the lemon sauce should be close to the temperature of the soup. If necessary, fold in a little more soup to achieve the correct temperature. Add egg sauce to soup, stirring vigorously as you add. Continue stirring until soup lightly coats the spoon. Do not allow the soup to boil or eggs will curdle. Remove from heat, add salt and pepper to taste, and serve at once.
Note: Leftovers may be brought to room temperature to serve. This soup does not reheat well.

SPANAKOPITTA
(Spinach—Cheese Pies)   *YIELD: Approximately 30, 2-inch squares*

2½ pounds fresh spinach or 4
  packages chopped frozen spinach
1 medium-sized yellow onion,
  finely chopped
1 bunch green onions, chopped
  with stems
2 tablespoons peanut oil
8 large eggs, well beaten
¾ cup small curd cottage cheese
¾ pound feta cheese, crumbled
2 scant tablespoons dill weed

1 scant tablespoon ground
  coriander
½ teaspoon salt
¼ teaspoon freshly ground black
  pepper
1 stick safflower margarine or
  butter, melted
1 pound sweet butter or safflower
  margarine
1 pound filo dough* (if frozen,
  thaw 48 hours in refrigerator
  before using)

Available at Greek or Middle Eastern grocery stores and some supermarkets.

1. *To prepare filling*: Wash spinach well. Cook fresh or frozen in a small amount of water just until fresh spinach is limp, or frozen spinach is thawed. Drain in a colander and squeeze out excess water. If using fresh spinach, chop coarsely. Put in a large bowl. Sauté onions in heated peanut

oil until limp. Mix with the spinach. Add the beaten eggs, cheeses, seasonings, and melted margarine or butter. Taste and adjust seasonings. Set aside.

2. Melt the pound of sweet butter. You may clarify it if you wish at this point (see *Index* "How to Clarify Butter") as this will help produce crisp filo leaves. Unclarified butter or margarine, however, is acceptable.

3. *To assemble Spanakopitta*: Remove filo dough from box and keep covered at all times with a lightly dampened cloth to prevent leaves from drying. Place a sheet of filo in a greased 10- by 14-inch pan. With a soft pastry brush, paint on a layer of melted butter and coat well, working as quickly as possible. Do not worry if a sheet tears as the next sheet will patch it. Repeat until you have brushed 12 sheets of filo. Spread spinach mixture over the top. Cover with remaining sheets of filo, following the same procedure as before, making sure each layer is brushed with butter.

4. Preheat oven to 325 degrees.

5. With a sharp knife, cut into 2-inch squares, penetrating halfway through the top layer of filo. Bake until golden brown and crisp—about 40 to 45 minutes. Let cool 10 minutes before cutting. Serve hot or at room temperature as an appetizer or main course.

SPANAKÓRIZO
(Spinach and Rice Pilaf)   *YIELD: 4 servings*

---

4 cups water
¼ teaspoon salt
½ cup uncooked long-grain brown or white rice
1 pound fresh spinach
¼ cup each: olive and peanut oil
½ medium-sized onion, chopped

Juice of 1 lemon
Salt and white pepper to taste
¼ teaspoon dried dill or mint—optional
Lemon wedges as garnish
Slices of feta cheese as garnish—optional

1. Bring water and ¼ teaspoon salt to a boil in a 2-quart saucepan. Add rice, reduce heat to low, cover with a lid, and simmer until rice is tender. Drain off excess liquid. Set rice aside.

2. Wash spinach well. Discard tough stems and blemished leaves. Tear into bite-sized pieces. Set aside.

3. Heat oils in a 3-quart saucepan. Sauté the onion until golden—about 10 minutes. Add the spinach and ¼ cup water. Cover and simmer until spinach wilts—about 5 minutes. Add lemon juice and rice. Heat until rice is warmed through, stirring frequently to prevent sticking. Season with salt, white pepper, and dill or mint. Serve hot or at room temperature as a side dish surrounded by lemon wedges and, if desired, slices of feta cheese.

TARAMASALATA
(Carp Roe Pâté)   *YIELD: 8 servings*

3 to 4 ounces *tarama** (salted carp
  roe)
2 slices stale or dried bread,
  crushed into fine crumbs
Juice of 3 lemons

2 tablespoons chopped onion or 2
  garlic cloves, minced—optional
¾ cup to 1½ cups olive oil
Chopped parsley

*Available at Greek specialty food shops.

1. Place the *tarama*, bread crumbs, lemon juice, and onion in a blender. Add ⅓ cup of the olive oil and blend until smooth. With blender on low speed, gradually add remaining oil in a slow thin stream until mixture is thick enough to hold its shape on a spoon. Refrigerate until ready to serve (it will thicken even more as it chills).
2. Place *Taramasalata* in a shallow dish. Sprinkle chopped parsley over the top. Surround with any of the following: warm bread, thin toast, whole grain crackers, black olives, or raw vegetables. Serve as an appetizer.
Note: *Taramasalata* will keep, covered in the refrigerator, for one week. If it becomes too salty, stir in a couple of tablespoons of plain low-fat yogurt or sour cream.

TYROPITTA
(Baked Cheese Triangles)   *YIELD: 36 triangles*

½ pound feta cheese, crumbled
½ pound pot cheese or creamed
  cottage cheese
3 to 5 eggs, well beaten
1 teaspoon each: dried oregano, dill
  weed, and chopped parsley
¼ teaspoon marjoram

Freshly ground pepper to taste
Salt to taste
½ pound filo dough* (if frozen,
  thaw 48 hours in the refrigerator)
½ cup safflower margarine or
  unsalted butter, melted

*Available at Greek and Middle Eastern groceries and many supermarkets.

1. Blend the cheeses together; mix thoroughly. Add eggs, one at a time, beating after each addition. Add seasonings; taste and adjust seasonings.
2. Remove filo from package and unfold. Count out 12 sheets (this makes ½ pound). With a sharp knife or kitchen shears, cut sheets into 3 equal parts. Stack and place strips under a damp cloth to prevent them from drying out.
3. Place 1 filo strip in front of you on a clean surface. Using a soft pastry brush, apply a coating of melted margarine. Place 1 heaping tablespoon of filling on one corner of the strip, leaving a ½-inch border. Fold adjacent corner over filling to make a triangle. Continue folding side to side in tri-

angle forms until the strip is used up. Tuck under any loose ends and seal the seam with melted margarine. Continue process with remaining filo sheets and filling. Refrigerate triangles as you go along, until ready to bake.

4. Preheat oven to 375 degrees.

5. Place triangles 1 inch apart on a lightly-greased baking sheet. Bake in a preheated oven on the middle rack until golden brown and crisp—about 25 to 30 minutes. Cool slightly before serving as an appetizer or main course. Leftovers may be reheated.

Variation: Replace half the feta cheese with grated Parmesan cheese.

Note: *Tyropitta*, like any filo pastry, will keep several days if covered and refrigerated. Or, they may be wrapped individually and frozen. Reheat on an ungreased baking sheet, in a preheated 350-degree oven, for approximately 10 minutes.

VILLAGER'S SALAD
YIELD: 4 to 6 servings

---

3 large firm tomatoes, cut into wedges	¼ cup red wine vinegar
	3 tablespoons olive oil
1 medium-sized zucchini, sliced	2½ tablespoons peanut oil
1 medium-sized green pepper, seeded and chopped	1 tablespoon dried oregano
	Salt and pepper to taste

Combine the tomatoes, zucchini, and green peppers. Combine the vinegar, oils, and seasonings. Toss with tomato mixture. Let stand at room temperature 30 minutes before serving.

Variations: Substitute 1 cucumber, peeled and sliced, for the zucchini. Or, add 6 to 8 *Kalamata* olives.

GREECE/RECIPE ANALYSIS CHART

Name of Recipe	Quantity	Calories	CHO gms.	Protein gms.	Total Fat gms.	Saturated Fat gms.	Choles-terol mg.	Dietary Fiber gms.
1. *Tyropitta* (Baked Cheese Triangles)	per serving	68	5 (29%)	3 (18%)	4 (53%)	1 (13%)	32	—
2. Feta Cheese Salad Dressing	per 2½-tbsp. serving	74	2 (11%)	3 (16%)	6 (73%)	2 (24%)	10	
3. *Soupa Avgolemono*	per serving	104	12 (46%)	5 (19%)	4 (35%)	2 (18%)	156	.1
4. Villager's Salad	per serving	144	7 (19%)	2 (6%)	12 (75%)	2 (13%)	—	1.1
5. Greek Salad Supreme	per serving	159	17 (43%)	7 (18%)	7 (39%)	1 (6%)	4	2.4
6. *Lahanika Psita* (Baked Green Vegetable Casserole)	per serving	174	19 (44%)	4 (9%)	9 (47%)	1 (5%)	—	1.5
7. *Soupa Faki* (White Bean Soup)	per serving	214	17 (32%)	5 (9%)	14 (59%)	2 (8%)	—	3.2
8. *Taramasalata*	per serving	225	5 (9%)	4 (7%)	21 (84%)	2 (8%)	—	—
9. *Skordalia*	per serving	242	10 (17%)	1 (2%)	22 (81%)	3 (7%)	—	.4
10. *Domates Yemistes me Rizi* (Baked Tomatoes Stuffed with Rice)	per serving	258	29 (45%)	4 (6%)	14 (49%)	2 (7%)	—	1.5
11. Greek Holi-day Bread	per slice	267	36 (54%)	6 (9%)	11 (37%)	3 (10%)	72	—
12. *Patato Salata* (Greek Hot Po-tato Salad)	per serving	314	34 (43%)	4 (5%)	18 (52%)	2 (6%)	—	1.2
13. *Faki Yiahni* (Lentil Soup)	per serving	330	37 (45%)	14 (17%)	14 (38%)	2 (5%)	—	2.4
14. *Kataifi*	per serving	349	36 (41%)	4 (5%)	21 (54%)	2 (5%)	—	1

Name of Recipe	Quantity	Calories	CHO gms.	Protein gms.	Total Fat gms.	Saturated Fat gms.	Choles- terol mg.	Dietary Fiber gms.
15. *Spanakórizo* (Spinach and Rice Pilaf)	per serving	371	26 (28%)	6 (6%)	27 (66%)	3 (7%)	—	.8
16. *Spanakopitta*	per serving	374	17 (18%)	9 (10%)	30 (72%)	8 (19%)	142	.5
17. Meatless *Moussaka*	per serving	394	31 (31%)	14 (14%)	26 (55%)	10 (23%)	132	2
18. *Galatobouryko*	per serving	410	46 (45%)	7 (7%)	22 (48%)	12 (26%)	130	.1
19. Greek Cheese Pie	per slice	500	27 (22%)	16 (13%)	36 (65%)	16 (29%)	249	.4
20. *Spaghetti me Tsigaristo Vootiro* (Pasta with Browned Butter Sauce)	per serving	548	58 (42%)	16 (12%)	28 (46%)	7 (11%)	13	1
21. Marinated Chicken with Lemon-Oregano Sauce	per serving	802	41 (20%)	47 (23%)	50 (57%)	9 (10%)	233	-

Numbers in parentheses (%) indicate percentage of total calories contributed by nutrient.

MENUS

LOW CALORIE SPECIALTIES
(500 to 700 calories per meal)

SOUPA AVGOLEMONO
SPANAKOPITTA
Steamed Squash with Lemon and Dill
Hot Anise Tea

Solanika Peppers
MEATLESS MOUSSAKA
Spinach Salad with Vinaigrette
Turkish Coffee

TYROPITTA (BAKED CHEESE TRIANGLES)
SPINACH AND RICE PILAF
GREEK SALAD SUPREME
Hot Mint Tea

●

LOW CHOLESTEROL MENUS
(Less than 50 mgs. of cholesterol per meal)

Solanika Peppers
PATATO SALATA (GREEK HOT
POTATO SALAD)
GREEK SALAD SUPREME
Pocket Bread
Honeydew Melon

Greek Olives
FAKI YIAHNI (LENTIL SOUP)
VILLAGER'S SALAD
Whole Grain Crackers
Dried Figs and Fresh Strawberries

TARAMASALATA
Raw Zucchini and Carrot Sticks
LAHANIKA PSITA (BAKED GREEN VEGETABLE CASSEROLE)
KATAIFI
Turkish Coffee

●

LOW SATURATED FAT SELECTIONS
(Less than 8 grams of saturated fat per meal)

SPAGHETTI ME TSIGARISTO
VOOTIRO (PASTA WITH
BROWNED BUTTER SAUCE)
Sliced Tomatoes and Green Onions
Greek Wine
Fresh Strawberries

SOUPA FAKI
(WHITE BEAN SOUP)
Sliced Cucumbers with
FETA CHEESE SALAD DRESSING
GREEK HOLIDAY BREAD
Iced Mint Tea

SKORDALIA with
Boiled Artichokes
DOMATES YEMISTES ME RIZI (BAKED TOMATOES STUFFED WITH RICE)
KATAIFI
Hot Anise Tea

HIGH PROTEIN MEALS
(30 or more grams of protein per meal)

FAKI YIAHNI (LENTIL SOUP)
GREEK CHEESE PIE
Sliced Cucumbers
Dried Figs and Walnuts
Greek Wine

**SOUPA FAKI
(WHITE BEAN SOUP)**
MEATLESS MOUSSAKA
GREEK SALAD SUPREME
GALATOBOURYKO

MARINATED CHICKEN WITH LEMON-OREGANO SAUCE
VILLAGER'S SALAD
KATAIFI
Turkish Coffee

•

WELL BALANCED LUNCH OR DINNER MENUS
(Selections that conform to recommendations in Dietary Goals for United States*)*

SOUPA AVGOLEMONO
GREEK SALAD SUPREME
GREEK HOLIDAY BREAD
Turkish Coffee

FAKI YIAHNI (LENTIL SOUP)
**LAHANIKA PSITA (BAKED GREEN
VEGETABLE CASSEROLE)**
Pocket Bread
Grapes and Bananas with Yogurt
Hot Tea

**SPAGHETTI ME TSIGARISTO VOOTIRO
(PASTA WITH BROWNED BUTTER SAUCE)**
DOMATES YEMISTES ME RIZI (BAKED TOMATOES STUFFED WITH RICE)
Feta Cheese with Sliced Cucumbers
Greek Wine

CHAPTER 7

HUNGARY
Noodles and Strudels

Culinary Essentials

Hungarian cooking challenges a wide range of your culinary skills. The novice can look like a pro by turning out exotic, but easy-to-make, cheese spreads and fruit salads. Sophisticated cooks will certainly want to try their hands at strudel-making, while the aspiring pastry chef will find Hungarian tortes an asset to any dessert repertoire.

Whether you intend to tackle simple or complicated creations, Hungarian recipes do not require expensive kitchen gear or difficult culinary techniques. A Dutch oven (a deep, heavy iron pot with a tight-fitting lid and side-handles) is ideal for poultry dishes, thick soups, and stews because it distributes heat evenly and seals in flavors. If you do not have one, a heavy 4½- to 6-quart pot is sufficient. Strudels usually require a cheesecloth, pastry brush, and baking sheet. To make the elegant *Sweet Potato Strudel*, you will also need a potato ricer or food mill.

Most of the ingredients used in this eastern European kitchen—baking chocolate, poppy seeds, sour cherries, and capers—are common supermarket items. You should not be deterred by names such as egg barley, Roman beans, or sauerkraut, for these too are available at grocery stores that stock Jewish or kosher foods. Although Hungarian foods are traditionally sautéed in lard, we prefer safflower or peanut oil, safflower shortening (available at health food stores), or rendered chicken fat.*

For those who want to discover new dimensions in ethnic cooking, Hungarian dishes are a good place to start. These novel preparations will introduce you to the gustatory pleasures of sour cream or yogurt-thickened

*See Seasoning Chart *in this chapter.*

casseroles. With the aid of rendered chicken fat, you will be able to transform plain boiled potatoes into sublime *Potato Pancakes*. The secrets to these recipes are fresh ingredients and proper cooking time.

Crêpe lovers will enjoy preparing Hungarian *palacsinta* or pancakes. Like the French crêpe, they are thin, light, slightly golden, and of eminently good flavor. There are limitless ways to serve these dainty cakes. Dessert *palacsintas* may be filled and rolled with apricot jam, walnuts, honey, sweetened pot cheese, or grated bittersweet chocolate. Sautéed cabbage, fried mushrooms, spinach, or grated cheese (cheddar or Parmesan) are commonly used for entrée pancakes.

Set bowls of black and white radishes, dill pickles, and pimientos on your Hungarian table for condiments. Soup, which follows a light appetizer such as the *Liptoí Cheese Ball*, can be accompanied by egg-rich *Poppy Seed Bread*, flaky croissants, or a mellow black bread.

For a salad course, select a cool and refreshing dish such as *Cucumbers Grand Mère*, *Fruit Salad with Poppy Seed Dressing*, potato salad, or marinated green peppers. Hungarian entrées are often flanked by a serving of *Egg Barley Casserole* or *Poppy Seed Noodles*, instead of rice or potato accompaniments.

If there is anything that rivals Hungarian gypsy music for capturing the soul, then it is an Hungarian dessert. End your meal on a sweet note with a pale and luminous *Sweet Potato Strudel* or magnificently rich *Csokolade Torta* iced with *Hungarian Chocolate Frosting*. They're playing your song.

Seasoning Essentials

The only way to impart an authentic aura to your Hungarian creations is to use imported Hungarian paprika, which comes in sweet and hot varieties. Do not confuse it with the standard paprika found on the supermarket spice rack which is harsher, less fragrant, and a poor substitute for the imported version.

Hungarian dishes have a spicier disposition than most of their Slavic counterparts, which can be attributed to the concentrated use of sweet Hungarian paprika. This fruity and mildly pungent member of the capsicum family is indispensable to the Hungarian cook—not only as a garnish but also in provocative alliances with other ingredients.

Sweet Hungarian paprika parades its versatility in vegetable mélanges, poultry dishes, soups, cheese spreads, egg combinations, and noodle casseroles. Its warm, persuasive flavor makes it a welcome addition to rich mixtures such as cream sauce, yogurt, or sour cream. Don't worry about adding a pinch too much—Hungarian cooks dole it out by the teaspoonful. Hot Hungarian paprika, used less frequently, will punctuate a dish more emphatically, much like cayenne pepper.

While imported paprika unites beautifully with most herbs and spices, it combines especially well with caraway seeds and garlic. These potent seasonings, along with ground black peppercorns, are combined in our *Spiced Hungarian Paprika*, a surefire blend for transforming otherwise bland

and unexciting foods into lively and tantalizing creations. You can also use this noble taste-enhancer to vary Hungarian recipes which rely solely upon paprika for their flavorings.

The discreet application of poppy seeds is also important to the art of seasoning Hungarian dishes. These tiny black seeds, which have an intriguing flavor and texture, are too often totally ignored or used exclusively as a topping for bread loaves. Experiment with the versatility of poppy seeds by dry-roasting them in a skillet over low heat. They will acquire a unique, nutlike flavor that makes them a splendid garnish for Hungarian noodles, fresh green vegetables, and fruit salad. Like the opium poppy, from which they are derived, poppy seeds can easily become an addiction.

HUNGARIAN SEASONING CHART

CARAWAY SEEDS have a stimulating and slightly acrid flavor which lightens heavy foods such as cabbage, sauerkraut, potatoes, and bean soups. These pungent crescents may be sprinkled over noodles or added to pickled beets. Tossed in salads or used in cheese spreads, they conjure up the licoricelike character of fennel seeds. Caraway seeds combine well with garlic, horseradish, and paprika. As a rule of thumb, add 2 teaspoons of caraway seeds to 3 cups shredded cabbage (for soups, salads, and strudels). The same amount may be added to the dough to make 2 loaves of bread.

DILL allies itself gracefully with vegetables, especially zucchini, cucumbers, and string beans. Teamed with fresh parsley and chives, dill is a popular seasoning for sour cream or yogurt-based sauces and salad dressings. Fresh dill is preferred to the dried variety because its flavor is more distinctive. But dried dill will acquire a new-born flavor when combined in equal proportions with fresh parsley. In general, 2 pounds of vegetables will take 1 to 2 tablespoons of freshly chopped dill or 1 to 2 teaspoons of dill weed. The same proportions should be used for 1 pint of sour cream or yogurt.

GARLIC donates its pungent flavor and incisive aroma to Hungarian soups and poultry dishes. Fresh garlic cloves are sometimes crushed and mingled with mushrooms, spinach, sauerkraut, or liver pâté. Occasionally, garlic salt is employed to doctor up lackluster foods.

HOT HUNGARIAN PAPRIKA is a ground, imported capsicum with a bittersweet flavor that is stronger than sweet Hungarian paprika, but milder than cayenne pepper. Use it in small doses like cayenne pepper when you want a more dominant and exciting flavor. It blends with any savory food. Hot Hungarian paprika is available at shops specializing in herbs and spices.

POPPY SEEDS lend a nutlike taste and crunchy texture to baked goods, especially yeast rolls and coffee cakes. As a filling for strudels or cakes, they are ground in a special poppy seed grinder or in a blender at high speed. As a garnish, the flavor of poppy seeds may be improved by roasting them in a dry skillet over low heat. Aligned with lemon rind and a pinch of sugar, the roasted seeds make a superb topping for noodles. Roasted or plain, they are an admirable addition to egg breads, fruit salads, dressings, rice, or fresh greens. To give your foods a "seedy" character, combine equal proportions of poppy, caraway, and sesame seeds.

RENDERED CHICKEN FAT is one of the greatest all-around cooking mediums with a much more exciting flavor than butter. It has the unique ability to intensify virtually any flavor with which it interacts. Bland foods, such as potatoes or egg barley, acquire a rich, warm taste when combined with chicken fat. It enhances baked chicken and is also the secret ingredient to superb chopped liver and matzo balls. When a recipe calls for rendered chicken fat, you may substitute butter, margarine, oil, or shortening, but the flavor will be severely compromised. Rendered chicken fat can be purchased at Jewish delicatessens and many grocery stores under the name *schmaltz*. Or you can make your own:

Wash 1 pound chicken fat and cut into 1-inch pieces. Place in a 2-quart saucepan with ¼ cup water. Bring to a boil, reduce heat to medium and boil gently until fat is melted and pieces begin to turn golden. Add 1 diced onion and 1 teaspoon salt. Cook until onions are browned and liquid turns to a deep yellow. Cool and strain through a fine sieve into a jar or plastic container. When covered and refrigerated, rendered chicken fat will keep several months. This recipe makes approximately 1 pint.

SPICED HUNGARIAN PAPRIKA BLEND has a warm and wonderful piquancy perfectly suited for perking up Hungarian specialties. Use in place of sweet Hungarian paprika when you want a more potent accent. This blend combines well with vegetables, sauerkraut, cheese spreads, and eggs. As a garnish, it should be used judiciously.

Combine and store in an airtight container:

- 1 tablespoon sweet Hungarian paprika
- 1 teaspoon ground black peppercorns
- ½ teaspoon garlic powder
- ¼ teaspoon cayenne pepper or hot Hungarian paprika
- ¼ teaspoon caraway seed

SWEET HUNGARIAN PAPRIKA is far superior to Spanish or American paprika. Its brilliant red hue and mild fruity flavor add color and character to foods without overwhelming them. The dishes in this cuisine which rely upon its spicy charm are myriad. One teaspoon to 1 tablespoon of sweet

Hungarian paprika will impart a deep reddish tone and zesty flavor to vegetables, stews, cheese spreads, and soups. As a garnish, it may be used lavishly. Paprika doesn't keep well; buy it in small amounts and store it in a cool, dry place. Avoid brownish paprika for surely it is stale and apt to give your dishes a musty aftertaste. Sweet Hungarian paprika is available at specialty food shops or stores that specialize in herbs and spices.

Other seasonings used in Hungarian cooking: parsley, white pepper, basil, marjoram, lemon rind, vanilla, cloves, cinnamon, horseradish, and orange rind.

Nutritional Essentials

Hungarian cooking is adaptable to a variety of dietary and nutritional preferences. Calorie-conscious cooks will be pleased that the recipes in this chapter contain an average of only 189 calories per serving, and of the 22 recipes, 7 have less than 100 calories per portion. The short and long of it is that even strict dieters may partake in Hungary's enticing culinary offerings.

For those trying to moderate their fat intake, there are eight delicious recipes in which the total fat constitutes 35% or less of the caloric content. And the protein-minded cooks can take advantage of two poultry recipes— *Chicken Fricassee* and *Chicken Paprikas*—which are plentiful in usable protein. Generally speaking, the Hungarian cuisine is best suited for people without specific dietary limitations.

Hungarian cooking brings to mind paprika, cabbage, and cucumbers. Paprika, perhaps the most vital ingredient of the Hungarian cuisine, arrived in Hungary with the Turks. A long, bright-red pepper now cultivated in Hungary, paprika belongs to the capsicum family which also includes as its members red peppers, sweet or bell peppers, and cayenne peppers. It is one of the richest sources of vitamin C—its claim to nutritional fame—and is also endowed with a substantial amount of vitamin A, fiber, and other minerals.

Cabbage is a principle ingredient in *Cabbage and Bean Soup* and *Strudel with Cabbage and Onions*. Commonly used in Hungarian cooking, raw cabbage has plenty of vitamin C, the early varieties of green-leaved vegetables having the greatest amount. This vegetable is also a good source of calcium, phosphorus, and potassium. One cup of shredded cabbage contains only 24 calories.

Cucumbers, noted for their crisp, crunchy texture and high water content (about 95%), are a refreshing addition to the weight-watcher's salad repertoire. While half-a-pound of cucumber contains only 35 calories, the same amount without skins contains only 25 calories. Given these vital statistics, weight-watchers should proceed directly to the *Marinated Cucumbers Grand Mère* or *Farmer's Salad*; a typical portion of these dishes will fill you with a mere 32 calories.

CABBAGE AND BEAN SOUP

YIELD: 5 quarts

1 pound pinto or Roman beans,
  soaked overnight
3 quarts water
2 tablespoons safflower margarine
  or butter

2 heaping tablespoons flour
1 tablespoon salt
½ teaspoon pepper
2 pounds sauerkraut
1 pint of plain yogurt or sour cream

1. Drain water from beans after they have soaked overnight. Place them in a 6-quart soup pot with 3 quarts of water. Bring to a boil, reduce heat, and simmer until tender—about 30 minutes.
2. In a small skillet, melt the margarine or butter over low heat. Add flour and stir until well blended. Cook a minute or two until the roux turns a rich, nut-brown color. Add salt and pepper.
3. Add the roux to the beans along with the sauerkraut and the juice it is packed in. Remove a few tablespoons of liquid from the soup pot and blend it with the yogurt or sour cream. Place mixture in a small saucepan over low heat until it is warm. Slowly add warm yogurt to the soup, stirring constantly. Do not allow soup to boil. Taste and adjust seasonings. Serve immediately or ladle into containers; refrigerate or freeze for later.
Note: This soup may be made a day ahead of serving so that the flavors have a chance to blend together.

CANTALOUPE SALAD WITH POPPY SEED DRESSING

YIELD: 6 servings

Salad:
  1 large cantaloupe, peeled, seeded,
    and cut into chunks
  2 ripe bananas, sliced
  2 large peaches, pitted and sliced
  ½ cup pitted and sliced cherries
    Butter lettuce

Dressing:
  ½ cup safflower mayonnaise
  1 tablespoon lemon juice
  1 tablespoon poppy seeds
  1 tablespoon apple or orange juice
  1 to 2 tablespoons honey

Mix fruit together and arrange on lettuce leaves. Place dressing ingredients in a blender. Whirl until smooth. Pour over fruit and serve immediately.
Variation: Substitute 1 tablespoon Cointreau, apricot brandy, or Amaretto for the apple juice.

CHICKEN FRICASSEE

YIELD: *Serves 6*

1 stewing hen, cut up (4½ to 5 pounds)
2 tablespoons safflower margarine, or rendered chicken fat*
2 large onions, diced
1 or 2 garlic cloves, pressed
*See Seasoning Chart.

1 tablespoon sweet Hungarian paprika
Salt and pepper to taste
Ground ginger and paprika
Water to cover

Wash chicken pieces, removing as much fat from them as possible. Pat dry. In a Dutch oven or large pot melt margarine or chicken fat. Add onions and garlic, sautéing until onions are golden brown. Mix the 1 tablespoon paprika with the sautéed onions. Add chicken and sprinkle well with salt, pepper, ground ginger, and paprika. Add enough water to cover chicken. Reduce heat, cover and simmer for 2 to 2½ hours or until chicken is tender. Add more water as necessary to maintain gravy. Serve with *Poppy Seed Noodles* (p. 182).

CHICKEN PAPRIKAS

YIELD: *6 servings*

2 tablespoons safflower margarine, or rendered chicken fat*
2 large yellow onions, chopped
2 garlic cloves, minced
1½ tablespoons sweet Hungarian paprika
1 stewing hen, cut up (5 pounds)
*See Seasoning Chart.

2 teaspoons salt
1 teaspoon ground white pepper
1 green pepper, chopped
1 large tomato, peeled, seeded, and chopped
Water to cover
1 cup plain yogurt or sour cream

1. In a Dutch oven or large pot melt the margarine or chicken fat. Brown the onions and garlic. Add paprika and stir to blend. Add the chicken and brown on all sides. Season with the salt and white pepper. Add the green pepper, tomato, and enough water to cover the chicken. Cook over medium heat, covered, 2 to 2½ hours or until tender.
2. Remove chicken with a slotted spoon and add yogurt or sour cream slowly to the gravy. Do not allow liquid to boil. Stir well, return the chicken to the pot; taste and adjust seasonings. Serve over plain-cooked or *Poppy Seed Noodles*. (p. 182)

CSOKOLADE TORTA
(Chocolate Cake)   *YIELD: 16 squares*

3½ squares unsweetened baking
   chocolate
½ cup water
3 egg whites, at room temperature
2¼ cups sugar
2½ cups cake flour, sifted

1 teaspoon baking soda
1 teaspoon salt
3 egg yolks, well beaten
1 cup orange juice
½ cup vegetable oil
1 teaspoon vanilla extract

1. Melt chocolate in the top of a double boiler over hot, not boiling, water. Remove from heat. Stir in the ½ cup water and set aside to cool.
2. Place egg whites in the small bowl of an electric mixer. At high speed, beat until soft peaks form. Continuing on high speed, sprinkle in ¾ cup of the sugar, 2 tablespoons at a time, and beat until marshmallowy in texture.
3. Preheat oven to 350 degrees.
4. Combine the remaining 1½ cups of sugar with the sifted flour, soda, and salt. Sift into the large mixing bowl. Make a well in the center. Put the beaten egg yolks, orange juice, vegetable oil, and the vanilla in the well. Beat at medium-high speed of the mixer just until blended. Add the melted chocolate. Blend. Do not overbeat. Fold in the egg whites.
5. Pour batter into a well-greased and lightly floured 9- by 13-inch baking pan. Bake in a preheated oven from 45 to 50 minutes or until toothpick inserted in center comes out clean.
Let cool before serving. This cake is excellent plain or iced with *Hungarian Chocolate Frosting* (p. 176). Cut into squares to serve.

FARFEL   *YIELD: 8 to 10 servings*

½ cup finely minced onion
2 tablespoons safflower margarine
   or rendered chicken fat*
2 packages egg drop *farfel***

1 stick safflower margarine or
   butter
½ pound fresh mushrooms, sliced
3 cups boiling vegetable or chicken
   stock
Salt and freshly ground white
   pepper

*See Seasoning Chart.
**Available in markets carrying Jewish or kosher foods.

1. Sauté the onion in the margarine or chicken fat until tender. Add the *farfel* and stir until brown. Transfer to a 9- by 12-inch baking dish.
2. Preheat oven to 350 degrees.
3. In the same skillet melt the margarine or butter. Sauté the mushrooms

for 5 minutes. Mix with the *farfel*. Pour in the boiling stock. Season to taste with salt and pepper.

4. Place in the oven and bake 1 hour or until liquid is absorbed. Fluff up with a fork before serving.

FARMER'S SALAD

YIELD: 2 servings

---

1 cucumber, peeled and sliced
6 green onions, chopped with tops
4 red radishes, sliced

3 heaping tablespoons plain yogurt
or sour cream
Salt and freshly ground pepper to
taste

Mix all ingredients together. Taste and adjust seasonings and serve chilled.

GOMBAVAL TOLTOTT PALACSINTA
(Mushroom-filled Pancakes)

YIELD: 4 stuffed pancakes

---

2 tablespoons safflower margarine
1 to 2 tablespoons safflower or
peanut oil
1 small onion, minced
½ pound fresh mushrooms, minced
¼ cup plain, low-fat yogurt
1 egg, well beaten

Sweet Hungarian paprika
Salt and freshly ground pepper
Fresh chopped or dried dill
4 *Crêpes* (p. 122)
¼ to ½ cup freshly grated Parmesan
cheese

1. Heat margarine and oil together in a large, heavy skillet until hot. Add onion and sauté until transparent but not brown. Add minced mushrooms and sauté until tender. Stir in yogurt and simmer 1 minute. Add beaten egg and stir constantly for 1 or 2 minutes until well blended. Season liberally with paprika, salt, pepper, and dill. Remove from heat and set aside.

2. Preheat oven to 350 degrees.

3. Place about 3 tablespoons of filling on the lower third of each crêpe and roll into cylinders. Place seam-side-down in an 8- by 8-inch baking dish. Sprinkle cheese over the top. Bake in a preheated oven until pancakes are warmed through and cheese has melted. Serve immediately, allowing 2 pancakes per person as an entrée or 1 pancake per person as a side dish. Variations: 1. Replace 1 tablespoon yogurt with 1 tablespoon dry sherry. 2. Replace mushrooms with ½ pound finely shredded cabbage or ½ pound steamed spinach.

HIDYJ-MEGGYLEVES
(Cold Sour Cherry Soup)   *YIELD: 6 to 8 servings*

3 cups hot water
½ cup honey (or to taste)
1 cinnamon stick
3 thin slices of lemon, cut in half

2 cups pitted fresh or canned sour
  cherries
1 tablespoon arrowroot or 4
  teaspoons cornstarch
¾ cup dry red wine
¼ cup yogurt or sour cream

1. In a 2-quart saucepan, bring the water, honey, cinnamon stick, lemon slices, and cherries to a boil. Reduce heat and simmer 20 minutes. Meanwhile blend arrowroot with a little water to make a paste.
2. Remove cinnamon stick and lemon slices. Slowly add arrowroot mixture, stirring constantly. Bring almost to a boil; reduce heat and simmer 2 minutes or until slightly thick, stirring constantly. Remove from heat; taste and adjust sweetness. Chill from 1 to 2 hours. Before serving, stir in the dry red wine. Spoon into soup bowls and garnish with a dollop of yogurt or sour cream. Serve as a first course or as a dessert.

HUNGARIAN CHOCOLATE FROSTING
YIELD: Frosting for 2, 9-inch layers or 1, 9- by 13-inch cake.

4 squares unsweetened baking
  chocolate
1¼ cups confectioners' sugar
2 tablespoons hot water (boiled
  water that has cooled slightly)

2 eggs
6 tablespoons unsalted butter or
  safflower margarine

Melt chocolate in the top of a double boiler over hot, not boiling, water. When chocolate is almost melted, remove from heat and stir until completely melted. Add sugar gradually, beating thoroughly with a wooden spoon. Add hot water and blend in well. Add eggs, one at a time, beating after each addition. Add butter, a little at a time, beating well until glossy. Spread evenly over cake.
Note: This frosting must be made by hand—it will not work if made with an electric mixer.

HUNGARIAN SWEET
POTATO STRUDEL

YIELD: 3 strudel rolls or 36, 1-inch slices

Filling:
- 1 large or 2 small sweet potatoes
- 6 eggs, separated
- 1 cup sugar
- Juice and rind of 1 lemon
- ½ teaspoon almond extract
- 2 teaspoons vanilla extract
- 1½ cups ground almonds or walnuts
- 1 cup crushed corn flakes or raisin bran cereal

Dough:
- 1 pound unsalted sweet butter
- 18 sheets (about ¾ pound) filo dough* (thaw 48 hours in the refrigerator if frozen)
- 6 tablespoons sugar
- ½ teaspoon cinnamon
- ¾ cup crushed corn flakes or raisin bran cereal

Available at Greek or Middle Eastern groceries and some supermarkets.

1. Place the sweet potato in a pot with enough water to cover. Boil until tender. Remove from heat, drain off water, and let cool. Peel potato and put through a ricer, sieve, or food mill.

2. Place egg yolks in a large mixing bowl and beat well. Add the sugar gradually, beating continually. Add the lemon juice, rind, extracts, nuts, the 1 cup crushed cereal, and riced sweet potato. Beat the egg whites until they form soft peaks; gently fold them into the potato mixture until no whites show. Set aside.

3. To make the dough, melt butter in a saucepan until it foams. Remove from heat. Pour through a cheesecloth-lined strainer into a bowl to remove the impurities. The remaining liquid is now clarified butter. Set aside—do not let butter solidify.

4. Unfold filo dough. Place one sheet on a 10- by 12-inch baking sheet; keep the other sheets covered with a slightly damp kitchen towel. With a soft pastry brush, coat the sheet thoroughly with melted butter. Continue this process with 5 more sheets. Combine the sugar and cinnamon. Sprinkle 2 tablespoons cinnamon-sugar mixture and ¼ cup of the crushed cereal over the top sheet of filo. Spread 2 cups of sweet potato filling evenly over a little more than half of the surface, leaving a 1½-inch margin on three sides. Carefully lift the edge (from the filled end) and roll up jelly-roll fashion, tucking in the sides as you roll. Seal the seam with melted butter. Set aside. Continue entire process to make two more rolls.

5. Preheat oven to 350 degrees.

6. Place rolls on a lightly greased baking sheet (you may be able to fit only 2 rolls on a sheet). Brush the tops with melted butter. Bake in a preheated oven until golden-brown and crisp, or until toothpick inserted in center comes out clean—about 35 to 40 minutes. Cool slightly, and cut crosswise into 1-inch slices.

Note: Baked strudel may be wrapped in foil and frozen for a later use. To reheat, thaw and place in a preheated 300-degree oven until warmed through.

KREPLACH
(Filled Noodle Triangles)   YIELD: *Approximately 32* kreplach

2 eggs
2 tablespoons water
2 cups all-purpose flour

Prune Filling,* Apricot Filling,*
or Cheese Filling (see recipe
below)
4 tablespoons melted margarine or
butter
¼ cup bread crumbs

Available at many supermarkets under Solo brand.

1. Mix eggs and water together in a mixing bowl with a fork. Add 1 cup of the flour. Mix well. Add just enough of the second cup to make a soft dough.
2. Place on a lightly floured board and knead until smooth and elastic. Cover and let dough rest ½ hour. Divide in half.
3. Roll out dough ⅛-inch thick and cut into 3-inch squares. Fill each square with 1 teaspoon of prune, apricot, or cheese filling. Fold in half diagonally to form triangles and pinch tightly together with lightly floured fingers.
4. Fill a 4-quart pot half full with water, to which ½ teaspoon of salt has been added. Bring to a boil. Drop in half of the *kreplach* and boil 10 minutes. Remove from water with a slotted spoon. Drain in a colander. Repeat process with remaining *kreplach*.
5. Preheat oven to 350 degrees.
6. Place *kreplach* in a buttered baking dish. Pour the melted margarine or butter over all. Turn to coat. Sprinkle with the bread crumbs. Bake for 30 minutes or until lightly browned, turning occasionally.

Cheese Filling:
½ pound farmer or pot cheese
1 egg, beaten
2 teaspoons sugar
½ teaspoon cinnamon

Mix all ingredients together thoroughly.

LIPTOÍ CHEESE BALL

YIELD: One cheese ball which generously serves 6 as an appetizer.

8 ounces Neufchâtel cheese or cream cheese
⅓ stick safflower margarine or butter
2 green onions, finely chopped
½ teaspoon dry mustard
1 teaspoon Dijon mustard or hot mustard

1 teaspoon anchovy paste (or to taste)
1 tablespoon beer—optional
Freshly ground pepper to taste
Paprika (preferably Hungarian paprika)

1. Soften cheese and margarine to room temperature. Blend together until smooth and creamy (this is best done in an electric mixer, which will make it fluffier). Add remaining ingredients, except paprika, and shape into a smooth ball. Chill several hours or overnight. Or you may tightly wrap the ball in plastic and freeze until needed.

2. Let the ball come to room temperature before serving. Sprinkle generously with paprika and place on a serving plate surrounded with fresh parsley sprigs. Serve with raw vegetables and dark bread or crackers as an appetizer.

Variation: Add 2 cloves pressed garlic or 1 teaspoon drained capers.

MARINATED CUCUMBERS GRAND MÈRE

YIELD: 6 to 8 servings

3 medium-sized cucumbers
Salt
1 large onion

1 cup apple cider or white vinegar
½ cup water
2 to 3 tablespoons sugar or honey

1. Peel and slice cucumbers into thin rounds. Place in layers in a glass bowl or baking dish and sprinkle each layer with salt. Cover with a plate and let stand 40 minutes.

2. Rinse cucumbers with cold water. Drain well and squeeze out as much liquid as possible. Pat dry with paper towels. Thinly slice the onion and separate into rings.

3. Place cucumbers in a ceramic or glass bowl and combine with the onion rings. Mix the vinegar, water, and sugar or honey together. Pour over the cucumbers and onions. Toss well. Cover with a lid and refrigerate for 6 hours or overnight.

4. To serve, remove cucumbers and onions from the liquid with a slotted spoon.

Variation: Add ½ cup plain yogurt or sour cream to the vinegar mixture and blend well.

MRS. SEIBOLD'S CREAM CHEESE DAINTIES* YIELD: 14 dozen

7½ cups all-purpose flour
2⅓ cups vegetable shortening
2½ cups cream cheese (20 ounces)
2 teaspoons salt

1 cup unsalted butter
Assorted jams: pineapple,
blueberry, cherry, and apricot
Powdered sugar to coat

1. Place all ingredients, except jams, in a large bowl and mix with a pastry blender until thoroughly combined. Form into a ball. Cover and chill 1 hour.
2. Preheat oven to 380 degrees.
3. Divide dough into six or seven portions. Roll out each portion into a ⅛-inch thick rectangle. Cut into 3-inch squares. In the center of each square, place ½ teaspoon of jam of your choice. Moisten edges with water and fold diagonally to form a triangle. Press edges together to seal.
4. Bake 15 minutes or until lightly browned. Remove from oven, then dust with powdered sugar after they have cooled. These cheese dainties freeze well.

*Note: This recipe can be cut in half.

MUSHROOM GOULASH YIELD: 6 servings

4 tablespoons safflower vegetable
shortening or margarine
1 yellow onion, chopped
2 garlic cloves, pressed
½ cup water
1½ tablespoons sweet Hungarian
paprika
1 large potato, boiled and cut into
large chunks
1 green pepper, seeded and cut into
strips

1 small zucchini, sliced
2 large tomatoes, peeled and
chopped
½ pound large mushrooms, thickly
sliced
1 tablespoon flour
½ cup of plain, low-fat yogurt or
sour cream
Salt and white pepper to taste
Spiced Hungarian Paprika Blend*
to taste—optional

*See Seasoning Chart.

Heat the shortening or margarine in a large soup pot. Sauté the onion until transparent. Stir in the garlic and water. Add the sweet paprika and vegetables. Simmer 10 to 15 minutes or until vegetables are tender, stirring occasionally. Combine the flour and yogurt or sour cream. Add to the pot and heat through, but do not boil. Season with salt, pepper, and Spiced Hungarian Paprika. Serve immediately with plain noodles sprinkled with poppy seeds or *Poppy Seed Noodles* (p. 182).

NANCY'S POPPY SEED EGG BREAD

YIELD: 2 loaves, approximately 16 slices each

3 tablespoons sugar
¼ cup safflower margarine or butter
3 teaspoons salt
1½ cups milk, scalded
½ cup very warm water
1 tablespoon sugar
2 packages dry active yeast
3 large eggs, well beaten
7¼ to 7½ cups flour
6 teaspoons poppy seeds

Topping:
1 egg, well beaten
2 tablespoons water
3 to 6 tablespoons poppy seeds

1. Combine the 3 tablespoons of sugar with the margarine and salt. Cover with scalded milk. Stir to dissolve margarine and cool to lukewarm. Combine the very warm water with 1 tablespoon of sugar. Sprinkle in yeast and let stand 5 minutes to "foam." Add to lukewarm milk. Stir in the beaten eggs and 3½ cups of the flour. Add remaining flour gradually until the dough leaves the sides of the bowl clean. Turn onto a lightly floured board and knead 5 minutes or until dough is smooth and elastic. If you can make a print in the dough with the palm of your hand without having it stick to your hand, then the dough has been kneaded long enough.
2. Shape dough into a ball and place in a greased bowl, turning dough to grease on all sides. Cover and let rise in a warm, draft-free place until doubled in bulk—about 45 minutes. Punch down and let rise again 20 minutes.
3. Divide dough into 2 equal pieces. Divide each piece into 3 equal pieces. Pat each piece into a 12- by 3-inch strip. Sprinkle 1 teaspoon of poppy seeds down the center of each strip. Roll widthwise to enclose seeds. Press a seam into the roll and pinch the ends together. Smooth out strips by rolling from side to side. Place 3 strips side-by-side and braid, beginning with the middle strip. Pinch and tuck ends under the loaf. Continue process with remaining 3 strips to form a second loaf. Place each loaf into a well-greased loaf pan. Combine the egg and water and brush the tops of each loaf. Sprinkle from 3 to 6 tablespoons of poppy seeds over the loaves. Let rise in pans for 45 minutes.
4. Preheat oven to 400 degrees.
5. Bake in a preheated oven 25 to 35 minutes or until nicely crusted and lightly browned on the bottom.

POPPY SEED NOODLES

YIELD: 6 to 8 servings

12 ounces medium-wide noodles
⅔ stick safflower margarine or
  butter
3½ tablespoons poppy seeds
½ cup slivered almonds, toasted—
  optional

2 tablespoons freshly squeezed
  lemon juice
Salt and freshly ground white
  pepper to taste

1. Place noodles in 4 to 6 quarts of boiling salted water. Cook until tender. Drain in a colander.
2. Melt the margarine or butter in a skillet over low heat. Add the poppy seeds, sliced almonds, and lemon juice. Toss with the hot noodles. Season to taste with salt and pepper.

POTATO PANCAKES

YIELD: Approximately 18 pancakes

4 large red potatoes, peeled
1 medium-sized onion
2 eggs, separated
2 tablespoons rendered chicken
  fat*
2 heaping tablespoons flour

½ teaspoon baking powder
1 teaspoon salt
¼ teaspoon pepper
  Peanut oil or rendered chicken
  fat* for frying

*See Seasoning Chart—*Strict vegetarians should omit this ingredient altogether, as there is no substitute that can be used in this recipe.*

1. Finely grate potatoes and onion into a large bowl. Drain off excess liquid to remove starch. Beat the egg yolks and stir them into the mixture. Add the chicken fat, flour, baking powder, salt, and pepper. Beat the egg whites until stiff and fold into the potatoes.
2. Heat 1 to 2 tablespoons of the oil or chicken fat in a heavy skillet until very hot. Drop the potato mixture by large spoonfuls into the heated oil. Fry until golden brown. Turn and brown the other side. Repeat process until all the batter is used. These taste best when eaten immediately.

SPENOTPUDDING

(Spinach Pudding Soufflé)

YIELD: 8 to 10 servings

1½ pounds fresh spinach
1 stick safflower margarine or
  salted butter
½ cup mild cheddar cheese

2 pounds small curd cottage cheese
6 eggs, well beaten
6 teaspoons whole wheat flour
  Salt and pepper to taste

1. Wash spinach. Cook in a small amount of water until tender. Drain and cool. Squeeze out any excess moisture. Chop finely.
2. Preheat oven to 350 degrees. Cut margarine and cheddar cheese into small pieces. Combine all the ingredients together and pour into a greased, 2-quart casserole. Bake 45 minutes in a preheated oven. Reduce heat to 300 degrees. Bake 10 to 15 minutes longer. Serve immediately as a main course or as a side dish.

STRUDEL WITH CABBAGE AND ONIONS   *YIELD: 8, 1½-inch slices*

---

1 head green cabbage (1¼ pounds)
1 large yellow onion
3 tablespoons safflower margarine, divided
¼ cup dark raisins
6 teaspoons brown sugar
½ to ¾ teaspoon salt
¾ teaspoon hot Hungarian paprika*

Freshly ground white pepper to taste
6 tablespoons unsalted butter
8 sheets (about ¼ pound) filo dough** (If frozen, thaw 48 hours in the refrigerator.)
½ cup bread crumbs

*See Seasoning Chart.
**Available at Middle Eastern or Greek groceries and some supermarkets.

1. Shred cabbage finely and set aside. Peel onion and slice into thin slivers. Heat 1 tablespoon of the margarine in a skillet. Sauté onion until lightly browned. Remove to a mixing bowl. Heat remaining margarine and sauté cabbage just until it loses its crispness. Remove and add to onion along with the raisins, sugar, and seasonings. Taste and adjust seasonings. Set aside.
2. Melt butter in a saucepan until it foams. Pour through a cheesecloth-lined strainer into a bowl to remove impurities. The liquid is now clarified butter.
3. Preheat oven to 400 degrees.
4. Unfold filo leaves. Place one sheet on a 10- by 12-inch baking sheet; keep remaining leaves under a slightly damp towel. Using a soft pastry brush, coat the sheet thoroughly with melted butter. Add another sheet and continue this process until all 8 sheets are used up. Sprinkle bread crumbs over the top sheet.
5. Spread cabbage mixture evenly over the surface, leaving a 1½-inch margin on all sides. Starting at one end, roll up jelly-roll fashion, folding sides in as you roll. Seal seam with melted butter. Place roll seam-side-down on a slightly greased baking sheet. Brush the top with melted butter. Bake in a preheated oven until lightly browned and crisp—about 20 to 30 minutes. Cool slightly and cut crosswise into 1½-inch slices. Serve as an appetizer or main course.
Variation: Add 1 to 2 teaspoons caraway seeds and 1 small apple, peeled, cored, and grated.

TÖK FÖZELEK
(Mari's Zucchini with Dill Sauce)   *YIELD: 4 to 6 servings*

2 pounds zucchini or summer
 squash
1 teaspoon salt
2 tablespoons vinegar
2 tablespoons safflower margarine
2 tablespoons flour
1 tablespoon sweet Hungarian
 paprika

1 tablespoon finely chopped fresh
 dill, or 1½ teaspoons dried dill
 weed
1 teaspoon minced onion
½ cup hot water
½ cup plain, low-fat yogurt or sour
 cream
Sweet Hungarian paprika and
 dill (fresh or dried) for garnish

1. Peel and cut the zucchini into julienne strips. Place in a bowl and sprinkle with salt and vinegar. Let stand 20 minutes. Rinse well and squeeze out excess moisture. Pat dry with paper towels and set aside.
2. Heat margarine in a 2-quart saucepan. Add flour and stir constantly with a wooden spoon until lightly browned. Remove from heat and stir in paprika, dill, and onion. Pour in hot water and stir vigorously until smooth. Add zucchini and mix well. Add a little water if necessary to thin out. Cook over low heat until barely tender—about 10 minutes. Fold in yogurt and blend until smooth. Serve immediately, garnished with paprika and dill.

HUNGARY/RECIPE ANALYSIS CHART

Name of Recipe	Quantity	Calories	CHO gms.	Protein gms.	Total Fat gms.	Saturated Fat gms.	Choles- terol mg.	Dietary Fiber gms.
1. Marinated Cucumbers *Grand Mère*	per serving	32	7 (86%)	1 (14%)	—	—	—	.3
2. Farmer's Salad	per serving	32	7 (86%)	1 (14%)	—	—	—	.6
3. Kreplach	each	54	7 (52%)	2 (15%)	2 (33%)	—	31	—
4. *Tök Fözelek* (Zucchini with Dill Sauce)	per serving	75	9 (48%)	3 (16%)	3 (36%)	1 (0%)	—	1.0
5. *Liptói* Cheese Ball	per 1-oz. serving	75	1 (5%)	2 (11%)	7 (84%)	3 (36%)	14	—
6. *Mrs. Seibold's* Cream Cheese Dainties	each	82	6 (29%)	1 (5%)	6 (66%)	2 (22%)	7	—
7. Potato Pancakes	each	97	11 (45%)	2 (8%)	5 (47%)	1 (9%)	37	.5
8. Cabbage and Bean Soup	per ¾-cup serving	106	17 (64%)	7 (26%)	1 (10%)	—	—	1.3
9. *Hidyj-Meg- gyleves* (Cold Sour Cherry Soup)	per serving	153	36 (94%)	2 (6%)	—	—	—	.2
10. *Nancy's* Poppy Seed Egg Bread	per slice	169	24 (57%)	5 (12%)	6 (31%)	1 (5%)	40	.2
11. *Gombaval Toltott Palacsinta* (Mushroom- filled Pancakes)	per serving	174	6 (14%)	8 (18%)	13 (68%)	3 (16%)	80	.6
12. Mushroom Goulash	per serving	187	24 (51%)	7 (15%)	8 (34%)	1 (5%)	—	2.2
13. *Hungarian* Sweet Potato Strudel	per slice	214	19 (36%)	3 (6%)	14 (58%)	7 (29%)	73	.2
14. Poppy Seed Noodles	per serving	242	34 (56%)	6 (10%)	9 (34%)	2 (7%)	—	.6

Name of Recipe	Quantity	Calories	CHO gms.	Protein gms.	Total Fat gms.	Saturated Fat gms.	Choles- terol mg.	Dietary Fiber gms.
15. Strudel with Cabbage and Onions	per serving	244	25 (41%)	4 (7%)	14 (52%)	7 (26%)	23	.9
16. Cantaloupe Salad with Poppy Seed Dressing	per serving	248	26 (42%)	2 (3%)	15 (55%)	3 (11%)	—	1.2
17. *Spenotpud- ding* (Spinach Pudding Soufflé)	per serving	257	6 (9%)	17 (26%)	18 (65%)	6 (22%)	183	.4
18. *Csokolade Torta*	per slice	283	43 (61%)	3 (4%)	11 (35%)	4 (13%)	59	.2
19. *Farfel*	per serving	290	36 (50%)	7 (10%)	13 (40%)	3 (9%)	4	.4
20. Chicken *Paprikas*	per serving	400	12 (12%)	52 (52%)	16 (36%)	6 (14%)	307	.9
21. *Csokolade Torta* with Hun- garian Chocolate Frosting	per slice	419	58 (55%)	4 (4%)	19 (41%)	9 (19%)	109	.3
22. Chicken Fricassee	per serving	546	3 (2%)	30 (22%)	46 (76%)	14 (23%)	131	.2

Numbers in parentheses (%) indicate percentage of total calories contributed by nutrient.

MENUS

LOW CALORIE SPECIALTIES
(500 to 700 calories per meal)

HIDYJ-MEGGYLEVES (COLD SOUR CHERRY SOUP)
NANCY'S POPPY SEED EGG BREAD
MRS. SEIBOLD'S CREAM CHEESE DAINTIES
Espresso

KREPLACH
FARMER'S SALAD
Steamed Green Peas
POTATO PANCAKES
Unsweetened Applesauce
Turkish Coffee or Hot Tea

White Radishes and Green Pepper Rings
CHICKEN FRICASSEE
MARINATED CUCUMBERS GRAND MÈRE
Sliced Oranges and Peaches
Iced Tea

•

LOW CHOLESTEROL MENUS
(Less than 50 mgs. of cholesterol per meal)

LIPTOÍ CHEESE BALL
Carrot and Raw Zucchini Strips
MUSHROOM GOULASH
POPPY SEED NOODLES
Sliced Peaches with Cointreau
Hot Herb Tea

Sliced Pimentos
White or Black Radishes
CABBAGE AND BEAN SOUP
Whole Grain Crackers
MARINATED CUCUMBERS GRAND MÉRE
Sliced Pears and Cherries
Iced Tea

STRUDEL WITH CABBAGE AND ONIONS
FARFEL
Steamed Broccoli
Fresh Raspberries and Plums
Turkish Coffee

LOW SATURATED FAT SELECTIONS
(Less than 8 grams of saturated fat per meal)

FARMER'S SALAD
STRUDEL WITH CABBAGE AND ONIONS
Steamed Green Beans Garnished with Fresh Dill
Fresh Cherries and Blueberries

White and Red Radishes
Whole Green Onions
Dill Pickles
CHICKEN PAPRIKAS
POPPY SEED EGG BREAD
Steamed Asparagus with Wedge of Lemon
Cantaloupe

LIPTOÍ CHEESE BALL
Whole Grain Crackers
KREPLACH
TÖK FÖZELEK (ZUCCHINI WITH DILL SAUCE)
MRS. SEIBOLD'S CREAM CHEESE DAINTIES
Hungarian Wine

●

HIGH PROTEIN MEALS
(30 or more grams of protein per meal)

SPENOTPUDDING (SPINACH PUDDING SOUFFLÉ)
Tossed Romaine and Celery Root Salad
FARFEL
NANCY'S POPPY SEED EGG BREAD
HUNGARIAN SWEET POTATO STRUDEL
Turkish Coffee

CHICKEN FRICASSEE
Green and Red Pepper Salad
Steamed Kohlrabi
Thin Slices of Dark Rye Bread
Fresh Cherries and Sliced Bananas
Hungarian Wine

CABBAGE AND BEAN SOUP
SPENOTPUDDING (SPINACH PUDDING SOUFFLÉ)
CANTALOUPE SALAD WITH POPPY SEED DRESSING
CSOKOLADE TORTA WITH HUNGARIAN CHOCOLATE FROSTING
Espresso

WELL BALANCED LUNCH OR DINNER MENUS
(Selections that conform to recommendations in Dietary Goals for United States*)*

**MARINATED CUCUMBERS
GRAND MÈRE
MUSHROOM GOULASH
POPPY SEED NOODLES
CSOKOLADE TORTA**
Turkish Coffee

**STRUDEL WITH CABBAGE AND
ONIONS
SOUR CHERRY SOUP
POTATO PANCAKES**
Unsweetened Applesauce
Iced Tea with Lemon

Dill Pickles
**FARMER'S SALAD
CHICKEN PAPRIKAS
POPPY SEED NOODLES**
Cantaloupe and Blueberries

CHAPTER 8

INDIA

Some Like It Hot

Culinary Essentials

An Indian feast brings forth an array of foods that will titillate your palate with brilliant colors, contrasting textures, and stimulating flavors. Jewel-like curries tempt the tastebuds with their sparkling yellow hue, while smooth yogurt salads are offset by the crisp accent of chopped cucumbers. Tastes are multifaceted with fiery green chilies, vibrant chutneys, and pungent coriander leaves providing some of the more lively touches. In short, Indian food is bursting with character.

Most Indian recipes are not as difficult as they appear. Occasionally, fifteen to twenty ingredients may be required for one preparation—a forbidding proposition to be sure! But upon close inspection, you will notice that many ingredients are seasonings, condiments, or garnishes. And despite their seemingly complex flavor, Indian dishes are among the easiest to master: anyone with basic cooking skills can produce an authentic dinner worthy of a raja's table.

Most of the vegetables, fruits, and nuts employed in this cuisine are available at large supermarkets. Cauliflower, eggplant, peas, and potatoes are favored ingredients; pistachio nuts, mangos, and dried currants also crop up frequently. *Ghee*,* or clarified butter, and peanut oil are traditional cooking mediums; safflower, corn, or sesame seed oils are also acceptable, but olive oil is never used in India. If you do not wish to make your own chutney—a hot-sweet condiment made of fruits or vegetables, spices, and vinegar—this article can be found ready-made at a well-stocked grocery store.

---

* See Seasoning Chart *in this chapter.*

A few imported items might require a visit to an Indian, gourmet, or health food store. For special occasions, you might try *basmati* rice, which has a nutlike taste and savory aroma. This long, hulled grain is treasured for its superior flavor and delicate texture. *Pappadums*, peppery lentil wafers that can be served in place of bread, are also worth trying. These crisp, tasty rounds are imported in packages and must be baked or fried in oil before serving. Spoon a little chutney over hot *pappadums* or use them to scoop up curried vegetables—fantastic food. Garnish-loving cooks will want a package of edible silver leaf to drape over Indian desserts as a decoration. Though it has no taste of its own, tissue-thin silver leaf dazzles the eye and connotes a memorable treat.

Indian meals are traditionally accompanied by a thick, souplike dish of spiced legumes made from *dahl* or split lentils. India boasts sixty varieties of *dahl*, each of which has its own color. Among the most popular are *moong dahl* (yellow), *masoor dahl* (orange), *urad dahl* (off-white), and *mung dahl* (green). If it is unavailable, you can usually substitute split or yellow peas, although the flavor will be somewhat different. *Dahl*-based dishes derive their distinguished flavor from fenugreek, cumin, or black mustard seed, any of which can be used singly or in combination with the others. Hot, sweet, or pungent nuances can also be imparted with the use of green chilies, pineapple, or fresh coriander leaves, respectively.

Because many Indian dishes require a long simmering time, heavy pots are the best kitchen utensils for this cuisine. To make *Chapatis*, Indian-style tortillas, you will need a flat griddle or cast-iron skillet and a rolling pin or long bottle. A *kadhai* or wok is the pot best suited for deep-frying and sautéing; a large heavy saucepan or skillet is acceptable, but a wok requires less oil and cooks more quickly and evenly.

One way to experience the entire spectrum of Indian flavors is to throw a curry party. A buffet table replete with curries and condiments fills the bill for easy entertaining: it looks enticing and exotic, but is simple to assemble. You need to prepare only a few appetizers and entrées, for it is the lavish assortment of condiments, for which this cuisine is renowned, that turns an unpretentious dinner into a sensual food odyssey.

Selecting an array of curry condiments lends itself to culinary ingenuity. A well-rounded and enticing assortment would include the panoply of Indian tastes: sweet (dates, currants, or toasted coconut); sour (quartered limes or tamarind*); cool (fried bananas or grated carrots); spicy (*pappadums*); and pungent (fresh coriander leaves or chopped onions). For a colorful and textural contrast, consider adding nuts, sieved hard-boiled eggs, sliced tomatoes, or fresh mint. Since frequent dipping into chutney is essential for curries and fried savories, you might include three or four different varieties, including a homemade *Peach and Mango Chutney*.

The mood for a more traditional sit-down dinner can be created with a

---

*See Seasoning Chart *in this chapter.*

few furnishings: an Indian print bedspread for a tablecloth; an incense burner to permeate the air with sandalwood; and recorded sitar music. Dinner is presented all at once rather than in courses. Customarily, each person is presented with a *thali*,* or round brass tray. On it are arranged several *katoris*,* tiny metal bowls filled with various sweet, savory, hot, and cold dishes. Typically, you would serve items such as *Moong Dahl*, *Chapati*, *Raita* (whipped yogurt salad), rice, and chutney. The featured entrée, perhaps a *Shrimp and Banana Curry* or *Spicy Eggplant with Yogurt*, is placed in the center. Lacking a *thali* or *katoris*, you can place several small bowls on individual dinner plates. Utensils may be offered, but Indians prefer to use their fingers, scooping up the food with unleavened breads (*Chapatis*, *Pooris* or *pappadums*) and sipping juices straight from the bowls.

Everyday meals conclude with something simple, like *Glazed Bananas* or a fruit platter comprised of fresh papayas, peaches, and mangos. More auspicious occasions can be honored with *Gajar Halva*, a creamy, saffron-tinged pudding, studded with almonds and garnished with silver leaf. And, if you enjoy after-dinner mints, chew on a few anise or fennel seeds to refresh your palate in true Indian fashion.

Seasoning Essentials

The preliminary step to preparing distinguished Indian fare is a simple one: Throw away any cans of commercial curry powder lurking in your cupboard. Replace it with an array of whole spices, a mortar and pestle for grinding, and, before long, you'll be on the road to discovering the refined art of Indian seasoning. It begins with *masalas*, custom-made spice formulas carefully calculated and tailored to suit each specialty as well as individual taste preferences. These freshly ground mixtures, which may vary from dish to dish, will enable you to elicit the precise degree of piquancy desired and leave the signature of singularity upon each creation.

In most minds, the word "curry" conjures up images of sweltering hot stews with muddy yellow hues. This misconception is largely due to the widespread use of commercial curry powder in this country. Indian cooks would never dream of using such a formulated blend because it lacks fragrance and renders the same color and character to everything it touches. Instead, they grind their own *garam masala* or "hot mixture" which allows them to control both the heat (curries are not always hot) and taste of a dish. Imported *garam masala* can usually be purchased in spice shops, but it will not rival the freshness of the homemade product. However, it will give you an idea of how much it does differ from commercial curry powder and it can be used for the sake of convenience. If *garam masala* is unavailable, and you can't do without a ready-made curry blend, try to find imported Madras Curry Powder, which is superior to most store-bought varieties.

Any of your favorite Indian spices may be used in *garam masala*, de-

---

* *Available from import shops or Indian food stores.*

pending upon how mild, fiery, fragrant, or exotic you want your dish to be. Options can be selected from the *Seasoning Chart*, including the list of secondary seasonings at the bottom of the chart. Hot food veterans will want a little cayenne pepper or dried chili peppers in their blend to unleash the heat of a curry. A pinch of ground fenugreek seeds, which exude a distinctive, slightly bitter taste, will please enterprising palates. And mace, allspice, or cinnamon can be enlisted by those who want a sweeter, more aromatic mixture.

Garam masala is usually added to a dish during the final stages of cooking or stirred in just before serving. It is a marvelous enhancer for cold foods such as yogurt and can also be sprinkled over cooked foods, much in the way we use salt and pepper. Of course, you should not rely exclusively upon this mixture to boost the flavor of your dishes. The spirit of many creations can also be lifted with bright green coriander leaves, pungent black mustard seeds, or tart tamarind juice.

Indians incorporate an incredible variety of flavorings into their food, many of which will be exciting additions to your seasoning repertoire. Once familiar with the characteristics of each, feel free to adjust proportions in any recipe. If you shy away from tongue-tingling foods, don't hesitate to substitute sweet (bell) peppers for vehement green chilies. Conversely, those who thrive on palate-paralyzing fare can step up the proceedings with a combination of minced ginger root, pressed garlic cloves, and freshly ground black peppercorns.

In any event, go slowly at first, spicing each dish a little at a time until you reach the correct balance. Remember, you can always add more if necessary, but there is no taking away. If everyone at your table is gasping, sweating, shoveling rice, or guzzling water, you can safely assume you have overdone it.

INDIAN SEASONING CHART

Note: To roast whole spices, place in a dry, heavy skillet over medium-low heat. Stir constantly until the seeds are lightly browned and exude a characteristic aroma. Only one variety should be roasted at a time. Pulverize with a mortar and pestle, blender, or electric coffee mill (one that is used exclusively for spices). Or, place on a chopping board and crush with a rolling pin until finely ground.

BLACK MUSTARD SEEDS* are essential to Indian cooking, lending a pleasantly pungent, almost nutlike flavor to vegetables, lentils, curried eggs, pickled foods, chutneys, and soups. These tiny pellets are usually placed whole into hot oil or *ghee* until they "pop," a distinctive sound that

---

* *Available at Indian food stores or spice shops.*

alerts the cook when the oil is ready for sautéing. Black mustard seeds are interchangeable with brown mustard seeds,* but not the common yellow mustard seeds, which are rarely used.

CARDAMOM has a sweet-sharp quality redolent of eucalyptus. Its attraction is its perfumelike scent and palate-stimulating effect. The white pods, commonly found in the supermarket, are prized for desserts, while the more fragrant green pods* are preferred for savory dishes. Brown cardamom pods,* which look like miniature coconuts, are filled with clusters of intensely aromatic seeds that are wonderful taste-producers. All three varieties can be used interchangeably. The white and green pods may be used whole in curries when you wish to heighten the aroma. Or, discard the pods of any variety and use the seeds alone which, when crushed, produce a stronger flavor. This spice marries especially well with rice, carrots, and yogurt. A dash of cinnamon and cloves will enrich cardamom's flavor and scent. Use discreetly—a small amount goes a long way.

CORIANDER leaves, available at Latin American and Oriental markets, are used extensively in curries and chutneys, adding a musty pungency that, for many, is an acquired taste. These bright green, fanshaped leaves are used like parsley, as an ubiquitous garnish, or as an addition to everything from appetizers to salads to vegetable dishes. Unless you are accustomed to its strong flavor, use sparingly. Coriander seeds are much milder and can be added lavishly to curries, rice *pilaū*, and other savory dishes. If there is one essential ingredient to *garam masala*, it is coriander seed. Like cumin, its flavor can be improved by dry-roasting.

GREEN CHILIES vary in piquancy from mild to exceedingly hot; Indians use the hot variety. Along with dried red chili peppers and cayenne pepper, green chilies control the heat of a curry. Before being added to a dish, they are usually pulverized or finely chopped. Fresh green chilies—*jalapeño*, *serrano*, or *güero*—are available at Latin American markets and some supermarkets. Wear rubber gloves to handle them as their volatile oils may sting the eyes or skin. Rinse in cold water, remove the stems, cut in half, and scrape out the seeds (which are the hottest part). Canned chilies may also be used. If peppers are unavailable, substitute sweet (bell) peppers and cayenne pepper to taste. The former may be used alone by those who want the flavor, but not the heat.

GINGER ROOT will be enjoyed by those who like their curries hot. It has an unmistakable flavor that is sweet, powerful, and biting. To shred, break off a knob, trim away the peel, and run along a flat-sided grater. A one-inch piece yields 1 tablespoon, a sufficient amount for seasoning 1 pound of

---

* *Available at Indian food stores or spice shops.*

vegetables, rice, or legumes. Refrigerated and wrapped in plastic, fresh ginger root will keep for several weeks. Ground ginger is not an acceptable substitute for fresh ginger.

RED CHILI PEPPERS and CHILI POWDER are usually found dried rather than fresh in Indian cookery. They are available at Latin American markets, spice shops, and some supermarkets and may be used to add fire and color to any dish in need of piquancy. Start with 1 teaspoon per pound of vegetables, yogurt, rice, or lentils, then add more as desired. Indian recipes frequently call for chili powder—this is not the commercial blend popularly used in Mexican cooking, but rather a finely ground powder of dried red chilies which you must pulverize yourself in a blender; cayenne pepper may be substituted in equal amounts.

TAMARIND is a mass of dried, dark-brown, seedless pods. Its juice, when extracted, is more tart and aromatic than vinegar and is commonly used as a souring agent for curries, *dahls*, and soups. Tamarind is available at Indian or Latin American groceries. To prepare: Macerate ½ cup tamarind in 1 cup hot water and let stand 1 hour. Strain and discard the pulp. The juice will keep indefinitely when stored in an airtight container. Lemon juice mixed with a pinch of brown sugar may be substituted. To season *dahls* or *rasam* (tart South Indian soups), add 1 tablespoon tamarind juice to 1 pound lentils or 1 quart broth. Try substituting this sour liquid for lemon juice in your favorite curry recipe.

CUMIN SEEDS are similar to caraway seeds in their shape and taste, but are stronger, warmer, and more biting. These pungent crescents are a popular addition to *garam masala* and vegetable curries. Ground roasted cumin, which imparts a racy flavor and deep, rich color, is excellent sprinkled over cooked and cold foods. Unroasted cumin has a much milder taste. Like many seasonings, cumin is welcome in small amounts, ruinous in excess.

FENUGREEK SEEDS* render a slightly bitter, but stimulating, flavor and aroma to lentils, curries and *garam masala*. When whole, these flat, yellow seeds can be used in small amounts to add an interesting texture to vegetables. To enhance their flavor, preroast them before using. A pinch of ground fenugreek perks up potatoes, eggplant, and okra. Spicewise, this unusual herb is compatible with fennel, black mustard, and cumin seed.

GARAM MASALA* is a mixture of freshly ground spices that should be used in place of curry powder to achieve an authentic Indian flavor. Ingredients and proportions are variable according to your preference, and you

---

* Available at Indian food stores or spice shops.

may use a different blend for each dish. A simple *masala* can be combined by pulverizing 2 parts roasted cumin seed, roasted coriander seed, and black peppercorns to 1 part cinnamon, cloves, and cardamom seed. Ideas for more elaborate *masalas* are listed below. Imported *garam masala* or Madras Curry Powder* may be substituted.

Mild Masala—Combine and pulverize, pass through a sieve, and store in an airtight container:

1   tablespoon roasted coriander seed
1½ teaspoons roasted cumin seed
1   teaspoon each: cardamom seed, black peppercorns, and cinnamon
½   teaspoon allspice

Hot Masala—Add to the above:

1   to 2 teaspoons dried red chili peppers or cayenne pepper
1   teaspoon each: turmeric and poppy seeds
¼   teaspoon roasted fenugreek seeds
⅛   teaspoon mace

GHEE* or clarified butter is the popular cooking medium in India. It may be made at home (see *Samneh*, p. 243) or purchased in a stronger form at Indian food shops. Spices and seasonings, such as garlic, ginger root, and black mustard seeds, are often cooked in *ghee* at the start of a recipe to meld their flavors. Safflower margarine, unclarified butter, or any vegetable oil, except olive oil, may be substituted.

TURMERIC or "poor man's saffron," is responsible for the golden color that characterizes many Indian dishes. Saffron is also used; it lends a prettier, more intense hue, but is also far more expensive. Though turmeric is not flavorless as many assume (it is slightly bitter), it is used more as a coloring agent than anything else. To give rice an attractive appearance, add 1 teaspoon of turmeric to the cooking water. When sautéing vegetables, remember that this powdered spice burns easily and there must be a sufficient amount of oil or *ghee* present to absorb it. In general, ½ to 1 teaspoon is enough to tint 1 pound of vegetables.

Other seasonings used in Indian cooking: cinnamon, cloves, nutmeg, mace, cayenne pepper, mint, paprika, black peppercorns, saffron, fennel seed, allspice, celery seed, lime, garlic, lemon grass, curry leaves, poppy seeds, bay leaves, rosewater, sesame seeds, dried mango powder, aniseed, and *asafoetida*.

Available at Indian food stores or spice shops.

Nutritional Essentials

Anyone who has eaten Indian food will tell you that it can be a dramatic and exotic experience. What's more, it's especially healthful for weight-watchers and individuals with heart disease or high blood pressure. In many ways, this ethnic kitchen can be considered the prototype for a low-cost, highly-seasoned, calorie-sparing diet. Perhaps more than any other country, India has evolved a sophisticated vegetarian repertoire consisting of lentil stews, vegetable curries, and dairy-based desserts and side dishes. Combining a number of eclectic ingredients into a single meal is the forte of this cuisine and assures a well-balanced diet.

Because Indian fare is flavored with a myriad of aromatic and pungent spices, rather than with heavy cheese sauces or an abundance of salt, this diet is low in calories, fat, and salt, as well as being virtually cholesterol-free. On the whole, the nutrient breakdown of the Indian recipes in this book would be looked upon favorably by most nutritionists as well as the Senate Subcommittee on Human Nutrition. An average serving contains a very acceptable 184 calories with 48%, 13%, and 35% of this total calorie intake being contributed by carbohydrates, protein, and fat, respectively. Except for Lebanese food, Indian portions—at 9 mgs. of cholesterol per average serving—are lower in this nutrient than any other culinary style discussed in this volume.

It should come as no surprise that Indian meals have a tendency to be low in protein. After all, the principal characters in this cuisine—eggplant, cauliflower, and potatoes—are not distinguished by their protein content. The substantial *quality* of eggplant makes some people look upon it as a main-dish item, but its protein content is actually quite low. It is not outstanding for any vitamin or mineral. Cauliflower, while much weaker nutritionally than its close relative broccoli, does boast respectable amounts of vitamins A and C. Potatoes are filling, but protein poor.

Of the vegetables and legumes which characterize this ethnic kitchen, only lentils—employed prolifically in Indian stews called *Dahl*—contain reasonable amounts of protein. Also rich in niacin, vitamin C, and iron, lentil protein is a nice complement to nuts, seeds, and dairy products, all of which crop up frequently in Indian recipes.

How then does the Indian cuisine make up for the lack of good vegetable protein? Principally by including protein-rich yogurt in main dishes. *Steamed Masala Cauliflower*, *Potato Curry Kashmiri*, and *Spicy Eggplant* all employ substantial amounts of yogurt, whose high-grade protein is a nice complement to the other ingredients in these dishes.

As pointed out in *Culinary Essentials*, a traditional Indian meal consists of a large number of small dishes, which assures that the deficient essential amino acids of one food group will be complemented by those from another. Fortunately, many of the desserts and side dishes—such as *Whipped*

Yogurt and Cucumber Salad and *Banana Raita*—contain nutritious dairy-based protein and are also low in the fat department.

Indian cooks selectively employ fruits and nuts to contrast with, or tone down, their fiery dishes. Fruit-wise, pineapple and mangos are brimming with substantial quantities of vitamins C and A. Nut-laced dishes such as *Cashew Vadas* and *Peach and Mango Chutney* are tailor-made for complementing the protein base of legume-centered dishes such as *Moong Dahl* or *Tomato Rasam*. Nuts, which are plentiful in tryptophan and the sulfur-containing essential amino acids, can be used to complement legumes, which are deficient in these protein-building blocks.

The important thing to remember is if you eat Indian food the way Indians do—a myriad of dishes with eclectic ingredients—you will be well on your way towards adopting a healthful, low-calorie diet that is quite adequate in protein.

SPICED ALMOND RICE

YIELD: 4 servings

1½ cups water
¼ teaspoon crushed saffron or ½ teaspoon turmeric
1 teaspoon salt
¾ cup long-grain brown rice
2 tablespoons safflower margarine or *ghee**
1 small onion, minced

2 garlic cloves, crushed
⅓ cup currants or raisins
⅓ cup chopped almonds, toasted
1 cup freshly cooked peas or broccoli
1 teaspoon *garam masala**
¼ teaspoon allspice
1 tablespoon lemon juice

*See Seasoning Chart.

1. In a 2-quart saucepan bring water, saffron, and salt to a boil. Slowly stir in rice and let it boil for 5 minutes. Cover with a tight-fitting lid and reduce temperature to low. Simmer for 45 minutes or until all the water is absorbed. Do not stir rice while cooking.
2. When rice is almost done, heat the margarine or *ghee* in a large skillet. Sauté the onion and garlic. Add rice, currants, almonds, peas, spices, and lemon juice. Sauté entire mixture over moderate heat for 10 minutes. Taste and adjust seasonings. Serve immediately.
Variation: Once the onion and garlic have been sautéed, all the ingredients may be placed in a lightly greased casserole dish and baked in a preheated, 350-degree oven for 25 minutes, rather than cooked in the skillet.

BANANA RAITA

YIELD: 4 to 6 servings

2 teaspoons safflower margarine or *ghee**
¼ to ½ teaspoon each: crushed cardamon seed, cayenne pepper, and grated ginger root

1 teaspoon cinnamon
2 large ripe bananas
3 cups plain yogurt

*See Seasoning Chart.

1. Melt the margarine or *ghee* in a small skillet. Add spices and stir for a few minutes over low heat until flavors are well blended. Set aside. Peel and mash bananas.
2. Place the yogurt in a blender and whip for 60 seconds, or whip in a bowl with a wire whisk. Combine with mashed bananas and spice mixture. Chill well before serving. *Raita* is a perfect accompaniment for hot curry dishes.

BASMATI RICE PILĀU KOH-I-NOOR

YIELD: 4 servings

1 teaspoon salt
1 teaspoon ground coriander seed
2 teaspoons ground cumin seed
¼ to ½ teaspoon ground cloves
  Crushed seeds of 1 black or 3
  white cardamom pods*
1 cup *basmati* rice**
  Water to cover

2 tablespoons safflower or peanut
  oil
2 medium-sized onions, finely
  chopped
1 teaspoon cooking oil
¼ cup water
½ cup boiling water
1 cinnamon stick

*See Seasoning Chart.
**Available at Far Eastern markets and some specialty food stores.

1. Combine the salt, coriander, cumin, cloves, and cardamom seeds and set aside. Place rice in a 3-quart saucepan. Cover with 2 inches of water. Bring to a boil and stir constantly until rice is tender on the outside and firm on the inside—about 5 minutes. Turn rice into a fine-mesh colander or strainer and rinse thoroughly with cold water. Wrap rice in a dry kitchen towel and set aside.
2. Wash and dry the 3-quart saucepan. Heat the 2 tablespoons of oil in the saucepan until hot. Add the onions and sauté 15 to 20 minutes or until almost black, stirring frequently to prevent burning. Stir in the reserved spices and mix well. Add ¼ cup water—it should sizzle when it hits the pan. Stir to make a paste. Remove from heat. Add the rice and gently combine with the onions and spices. Return to heat and add ½ cup boiling water and cinnamon stick. Cover with a tight-fitting lid and simmer over very low heat until the water is absorbed. Rice will stick partially to the bottom. Remove cinnamon and serve immediately.

CASHEW VADAS
(Deep-fried Cashew Balls)

YIELD: approximately 16 vadas

1 cup chopped, unsalted cashew
  nuts
1 cup water
2 tablespoons sweet red bell
  pepper
1 teaspoon ground coriander seed
1 tablespoon grated or chopped
  ginger root

1 teaspoon salt
1 quart vegetable oil for deep
  frying
Peach and Mango Chutney
(p. 206), or any fruit or mint-
flavored chutney

1. Soak cashews in water for 45 minutes. Drain off excess liquid. In a blender, combine cashew nuts, red pepper, coriander, and ginger. Blend to a thick paste, adding water a little at a time as needed for a thick, smooth consistency. Transfer to a bowl, add salt, and mix thoroughly.

2. Place oil in a deep heavy saucepan. Heat to 375 degrees (if you don't have a thermometer, drop a bread cube into the hot oil for exactly 60 seconds—if it browns, the oil is ready). Drop cashew paste, carefully, by tablespoons into the hot oil. You may fry up to ten *vadas* at a time; fry until golden brown. Let cool slightly and serve with chutney as an appetizer.

CHAPATIS or POORIS
(Indian-style Tortillas)   YIELD: 12 chapatis or pooris

---

1 cup whole wheat flour
1 cup unbleached white flour
½ to 1 teaspoon salt

2 tablespoons corn or peanut oil—
  optional
½ to 1 cup water
3 tablespoons safflower margarine
  or *ghee*,* melted

*See Seasoning Chart.

1. Sift the flours and salt into a large mixing bowl. Add the oil and rub it in with your fingertips until thoroughly blended. Add ½ cup water and knead it into the flour with both hands. Continue kneading 5 to 10 minutes, adding additional water, a little at a time, only as necessary to obtain the correct consistency—a stiff and elastic, but not sticky, dough. Place dough in a lightly-greased bowl; turn once to oil the surface. Cover with a towel and let rest 1 hour at room temperature.
2. Divide dough into 12 equal pieces. With a rolling pin, roll each piece into a thin circle, turning it an inch or so in a clockwise direction to keep a uniform shape. It is best to roll and fry *chapatis* in groups of four to prevent them from drying out.
3. Heat a dry griddle or heavy skillet until hot but not smoking. Cook *chapatis*, one or two at a time, on one side until brown spots appear on the surface; turn and lightly brown the other side. When finished, *chapatis* should be lightly browned and pliable, but not tough or crisp. Remove from griddle, brush lightly with melted margarine or *ghee*, and serve hot.
Variation: To make *Pooris* (deep-fried puffed *chapatis*): Prepare *chapatis* as above adding ⅓ teaspoon ground cumin and ¼ teaspoon cayenne pepper to the flour. Heat 2 cups vegetable oil in a wok, deepfryer, or large heavy saucepan until a small piece of dough, when added to the oil, immediately bubbles to the surface. Add *pooris*, 4 at a time, and fry until lightly browned on both sides, turning several times with tongs once they rise to the surface. Do not worry if all *pooris* do not puff—the taste remains the same even if they are flat. Drain on paper towels and serve hot.

CHEESE AND CHUTNEY SPREAD

YIELD: Serves 6 as an appetizer

8 ounces Neufchâtel cheese or
   cream cheese
½ cup *Peach and Mango Chutney*
   (p. 206) or any fruit chutney
1 teaspoon *garam masala**
See Seasoning Chart.

½ teaspoon ground ginger
¼ teaspoon dry mustard
¼ cup chopped toasted almonds
Grated coconut or chopped
   peanuts

Allow cream cheese to soften at room temperature. Add the chutney, *garam masala,* ginger, and dry mustard and cream together. Fold in almonds last. Spread out thinly on a plate and garnish, if desired, with grated coconut or chopped peanuts. This spread is delicious on crackers, *Chapatis* (p. 202), or any Indian flat bread.

CUCUMBER RAITA

(Whipped Yogurt and Cucumber Salad)   *YIELD: 6 servings*

2 cups plain yogurt
1 cucumber, thinly sliced (peel if
   waxed)
1 teaspoon *garam masala**
½ teaspoon salt
See Seasoning Chart.

Pinch of cayenne pepper
½ cup raisins—optional
Fresh coriander leaves as
   garnish—optional

Place yogurt in a bowl and whip with a wire whisk until smooth and fluffy. Stir in cucumbers, spices, and raisins. Chill before serving. Garnish with coriander leaves if desired. *Raita* is a perfect accompaniment for a hot curry. Variations: 1. Any of the following may be substituted for the cucumber: 1 large grated carrot, 6 grated radishes, or 1 diced tomato, combined with ⅓ cup grated onion.
2. Substitute ¼ cup ground peanuts for the raisins.
3. Substitute for the *garam masala*: ½ teaspoon ground cumin, ½ teaspoon chili powder (see *Seasoning Chart*), and a pinch of black pepper.

GAJAR HALVA
(Sweet Carrot Dessert)   *YIELD: 6 servings*

1 pound carrots, finely grated
3 cups milk
1 cup light cream
¼ cup safflower margarine or *ghee**
¾ to 1 cup dark brown or white
   sugar
½ cup blanched almonds, finely
   ground
¼ cup raisins—optional
⅛ teaspoon powdered saffron—
   optional
Seeds of 10 cardamom pods,
   crushed
*See Seasoning Chart.
***Available at Far Eastern markets.*

Garnishes—optional
¼ cup shelled and unsalted
   pistachio nuts
¼ cup chopped almonds, toasted
Edible silver leaf**

1. Combine carrots, milk, and cream in a heavy 2-quart saucepan. Bring to a boil, stirring constantly. Reduce heat and simmer, stirring frequently, for 1 hour, or until mixture is thick enough to heavily coat a spoon.
2. Add margarine or *ghee*, sugar, ground almonds, and raisins, stirring constantly. Bring to a boil, reduce heat, and add the saffron and cardamom. Continue cooking over low heat 15 minutes or until mixture pulls away from the sides of the pan. Stir frequently to prevent mixture from sticking. Spoon into individual dessert bowls, cover, and chill. Just before serving, garnish with chopped nuts and silver leaf.

GINGER SPICE TEA
                                                              YIELD: 4 servings

½ -inch piece ginger root
10 whole cloves
2 tablespoons grated orange peel

3 cinnamon sticks
8 cardamom seeds
1 quart water

Bring all the ingredients to a boil in a 2-quart saucepan. Turn off heat, cover, and let stand for 30 minutes. Strain and pour into a teapot which has been rinsed several times with boiling water. Sweeten to taste with honey or sugar if desired.

GLAZED BANANAS

YIELD: 6 servings

6 small firm bananas
Juice of 2 small oranges
¼ cup each: finely chopped cashew
  nuts and blanched toasted
  almonds
⅓ to ½ cup dark brown sugar,
  firmly packed
*See Seasoning Chart.

¼ cup safflower margarine or *ghee**
½ to 1 teaspoon ground cardamom
  seed
⅛ teaspoon powdered ginger
Pinch of cayenne pepper

1. Preheat oven to 375 degrees.
2. Peel bananas and cut in half lengthwise. Place cut-side-down in a shallow baking dish. Cover with orange juice and sprinkle with nuts and sugar. Melt the margarine or *ghee* in a skillet and stir in the spices. Pour over bananas and place in a preheated oven until warmed through, basting occasionally. Serve as a dessert.

MOONG DAHL
(Lentils with Spices)

YIELD: 6 servings

1 cup *moong dahl** or yellow split
  peas, soaked 1 hour in 2 cups
  water
1 cup red or brown lentils
5 to 6 cups water
1 teaspoon turmeric
1 teaspoon salt
3 tablespoons peanut oil or *ghee***
½ teaspoon black mustard seed**
1 large onion, chopped
*Available at Far Eastern markets and health food stores.
**See Seasoning Chart.

1 small (fresh or canned) hot green
  chili, seeded and chopped—
  optional
1 inch fresh ginger root, grated
4 garlic cloves, minced
1 to 2 teaspoons *garam masala***
2 tablespoons chopped fresh
  coriander, or 2 teaspoons dried
  coriander leaves
Salt to taste

1. Drain water off *moong dahl*. Combine with lentils, water, turmeric, and the 1 teaspoon salt in a heavy saucepan. Bring to a boil, reduce heat, and simmer until tender—about 20 or 30 minutes.
2. Meanwhile, heat the oil or *ghee*. Add the mustard seed. When seeds start to crackle add the onion, chili, ginger, and garlic. Sauté, stirring frequently, 5 to 10 minutes or until onion and garlic are translucent. Add *garam masala* and coriander and cook 1 more minute. Add spice mixture to lentils. Season to taste with salt. Serve hot.
Variation: Add 1 cup pineapple chunks to cooked *dahl* or add 2 tablespoons each: shredded coconut, golden raisins, and toasted cashews.

PAKISTANI VEGETABLE CURRY   YIELD: *4 large servings*

1 tablespoon safflower or peanut
  oil
2 medium-sized onions, finely
  chopped
1 large garlic clove, finely chopped
1 tablespoon hot *garam masala** or
  imported Madras Curry Powder
2 teaspoons ground coriander
1 teaspoon ground cumin seed
1 teaspoon salt

1 tablespoon flour
1 heaping tablespoon tomato paste
Ground seeds of 1 black,* or 2
  white, cardamom pods
¼ cup water
4 medium-sized tomatoes, skinned
  and puréed
1½ cups hot water
1 large red potato, cubed
2 pounds broccoli, cut into
  flowerets

*See Seasoning Chart.

1. Heat the oil in the bottom of a large soup pot until hot. Add the onions and sauté 15 to 20 minutes or until almost black, stirring frequently to prevent burning. Add the garlic, *garam masala* or curry powder, coriander, cumin, salt, and flour. Stir well to blend. Push the onions and spices to one side. Add the tomato paste in the cleared space and brown it slightly. Combine with onions, spices, and cardamon seeds. Add ¼ cup water and stir to make a thick paste. Stir in the puréed tomatoes and simmer 5 minutes.
2. Gradually stir in the 1½ cups hot water. Stir constantly until water is thoroughly blended into the mixture. Add the potato and simmer 10 minutes. Add the broccoli and simmer 10 minutes longer or until vegetables are tender. Serve over *Basmati Rice Pilāu* (p. 201), brown rice, or white rice. Variations: Replace broccoli with any of the following: 1 large cauliflower (broken into flowerets) and ½ cup fresh shelled or frozen peas; 1 large cubed eggplant and 1 large sliced green pepper; 2 large sliced zucchini squash and 1 small cubed eggplant; or 1 pound stemmed and sliced okra (increase garlic to 3 cloves).

PEACH AND MANGO CHUTNEY   YIELD: *4 half-pint jars, (8 ounces each)*

4 cups peeled, pitted, and sliced
  fresh peaches
2 cups peeled, pitted, and sliced
  fresh mangos or fresh pineapple
½ cup each: chopped dates and
  currants
2 crushed garlic cloves
½ cup brown sugar
¼ cup water

2 tablespoons lime or lemon juice
¾ cup vinegar
¼ teaspoon each: salt and cayenne
  pepper
1½ teaspoons mustard seed
¾ teaspoon ground ginger
½ teaspoon allspice
¼ cup chopped almonds or
  pistachio nuts

Combine all the ingredients, except the nuts, in a Dutch oven or large pot. Cover and simmer for 30 minutes. Stir frequently to prevent sticking. Uncover, add nuts, and cook 30 minutes more or until most of the liquid is absorbed. Pack into hot, sterilized jars. Seal and store in the refrigerator.

PHULGOBI DAM
(Steamed Masala Cauliflower)   *YIELD: 4 servings*

---

1 medium-sized cauliflower
1 tablespoon peanut oil
1 large onion, chopped
2 to 4 garlic cloves, pressed
2 teaspoons grated ginger root
¼ teaspoon ground cardamom seed
¼ teaspoon turmeric
4 whole cloves

¼ teaspoon cayenne pepper
1 teaspoon *garam masala**
1 teaspoon ground coriander or 2
  tablespoons fresh chopped
  coriander
6 black peppercorns
5 blanched almonds, finely ground
2 tablespoons peanut oil or *ghee**
1 cup plain, low-fat yogurt

*See Seasoning Chart.

1. Wash the cauliflower, separate into flowerets, and place in a vegetable steamer with ½ inch water. Cover and steam over medium-low heat until just tender—about 6 minutes.
2. Meanwhile, heat the 1 tablespoon of oil in a skillet until hot. Sauté the onion until transparent. Add the garlic and ginger root. Sauté briefly. Remove from heat and set aside. Grind the spices and almonds together in a mortar with a pestle or spice grinder until fine. Heat the 2 tablespoons of peanut oil or *ghee* in a skillet until hot. Add spice and almond mixture and stir to blend the flavors. Stir in the onion mixture and yogurt.
3. Drain liquid off the cauliflower. Return to saucepan, cover with yogurt sauce, and warm through. Serve immediately as a main course or side dish.
Variation: Replace cauliflower with 1 pound string beans, broccoli, new potatoes, mushrooms, green peas, or bananas.

POTATO CURRY KASHMIRI

YIELD: 6 servings

3 tablespoons peanut oil or *ghee**
1 teaspoon each: cumin seed,
  turmeric, black mustard seed*
½ to 1 teaspoon cayenne pepper
1 teaspoon grated ginger root
2 to 4 garlic cloves, crushed
2 medium-sized red potatoes,
  peeled and cubed
*See Seasoning Chart.

1 medium-sized cauliflower, cut
  into flowerets
1 medium-sized onion, diced
1 cup water
1 cup fresh shelled or frozen peas
¾ cup plain or apple yogurt
½ cup dried currants or raisins—
  optional

1. In a large skillet, heat the peanut oil or *ghee* over medium-low heat. Add the spices and garlic, stir well, and simmer for a minute to let the flavors blend. Add potatoes, cauliflower, and onion; stir well to coat with spices. Add water, cover with a tightly-fitting lid, and simmer 20 minutes.
2. Add peas, yogurt, and currants. Simmer from 10 to 12 minutes, uncovered, stirring frequently. Serve immediately. Leftovers may be reheated.

QUICK CURRIED TOMATOES

YIELD: 2 to 4 servings

2 tablespoons safflower margarine,
  or *ghee**
1 teaspoon ground coriander
¼ teaspoon ground cumin
*See Seasoning Chart.
**See Seasoning Chart *under red chili peppers.*

¼ teaspoon chili powder**
1 tablespoon brown sugar
2 large, firm but ripe, tomatoes

Heat margarine or *ghee* in a 9-inch skillet. Add seasonings and stir for a few minutes over low heat until flavors are well blended. Slice tomatoes first in half and then in quarters. Add to skillet and simmer until tomatoes are soft—about 10 minutes. Serve as a side dish.

SHRIMP AND BANANA CURRY

YIELD: 6 servings

2 tablespoons safflower margarine
or *ghee**
½ to 1 teaspoon cayenne pepper
½ teaspoon ground coriander seeds
⅓ teaspoon each: turmeric, ground
cumin seed, and ground fenugreek seed
1 teaspoon *garam masala**
2 teaspoons grated ginger root
1 tablespoon vinegar
½ teaspoon ground allspice
½ teaspoon salt
*See Seasoning Chart.

4 garlic cloves, pressed
2 medium-sized onions, minced
1 pound fresh shrimp, shelled and
deveined
1 cup apple juice or coconut milk
1 tablespoon cornstarch
½ teaspoon water
2 large, firm (but ripe) bananas,
peeled and cut into ½-inch slices
1 tablespoon fresh lemon juice
Grated coconut, currants, and
unsalted peanuts as condiments

1. Heat the margarine in a large skillet. Add all the seasonings up to the garlic. Stir well to blend flavors for 1 minute. Add the garlic and onions. Sauté until onions are transparent. Add the shrimp and cook, stirring constantly, until they are barely pink.
2. Add apple juice or coconut milk along with the cornstarch dissolved in the water. Stir constantly over medium-low heat until mixture is thick and smooth. Toss the bananas with the lemon juice and add, cooking only long enough to heat bananas through.
3. Transfer to a serving dish. Place coconut, currants, and peanuts in individual bowls and serve alongside this dish as condiments. Serve with rice and chutney if desired.

TOMATO RASAM
(Tart and Spicy South Indian Soup)

YIELD: 4 servings

3 cups water
½ cup yellow split peas or lentils
½ teaspoon salt
1 pound tomatoes, fresh or canned
1 cup water
1 cup chopped fresh coriander, or 3
tablespoons dried coriander
leaves
2 garlic cloves, mashed
½ teaspoon cumin seed
*See Seasoning Chart.

½ teaspoon turmeric
6 black peppercorns
1 small (fresh or canned) hot green
chili, seeded and chopped
Salt and freshly ground pepper to
taste
1 tablespoon peanut oil
1 teaspoon black mustard seed*
4 tablespoons chopped onion
Juice of ½ lemon

1. Place 3 cups water in a 3-quart saucepan. Bring to a boil and add the split peas or lentils and salt. Cook over medium heat until legumes are tender—about 20 minutes. Remove from heat and set aside.
2. If using fresh tomatoes, dip them in boiling water for 10 seconds. Slip off skins and remove cores. If using canned tomatoes, drain off excess liquid. Place tomatoes in a blender and purée. Add to legumes along with 1 cup water and the coriander. Return to stove over low heat.
3. Pound garlic, cumin, turmeric, peppercorns, and green chili to a paste in a mortar with a pestle. Add to soup and season to taste with salt and pepper. Simmer 15 minutes.
4. Heat peanut oil in a small skillet until hot. Add the mustard seed. When seeds start to "pop," add the onion and sauté until transparent. Add to soup. Add lemon juice, stir to blend, and serve hot.

WILL'S SPICY EGGPLANT WITH YOGURT   YIELD: 4 to 6 servings

---

2 large eggplants	3 garlic cloves, chopped
2 medium-sized tomatoes	1 teaspoon salt
6 tablespoons plain, low-fat yogurt	1½ teaspoons turmeric
3 tablespoons peanut oil	1 teaspoon each: chili powder,**
1 teaspoon black mustard seed*	cumin seed, and ground
	coriander seed

*See Seasoning Chart.
**See Seasoning Chart *under red chili peppers.*

1. Preheat oven to 350 degrees.
2. Wash and pierce the eggplants in several places. Place on a baking sheet and set in the oven 20 or 30 minutes, turning them every 10 minutes. When baked (they will have swelled considerably), remove from oven and peel off the skins. Place eggplants in a large mixing bowl and coarsely mash them. Set aside.
3. Chop the tomatoes and set aside. In a small bowl, mix the yogurt with enough water to acquire the consistency of heavy cream. Set aside.
4. Heat the oil in a large, heavy or cast-iron skillet until hot. Add the mustard seeds and garlic. When mustard seeds stop crackling or popping, add the chopped tomatoes and sauté 2 minutes. Add the mashed eggplant, salt, and remaining spices. Stir briskly to mix thoroughly, and sauté 5 minutes. Stir in the yogurt. Cover with a tight-fitting lid and simmer 10 minutes. Taste and adjust seasonings. Serve with rice or *Chapatis* (p. 202).
Variation: Stir leftover cooked chicken, cut into small cubes, into the mixture during the final 10 minutes of simmering.

INDIA/RECIPE ANALYSIS CHART

Name of Recipe	Quantity	Calories	CHO gms.	Protein gms.	Total Fat gms.	Saturated Fat gms.	Choles-terol mg.	Dietary Fiber gms.
1. Ginger Spice Tea	per cup	—	—	—	—	—	—	—
2. Cucumber *Raita*	per serving	48	7 (58%)	5 (42%)	—	—	1	.25
3. Peach and Mango Chutney	per table-spoon	52	11 (85%)	2 (15%)	—	—	—	.3
4. Quick Curried Tomatoes	per serving	81	8 (40%)	1 (5%)	5 (55%)	1 (0%)	—	1.0
5. *Chapatis*	each	90	16 (71%)	2 (9%)	2 (20%)	—	—	.3
6. Banana *Raita*	per serving	114	17 (60%)	7 (25%)	2 (15%)	—	1	—
7. *Will's* Spicy Eggplant with Yogurt	per serving	123	12 (39%)	3 (10%)	7 (51%)	1 (7%)	1	2.2
8. Pakistani Veg-etable Curry	per serving	143	24 (67%)	5 (14%)	3 (19%)	—	—	2.0
9. Potato Curry Kashmiri	per serving	151	17 (45%)	5 (13%)	7 (42%)	1 (6%)	1	1.0
10. Tomato *Rasam*	per serving	156	22 (56%)	8 (21%)	4 (23%)	—	—	1.2
11. Cashew *Vadas*	per serving	158	5 (13%)	3 (8%)	14 (79%)	2 (11%)	—	.3
12. Cheese and Chutney Spread	per serving	168	10 (24%)	5 (12%)	12 (64%)	6 (32%)	29	.3
13. Shrimp and Banana Curry	per serving	188	23 (49%)	15 (32%)	4 (19%)	1 (5%)	94	.7
14. *Phulgobi Dam* (Steamed Mas-ala Cauliflower)	per serving	230	12 (21%)	5 (9%)	18 (70%)	4 (16%)	1.0	.8
15. Basmati Rice Pilāu *Koh-i-noor*	per serving	272	45 (66%)	5 (7%)	8 (27%)	—	—	.7
16. *Moong Dahl* (Lentils with Spices)	per serving	300	43 (57%)	16 (21%)	7 (22%)	1 (3%)	—	1.2

Name of Recipe	Quantity	Calories	CHO gms.	Protein gms.	Total Fat gms.	Saturated Fat gms.	Cholesterol mg.	Dietary Fiber gms.
17. Spiced Almond Rice	per serving	316	46 (58%)	8 (10%)	11 (32%)	3 (9%)	—	1.6
18. Glazed Bananas	per serving	360	50 (56%)	4 (4%)	16 (40%)	3 (8%)	—	1.0
19. *Gajar Halva* (Sweet Carrot Dessert)	per serving	447	52 (47%)	8 (7%)	23 (46%)	9 (18%)	40	1.1

Numbers in parentheses (%) indicate percentage of total calories contributed by nutrient.

MENUS

LOW CALORIE SPECIALTIES
(500 to 700 calories per meal)

WILL'S SPICY EGGPLANT WITH YOGURT
Steamed Rice Garnishes with Fresh Coriander
CHAPATIS
Sliced Peaches and Bananas
Iced Mint Tea

POTATO CURRY KASHMIRI
Mint Chutney
BANANA RAITA
Fresh Pineapple
GINGER SPICE TEA

QUICK CURRIED TOMATOES
PHULGOBI DAM (STEAMED MASALA CAULIFLOWER)
Radish Raita
Fresh Mangos and Papayas
Hot Herb Tea

●

LOW CHOLESTEROL MENUS
(Less than 50 mgs. of cholesterol per meal)

PAKISTANI VEGETABLE CURRY
Steamed Rice
WILL'S SPICY EGGPLANT WITH YOGURT
Sliced Apples and Dates
GINGER SPICE TEA

CASHEW VADAS
POTATO CURRY KASHMIRI
PEACH AND MANGO CHUTNEY
GLAZED BANANAS

SPICED ALMOND RICE
QUICK CURRIED TOMATOES
PHULGOBI DAM (STEAMED MASALA CAULIFLOWER)
Fresh Pineapple and Mangos
Hot Herb Tea

LOW SATURATED FAT SELECTIONS
(Less than 8 grams of saturated fat per meal)

CASHEW VADAS
PEACH AND MANGO CHUTNEY
TOMATO RASAM
PHULGOBI DAM (STEAMED MASALA CAULIFLOWER)
Sliced Oranges and Papayas

CUCUMBER RAITA
MOONG DAHL (LENTILS WITH SPICES)
BASMATI RICE PILĀU KOH-I-NOOR
Sliced Carrots and Radishes
GLAZED BANANAS

SHRIMP AND BANANA CURRY
CHAPATIS
Steamed Peas
Plain Yogurt
GINGER SPICE TEA

●

HIGH PROTEIN MEALS
(30 or more grams of protein per meal)

SHRIMP AND BANANA CURRY
Fruit Chutney
Steamed Rice
CUCUMBER RAITA
GAJAR HALVA (SWEET CARROT DESSERT)

MOONG DAHL (LENTILS WITH SPICES)
PAKISTANI VEGETABLE CURRY
BASMATI RICE
Tomato, Onion and Radish Salad
GLAZED BANANAS

CHEESE AND CHUTNEY SPREAD
TOMATO RASAM
POORIS
SPICED ALMOND RICE
BANANA RAITA

●

WELL BALANCED LUNCH OR DINNER MENUS
(Selections that conform to recommendations in Dietary Goals for United States*)*

CUCUMBER RAITA
MOONG DAHL (LENTILS WITH SPICES)
PAKISTANI VEGETABLE CURRY
GLAZED BANANAS
Mint Tea

CARROT RAITA
POTATO CURRY KASHMIRI
CHAPATIS
GINGER SPICE TEA

TOMATO RASAM
SHRIMP AND BANANA CURRY
Steamed Rice
GAJAR HALVA (SWEET CARROT DESSERT)
Orange Spice Tea

CHAPTER 9

ITALY
Favorite Pasta Time

Culinary Essentials

Some palates you just can't please. Give them a French creation, and they say "too rich." Szechuan food? "Too spicy." How about a Polish dish? "Too bland." But mention an Italian meal, and you'll be met with nothing but sighs of approval. That the whole world loves Italian food is no surprise. Smoky sharp cheeses, glistening platters of *antipasto* and fluffy, golden egg *frittatas* are enough to tempt even the most jaded appetite.

Assembling ingredients for an Italian meal should pose few problems. Grocery stores carry the basics, and Italian delicatessens purvey imported items such as cheeses, olives, and Amaretto (an almond-flavored liqueur). For general purposes, stock your shelves with virgin olive oil, red wine vinegar, canned Italian tomatoes, garbanzo beans, tuna, and assorted dried noodles. An adequate supply of these items will make it easier to enhance an Italian recipe or throw together a dinner for unexpected company.

With the recent surge in nutritional consciousness, white pasta, like white bread, has almost disappeared from the American table. Instead, nutritious noodles, fashioned from whole grain flours or flavored with vegetable purees, occupy a prominent position on Italian menus. These rich-tasting pastas, available at Italian markets, specialty food stores, and supermarkets, can be used to produce simple, nourishing, and low-cost main dishes. Whole wheat and spinach noodles are the most popular, but you will also enjoy exotic varieties made with tomato purée, carrots, or Jerusalem artichoke flour.

Whole grain pasta comes in an enticing array of shapes and sizes, from small grooved shells to giant hollow tubes. Innovative cooks will find these colorful noodles an ideal backdrop for simple sauces. Tan-colored ribbons of whole wheat *fettucine*, for example, need nothing more for show than a dressing of thick cream and fresh parsley. A nest of buckwheat spaghetti can be embellished with cauliflower and bathed in hot olive oil and garlic. Or, you might find jade-green spinach noodles the perfect foil for a tomato-red sauce.

Your ability to create exciting pasta dishes will be enhanced by a little cheese expertise. Rule number one: Avoid pregrated Parmesan or Romano—its dull flavor and cornmeal texture will do nothing to improve the quality of your meals. Rather, look for an imported variety that is hard, slightly golden in color, and properly aged; buy small amounts, keep refrigerated, and grate as needed. Good Parmesan has a nutty, slightly sweet taste; aged *Pecorino Romano* is sharper, coarser, and somewhat salty in flavor.

Experiment with the more unusual imported Italian cheeses, using them in moderation to accent pasta, eggs, vegetables, or salads. *Gorgonzola*, a pale, crumbly cheese, finely veined with blue and pleasantly sharp in taste, will give salads or stuffed mushroom caps superior flavor. Buttery, nutlike *Fontina* blends beautifully with fresh fruit or eggs. The next time you prepare pasta, grate full-bodied *Asagio* or pungent *Caciocavallo* over the top for a change of pace from the more common Parmesan cheese. Varying cheeses as you would seasonings gives even simple dishes a tantalizing foreign flavor.

While nothing frivolous is needed in the utensil department, certain kitchen equipment is integral to this cuisine. To cook pasta, you will need a heavy 6½-quart pot for boiling and a large colander for draining. Stainless steel "pasta tongs" or metal kitchen tongs should be on hand to lift strands of spaghetti or *fettucine* into serving bowls. Sauce-making requires a ladle, long-handled wooden spoon, and several heavy saucepans of varying capacity. Those who like sauces with a well-defined garlic flavor will find a cast-aluminum garlic press indispensable. Although a food processor is unsurpassable for quick-grating hard cheese, a hand-operated grater is an inexpensive and efficient alternative. Recommended options include a stainless steel four-sided grater; a small, rotary, cylinder-shaped grater; or a modern two-piece plastic grater used like a hand-cranked pepper mill.

Much of the fun in this cuisine lies in creating an atmosphere of warmth and good spirits. A simple linen tablecloth bedecked with red nappery, dripping white candles, and a carafe of Italian wine will set the stage. Place *Antipasto Supreme*, a variety of tidbits dressed with oil, vinegar, and herbs, in the center of the table. Sesame-studded bread sticks or warm, crusty Italian bread make an ideal companion for this traditional appetizer.

The next course can be either a bountiful bowl of *Minestrone Milanese*, Italy's famous vegetable and bean soup, or a dish of lightly sauced pasta. Accompany entrées with an innovative salad and steamed vegetables garnished with herbs or pine nuts. Fresh fruit and cheese comprise dessert for everyday meals, but special occasions call for a glorious creation such as *Cassata alla Siciliana*, a rich cake, layered with almond-flavored pound cake, chopped chocolate, nuts, and thick, cinnamon-tinged cream. Or, you might enjoy *Poached Pears* simmered in honeyed red wine and adorned with whipped cream and crushed mint leaves. Finally, serve espresso or hot anise tea—a classic ending to a modern Italian meal.

Seasoning Essentials

The dullest Italian dishes are those that lack any flavor other than basil, oregano, or garlic. If you want to give your creations a unique taste, you must seek additional seasonings because their character is all too familiar in this cuisine.

A tomato sauce is perfect for practicing your seasoning powers. To impart an elusive flavor with licoricelike undertones, add a teaspoon of fennel or anise seed. You can give your sauce a peppery personality with a good pinch of cayenne pepper and ground coriander seed. Or, if you prefer a faintly sweet taste, enlist a little dark honey and ground cloves.

Try not to get too heavy-handed with any seasoning. The most exciting sauces do not have one dominant taste, but rather subtle hints of several different flavors. Aniseed and garlic, for example, have the ability to overpower a sauce. Strongly flavored herbs such as these should always be added a little at a time until the desired flavor is reached.

One way to ensure a delicate balance of herbs is to make your own *Italian Seasoning* blend. You can use this well-balanced mixture—which is accented with coriander, rosemary, and dried red chili pepper—when you are in need of interesting, yet contrasting flavors. A moderate amount will do wonders for a tossed salad, vegetable soup, or egg-based *frittata*. *Italian Seasoning* has a great affinity for garlic. You can count on this "dynamic duo" to brighten up almost any lackluster dish imaginable.

Fresh cloves of garlic are far superior to garlic powder. When you want a sharp, well-defined flavor, sieve the whole, peeled cloves through a garlic press; minced garlic is not as forthright and best suited for delicate dishes. Save the powder for perking up a dish at the last minute when it is inconvenient to use the press.

On the subtler side, you will find nutmeg, which also plays an important role in Italian cooking. Add a pinch of this aromatic spice to any spinach or mushroom dish and the flavor will improve. Bland cheeses, such as ricotta, also benefit from a touch of nutmeg. If you want to give a cream-enriched pasta dish an air of elegance, crown it with freshly grated whole nutmeg. Whenever possible, you should try to grate your own, as pre-ground nutmeg can lose its precious qualities with prolonged shelf life.

Unfortunately, fresh basil, another integral member of the Italian kitchen is not available in our markets. Unless you grow your own, you will have to make do with the dried variety which is less fragrant and distinctive. Since the compromise must be made, seek out a reliable shop specializing in bulk herbs, where you are likely to encounter the freshest dried basil available.

True basil aficionados put a little of it in everything. Often, it is used in combination with the more pungent dried oregano leaf. You will find this titillating twosome great for enhancing vinaigrettes and soups. However, heed a word of caution concerning oregano—too much of it will turn a dish bitter.

ITALIAN SEASONING CHART

ANISE SEEDS have a sweet licoricelike flavor. When crushed, a small amount will give a tomato or pizza sauce an unusual aroma and taste. Whole aniseed is a fine addition to poached pears or Italian bread. For a splendid taste treat, press ½ teaspoon of seeds into a halibut steak and brush the surface with olive oil before baking. To end an Italian meal with a delightful tea, steep 2 teaspoons aniseed in 4 cups boiling water; add honey and lemon juice to taste.

BASIL is the most ubiquitous herb in this cuisine. It will lend a fantastic flavor and scent to almost any dish employing tomatoes. This delicate herb is a great enhancer for Italian vegetables such as peas, asparagus, or cauliflower and is exceptional with artichokes or eggplants. In combination with oregano or garlic, basil does wonders for soups, pastas, fava beans, and vinaigrettes. Fresh basil, which is more potent and fragrant than the dried leaves, should be used whenever possible.

FENNEL seeds exude an aroma reminiscent of aniseed. They are a popular addition to bread sticks and bean soups and will give a unique personality to tomato-based sauces. Fresh fennel root, available seasonally in some supermarkets, can be cut into julienne strips and tossed with a vinaigrette as a salad. When sautéed in oil and seasoned with garlic, fresh fennel makes a superb side dish.

GARLIC is responsible for the pungent flavor that characterizes the heartier foods in this cooking style. Many cooks feel that an Italian dish can never have too much garlic, and amounts can be increased in most dishes if desired. When you want a mild flavor, use minced garlic cloves; a more biting flavor can be achieved with a garlic press. Use fresh garlic for general cooking purposes—the powder can be used to doctor up a dish at the last minute, but its use in the kitchen should be restricted.

ITALIAN SEASONING is the best all-purpose blend for this cuisine. Ready-made Italian Seasoning can be found in most supermarkets, but your own mixture will be much livelier. Proportions are flexible and may be adjusted according to your taste preferences or whims. Toss this delightful seasoning into a standard green salad before adding the vinaigrette for a well-herbed flavor. Or, add a moderate amount to soups, sauces, vegetables, or seafood. To make a delectable spread for Italian or French bread, combine 1½ tablespoons Italian Seasoning with 4 tablespoons softened safflower margarine or butter; add pressed cloves of garlic to taste.

Combine and store in an airtight container:

4 tablespoons dried basil
2 tablespoons dried oregano
1 tablespoon thyme
½ teaspoon rosemary, ground coriander seed, and dried red chili flakes
⅓ teaspoon fennel seed and sage

NUTMEG has a pronounced scent and delicate taste. It is used, somewhat arbitrarily, to season both sweet and savory dishes. To elevate the status of a humble, cream-sauced pasta dish, grate a little nutmeg over the top. This gentle-natured spice can profoundly influence the flavor of spinach, mushrooms, or bland cheeses such as ricotta. To give a dish a biting quality, add a pinch of ground nutmeg and cayenne pepper.

OREGANO is also called *wild marjoram*. Its robust flavor, which falls somewhere between sage and sweet marjoram, is essential to this cuisine; without it many dishes would lose the pleasingly pungent taste that is an attribute of this seasoning. Oregano blends admirably with zucchini, olives, eggplant, tomatoes, and beans. Use discreetly, as too much will give a dish a bitter aftertaste. In general, oregano combines well with other herbs.

Other flavorings found in Italian cookery: thyme, spearmint, rosemary, bay leaves, tarragon, saffron, cinnamon, cloves, coriander, parsley, sage, dried red peppers, sweet marjoram, celery seed, borage, and juniper berries.

Nutritional Essentials

Visions of herb-spiked tomato sauce covering a wealth of tender noodles is enough to make the mouth of any pasta-lover water. With all the virtues of Italian cooking, one can be prone to repeated attacks of gastronomical gluttony. But, if you are willing to concentrate more on the use of fresh vegetables, low-fat cheeses, and whole grain pastas and less on cream, bread, and white noodles, you can enjoy this popular cuisine without an excessive intake of calories.

One special feature of Italian cooking which makes it amenable to nutritional manipulation is the availability of whole grain pastas. You can substantially fortify your noodle dishes by using natural grain products.

Wheat-soy macaroni, for example, is very high in protein, while buckwheat spaghetti is lower in calories than white "enriched" spaghetti. By substituting whole wheat lasagne noodles for the common white flour variety, you can increase the protein content of your dish by about 20 percent. The artichoke noodle, made from soy powder and Jerusalem artichoke flour is especially nutritious; it is low in carbohydrates and higher in both protein and iron than even the whole wheat varieties. Spinach noodles, also plentiful in protein and iron, are another tasty addition to any pasta concoction. Whole wheat, wheat-soy, and spinach-based pastas also contain more dietary fiber than white noodle varieties.

Homemade pasta can be formulated to satisfy your nutritional preferences. We have provided a basic recipe to familiarize you with this health-minded cooking skill. Protein considerations prevailed while we were perfecting the *Wheat Soy Fettucine Noodles*; as a result, one serving will supply 22 grams of protein, whereas the same amount of white noodles yields only 7 grams.

Although Italian meals are a delicate balance of spices and sauces, you can use whole grain pasta in any noodle dish without compromising the quality of your meal. Also be aware that pasta cooked *al dente* (tender yet firm) will provide almost 30 percent more protein than soft-cooked noodles, but is also higher in calories. Still another way to increase the protein potential of meatless Italian recipes is to combine pasta with milk or cheese products, as we have done in the *Rigatoni with Cauliflower* and *Walnut Mushroom Lasagne*.

The Italian cuisine, because it relies heavily upon dairy products, can easily provide high-protein meals. Some cheeses employed in this culinary style—Ricotta, Mozzarella, and Parmesan—are among the most desirable dairy foods; they are extremely high in usable protein, yet relatively low in total fat content. Although Italian recipes tend to be high in calories, proper planning will enable you to prepare meals that are calorie-sparing, high in protein, rich in vitamin B_{12} and calcium, and moderate in fat. In general, the secret to the nutrition balancing of this type of meal is to combine a low-fat, cheese-oriented entrée with a high-fiber side dish.

The Italian kitchen is endowed with several low-fat cheeses which have nutritional advantages for both protein- and calorie-conscious cooks. As an example, low-fat Ricotta (less than 10 percent fat) is a fine substitute for high-fat cream cheese and can also be used as a sandwich spread, noodle stuffing, or dessert-making cheese. Those on restricted diets might try defatted cottage cheese (also called pot cheese) as a low-fat filling for tubular noodles or lasagne. Other protein-rich varieties include Parmesan, Mozzarella, and *Fontina*, all of which are moderate in fat content (less than 40 percent total fat). Parmesan cheese, in particular, is higher in grams of usable protein than any other cheese and, for this reason, should be used liberally in Italian cooking.

Because of their cheese content, dishes such as *Mushroom Pan Pizza*,

Minestrone Milanese, Rigatoni with Cauliflower, Asparagus Frittata, and *Walnut Mushroom Lasagne* are all rich in protein. The *Mushroom Pan Pizza* deserves special mention because, unlike many pizza recipes, this one is more than a dish of "empty calories." By adding soy flour to a whole wheat pizza crust, we have boosted its protein content by about 20 percent. One slice will provide about two-thirds of your total daily protein allowance.

The protein make-up of Italian recipes can also be increased by adding nuts to a tomato- or cheese-based sauce. For example, you can increase the protein content of one quart of tomato sauce by seven grams if you add one-half pound of chopped walnuts. You can choose between black and English walnuts, both of which are excellent sources of polyunsaturated fat. The former are somewhat higher in protein and lower in calories than the latter, but not as flavorful.

Combining nuts with vegetables is the trick to increasing the usable protein content of *Broccoli Pignolia with Raisins.* Because of the inclusion of pine nuts, this moderately caloric dish has a substantial protein base. The nutritional virtue of the pine nut is that its protein-to-calorie ratio is greater than that of any nut known. As a general rule, adding nuts to Italian salads, sauces, and *antipasto* is a reliable way to fortify the protein base of dishes in this cuisine.

The Italian kitchen will also provide many opportunities to augment your intake of dietary fiber. *Honey-Spiced Pears, Antipasto Supreme,* and *Garbanzo Bean and Gorgonzola Cheese Salad* are all good sources of fiber; these selections are versatile enough to be included in your Italian meals on a regular basis.

In general, our Italian recipes are not excessive in their fat content. Most entrées deliver about 7 to 11 percent of their total caloric content as saturated fat, which is a reasonable amount, even for those people who are trying to cut down on their fat intake. The *Asparagus Frittata,* however, is high in saturated fat and cholesterol and should be eaten only on occasion by those who are following a restricted diet.

This cooking style has many nutritional virtues, but the use of one particular ingredient needs some modification. Virgin olive oil, precious for the subtle, but distinctive flavor it imparts to this cuisine, is very low in polyunsaturated fats. There is no need, however, to eliminate it from your diet altogether. By combining olive oil with safflower, or other vegetable oils, which are mild in flavor and abundant in polyunsaturated fats, you can prepare an oil with a more acceptable fat composition.

We have tried to introduce you to both the nutritional assets as well as the drawbacks of the Italian cuisine, so that you will be able to make sensible food and recipe choices. It should be apparent that, while high in protein, Italian meals have a tendency to be rich in fat and calories. Our recommendation is that you use low-fat cheeses such as Ricotta and Mozzarella whenever possible to help prevent an excessive caloric intake. If you are active enough to maintain an ideal body weight, you can enjoy some of the high-fat cheeses such as *Gorgonzola*, *Bel Paese*, and *Taleggio*. Also explore the possibilities of whole grain pastas, which will provide more fiber and protein than their white noodle counterparts. On the whole, you can count on our Italian recipes to supply substantial amounts of balanced protein, vitamin B_{12}, and calcium without an excessive number of calories.

ANTIPASTO SUPREME

YIELD: 12 small servings

1 package frozen artichoke hearts
2 carrots, sliced
1 small head cauliflower, separated
   into flowerets
2 ribs celery, diced
1 green pepper, seeded and sliced
4 ounces pimiento olives
4 ounces black pitted olives
1 cup fresh string beans, broken
   into thirds

1 cup mushrooms
¾ cup wine vinegar
¼ cup olive oil
¼ cup safflower oil
2 tablespoons honey
1 teaspoon salt
¼ teaspoon cayenne pepper
¼ cup water
¾ cup flaked white tuna—optional

Combine all ingredients, except optional tuna, and place in a soup pot. Bring to a boil over medium heat, reduce heat to low, and simmer for 10 minutes uncovered. Remove from heat and allow to cool. Transfer mixture to a bowl and marinate in refrigerator for 2 days, stirring occasionally. Before serving, add flaked tuna if desired. Serve as an appetizer or salad.

APPLE SPINACH SALAD WITH SWEET AND SOUR DRESSING

YIELD: 6 servings

1 pound spinach
2 medium-sized Red Delicious
   apples, cored and chopped, but
   not peeled
1 small red onion
¼ cup each: olive and safflower oil
   or peanut oil

2 tablespoons apple cider vinegar
½ teaspoon salt
⅛ teaspoon cayenne pepper
½ teaspoon dry mustard
2 garlic cloves, pressed
2 to 3 teaspoons honey

Wash spinach thoroughly to remove sand. Remove stems and tear into bite-size pieces. Add chopped apples. Slice onion into very thin rings and add to spinach. Heat remaining ingredients in a saucepan and bring to a boil. Remove from heat, pour over salad, and serve immediately.

ASPARAGUS FRITTATA

YIELD: 4 servings

6 large eggs
2 to 3 tablespoons milk
Salt and freshly ground pepper to
taste
½ teaspoon dried basil
Pinch of nutmeg
1 tablespoon chopped fresh parsley
2 tablespoons grated Romano or
Parmesan cheese, divided

1 tablespoon safflower oil or olive
oil
1 tablespoon butter
1 scallion, chopped with top
½ pound asparagus, cooked and cut
into bite-size pieces
Few squirts fresh lemon juice
4 ounces cubed Fontina or Swiss
cheese

1. Preheat oven to 425 degrees.
2. Beat together the eggs, milk, salt, pepper, basil, nutmeg, parsley, and 1 tablespoon of the Romano or Parmesan cheese until frothy. Heat oil and butter in a large ovenproof skillet; sauté the scallion. Pour in egg mixture, give one quick stir, and cook over low heat. With a spatula, lift the edges of the omelet after it has cooked several minutes to allow uncooked egg to run underneath.
3. When eggs are set on the bottom, but soft on the top, remove from heat. Distribute the asparagus, lemon juice, cubed Fontina, and remaining table-spoon of Romano or Parmesan cheese across the top. Place skillet in a pre-heated oven. Bake until cheese melts. Serve immediately as a side dish or cut into strips as an appetizer.

BROCCOLI PIGNOLIA WITH RAISINS

YIELD: 6 servings

3 pounds fresh broccoli, cut into
large sprigs
4 tablespoons safflower margarine
or butter

½ cup yellow raisins
3½ ounces pignolia nuts
2 tablespoons lemon juice

In a pot, steam broccoli in salted water until tender, but firm. While broc-coli is cooking, melt the margarine in a skillet. Add the raisins and nuts and sauté until nuts are golden brown. Stir in lemon juice. Drain broccoli and combine with the pignolia sauce. Serve immediately as a side dish.

CASSATA ALLA SICILIANA
(Sicilian Cream Cake with Chocolate and Almonds)   *YIELD: 20 squares*

1 quart whole milk
2 cinnamon sticks, broken in half
4 tablespoons sugar
4 tablespoons cornstarch

2, 1-pound *Pound Cakes* **(p. 230)**
2 teaspoons cinnamon
2 cups chopped milk chocolate
1½ cups toasted almonds, chopped

1. *To prepare milk cream*: Set aside 1 cup of milk. Heat in a saucepan 3 cups of milk and cinnamon sticks over low flame for 30 minutes, stirring frequently but not constantly. Do not boil. Remove milk, strain, and return to saucepan over low flame. Stir sugar and cornstarch into reserved cup of milk until dissolved. Add to saucepan and stir constantly until thick. Again, do not boil. When thick, remove from heat and set aside.

2. *To assemble*: Cut pound cakes lengthwise into ½-inch-thick slices. Arrange enough slices to cover the bottom of an 8- by 10- by 2-inch baking pan. Cover with half of the milk cream. Sprinkle with half the cinnamon, chocolate, and nuts. Arrange another layer of cake over filling and top with remaining milk cream, cinnamon, chocolate, and nuts. Cover and refrigerate for at least 4 hours. Cut into squares and serve. Leftovers will keep refrigerated several days.

GARBANZO BEAN AND GORGONZOLA CHEESE SALAD
YIELD: 6 servings

1 small head romaine lettuce, torn
   into bite-size pieces
½ pound string beans, sliced and
   steamed until tender
2 cups cooked garbanzo beans
1 small red onion, sliced into very
   thin rings
½ cup yellow raisins
1 sweet red bell pepper, sliced
½ cup raw peas, or substitute 6
   artichoke hearts, sliced

½ cup peanut oil
2½ tablespoons red wine vinegar
1 teaspoon Dijon mustard
1 garlic clove, mashed
   A few drops lemon juice
⅛ teaspoon honey
¼ teaspoon basil
6 tablespoons crumbled
   Gorgonzola or Roquefort cheese
1 cup croutons

Combine in a salad bowl the romaine, string beans, garbanzo beans, red onion, raisins, red pepper, and peas or artichoke hearts. Place the oil, vinegar, mustard, garlic, lemon juice, honey, and basil in a jar and shake well. Toss salad ingredients with enough dressing to coat lightly. Sprinkle Gorgonzola or Roquefort cheese and croutons on top and serve immediately.

HONEY-SPICED PEARS

YIELD: 6 servings

2 cups dry red wine
¾ cup honey
2 tablespoons fresh lemon juice
2 cinnamon sticks
8 whole cloves

¼ teaspoon anise seed—optional
6 fresh Bartlett pears, cored and
halved
Chopped almonds or walnuts
Crushed mint—optional

In a large pot combine the wine, honey, lemon juice, cinnamon sticks, cloves, and anise. Reduce heat to low, add the pears, and simmer 10 minutes, turning fruit occasionally. Remove from heat and allow pears to cool in syrup. Lift pears from syrup with a slotted spoon and transfer to individual serving dishes, allowing 2 halves per dish. Spoon a little syrup over each pear and garnish with nuts and mint.
Variation: Top each half with a spoonful of whipped cream. Sugar may be substituted for the honey if desired.

ITALIAN DRESSING

YIELD: Approximately ¾ cup

2 tablespoons white or red wine
vinegar
1 garlic clove, crushed
½ teaspoon salt

¼ teaspoon freshly ground pepper
6 tablespoons olive oil (or part
peanut oil)
¼ cup freshly grated Parmesan
cheese

Beat the vinegar, garlic, salt, and pepper in a small bowl with a wire whisk. Add the oil and beat until creamy. Add the Parmesan cheese and blend well.

MARINARA SAUCE

YIELD: Approximately 3 quarts or 12 cups

2 bunches green onions with tops
2 tablespoons olive oil
½ pound fresh mushrooms
9 cups tomato sauce with tomato
bits
2 cups dry red wine

1 small jalapeño pepper, finely
chopped
10 to 15 pimiento olives, sliced
10 to 15 pitted black olives, sliced
4 bay leaves
½ teaspoon each: rosemary, thyme,
oregano, and garlic powder

Cut up the onions and tops into ¼-inch pieces. Sauté lightly in the oil. Quickly wash the mushrooms and pat dry. Cut into halves. Add to the onions and sauté 3 or 4 minutes. Transfer onions, mushrooms, and any pan juices to a 6-quart soup pot. Add the tomato sauce, wine, jalapeño pepper, green and black olives, and bay leaves. Crush the rosemary, thyme, and oregano with a pestle or spoon until finely pulverized. Add to the sauce with the garlic powder. Cover and cook on a low flame from 3 to 4 hours. Stir every 15 minutes to prevent sauce from sticking to the bottom of the pot. Mixture will be thick. Add a little more wine if a thinner consistency is preferred. Taste and adjust seasonings. Serve over any pasta. Leftovers may be poured into plastic quart containers and frozen.

MINESTRONE MILANESE

YIELD: Approximately 3 quarts or 12, 1-cup servings

¼ cup each: dried kidney beans and dried garbanzo beans
2½ quarts *Vegetable Broth* (p. 383)
2 tablespoons peanut oil
1 large onion, chopped
2 garlic cloves, finely chopped
2 leeks, chopped (white part only)
2 cups (1-pound can) Italian plum tomatoes
2 small potatoes, cubed with peels
1 zucchini, cut into thick slices
1 large carrot, cut into thick slices
1 cup string beans, trimmed and sliced

⅓ cup long-grain rice or macaroni shells*
1 bay leaf
½ teaspoon each: fennel seed, thyme, rosemary, and crushed red chili pepper
1 teaspoon marjoram, basil, or oregano
Salt and pepper to taste
1 cup shredded cabbage
1 cup fresh or frozen peas— optional
1 cup grated Parmesan cheese

1. Soak beans in 2 cups of water overnight. Or bring water to a boil, add beans, and boil 2 minutes. Remove from heat and let stand 1 hour. Drain off water and place in a large heavy pot with the vegetable broth. Bring to a boil, reduce heat, and simmer 45 minutes, adding more broth or water if necessary.

2. Heat oil in a saucepan. Sauté the onion, garlic, and leeks. Add the tomatoes and stir to break up. Add this to the beans along with the potatoes, zucchini, carrot, string beans, and rice. Bring to a boil and reduce heat to low. When boiling subsides, add the bay leaf, seasonings, salt, and pepper. Simmer 25 minutes. Add the cabbage and peas the last 10 minutes of cooking time; taste and adjust seasonings at this point. Stir in the Parmesan cheese just before serving. Leftovers may be frozen in plastic containers.

*Note: Macaroni shells should be added the last 10 minutes, along with the cabbage and peas.

MOUSSE ALLA RICOTTA

YIELD: 6 servings

½ pound ricotta cheese
½ cup honey or superfine sugar
½ cup ground carob or chocolate
    chips

1 cup whipping cream
2½ teaspoons finely grated orange
    peel
1 tablespoon orange or anise-
    flavored liqueur—optional

Cream together the cheese and honey. Fold in carob (you may grind it in a blender). Beat whipping cream with an electric beater or wire whisk until soft and fluffy. Fold into mixture along with orange peel and liqueur. Divide between 6 dessert bowls or stemmed glasses and chill at least 3 hours before serving.

MUSHROOM PAN PIZZA

YIELD: 8 slices

Crust:
⅔ cup warm water (110 degrees)
1 teaspoon sugar
1 package yeast
1 beaten egg
1 tablespoon each: olive and
    safflower oil
1 teaspoon each: Italian Seasoning
    and salt
¾ cup each: whole wheat and
    unbleached white flour
½ cup soy flour or unbleached white
    flour

Sauce:
1 teaspoon each: olive and
    safflower oil
1 garlic clove, pressed
¼ cup chopped onion
1 rib celery, diced
1 small carrot, thinly sliced
12 ounces tomato sauce (*Walnut
    Mushroom Sauce*, p. 233, may be
    substituted)
1 heaping tablespoon tomato paste
¼ teaspoon each: basil and dried
    oregano
⅛ teaspoon crushed rosemary

Topping:
1 to 2 tablespoons safflower oil or
    margarine
½ pound mushrooms, sliced
1 small onion, sliced into rings
½ pound grated mozzarella cheese
2 small tomatoes, sliced (preferably
    fresh pear-shaped tomatoes)
    Grated Parmesan cheese

1. *To prepare crust*: Combine warm water and sugar in a small bowl. Add the yeast and stir until dissolved. Let stand 5 minutes or until foamy. Pour into a large mixing bowl and combine with the beaten egg, oils, seasoning, and

salt. Add 1 cup of the flour and beat 100 strokes. Add remaining flour and stir to make a smooth dough. Knead for a few minutes on a floured board.

2. Shape dough into a ball and place it in a large bowl. Brush the surface with oil, cover bowl with a cloth, and let rise in a warm spot until doubled in bulk—about 1 hour.

3. Punch dough down and pat it into a well-greased pizza pan. Shape it as you would a pie crust with a thin bottom and thick, well-rounded sides. Brush the surface with oil and let rise in the pan for 20 minutes while assembling the sauce.

4. *To prepare sauce*: Put the 2 teaspoons oil in a large saucepan over medium heat. Sauté the garlic, onion, celery, and carrot. Add tomato sauce, paste, basil, oregano, and rosemary. Reduce heat and simmer about 10 minutes. Taste and adjust seasonings. Set aside.

5. Preheat oven to 400 degrees.

6. *To prepare topping*: Heat the 2 tablespoons of oil in a skillet. Sauté the mushrooms and onion rings. Set aside. Be sure cheese is grated and tomatoes are sliced.

7. *To assemble pizza*: Bake dough for 15 minutes. Remove from oven and spread sauce evenly across the surface. Spread mushrooms and onions over sauce. Cover with half of the grated cheese. Place sliced tomatoes over cheese and cover with remaining grated cheese. Top with Parmesan cheese. Return to oven until cheese melts—about 10 or 12 minutes.

POLLO ALLA CACCIATORA
(Chicken with Wine and Tomato Sauce)   *YIELD: 8 servings*

---

3 tablespoons olive oil
6 tablespoons safflower margarine or butter
2 chickens, cut up (3 pounds each)
2 large onions, finely chopped
1 large green pepper, finely chopped
3 garlic cloves, minced
1¼ teaspoons salt

½ teaspoon each: pepper, thyme, rosemary, and basil
4 cups Italian pear-shaped tomatoes, coarsely chopped (with juice)
3 tablespoons tomato paste
1 tablespoon wine vinegar
1 cup dry red wine
1 small jar pimiento olives— optional

Heat oil and margarine in a large skillet and sauté the chicken pieces until golden brown on both sides. Add the onions, green pepper, garlic, and seasonings. Cook until the onions are transparent. Transfer to a 5- or 6-quart Dutch oven. Add the Italian tomatoes, tomato paste, and vinegar. Bring to a boil, cover, and cook over low heat 30 minutes. Add the wine and simmer for 30 minutes more or until chicken is tender. Add the drained olives. Cook 2 or 3 minutes longer. Serve over rice or noodles.

POUND CAKE

YIELD: 2, 1-pound loaves or 24 slices

---

1 cup softened safflower margarine
  or sweet butter
2½ cups sugar
6 eggs
1 teaspoon almond extract
1 teaspoon lemon extract
1 teaspoon vanilla extract

2 teaspoons grated orange peel
3 cups cake flour
¼ teaspoon baking soda
½ teaspoon salt
1 cup plain yogurt
½ cup orange juice or almond-
  flavored liqueur

1. Preheat oven to 325 degrees.
2. In large bowl of mixer, cream together margarine or butter and sugar until lemony in color and fluffy. Add eggs one at a time, beating well after each addition. Add the extracts and orange peel.
3. Sift the flour, baking soda, and salt together. Alternately add the dry ingredients with the yogurt and orange juice (or the liqueur) into the batter. Blend thoroughly. Pour into 2, well-greased 9- by 5-inch loaf pans.
4. Bake for 1 hour or until cakes test done. Cool 10 to 15 minutes. Turn out on a cake rack to finish cooling. It is best to let pound cake stand 24 hours before slicing.

RIGATONI WITH CAULIFLOWER

YIELD: 6 servings

---

1 small head cauliflower
12 ounces whole wheat rigatoni or
  large macaroni noodles
4 tablespoons safflower margarine
  or butter, melted
2 to 3 large garlic cloves, pressed

½ teaspoon freshly grated nutmeg
2 tablespoons fresh, or 2 teaspoons
  dried, basil
1 cup half-and-half or heavy cream
½ cup grated Parmesan cheese
½ cup chopped parsley

1. Remove stalk from cauliflower and discard. Break into flowerets and steam in salted water until tender, but firm. Drain in a colander and rinse with cold water to stop the cooking process. Set aside.
2. Cook rigatoni in 4 to 6 quarts of boiling salted water until *al dente* (tender but firm). Drain in a colander.
3. In a large saucepan, combine all the ingredients except the parsley. Bring to a quick boil, reduce heat to low, and simmer about 5 minutes or until sauce begins to thicken. Transfer to a serving dish and garnish with parsley. Serve immediately.
Variation: Replace cauliflower with broccoli or use a combination of both.

SALATA DI MICHAEL REEDY
(Italian Salad Supreme)   *YIELD: 6 servings*

Salad:

1 head iceberg or romaine lettuce,
washed, drained, and patted dry
½ Bermuda onion, thinly sliced into
rings
6 ounces marinated artichoke
hearts, drained

6 hearts of palm—optional
4 ounces chopped pimientos, or 1
tomato, sliced
Italian Dressing (p. 226)

Remove outer leaves from lettuce using only the firm part of the head. Break into bite-size pieces. Put into a salad bowl. Cut onion rings and artichoke hearts into quarters. Arrange over lettuce. Slice hearts of palm into ¼-inch pieces. Combine with pimientos or tomato and add to salad. Toss lightly with *Italian Dressing*.

SPINACH FRITTATA
                                  YIELD: 9 pancakes or frittatas

½ pound fresh spinach
5 large eggs
2 to 4 large garlic cloves, pressed
¼ cup seasoned breadcrumbs

¼ cup grated Parmesan cheese
½ teaspoon salt (or to taste)
⅛ teaspoon pepper (or to taste)
3 tablespoons peanut or safflower
oil for frying

1. Wash spinach well and remove the stems. Cook in a small amount of boiling water or steam in a vegetable steamer until tender. Drain in a colander and cool. Squeeze out any excess moisture and chop leaves finely.
2. In a large bowl, beat the eggs well. Stir in the spinach, garlic, breadcrumbs, cheese, salt, and pepper. Mix together; taste and adjust seasonings. Mixture should have a distinct garlic flavor—add more if necessary.
3. Heat oil in a large heavy skillet. Drop ¼ cup of the mixture for each pancake into hot oil. Brown lightly. Turn and cook until the second side is brown and pancakes are puffy. Repeat process until all the batter is used, adding oil as necessary to prevent sticking. Serve *frittatas* as soon as they come out of the skillet or place them in a warm oven until ready to serve.

TONY'S ITALIAN POTATOES

YIELD: 4 servings

1½ pounds small new potatoes
1½ tablespoons peanut oil
1½ tablespoons olive oil
  1 large onion, thinly sliced

Salt to taste
Freshly ground pepper to taste
12 black Italian olives

1. Boil potatoes, unpeeled, until tender but not bursting. Drain. Peel and slice into ⅛-inch rounds.
2. Heat peanut and olive oil in a large heavy skillet. Add potatoes. Sauté until brown on both sides. Add onion and sauté until tender. Season to taste with salt and pepper. Sprinkle olives, cut into segments, over potatoes. Heat and serve.
Variation: For potatoes with a heavier garlic flavor, press 2 or 3 garlic cloves into the hot oil before adding the potatoes.

TONY'S TOMATO AND ANCHOVY SALAD

YIELD: 4 servings

Salad:
  4 firm ripe tomatoes, stemmed
12 thin slices red onion, separated
    into rings
  8 anchovy fillets
  4 teaspoons finely chopped shallots
  4 teaspoons coarsely chopped
    parsley
    Salt
    Freshly ground black pepper
    Dried oregano

Oil and Vinegar Dressing:
  3 tablespoons red wine vinegar
  1 garlic clove, mashed
  ½ teaspoon salt
  ¼ teaspoon pepper
  9 tablespoons light Italian olive oil

1. Cut each tomato into 5 slices. Arrange 5 slices on each of 4 salad plates in an overlapping row or circle. Top each with slices of red onion and 2 anchovy fillets. Sprinkle 1 teaspoon shallots and 1 teaspoon chopped parsley over each portion. Sprinkle each with salt, a few turns of the pepper mill, and a good pinch or two of oregano.
2. Combine all ingredients for the dressing in a screw-top jar. Shake vigorously until well blended. Spoon enough dressing over each salad to coat well—approximately 3 tablespoons.

WALNUT MUSHROOM LASAGNE

YIELD: 9 servings

Walnut Mushroom Sauce:
1 large onion, chopped
   Safflower oil for sautéing
2 garlic cloves, pressed
1 large green pepper, seeded and
   chopped
1 pound mushrooms, sliced
½ pound walnuts, chopped
1 large can tomato paste
1 large (No. 2½) can pear-shaped
   tomatoes, chopped with juice
2 teaspoons dried oregano
2 teaspoons Italian Seasoning
   Salt and pepper to taste

Lasagne:
1½ pounds low-fat ricotta cheese
1 egg, beaten
16 ounces whole wheat or spinach
   lasagne noodles
12 ounces mozzarella cheese
   Parmesan cheese, grated

1. *To prepare sauce*: In a large pot, brown the onion in oil. Remove with a slotted spoon and set aside. Sauté garlic, green pepper, mushrooms, and walnuts and set aside with onion. Place tomato paste in pot and stir until slightly browned. Add pear-shaped tomatoes with juice and the onion-walnut mixture. Add seasonings and simmer 30 minutes. Taste and adjust seasonings.

2. *To prepare noodles*: Mix ricotta cheese with egg and set aside. Boil lasagne noodles in 6 quarts of water with 2 teaspoons of salt. When noodles are just tender, remove from burner. Leave them in the hot water and they will stay flexible while assembling the casserole.

3. Preheat oven to 350 degrees.

4. *To assemble lasagne*: On the bottom of a 9- by 13-inch oblong pan, put a ladleful of sauce. Then add a layer of noodles. Cover with ⅓ of the ricotta cheese. Cut mozzarella cheese into slices. Layer on top of the ricotta, then cover with a layer of sauce. Repeat process until casserole is full, ending with the sauce on top. Sprinkle lightly with grated Parmesan cheese.

5. Bake in a preheated oven 35 or 45 minutes or until casserole is browned and bubbling and sauce is not runny. Cut into squares and serve hot.

WHEAT SOY FETTUCINE NOODLES

YIELD: Approximately ¾ pound of noodles or 4 servings

3 large egg yolks
1 large egg
2 tablespoons water
1 teaspoon safflower oil

½ teaspoon salt
½ cup unbleached white flour
1 cup whole wheat flour
¼ cup soy flour

1. Combine together the egg yolks, whole egg, water, oil, and salt. Place the unbleached white flour, ¾ cup of the whole wheat flour, and the soy flour in a large mixing bowl. Stir to blend the flours. Make a well in the center of the flour and pour in the egg mixture. Stir with a fork until all the flour is moist. Shape into a ball. Sprinkle remaining ¼ cup whole wheat flour on a board and knead dough until smooth. Add more flour if too sticky, but do so sparingly. Wrap dough in plastic and chill 1 hour.

2. Divide dough into 4 equal pieces. With a rolling pin, roll each piece as thinly as possible. Trim ends to make a uniform rectangle. Repeat with remaining portions. Roll each strip up like a jelly roll. With a sharp knife, cut strips into ¼-inch pieces. Unroll each strip and lay out on floured waxed paper for about 30 minutes. Wrap noodles in plastic and refrigerate until ready to use.

3. *To cook noodles*: Drop noodles into 4 quarts of boiling salted water. Fresh noodles will cook in just a few minutes. Drain and toss with *Marinara Sauce* (p. 226), *Walnut Mushroom Sauce* (p. 233), or your favorite sauce. If you don't want to use any sauce at all, combine noodles with sautéed vegetables and top with freshly grated Parmesan cheese.

ZUCCHINI AL LIMONE
(Zucchini with Lemon)   *YIELD: 4 servings*

---

2 large firm zucchini	Juice of ½ lemon
¼ cup water	½ teaspoon salt
4 tablespoons safflower margarine, cut into pieces	¼ teaspoon freshly ground white pepper

1. Wash and slice unpeeled zucchini into ¼-inch rounds. Place in a heavy saucepan with the water. Bring to a boil. Reduce heat to simmer, cover, and cook until zucchini is opaque. Do not overcook.

2. Turn off burner. Remove pot from heat and drain off any remaining liquid. Dot zucchini with margarine. Sprinkle with lemon juice and seasonings. Return the still warm water. Cover and let stand for 5 minutes before serving.

Variation: Use 1 pound of fresh asparagus in place of the zucchini.

ITALY/RECIPE ANALYSIS CHART

Name of Recipe	Quantity	Calories	CHO gms.	Protein gms.	Total Fat gms.	Saturated Fat gms.	Cholesterol mg.	Dietary Fiber gms.
1. Marinara Sauce	per cup	100	13 (52%)	3 (12%)	4 (36%)	—	—	1.0
2. Spinach *Frittata*	each	126	3 (10%)	6 (19%)	10 (71%)	3 (21%)	175	.2
3. *Zucchini al Limone*	per serving	131	6 (18%)	2 (6%)	11 (76%)	2 (14%)	—	1.0
4. Antipasto Supreme	per serving	144	12 (34%)	6 (16%)	8 (50%)	2 (12%)	—	3.6
5. Minestrone Milanese	per 1-cup serving	177	22 (50%)	11 (25%)	5 (25%)	1 (5%)	1	1.0
6. Apple Spinach Salad with Sweet and Sour Dressing	per serving	186	13 (28%)	2 (5%)	14 (67%)	1 (5%)	—	1.0
7. Pound Cake	per slice	189	23 (49%)	4 (8%)	9 (43%)	3 (14%)	55	.1
8. Broccoli Pignolia with Raisins	per serving	219	21 (40%)	9 (16%)	11 (44%)	1 (4%)	—	1.0
9. *Salata di Michael Reedy* (Italian Salad Supreme)	per serving	219	7 (13%)	5 (9%)	19 (78%)	4 (16%)	1	1.5
10. Honey-Spiced Pears	per serving	245	38 (62%)	3 (5%)	9 (33%)	—	—	3.0
11. *Mousse Alla Ricotta*	per serving	274	34 (50%)	5 (8%)	13 (42%)	5 (16%)	60	.02
12. *Tony's Italian Potatoes*	per serving	284	27 (38%)	4 (6%)	18 (56%)	3 (10%)	—	1.3
13. *Cassata Alla Siciliana*	per serving	320	29 (36%)	8 (10%)	19 (54%)	7 (20%)	72	.1
14. Wheat Soy Fettucine Noodles	per serving	326	34 (42%)	22 (26%)	14 (32%)	3 (8%)	225	1.0
15. Asparagus *Frittata*	per serving	341	5 (6%)	33 (39%)	21 (55%)	8 (21%)	360	.1

Name of Recipe	Quantity	Calories	CHO gms.	Protein gms.	Total Fat gms.	Saturated Fat gms.	Choles- terol mg.	Dietary Fiber gms.
16. *Tony's* Tomato and An- chovy Salad	per serving	354	16 (18%)	5 (6%)	30 (76%)	3 (8%)	—	1.2
17. Mushroom Pan Pizza	per slice	367	22 (24%)	36 (40%)	15 (26%)	5 (11%)	2	1.1
18. Rigatoni with Cauliflower	per serving	417	49 (46%)	17 (16%)	17 (38%)	4 (9%)	20	1.0
19. Garbanzo Bean and Gorgonzola Cheese Salad	per serving	431	46 (43%)	10 (9%)	23 (48%)	4 (8%)	—	2.5
20. *Pollo Alla Cacciatora*	per serving	445	10 (9%)	45 (40%)	25 (51%)	7 (14%)	275	.9
21. Walnut Mushroom Lasagne	per serving	639	50 (32%)	31 (20%)	35 (48%)	8 (11%)	28	2.0

Numbers in parentheses (%) indicate percentage of total calories contributed by nutrient.

MENUS
LOW CALORIE SPECIALTIES
(500 to 700 calories per meal)

MINESTRONE MILANESE
TONY'S ITALIAN POTATOES
**APPLE SPINACH SALAD WITH
SWEET AND SOUR DRESSING**
Hot Mint Tea

SPINACH FRITTATA
**GARBANZO BEAN AND
GORGONZOLA CHEESE SALAD**
Cantaloupe with Wedge of Lime
Hot Espresso

ANTIPASTO SUPREME
BROCCOLI PIGNOLIA WITH RAISINS
Herbed Rice
Broiled Tomato Slices with Fresh Basil
Sliced Tangelos
Hot Anise Tea

●

LOW CHOLESTEROL MENUS
(Less than 50 mgs. of cholesterol per meal)

MUSHROOM PAN PIZZA
**SALATA DI MICHAEL REEDY
(ITALIAN SALAD SUPREME)**
Crenshaw Melon
Chilled Apple Cider

**TONY'S TOMATO AND ANCHOVY
SALAD**
Boiled Artichokes
TONY'S ITALIAN POTATOES
Fresh Raspberries and Apricots

Fresh Garden Salad with Vinaigrette
ZUCCHINI AL LIMONE
WALNUT-MUSHROOM LASAGNE
HONEY-SPICED PEARS
Iced Coffee with Cinnamon Sticks

●

LOW SATURATED FAT SELECTIONS
(Less than 8 grams of saturated fat per meal)

Pickled Peppers
MINESTRONE MILANESE
**APPLE SPINACH SALAD WITH
SWEET AND SOUR DRESSING**
Plain Bread Sticks
MOUSSE ALLA RICOTTA

**WHEAT SOY FETTUCINE
NOODLES with
MARINARA SAUCE**
**BROCCOLI PIGNOLIA WITH
RAISINS**
Persian Melon and Figs
Iced Tea with Lemon

TONY'S TOMATO AND ANCHOVY SALAD
RIGATONI WITH CAULIFLOWER
Sliced Green Pepper Rings
Red Grapes and Apricots
Italian Wine

HIGH PROTEIN MEALS
(30 or more grams of protein per meal)

WALNUT-MUSHROOM LASAGNE
Fresh Fennel Salad with Vinaigrette
Sliced Plums and Peaches
Italian Wine

Sliced Tomato and Garbanzo Bean
Salad
ASPARAGUS FRITTATA
ZUCCHINI AL LIMONE
CASSATA ALLA SICILIANA
Iced Espresso

POLLO ALLA CACCIATORA
SALATA DI MICHAEL REEDY (ITALIAN SALAD SUPREME)
Spumoni
Hot Tea with Lemon

●

WELL BALANCED LUNCH OR DINNER MENUS
(Selections that conform to recommendations in Dietary Goals for United States*)*

MINESTRONE MILANESE
WHEAT-SOY FETTUCINE
NOODLES with
MARINARA SAUCE
HONEY-SPICED PEARS
Hot Anise Tea

Sesame Bread Sticks
ANTIPASTO SUPREME
RIGATONI WITH CAULIFLOWER
Sliced Pears and Strawberries
Chilled Apple Juice

MUSHROOM PAN PIZZA
Fresh Green Salad with Vinaigrette
Casaba Melon with Wedge of Lemon
Red Wine

CHAPTER 10

LEBANON
Open Sesame!

Culinary Essentials

If you have an adventurous palate, you will enjoy the unusual contrast of tastes offered by the Lebanese cuisine. The Turkish influence on this cooking style encourages the interplay of dissimilar flavors—sweet mint is set against tangy yogurt; nutty *tahini* complements fruity olive oil; and plain chick-peas are a perfect foil for potent garlic. Lebanese food is well spiced but not hot, and lemon juice is vital to its stimulating character.

Don't let exotic names like fava beans, *tahini*,* or bulgur alarm you. These items are adaptable, moderately priced, and easy to find at Middle East, Greek, or specialty food stores, as well as many large supermarkets. Fava beans can be tossed with lemon juice, minced garlic, and parsley for a simple salad or savored in a spicy dip called *Ful Moudammas*. You can add these dark brown legumes to soups, stuffed vegetables, or bean patties; once addicted to their meaty flavor, you'll always want a supply on hand. Also known as broad beans, fava beans are available canned or dried; garbanzo beans (chick-peas) may be substituted if necessary.

Tahini, a nutty-flavored paste made from sesame seeds, is worth discovering. Although this beige-colored spread is of the same consistency as peanut butter, its role in the Lebanese kitchen goes way beyond that of a sandwich filling. You can stir *tahini* into puréed garbanzo beans to make a mellow dip called *Hummous B'Tahini*. When *tahini* is mashed with garlic and thinned with lemon juice, it becomes *Tahini Sauce*, a versatile topping that can dress steamed vegetables, baked fish, or tossed salads. You will

---

*See Seasoning Chart *in this chapter.*

find *Tahini Sauce* an exciting alternative to a cheese sauce for general cooking purposes.

Bulgur, or cracked wheat, is a mainstay of the Lebanese table. You can fashion an interesting side dish from this crunchy grain by preparing it exactly as you would white rice. To make wheat pilaf, a popular accompaniment for Arabic entrées, boil bulgur in broth (instead of water) and mix with sautéed onions, mushrooms, and herbs. Salad devotees will want to try *Taboulee*, a refreshing blend of (soaked) bulgur, tomatoes, mint, cucumbers, and radishes. Or, sample this versatile ingredient in *Potato Kibbe*, a mock lamb loaf enhanced with walnuts, onions, and cinnamon.

Once your kitchen is stocked with staples, you need only a few basic kitchen tools to prepare a plethora of delicious recipes. A blender or food processor is essential for smooth-textured dips made from beans or *tahini*. Colorful bowls or platters are useful for enhancing the presentation of these superb-tasting, but bland-colored purées. Since fresh lemon juice is used frequently, an inexpensive hand juicer is a worthwhile investment.

A Lebanese feast is exciting from the first bite of *mezza*, a variety of small-portioned appetizers that can turn a simple meal into a feast of prodigal proportions. This array of creamy spreads and pick-up foods is perfect for experiencing the variety of Lebanese flavors, which range from tart to sweet to biting.

If you're planning a full-course Lebanese dinner, limit the *mezza* to a few simple items like *feta* cheese, Greek olives, and *Hummous B'Tahini*. For a more elaborate selection, you might include several sauces or dips made from fava beans, mashed eggplant, or *tahini*; hot pita bread and raw vegetables should accompany these spicy purées. Salads are as popular as *mezza*, as are savory pastries such as *Sabanikh*, an allspice-perfumed spinach pie. Nuts, cucumber sticks, tomato wedges, and plain yogurt are also favored inclusions. Depending upon how many items you wish to serve, *mezza* can be a complete dinner.

Arabic bread, also known as pita or pocket bread, occupies an important position in the Lebanese cuisine. When sliced in half, this slightly puffed round has a pocket that somewhat resembles a soft taco shell. It can be made at home (see *Whole Wheat Arabic Bread*) or purchased ready-made at Middle East or Greek stores and many supermarkets. You can make a delectable Mideast sandwich by stuffing pita with crumbled *Potato Kibbe*, *Taboulee Salad*, sliced avocados, or fried bean patties (*felafel*). Customarily, Arabic bread is used to scoop up Lebanese food instead of a knife and fork. If you have ever tried to master the art of eating with chopsticks, you will find this method just as challenging!

To end a meal in true Lebanese fashion, serve a strong brew of black coffee in demitasse cups; pass around a pitcher of orange blossom water,*

---

*See Seasoning Chart *in this chapter.*

and let everyone put a few drops in their cups. Accompany this with a platter of pistachio nuts, dried apricots, and sticky dates. Could Ali Baba have had it any better?

Seasoning Essentials

The Lebanese cuisine is unique in that it does not rely upon dairy products to enhance the flavor of its dishes. Adventures with Lebanese cooking will enable you to transform bland ingredients, such as eggplant or beans, into exotic creations without the aid of cheese, eggs, or cream. This culinary feat is performed with an amalgam of seasonings, *tahini*, and lemon juice.

The intriguing flavor that characterizes many Lebanese dishes is derived from a blend of *tahini* (sesame seed paste), lemon juice, and garlic. You can use this combination to season puréed garbanzo beans, mashed eggplant, plain yogurt, or broiled fish. Unite this illustrious trio with parsley and you have *Tahini Sauce*, a fantastic dip for hot or cold vegetables and pita bread.

Whenever a recipe calls for garlic, feel free to adjust its proportion according to your tastebuds. For example, if you are a bona fide garlic lover, add it to your heart's delight. Conversely, those who find this pungent herb less than enchanting can either scale down the quantity called for or eliminate it altogether. When you want a sauce or dip that is neither bland nor garlic-flavored, add a pinch of potent herbs such as cumin or coriander; cayenne pepper or Tabasco sauce in small amounts will also provide piquancy.

Lemon juice is celebrated in many Lebanese dishes because of its amazing ability to unify flavors. Soups made with lentils and Swiss chard can be greatly enhanced if the juice of several lemons is added just before serving. Vegetable dishes prepared with spinach, eggplant, or squash will also benefit from a good dose of this tangy citrus fruit. Don't be timid—when used lavishly, lemon juice will make a dish shine.

Another unique feature of this Arabic kitchen is the special treatment of allspice and cinnamon. Many countries restrict the use of these aromatic spices to pastry dough and baked goods. In Lebanon, however, these distinguished spices lend personality to entrées, salads, and side dishes. You can be assured success by adding a good pinch of allspice or cinnamon to spinach pies, cracked-wheat salads, rice pilaf, or *kibbe*.

Mint also plays an important role in seasoning Lebanese foods. Cherished for its lovely fragrance and seductively sweet flavor, this herb is used in a myriad of Lebanese dishes. When added to *Eggplant Salad Bulus* or *Fatouch* (Bread Salad), it tames the powerful taste of onions and parsley. It will temper the tang of plain yogurt or complement the coolness of a cucumber. In the event that you have "out-garlicked" yourself during a meal, fresh mint leaves may save your social grace; they provide one of the best breath fresheners known.

LEBANESE SEASONING CHART

ALLSPICE resembles a mixture of cloves, cinnamon, and nutmeg with cloves being the dominant flavor. This fragrant spice is responsible for the subtly sweet undertone that characterizes many Lebanese dishes. A good pinch will impart an interesting flavor to farinaceous, bean, or cracked-wheat dishes. It will give an agreeable flavor to stuffed grape leaves, puddings, *taboulee* salad, and spinach. In general, allspice can be added sparingly to highly seasoned dishes or added in moderate amounts to bland foods. When unavailable, substitute equal proportions of ground cloves, cinnamon, and nutmeg.

BASIL can be used arbitrarily to accent the flavor of dishes employing tomatoes, lentils, potatoes, eggplants, or cracked wheat. You can unleash basil's pungent quality by using it in the presence of garlic and lemon juice. This delicate herb also harmonizes well with mint.

CINNAMON is favored in a variety of entrées including stuffed squash, potato *kibbe*, rice pilaf, and stuffed grape leaves. In small amounts, ground cinnamon will add a soft fragrance and spicy quality to a tomato sauce, vegetable or bean soup, omelet, or cracked-wheat dish. When combined with cayenne pepper, it is perfect for enlivening eggs, yogurt, potatoes, or tomatoes. Add a cinnamon stick when simmering your favorite Lebanese vegetable for a surprisingly good taste.

CUMIN is a great culinary herb with a distinctive and powerful taste. It combines especially well with ground coriander and is mostly used in dishes using beans or legumes. In general, 1 teaspoon of ground cumin seed is sufficient to season 2 cups of beans. A few drops of Tabasco sauce or a good pinch of cayenne pepper will help intensify the sharpness of this penetrating herb.

GARLIC seems to crop up in every type of Lebanese preparation except desserts and baked goods. This pungent seasoning is used liberally to season soups, sauces, dips, savory pastries, and seafood. It is not unusual to find a dish flavored with nothing more than garlic, lemon juice, salt, and pepper. In general, 1 pound of vegetables or beans will use 2 to 4 cloves of fresh garlic.

LEBANESE HERB BLEND is an all-purpose seasoner for vegetables, salads, and soups. About 1 teaspoon should be sufficient to flavor a dish that will serve four persons.

Combine and store in an airtight container:

⅓ cup freshly dried parsley
¼ cup sesame seeds
1 tablespoon garlic salt
1½ teaspoons dried mint
1 teaspoon each: allspice and cayenne pepper

LEMON JUICE has an affinity with most Lebanese vegetable and bean dishes. A squeeze of this tangy citrus fruit goes into everything from appetizers to desserts. To put a finishing touch on soups, rice pilaf, spinach, or lentils, add lemon juice to taste just before serving. Salad dressings in this cuisine have a distinct lemony flavor—proportions are usually 2 parts lemon juice to 1 part olive or peanut oil. Dips such as *hummous b'tahini* and *tahini* sauce can use as much as ½ cup of lemon juice. One lemon yields 3 to 4 tablespoons or ¼ cup juice, plus 2 teaspoons grated rind.

MINT adds a lovely scent and refreshing taste to salads, feta cheese dishes, and stuffed vegetables. It is often used in combination with mashed garlic and salt to flavor yogurt-based salads and sauces; proportions are usually 1 tablespoon dried or 3 tablespoons finely chopped fresh mint to 2 cups of yogurt. Mint is almost always added to Lebanese salads made with tomatoes, cucumbers, cracked wheat, or bread. Do not be deceived by the gentle nature of mint. Its flavor is quite distinctive and noticeable. If you are not overly fond of this herb, either omit it or decrease the amount by half in any recipe.

ORANGE BLOSSOM WATER is a fragrant liquid made from distilled orange blossom petals. Lebanese cooks use it the same way American cooks use vanilla extract—to perfume desserts, baked goods, and occasionally, fruit salads. A few drops in a cup of mint tea or black coffee is delightful. Orange blossom water is available at Greek or Middle Eastern groceries, delicatessens, and some supermarkets.

SAMNEH is also called clarified butter, which means that all the impurities have been removed. It has a stronger flavor than regular butter, and therefore, can be used in smaller amounts. Because the impurities have been removed, clarified butter does not burn easily which makes it excellent for sautéing. Safflower margarine, vegetable oil, or unclarified butter may be substituted.

To prepare: Place 1 stick of unsalted butter or safflower margarine in a saucepan over low heat. Simmer 5 to 10 minutes. Remove from heat, skim off top foam and discard. Strain through a cheesecloth-lined strainer into a clean container. Discard any milky residue that remains in the pan. *Samneh* or clarified butter will keep several weeks without refrigeration.

TAHINI is made from ground sesame seeds and has the same consistency as peanut butter. It is frequently added to dips and sauces and is responsible for the nutty flavor that characterizes many Lebanese dishes. *Tahini* combines well with garlic—you can use 2 or 3 cloves of fresh garlic in any sauce or dip that calls for ½ cup *tahini*. An unusual dip for Arabic bread can be made by combining 2 tablespoons *tahini* with ½ cup carob syrup (available at health food stores). Look for this delicious sesame seed paste at Middle Eastern groceries, delicatessens, or specialty food shops. Stir in any oil that has risen to the top before using. To make your own *tahini*, stir 6 tablespoons sesame seed or peanut oil into 1 cup ground and toasted unhulled sesame seeds until it takes on the consistency of peanut butter. Add salt to taste and store, covered, in the refrigerator.

ZA'ATAR is a hybrid of oregano and marjoram that grows wild on the Mediterranean shores. It is available dried at many Middle Eastern markets and some spice shops. You can sprinkle *za'atar* over plain yogurt or *labna* (yogurt cheese) as a unique and tasty garnish. To make an excellent dip for Arabic bread, place ½ cup *za'atar* in a bowl and add enough olive or peanut oil to make a sauce that is thinner than a paste, but not runny. Serve with olives.

Other seasonings found in Lebanese cooking: coriander, cayenne pepper, cloves, ginger, saffron, paprika, parsley, turmeric, and marjoram.

Nutritional Essentials

The culinary creations of the Lebanese cuisine are, on the average, lower in saturated fats and calories than selections from most other ethnic diets. By virtually eliminating cheese, eggs, and high-fat dairy products and relying more upon beans, seeds, and low-fat yogurt as protein sources, this Arabic kitchen is able to offer a well-balanced diet which is (1) high in dietary fiber, (2) adequate in protein, and (3) low in total fat and cholesterol. In addition, the fat composition of this diet is over 90 percent polyunsaturated.

From a nutritional point of view, meatless Lebanese cooking has something specific to recommend for individuals who need to moderate their cholesterol and saturated fat intake. Many of these recipes will also be helpful for diabetics and overweight individuals, as well as others who wish to explore innovative low-calorie substitutions for their diet. Generally speaking, the selections from this cuisine will guarantee a fiber, protein, and nutrient intake which can, at the very least, maintain good health and possibly prevent heart disease.

Because this cooking style rarely employs high biologic value foods such as eggs, cheese, and milk, your essential protein intake will be derived largely from food combinations and meals which employ the concept of mutual amino acid supplementation or "protein complementation." In this and other vegetarian diets, in which essential amino acids are derived predominantly from a plant- (rather than dairy-) centered diet, attention to this facet of protein nutrition becomes relatively more important. As we introduce you to the eclectic food items of the Lebanese kitchen, try to make note of those combinations which are able to furnish balanced protein.

Complementary protein combinations which you will use in this cuisine include (1) bean and sesame seed, (2) wheat and sesame seed, and (3) bean and wheat. Lentils, garbanzo beans (chick-peas), and fava beans (similar to lima beans) are the most popular legumes. Unfortunately, they are among the poorer sources of usable protein within the bean group, being relatively deficient in the amino acids tryptophan and methionine, but rich in lysine and isoleucine. However, you can increase the protein potential of legume-centered recipes such as *Lentil Lemon Soup*, *Adeece Howeed* (lentils with spinach), and *Stuffed Acorn Squash* by serving them along with recipes containing sesame seeds, such as *Cauliflower with Tahini Sauce* and *Hummous B'Tahini*. What makes these recipe combinations nutritionally favorable is the fact that sesame seeds, unlike lentils and beans, are deficient in lysine and isoleucine, but rich in tryptophan and methionine.

A legume-oriented diet such as this one has the advantage of being very low in saturated fat. In addition, the liberal use of sesame seeds and safflower oil (which may be substituted for olive oil) will provide a significant amount of polyunsaturated fat. Many of our Lebanese recipes contain less than 1 percent saturated fat, which means they can be freely incorporated into any diet, even one that is restricted in fat and cholesterol intake.

Versatile and nutritious sesame seeds play a central role in this Mideast kitchen. They can be sprinkled over a cracked wheat or eggplant salad, used in desserts, or ground into *tahini*, a versatile paste reminiscent of peanut butter. As mentioned earlier, sesame seeds are lacking two of the essential amino acids, but when complemented with wheat or beans, they constitute an excellent source of usable protein.

Tahini contains significantly more fiber, calcium, phosphorus, thiamine, riboflavin, and iron when it is made from unhulled, rather than hulled, sesame seeds. In fact, unhulled sesame seeds are one of the richest sources of dietary fiber, containing 6.3 grams per 3.5 ounce serving. With respect to fat composition, *tahini* has a high polyunsaturated to saturated fat ratio. For these reasons, sesame seed butter is preferable to some of the other nut butters, such as peanut, which are lower in polyunsaturates and slightly higher in saturated fat content.

Carob powder, also called St. John's Bread, is a highly nutritious addition to the *Carob Date Loaf*. For all its virtues, carob is an untapped food source in most diets. This wonderful chocolate substitute, native to the Mediterranean coast, is one of the only confectionary items that can boast both a low calorie content as well as a nutritive value equivalent to that of many whole grain products.

The carbohydrate content of carob powder is about 50 percent. It contains as much thiamine as asparagus or strawberries, the same amount of niacin as lentils, and more vitamin A than eggplant, just to mention a few of its nutritional assets. Compared to chocolate or cocoa, carob has less than half the calories and more than twice the amount of calcium. As far as fat content is concerned, cocoa and chocolate are extremely high (about 50 percent) while carob is almost fat-free, which makes it an ideal flavoring for those on restricted diets.

Because carob has natural sweetening abilities, you can reduce the recommended amount of honey or sugar in most dessert recipes by 25 percent if you substitute carob for cocoa or unsweetened chocolate. For these reasons, try to incorporate this food into your cooking endeavors. As a rule, you may use it as a direct replacement for cocoa in equal proportions. Three tablespoons of carob powder, plus 1 tablespoon of water, can also replace one square of unsweetened chocolate.

The Lebanese kitchen offers an exciting selection of healthful recipes. Familiarity with some of the more unusual foods and methods of preparation used in this cuisine will surely expand your culinary and nutritional horizons. Learn especially to exploit the dietary benefits of sesame seeds, fava beans, garbanzo beans, carob powder, and bulgur.

In general, these selections are adequate, but not as high in protein as diets which rely more upon dairy products for cooking purposes. As a result, complementation of essential amino acids is important and necessary to furnish high-grade protein. The principal advantage of Lebanese recipes is that they are low in total and saturated fat, low in calories, and high in fiber. Many medical experts believe, as we do, that this type of diet may prevent atherosclerosis, certain cancers, and other diseases thought to be associated with high-fat, low-fiber Western diets.

A word of caution is in order concerning the use of fava beans by a very small group of individuals, usually of Mediterranean descent, who have a genetically determined enzyme deficiency of Glucose-6-Phosphate-dehydrogenase (G-6-P-D). A minority of people with this rare defect are exquisitely sensitive to fava beans and are subject to serious hemolytic crises. Individuals with this disorder must be certain to avoid this food at all costs.

ADEECE HOWEED
(Lentils with Spinach)   *YIELD: 6 servings*

---

2 tablespoons sesame or safflower
  oil
1 small onion, minced
3 cups water
1 cup uncooked lentils
1 large potato, cubed
2 small yellow squash, cubed

⅛ teaspoon each: allspice and cloves
2½ teaspoons salt
1 pound spinach, washed,
  stemmed, and torn into bite-size
  pieces
Juice of 1½ lemons

1. Heat the oil in a small skillet. Add the onion and sauté until browned. Set aside. Place the water and lentils in a 2½-quart saucepan. Bring to a boil, reduce heat to low, and simmer 40 minutes.
2. Add the potato and simmer until almost tender. Add the squash, sautéed onion, and seasonings. Simmer until squash is tender, but still firm. Taste and adjust seasonings. Add spinach and lemon juice. Simmer 2 minutes or until spinach wilts. Serve immediately as a side dish.

BAQLAWA
(Layered Nut-filled Pastry)   *YIELD: Approximately 30, 2-inch pieces*

Filling:
1½ pounds walnuts, coarsely ground
1½ cups sugar
  1 tablespoon orange blossom
    water*
  1 tablespoon rose water*

Pastry:
  1 pound safflower margarine or
    unsalted butter
  1 pound filo dough* (if frozen,
    thaw 48 hours in the refrigerator
    before using)

Orange-Rose Flower Syrup:
  2 cups sugar
  1 cup water
  1 tablespoon orange blossom
    water**
  1 tablespoon rose water
    Juice of ½ lemon

  Available at Greek or Middle Eastern grocery stores.
**See Seasoning Chart.*

1. Thoroughly combine ingredients for filling and set aside.
2. Melt the margarine or butter in a saucepan over low heat.
3. *To assemble baqlawa:* Remove filo dough from box and keep covered at all times with a damp cloth to prevent leaves from drying. Place a sheet of filo in a well-buttered 10- by 14-inch pan. With a soft pastry brush, paint the filo with the melted margarine or butter and coat well. Repeat process until you have 6 layers. Cover with half of the filling.

4. Add another 6 layers of filo, brushing each one thoroughly with the melted margarine or butter. (Don't worry if dough tears occasionally). Cover with remaining filling. Add final 8 layers of dough, repeating process. Tuck under any loose ends around the edges like a pie crust.

5. Preheat oven to 300 degrees.

6. With a sharp knife, cut the pastry diagonally into 2- or 3-inch diamond shapes, penetrating only as far as the bottom layer of nuts. Bake until golden brown—about 45 minutes. Remove from oven and let stand until cool.

7. *To prepare syrup*: In a saucepan combine the sugar, water, orange flower, and rose water together. Bring to a boil over medium heat and add the lemon juice. Boil gently 20 minutes or until syrupy. Pour the hot syrup very gradually over the cooled *baqlawa*, allowing syrup to saturate layers. It is best to let the pastry rest 6 hours or overnight at room temperature to absorb the syrup, although this is not absolutely necessary. Cut with a sharp knife all the way through the pastry to serve.

CAROB DATE LOAF

YIELD: 1 loaf or 16 slices

1 cup pitted dates, cut up
1½ teaspoons baking soda
½ teaspoon salt
¼ cup carob powder
3 tablespoons safflower shortening
¾ cup, plus 1 tablespoon, boiling water

2 large eggs, well beaten
1 teaspoon orange blossom water* or vanilla extract
¾ cup honey (warmed to pouring consistency)
1¼ cups whole wheat flour

*See Seasoning Chart.

1. Place the dates, baking soda, salt, and carob powder in a mixing bowl. Toss lightly with a fork. Add the shortening and boiling water, but do not stir. Let stand 20 minutes.

2. Preheat oven to 350 degrees.

3. Combine the eggs and orange blossom water or vanilla. Add the honey and flour, stirring until well blended. Add date mixture, stirring just to blend. Pour into a well-greased 9- by 5-inch loaf pan. Bake 45 minutes or until toothpick inserted comes out clean. Let cool before removing from pan. Serve plain or top each slice with plain yogurt sweetened with a little honey.

Variation: Replace carob powder with ¾ cup chopped walnuts. Decrease the amount of boiling water by 1 tablespoon and replace the honey with 1 cup sugar.

CAULIFLOWER WITH TAHINI SAUCE

YIELD: 4 servings

1 large head cauliflower, separated
   into flowerets
2 cups water

1 teaspoon lemon juice
Tahini Sauce **(p. 256)***

Place cauliflower, water, and lemon juice in a large saucepan. Bring to a quick boil, reduce heat, and simmer until tender but firm. Or, place flowerets in a vegetable steamer with ½-inch water and steam until tender. Drain in colander. Place in a serving dish and toss with enough *Tahini Sauce* to coat lightly. Serve hot or cold. If hot, serve as a side dish, or allow to cool and serve as a salad or *mezza* dish.
*Note: If refrigerated, let stand at room temperature before serving.

EGGPLANT SALAD BULUS

YIELD: 4 servings

1 large eggplant
1 small onion, finely diced
1 medium-sized tomato, sliced into
   thin wedges
2 tablespoons chopped parsley

Garlic salt and cayenne pepper to
   taste
2 tablespoons olive oil
1 tablespoon vinegar or lemon
   juice
1 to 2 teaspoons crushed dried
   mint—optional

1. Preheat oven to 350 degrees.
2. Pierce eggplant in several places. Set on a baking sheet and bake in a preheated oven from 20 to 30 minutes or until skin splits. Turn eggplant every 10 minutes while baking. Remove from oven. Cool.
3. Peel and dice eggplant. Combine with onion, tomato, and parsley. Season with garlic salt and cayenne pepper. Combine oil and vinegar and toss with eggplant. Fold in mint if desired. Chill before serving.
Variation: Replace garlic salt and cayenne pepper with 2 cloves garlic, peeled and finely minced. Season to taste with salt and freshly ground pepper.

FATOUCH
(Lebanese Bread Salad)   *YIELD: 6 servings*

1 cucumber (peel, if waxed)
1 small head romaine lettuce
2 stale pita bread* or 3 thin slices
  bread
2 to 3 firm ripe tomatoes, diced
20 sprigs fresh parsley
1 bunch green onions, finely
  chopped
½ cup lemon juice
⅛ cup olive oil

⅛ cup sesame oil
Salt to taste
½ teaspoon freshly ground pepper
1 to 2 garlic cloves, pressed—
  optional
1½ tablespoons chopped fresh mint
  leaves or 2 teaspoons dried mint
1 tablespoon chopped fresh
  coriander—optional

Available at Greek and Middle Eastern groceries.

1. Slice cucumber. Sprinkle with salt and set in a colander to drain for ½ hour. Rinse well and pat dry. Chop finely. Wash romaine. Drain on towels. Tear into bite-size pieces. Toast the pita or bread. Break into small pieces.
2. Combine in a salad bowl the cucumber, romaine, toasted bread pieces, tomatoes, parsley, and green onions. Combine remaining ingredients in a screw-top jar. Shake vigorously to blend and toss with salad. Serve immediately.
Variations: Add 6 diced radishes or 1 sweet red pepper, seeded and chopped.

FUL MOUDAMMAS
(Spicy Fava Bean Spread)   *YIELD: 2 cups or 4 servings*

2 cups cooked fava beans (available
  in cans)
2 to 4 tablespoons water
1 large garlic clove, minced
1 teaspoon ground cumin, divided

½ teaspoon ground coriander,
  divided
½ teaspoon Tabasco sauce, divided
Olive oil
Sliced cucumbers and hot
  peppers for garnish

1. In a blender, purée 1 cup of fava beans with the water, garlic, ½ teaspoon of the cumin, ¼ teaspoon of the coriander, and ¼ teaspoon of the Tabasco. Set aside.
2. In a bowl, coarsely mash remaining 1 cup fava beans along with remaining ½ teaspoon cumin, ¼ teaspoon coriander, and ¼ teaspoon Tabasco. Add puréed beans and combine thoroughly.
3. *To serve*: Spread mixture evenly on a dinner-size plate. Drizzle a little olive oil over the top and garnish with diagonally sliced cucumbers and hot peppers. Serve with Arabic bread or sesame crackers.

HUMMOUS B' TAHINI
(Garbanzo Bean Spread)   *YIELD: 2 cups or 4, ½-cup servings*

1 15½ ounce can garbanzo beans
2 tablespoons *tahini**
  Juice of 1 large lemon
2 garlic cloves
½ to 1 teaspoon Tabasco sauce
**See* Seasoning Chart.

½ to 1 teaspoon each: ground cumin
  and coriander
Olive oil
Chopped parsley
Paprika

Drain half the liquid off the garbanzo beans. Place remaining liquid and beans in a blender along with the *tahini*, lemon juice, garlic, Tabasco, cumin, and coriander. Purée until smooth. Taste and adjust seasonings. Spread on a plate or place in a bowl to serve. Drizzle olive oil over the top and garnish with parsley and paprika. Accompany with Arabic bread, whole grain crackers, or raw vegetables.

MIREILLE'S ADASS BI HAMOD
(Lentil Lemon Soup)   *YIELD: 8 to 10 servings*

1 pound (2 cups) brown lentils,
  washed
½ pound Swiss chard
  Salt, pepper, and ground
  cinnamon to taste

6 tablespoons safflower margarine
  or butter
6 garlic cloves, pressed
3 tablespoons ground coriander
  seed
  Juice of 4 lemons

1. Place the lentils, Swiss chard, salt, pepper, and cinnamon in a large pot. Cover with 2 to 3 quarts of water. Bring to a boil, reduce heat, and simmer 1½ hours or until lentils are tender, adding more water as needed (in a pressure cooker this will take only 20 or 30 minutes).
2. Heat the margarine or butter in a small skillet. Sauté the garlic. Add the coriander and lemon juice and stir mixture into lentils. Taste and adjust seasonings. Serve hot in the winter and cold in the summer.

PISTACHIO DATE CRESCENTS   *YIELD: 50 dainty cookies*

½ cup sweet butter or safflower
  margarine, softened
½ cup sugar
2 egg yolks
2 tablespoons orange flower water*
  or 1 tablespoon vanilla
**Available at Greek or Middle Eastern grocery stores.*

1½ cups sifted unbleached white
  flour
½ cup chopped dates
½ cup ground pistachio nuts
  Sifted confectioners' sugar—
  optional

1. Preheat oven to 400 degrees. Adjust rack to middle.
2. Cream together the butter, sugar, egg yolks, and orange flower water (if using an electric mixer beat at speed #2). Beat in the flour. Fold in dates and nuts by hand. Be sure ingredients are thoroughly blended.
3. Roll 1 teaspoon of cookie mixture at a time between the palms of your hands. Shape into crescents. Place on a greased baking sheet. Bake 10 to 12 minutes or until crescents are lightly browned at the edges. When cool, dust with confectioners' sugar.

PISTACHIO RICE PILAF

YIELD: 6, ½-cup servings

¼ cup dried currants	½ cup pistachio nuts
1 cup long-grain brown rice	Salt
2 cups water or vegetable broth	Cinnamon
¼ cup dried apricots, cut into strips	

1. Soak currants for 15 minutes in warm water. Drain and set aside. Wash rice and drain. Place in a skillet over medium heat and stir around until it is dry and lightly browned (be careful not to burn!).
2. Place toasted rice in a 1½-quart saucepan and cover with water or broth. Bring to a boil, reduce heat to low, and cover with a tight-fitting lid. After rice has simmered for about 25 minutes, place the currants, apricots, and nuts on top of the rice (do not stir in). Return the lid and continue simmering 20 minutes or until rice is tender and water is absorbed. Remove from heat and let stand 2 minutes. Turn into a serving dish. Season with salt and sprinkle cinnamon over the top.

POTATO AND WALNUT KIBBE
(Mock Lamb Loaf)

YIELD: 8 servings

1½ cups bulgur (cracked wheat)	4 medium-sized, red-skinned potatoes, boiled and coarsely mashed
2 teaspoons salt	
2 tablespoons basil	
½ teaspoon each: cinnamon and allspice	¼ cup tomato sauce, ketchup, or barbecue sauce
½ cup finely chopped onion	1 large onion, coarsely chopped
½ cup finely chopped walnuts	½ cup vegetable or peanut oil, divided

1. Place bulgur in a bowl and cover with water. Let stand 30 minutes. Do not drain. Remove bulgur a handful at a time to another bowl, squeezing out excess water between your palms.
2. Combine the bulgur, salt, basil, cinnamon, allspice, the ½ cup finely chopped onion, walnuts, potatoes, and tomato sauce. Knead the mixture into a soft dough. Taste and adjust seasonings.

3. Preheat oven to 350 degrees.

4. Place the coarsely chopped onion in the bottom of an 8- by 10-inch baking dish (or any small oblong pan). Cover with ¼ cup of the oil. Pat bulgur mixture evenly into the dish. Drizzle remaining oil around the edges. Bake in preheated oven from 35 to 40 minutes. Cut into squares and serve hot or at room temperature as a main course.

RIZ BISH SHIRIYYI
(Rice with Vermicelli)   *YIELD: 4 servings*

---

3 tablespoons safflower margarine
  or *samneh**
¼ pound whole wheat vermicelli
  noodles, broken in half

*See Seasoning Chart.

1 cup raw, long-grain rice
1 vegetable or chicken bouillon
  cube
2½ cups boiling water
  Salt to taste

Melt margarine or *samneh* in a heavy skillet or saucepan. Add the noodles and sauté until lightly browned, turning frequently. Add the rice and sauté with vermicelli for several minutes. Dissolve bouillon in the boiling water. Pour over rice and vermicelli, cover with a tight-fitting lid, and simmer 20 minutes or until rice and noodles are tender. Season with salt and serve immediately as a side dish.

SABANIKH
(Spinach Pies)   *YIELD: 50, 3-inch pies or 25, 6-inch pies*

Dough:
  3 cups all-purpose flour
  ¼ cup each: peanut and olive oil
  ½ teaspoon yeast dissolved in 2
    teaspoons warm water
  1 teaspoon salt
  1 cup lukewarm water

Filling:
  1 pound fresh spinach
  1 cup chopped onion (may use part
    green onions with tops)
  5 tablespoons lemon juice
  ¼ cup each: peanut and olive oil
  ¼ pound feta cheese (preferably
    Bulgarian feta)
  1¼ teaspoons salt
  1½ teaspoons allspice

1. *To prepare dough:* Combine the flour, peanut and olive oils, yeast dissolved in water, and salt until well blended. Add the water. Gather together to form a soft dough. Do not knead. Cover with a towel. Let rise in a warm, draft-free place for 2 hours.

2. *To prepare filling:* Wash and drain the spinach. Discard stems and any

blemished leaves. Finely chop spinach and combine with remaining ingredients, mixing well.

3. *To roll out and fill dough*: Roll out dough ⅛-inch thick on a lightly floured board. Cut into 3- or 6-inch rounds. Fill 3-inch rounds with 1 teaspoon filling and 6-inch rounds with 1 tablespoon filling. Fold in half and pinch together with lightly floured fingers. Press all around the edges with a fork.

4. Preheat oven to 350 degrees.

5. Place spinach pies on a greased baking sheet. Bake in a preheated oven 30 minutes or until lightly browned.

SALATA LEBANEE
(Yogurt Salad)   YIELD: *4 servings*

---

1 pint plain whole milk yogurt*
2 small cucumbers, peeled and
  seeded
Juice of ½ lemon
1 garlic clove, pressed
1 tablespoon olive oil

Salt and freshly ground pepper to
taste
1½ tablespoons chopped fresh mint
  or 1 teaspoon dried mint—
  optional

*You can use low-fat yogurt, but the consistency will be thinner.

1. Line a colander with a damp cheesecloth. Stir the yogurt and pour into the cheesecloth. Place colander on a plate to catch the whey, and refrigerate 1 to 2 hours while draining.

2. Cut the cucumbers in half. Slice into ¼-inch pieces. Place drained yogurt in a bowl. Combine with cucumbers and remaining ingredients. Serve as a salad or *mezza* dip. (Chop the cucumbers instead of slicing them if you are using this for a dip.)

Note: To make *Labna*, or yogurt cheese, prepare yogurt as in step 1, adding ¾ teaspoon salt. Let drain overnight or tie the corners of the cheesecloth into a bundle and hang from a faucet until the whey drains away, leaving a thick yogurt-cheese. *Labna* is an excellent substitute for cream cheese.

STUFFED ACORN SQUASH   YIELD: *Serves 4*

---

2 medium-sized acorn squash
3 cups cooked garbanzo or fava
  beans (or a combination of both)
1¼ teaspoons each: ground cumin,
  coriander, and garlic powder
½ teaspoon each: turmeric and
  crushed dried red chilies

2 green onions, finely chopped
  with tops
½ cup minced parsley
1 teaspoon salt
Pepper to taste

1. Cut squash in half and remove seeds. Place cut-side-up in a large pot filled with an inch of water. Cover and steam over medium-low heat until squash is tender, about 15 to 20 minutes.

2. Meanwhile, prepare filling. Mash beans until smooth and combine with remaining ingredients. Taste and adjust seasonings. If you do not have dried chili peppers, substitute cayenne pepper or Tabasco sauce to taste.

3. Preheat oven to 350 degrees.

4. Fill each squash cavity with ¾ cup filling. Bake in preheated oven for 35 to 40 minutes. Serve immediately as a main course or side dish. To serve 6, add another squash and reduce filling to ½ cup per squash.

Variation: Serve the squash with a mildly seasoned tomato sauce.

STUFFED CORNISH HENS

YIELD: 6 stuffed hens

---

6 Cornish hens
Salt, pepper, allspice
½ cup orange juice
1 teaspoon almond extract
½ cup yellow raisins
3 tablespoons safflower oil or
margarine
½ cup diced onion
½ cup diced celery
1 large apple, coarsely chopped
3 cups cooked rice

1 teaspoon each: salt, allspice, and
cinnamon
½ teaspoon each: white pepper and
cumin
¼ teaspoon each: ginger and
nutmeg
2 tablespoons orange flower water*
2 tablespoons pine nuts

Orange Glaze:
1 cup orange juice
½ cup apricot preserves
1 teaspoon lemon juice

* Available at Greek or Middle Eastern grocery stores.

1. Wash hens. Sprinkle with salt, pepper, and allspice. Set aside. Combine the ½ cup orange juice and almond extract. Pour over raisins and set aside.

2. *To combine filling:* Heat oil in a skillet and sauté onion until tender. Add celery and chopped apple. Sauté 3 minutes. Mix with rice and spices. Stir in orange flower water, pine nuts, and reserved raisins with juice.

3. *To prepare glaze:* Boil glaze ingredients together in a saucepan over medium heat, stirring constantly, until slightly thick. Leave on very low heat, stirring occasionally, while stuffing the hens.

4. *To stuff and bake hens:* Preheat oven to 350 degrees. Fill cavities of hens with 4 heaping tablespoons of rice mixture. Secure with a toothpick. Tie the legs together. Place in a roasting pan. Bake in a preheated oven 45 minutes, covered, basting with orange glaze every 10 minutes. Uncover. Bake 15 minutes longer or until hens are golden brown. When hens have 5 more minutes to bake, pour remaining glaze over all.

TABOULEE SALAD

YIELD: 4 to 6 servings

1 cup bulgur wheat
1 cucumber, diced
2 tomatoes, diced
1 or 2 green onions with tops,
   minced
15 to 20 sprigs fresh parsley
10 radishes, diced

½ cup lemon juice
¼ cup olive oil
½ teaspoon salt
½ teaspoon pepper
1 to 3 teaspoons crushed mint
   leaves

1. Place bulgur in a bowl and cover with water. Transfer to another bowl a handful at a time, squeezing out as much water as possible between your palms. Let stand for 3 hours (it will still be a little moist after you have squeezed the water out).
2. Add the cucumber, tomatoes, green onions, parsley, and radishes to the wheat. Combine the lemon juice, olive oil, salt, pepper, and mint leaves. Taste and adjust seasonings. Toss with other ingredients. Serve immediately.

TAHINI SAUCE

YIELD: Approximately 1 cup or 4 servings

½ cup *tahini**
½ cup water
   Juice of 1 lemon
**See* Seasoning Chart.

½ cup finely chopped parsley
1 large garlic clove, minced
¼ teaspoon salt

Purée *tahini* and water in a blender until smooth. Add remaining ingredients; taste and adjust amounts of lemon juice, garlic, and salt to your taste. Serve as a dressing for vegetables, grilled fish, or salads. To serve as a dip, drizzle olive oil over the top and garnish with sliced cucumbers and hot peppers. This will keep one week refrigerated.
Variation: Add 1 ripe, mashed avocado to the blender.

WHOLE WHEAT ARABIC BREAD

YIELD: 12 individual pocket breads

1 package yeast
½ cup warm water (110 degrees)
2 tablespoons sugar, divided
2 cups water

4 cups unbleached white flour
2 to 3 cups whole wheat flour
2½ teaspoons salt
1 tablespoon soft butter

1. Soften yeast in ½-cup of warm water mixed with 1 tablespoon of the sugar. Let stand 5 minutes.

2. In a large bowl combine yeast mixture with 2 cups water, the flours, salt, and the remaining tablespoon of sugar. Combine thoroughly using a large wooden spoon, making certain all the liquid is mixed into the flour. Knead until the dough becomes a smooth ball and the sides of the bowl are clean. Add more flour if necessary.

3. Shape dough into a smooth ball and place in a large, lightly oiled bowl. Rub butter across the top, cover with a towel, and set in a warm place to rise until doubled in bulk—about 2 hours.

4. Punch down dough to let air escape. Break off 12 handful-size pieces of dough. Roll each piece into a smooth ball, cover and let rise ½ hour.

5. Preheat oven to 400 degrees. Remove bottom rack from oven.

6. Roll or pat each ball into a circle ¼-inch thick. Be certain that there are no creases in the dough and that the sides are not thicker than the middle. Cover circles with a damp cloth to prevent drying out. Place two flat circles at a time on the bottom of the oven for 5 minutes or until they puff up. Pop under the broiler for about 2 minutes just to lightly brown the top. Repeat until all circles are baked. Watch your oven temperature as opening and closing the oven will allow hot air to escape. Bread may be eaten warm or cold and may also be frozen and reheated.

Note: To stuff this bread with *felafel* (deep-fried bean patties) or any other filling, cut the bread in half and open into a pocket.

LEBANON/RECIPE ANALYSIS CHART

Name of Recipe	Quantity	Calories	CHO gms.	Protein gms.	Total Fat gms.	Saturated Fat gms.	Choles- terol mg.	Dietary Fiber gms.
1. Pistachio Date Crescents	each	59	7 (47%)	1 (7%)	3 (46%)	1 (15%)	18	.10
2. *Sabanikh* (Spinach Pies)	one 3-in. pie	73	6 (33%)	1 (5%)	5 (62%)	1 (12%)	2	—
3. *Ful Moudam-mas* (Spicy Fava Bean Spread)	per ½-cup serving	108	13 (48%)	5 (19%)	4 (33%)	—	—	1.0
4. Eggplant Salad *Bulus*	per serving	114	13 (46%)	2 (7%)	6 (47%)	—	—	1.0
5. *Salata Lebanee*	per serving	124	9 (29%)	4 (13%)	8 (58%)	3 (22%)	13	—
6. *Hummous B'Tahini*	per ½-cup serving	125	14 (48%)	6 (19%)	5 (33%)	—	—	1.0
7. *Fatouch* (Lebanese Bread Salad)	per serving	150	13 (35%)	2 (5%)	10 (60%)	1 (6%)	—	.7
8. Cauliflower with *Tahini* Sauce	per serving	168	15 (36%)	9 (22%)	8 (42%)	—	—	2.4
9. *Tahini* Sauce	per ¼-cup serving	186	7 (15%)	6 (14%)	15 (71%)	—	—	2.5
10. *Mireille's Adass Bi Hamod* (Lentil Lemon Soup)	per serving	235	31 (53%)	12 (20%)	7 (27%)	1 (4%)	—	1.0
11. *Taboulee* Salad	per serving	249	37 (59%)	5 (8%)	9 (33%)	1 (4%)	—	1.4
12. Whole Wheat Arabic Bread	each	254	48 (76%)	11 (17%)	2 (7%)	—	2	1.0
13. *Riz Bish Shiriyyi* (Rice with Vermicelli)	per serving	277	32 (47%)	17 (25%)	9 (28%)	5 (15%)	—	.40
14. Pistachio Rice Pilaf	per ½-cup serving	281	33 (47%)	15 (22%)	10 (31%)	—	—	.90

Name of Recipe	Quantity	Calories	CHO gms.	Protein gms.	Total Fat gms.	Saturated Fat gms.	Choles-terol mg.	Dietary Fiber gms.
15. *Adeece Howeed* (Lentils with Spinach)	per serving	305	53 (70%)	12 (16%)	5 (14%)	—	—	2.0
16. Carob Date Loaf	per slice	314	58 (75%)	7 (9%)	6 (16%)	—	31	1.0
17. Potato and Walnut *Kibbe*	per serving	368	40 (44%)	7 (8%)	20 (48%)	2 (5%)	—	2.5
18. *Baqlawa*	per serving	398	36 (36%)	5 (5%)	27 (59%)	3 (7%)	—	.5
19. Stuffed Acorn Squash	per serving	405	71 (70%)	19 (19%)	5 (11%)	—	—	5.0
20. Stuffed Cornish Hens	per hen	1118	37 (13%)	85 (30%)	70 (57%)	23 (19%)	293	.7

Numbers in parentheses (%) indicate percentage of total calories contributed by nutrient.

MENUS

LOW CALORIE SPECIALTIES
(500 to 700 calories per meal)

FATOUCH (LEBANESE BREAD SALAD)
SABANIKH (SPINACH PIES)
SALATA LEBANEE
PISTACHIO DATE CRESCENTS
Hot Mint Tea

POTATO AND WALNUT KIBBE
EGGPLANT SALAD BULUS
Steamed Zucchini with Lemon
Baked Apples
Turkish Coffee

CAULIFOWER WITH TAHINI SAUCE
TABOULEE SALAD
Persian Melon
Plain Yogurt
Iced Tea

•

LOW CHOLESTEROL MENUS
(Less than 50 mgs. of cholesterol per meal)

TAHINI SAUCE
Raw Vegetable Sticks
Pocket Bread
SABANIKH (SPINACH PIES)
CAROB DATE LOAF
Turkish Coffee

MIREILLE'S ADASS BI HAMOD (LENTIL LEMON SOUP)
Sesame Crackers
SALATA LEBANEE
CAULIFLOWER WITH TAHINI SAUCE
Figs, Dates and Dried Apricots
Iced Mint Tea

POTATO AND WALNUT KIBBE
Sliced Radishes and Green Peppers
Avocado Wedges Garnished with Parsley
BAQLAWA
Hot Tea with Lemon

LOW SATURATED FAT SELECTIONS
(Less than 8 grams of saturated fat per meal)

HUMMOUS B'TAHINI
Raw Carrot and Zucchini Sticks
**MIREILLE'S ADASS BI HAMOD
(LENTIL LEMON SOUP)**
Plain Yogurt
Baked Apples
Hot Mint Tea

**STUFFED ACORN SQUASH
EGGPLANT SALAD BULUS**
Baked Turnips
Cantaloupe
Turkish Coffee

**WHOLE WHEAT ARABIC BREAD
ADEECE HOWEED (LENTILS WITH SPINACH)**
Sliced Tomatoes and Avocados
Fresh Pomegranates
White Wine

•

HIGH PROTEIN MEALS
(30 or more grams of protein per meal)

Feta Cheese and Sliced Tomatoes
**MIREILLE'S ADASS BI HAMOD
(LENTIL LEMON SOUP)
WHOLE WHEAT ARABIC BREAD
TABOULEE SALAD
PISTACHIO DATE CRESCENTS**

**STUFFED ACORN SQUASH
PISTACHIO RICE PILAF**
Sliced Cucumbers Garnished with
Fresh Mint
CAROB DATE LOAF
White Wine

**SALATA LEBANEE
CAULIFLOWER WITH TAHINI SAUCE
RIZ BISH SHIRIYYI (RICE WITH VERMICELLI)
BAQLAWA**
Turkish Coffee

•

WELL BALANCED LUNCH OR DINNER MINEUS
(Selections that conform to recommendations in Dietary Goals for United States)

**FUL MOUDAMMAS (SPICY FAVA
BEAN SPREAD)
TABOULEE SALAD
WHOLE WHEAT ARABIC BREAD
CAROB DATE LOAF**
Turkish Coffee

**RIZ BISH SHIRIYYI (RICE WITH
VERMICELLI)
STUFFED ACORN SQUASH**
Pocket Bread
Sliced Tomatoes
Iced Tea

**HUMMOUS B'TAHINI
ADEECE HOWEED (LENTILS WITH SPINACH)**
Sliced Cucumber with Mint
Dried Figs and Pistachio Nuts
Red Wine

CHAPTER 11

MEXICO
Tortilla Flats

Culinary Essentials

There's more to Mexican gastronomy than pouring bottled hot sauce over a cold, hastily stuffed, taco shell. This exciting culinary style employs a myriad of colorful ingredients, and with just a few cooking concepts under your apron, you will be turning yellow corn, black beans, and tan-freckled tortillas into a glorious array of ruggedly-shaped and highly-seasoned creations. Once inured to making your own fresh sauces from tomatoes, vibrant red chili powder, and green Mexican tomatoes, you'll never settle for a bottled imitation again.

Collecting ingredients for this foreign kitchen will require some perseverance, especially if you go the "authentic route." Fortunately, most grocery stores have an aisle devoted to Mexican foods, but any items unavailable at your supermarket are virtually always stocked by Latin American markets.

Those habituated to Mexican cooking will want to acquire a few of the essential foods that constitute the backbone of this ethnic cuisine: canned Mexican green tomatoes (also called *tomatillos enteros* or *tomatitos verdes*) should be on hand to make *Salsa Verde*, a piquant green sauce that brings life to everything from eggs to enchiladas; tinned peppers, most notably *jalapeños* and mild green chilies, will invigorate sauces, dips, and tortilla dishes; pumpkin seeds (*pepitas*) are perfect for thickening sauces, adding crunch to steamed vegetables, or garnishing a cheese spread.

There is no such thing as a well-stocked Mexican kitchen without corn tortillas. Occasionally, they can be purchased hot off the (tortilla) press. This is far and away the optimal way to experience the unique flavor and texture of tortillas, but if unavailable fresh, the next best alternative is the packaged variety, which can be frozen for future use without much compromise in flavor. By all means, avoid canned tortillas, which are totally devoid of character.

To complete your Mexican shelf, you will want to stock several varieties of dried or canned beans, used in prodigious amounts to make hardy soups and *Frijoles Refritos* (refried beans), the omnipresent Mexican side dish. Pink, pale yellow, and black beans (also called turtle beans or *frijoles negros*) are the most authentic, but pinto or red kidney beans can be substituted in most recipes.

Some Latin markets carry imported cheeses that will lend an enticing flavor and unqualified authenticity to your dishes. *Queso Blanco* (also known as *Queso Fresco*) is a moist, white cheese that is similar in taste to mildly salted ricotta. *Queso Blanco* crumbles easily and is excellent in enchiladas or as a garnish for vegetable salads. *Queso Añejo*, shaped in a round and sprinkled with paprika, is also crumbly and features a slightly sour taste. Ideal for *Chilies Rellenos*, *Queso Añejo* can also be sprinkled over refried beans, tostados, and tacos; you'll be delighted with the results. *Chihauhau* and *Queso Supremo* are stringy, white cheeses that taste like a cross between Mozzarella and Monterey Jack; these two varieties are good choices for baked casseroles such as *Chilequiles*. Generally, imported Mexican cheeses can be used interchangeably. When the real stuff is not available, the best substitutes are Mozzarella, farmer's cheese, Monterey Jack, Armenian string cheese, and Muenster.

Assembling kitchen equipment is much easier than stocking your shelves with the eclectic foods required for Mexican cooking. No elaborate utensils are required. With a battery of cast-iron skillets and earthenware pots—excellent conductors of heat and therefore perfect for the long-simmering soups and stews that typify this cuisine—you'll be ready to tackle almost any Mexican recipe. A wooden bean masher is nice to have for making refried beans, but a potato masher will suffice. Enchilada lovers wishing to preserve the beauty and integrity of their sauce-smothered tortillas will find small, oval gratin dishes a worthwhile investment. They allow you to bake enchiladas individually and thereby avoid the mangling process that inevitably occurs when removing tightly packed tortillas from a large baking pan.

Cooks who like experimentation will feast on the permutations that Mexican recipes can undergo. Most dishes of this cuisine can take on a new personality with a few minor changes. Consider the enchilada. First fried lightly in oil and then stuffed, rolled, sauced, and baked, these tortillas can easily be modified to suit your culinary whims. Crunchy *Pine Nut Enchiladas*, for instance, have a touch of the exotic, while *Guacamole Enchiladas*, ozzing with avocados and tomatoes, are light and refreshing. *Cheese-Bean Enchiladas* are the heartiest variation on the stuffed-tortilla theme. The permutations are endless and limited only by your imagination.

Your Mexican fiesta should commence with an array of sumptuous fruit. Any seasonal fruit will do, but sliced mangos, guavas, oranges, papayas, and pineapples will lend a tropical touch. To embellish the presentation, you might mound clusters of almonds, hazelnuts, and pumpkin seeds in the center of your plate, and then garnish the whole affair with wedges of fresh limes.

Soup is the appropriate second course. Chilled *Gazpacho*, bolstered by a tart and chunky blend of tomatoes, cucumbers, and green peppers is a fine selection for balmy summer nights. On wintry evenings, you will do better with *Sopa de Frijoles Negros*, a rich purée of black beans enriched with cream and spiced with cumin and oregano. Accompany either of these time-honored specialties with hot tortillas, sesame-studded *Toasted Bread Rounds* or *Bolillos* (wonderful hard-crusted rolls reminiscent of French bread).

Tasty, inexpensive, and easy to find, corn tortillas are an essential part of any Mexican meal. These "little cakes" are versatile—rivaled only by Arabic pocket bread—and can be filled with anything from shredded chicken to mashed avocados. Corn tortillas can be rolled (enchiladas), folded (tacos), and fried (tostadas), while soft-flour tortillas, when folded and stuffed, become burritos or *flautas*. Tortillas can be layered in casseroles (*chilequiles*) like lasagne noodles or simply sent warm to the table as a "bread course." Soft-flour tortillas are available in white and whole wheat varieties; the latter are more nutritious, without compromising the Mexican essence of a meal.

Garnishes hold a distinguished spot on the Mexican table. Tradition dictates that you rim your entrées with finely shredded lettuce in order to cool down and contrast with spicy foods. Alfalfa sprouts, while not an authentic south-of-the-border ingredient, also make an attractive and tasty garnish for tortilla or avocado dishes. Olives, pimientos, fresh coriander, and radishes also make colorful and tasty accompaniments.

A Mexican plate is not complete without *Salsa Piquante**, a fiery, cold tomato sauce amply packed with serrano chili peppers. This stimulating mixture, which may be spooned over everything from eggs to steamed vegetables, will be appreciated especially by those daring souls who feel their food is never hot enough. *Jalapeño* peppers, the national condiment, are also a must. Place them in a bowl, surround with sliced carrots, and let the fiesta begin!

Seasoning Essentials

Many cooks in this country hold the misconception that all Mexican dishes are spicy-hot. Nothing could be further from the truth. While it is true that some of the finest and most popular Mexican offerings are bursting with the taste of vehement chili peppers, many dishes acquire their superb flavor from much more delicate spices such as cinnamon and nutmeg,

---

*See Seasoning Chart *in this chapter.*

or from taste enhancers such as tangy lime juice. Pungent herbs, most notably fresh coriander and *epazote*, also play an important role.

Mexican specialties generally range in heat from mildly piquant to palate-paralyzing. Exactly where a dish falls on this spectrum depends largely upon how *you* choose to spice it. For example, if you are in pursuit of explosive flavors, fresh or tinned hot green chilies will meet the challenge. Conversely, when preparing a meal for timid tongues, you can rely upon gentle-natured herbs such as oregano, cumin, or thyme. Unless used in minute quantities, assertive seasonings such as cayenne pepper, fresh garlic, and coriander should be reserved for adventurous eaters.

Among the seasonings commonly used in this cuisine, none will repay meticulous study and experimentation better than chili peppers. Mexico boasts over 50 species of fresh and dried chilies, varying in potency from subdued to volcanic. Several of these unique peppers can usually be found at Latin American or Oriental groceries, and occasionally, at your neighborhood supermarket. Size is the best yardstick for judging the heat potential of chilies with which you may not be familiar: Large peppers generally range from mild to hot; small varieties (1 to 2 inches) are hot to feverish; and tiny ones range from sweltering to unbearable. Most shopping outlets carry canned *serrano* and *jalapeño* peppers, ground cayenne (red) pepper, and dried red pepper flakes, all of which admirably impart a sufficient amount of heat to any dish.

Dried red chili peppers, which can be used interchangeably with fresh red (hot) peppers, are full of surprises. Their value in Mexican cooking lies not only in the peculiar flavor of the pod but, more importantly, in that of the seeds. As a rule, dried red chili peppers should be soaked in boiling water for 30 minutes before using. They can then be added to long-simmering bean dishes, sauces, corn casseroles, and vegetable medleys. Whole dried red peppers will keep indefinitely without losing their fierce bite. They are to be handled carefully as their "dust" may be irritating to mucous membranes. Rubber gloves should also be worn when handling them.

Whenever one of your Latin creations is lacking an indefinable quality, you can almost always call upon coriander to provide the missing link. This pungent herb is guaranteed to impart the seductively elusive flavor that characterizes "authentic" Mexican dishes. Fresh coriander (*cilantro*) is preferable. It has the appearance of flat-leafed parsley and is imbued with a strong aroma and pronounced flavor. This exciting herb will make your Mexican meals something to write home about. Use it in small amounts at first, as you may find *cilantro* an acquired taste.

Epazote, a dry crumbly herb found almost exclusively in Latin American markets, is another ticket to making Mexican fare taste authentic. A small amount of this highly pungent seasoning can make the difference between a run-of-the-mill and extraordinary refried bean dish. A fine addition to *Chilies Rellenos*, *epazote* can also be used in any tortilla-based casserole.

Whether hot, mild, or pungent, your Mexican dishes will almost always benefit from a touch of lime juice. This spring-green citrus fruit is customarily served as a garnish, which is then squeezed liberally over steamed vegetables (especially corn), salads, seafood, fresh fruit, and raw nuts. Lime is a refreshing alternative to lemon juice. Try it for seasoning sliced tomatoes, baked fish, or your favorite *guacamole* dip. A few trial-and-error experiences with fresh lime juice will convince you of its special place in Mexican cooking.

MEXICAN SEASONING CHART

ANISE is an aromatic herb reminiscent of licorice. A few crushed seeds will lend a unique flavor and aroma to fish soups, vegetable stews, or enchilada sauce. In pastries and puddings, this distinctive flavoring combines well with cinnamon, lemon peel, or orange rind.

CAYENNE PEPPER is made from finely ground red chili peppers. As a seasoning, this scarlet red powder is unrivaled in its ability to heighten flavors. Use sparingly as it is exceedingly hot. Start with no more than ¼ to ½ teaspoon in any dish that does not specify proportions; increase the amount, judiciously, until the desired piquancy is reached. When called for in small amounts, cayenne pepper is the best substitute for fresh or dried chili peppers. Avoid cayenne that has a dull, orange-red hue, for surely it is stale and insipid.

CORIANDER is also called *Cilantro*. The fresh herb, which tastes something like a cross between sage, orange peel, and cumin, is one of the keys to imparting an "authentic" Mexican flavor. Use it as you would fresh parsley, but in smaller amounts. A few chopped leaves will turn an average *guacamole* into something extraordinary. With seafood, tomatoes, or rice, it is superb. Fresh coriander can be found at Latin American or Oriental markets.
Dried coriander leaves, available at spice shops and some supermarkets, are less pungent and fragrant than fresh *cilantro*. They can be used, however, to season avocados, vegetables, sauces, or long-simmering dishes.
Coriander seed has a clean aroma and pungent taste that is quite different from the fresh or dried variety. It imparts an agreeable flavor to both starchy and protein foods such as corn, lentils, rice, and eggs. Despite their differences, all forms of coriander blend favorably with garlic, cumin, oregano, onions, and chili peppers.

CUMIN is also called *Comino*. It has a pleasant bite reminiscent of caraway seed. This pungent herb is indispensable to tomato-based dishes and is a fine enhancer for beans, rice, chicken, and potatoes. Cumin is especially complementary with coriander, and the two can be used interchangeably in most recipes.

DRIED RED CHILIES are frequently added to Mexican sauces and chicken dishes. They vary in size, color, shape, and potency, and in general, can be found at Latin American markets and some specialty food shops. Unless called for whole, they are usually torn into small pieces and soaked in boiling water from ten to thirty minutes before being used; 1 cup water is sufficient for 6 medium-sized chilies. Most supermarkets carry dried red pepper flakes which may be used like cayenne pepper. The most popular varieties used in Mexican cooking are listed below.

Ancho—a dark reddish-brown chili that is flat, wide, and wrinkled. Its flavor is robust, but mild.

Mulato—a brownish-red pepper that is larger and more pungent than the *ancho* chili. It is not uncommon for a dish to call for both *ancho* and *mulato* chilies for their flavors are quite complementary.

Pasilla—a long slender pepper with a mahogany-black color, also known as *Chile Negro*, it has less flavor but more pungency than either the *ancho* or *mulato* chili.

EPAZOTE is a pungent herb popular in bean and tortilla dishes. Along with fresh coriander, this distinctive dried herb will impart an "authentic" quality to your Mexican dishes. It is usually available at Latin American markets and is sometimes found under the name "Jerusalem oak *pazote*." Add ¼ to ½ teaspoon to 1 pound of beans or 1 quart sauce for tortilla-based dishes such as *chilequiles*. *Epazote* will also give the stuffing for *chilies rellenos* a unique flavor—add 1 tablespoon per 4 chilies.

FRESH GREEN CHILI PEPPERS come in over 60 varieties, ranging from sweet to hot, in Mexico. The test of excellence of many sauces and tortilla dishes is the manner in which the chili flavor has been made to blend with, enhance, and modify that of the other ingredients. To seed and stem fresh chilies, rinse them under cold water, tear out stem, and break in half. Scoop out and discard the seeds (the hottest part) and, if desired, trim away any fleshy ribs or veins. Always wear rubber gloves when handling fresh chilies; never touch your eyes or face before washing your hands well with cold water. When fresh chilies are unavailable, tinned *jalapeño* or mild green chilies can be found in most grocery stores. Rinse canned chilies in cold water before using. The most popular chilies used in Mexican cooking are listed below.

Jalapeño—a medium-sized, forest-green chili with a smooth skin. It is intensely sharp and should be added cautiously to any dish.

Poblano—a large, tapering, dark-green chili that ranges from mild to moderately hot in flavor. It is the preferred variety for *chilies rellenos*, although a sweet bell pepper may be substituted.

Serrano—a small, tapering, bright-green chili with an extraordinarily sharp flavor. Use judiciously.

LIME JUICE has a wonderful tang that blends beautifully with the staples of this cuisine. This luscious citrus juice can be used as a pleasant alternative to lemon juice in almost any recipe. When squeezed over fresh fruit, raw vegetables, or corn, lime juice imparts a most refreshing taste that cannot be duplicated by any other seasoning.

MEXICAN CHILI POWDER can be used in any recipe that calls for chili powder. A good pinch of this homemade blend will do wonders for beans, corn-stuffed peppers, eggs, or avocado spreads.

Finely grind in a blender and store in an airtight container:

    1   dried red chili pepper, crushed, or 1 teaspoon cayenne pepper
    1   dried *ancho* chili, stemmed, seeded, and crushed
    1½ teaspoons cumin seed
    1   teaspoon dried oregano
    ¾   teaspoon coriander seed
    ½   teaspoon each: salt and garlic powder

OREGANO is also called *Mexican Sage*. It is used extensively in this cuisine to harmonize with tomatoes and chilies. This pungent herb will also enliven bean or rice dishes. Sprinkle dried oregano over onions while they are sautéing, and they will acquire a fantastic taste.

SALSA PIQUANTE is the quintessential hot sauce for this cooking style. It may be spooned over seafood, burritos, tostados, or tacos, or used as a dip for tortilla chips. Although this nippy sauce is best the day it is prepared, it will keep two days if covered and refrigerated. If a hotter taste is desired, increase the amount of chili peppers.

Combine all ingredients and pour into a bowl:

    1   *serrano* or *jalapeño* pepper, seeded and finely diced
    2   large ripe tomatoes, peeled and finely diced
    ½   small onion, finely diced
    1   tablespoon fresh coriander (optional)
        Salt and pepper to taste
        Pinch of sugar

Other seasonings found in Mexican cookery: cinnamon, marjoram, garlic, thyme, bay leaves, vanilla, cloves, ginger, *achiote* seeds, nutmeg, parsley, saffron, mint, and paprika.

Nutritional Essentials

Mexican cooking is characterized by wholesome, highly seasoned meals that tend to be higher in calories than offerings from most other ethnic cuisines. If you watch your serving size and number of portions, you will find this cuisine to be rich in complex carbohydrates, high in protein, and plentiful in vitamins and calcium. Some Mexican dishes, while high in total fat content, are relatively low in saturated fat. For the most part, this tendency reflects the fat composition of vegetable oils used in this style of cooking.

Mutual supplementation of essential amino acids in the Mexican cuisine relies upon food combinations that have been used since pre-Columbian times. It is important to realize that corn (maize), the grain staple of this culinary style, is deficient in the amino acids lysine and isoleucine. Consequently, dishes made with corn tortillas, corn flour (*masa harina*), or corn kernels should be served with foods such as beans, cheese, or nuts, which are abundant in these two essential amino acids. Examples of complementary combinations in Mexican cooking include tortillas and beans (*Cheese-Bean Enchilada*), fresh corn and cheese (*Corn-Stuffed Peppers*), and tortillas and pignolia nuts (*Pine Nut Enchilada*).

More than just a bread equivalent, the corn tortilla plays a pivotal role in this culinary style. Although the usable protein content of a five-inch tortilla is a mere 1.5 grams, its protein-to-calorie ratio is nearly equivalent to that in a slice of whole wheat bread. When tortillas are eaten with beans, cheese, milk, eggs, or selected nuts, the usable protein content of your meal will be enhanced considerably. With respect to mutual supplementation of amino acids, beans are more complementary with corn tortillas (42 percent increase in grams of usable protein) than with whole wheat tortillas (32 percent increase in grams of usable protein). The latter, on the other hand, are substantially better than corn tortillas for supplementation with cheese, milk, and nuts. These nutritional concepts are illustrated in the following recipes: *Essential Bean Burritos* (cheese with whole wheat), *Avocado Flautas* (wheat tortilla with yogurt), and the *Cheese-Bean Enchilada* (corn tortillas with beans).

By perusing the recipe analyses at the end of this section you will notice that beans constitute an important source of complex carbohydrates, fiber, and protein in the Mexican diet. Because these legumes are deficient in the amino acids methionine and tryptophan, you should complement them with dairy products, corn, wheat, nuts, or seeds.

Perhaps nothing is more important for the nutrition-minded Latin cook than learning to make flavorful *Frijoles Refritos* (refried beans). This time-honored Mexican mainstay is an important source of low-fat protein and is frequently used as a side dish or stuffing. By strategically wrapping a tortilla blanket around these mashed legumes and lacing the inside with cheese and yogurt, you can create a highly nutritious dish called *Essential*

Bean Burritos. Two of these tasty, high-fiber Mexican sandwiches will almost provide an adult's total daily protein allowance.

By now it should be clear that much of the protein revenue in this cuisine is derived from bean/cheese, bean/wheat, and bean/corn combinations. Other nonlegume sources of this essential nutrient include fish (*Huachinango*), eggs (*Huevos Revueltos Yucatán*), and nuts and seeds (*Corn Stuffed Peppers*). The *Pepita Pleaser,* a nut-studded cheese appetizer, is also quite protein-rich. This is because pumpkin seeds (*pepita* nuts), good suppliers of usable protein even when eaten alone, are nicely supplemented by the lysine-rich cheese base of this dish. Pumpkin seeds are an interesting and nutritious Mexican ingredient which you can use in a number of ways: to thicken enchilada sauce, as a flavor enhancer for vegetable dishes, or as the crowning touch for *guacamole*. In addition to providing protein, these seeds are higher in iron and vitamin B_6 than most other nuts and seeds.

The *liquado,* a popular Mexican beverage resembling a "smoothie," is another reasonably good source of protein. This nourishing milk-fruit creation, unlike caffeine- or sugar-laden soft drinks, can make a significant nutritional contribution to any Mexican meal. One large glass of *Banana Milk Liquado* contains about 7 grams of protein and a mere 189 calories.

The *liquado* will give you the opportunity to utilize an array of milk and fruit or juice and fruit combinations such as: pineapple juice/coconut milk, strawberry/orange juice, melon/milk, and banana/orange juice. Depending upon which fruits you select, your beverage can be abundant in vitamin A (papaya, canteloupe or watermelon) or vitamin B_6 and potassium (bananas). *Liquados* made with melons and skimmed or 2 percent milk are great for calorie-watchers. Guavas and strawberries will help in the vitamin C department, while the addition of *tamarind* will boost your dietary fiber intake considerably. In Mexico, the *liquado* is often blended with watercress, which is strained before serving. This simple manipulation increases the thiamine, vitamin A, and iron content of each serving. You can always fortify the protein and vitamin content of your milk-fruit drink by adding a little carob powder (see *Nutritional Essentials* in the Lebanon chapter), wheat germ, powdered milk, or Tiger's milk.

The role of fresh fruits in Mexican meals is an important one and should not be underestimated. They not only provide a tangy or sweet contrast to spicy dishes, but are also a nutritious source of complex carbohydrates. Calorie-counters will note that two fruit selections from the *Mexican Fruit Platter* contain an average of only 114 calories.

The avocado is a commonly used Mexican ingredient deserving special mention. You can satisfy 20 percent of an adult's recommended dietary allowances for iron, magnesium, vitamin C, and vitamin E by consuming one average-sized avocado. Moreover, its fat content is 96 percent polyunsaturated. Considering these attributes, a calorie content of 300 is not unreasonable. You will also save calories by combining these "alligator pears" with fresh vegetables or yogurt, rather than high-fat dairy products. *Avo-*

cado Flautas employ this cooking concept and, as a result, contain only 218 calories per serving.

Just about everyone will enjoy the satisfying, well-spiced creations of Mexican cooking. As a rule, meals of this cuisine are very high in usable protein and other nutrients, but unfortunately are also higher in calories and fat than offerings from most other foreign kitchens. Overconsumption of fat and food energy is especially likely to occur if you rely upon high-fat cheeses such as cheddar in your south-of-the-border specialties. This cooking practice appears to be an American adulteration of Latin cooking, since most native enchilada and tortilla dishes are, in fact, made with low-fat *Queso Blanco*. This mild, white cheese (less than 15 percent fat) most closely resembles ricotta in flavor. We have tried to use tasty, yet low-calorie cheeses in our Mexican recipes to combat the calorie-rich tendencies of this cuisine.

Another way to indulge in Mexican meals without insulting your body weight is to alternate between cheese, bean, and avocado-based tortilla stuffings. For convenience, we have offered a number of enchilada and burrito variations which, as you will notice, differ substantially in their calorie content.

AVOCADO FLAUTAS*

YIELD: 12 large flautas

3 medium-sized ripe tomatoes,
    skinned and finely chopped
2 to 3 garlic cloves, pressed
2 green onions, chopped with tops
4 medium-sized ripe avocados,
    peeled and pitted
    Juice of 1 lime or lemon
¾ teaspoon salt

¼ teaspoon cayenne pepper
½ teaspoon Tabasco sauce
12 large soft-flour tortillas
    (preferably made with whole
    wheat)
12 ounces plain, low-fat yogurt or
    sour cream
    Paprika
    Alfalfa sprouts for topping

1. *To prepare filling*: In a large mixing bowl, combine tomatoes, garlic, and green onions. Mash in avocados. Add lime or lemon juice, salt, cayenne pepper, and Tabasco. Taste and adjust seasonings. If spicier taste is desired, add more Tabasco or cayenne pepper.
2. *To assemble*: Fill one end of each tortilla with about ½ cup of filling and roll up. Place side by side in an oblong baking dish or on a cookie sheet. Stir yogurt or sour cream until creamy and spread a few tablespoons over each *flauta*. Sprinkle generously with paprika.
3. Preheat oven to 350 degrees.
4. Heat *flautas* for 15 minutes or until warmed through (not piping hot). Top each *flauta* with a handful of sprouts to serve.
Variation: Cover *flautas* with *Salsa Verde* (p. 284) before placing in the oven.

Note: You can use the filling for Avocado Flautas as a guacamole dip. If desired, add 1 tablespoon fresh chopped, or 1 teaspoon dried, coriander leaves.

BANANA MILK LIQUADO

YIELD: 4 servings

3 cups ice-cold skimmed milk
2 large ripe bananas, sliced

2 tablespoons honey
4 whole strawberries

Place milk, bananas, and honey in a blender. Whirl until smooth. Pour into 4 chilled glasses and float a whole strawberry in each glass. This serves as an excellent before-dinner drink or a late-night nourisher.
Variations: 1. Replace bananas with fresh papaya, strawberries, or melon.
2. Replace milk with pineapple or orange juice.
3. Replace skimmed milk with either 2 percent low-fat or whole milk.
4. Add 2 tablespoons plain yogurt.

CORN-STUFFED PEPPERS

YIELD: 6 servings

6 medium-sized green peppers
2 tablespoons corn oil
1 small onion, finely chopped
1 cup fresh corn kernels
1 to 2 medium-sized tomatoes,
   seeded and chopped
1 cup cooked, diced green beans
¼ cup chopped almonds

2 teaspoons pumpkin seeds—
   optional
½ to 1 teaspoon salt
Pinch of marjoram, thyme, and
   cayenne pepper
¼ to ½ teaspoon Tabasco
1½ cups grated *Queso Blanco* or
   mozzarella cheese
Sesame seeds for topping

1. Remove tops and seeds from green peppers. Place the peppers in a large soup pot filled with an inch of water over medium heat. Cover with a lid and steam for a few minutes until peppers soften slightly, but are not tender. Remove peppers from pot and set aside.
2. Preheat oven to 350 degrees.
3. Place the corn oil in a frying pan over medium heat and brown the onion. Combine with corn, tomato, cooked green beans, almonds, pumpkin seeds, salt, marjoram, thyme, cayenne pepper, Tabasco, and cheese. Taste and adjust seasonings. Fill peppers with vegetable mixture and sprinkle sesame seeds on top. Place in an oblong baking dish and bake in a preheated oven for 25 minutes.
Variation: Cover peppers with *Enchilada Sauce* (p. 278) or *Salsa Verde* (p. 284) before baking.

CHILIES RELLENOS RUBALCAVA

YIELD: 8 servings

Chilies:
8 fresh, large chilies *poblanos** or
   green bell peppers
   Salt
½ pound aged white cheese such as
   *Queso Añejo,** *Chihuahua,**
   crumbled farmer cheese, or
   Monterey Jack
1 small onion, finely chopped
2 sprigs *cilantro** or parsley, finely
   chopped

Sauce:
4 to 5 fresh firm tomatoes,
   quartered
2 sprigs *cilantro* or parsley, finely
   chopped
1 garlic clove, crushed
½ teaspoon salt
2 tablespoons peanut oil

Batter:
4 eggs, separated
Peanut oil for frying

*Available at Latin American markets.

1. *To prepare chilies*: Pierce the chilies with a long-handled fork. Roast over a gas flame, turning frequently until the skins begin to blister and blacken. Or, place on a baking sheet and broil on the second rack from the top, turn-

ing frequently until blistered and black. When roasted, place in a bread basket lined with a damp linen napkin or kitchen towel. Cover to keep moist. As they cool, peel off the skins with your hands or rub with the napkin. Carefully make a slit on one side and remove the seeds and veins. Sprinkle the insides with a little salt. If using bell peppers, roast as above. Slice off the tops, remove the seeds, and reserve tops for lids when peppers are filled.

2. Grate the cheese. Combine with the onion and *cilantro*. Stuff each pepper with the cheese mixture.

3. *To prepare sauce*: Place the tomatoes, *cilantro*, garlic, and salt in a blender and purée. Heat the peanut oil in a deep skillet. Add the purée and sauté 3 to 4 minutes to blend flavors. Set aside.

4. *To prepare batter*: Beat the egg whites with a wire whisk until stiff peaks form. Add the egg yolks, one at a time, and beat gently until blended.

5. Heat enough peanut oil in a 1½-quart saucepan to cover a chili (about 1½ inches deep). When oil is just smoking, dip each chili into the beaten egg mixture and place one by one into the hot oil—this will seal the split end (bell peppers must be turned in the oil to cook on all sides). Drain on paper towels. Add the chilies or peppers to the tomato sauce. Taste and adjust seasonings. Return sauce to stove, cover, and simmer 20 minutes. Serve with buttered rice.

CHILEQUILES MARANZE
(Tortillas Layered with Cheese and Chili Sauce)   YIELD: 12 servings

---

Chili Sauce:
  4 to 5 cups fresh chopped tomatoes
    (or canned and drained)
  2 tablespoons safflower or peanut
    oil
  1 large onion, chopped
  4 garlic cloves, minced
  4 whole mild green chilies, seeded
    and chopped (fresh or canned)
  ½ teaspoon each: basil and dried
    oregano
  2 tablespoons chili powder (or to
    taste)

Tortillas:
  1 dozen corn tortillas
  ¼ cup safflower oil for frying
  ¼ cup peanut oil for frying

Filling:
  ½ pound fresh mushrooms, sliced
    and sautéed—optional
  2 zucchini, sliced and sautéed—
    optional
  6 whole mild green chilies, seeded
    and chopped
  2 cups grated *Queso Blanco*,*
    mozzarella, or Monterey Jack
    cheese
  2 cups plain yogurt or sour cream
    Paprika

Available at Latin American markets.

1. *To prepare sauce*: Place half the tomatoes in a blender and coarsely purée. Heat oil in a 3-quart saucepan and sauté the onion and garlic. Add toma-

toes, chilies, and seasonings. Simmer 15 to 20 minutes, stirring occasionally. Taste and adjust seasonings. Sauce should be spicy-hot as some of the heat from the spices will dissipate when baked.

2. Cut tortillas in half and then in fourths. Heat safflower and peanut oil in a 7-inch skillet until smoking. Reduce heat a little and drop 4 tortilla quarters at a time in the hot oil until they puff. Remove with tongs to paper towels to drain. Pat well with clean paper towels to remove excess oil.

3. Preheat oven to 350 degrees.

4. *To assemble*: If using mushrooms and zucchini, combine them with the chopped chilies. In a 9- by 13- by 2-inch baking dish, make alternate layers of tortillas, sauce, chili mixture, and cheese, until all ingredients are used up, finishing with grated cheese on top. Bake in a preheated oven until bubbly—about 20 minutes. Remove from oven. Stir yogurt until smooth and creamy. Spread over the top and return to oven until set—5 to 10 minutes. Remove from oven, garnish with paprika, cut into squares, and serve immediately.

COCONUT-HONEY ICE CREAM BALLS
YIELD: 4 servings

---

4 scoops vanilla-honey ice cream
1 cup finely chopped filberts,
    almonds, or pumpkin seeds

1 cup grated fresh, or
unsweetened, coconut
Kahlúa for topping

1. Make rounded balls of ice cream with an ice-cream scoop. Place nuts and coconut in separate bowls. Quickly roll each ice cream ball first in nuts and then in coconut. Wrap each ball in a plastic bag and freeze until ready to use. This may be done several days before you plan to serve them.

2. *To serve*: Place each ball in a long-stemmed glass and top with a few tablespoons of Kahlúa.

DOÑA GRACIELA'S BOLILLOS
(Mexican Rolls)
YIELD: 14 bolillos

---

3 to 3½ cups unbleached white
    flour, unsifted
4 teaspoons sugar
1½ teaspoons salt
1 package active dry yeast

2 tablespoons margarine or butter,
softened to room temperature
1¼ cups warm water (120 to 130
degrees)
1 egg white, slightly beaten
1 tablespoon cold water

1. *To assemble dough in an electric mixer without a dough hook*: Mix 1 cup of the flour, sugar, salt, and yeast in large bowl of the mixer. Add softened margarine and warm water. Beat 2 minutes at medium speed. Add 1 more cup of the flour. Beat 2 minutes at high speed. With a wooden spoon, stir in

enough of the remaining flour to make a soft dough. Place dough on a lightly floured board and knead 10 to 12 minutes or until smooth and elastic. Proceed to Step 2.

To assemble dough in an electric mixer with a dough hook: Put yeast and warm water in warmed bowl of mixer. Stir to dissolve yeast. Add sugar, salt, margarine, and 3¼ cups of the flour. Attach bowl and dough hook. Beat and knead according to manufacturer's instructions for making French bread. Add remaining ¼ cup of flour if dough does not leave sides of bowl. Dough will be sticky. Proceed to Step 2.

2. Form dough into a ball and place in a well-greased bowl. Turn once to coat top. Cover tightly with plastic wrap or foil. Set in a warm, draft-free place and let rise until doubled in bulk (about 1 hour).

3. Stir dough down. Put on lightly floured board. Cover with a towel and let rest 10 minutes. Divide dough into 14 equal portions. Shape each into individual oval loaves about 5 inches long. Pinch and twist ends. Place rolls about 3 inches apart on greased and floured baking sheets. Cover with towels and let rise again in a warm, draft-free place (45 minutes to 1 hour).

4. Preheat oven to 400 degrees.

5. When rolls have doubled in size, with a sharp knife make a lengthwise cut, ¼-inch deep, across the top. Fill a large pan with boiling water and place on the bottom rack of the oven. Place pan of rolls on rack directly above and bake from 20 to 25 minutes. (Cover with foil after 15 minutes if rolls are browning too quickly). Remove from oven. Brush tops and sides well with slightly beaten egg white combined with the tablespoon of cold water. Return to oven and bake from 5 to 10 minutes longer or until golden brown and nicely crusted. Cool on a wire rack.

EMPANADITAS
(Miniature Cheese Pies)   YIELD: 48 empanaditas

---

1 cup 2% low-fat or whole milk	⅓ cup vegetable shortening
1 teaspoon salt	12 ounces mozzarella cheese
2½ cups unbleached white flour (may use part whole wheat)	½ cup minced mild green chilies—optional
1 egg, well beaten	Safflower or peanut oil for frying

1. In a small saucepan warm the milk and salt to 105 degrees (baby-bottle temperature). Sift the flour onto a large cutting board. Make a well in the center. Put in the beaten egg and shortening. Work them into the flour with your hands until crumbly. Add the milk and continue working it into the mixture until it forms a soft ball. Knead for 5 minutes until dough is pliable and elastic, slapping it occasionally on the board. Cut into 3 equal portions and cover with a towel.

2. Cut cheese into 16 equal slices and cut each slice into 3 strips. Fold each strip in half. Set aside on a plate.

3. Thinly roll one portion of the dough at a time, with a floured rolling pin,

into a 16- by 16-inch square. Cut into 16 rounds, 4 inches in diameter. Place one folded strip of cheese below the center of each round and top with ½ teaspoon minced chilies. Moisten edges of each circle with milk and fold in half. Pinch edges together firmly with thumb and index finger. Then with a fork firmly press edges down all around. Repeat process until all dough is used.

4. Pour oil 1-inch deep into a large heavy skillet. Heat to 375 degrees or until very hot, but not smoking. Fry *empanaditas*, 8 to 10 at a time, until lightly browned and puffy. Turn occasionally with tongs. Drain on paper towels. Serve warm.

AUTHENTIC ENCHILADA SAUCE
YIELD: 1 quart

---

2 tablespoons whole wheat flour
1 tablespoon ground toasted sesame seeds—optional
¼ cup peanut oil
3 rounded tablespoons powdered red chili pepper*
3 cups water, divided

4 heaping tablespoons tomato paste, divided
1 tablespoon each: salt, ground cumin, ground coriander, and dried oregano
Fresh pressed garlic to taste
1 tablespoon pulverized *jalapeño* chili pepper—optional

1. Place the flour, sesame seeds, and oil in a saucepan over medium-low heat. Stir to dissolve the flour in the oil and cook about 2 minutes, being careful not to brown the flour. Add powdered red chili pepper and stir to make a paste the color of brick-red. Add 1 cup of the water and 2 heaping tablespoons of the tomato paste, stirring well until all the lumps are dissolved.

2. Add another cup of the water, a little at a time, stirring constantly with each addition. Simmer a few minutes until the sauce begins to thicken. Slowly add the remaining cup of water and tomato paste, stirring constantly. Simmer about 5 minutes, stirring occasionally. If thinner sauce is desired, add another ½ to 1 cup water.

3. Add seasonings and at least 2 large cloves of garlic that have been run through a garlic press. If the sauce is too hot, you may need a little more salt. If it isn't hot enough, add a little cayenne pepper or *jalapeño* chili pepper. This sauce may be served immediately or reheated when necessary. It should be stored, covered, in the refrigerator and will keep at least 2 weeks. Leftover sauce may be served on *Huevos Yucatán* (p. 281), *Essential Bean Burritos* (p. 279), tacos, tostados, or any egg, bean, or vegetable dish desired.

*Note: This is not cayenne or red pepper. It is a mildly piquant, ground, red chili powder distributed by Mojave. Look for it in Mexican markets or the section in the grocery store that carries Mexican spices and products. If unavailable, substitute a mild California chili powder, powdered ancho, or mulato chilies, all available in specialty shops.

ESSENTIAL BEAN BURRITOS

For each burrito:
½ cup *Frijoles Refritos* (the
following recipe) or any refried
beans
1 soft whole wheat or white flour
tortilla
¼ cup grated cheese

1 green onion, chopped with tops
2 tablespoons chopped mild green
chilies
1 tablespoon plain low-fat yogurt
or sour cream
Enchilada Sauce (p. 278) or *Salsa
Verde* (p. 284)—optional

1. Preheat oven to 300 degrees.
2. Spread beans evenly over the tortilla. Sprinkle the cheese, onion, and chilies over the top. Spread the yogurt or sour cream in the center. Roll up like a jelly roll and place on a baking sheet or in an oblong baking dish. Cover if desired, with *Enchilada Sauce* or *Salsa Verde*. Bake until warmed through—about 20 minutes. For variation, add sautéed mushrooms or left-over vegetables.

FRIJOLES REFRITOS
(Refried Beans)   YIELD: 8, ½-cup servings

2 cups pinto, black, pink, or red
Mexican beans, washed well
8 cups water
1 small onion, coarsely chopped
2 teaspoons salt

2 tablespoons safflower or peanut
oil
⅛ to ¼ teaspoon crushed red chili
pepper or *epazote**—optional
1 cup crumbled *Supremo*,* grated
Chihuahua,* or mozzarella cheese

**Available at Latin American markets.*

1. *To prepare beans:* In a heavy pot, place beans, water, and ½ of the chopped onion. Bring to a boil, reduce heat to low, cover and simmer without stirring until beans are tender (about 2 to 2½ hours). Add boiling water, if necessary during cooking, to keep beans covered.
2. Stir in salt and allow beans to cool. Do not drain excess liquid (bean broth). If you are not preparing refried beans immediately, refrigerate to prevent souring. They will keep this way for several days.
3. *To prepare frijoles refritos:* Drain and reserve liquid from beans. In a large bowl or crock, mash beans with about ½-cup reserved bean broth, or purée in blender, a little at a time. Set aside.
4. In a large skillet, heat oil over medium-high flame. Add beans, remaining chopped onion, dried chili pepper, and ½-cup of the crumbled or grated cheese. Fry for about 10 minutes, stirring frequently. Sprinkle remaining ½-cup cheese on top, reduce heat to low, and cover until cheese melts. Serve immediately. Top with plain yogurt if desired. Leftovers will keep for several days if refrigerated. *Frijoles* may also be frozen.

GAZPACHO
YIELD: Approximately 2 quarts or 8 to 10 servings

1 pound ripe tomatoes, peeled,
    seeded, and diced
2 cucumbers, peeled and diced
2 green peppers, seeded and diced
1 medium-sized onion, diced
2 garlic cloves
2 sprigs parsley
1 tablespoon cottage cheese

1½ quarts (48 ounces) tomato juice
1 tablespoon each: peanut and
    olive oil
3 tablespoons red wine vinegar
Salt to taste
½ teaspoon freshly ground pepper
Dash cayenne pepper
Diced tomatoes, cucumbers,
    green peppers, and croutons as
    garnish

Finely chop the tomatoes, cucumbers, green peppers, onion, garlic, parsley, and cottage cheese in a food processor or by hand. Ingredients should not be puréed. Stir in the tomato juice, olive and peanut oils, and wine vinegar. Add the salt, freshly ground pepper, and cayenne. Taste and adjust seasonings. Chill until very cold. Serve in chilled soup bowls. Bowls of diced tomatoes, cucumbers, green peppers, and croutons should be passed around to spoon over as a garnish.

HUACHINANGO EN SALSA MEXICANA
(Baked Red Snapper with Mexican Sauce)
YIELD: 4 servings

Salsa Mexicana:
2 tablespoons corn or peanut oil
½ cup each: diced onion, celery, and
    green pepper
2 garlic cloves, crushed
1 bay leaf
6 whole cloves
2 teaspoons each: chopped parsley
    and salt
2½ cups stewed tomatoes, chopped
2 tablespoons whole wheat or all-
    purpose flour

Fish:
1 red snapper (3 pounds)
Salt, cayenne pepper, oregano,
    and garlic powder
½ stick safflower margarine or
    butter, melted

1. *To prepare sauce*: Heat the oil in a 2-quart saucepan over medium heat. Sauté the onion, celery, and green pepper. Add the remaining ingredients except the flour. Cook over low heat about 10 minutes, stirring occasionally. Remove bay leaf and cloves and discard. Dissolve flour in enough water to make a paste and stir into sauce. Simmer 5 minutes or until sauce thickens, stirring frequently. Remove from heat and set aside.
2. Preheat oven to 400 degrees.

3. *To prepare fish*: Line a greased, shallow baking dish with 2 sheets of aluminum foil that extend 2 inches beyond the end of the dish. Lightly grease the foil. Rub the snapper on the inside and out with the salt, cayenne pepper, oregano, and garlic powder. Place on the foil and brush with melted margarine. Bake uncovered in a preheated oven for 20 minutes, basting frequently. Cover with *Salsa Mexicana* and bake 20 minutes longer or until fish flakes easily when tested with a fork. Remove from oven. Using the extended foil as handles, transfer fish to a heated serving platter.

HUEVOS ASADOS CON QUESO
(Baked Eggs with Cheese)   *YIELD: 8 servings*

4 ounces mild green chilies, chopped
4 cups shredded *Chihuahua** or Monterey Jack cheese
*Available at Latin American markets.

6 large eggs, separated
1 cup milk
1 quart *Enchilada Sauce* (p. 278)

1. Grease a 9- by 13-inch oblong pan. Spread half of the chilies on the bottom and cover generously with a layer of cheese. Repeat layering again, first with chilies, and then the remaining cheese.
2. Preheat oven to 350 degrees.
3. Beat egg yolks well. Add milk and beat well again. Beat whites until stiff, but not dry. Carefully fold the whites into the yolk-milk mixture. Pour over chilies and cheese and bake in a preheated oven for 45 minutes.
4. Remove from oven and cover with *Enchilada Sauce*. Return to oven for 15 minutes. Remove from oven, cool slightly, and cut into squares to serve.

HUEVOS REVUELTOS YUCATÁN
(Scrambled Eggs Yucatán Style)   *YIELD: 6 servings*

3 tablespoons peanut oil
½ cup diced onion
¼ cup diced zucchini
¼ cup milk
⅓ cup safflower mayonnaise
8 large eggs, lightly beaten

¼ teaspoon ground cumin
2 tablespoons chopped pimiento or sweet red bell pepper
1 avocado, peeled and sliced for garnish
Enchilada Sauce (p. 278), or any enchilada sauce—optional

1. Heat the oil in a large skillet over medium heat. Add the onion and zucchini and sauté until tender. Combine milk with mayonnaise and stir in the eggs, cumin, and pimiento.
2. Pour egg mixture into a skillet; reduce heat slightly. Cook slowly, stirring occasionally, until eggs are set, but moist. To serve, transfer to a heated

platter and garnish with avocado slices. If you have any leftover enchilada sauce on hand, warm it in a saucepan. Pour it into a bowl or gravy boat and serve as an accompaniment to spoon over the eggs.

MEXICAN FRUIT PLATTER

Attractively arrange on a platter any of the following fruits. Surround with fresh lime wedges.

Banana	Pineapple
Cantaloupe	Strawberry
Guava	Tangerine
Honeydew melon	Ugli
Mango	Watermelon
Papaya	White Sapote

PAN DULCE
*(Mexican Sweet Buns)**   *YIELD: 14 sweet buns*

Dough:
- 1 cup 2% low-fat milk
- 6 tablespoons safflower margarine
- 1 teaspoon brown sugar
- 1 package active dry yeast
- 1 teaspoon salt
- ½ cup, plus 2 tablespoons, firmly packed brown sugar
- 1 cup whole wheat flour, sifted
- 2 eggs
- 2¾ to 3¼ cups unbleached white flour, unsifted

Vanilla Streusel: (for 7 buns)
- ½ cup, plus 2 tablespoons, firmly packed brown sugar
- ⅔ cup, less 2 tablespoons, whole wheat flour, unsifted
- ½ teaspoon grated lemon rind— optional
- 4 to 5 tablespoons safflower margarine at room temperature
- 1 egg
- ½ teaspoon vanilla extract

Chocolate Streusel: (for 7 buns)
- ½ cup, plus 2 tablespoons, firmly packed brown sugar
- ⅔ cup, less two tablespoons, whole wheat flour, unsifted
- 2 tablespoons ground semisweet chocolate
- ½ teaspoon cinnamon
- 4 to 5 tablespoons safflower margarine at room temperature
- 1 egg

Egg Wash:
- 1 egg yolk
- ½ teaspoon water or milk

1. *To prepare dough*: Heat milk, margarine, and 1 teaspoon brown sugar until warm—about 115 degrees. Pour into the large bowl of a mixer. Sprinkle in yeast, stir to dissolve, and let stand 5 minutes to "sponge." Add salt, remaining brown sugar, and 1 cup whole wheat flour. Beat 2 minutes at medium speed until smooth. Add eggs one at a time, beating after each addition. Add 2¼ to 2½ cups white flour, ½ cup at a time, until beaters stop turning or batter is smooth. Remove bowl and scrape down beaters. Beat in enough flour (½ to ¾ cup) to make a stiff dough. Turn out on a lightly floured board and knead 5 to 10 minutes until smooth, elastic, and non-sticky. Shape into a ball and place in an oiled bowl, turning once to coat the surface. Set in a warm, draft-free spot until doubled in bulk—about 1½ hours. About 10 minutes before punching dough down, prepare streusel (crumbly flour, butter, and sugar mixture).

2. *To prepare streusels*: For vanilla streusel, mix in a bowl the sugar, flour, and lemon rind. Cut in margarine with a pastry blender or work in with fingertips until coarse and crumbly. Beat egg with vanilla and stir in, making sure dry ingredients are moistened. Pack lightly into a cup and set aside. Prepare chocolate streusel the same way, replacing ground chocolate and cinnamon for the lemon rind and vanilla.

3. *To shape Pan Dulce*: Punch down dough and turn out on a lightly floured board. Knead 1 minute. Divide into 14 equal portions and roll each into a smooth ball. Cover with a damp towel to prevent drying out. To shape into *Corn Ears*: Roll 7 balls, one at a time, as thinly as possible, into oval shapes. Stretch the sides if necessary to achieve desired shape. Measure out 2 tablespoons of either filling. Break into pea-size lumps and sprinkle over dough. Roll up jelly-roll fashion; pinch edges together, and tuck under. Make deep slashes across the top. To shape into *Horns*: Roll out 7 balls into oval shapes and fill as in *Corn Ears*. Roll up jelly-roll fashion halfway; fold outer edges toward center to form a triangle and continue rolling up. Pinch edges together to seal. Place rolled buns 2 inches apart on 2 well-greased baking sheets. Place in a warm spot and let rise from 30 to 45 minutes.

4. *To bake*: Preheat oven to 350 degrees. Prepare egg-wash by beating the egg yolk with water. Brush lightly over the top of the buns. Place in a preheated oven 12 to 15 minutes or until golden brown. Be sure not to overbake or buns will dry out. Leftovers may be wrapped in foil and reheated in a 300-degree oven.

Note: Unbleached white flour may be substituted for whole wheat flour throughout the recipe if desired.

PEPITA PLEASER
YIELD: 4 servings

---

8 ounces Neufchâtel or cream
  cheese
½ small onion, grated

1 to 2 tablespoons milk
1 cup pepitas (pumpkin seeds)
Dash cayenne pepper

1. Combine cheese and onion and cream them together. Add just enough milk to make a mixture of spreading consistency. Place mixture in the center of a round plate. Flatten into a circle about ½-inch thick. Place in refrigerator and chill until firm (about 1 or 2 hours).

2. *To serve*: Remove cheese from refrigerator. Add a dash of cayenne pepper to the pumpkin seeds and sprinkle them on top of the cheese spread. Surround with stoneground tortilla chips and serve as an appetizer. This recipe may be easily doubled to serve more people.

SALSA VERDE
(Green Tomato Sauce)   YIELD: *Approximately 1¾ cups or 4 servings*

---

1 12-ounce can *tomatillos enteros*
   (Mexican green tomatoes)*
2 green onions, chopped with tops
2 tablespoons chopped fresh
   coriander (*cilantro*)* or 1
   teaspoon ground coriander
½ teaspoon dried oregano

2 to 3 garlic cloves, cut into fourths
½ teaspoon salt
⅛ teaspoon pepper
1 fresh or tinned *jalapeño* or
   serrano chili, seeded and finely
   chopped

Available at Latin American markets and some supermarkets.

Drain off half of the liquid from the tomatoes and discard. Place tomatoes and remaining liquid in a blender with remaining ingredients. Purée until smooth. Use as a sauce for cheese, bean, or chicken enchiladas, eggs, stuffed vegetables, burritos, *flautas*, etc.

SOPA DE FRIJOLES NEGROS
(Black Bean Soup)   YIELD: *Approximately 10 servings*

---

1 pound black beans
1 bay leaf
2 sprigs parsley
1 tablespoon salt
3 tablespoons safflower or peanut
   oil
2 medium-sized onions, diced
2 large garlic cloves, minced

2 quarts vegetable or chicken stock
1 teaspoon dried oregano
1½ teaspoons ground cumin seed
1 tablespoon safflower margarine
   or butter
½ cup heavy cream, whipped for
   garnish
Toasted Bread Rounds (p. 285)—
   optional

1. Soak beans overnight in enough water to cover, plus 4 cups. The following day, pour the beans, soaking water, bay leaf, parsley, and salt into a 3-quart pot. Bring to a boil, reduce heat, and simmer until tender—about 2 to 3 hours—adding more water if necessary.

2. Heat the oil in a soup pot until hot. Brown the onions. Add the garlic

and quickly sauté. Add the stock, oregano, and cumin. Bring to a boil, reduce heat, and simmer 10 minutes.

3. Drain the beans and add to the stock. Taste and adjust seasonings. Stir in the margarine or butter. Simmer 20 minutes longer.

4. Ladle soup into bowls. Garnish each with a dollop of whipped cream. Accompany with a basket of toasted bread rounds if desired.

TOASTED BREAD ROUNDS
YIELD: Serves 8 to 10

---

1 loaf French bread or 4 *Bolillos*
(p. 276)
1 stick safflower margarine, melted
Garlic powder

4 ounces *Queso Añejo,** crumbled,
or ½ cup grated Parmesan cheese
2 tablespoons sesame seeds

**Available at Latin American markets.*

1. Preheat oven to 325 degrees.
2. Cut the bread into ½-inch slices. Brush each with melted margarine. Sprinkle with garlic powder and cheese. Garnish tops with sesame seeds.
3. Place on an ungreased baking sheet. Bake 15 to 20 minutes or until golden. Serve warm as a bread accompaniment to any soup.

THE GREAT ENCHILADA CASSEROLE
YIELD: 12 enchiladas

Corn or peanut oil
12 corn tortillas
4 to 5 cups grated mozzarella
cheese
1 cup minced onion, sautéed
½ cup chopped black olives
4 ounces chopped green chilies

8 ounces plain, low-fat yogurt or
sour cream
Enchilada Sauce (p. 278) or 1
quart any enchilada sauce
1 large tomato, chopped
2 green onions, chopped with tops
Shredded lettuce—optional

1. *To prepare tortillas*: Pour oil in a small skillet, about ¼-inch deep. Heat oil over medium heat until barely smoking and reduce heat to low (this prevents the oil from tasting "raw"). Using tongs, drop in tortillas, one at a time, for just a few seconds until they puff slightly. Remove and drain well on paper towels (pat well with the towels to remove as much excess oil as possible).

2. Preheat oven to 350 degrees.

3. *To prepare filling*: Place approximately ⅓-cup grated cheese, 1 tablespoon sautéed onion, 1½ teaspoons chopped olives, and a sprinkling of green chilies on one end of a tortilla and roll it up. Repeat until all tortillas are filled and rolled. Reserve any leftover filling.

4. *To assemble casserole*: Place 8 tortillas, side by side, in an oblong baking dish; the remaining 4 will fit into an 8- by 8-inch square pan. Or, if you own

individual enchilada dishes, place 2 tortillas in each dish. Place yogurt in a bowl and whip it with a fork until nice and fluffy. Spread a layer over the tortillas and pour over enough sauce to cover all. Sprinkle any remaining filling along with the chopped tomato and green onions on top. Bake in a preheated oven until hot, about 15 to 20 minutes. Serve surrounded with shredded lettuce if desired. Leftovers may be frozen.

Variations: 1. *Cheese-Bean Enchiladas*: Reduce the amount of cheese in each enchilada to ¼ cup, eliminate black olives, and add a few tablespoons of refried beans to each tortilla.

2. *Guacamole Enchiladas*: Reduce the amount of cheese in each enchilada to ¼ cup and add ¼ cup guacamole or *Avocado Flauta* (p. 273) filling to each tortilla.

3. *Pine-nut Enchiladas*: Replace black olives with ½-cup pine nuts and replace green chilies with 1 cup chopped, sautéed mushrooms.

TORTA DE CHOCOLATE
(Mexican Chocolate Torte)   YIELD: 14 *servings*

Pastry:
2¼ cups all-purpose flour
2 tablespoons sugar
½ teaspoon salt
½ cup cocoa
1 cup chilled safflower margarine
 or butter, cut into 1-inch pieces
2 eggs, slightly beaten
 Grated rind of ½ lemon
1 tablespoon ice water

Filling:
11 ounces semisweet chocolate
 pieces
2⅔ tablespoons light cream
5 tablespoons safflower margarine
 or butter
4 egg yolks
1½ teaspoons vanilla extract or dark
 rum
1 cup sliced almonds, toasted

1. *To prepare pastry*: Sift the flour, sugar, salt, and cocoa together into a large mixing bowl. Cut in the margarine or butter pieces with a pastry blender or two knives until pieces are the size of peas. Gently stir in the eggs and lemon rind with a wooden spoon to form a soft dough. Add the ice water, only if necessary, to moisten the dough a little more. Gather into a ball and divide into 4 equal pieces. Roll each piece into a ball, wrap in waxed paper, and chill 2 hours.

2. Preheat oven to 325 degrees.

3. Remove one ball at a time from the refrigerator. Roll between two pieces of waxed paper to a 9-inch circle. Slide onto a cookie sheet. Carefully remove the top layer of waxed paper. Place a 9-inch plate over the circle and cut around it. Trim off excess dough and reserve. Remove plate. Patch any tears or uneven edges with excess dough. Prick well with a fork to prevent dough from puffing while baking.

4. Bake in a preheated oven from 6 to 8 minutes or until pastry is as firm as a soft brownie. Remove to a wire rack to cool. Carefully peel off bottom layer of waxed paper. Repeat process with remaining dough. It is impor-

tant during the entire process to work as quickly as possible to prevent dough from becoming too soft to roll or peel off waxed paper. If this happens, chill again 15 minutes.

5. *To prepare filling*: Place the chocolate, cream, and margarine in the top of a double boiler. Stir over hot, but not boiling, water until chocolate and margarine are melted. Beat egg yolks in a bowl until thick and lemon-colored. Stir 6 tablespoons of the chocolate mixture very gradually into the yolks. This will prevent the yolks from curdling in the hot chocolate. Add yolks to chocolate mixture, stirring constantly until thoroughly blended. Remove from heat and stir in the vanilla or rum and half of the toasted almonds.

6. *To assemble torte*: Place 1 layer of pastry on a dessert plate. Spread a thick layer of filling evenly over the pastry. Repeat process with remaining layers of pastry and filling, ending with filling on top. Sprinkle remaining nuts over the top. Spread any remaining filling around the sides. Refrigerate 15 to 30 minutes to firm up chocolate filling. This is a very rich torte—cut into thin slices to serve.

Variation: Cut the amount of filling in half. Cover the first and third layers of pastry with apricot or raspberry preserves. Cover the second and fourth layers with chocolate filling. Sprinkle nuts on top as above.

MEXICO/RECIPE ANALYSIS CHART

Name of Recipe	Quantity	Calories	CHO gms.	Protein gms.	Total Fat gms.	Saturated Fat gms.	Choles- terol mg.	Dietary Fiber gms.
1. *Salsa Verde* (Green Tomato Sauce)	per serving	31	7 (88%)	1 (12%)	—	—	—	1.0
2. *Empanaditas* (Miniature Cheese Pies)	each	78	6 (32%)	2 (10%)	5 (58%)	2 (23%)	12	0
3. Gazpacho	per ¾-cup serving	108	13 (48%)	3 (11%)	5 (41%)	1 (8%)	—	1.2
4. *Doña Graciela's Bolillos* (Mexican Rolls)	each	110	20 (73%)	3 (11%)	2 (16%)	—	—	—
5. Mexican Fruit Platter	per serving	114	27 (98%)	1 (1%)	1 (1%)	—	—	2.0
6. Authentic En- chilada Sauce	per ½-cup serving	132	23 (69%)	2 (1%)	5 (30%)	2 (9.0%)	—	.10
7. Banana Milk *Liquado*	per glass	188	40 (85%)	7 (15%)	—	—	6	.1
8. Toasted Bread Rounds	per serving	192	16 (33%)	5 (10%)	12 (57%)	3 (14%)	1	—
9. *Sopa de Frijoles Negros* (Black Bean Soup)	per ¾-cup serving	214	29 (54%)	11 (21%)	6 (25%)	1 (4%)	—	2.0
10. Avocado *Flautas*	each	218	22 (40%)	5 (10%)	12 (50%)	2 (8%)	8	.8
11. *Frijoles Refritos*	per ½-cup serving	255	33 (52%)	15 (24%)	7 (24%)	—	2	3.0
12. Corn-Stuffed Peppers	per pepper	267	20 (30%)	15 (22%)	14 (48%)	3 (10%)	3	3.0
13. Pepita Pleaser	per serving	276	8 (12%)	18 (26%)	19 (62%)	6 (19%)	45	.8
14. Coconut- Honey Ice Cream Balls	per scoop	284	21 (30%)	5 (7%)	20 (63%)	7 (22%)	75	1.0
15. *Chilequiles Maranze*	per serving	292	28 (38%)	9 (12%)	16 (50%)	4 (13%)	16	2.0

Name of Recipe	Quantity	Calories	CHO gms.	Protein gms.	Total Fat gms.	Saturated Fat gms.	Choles-terol mg.	Dietary Fiber gms.
16. *Chilies Re-llenos Rubalcava*	per serving	293	14 (19%)	12 (16%)	21 (65%)	7 (22%)	179	2.0
17. *Huevos Asados Con Queso* (Baked Eggs with Cheese)	per serving	305	5 (7%)	15 (20%)	25 (73%)	8 (24%)	264	.2
18. *Huevos Re-vueltos Yucatán* (Scrambled Eggs Yucatán Style)	per serving	315	7 (9%)	11 (14%)	27 (77%)	5 (14%)	362	.8
19. *Huachinango en Salsa Mexicana* (Baked Red Snapper with Mexican Sauce)	per serving	348	12 (14%)	47 (54%)	12 (32%)	—	30	1.3
20. Guacamole Enchiladas	each	373	33 (35%)	22 (24%)	17 (41%)	2 (5%)	4	1.7
21. The Great Enchilada Casserole	each	380	23 (25%)	24 (26%)	21 (49%)	10 (24%)	5	.7
22. Cheese-Bean Enchiladas	each	402	23 (23%)	28 (28%)	22 (49%)	10 (24%)	4	2.2
23. *Torta de Chocolate*	per serving	440	34 (31%)	6 (5%)	32 (64%)	9 (18%)	134	.4
24. *Pan Dulce* with Chocolate Streusel	1 sweet bun	478	75 (63%)	9 (8%)	16 (29%)	3 (6%)	113	.8
25. *Pan Dulce* with Vanilla Streusel	1 sweet bun	484	75 (62%)	10 (8%)	16 (30%)	1 (2%)	187	.8
26. Pine-nut Enchiladas	each	516	32 (25%)	34 (27%)	28 (48%)	6 (10%)	5	2.0
27. Essential Bean Burritos	each	587	68 (47%)	27 (19%)	23 (34%)	4 (8%)	4	5.0

Numbers in parentheses (%) indicate percentage of total calories contributed by nutrient.

MENUS

LOW CALORIE SPECIALTIES
(500 to 700 calories per meal)

MEXICAN FRUIT PLATTER
AVOCADO FLAUTAS
Alfalfa Sprouts and Sliced Tomatoes
**COCONUT-HONEY ICE CREAM
BALLS**

GAZPACHO
**HUACHINANGO EN SALSA
MEXICANA**
**(BAKED RED SNAPPER WITH
MEXICAN SAUCE)**
**DOÑA GRACIELA'S BOLILLOS
(MEXICAN ROLLS)**
Fresh Papaya with Wedge of Lime

SOPA DE FRIJOLES NEGROS (BLACK BEAN SOUP)
HUEVOS REVUELTOS YUCATÁN
(SCRAMBLED EGGS YUCATÁN STYLE) with
SALSA VERDE (GREEN TOMATO SAUCE)
Steamed Tortillas
Sliced Mangos and Pears

●

LOW CHOLESTEROL MENUS
(Less than 50 mgs. of cholesterol per meal)

GAZPACHO
PINE-NUT ENCHILADA
Alfalfa Sprouts
Steamed Zucchini with Lemon
Cantaloupe

**THE GREAT ENCHILADA
CASSEROLE**
FRIJOLES REFRITOS
Shredded Lettuce
Green and Red Pepper Rings
Sliced Bananas and Oranges

CORN-STUFFED PEPPERS with
SALSA VERDE (GREEN TOMATO SAUCE)
Sliced Avocados with Fresh Coriander
Tangerines and Ugli Fruit
Chilled Apple Juice

LOW SATURATED FAT SELECTIONS
(Less than 8 grams of saturated fat per meal)

CHILEQUILES MARANZE
FRIJOLES REFRITOS
Shredded Lettuce and Grated Carrot
Salad
Watermelon

BANANA MILK LIQUADO
GUACAMOLE ENCHILADAS
Steamed Rice
Fresh Papaya with Wedge of Lime

Jalapeño Peppers
SOPA DE FRIJOLES NEGROS (BLACK BEAN SOUP)
DOÑA GRACIELA'S BOLILLOS (MEXICAN ROLLS)
Fresh Pineapple and Oranges
Iced Mint Tea

•

HIGH PROTEIN MEALS
(30 or more grams of protein per meal)

Freshly Squeezed Orange Juice
**PAN DULCE WITH VANILLA
STREUSEL**
**HUEVOS ASADOS CON QUESO
(BAKED EGGS WITH CHEESE)**
FRIJOLES REFRITOS
Fresh Strawberries

Jalapeño Peppers
ESSENTIAL BEAN BURRITO
Sliced Radishes and Carrot Sticks
STRAWBERRY MILK LIQUADO

PEPITA PLEASER
CORN-STUFFED PEPPERS
Honeydew Melon
TORTA DE CHOCOLATE
Coffee or Hot Tea

WELL BALANCED LUNCH OR DINNER MENUS
(Selections that conform to recommendations in Dietary Goals for United States*)*

GAZPACHO
FRIJOLES REFRITOS
GUACAMOLE ENCHILADAS
BANANA MILK LIQUADO

MEXICAN FRUIT PLATTER
SOPA DE FRIJOLES NEGROS
(BLACK BEAN SOUP)
HUACHINANGO EN SALSA
MEXICANA
(BAKED RED SNAPPER WITH
MEXICAN SAUCE)
PAN DULCE WITH CHOCOLATE
STREUSEL
Coffee

PAPAYA MILK LIQUADO
CHILEQUILES MARANZE
Steamed Tortillas
Iced Tea

CHAPTER 12

POLAND
From Chopin to Cake Pan

Culinary Essentials

Take a group of root vegetables like potatoes, turnips, beets, and carrots. Combine them with a few dried mushrooms and a handful of barley. Add a dollop of sour cream and a sprinkling of dill and you have the recipe for a Polish diet. There's nothing fancy about this cuisine, and to appreciate it is to recognize the resourcefulness of cooks confronted with a minimum of fresh produce and tighter purse strings. Although the hearty affairs that characterize the Polish kitchen do not scale the heights of culinary *hauteur*, they're perfect if you're searching for simple, satisfying foods.

Both the novice and budget-minded cook will find solace in Polish cooking. The former will be relieved that most dishes are as easy to assemble as an all-American casserole. The latter will delight in the fact that recipes primarily call for low-cost ingredients like cabbage, unseasoned bread crumbs, eggs, green onions, and pot or cottage cheese.

Epicureans can be appeased with dried Polish mushrooms, which are tastier, meatier, and more exotic than the cultivated variety. Although they are only obtainable at imported food shops and a bit costlier than fresh mushrooms, nevertheless the culinary virtuosity of these imported delicacies is more than ample compensation. You can sauté, stuff, or pickle them like fresh mushrooms or add them to soups, sauces, and stews. But remember, unless placed in a long-simmering dish where they will soften, dried mushrooms must be soaked from thirty to sixty minutes before using; once reconstituted, they will keep several days refrigerated. If necessary, dried Italian or French mushrooms may be substituted, but not the Chinese variety which have a stronger taste.

When the "white-rice-for-dinner routine" has got you in a blue funk, do as the Poles do: Think barley! This ancient grain, with its creamy texture and nutty flavor, can serve as a perfect change of tempo. When cooked like rice, barley can be employed in many felicitous ways. Toss it with sautéed mushrooms, onions, and a handful of freshly chopped dill for a side dish with Eastern European overtones. When you're looking for a unique stuffing for cabbage leaves or capon, this robust grain fills the bill. Or, you might enjoy *Krupnik*, a renowned Polish soup that takes its wholesome goodness from barley, potatoes, and dried mushrooms. Accented by the spirited flavors of dill and parsley, this stout pottage makes an excellent repast on wintry evenings, especially when accompanied by thick wedges of *Dark Rye Bread* and farmer's cheese.

Poles are inordinately fond of noodles and prepare them in fantastic ways. When blended with chopped apples and brown sugar, or sour cream and honey, and baked until lightly browned, boiled egg noodles are suitable for serving with almost any nonstarchy Polish entrée. *Noodle Molds*, individual "cakes" rich with yogurt and golden raisins, offer admirable support for light courses composed of fruit or vegetables. *Ravioli* lovers will relish *Pierogi*, the Polish version of this Italian favorite. Shaped into crescents and boiled until tender, these delicate little morsels can be filled in a variety of ways with potatoes and cheese, fresh blueberries, or smoky-flavored sauerkraut; a side dish of plain yogurt or sour cream, to be spooned over as desired, provides the finishing touch.

When you prepare vegetables Polish-style, don't expect complex sauces or lavish embellishments. Most often, they are served "à la Polonaise," which means simply adorned with bread crumbs and butter and brightened with a squeeze of lemon juice. You can annoint steamed string beans, asparagus, baby carrots, or whole leaves of Savoy cabbage in a similar fashion, or try our version of *Brussels Sprouts Polonaise*. Potatoes, on the other hand, usually receive another treatment—a smattering of sour cream, sautéed onions, and fresh dill. If you are in an upbeat mood, you might orchestrate something a little more time consuming such as *Potato and Mushroom Casserole*. This stalwart mélange, touched with cream and allspice, illustrates well peasant cookery at its heartiest.

Capturing the spirit of a Polish meal is as important as presenting authentic flavors. A pastel-colored or hand-embroidered tablecloth, bedecked with vases of lilies-of-the-valley, and the recorded sound of a Chopin nocturne softly playing in the background will set the stage. A basket of warm *razowy chleb* (pumpernickel bread) is always present for dinner as is a bowl of pickled or creamed herring, sliced cucumbers with sour cream, pot cheese, and iced Polish vodka.

If you plan to serve several courses, begin with something light, perhaps *Stuffed Eggs from Warsaw* and *Cwikla*, a caraway-flecked, pickled beet relish. Salads are not the delicate, leafy lettuce combinations we know well (weather-sensitive produce is very expensive in Poland and rarely used), but rather novel mixtures comprised of knob celery, potatoes, cabbage, or cottage cheese.

When it comes to desserts, however, Polish foods move out of the realm of the robust and into the realm of the elegant. Conclude your dinner on a high note with either the raisin-studded *Apple-Apricot Cake* or the sinfully delicious *Mocha-Walnut Torte*. Either one should rate a rave review.

Seasoning Essentials

How many times have you spoiled an Indian curry or Szechuan stir-fry because you got carried away with the hot chili peppers? If the answer is "too many times," you're apt to find Polish cooking a good shelter from seasoning disasters. A limited number of herbs and spices are employed in this cuisine, and the favored few—caraway, horseradish, dill, and cinnamon—are used in judicious amounts.

Caraway seeds make an invaluable contribution to this heartwarming culinary style. The novice can sprinkle them over almost any cabbage, beet, or sauerkraut preparation and be assured a harmonious alliance. Adventurous cooks can transform turnips, cauliflower, or carrots into a novel side dish with a good pinch of these pungent crescents. And bread-bakers will find them crucial to the success of a good dark rye or pumpernickel.

If you have relegated horseradish to a condiment bowl, the Polish cuisine might convince you otherwise. This forthright seasoning is highly esteemed in Eastern European kitchens for its ability to enhance sauces and relishes. You can ennoble a basic white sauce or strengthen an insipid beet relish with just a smidgen of this zestful herb. Stir it into sour cream and you have a memorable topping for potatoes or baked fish.

Although commercial horseradish can be used in most Polish recipes, try to use the fresh variety when available. Fresh horseradish should be washed well and, if the outer skin seems tough or discolored, scraped lightly. To use, grate finely or shred with a sharp knife. Try to keep the pieces as small as possible; eating a chunk of horseradish root is a sensation comparable to biting a clove of raw garlic. Be sure to grate just before using, as the pungency of fresh horseradish diminishes rapidly once exposed to air.

The ubiquitous role of cinnamon, nutmeg, and allspice reflects the Polish affinity for delicate flavors. Depending upon how much you are in the mood to experiment, you can use these aromatic spices interchangeably or in combination. Those who want the spiciness of a dish to really shine through might try the *Polish Spice Blend*, which could be called the Eastern European analogue to American pumpkin-pie spice. This highly perfumed mixture, accented with mace and ginger, can be counted on to brighten the flavor of almost any fruit soup, sweet noodle pudding, or spice cake.

POLISH SEASONING CHART

CARAWAY is responsible for the warm, pronounced flavor associated with some of the more robust Polish dishes. These bow-shaped seeds blend exotically with hearty vegetables like cauliflower, turnips, and carrots. This pleasantly pungent seasoning can be tossed with boiled noodles and sauerkraut or sprinkled over baked apples and turnips. In dark breads, such as rye or pumpernickel, caraway seeds are a welcome addition; 1 tablespoon per loaf is sufficient enough to add a lovely scent and flavor without overwhelming.

DILL is the only herb used in this cooking style with any frequency. Fresh dill is available in many supermarkets near the end of summer. The status of a salad dressing, sauce, soup, egg, or fish preparation can be raised with the addition of freshly chopped dill leaves. Start with 2 tablespoons fresh, or 2 teaspoons dried, dill to enhance 1 cup of sour cream- or yogurt-based sauces or ¼ cup Polonaise sauce; a quart of soup fashioned from mushrooms, cucumbers, beets, or potatoes will need at least 3 tablespoons fresh, or 3 teaspoons dried, dill. Tufts of feathery dill leaves make a beautiful garnish and are a welcome change on a dinner plate from a sprig of parsley. As a rule, dill is not combined with other seasonings in this cuisine with the exception of salt, pepper, parsley, or horseradish.

HORSERADISH finds its way into everything from cream sauces to pickled beet relish. Horseradish sauces in particular are quite popular in Poland and are usually made with a base of dairy or sour cream. Fresh horseradish root, native to Eastern Europe, can be found in the produce section of many large supermarkets. When uncooked, it is quite pungent, but its potency diminishes rapidly once grated. In most recipes, the root is interchangeable with prepared horseradish, which is readily available at even small grocery stores. As a rule, 1 tablespoon of the freshly grated root is equivalent to 4 teaspoons of the prepared variety. Either one can be mixed into grated apples to make a tasty condiment for fish, chicken, or stuffed eggs.

JUNIPER BERRIES are the bluish-gray fruit of the juniper tree. When dried, they are extremely aromatic and have a bittersweet taste. Though readily available on most spice racks, juniper berries receive little attention from American cooks. In Poland, a few crushed berries are a popular addition to cooked sauerkraut or cabbage. Most often, they are utilized in bread stuffings for chickens or capons; enthusiasts will use anywhere from 15 to 20 crushed berries for 2 cups of stuffing. When combined with garlic and brandy, juniper berries will impart an elusive and sublime flavor to Polish liver pâtés.

POLISH SPICE BLEND can be called upon when you want to give sweet noodle dishes, fruit soups, or baked cabbage a delicate, spicy flavor. As long as you don't go overboard, this fragrant blend can be added fearlessly to black bread pudding, egg custard, *baba au rhum*, or fruit compote. A good pinch will enliven a pâté or fruit filling for *pierogi*. You can substitute this blend for cinnamon in most recipes.

Combine and store in an airtight container:

2   tablespoons ground Ceylon cinnamon
1   teaspoon each: nutmeg and ginger
¾   teaspoon allspice
¼   teaspoon mace

Other seasonings found in Polish cookery: marjoram, basil, paprika, parsley, mustard seed, poppy seed, garlic, thyme, cinnamon, bay leaves, allspice, mace, ginger, nutmeg, and celery seed.

Nutritional Essentials

When nutritionists and epidemiologists discuss ethnic diets which are exemplary of healthful eating patterns—i.e., moderate in calorie content, adequate in vitamins and protein, low in fat and cholesterol—the cuisines of India, China, and the Middle East come to mind. Polish cooking, however, perhaps because it is not as well known, has received little attention regarding its dietary virtues, which are on par with the more exotic diets cited above.

The Polish recipes in this chapter are distinguished for being lower in calories than those of any other cuisine represented in this volume. Averaging only 134 calories per serving, a large number of the dishes also conform to guidelines set forth by the *Dietary Goals for the United States*: 45 percent of the total caloric content is derived from carbohydrates, 15 percent from protein, and 40 percent from fat, of which only 13 percent is saturated. Because this style of cookery takes advantage of wholesome foods which are high in complex carbohydrates but low in fat—potatoes, mushrooms, cabbage—it will meet the approval of calorie-counters and fat-conscious cooks alike.

Poland, along with Germany, leads Europe in potato production. As one of the world's most important vegetables, potatoes have kept entire nations alive during stress, and when imaginatively prepared, can add character (and abundant nutrients) to a Lucullan feast.

Unfortunately, when it comes to dieting, few foods have been as maligned as the potato. It has taken the blame for the additional calories lavished on it by cooking oils, butter, cheeses, and cream. If the truth be told, this tuber can play an integral part in the dieter's repertoire. A medium-sized potato contains only 90 calories, or about as much as an orange, an apple, or a single slice of buttered toast. Ultimately, the number of calories in a potato dish depends not only upon the embellishments, but the manner in which it is prepared. One potato, French fried, contains about 360 calories; when pan fried, 240; and when boiled, only 71 calories. As a rule, Slavic cookery employs this humble food in its simplest (usually nonfried) form, and thus takes advantage of its low calorie content.

Potatoes contain a good amount of vitamin C, as well as some iron, B vitamins, phosphorus, and other minerals. Whenever possible, serve them in their skins inasmuch as most of the nutrients are concentrated in the layer beneath. A substantial amount of this vegetable's vitamin C content is lost during cooking; still more is lost if cooked potatoes are stored for later use.

The Polish cuisine, perhaps more than all others, glamorizes the potato in a number of dishes, which are nutritionally beyond reproach. The potato-based recipes, for the most part, are *not* embellished by high calorie oils, butter, or cream, resulting in an average calorie count of 54 to 222 per serving in the following dishes: *Pierogi, Boiled Potato Dumplings, Vegetable Barley Soup,* and *Potato and Mushroom Casserole.* Additionally, each of these preparations is accompanied by a dairy item—yogurt, sour cream, or milk—which complements the essential amino acid make-up of potato protein. On the whole, potatoes and Polish cooking are inseparable. The result is a nutritious marriage, yielding satisfying, low-calorie, low-fat creations that have a place in any health-oriented diet.

After the potato, the mushroom, more than any other food, is the mainstay of the meatless Polish cuisine. These tasty fungi, while having minimal nutritive value, are valuable to dieters for they give a feeling of a full meal, with only a small number of calories. Largely composed of water, mushrooms contain only about 103 calories per pound. You will find them used in combination with a number of vegetables to produce satisfying low-calorie dishes such as *Mushroom Cutlets* and *Cauliflower with Dried Mushroom Sauce.*

Finally, Polish cooking calls upon many dairy items, particularly sour cream and cottage cheese, to supplement or to serve as ingredients for main dishes. Because of the high calorie count of sour cream, we have chosen to substitute yogurt in many of the recipes. Cottage cheeses are also available in high and low-fat varieties. The following chart of nutritive values of cottage cheeses, yogurts, and sour cream will help you determine the item most suitable to your dietary needs.

Nutritive Values of Sour Cream, Cottage Cheeses, and Yogurts
(Values per one-cup servings)

Nutrient:	Sour Cream	Cottage Creamed	Cottage Dry Curd (unsalted)	Cottage Low Fat (1% Milk)	Skim-Milk Yogurt	Whole-Milk Yogurt	Lowfat Yogurt Plain	Lowfat Yogurt Fruited
Calories	454	217	123	164	127	139	144	239
Protein, Grams	7	26	25	28	13	8	12	11
Fat, Grams	44	10	1	2	.5	7	4	3
Saturated Fat Grams	42	6	—	1.3	—	5	2	2
Carbohydrate Grams	8	3	3	6	17	11	16	42
Cholesterol Milligrams	112	10	10	10	4	29	14	12
Sodium Milligrams	96	850	19	918	174	105	159	147
Calcium Milligrams	240	230	180	120	452	274	415	383

BRUSSELS SPROUTS POLONAISE

YIELD: 4 servings

1 pound Brussels sprouts
2 tablespoons safflower margarine
  or butter
2 teaspoons lemon juice

½ teaspoon salt
¼ teaspoon white pepper
2 tablespoons bread crumbs

Place Brussels sprouts in a saucepan with a small amount of lightly salted water to which a good pinch of sugar has been added. Bring to a boil, cover, and cook 5 to 8 minutes or until just tender. Drain and keep warm. Heat the margarine or butter in a skillet. Add the lemon juice, salt, and pepper. Pour over the Brussels sprouts and sprinkle bread crumbs on top. Serve immediately.
Variation: Replace Brussels sprouts with string beans, cauliflower, kohlrabi, Savoy cabbage, carrots, or leeks.

CAULIFLOWER WITH
DRIED MUSHROOM SAUCE

YIELD: 4 to 6 servings

1 large head cauliflower
1 ounce dried Polish mushrooms
1 small onion, finely chopped
2 cups vegetable or chicken stock
3 tablespoons safflower margarine
  or butter

3 tablespoons flour
Salt and pepper to taste
½ cup plain, low-fat yogurt or sour
  cream
2 tablespoons chopped parsley

1. Place cauliflower, stem-end-down, in a large pot of boiling salted water. Cover and cook gently for about 15 minutes or until tender but compact and firm. Drain thoroughly and let cool slightly. Meanwhile prepare sauce.
2. Place mushrooms, onion, and stock in a saucepan. Bring to a boil, reduce heat, and simmer until mushrooms are tender. In another saucepan stir the margarine or butter and flour over moderate heat for 3 to 5 minutes without browning. Slowly add mushroom-stock mixture, stirring constantly. Bring to a boil and continue to stir until thickened. Season to taste with salt and pepper. Remove from heat and stir in the yogurt or sour cream and parsley. Place cauliflower in a serving dish and cover with mushroom sauce.
Variation: Replace yogurt or sour cream with 2 tablespoons lemon juice (or to taste).

CHICKEN SOUP

YIELD: 8 cups chicken soup

1 stewing hen, cut up (5 pounds)
Salt
2½ quarts water
1 large onion
1 bay leaf

2 teaspoons salt
4 carrots
2 sprigs fresh parsley
2 ribs celery, cut in halves

1. Clean and remove excess fat from chicken pieces. Wash and pat dry. Sprinkle with salt. Put into a soup pot with the water. Bring to a boil and remove any surface scum with a slotted spoon. Cook for 1 hour over medium heat.
2. Add the onion, bay leaf, salt, and carrots. Tie parsley and celery together with white thread and add to soup pot. Simmer 1½ hours or until chicken is tender. Taste and adjust seasonings. Remove chicken and vegetables. Discard onion, bay leaf, parsley, and celery. Reserve carrots and chicken.* Strain soup through a fine sieve into quart containers. Chill in the refrigerator until fat congeals on top.
3. *To serve*: Remove congealed fat from chilled stock. Reheat soup with carrots. Serve over boiled noodles if desired. Soup may be frozen and thawed before reheating.

Note: Reserved chicken can be reheated with soup or saved for other uses such as chicken crêpes, salads, etc.

CHOPPED CHICKEN LIVERS

YIELD: Approximately 3 cups

3 tablespoons safflower margarine
  or rendered chicken fat
1 pound chicken livers
2 medium-sized onions, sliced
1 small onion
6 eggs, hard boiled

1 teaspoon salt
½ teaspoon pepper
Pinch of sugar
4 tablespoons rendered chicken fat
Parsley—optional
Whole grain crackers or rye bread

1. Heat the 3 tablespoons of margarine or fat in a large heavy skillet. Sauté the livers until brown. Add the sliced onions. Cook until livers are no longer pink in the center. Cool. Reserve pan juices.
2. Chop the liver and onions in a wooden bowl or put through a grinder. Chop the small onion and the eggs. Mix all together. Add the reserved pan juices, salt, pepper, sugar, and enough of the chicken fat to hold ingredients together. Taste and correct seasonings.
3. Put into a fluted mold or glass bowl. Refrigerate. To serve, unmold onto a glass platter. Garnish with parsley on top. Surround with crackers or rye bread.

CWIKLA
(Pickled Beet Relish)

YIELD: *Approximately*
5 cups or 10 servings

---

10 medium-sized beets, cooked and
   cooled
3 tablespoons grated horseradish
   root
2 teaspoons caraway seed

1½ tablespoons brown sugar
1 cup apple cider vinegar
½ cup water
1 tablespoon salt

Remove skins from cooked beets. Grate coarsely. Combine with horse-radish and caraway seed. Place brown sugar, vinegar, water, and salt in a saucepan. Bring to a boil and pour over beets. Refrigerate overnight. This will keep up to a week refrigerated. Serve as a condiment to Polish meals.

DARK RYE BREAD •

YIELD: *1 loaf or 16 servings*

---

2 tablespoons safflower margarine
   or butter
½ cup light molasses
2 teaspoons salt
2 tablespoons caraway seed
1 cup milk, scalded
½ cup warm water (110 degrees)
½ teaspoon sugar

2 packages dry active yeast
2 cups rye flour
4 tablespoons cocoa
1 cup whole wheat flour
1½ cups unbleached white flour
Cornmeal
Melted margarine or butter—
   optional

1. Place the margarine, molasses, salt, and caraway seed in a large mixing bowl. Cover with scalded milk and cool to lukewarm. Combine the warm water and sugar. Sprinkle in yeast and let stand 5 minutes to "foam." Combine yeast with the lukewarm milk. Mix the rye flour and cocoa together. Add to the milk and beat 100 strokes. Add the wheat flour and unbleached white flour gradually to form a stiff dough.
2. Turn dough out onto a lightly floured board and knead 10 to 15 minutes or until smooth and elastic, adding more flour if necessary to prevent stickiness. Shape into a ball and place in a greased bowl. Turn dough once to grease the top. Cover and place in a warm, draft-free spot until doubled in bulk—about 2 hours.
3. Punch down dough and shape into a round loaf. Place on a greased, round baking sheet sprinkled liberally with cornmeal. Let rise 45 minutes.
4. Preheat oven to 375 degrees.
5. Bake 35 to 40 minutes or until the bottom sounds hollow when tapped. Brush with melted margarine or butter 5 minutes before done if a more tender crust is desired.

DORKA'S APPLE-APRICOT CAKE

YIELD: 12 to 14 servings

Dough:
- 1 cup unbleached or all-purpose flour
- 1½ teaspoons baking powder
- ½ cup, plus 2 tablespoons, sugar
- 1 stick safflower margarine or butter, softened at room temperature
- ½ teaspoon vanilla extract
- 1 large egg

Filling:
- 8 large cooking apples, peeled, cored, and coarsely chopped
- ¼ cup fine unseasoned bread crumbs
- ½ cup raisins
- ½ cup apricot preserves or orange marmalade
- 3 tablespoons brown sugar
- 2 tablespoons bread crumbs for topping

1. *To prepare dough*: Sift the flour and baking powder into a large mixing bowl. Stir in the sugar. Add the margarine or butter, cut into 1-inch pieces. Work in with a fork or pastry blender until mixture resembles coarse meal. Add the vanilla. Make a small well in the center of the mixture and break in the egg. Stir in with a wooden spoon. Gather dough into a ball and knead a few minutes. If necessary, add a little flour while kneading to form a soft, but not sticky, dough. Cover and set aside.

2. *To prepare filling*: Combine in a bowl the apples, bread crumbs, raisins, preserves, and brown sugar. If mixture is too sticky, add more bread crumbs.

3. Preheat oven to 350 degrees.

4. *To assemble*: Grease and flour a 9-inch spring-form pan. Break off ⅔ of the dough and pat it evenly into the bottom of the pan bringing it up about an inch on the sides. Pour filling over the dough, spreading with a spatula to insure evenness. Roll out remaining dough ¼-inch thick. Cut into finger-size strips. Place strips around the edges of the fruit filling. Arrange any remaining strips decoratively over the top. Sprinkle 2 tablespoons bread crumbs over the top. Bake in a preheated oven 1 hour and 20 minutes or until edges are golden brown and have pulled away from the sides. Remove from oven and gently run a knife around the edges to separate any cake that sticks to the sides. Cool ½ hour before removing from pan.

FARMER'S SALAD

YIELD: 4 servings

- 12 ounces creamed cottage cheese
- 5 red radishes
- 4 green onions
- 1 cucumber (peel if waxed), or large dill pickle
- Salt and pepper to taste

Place the cottage cheese in a bowl and stir to separate curds. Wash and dice the radishes. Dice the green onions with green tops. Dice the cucumber.

Combine the vegetables and cottage cheese. Season to taste. Chill before serving.

Variation: Add 1 tomato, diced, 2 hard-boiled eggs, diced, and ½ cup sour cream or plain yogurt.

KARTOFLANE KLUSKI
(Boiled Potato Dumplings)   *YIELD: Serves 6*

---

1 pound red potatoes, peeled, boiled, and cooled
1 tablespoon safflower margarine
1 small onion, minced
2 eggs, beaten
1 tablespoon chopped fresh parsley

1½ tablespoons fine dry bread crumbs
2 to 4 tablespoons flour (or as needed)
Salt and pepper to taste

1. Place boiled potatoes in a large bowl and mash. Melt margarine in a skillet and sauté the onion until transparent. Add to the potatoes, along with the eggs and parsley. Beat well with a wooden spoon. Add bread crumbs and flour. Add more flour if needed to make a stiff dough. Season with salt and pepper. With floured hands, shape dough into balls about 1½ inches in diameter.

2. Drop balls, 6 to 9 at a time, into a large pot of boiling water. Boil gently 12 minutes or until dumplings float to the top. Remove with a slotted spoon to a colander to drain off excess water. Serve plain or with melted margarine and bread crumbs if desired. To add to clear soups, place in a soup tureen and cover with hot soup just before serving.

Variation: *Potato Croquettes*: Shape potato mixture into patties instead of dumplings. Do not boil. Dip in seasoned bread crumbs and fry in hot safflower margarine or peanut oil until golden-brown on both sides.

KOTLETY z GRZBOW
(Mushroom Cutlets)   *YIELD: 6 to 8 cutlets*

½ pound fresh mushrooms
1 small onion
2 tablespoons safflower margarine or butter
¼ teaspoon allspice
1 cup stale bread cubes
¼ cup milk
1 egg, beaten

2 teaspoons chopped parsley
Salt and pepper to taste
¼ to ½ cup fine bread crumbs
3 tablespoons safflower margarine for frying
Plain, low-fat yogurt or sour cream

1. Wash the mushrooms and pat dry. Chop finely and set aside. Mince the onion. Heat the margarine or butter in a skillet and sauté the mushrooms and onion 5 to 10 minutes. Season with allspice. Set aside.
2. Soak the bread cubes in milk 8 minutes. Squeeze out any excess liquid. Add to sautéed mixture along with the egg, parsley, salt, and pepper. Shape into patties using about 3 tablespoons of mixture for each. Dip in bread crumbs and fry in hot margarine until golden-brown on each side. Top each with a dollop of yogurt or sour cream and serve hot as a main course.

KRUPNIK
(Vegetable Barley Soup)

YIELD: 2 to 2½ quarts or 8 to 10 servings

2 cups water
½ cup barley
2 tablespoons safflower margarine or butter
2 medium-sized potatoes, diced
2 large carrots, sliced
1 large onion, chopped
10 dried Polish mushrooms (or substitute 1 cup sliced, fresh mushrooms)

6 cups vegetable or chicken stock
2 tablespoons chopped fresh dill or 2 teaspoons dill weed
¼ cup chopped fresh parsley
Salt and freshly ground pepper to taste
Sour cream—optional

Bring 2 cups water to a boil in a large soup pot. Add the barley and margarine and cook until barley swells and is barely tender. Add the potatoes, carrots, onion, mushrooms, and stock. Bring to a boil and cook over medium heat 20 minutes or until potatoes and mushrooms are tender. Season with dill, parsley, salt, and pepper. Taste and adjust seasonings. Serve hot. Top each portion, if desired, with a dollop of sour cream.

NOODLE MOLDS

YIELD: Approximately 16 noodle molds

16 ounces medium-wide noodles
6 eggs, well beaten
½ stick safflower margarine, melted
½ cup granulated or brown sugar
1 cup plain yogurt or sour cream

Salt and pepper to taste
8 ounces cottage cheese
½ to 1 cup yellow raisins
½ stick safflower margarine

1. Cook noodles in 4 quarts boiling salted water until tender, but firm. Drain in colander. Put noodles back into pot. Stir in the beaten eggs and mix well. Add the melted margarine, sugar, yogurt, salt, and pepper to taste. Return to burner and cook 2 minutes stirring constantly over me-

dium heat. Remove from heat. Stir in cottage cheese and raisins. Blend all ingredients together.

2. Preheat oven to 350 degrees. Fill a 16-cup muffin tin to the top. Wipe the outside of each cup with a damp cloth to remove any excess mixture.

3. Melt remaining ½ stick margarine and pour a little over each noodle mold. Bake 15 minutes in a preheated oven. Reduce heat to 325 degrees and bake 45 minutes more. Remove from oven. Run sharp knife around the edges to loosen. Lift out carefully and serve hot. Leftovers may be reheated.

Variations: Add any of the following: 1 tablespoon vanilla extract, 1 teaspoon grated lemon or orange rind, 1 teaspoon cinnamon, or 2 tablespoons chopped filberts. If desired, dust tops of baked noodle molds with powdered sugar.

PIEROGI
(Potato and Cheese Dumplings)   YIELD: *Approximately 30 pierogi*

Filling:
  1 pound red potatoes, peeled
  2 tablespoons safflower or peanut
    oil
  1 large onion, minced
  ½ pound pot, farmer, or dry cottage
    cheese
    Salt and pepper to taste
  1 teaspoon dill weed—optional
  1 teaspoon garlic powder—
    optional

Dough:
  2 cups all-purpose flour
  ½ teaspoon salt
  2 eggs
  ⅓ to ½ cup very warm water (may
    use part milk)

1. *To prepare filling*: Place potatoes in a pot with enough water to cover. Boil until tender. Drain and mash while hot. Heat oil in a skillet. Sauté the onion 10 minutes or until golden-brown. Add to potatoes. Add the cheese and seasonings. Combine thoroughly and set aside.

2. *To prepare dough*: Place flour in a large mixing bowl. Make a well in the center. Drop salt and eggs in the center. Add water gradually and mix with a wooden spoon. Knead with your hands until dough is soft and of rolling consistency. Cover with a warm bowl and let dough rest 10 to 15 minutes.

3. *To assemble pierogi*: Divide dough into 3 equal parts. Keep 2 parts covered with a damp towel or refrigerated while rolling the third part on a lightly floured board. Roll dough as thinly as possible. Cut into 2½-inch circles with a cookie cutter, sharp knife, or pastry wheel. Place 1 tablespoon filling below the center of each circle. Fold over. Moisten the edges lightly with water and press together to seal. Continue process until all dough and filling is used up.

4. *To boil pierogi*: Bring 3 quarts lightly salted water to a boil. Drop *pierogi*, 6 to 8 at a time, in the water. Boil gently 5 minutes or until they float to the surface. Remove with a slotted spoon. Serve immediately or keep in a low (200-degree) oven until ready to serve. Accompany, if desired, with melted safflower margarine, plain yogurt or sour cream. Serve as a main course or side dish.

Variations: *Blueberry Pierogi*: Replace the potato-cheese filling with 2 cups fresh blueberries. Place 1 teaspoon berries below the center of each circle. Sprinkle with sugar. Fold over, seal, and boil as above. Serve with plain yogurt or sour cream, sweetened if desired.

Sauerkraut Pierogi: Heat 1 tablespoon safflower margarine in a skillet. Add 1½ cups finely chopped, thoroughly drained and squeezed sauerkraut. Season with a dash of pepper and 1 teaspoon caraway seed. Cook 10 minutes over low heat, stirring occasionally. Remove from heat, stir in 2 tablespoons plain yogurt or sour cream, and let cool. Use 1 tablespoon on each circle in place of the potato-cheese filling.

POTATO AND MUSHROOM CASSEROLE

YIELD: 6 to 8 servings

6 medium-sized red potatoes, boiled in their jackets and cooled
3 tablespoons safflower margarine or butter
2 tablespoons peanut oil or safflower margarine
1 large onion, diced
½ pound fresh mushrooms, sliced
Salt and pepper to taste
⅛ teaspoon allspice
1 cup milk or light cream
2 eggs, well beaten

1. Preheat oven to 350 degrees.
2. Thinly slice boiled potatoes. Set aside. Heat the margarine and oil in a large skillet. Sauté the onion and mushrooms. Season with salt, pepper, and allspice.
3. In a greased 2½- or 3-quart casserole dish, put a layer of potatoes. Cover with a layer of the sautéed mixture. Continue layering until all ingredients are used up, ending with a layer of potatoes on top. Combine the milk and eggs. Pour over casserole. Bake in a preheated oven 20 to 30 minutes or until eggs are set. Serve hot.

Variation: Eliminate eggs and milk. Stir ½ cup plain, low-fat yogurt or sour cream into the sautéed mixture. Spread another ½ cup yogurt or sour cream on top of the final layer of potatoes. Bake until bubbly and heated through.

RED CABBAGE AND APPLE SALAD
YIELD: 4 servings

2 cups shredded red cabbage
Salt
1 Red or Golden Delicious apple,
coarsely grated

2 tablespoons lemon juice
1½ tablespoons sugar or honey

Place cabbage in a bowl. Sprinkle lightly with salt and let stand 10 minutes. Transfer to a colander and squeeze out as much excess liquid as possible. Return to bowl and combine with grated apple. Combine lemon juice and sugar or honey and pour over cabbage. Toss well and chill before serving.

ROSE'S MOCHA-WALNUT TORTE
YIELD: 10 to 12 servings

Cake:
6 egg yolks
½ pound confectioners' sugar
2 cups finely chopped walnuts
Grated rind of ½ lemon
1 teaspoon lemon juice
6 egg whites, at room temperature
Pinch of salt

Mocha Butter Cream:
1 egg yolk
2 tablespoons confectioners' sugar
1 stick sweet butter, softened at
room temperature
2 tablespoons cocoa
2 teaspoons instant coffee
1 tablespoon hot water

Garnishes:—optional
Chopped walnuts
Grated chocolate

1. *To prepare cake*: Grease and flour a 9-inch spring-form pan. Beat egg yolks in the small bowl of an electric mixer at high speed 3 minutes. Add the sugar gradually, and beat 5 to 7 minutes or until very thick and smooth. Add the walnuts, lemon rind, and lemon juice at low speed. Remove beaters and thoroughly wash and dry them. In large bowl of mixer, beat egg whites at medium speed until frothy. Add the pinch of salt and beat at high speed until stiff peaks are formed. Fold 3 tablespoons whites into the yolk mixture to lighten it. Gently fold in remaining whites. Pour into spring-form pan.
2. Place cake on the middle rack of the oven. Set temperature at 350 degrees. Bake 35 minutes. Open door slowly. Insert a toothpick—if it comes out clean, the cake is done. (If cake is not done, bake another 5 or 10 minutes.) Do not remove from oven. Turn off heat, leave door partially open, and allow cake to cool in oven. Remove from pan before icing.
3. *To prepare butter cream*: Beat egg yolk with sugar. Add butter in small pieces, beating constantly. Add cocoa gradually, beating continually. Add the coffee, dissolved in the hot water, and beat in thoroughly. Taste and

adjust for sweetness. Spread evenly over the top and sides of cake. Decorate, if desired, with chopped walnuts and grated chocolate. Serve at room temperature.

STUFFED EGGS
FROM WARSAW

YIELD: 4 servings

---

4 hard-boiled eggs, peeled
1 tablespoon chopped parsley or 2
  teaspoons dill weed
1½ to 2 tablespoons chopped green
  onion
4 tablespoons plain, low-fat yogurt
  or sour cream

Salt and pepper to taste
1 egg white
2 tablespoons bread crumbs
2 to 3 tablespoons safflower
  margarine or butter

Cut the eggs in half lengthwise. Scoop out the yolks and press through a strainer. Combine sieved yolks with the parsley, green onion, and yogurt or sour cream. Season to taste with salt and pepper. Refill egg whites. Beat raw egg white until frothy and brush over the stuffed side of the eggs. Sprinkle with bread crumbs. Melt the margarine in a 9-inch skillet. Fry the eggs, stuffed-side-down, until golden-brown. Serve as a first course or breakfast dish.

POLAND/RECIPE ANALYSIS CHART

Name of Recipe	Quantity	Calories	CHO gms.	Protein gms.	Total Fat gms.	Saturated Fat gms.	Cholesterol mg.	Dietary Fiber gms.
1. Chicken Soup		—	—	—	—	—	—	—
2. *Cwikla* (Pickled Beet Relish)	per serving	32	7 (88%)	1 (12%)	—	—	—	.4
3. Red Cabbage and Apple Salad	per serving	41	9 (88%)	1 (12%)	—	—	—	.4
4. *Pierogi*	each	54	9 (67%)	2 (15%)	1 (18%)	—	19	.1
5. Farmer's Salad	per serving	96	7 (29%)	15 (63%)	1 (8%)	—	—	1.0
6. Cauliflower with Dried Mushroom Sauce	per serving	103	11 (43%)	3 (12%)	5 (45%)	1 (9%)	—	.7
7. *Kartoflane Kluski* (Boiled Potato Dumplings)	per serving	106	15 (56%)	5 (19%)	3 (25%)	1 (8%)	105	—
8. Brussels Sprouts Polonaise	per serving	113	11 (39%)	6 (21%)	5 (40%)	1 (8%)	—	1.8
9. *Krupnik* (Vegetable Barley Soup)	per 1-cup serving	118	19 (64%)	4 (14%)	3 (22%)	1 (7%)	—	1.0
10. *Kotlety z Grzbow* (Mushroom Cutlets)	per cutlet	120	15 (50%)	6 (20%)	4 (30%)	1 (8%)	40	—
11. Dark Rye Bread	per slice	171	32 (75%)	4 (9%)	3 (16%)	1 (5%)	2	.3
12. Stuffed Eggs *from Warsaw*	per serving	179	3 (7%)	8 (18%)	15 (75%)	4 (20%)	315	—
13. Chopped Chicken Livers	per ¼-cup serving	188	5 (11%)	11 (23%)	14 (67%)	11 (53%)	372	.2
14. Potato and Mushroom Casserole	per serving	222	27 (49%)	6 (11%)	10 (40%)	2 (8%)	72	1.2

Name of Recipe	Quantity	Calories	CHO gms.	Protein gms.	Total Fat gms.	Saturated Fat gms.	Choles- terol mg.	Dietary Fiber gms.
15. Noodle Molds	per mold	231	29 (50%)	8 (14%)	9 (36%)	2 (8%)	107	.1
16. *Dorka's* Apple-Apricot Cake	per serving	247	44 (71%)	2 (3%)	7 (26%)	1 (4%)	22	1.0
17. *Rose's* Mocha-Walnut Torte	per serving	332	24 (29%)	5 (6%)	24 (65%)	7 (19%)	204	—

Numbers in parentheses (%) indicate percentage of total calories contributed by nutrient.

MENUS

LOW CALORIE SPECIALTIES
(500 to 700 calories per meal)

CHICKEN SOUP with Carrots
DARK RYE BREAD
PIEROGI
Sliced Apricots with Low-Fat Yogurt
Hot Tea with Lemon

CWIKLA (PICKLED BEET RELISH)
STUFFED EGGS FROM WARSAW
**POTATO AND MUSHROOM
CASSEROLE**
Sliced Bananas and Cherries
Iced Tea

Baked Pike with Lemon and Horseradish
RED CABBAGE AND APPLE SALAD
Steamed Kohlrabi
KARTOFLANE KLUSKI (BOILED POTATO DUMPLINGS)
Baked Apples
Coffee

●

LOW CHOLESTEROL MENUS
(Less than 50 mgs. of cholesterol per meal)

Radish, Green Pepper and Tomato
Platter
**KRUPNIK (VEGETABLE BARLEY
SOUP)**
DARK RYE BREAD
Boiled Artichoke with Wedge of
Lemon
Sliced Plums

Sauerkraut Sprinkled with Caraway
seeds
**CAULIFLOWER WITH DRIED
MUSHROOM SAUCE**
String Beans with Dill
Fresh Fruit Salad
Orange Spice Tea

Dill Pickles and Sliced Cucumbers
PIEROGI
Steamed Peas and Carrots
DORKA'S APPLE-APRICOT CAKE
Coffee

LOW SATURATED FAT SELECTIONS
(Less than 8 grams of saturated fat per meal)

CAULIFLOWER WITH DRIED MUSHROOM SAUCE
Baked Potato with Chives
Sliced Cucumbers and Dill Pickles
DORKA'S APPLE-APRICOT CAKE

KARTOFLANE KLUSKI (BOILED POTATO DUMPLINGS)
KOTLETY Z GRZBOW (MUSHROOM CUTLETS)
BRUSSELS SPROUTS POLONAISE
Sliced Pears with Orange Liqueur

CWIKLA (PICKLED BEET RELISH)
PIEROGI
FARMER'S SALAD
ROSE'S MOCHA-WALNUT TORTE

●

HIGH PROTEIN MEALS
(More than 30 grams of protein per meal)

CHOPPED CHICKEN LIVERS
Whole Grain Crackers
NOODLE MOLDS
BRUSSELS SPROUTS POLONAISE
Sliced Apples with Yogurt

FARMER'S SALAD
POTATO AND MUSHROOM CASSEROLE
DARK RYE BREAD
ROSE'S MOCHA-WALNUT TORTE

STUFFED EGGS FROM WARSAW
KRUPNIK (VEGETABLE BARLEY SOUP)
Pot Cheese with Radishes and Dill Pickles
Pumpernickel Bread
Blueberries and Sour Cream

●

WELL BALANCED LUNCH OR DINNER MENUS
(Selections that conform to recommendations in Dietary Goals for United States)

RED CABBAGE AND APPLE SALAD
POTATO AND MUSHROOM CASSEROLE
DORKA'S APPLE-APRICOT CAKE
Rose Hips Tea

FARMER'S SALAD
PIEROGI
NOODLE MOLDS
ROSE'S MOCHA-WALNUT TORTE
Coffee

KRUPNIK (VEGETABLE BARLEY SOUP)
DARK RYE BREAD
KOTLETY Z GRZBOW (MUSHROOM CUTLETS)
Blueberries with Yogurt
Orange Spice Tea

CHAPTER 13

RUSSIA

A Borsch You Can't Beet

Culinary Essentials

When you find yourself singing the "kitchen-rut blues," why not try Russian cooking for a change? Granted, this cuisine does not rival the sophisticated saucing of the French or the complex spicing of the northern Chinese. Still, there are praises to be sung for the likes of *Eggplant Caviar*, *Russian Black Bread*, and *Kugelis* (a Lithuanian pudding of grated potatoes).

Russian cooking, with its love for pungent cabbage stews, thick porridge, pickled vegetables, strong cheeses, and dark, coarse-grained breads, is not designed for those with small appetites. The food is robust, nourishing, and filling. Think of a Russian meal as you would a good spy novel—there are enough contrasting elements to keep you intrigued and, upon completion, a feeling of satisfaction prevails.

This hearty cuisine is easily adaptable to American kitchens. Most ingredients—root vegetables, sauerkraut, *kasha*, and sunflower seed oil—are available at large supermarkets. Ready-made products such as canned *borsch* (beet soup) and pumpernickel bread (similar to black bread) can be used as alternatives to the homemade versions. These items may be found in Jewish delicatessens and grocery stores with kosher food sections.

Much of the action in this cooking style revolves around grating or slicing. If you do not own a food processor, a high-quality peeler, a vegetable or paring knife, and a flat-sided Mandolin (a narrow, oblong wooden board on which assorted cutting blades are attached) are your best tools. Because Russian dishes are not especially colorful, you may wish to collect a few gadgets that will help provide decorative touches: an egg-slicer, a parsley-mincer for freshly chopped herbs, or a radish rose-cutter.

Classically, a Russian meal begins with *zakusky*, an assortment of "small bites" that can match a Scandinavian *smörgåsbrod* in variety, tastes, and seasonings. Good food, plenty of vodka, and endless toasts help make this feast of appetizers one of the most convivial of Russian dining customs.

Your *zakusky* may consist of a few simple selections such as marinated herring, smoked salmon, pot cheese, or cooked vegetable salads. For a copious buffet, you might enjoy preparing *Pickled Mushrooms, Sweet and Sour Stuffed Cabbage,* or *Chopped Eggs with Mushroom "Caviar."* To add color and piquancy, include dill pickles, pearl onions, horseradish, *Tilsiter** (a Havarti-like cheese with a sour tang), or *Brindza** (a salty-sharp sheep's milk cheese).

Hot or cold soups, which follow *zakusky*, reflect the Russian penchant for tart flavors. One of the most popular is Ukrainian-style *Borsch*, a rosy-toned beet soup laden with cabbage and fortified with sour cream or yogurt. Like most Russian soups, it is so packed with ingredients that it qualifies as a meal in itself, especially when accompanied by thick wedges of black bread.

It is hard to imagine a Russian feast without *kasha* (buckwheat groats). Like rice, *kasha* is incredibly versatile. Once you master the basic preparation (steaming or baking), the possibilities are myriad. *Kasha* may be sweet or savory, tossed with eggs, or fried with onions. It mixes well with noodles, fruit compotes, or soups, and can turn leftovers into a tempting dish.

Soft, warm colors and simple serving pieces will work well for your Russian table. Fill bowls with hard-boiled eggs, dyed in bright colors, to recreate a cheerful Ukrainian setting. A basket of pumpernickel, rye bread, or bagels is usually provided for soaking up juicy soups and stews; scallions, black olives, and radish roses help round out the meal. For a special after-dinner beverage, serve hot tea sweetened with a spoonful of black currant jam.

Seasoning Essentials

Many ingredients found in Russian cooking are vibrant and imbued with natural flavors of their own. Recipes that are packed with horseradish, mustard, sour cream, yogurt, or sauerkraut require only modest seasonings. Sometimes a handful of freshly chopped parsley and a liberal dose of salt and pepper are sufficient to bring a dish to its completion.

The role of herbs and spices in this cuisine is simply to contrast or harmonize with the essence of foods already present in a dish. Bay leaf, for example, sees limited action, but its task is an important one—to offset the blatant flavor of cabbage as well as to neutralize its cooking odor.

If there is one taste-enhancer that figures prominently in this style of cooking, it is dill. This versatile, parsley-like herb is your greatest ally when it comes to enlivening the ubiquitous root vegetables. Humble foods—

---

*Available at imported cheese shops.

beets, parsnips, turnips, or potatoes—are assured a new authority under a mantle of sour cream and dill. Used wisely and discreetly, it will heighten lackluster flavors without sacrificing its own subtle pungency.

The *Russian Herb Blend*, which exploits the talents of dill, is designed to help you add savor to your meals with ease. Try it in place of salt in your favorite Russian vegetable or egg dish and see how they improve. Rice, soups, and broiled fish will also benefit from this pleasantly balanced and salty mixture.

Remember, Russian dishes do not require heavy-handed spicing. Condiments such as capers, dill pickles, parsley, mustard, and lemon wedges blend wonderfully with the staples of this cuisine and are effective in bringing out and enhancing their intrinsic flavors.

RUSSIAN SEASONING CHART

BAY LEAVES have a pungent flavor and sweet balsam scent that is liberated slowly when exposed to the heat of long-simmered dishes. Russian cooks prize this fragrant herb for its ability to offset tastes that are potentially overbearing such as those found in cabbage-based soups, sauerkraut dishes, and fish stews. Use sparingly; one or two leaves are sufficient to season a pot of soup or an entire casserole.

CLOVES have the unique ability to season both sour and sweet foods. The warm spiciness of ground cloves tempers the tang of beets and sauerkraut while the sharpness of whole cloves provides a rich aroma for pickled mushrooms, poached fish, and vinegar-brined vegetables. A pinch of cloves and a splash of brandy are delightful additions to honey cake, sweetened pot cheese, or dried fruit soup. Use judiciously as this potent spice can easily dominate or ruin a dish.

CORIANDER is also called *Kindza*. Widely used in Southern Russia, it lends a curious accent to tomato sauce, chicken soup, kidney bean salad, or stewed lentils. The musty quality of coriander is best appreciated when combined with dill or garlic in this cooking style. Freshly chopped or dried coriander leaves are a superb addition to mildly garlicked eggplant caviar. Fresh coriander is available at Latin American and Oriental markets.

DILL has a zestful personality comparable to fresh parsley. Freshly chopped dill leaves blend perfectly with the staples of this cuisine—sour foods, root vegetables, and thick, hearty soups. Dried dill weed, though not as distinctive as fresh dill, is an acceptable substitute. This versatile herb is popularly used in Russian dishes containing mushrooms, yogurt, sour cream, eggplant, pumpkin, sorrel, eggs, or potatoes. For optimum flavor, add dill to a dish just before it is removed from the heat.

TARRAGON that is native to Russia is less delicate than French tarragon. Russian cooks prefer the latter when available to them. With its licoricelike undertones, tarragon is best suited in this cuisine to seasoning fish, especially sole and halibut. Occasionally, the dried leaves are stirred, along with fresh parsley, into a mayonnaise-based dressing.

RUSSIAN HERB BLEND is a marvelous all-purpose seasoner for potatoes, noodles, fish, hard-boiled eggs, salads, rice, cucumbers, stuffed cabbage filling, soups, and root vegetables. Use in place of salt but not pepper.

Combine and store in an airtight container.

  2 tablespoons dill weed
  1 tablespoon coarse (kosher) salt
  1 teaspoon dried onion flakes
  ½ teaspoon garlic powder
  ¼ teaspoon summer savory or thyme

Other seasonings found in Russian cookery: caraway seed, poppy seed, horseradish, paprika, parsley (root and leaves), nutmeg, garlic, allspice, ginger, lemon rind, saffron, fennel seed, thyme, cinnamon, summer savory, cardamom, mint leaves, and cayenne pepper.

Nutritional Essentials

It has been said that Russian women are endowed with beautiful complexions because they consume large quantities of cabbage. Fact or fancy, it is unlikely that this sturdy vegetable will become a serious competitor against Helena Rubinstein's facial packs. This controversy aside, there are good reasons for familiarizing yourself with wholesome Russian fare, whose wonderfully low-calorie content is guaranteed to keep your face on the nice and slim side.

Boasting about 150 calories per serving portion, the Russian recipes in this book rank lower in this department than all other ethnic dishes except those of Poland. What's more, and perhaps ironic, is that the caloric composition of our Russian recipes conforms closely to the *Dietary Goals for the United States*! Carbohydrates and fat each contribute about 40 percent of the caloric intake, with protein providing the remaining 20 percent. This is a healthy balance of nutrients, and furthermore, the cholesterol content is a very acceptable average of 43 mgs. per offering.

Russian cookery makes great use of hearty vegetables such as cabbage, turnips, and beets. These foods are great for making interesting, filling dishes with a reasonable caloric content. Consider that *Sweet and Sour Cabbage, Beets Igdaloff*, and *Borsch Ukraïnsky* deliver only 28, 52, and 106 calories per serving respectively. You could not ask for a more satisfying low-calorie diet, and besides, what better way is there for getting "back to your roots"?

Raw beets, distinguished by their deep maroon color, are a good source of vitamin C and a fair source of vitamin A, much of which is lost during cooking. Leafy beet *tops*, on the other hand, are not only a good source of calcium and iron, but are an excellent source of vitamin A, one-half cup yielding over twice the adult daily requirement. While our Russian recipes do not call for beet greens, you may add them to your favorite green salads or cook them like spinach.

White and green cabbage will provide more than one-half of your daily vitamin C needs. Though turnips have less to offer nutritionally than both beets and cabbage, they are extremely low in calories.

The Russian diet is replete with a number of dairy items—sour cream, pot cheese (uncreamed dry curd cottage cheese), creamed cottage cheese, yogurt, and *Brindza* (feta-like goat cheese)—which provide high-grade protein without excessive quantities of fat. Furthermore, by combining into a single meal dairy dishes such as *Yogurt Soup* or *Cheese Blintzes* with grain-based recipes such as *Russian Black Bread* or *Kasha and Shells*, you can prepare well-balanced offerings that take advantage of protein complementation.

Frequently, you will be able to substitute low-fat, low-calorie dairy foods for richer items: Neufchâtel cheese for cream cheese; yogurt for sour cream; or pot cheese for creamed cottage cheese. Learning to make these culinary substitutions is an art worth cultivating, for the calorie and fat savings can be substantial. A cup of pot cheese, for example, contains only 172 calories of which only 9 (or about 5 percent of the total) are derived from fat. This is a 20 percent fat and calorie saving over cottage cheese. Similarly, by using yogurt instead of sour cream, you will spare yourself about 200 calories per cup, increase your protein intake slightly, and reduce your fat intake by an impressive 80 percent. Yogurt prepared from skimmed milk is even lighter in the fat and calorie department. If you are not enamored with the taste of yogurt (the Russians love it according to TV commercials), you can always combine it in equal proportions with sour cream.

Many nutrition-conscious cooks are not aware that a delicious low-calorie, low-fat cream cheese, Neufchâtel, is widely available as a cream cheese substitute. You can appreciate this soft, creamy-smooth cheese—which is almost indistinguishable in taste from cream cheese—in recipes for *Cheese Noodle Soufflé*, *Cream Cheese with Sardines and Red Onions*, and *Cheese Blintzes*.

Kasha or buckwheat groats, the grain staple of this cuisine, is similar in protein and calorie content to wheat flour. Ideally, *kasha*-based dishes should be served along with kefir,* buttermilk, or yogurt to increase the protein make-up of your meal.

Russian beverages have long been touted for their health-giving properties. The Russian centenarians of Georgia have celebrated vodka as a youth potion. Interestingly, one epidemiologic study suggests that a small daily intake of alcohol may protect people from heart disease. So, the old folks

---

Available at health food stores.

may not be as senile as they seem! Less controversial are the benefits of popular Russian drinks such as vitamin C-rich cranberry juice and rose hips tea as well as high-protein, low-calorie beverages such as kefir (a yogurtlike drink) and buttermilk, which can be served with almost any meal.

ARMENIAN FISH PLAKI SAUCIER

YIELD: 4 to 6 servings

1½ pounds white-fleshed fish fillets such as cod, halibut, or haddock
2 tablespoons each: peanut and olive oil
1 large onion, chopped
1 to 2 garlic cloves, pressed
¼ cup fresh chopped parsley or 3 tablespoons fresh chopped dill
1 cup fresh or canned tomatoes, chopped
Salt and pepper to taste
¼ cup lemon juice
½ cup bread crumbs
6 round lemon slices

1. Preheat oven to 350 degrees.
2. Arrange fillets in a greased, shallow 10- by 10-inch baking dish. Heat the oils in a saucepan. Sauté the onion over medium heat 5 minutes or until soft, but not brown. Add the garlic, parsley or dill, tomatoes, salt, pepper, lemon juice, and bread crumbs. Bring to a slow boil and pour immediately over the fillets. Arrange lemon slices over the top. Bake in a preheated oven 40 minutes or until fillets are fork-tender.
Variations: Thinly sliced carrots, diced celery, or sautéed diced potatoes may be added to the sauce.

BAKLAJANAYA IKRA
(Russian Eggplant Caviar)

YIELD: 6 to 8 servings

1 pound eggplant
8 tablespoons peanut or sunflower seed oil, divided
2 to 3 yellow onions, finely chopped
6 ounces tomato paste
Salt and freshly ground pepper to taste
3 garlic cloves, crushed

1. Peel eggplant and cut into ½-inch rounds. Sprinkle each slice with salt. Place in a colander and cover with a weighted plate. Let stand 30 minutes to remove bitterness. Rinse well and pat dry. Dice each round.
2. Heat 5 tablespoons of the oil in a heavy 9-inch skillet. When hot add the eggplant and sauté 8 minutes or until dark in color and tender. Add more oil if necessary to prevent sticking. Transfer to a mixing bowl to cool. Heat the remaining oil in the same skillet and sauté the onions until golden-brown—about 10 minutes. Combine with eggplant. Stir in the tomato paste, salt, pepper, and garlic. Taste and adjust seasonings. If a more pronounced garlic flavor is desired, season with additional crushed cloves.
3. Preheat oven to 350 degrees.
4. Place eggplant mixture in a well-greased loaf pan. Bake 40 to 50 minutes. Cover with foil after 25 minutes of baking to prevent the top from overcooking. Serve hot as an appetizer with dark bread, French bread, or whole grain crackers.

BEETS IGDALOFF

YIELD: 4 servings

6 medium-sized beets with fresh
leafy tops
Salt to taste
Freshly ground white pepper to
taste

1 teaspoon prepared horseradish **or**
1 tablespoon lemon juice—
optional
½ cup plain, low-fat yogurt or sour
cream

1. Preheat oven to 350 degrees.
2. Wash the beets, but do not peel. Trim off leafy stalks, leaving 1 or 2 inches attached to the beet tops. Place in a 9- by 13- by 2-inch baking pan. Bake, uncovered, 1 to 2 hours or until tender. Do not pierce beets unnecessarily with a fork to check for tenderness as beets will "bleed."
3. Remove beets and let cool until they can be handled. Peel and thinly slice. Sprinkle with salt and white pepper. Place in a well-greased 2½-quart casserole. Combine horseradish or lemon juice with yogurt or sour cream. Pour over beets and return to the oven until bubbling. Serve hot.

BLINCHATIYE PIROSHKI S TVOROGOM

(Cheese Blintzes) *YIELD: 10 filled pancakes*

Pancakes:
1 egg
1¼ cups water or milk
¼ teaspoon salt
½ cup unbleached white flour
2 tablespoons safflower oil or
margarine, melted
1 to 2 tablespoons safflower
margarine or butter for frying

Filling:
8 ounces Neufchâtel cheese or
cream cheese, softened at room
temperature
½ pound dry cottage cheese (also
called farmer's or pot cheese)
1 egg, well beaten
1 tablespoon melted safflower
margarine
2 tablespoons sugar or honey
1 teaspoon vanilla extract
¼ teaspoon cinnamon
¼ cup white raisins—optional

1. *To prepare pancakes:* Beat the egg well in a mixing bowl. Add ¼ cup of the water, salt, and flour. Mix until there are no lumps. Add remaining cup of water very gradually. Beat well.
2. Brush the bottom of a 7-inch skillet with oil or melted margarine. Heat until a drop of water forms a ball—the skillet is now ready. Add a scant ¼ cup batter, quickly turning skillet from side to side to coat bottom. Lightly brown pancake on one side and remove to a clean towel or plate. Continue process until all the batter is used, brushing skillet with oil each time.
3. *To prepare filling:* Place cream cheese in a bowl and stir with a wooden spoon until smooth and creamy. Add remaining ingredients and mix well.

4. *To assemble pancake pies*: Place 2 heaping tablespoons of filling in the center of the browned side of a pancake. Fold over a flap to cover filling, then fold in each side and roll up into a parcel, making a *blintze* or *piroshki*.
5. *To serve*: Melt 2 tablespoons margarine in a large skillet. Add *piroshkis* and brown lightly on both sides. Serve with plain yogurt or sour cream, mixed with sugar or honey, to taste. Fresh fruit or preserves also make a nice accompaniment.

BORSCH UKRAÏNSKY
(Ukrainian-Style Beet Soup)　　　　　　　　*YIELD: Approximately 10 servings*

---

2 medium-sized beets, peeled and grated
1 turnip or parsnip, grated
2 carrots, grated
4 tablespoons safflower margarine
1 large onion, chopped
7 cups (1 medium-sized head) shredded cabbage
6 cups vegetable or chicken stock
4 vegetable-stock bouillon cubes*—optional
¾ pound new potatoes, diced
Juice of 2 large lemons

3 medium-sized fresh tomatoes, chopped, or ½ cup tomato puree
2 bay leaves
2 garlic cloves, minced, or 1 teaspoon garlic powder
½ to ¾ teaspoon pepper
1 teaspoon salt
2 teaspoons brown sugar
½ to 1 cup plain, low-fat yogurt or sour cream
3 teaspoons flour
Freshly ground pepper

Available at specialty food stores and many supermarkets.

1. Combine the grated beets, turnip, and carrots in a bowl. Heat half the margarine in a skillet until hot. Sauté the onion and combine with beet mixture. Heat remaining margarine and sauté the cabbage. Add to beet mixture and set aside.
2. Bring stock to a boil in a large soup pot. Add vegetable cubes and stir until dissolved. Add potatoes and boil slowly 15 minutes. Stir in beet mixture and sautéed cabbage. Add lemon juice, tomatoes, bay leaves, garlic, pepper, salt, and sugar. Cook until cabbage is almost tender. Combine yogurt or sour cream with the flour and add to pot. Reduce heat to low and simmer 5 to 10 minutes longer. Cabbage should be tender, but not soggy.
3. Spoon *borsch* into individual bowls. Top each serving with freshly ground pepper.

CHEESE NOODLE SOUFFLÉ

YIELD: 12 servings

8 ounces medium-wide, flat egg
noodles
8 ounces Neufchâtel cheese or
cream cheese
16 ounces small curd cottage cheese
1 pint plain yogurt or sour cream

½ cup raisins
6 large eggs
1 tablespoon vanilla
1 cup sugar
1 teaspoon cinnamon
½ cup ground nuts

1. Bring 4 quarts of salted water to a boil and cook the noodles until tender.
Drain noodles. Cut cream cheese into cubes and toss with warm noodles
along with cottage cheese, yogurt or sour cream, and raisins. Set aside.
2. Preheat oven to 350 degrees.
3. Beat the eggs and vanilla in a mixer until frothy. Add sugar gradually
and beat for 5 minutes. Add to noodle mixture and pour into a 9- by 13-inch
oblong baking dish. Bake in a preheated oven for 30 minutes. Remove from
oven and sprinkle combined cinnamon and nuts over the top. Return to
oven for another 30 minutes. Cut into squares and serve immediately. Leftovers may be wrapped in foil and reheated.

CHICKEN ON A
BED OF VEGETABLES

YIELD: 4 servings

1 large onion, sliced
2 carrots, diced
1 rib celery, diced
Pepper to sprinkle over
vegetables

1 fryer, cut up (2½ pounds)
1 heaping teaspoon salt
½ teaspoon garlic powder
Pepper to taste
Paprika

1. Preheat oven to 325 degrees. Make a bed of the diced vegetables on the
bottom of a roasting pan. Sprinkle lightly with pepper.
2. Clean chicken pieces. Wash and pat dry. Mix together the salt, garlic
powder, pepper, and paprika. Sprinkle over chicken. Place chicken over
vegetables. Bake 1 hour, covered, in preheated oven. Remove from oven
and turn chicken. Bake, uncovered, 30 minutes longer. Turn again and
bake until brown.

CHOPPED EGGS
WITH MUSHROOM "CAVIAR"

YIELD: *Serves 8 to 10*

Caviar:
1½ cups Pickled Mushrooms (p. 328)
  or 6 ounces dried mushrooms*
1 medium-sized yellow onion
1 to 2 tablespoons sunflower seed
  or safflower oil
1 garlic clove, pressed or minced
Juice of ½ lemon
Salt and freshly ground pepper to
  taste

Eggs:
8 large, hard-boiled eggs
1 small yellow onion, finely
  chopped
½ cup safflower mayonnaise—
  approximately
Salt and freshly ground pepper to
  taste
½ pint sour cream

Garnishes:
1 cucumber, thinly sliced (peel if
  waxed)
Pumpernickel bread, thinly
  sliced

Dried mushrooms must be covered with boiling water and soaked 30 minutes. Drain and cut off tough stem-ends before using.

1. *To prepare "caviar"*: Rinse pickled or reconstituted dried mushrooms and chop very finely. Mince the onion. Heat the oil in a small skillet until hot. Add the garlic and sauté 10 seconds. Add the onion and fry until lightly browned. Add mushrooms and sauté until tender. Remove from heat and transfer to a bowl to cool. Season with lemon juice, salt, and pepper.
2. *To prepare eggs*: Place hard-boiled eggs in a bowl and chop finely. Add the chopped onion. Add the ½-cup mayonnaise or just enough to hold the mixture together (depending upon the size of your eggs). Season to taste with salt and pepper. Beat the sour cream to spreading consistency. Mound the eggs in the center of a platter. Spread on sour cream like icing.
3. *To serve*: Make a small well in the center of the egg mixture. Place the "caviar" in the well. Surround the mound with sliced cucumbers and pumpernickel bread. Let each person make a sandwich of bread, cucumber, egg mixture, and finally, the "caviar." Serve as an appetizer.
Variation: Eliminate mushroom caviar and fill the center of the mound with black caviar or sliced black olives or serve the eggs and garnishes alone.

CREAM CHEESE WITH
SARDINES AND RED ONIONS

YIELD: *8 servings*

8 ounces Neufchâtel cheese or
  cream cheese
1 tin of sardines, drained
  (preferably crosspacked)

¼ cup coarsely chopped red onion
Russian Black Bread (p. 329),
  pumpernickel bread, bagels, or
  crackers

Bring cheese to room temperature. Place on a serving platter. Lay sardines across the cheese. Sprinkle onions on top. Serve as an appetizer with black bread, pumpernickel, bagels, or crackers.

KASHA AND SHELLS

YIELD: 10 to 12 servings

1 cup *kasha*
1 whole egg, beaten
2 tablespoons safflower margarine or rendered chicken fat
2 tablespoons sunflower seed oil or peanut oil

2 cups finely chopped onions
2 cups boiling water or chicken stock
Salt and pepper to taste
8-ounce package shell noodles

1. Preheat oven to 350 degrees.
2. Place *kasha* in a 2-quart saucepan. Set in oven to warm. When *kasha* is warm to the touch, stir in the egg. Return to oven until egg is cooked. Break up the cooked egg with a wooden spoon. Add the margarine or chicken fat. Return to oven again until *kasha* is brown. Remove from oven. Set aside.
3. Heat sunflower seed oil or peanut oil in a heavy skillet. Add onions and sauté until golden. Add to *kasha*, along with the boiling water or stock. Cook over medium heat until mixture begins to thicken. Season to taste with salt and pepper. Transfer to a 2-quart casserole. Cover and bake 30 minutes or until liquid is absorbed.
4. Cook shells according to directions on the package. Drain and toss with *kasha*. Taste and adjust seasonings.

KUGLIS NATASHA
(Natalie's Potato Kugel)

YIELD: 6 to 8 servings

2 pounds red potatoes
1 medium-sized onion
1 large carrot
2 to 4 eggs, well beaten
½ cup unbleached or all-purpose flour

1 teaspoon salt (or to taste)
¼ teaspoon pepper (or to taste)
3 tablespoons peanut oil, safflower margarine, or rendered chicken fat

1. Preheat oven to 350 degrees.
2. Grate potatoes into a large bowl. Pour off excess liquid. Grate onion and carrot into the potatoes. Add the remaining ingredients. Spoon into a well-greased 2-quart casserole. Bake in a preheated oven, uncovered, for 90 minutes or until the top is browned and the edges look crisp.
Variation: Drop mixture into well-greased muffin tins and bake at 350 degrees for 1 hour.

LEKAKH
(Honey Spice Cake)

YIELD: Approximately 20, 2½-inch squares

1 pound honey, warmed to pouring
  consistency
½ cup sugar
½ cup safflower oil
1 tablespoon vegetable shortening
3 eggs
  Grated rind of 1 small lemon
3 cups all-purpose flour (may use
  part whole wheat)
2 rounded teaspoons double-acting
  baking powder

1 teaspoon baking soda
  Pinch of salt
1 teaspoon each: cinnamon and
  allspice
¼ teaspoon each: cloves and ginger
1 cup strong black coffee, cooled
  Juice of ½ lemon
1 tablespoon brandy—optional
12 to 15 walnut halves

1. In the large bowl of a mixer, cream together the honey, sugar, oil, and shortening until well blended. Add the eggs, one at a time, beating after each addition. Stir in grated lemon peel.
2. In another bowl, sift together the dry ingredients. Mix the coffee, lemon juice, and brandy together. Alternately add the flour and liquid to the egg batter, beginning and ending with the flour.
3. Preheat oven to 300 degrees. Pour batter into a greased and floured 9- by 12-inch baking pan. Arrange walnuts attractively over the top. Bake on the middle rack 45 to 50 minutes or until toothpick inserted in center comes out dry. Cool and cut into squares.

LEMON-EGGPLANT SPREAD

YIELD: 6 to 8 servings

2 small eggplants
2 tablespoons sunflower seed oil or
  safflower margarine
1 medium-sized yellow onion,
  chopped
1 teaspoon salt
½ teaspoon pepper

1½ teaspoons honey or 2 teaspoons
  brown sugar
3 tablespoons lemon juice
⅓ cup tomato paste
  Pumpernickel bread or whole
  grain crackers

1. Peel eggplants and cut into slices. Salt each slice and place in a colander 30 minutes to drain and remove bitterness. Rinse well and pat dry with paper towels.
2. Cut eggplants into ½-inch cubes. Place in an enamel or stainless steel saucepan and add enough water to cover. Cook over medium heat until tender—about 5 minutes.
3. Heat oil or margarine in a skillet and sauté chopped onion until transparent. Toss with cubed eggplant and season with salt, pepper, honey or brown sugar, and lemon juice. Place ⅓ of eggplant mixture in a blender,

along with the tomato paste, and purée until smooth. Add remaining egg-plant mixture, a little at a time, until smooth. Add a little water or oil for puréeing if necessary. Taste and adjust seasonings.

4. *To serve*: Warm purée in a skillet over very low heat. Spread on a plate and surround with pumpernickel bread or whole grain crackers.

MATSUNABUR

(Armenian Yogurt Soup)   *YIELD: 6 to 8 servings*

---

1 large cucumber	1 garlic clove, crushed
Salt	1 cup light cream
1½ cups water or chicken stock	1 teaspoon dill weed
1½ cups plain yogurt	Salt and pepper to taste
1 cup tomato juice	1 large tomato, peeled, seeded, and
Juice of ½ lemon	diced
	Plain yogurt

1. Peel and slice the cucumber into thin rounds. Sprinkle with salt. Set aside in a covered bowl for 20 minutes.

2. Combine the water or stock, 1 cup of the yogurt, tomato juice, lemon juice, and garlic. Blend well. Stir in the cream and dill weed. Season to taste with salt and pepper. Rinse cucumber under cold, running water. Pat dry with paper towels. Add to the soup mixture along with the tomato. Taste and adjust seasonings. Stir well and chill.

3. To serve, garnish each serving of chilled soup with a dab of yogurt and a sprinkling of dill weed.

PICKLED MUSHROOMS

YIELD: Approximately 3 cups or
6 to 8 servings

½ cup water	2 tablespoons whole black
1 cup distilled white or red wine	peppercorns
vinegar	1 bay leaf
2 to 3 teaspoons salt	2 garlic cloves, crushed
1 sprig fresh dill—optional	1 pound fresh small mushrooms,
3 whole cloves	washed well with stems removed

Bring the water, vinegar, and salt to a boil in a heavy 2-quart saucepan. Add remaining ingredients. Reduce heat to low and simmer uncovered, 12 minutes, stirring occasionally. Remove from heat and cool. Place in a crock or glass jar and refrigerate, covered, at least 2 days. This will keep up to two weeks refrigerated. Serve as a condiment or appetizer.

RUSSIAN BLACK BREAD

YIELD: 2 loaves

3 cups rye flour
1 cup whole wheat flour
2 cups bran flakes or bran cereal, crushed
2 packages active dry yeast
2 tablespoons caraway seed, crushed
½ teaspoon fennel seed
1½ teaspoons brown sugar
1 teaspoon salt
2 teaspoons instant coffee
2 teaspoons onion flakes or powder
2½ cups water
¼ cup each: light molasses and vinegar
4 tablespoons softened safflower margarine or butter
2 tablespoons cocoa
2½ to 3 cups unbleached white flour
1 slightly beaten egg white

1. Combine in a mixing bowl the rye flour, wheat flour, bran flakes, dry yeast, caraway seed, fennel seed, brown sugar, salt, instant coffee, and onion flakes.
2. In a saucepan, heat together the water, molasses, vinegar, margarine, and cocoa until just warm (115 degrees), stirring constantly, until margarine is almost melted. Add to dry mixture and beat well (if using an electric mixer, beat one-half minute at low speed, then 3 minutes at high speed). Gradually add unbleached white flour by hand, ½ cup at a time, to make a soft dough. Beat about 3 more minutes.
3. Turn dough out on a lightly floured surface. Cover with a large bowl and allow dough to rest for 10 minutes. Knead until smooth and elastic, about 10 minutes, adding additional flour only when necessary.
4. Shape dough into a ball and place in a large, lightly greased bowl, turning once to coat the surface. Cover with a hot damp towel and let rise in a warm, draft-free place until doubled in bulk, about 1 to 1½ hours.
5. Punch dough down and return to lightly floured board. Divide in half and shape into two loaves. Place in 2, well-greased, 8-inch layer cake pans or 2, well-greased, loaf pans. Cover with plastic wrap and let rise till nearly doubled in bulk, about 1½ hours.
6. Preheat oven to 350 degrees. Bake loaves for 25 minutes, remove from oven, and brush with egg white. Return to oven and bake 20 minutes more or until done.

SALAT OLIVIYE
(Vegetable Salad)   *YIELD: 6 servings*

4 medium-sized red potatoes,
  boiled, cooled, and diced
2 carrots, cooked, cooled, and
  diced
½ cup green peas, cooked and
  cooled
1 cucumber, peeled and diced
½ cup diced apple
1 to 2 teaspoons dill weed
  Salt and pepper to taste

¼ cup safflower mayonnaise
¼ cup plain, low-fat yogurt or sour
  cream
1 teaspoon Dijon mustard

Garnishes:
  Leaf lettuce
1 hard-boiled egg
1 black olive

1. Combine the potatoes, carrots, peas, cucumber, apple, dill, salt, and pepper. Chill before serving.
2. Combine the mayonnaise, yogurt or sour cream, and mustard to make a dressing. Toss with salad, just enough to moisten. Place on a flat platter and surround with leaf lettuce. To decorate: Remove the yolk from the hard-boiled egg and place it in the center of the salad. Cut remaining egg white into strips and surround the yolk to make a daisy pattern. Slice a piece of olive and place it in the center of the yolk. Serve immediately.
Variation: Add any of the following items: chopped dill pickle, herring, shredded chicken, cooked and diced beets, or chopped onion.

SONIA'S KAMISH BREAD
(Crisp Almond Cookies)   *YIELD: Approximately 50 cookies*

4 cups unbleached white flour
1 teaspoon double acting baking
  powder
⅛ teaspoon salt
1 cup sugar
4 eggs
½ cup vegetable oil
1 teaspoon pure lemon extract*

½ teaspoon almond extract—
  optional
1 teaspoon vanilla extract
½ cup chopped almonds or walnuts
½ cup yellow raisins
3 teaspoons sugar
1 teaspoon cinnamon

1. Sift flour, baking powder, and salt into a mixing bowl. Set aside. Place sugar in another bowl; add eggs, one at a time, beating after each addition. Add the oil and extracts, mixing thoroughly.
2. Combine the nuts and raisins. Alternately add the dry ingredients and nut-raisin mixture to the sugar-egg mixture until well blended. Turn out on a lightly floured board and knead well. Place in a bowl and let rest, covered, for 10 minutes.
3. Preheat oven to 350 degrees.
4. Divide dough into 4 equal portions. Pat each piece into an oblong slab

about ¾-inch high and 1¾ inches wide. Place 2 inches apart on a well-greased baking sheet. Bake 20 minutes or until slightly golden on top. Remove from oven and transfer to a large cutting board. Slice each piece diagonally into ½-inch pieces. Sprinkle with cinnamon and sugar. Return to baking sheet, cut-side-down. Bake 5 minutes on each side or until lightly browned. Do not let them brown too much as they will crisp when cool. Cool on wire racks.

*Note: The rind of ½ lemon, plus 1 teaspoon lemon juice, may be substituted for the extract.

SWEET AND SOUR STUFFED CABBAGE   YIELD: Approximately 18 stuffed cabbage leaves

---

1 large head green cabbage	Salt and pepper to taste
	½ cup currants—optional
Rice and vegetable filling:	¼ cup chopped walnuts—optional
1½ cups cooked rice	
1 small onion, diced	1 small head green cabbage
2 garlic cloves, crushed	1 cup dried pitted prunes
1 rib celery, diced	1 pound sauerkraut, drained
½ green pepper, seeded and chopped	2 cups chopped tomatoes .
¼ cup sliced mushrooms	2 cups tomato sauce
4 tablespoons soy sauce	Juice of 2 large lemons
½ teaspoon sage	⅓ to ½ cup honey or brown sugar

1. *To prepare cabbage*: Remove the core and tough outer leaves of the large head of cabbage and discard them. Put cabbage in a pot with enough water to cover. Parboil only until leaves are pliable—about 5 minutes. If your pot isn't large enough to cover cabbage, turn halfway through cooking. When pliable, remove from heat and leave in hot water. Carefully remove a few leaves at a time and set them aside on a plate. For easier rolling, trim the thick center rib of the leaf with a paring knife, being careful not to break the leaf.

2. *To prepare filling and roll leaves*: Combine ingredients for the filling in a bowl. Taste and adjust seasonings. Place 2 tablespoons of filling in the lower part of the leaf. Roll up just enough to cover the filling. Fold both sides toward the center and continue rolling all the way up. Secure with a toothpick. Continue process with remaining leaves.

3. Preheat oven to 350 degrees.

4. Remove core, and coarsely cut up the small head of cabbage. Distribute evenly over the bottom of a roasting pan. Place cabbage rolls 1 inch apart over cabbage bed. Cover with pitted prunes and sauerkraut. Combine chopped tomatoes, tomato sauce, lemon juice, and honey (or brown sugar). Pour over sauerkraut and prunes and shake pan gently. Cover with a lid and place in a preheated oven. Bake 1½ to 2 hours or until cabbage rolls are tender and liquid is reduced. If sauce is too thin, dissolve 2 teaspoons cornstarch in ½ cup water and add to roaster. Bake 10 to 15 minutes longer.

5. Serve hot as a main course. Leftovers may be frozen in plastic containers or reheated the following day.

RUSSIA/RECIPE ANALYSIS CHART

Name of Recipe	Quantity	Calories	CHO gms.	Protein gms.	Total Fat gms.	Saturated Fat gms.	Choles-terol mg.	Dietary Fiber gms.
1. Sweet and Sour Stuffed Cabbage	per cabbage leaf	28	6 (86%)	1 (14%)	—	—	—	.4
2. Pickled Mushrooms	per serving	28	5 (71%)	2 (29%)	—	—	—	.6
3. Beets *Igdaloff*	per serving	52	10 (77%)	3 (23%)	—	—	—	.6
4. Lemon-Egg-plant Spread	per serving	80	9 (45%)	2 (10%)	4 (45%)		—	1.0
5. *Sonia's Ka-mish Bread*	per rusk	87	13 (60%)	2 (9%)	3 (31%)	—	24	.3
6. *Matsunabur* (Armenian Yogurt Soup)	per serving	98	8 (37%)	4 (16%)	5 (47%)	4 (37%)	21	.3
7. Cream Cheese with Sardines and Red Onions	per serving	100	2 (8%)	5 (20%)	8 (72%)	4 (36%)	22	—
8. *Russian* Black Bread	per slice	102	18 (71%)	3 (12%)	2 (17%)		—	.4
9. *Borsch Ukraïnsky*	per serving	106	19 (72%)	3 (11%)	2 (17%)		—	1.5
10. Chopped Eggs with Mushroom Caviar	per serving	163	2 (5%)	5 (12%)	15 (83%)	5 (28%)	216	—
11. *Baklajanaya Ikra* (Russian Eggplant Caviar)	per serving	170	9 (21%)	2 (5%)	14 (74%)	2 (11%)	1	.8
12. *Blinchatiye Piroshki S Tvorogom* (Cheese Blintzes)	each	176	9 (20%)	8 (18%)	12 (62%)	5 (26%)	81	—
13. *Kuglis Natasha* (Natalie's Potato Kugel)	per serving	177	24 (54%)	5 (11%)	7 (35%)	2 (10%)	103	.5

Name of Recipe	Quantity	Calories	CHO gms.	Protein gms.	Total Fat gms.	Saturated Fat gms.	Choles-terol mg.	Dietary Fiber gms.
14. Kasha and Shells	per serving	191	27 (57%)	5 (10%)	7 (33%)	1 (5%)	31	1.0
15. *Salat Oliviye*	per serving	196	27 (55%)	4 (8%)	8 (37%)	1 (5%)	—	1.0
16. *Lekakh* (Honey Spice Cake)	per square	236	38 (64%)	3 (5%)	8 (31%)	1 (4%)	41	.1
17. Armenian Fish Plaki *Saucier*	per serving	242	14 (23%)	24 (40%)	10 (37%)	1 (4%)	15	.5
18. Cheese Noo-dle Soufflé	per serving	288	31 (43%)	14 (19%)	12 (38%)	6 (19%)	178	.2
19. Chicken on a Bed of Vegetables	per serving	394	13 (13%)	45 (45%)	18 (42%)	5 (11%)	81	1.0

Numbers in parentheses (%) indicate percentage of total calories contributed by nutrient.

MENUS

LOW CALORIE SPECIALTIES
(500 to 700 calories per meal)

BORSCH UKRAÏNSKY
BLINCHATIYE PIROSHKI S
TVOROGOM
(CHEESE BLINTZES)
Low-Fat Yogurt and Black Currant
Preserves
Fresh Strawberries
Bilberry Tea with Lemon

CHOPPED EGGS WITH
MUSHROOM CAVIAR
Thin Slices of BLACK BREAD
SWEET AND SOUR STUFFED
CABBAGE
Fresh Blueberries and Pears
Orange Spice Tea

PICKLED MUSHROOMS
Radish, Dill Pickle and Green Onion Platter
CHEESE NOODLE SOUFFLÉ
Fresh Fruit Salad
SONIA'S KAMISH BREAD
Rose Hip Tea with Lemon

•

LOW CHOLESTEROL MENUS
(Less than 50 mgs. of cholesterol per meal)

Dill Pickles
BORSCH UKRAÏNSKY
Bagels with Pot Cheese
Sliced Tomato, Onion and Cucumber
Platter
Cranberry Juice

CREAM CHEESE WITH SARDINES
AND RED ONIONS
RUSSIAN BLACK BREAD
SALAT OLIVIYE
Sauerkraut Sprinkled with Caraway
Seeds
Chilled Cider

BAKLAJANAYA IKRA (RUSSIAN EGGPLANT CAVIAR)
Rye Crackers
MATSUNABUR (ARMENIAN YOGURT SOUP)
SWEET AND SOUR STUFFED CABBAGE
Sliced Pears with Dried Currants
Russian Tea

LOW SATURATED FAT SELECTIONS
(Less than 8 grams of saturated fat per meal)

CREAM CHEESE WITH SARDINES AND RED ONIONS
Pumpernickel Bread
SWEET AND SOUR STUFFED CABBAGE
Sliced Cucumbers and Green Peppers
Fresh Apricots and Apples

Tossed Cabbage, Apple and Celery Salad
ARMENIAN FISH PLAKI SAUCIER
Steamed Kasha
Fresh Raspberries with Low-Fat Yogurt
Iced Rose Hips Tea

LEMON-EGGPLANT SPREAD
Dark Rye Bread
KUGLIS NATASHA (NATALIE'S POTATO KUGEL)
BEETS IGDALOFF
LEKAKH (HONEY SPICE CAKE)

●

HIGH PROTEIN MEALS
(30 or more grams of protein per meal)

MATSUNABUR (ARMENIAN YOGURT SOUP)
ARMENIAN FISH PLAKI SAUCIER
RUSSIAN BLACK BREAD
Steamed String Beans with Walnuts
Fresh Raspberries
Linden Blossom Tea

CHEESE NOODLE SOUFFLÉ
KASHA AND SHELLS
KUGLIS NATASHA (NATALIE'S POTATO KUGEL)
SONIA'S KAMISH BREAD (3 pieces)
Coffee

CHICKEN ON A BED OF VEGETABLES
Baked Potatoes and Mushrooms
BEETS IGDALOFF
LEKAKH (HONEY SPICE CAKE)
Red Wine

WELL BALANCED LUNCH OR DINNER MENUS
(Selections that conform to recommendations in Dietary Goals for United States*)*

PICKLED MUSHROOMS
LEMON-EGGPLANT SPREAD
Whole Grain Crackers
KUGLIS NATASHA (NATALIE'S POTATO KUGEL)
LEKAKH (HONEY SPICE CAKE)
Coffee

BORSCH UKRAÏNSKY
KASHA AND SHELLS
CHICKEN ON A BED OF VEGETABLES
SONIA'S KAMISH BREAD
Russian Tea

BEETS IGDALOFF
CHEESE NOODLE SOUFFLÉ
Tossed Apple, Plum and Apricot Salad
Sliced Cucumbers
Linden Blossom Tea

CHAPTER 14

SCANDINAVIA
Oat Cuisine

Culinary Essentials

The next time you crave a light meal imbued with flavors as cool and clean as an arctic glacier, consider the foods of Scandinavia: an enticing blend of Swedish, Danish, Finnish, and Norwegian cooking. This simple, down-to-earth style, free of elaborate, weighty, or complex recipes, will refresh your palate with fennel-fragrant breads, crisp cucumber salads, cold fruit soups, and tart lingonberry jams. The delicate creations of the Nordic kitchen display a palette of colors, and, when placed side-by-side, the pink flesh of salmon, the yellow skin of a rutabaga, and the rust-brown rind of goat cheese are as captivating as a magnificent sunset.

Most Scandinavian recipes call for familiar ingredients like apples, currant jelly, red cabbage, and cucumbers; cooking techniques rarely go beyond the basics and nothing fancy is required in the way of kitchen utensils. With the exception of dried brown beans and split yellow peas, you will find that legumes, noodles, and rice are rarely found in Northern cooking. Instead, new potatoes, boiled and adorned with dill or horseradish sauce, will be the ubiquitous sidekick for your savory entrées. And make room for versatile whole grains: tangy rye flour and crunchy rolled oats team up with molasses, brown sugar, and grated orange rind in an array of baked goods and yeast breads. You might also want to stock your shelves with *flatbrød*, imported crackers that add a Scandinavian touch to any meal. *Flatbrød*, which ranges from brittle "hardtack" to paper-thin "crisp bread" to thick rounds of "*knäcker bröd*," is available at most well-stocked supermarkets and delicatessens.

Though there are many Scandinavian specialties worthy of praise, it is the *smörgàsbrod*, or "bread and butter table," that has earned this cuisine its well-deserved fame. This sumptuous array of pickled and pungent snacks originated in the Viking era when epicureans staged elaborate food festivals, or what might be called "medieval state fairs," to proudly display their regional creations. Time has not eroded tradition, for the *smörgàsbrod* of today is made with just as much pride and enthusiasm as it was then.

Although you may prepare a three or four course sit-down dinner, a *smörgàsbrod* is the best way to experience the diverse textures and pure, sweet-tart flavors that embody this culinary style. In its most popular form, a *smörgàsbrod* is an infinite assortment of cold and hot foods spread out on a table, buffet-style. Variety is the key to its success, and though selections may change according to your creative instincts, several kinds of Scandinavian bread, fish, salad, and open-faced sandwiches will ensure satiation for both easy-to-please and divergent appetites. And if you adhere to tradition, each course should be washed down with gulps of ice-cold *aquavit*, a fiery caraway-flavored spirit distilled from barley or potatoes.

To ease your work load, plan a *smörgàsbrod* that utilizes ready-made items: pickled herring, smoked whitefish, sliced beets, hard-boiled eggs, or imported *flatbrød* would grace any collection of pick-up foods, while lingonberry jam, sharp mustards, horseradish, and dill pickles are favored condiments. A few time-honored recipes—*Gravlax* (Salmon Marinated in Dill) and *Herring with Sour Cream and Apples*—must be assembled several days in advance, which eliminates some of the last-minute preparation time. If you'd like to include homemade bread, orange-scented *Swedish Limpá*, cream-enriched *Rieska*, or molasses-tinged *Farmer's Oatmeal Bread* can be baked a day ahead and reheated when necessary. With a well-organized cooking schedule, you will have plenty of time to set your table and simmer a hot dish like sweet and sour *Braised Red Cabbage* before the feast begins.

Cheese figures prominently in the *smörgàsbrod* theme, and those who are unfamiliar with the smooth and golden Scandinavian varieties will find them exceptionally pleasing. Swiss cheese devotees will enjoy *Samsoe*, *Tybo*, or *Danbo*, all of which have a firm, tiny-holed texture. These mellow, nutty-flavored types are superb partners for sliced tomatoes and smoked fish. *Havarti*, characterized by a creamy consistency and mildly pungent taste, is fantastic on rye bread, especially when moistened with a dab of sharp mustard. Piquant and crumbly *Mycella*, or Danish blue cheese, pairs nicely with cool cucumbers, while *Esrom* (reminiscent of *Port du Salut*) and salty *Edam* are fine accompaniments for *flatbrød*. *Gjetost*, made of cow's and goat's milk, can be served with fresh fruit or featured in an unusual dish called *Asparagus with Gjetost Sauce*. While most Scandinavian cheeses are mild enough to suit even fastidious palates, *Gjetost*, with its grainy texture and caramel-sweet aftertaste, is definitely for willing experimenters.

As might be surmised, once you have sufficiently raided the *smörgàsbrod* table, there is little room for dessert; a cluster of grapes and a rich cheese, like *Crema Dania* or Danish *Camembert*, are often the culmination of this copious meal. Pastry-makers can reserve their sumptuous treats for another festive occasion—the Finnish "coffee table *smörgåsbrod.*" According to custom, this procession of baked goods boasts at least seven distinguished items, including a sweet yeast bread, an uniced cake, and an assortment of cookies. If desired, you may scale down the presentation to three selections such as a walnut-studded *Apple Cake*, deeply-spiced *Ginger Snaps*, and *Pulla*, a cardamom-perfumed coffee cake braided into a long loaf. Regardless of how many desserts you wish to offer, only one specialty should be served at a time and savored with a rich cup of coffee.

Seasoning Essentials

The Scandinavian penchant for pure, sparkling flavors is reflected in their selection of seasonings as well as in their food preferences. This unpretentious style employs only a limited number of herbs and spices with any regularity, and the chosen few—allspice, caraway, cardamom, cinnamon, dill, and fennel—are all known for their ability to penetrate selected ingredients with a pristine sharpness.

Vegetable preparations exemplify an important aspect of this cuisine: a capacity to allow the natural flavors of a dish to identify themselves. For instance, most people tend to smother rutabagas, with their turniplike pungency, in a galaxy of seasonings. Respect for this maligned root vegetable is demonstrated in the classic *Finnish Rutabaga Casserole*, where only a touch of cardamom or nutmeg is called upon for refinement. Boiled new potatoes, commonly slathered with butter or sour cream, are lovely to the Scandinavian eye with little more than a crown of fresh dill. And a mere pinch of cinnamon or cloves is considered adequate in this elemental style for accentuating a whole head of red cabbage.

While the amount of seasonings utilized in vegetables as well as fish preparations is downplayed, the baked goods of these Northern kitchens are bursting with lively flavors. Scandinavian rye breads, deeply perfumed with the essence of caraway and fennel seeds, are considered among the best in the world. The *Seasoning Chart* will provide a few tips on how to strategically combine these herbs with orange or lemon peel to achieve the characteristic effect; with a little practice, you can instill your own creations with the same tantalizing qualities that have won Scandinavian breads such high acclaim.

With the help of fennel seed, caraway seed, and grated orange peel, as well as cardamom and nutmeg, we have devised a *Scandinavian Spice Blend* especially suited for bread-baking. Without having to guess proportions, you can rely upon a teaspoon of this aromatic mixture to give an individual and attractive personality to each loaf.

SCANDINAVIAN SEASONING CHART

ALLSPICE is one of nature's most aromatic seasonings. These tiny, sun-dried berries, derived from a West Indian tropical evergreen, are naturally endowed with the flavor of cloves, cinnamon, and nutmeg all rolled into one. This warm, sweet-savory spice is highly prized in Scandinavian countries, especially Finland. The whole berries frequently team up with bay leaves, mustard seed, or dill to season poached, marinated, or pickled fish; approximately 6 berries are sufficient for 1 pound of seafood. Ground allspice will add dramatic new dimensions to soups made with cabbage, cauliflower, or potatoes. To get an idea of its character, start with ¼ to ½ teaspoon to 1 cup of soup. For optimum flavor, allspice should be bought whole and freshly ground like most spices.

CARAWAY SEEDS impart a clean-tasting pungency that blends beautifully with light, cool Scandinavian flavors. The pronounced aniselike taste of these tiny crescents is particularly effective in breads made with rye flour. Depending upon your love of this distinctive seasoning, you may use anywhere from 1 teaspoon to 1 tablespoon per loaf; a teaspoon of grated lemon peel will add a lovely sparkle to any caraway-flavored bread. Caraway also goes well with all kinds of cabbage dishes. You may sprinkle it over soups or add it liberally to baked cabbage. But, generally speaking, 1½ tablespoons is enough to season one medium-sized head. A tasty cheese for the *smörgåsbrod* table can be made by stirring caraway seeds into softened cream cheese; less ambitious cooks can buy *Tybo* cheese studded with caraway.

CARDAMOM could be called the quintessential seasoning for the Nordic kitchen. It is the lavish use of this aromatic, but pungent, spice that distinguishes the baked goods of Scandinavia from others in the world. Ground cardamom seed, which is reminiscent of ginger but less nippy, will give a beguiling personality to sweet yeast breads, holiday buns, or coffee cake. To give baked goods a subtle cardamom accent, use ½ to 1 teaspoon per loaf or cake; at least 1 tablespoon is needed to produce a well-defined character. Add cardamom and grated orange peel to your favorite pancake or waffle batter for a Scandinavian touch. As a rule, this versatile flavoring works well in combination with cinnamon, cloves, nutmeg, ginger, fennel, allspice, or lemon.

CINNAMON plays a traditional role in this cuisine, scenting and flavoring breakfast foods, baked goods, and desserts. Like vanilla, which is found in similar dishes, it has the unique ability to intensify the taste of chocolate, fruit, or anything that is inherently sweet. A good pinch of this ground spice will improve the quality of oatmeal porridge, pancakes, stewed rhubarb, apple cake, and countless other dishes. A stick of cinnamon, which exudes a lovely perfume, can be simmered in fruit soup or rice pudding and removed before serving.

DILL acquired its name from the Norse word *dilla* which means "to soothe" or "lull." This gentle-natured herb is responsible for the delicate but robust bouquet that is the signature of this cooking style. Dill refreshes the palate in various ways. The dried herb lends intrigue to marinated beets, pickled mushrooms, whipped horseradish sauce, and potato salad. Feathery tufts of fresh dill make a beautiful garnish for fish or new potatoes; chopped fresh dill is a marvelous enhancer for cucumbers or mustard sauce. Stir a few dill seeds into a sour cream-based sauce, a cabbage dish, or the poaching liquid for fish and you'll be rewarded with tastes that shine. As a rule, dill is not integrated with other herbs in this cuisine, although it does seem to enjoy the company of mustard, horseradish, parsley, and occasionally, bay leaf or allspice.

FENNEL SEEDS taste somewhat like a cross between licorice and celery. In many schools of cooking, they would be a preferred seasoning for seafood preparations, but in this cuisine they are mated with floury foods—breads, rolls, cookies, and pastries. In most Scandinavian recipes, this zesty seasoning is interchangeable with anise seed and compatible with caraway seeds, lemon rind, and grated orange peel. One loaf of bread can be flavored with up to 1 teaspoon of fennel seeds.

SCANDINAVIAN SPICE BLEND is designed to be an all-purpose seasoning for rye, graham, or buttermilk bread. This vibrant and distinctive mixture works especially well when molasses or brown sugar is incorporated into the bread dough. Use ½ to 2 teaspoons to season 1 loaf.

Combine ingredients listed below and store in an airtight container. To use, measure out the desired amount and combine with equal proportions of grated orange peel.

- 4 tablespoons fennel seed
- 2 teaspoons caraway seed
- 1 teaspoon ground cardamom seed
- ½ teaspoon nutmeg
- ¼ teaspoon mace

Other seasonings found in Scandinavian cookery: nutmeg, thyme, bay leaf, anise, poppy seed, cloves, ginger, saffron, tarragon, horseradish, white pepper, parsley, and curry powder.

Nutritional Essentials

If you enjoy light, wholesome meals, that are plentiful in their use of dairy and grain foods, Scandinavian cookery has much to offer. Along with

India, the specialties of this cuisine have the third lowest average calorie content per dish. Saturated fat calories account for about 15 percent of the total, which reflects the use of dairy foods in this style of cooking. Overall, the Scandinavian diet is compatible with healthful eating, and can easily be adapted to low-calorie programs.

Cheeses and hearty grain-based dishes are predominant in the Nordic kitchen. Of the cheeses, *Gjetost*, a grainy, almost buttery cheese, is one of the most popular. A one-ounce portion contains 132 calories of which only 12 percent is protein. The majority of calories are in the form of fat and carbohydrates, the latter being derived from sugar which is added to the milk whey during cheese manufacture. Other Norwegian and Danish cheeses, along with their fat content, are presented in the table at the end of this section.

In addition to cheese, there are a number of other dairy products which you can use in Scandinavian cooking. Because the nutritional make-up of most items reflects the nutrient composition of the milk from which they are manufactured, it is extremely helpful to know the values for a number of different products:

1. *Whole Milk* is a fresh fluid that contains between 3.25 and 4 percent milk fat. It is usually fortified with vitamin D and sometimes vitamin A. Milk protein is high in all the essential amino acids, especially lysine.
2. *Skim Milk*, from which much of the fat has been removed, is the milk of choice for calorie-watchers and those who must restrict their saturated fat and cholesterol intake. This kind of milk, which can substitute for whole milk in baking or cooking, contains all the protein of whole milk. Both "partially skim," containing 2 percent fat, and "skim," containing 1 percent fat, are available.
3. *Buttermilk*, which is made by fermenting whole or skim milk with lactic acid bacteria, is generally lower in fat and calories than whole milk.
4. *Cream* is classified as "light" or "heavy" depending upon the amount of fat it contains. The former is generally up to 30 percent fat, while the fat content of the latter is about 36 percent.
5. *Half-and-Half*, a mixture of cream and milk, is about 12 percent fat.
6. *Sour Cream* is made from sweet cream and has an 18 to 20 percent fat content.

The average carbohydrate content of Scandinavian dishes is 50 percent, which is higher than that of any other cuisine in this book, except the Lebanese. Because carbohydrates contribute only 4 calories per gram (whereas fat contributes 9 calories per gram), dishes which are plentiful in this nutrient (but low in fat) tend to be low in calories. This explains why Scandinavian dishes are calorie-sparing. Most of the carbohydrate content in *Lefse*, *Farmer's Oatmeal Bread*, *Finnish Flat Bread*, and *Swedish Pancakes* is derived from grains and potatoes. Commercial *flatbrød*, sesame crackers, and rye crisps also make tasty, low-fat, high-carbohydrate Scandinavian meal accompaniments.

Seafood is an important source of protein, vitamins, and minerals in the Scandinavian diet. Dishes such as *Herring with Sour Cream* and *Salmon Marinated in Dill* are protein-rich and low in calories. As a rule, you can expect seafood dishes to be excellent sources of high-quality protein, important minerals, and essential B vitamins. Furthermore, fish is generally low in fat, and what fat is present is usually of the polyunsaturated type.

Fishery products make excellent additions to the weight-watcher's menu. Lean-meat varieties such as haddock, sole, cod, and flounder contain only 80 calories in a 3½-ounce (100 grams) serving. Salmon, popular in Scandinavian cooking, has a fat content of 14 percent and contains about 200 calories in a 3½-ounce serving. Shellfish tend to be lean but are higher in cholesterol than regular fish. Carbohydrates are totally absent from fish and occur in very small amounts in shellfish. Both fresh-water and salt-water fish have a low sodium (salt) content, but in shellfish the salt content is medium-high.

AUNT JUNE'S
NORWEGIAN APPLE CAKE

YIELD: 16 squares

2 cups unbleached white flour
1 teaspoon salt
1 teaspoon baking soda
2 teaspoons baking powder
1 cup Wesson oil
2 cups sugar

2 eggs
1 teaspoon vanilla extract
3 medium-sized Jonathan apples,
   peeled, cored, and cut into
   eighths
½ cup chopped walnuts
½ cup raisins

1. Preheat oven to 350 degrees.
2. Sift the flour, salt, baking soda, and baking powder into a mixing bowl. Place the oil and sugar in the large bowl of an electric mixer and beat thoroughly. Add the eggs, one at a time, beating after each addition. Add the vanilla. Beat in the dry ingredients gradually until batter is very thick and smooth. Lift out beaters and scrape down with a rubber spatula. Fold in apples, nuts, and raisins by hand.
3. Spread batter evenly into a well-greased 9- by 13- by 2-inch baking dish. Bake in a preheated oven 50 minutes or until top is lightly browned and toothpick inserted in center comes out clean. Cool and cut into squares. This cake will keep well for several days if covered.

BOILED NEW POTATOES WITH
WHIPPED HORSERADISH SAUCE

YIELD: 6 servings

Sauce:
½ cup whipped cream or *Crème
   Fraîche* (p. 124)
1 teaspoon Dijon mustard
2 tablespoons freshly grated
   horseradish root
½ teaspoon dill weed or 1½
   teaspoons fresh chopped dill
   Dash liquid hot pepper—
   optional
   Salt to taste

2 pounds new potatoes
2 tablespoons minced fresh parsley

1. *To prepare sauce*: Place the whipping cream or *Crème Fraîche* in the small bowl of an electric mixer. Beat with chilled beaters until stiff enough to mound. Fold in remaining ingredients and mix thoroughly. Transfer to a bowl and set aside.
2. Peel potatoes if desired. Place in large pot with salted water to cover. Boil until tender. Drain well. Transfer to a serving bowl and toss with the

whipped horseradish sauce. Sprinkle with minced parsley and serve immediately.

Variation: Replace whipping cream with ¾ cup plain yogurt or sour cream.

BRUNA BONER
(Brown Beans, Swedish Style)   *YIELD: 8 servings*

1 pound imported Swedish dried brown beans,* soaked overnight in cold water Water to cover 1 cinnamon stick 1 tablespoon safflower margarine	2 tablespoons white vinegar 2 tablespoons light molasses, Karo syrup, or brown sugar 1½ teaspoons salt (or to taste) 2 tablespoons flour for thickening if necessary

* Available at Swedish delicatessens and some supermarkets.

Do not drain beans after overnight soaking. Place in a 3-quart saucepan with enough water to cover. Add the cinnamon stick, margarine, vinegar, and molasses. Bring to a boil, reduce heat, partially cover, and simmer 1 to 2 hours or until beans are tender, brown, and thick. Taste beans occasionally—they should have a liquidy, not dry, taste. If too much liquid evaporates during cooking, add more water as needed. If mixture is not thick enough stir in the flour. Add salt as needed to taste. For sweeter beans, double the amount of molasses. Serve hot as a side dish.

ASPARAGUS WITH GJETOST SAUCE   *YIELD: 4 servings*

2 pounds fresh asparagus *Sauce:* 3 tablespoons safflower margarine or butter 2 small onions, minced ½ cup sour cream ½ cup milk 1 cup grated *Gjetost* cheese*	2 tablespoons lemon juice 1 teaspoon dill weed or 1 tablespoon chopped fresh dill 1 teaspoon Dijon mustard Salt and freshly ground pepper to taste

* Available in most supermarkets.

1. *To prepare asparagus*: Break each asparagus spear as far down as it snaps easily. Discard tough ends. Place in a vegetable steamer with 1 inch water. Steam until tender, but firm. Or, stand stalks in the lower part of a double boiler or deep kettle. Add 2 inches of boiling salted water, cover, and cook until tender—about 10 to 13 minutes.

2. *To prepare sauce*: Heat the margarine or butter in a small saucepan. Sauté the onions until transparent. Stir in the remaining ingredients and simmer

over low heat, stirring constantly, until cheese is melted and sauce is bubbly.

3. *To serve*: Transfer asparagus to a serving dish and cover with sauce. This dish goes well with boiled new potatoes and marinated cucumbers.

Note: *Gjetost Sauce* is also delicious with poached or broiled cod fillets.

BRAISED RED CABBAGE
YIELD: 8 servings

1 head red cabbage (3 pounds)
3 tablespoons safflower margarine or butter
2 apples, pared, cored, and chopped
1 medium-sized red onion, minced
⅓ cup red wine vinegar
⅓ cup honey

1 teaspoon salt
¼ teaspoon powdered cloves
½ teaspoon freshly ground pepper
1 to 1½ cups water
1 tablespoon flour
1 tablespoon safflower margarine or butter
½ cup red currant jelly

1. Cut cabbage into quarters. Wash and drain. Remove the core and tough ribs. Shred cabbage coarsely. Melt the 3 tablespoons margarine or butter in a Dutch oven or large pot. Add the chopped apples and onion. Sauté 3 to 4 minutes. Add shredded cabbage and toss to coat with margarine. Pour the vinegar and honey over cabbage and mix thoroughly.

2. Cover the pot and cook 10 minutes. Add the salt, cloves, pepper, and 1 cup of water. Cover again and simmer over low heat from 30 to 40 minutes. Add remaining water if needed.

3. Blend the flour and 1 tablespoon of margarine or butter together. Form into small balls. Add to cabbage. Cook 20 minutes or until cabbage is tender and sauce has thickened. Stir in currant jelly until melted.

FARMER'S OATMEAL BREAD
YIELD: Two loaves, containing approximately 14 servings each.

1 cup rolled oats
1 pint boiling water or skimmed milk
1 package dry active yeast
¼ cup lukewarm water
2 tablespoons dark molasses
5 to 5½ cups unbleached white flour

2 tablespoons sugar
1 tablespoon safflower margarine or butter, melted
1 teaspoon salt
Melted margarine or butter—optional

1. Place oats in a large mixing bowl. Cover with boiling water. Let stand until cool—about 20 minutes.

2. Dissolve yeast in lukewarm water. Let stand 5 minutes to "foam." Add molasses to cooled oatmeal along with 1 to 2 cups of the flour. Beat well. Add the yeast, sugar, melted margarine, and salt. Beat well. Add enough of the remaining flour to form a soft dough. Knead 10 minutes or until smooth and elastic; the dough will spring back when pressed with your finger. Place in a clean, well-greased bowl. Cover and let rise until doubled—about 1 to 2 hours. Punch down, knead 10 times more, and divide into 2 equal parts. Cover and let rest 5 minutes.

3. Shape each piece of dough into a round loaf. Place into 2 well-greased, 9-inch pie plates. Prick tops well with a fork and let rise 40 to 60 minutes.

4. Preheat oven to 400 degrees. If using glass pie plates, reduce temperature by 25 degrees.

5. Brush tops with melted margarine or butter. Bake in a preheated oven 30 minutes or until done. Cool on wire racks.

GRAVLAX
*(Swedish Salmon Marinated in Dill)**   *YIELD: 8 to 12 servings*

---

2 pounds fresh (not frozen) salmon, center-cut	¼ cup sugar
1 tablespoon finely chopped fresh dill—no substitute	½ teaspoon freshly ground white pepper
2 tablespoons coarse (kosher) salt	Fresh dill for garnish
	Lemon wedges for garnish

Must be prepared 48 hours in advance.

1. Clean fish and rinse well with cold water. Pat dry with paper towels. Cut along the back with a sharp knife and carefully remove the bone to divide into 2 fillets (you may also ask your fish dealer to perform this task). Remove any small bones.

2. Place 1 fillet, skin-side-down, in a square glass baking dish. Sprinkle with chopped dill, salt, and sugar. Top with the other fillet, skin-side-up. Place a heavy cutting board or plate, topped with canned food to act as a weight, over fish. Refrigerate at least 48 hours. Salmon is "cooked" when orange in color and flaky in texture.

3. *To serve*: Wipe off seasonings and cut fillets diagonally, away from the skin, into thin slices. Arrange on a platter surrounded by fresh dill and lemon wedges. Serve with *Whipped Horseradish Sauce* (p. 344), or sour cream blended to piquancy with Dijon mustard, as an appetizer, *smörgåsbrod* item, or sandwich on hot buttered toast.

Variation: Replace 2 tablespoons sugar with cognac and add ½ teaspoon ground allspice along with the chopped dill and salt.

HERRING WITH
SOUR CREAM AND APPLES*

YIELD: Serves 8

1 pint jar herring fillets packed in
  wine sauce
1 cup sour cream
  Sugar (about 1 teaspoon)
Must be prepared 4 days in advance.

1 small onion, thinly sliced
1 small Red Delicious apple,
  peeled, cored, and thinly sliced
1 small cucumber, thinly sliced

Place the herring in a colander, discarding any pieces of onion from the jar. Rinse well and pat dry with paper towels. Stir sour cream to a spreading consistency. Spread a layer of sour cream in the bottom of a wide-mouth quart jar. Sprinkle with about ⅛ teaspoon sugar. Then add alternate layers of herring pieces, onion rings, apples, and cucumber slices. Repeat process beginning with sour cream and continue until all ingredients are used, reserving some of the sour cream for the top. Spread top with remaining sour cream and a little sugar. Cover with a tight-fitting lid and shake vigorously 20 seconds. Refrigerate 4 days before serving to let flavors develop. Turn out into a serving bowl and stir to break up the layers. Serve as an appetizer accompanied by Scandinavian breads or crackers.

KAURALASTUT
(Oatmeal Lace Cookies)

YIELD: Approximately 48 cookies

1 cup quick-cooking oats
1½ cups dark brown sugar, firmly
  packed
1 egg, well beaten

1 teaspoon vanilla extract
½ teaspoon salt
1½ cups melted safflower margarine
  or butter

1. Preheat the oven to 350 degrees.
2. Place oats in a blender and finely grind. Transfer to a bowl and combine with remaining ingredients. Beat well until batter is dark brown in color. Drop by teaspoonfuls 2 to 3 inches apart, on a lightly greased cookie sheet. Bake 12 minutes in a preheated oven. Remove with a metal spatula while still warm. Cool on wire racks. If cookies should harden on the baking sheet, return them to the oven for a few seconds until they are soft enough to remove. Cool and store in a closed cookie jar or tin.

KURKKUSALAATTI
(Finnish Cucumber Salad)   *YIELD: 6 to 8 servings*

2 large cucumbers
Salt
2 small onions, thinly sliced and
   separated into rings
½ cup each: plain low-fat yogurt
   and sour cream

¼ cup light cream (half-and-half)
1 tablespoon white distilled
   vinegar
Freshly ground pepper to taste

Peel cucumbers if waxed. If not, score lengthwise with the tines of a fork to make shallow ridges. Slice thinly, place in a bowl, and sprinkle with salt. Cover with a plate and let stand at room temperature for 45 minutes. Drain, rinse well, and squeeze out as much liquid as possible. Pat dry and combine with onion rings. Combine remaining ingredients and pour over cucumbers. Chill before serving.

LANTTALAATIKKO
(Finnish Rutabaga Casserole)   *YIELD: 6 servings*

4 cups peeled and diced rutabaga
   or turnips
   Boiling water
1 teaspoon salt
1 teaspoon sugar
2 tablespoons safflower margarine
   or butter, divided
1 to 2 tablespoons minced green
   onion

1½ cups bread crumbs, divided
1 cup light cream
⅛ teaspoon nutmeg
¼ teaspoon dry mustard
   Salt and freshly ground pepper to
   taste
2 eggs, well beaten
¼ to ½ cup grated *Gjetost* or sharp
   cheddar cheese—optional

1. Place diced rutabaga in a saucepan. Cover with an inch of boiling water to which the salt and sugar have been added. Cover and boil gently until tender—about 12 to 15 minutes. Drain and mash until fluffy. Add half the margarine or butter and green onion. Add 1 cup of the bread crumbs, cream, and seasonings. Taste and adjust seasonings. Add beaten eggs.
2. Preheat oven to 325 degrees.
3. Place mixture in a well-greased, 2-quart casserole dish. Sprinkle remaining ½ cup bread crumbs on top. Dot with remaining margarine or butter. Bake in a preheated oven 55 minutes. Sprinkle cheese over the top and bake 5 minutes longer. Serve as a main course or side dish.

MRS. BJORN'S LEFSE
(Norwegian Potato Pancakes)

*YIELD: Approximately
28 lefse or potato pancakes*

2½ to 3 pounds potatoes
1 tablespoon sugar
1½ teaspoons salt
½ cup light cream (half-and-half)

⅓ cup safflower margarine or butter
1½ to 2 cups unbleached white flour
(may use part rye flour)

1. *To prepare potatoes*: Peel potatoes and cut into chunks. Place in a pot with enough water to cover. Boil until tender. Drain and measure out 4 cups. Place in a bowl and mash while hot with the sugar and salt. Heat cream and butter in a small saucepan to the boiling point. Add to potatoes and mix well. Place in refrigerator to cool.
2. *To roll out lefse*: When dough has cooled, stir in 1½ cups flour or enough to make a smooth, nonsticky dough. Turn out portions of dough onto a floured board and roll with an ordinary rolling pin (preferably one covered with a stockinet) or *lefse* rolling pin (with lengthwise grooves) into very thin circles about 8 inches in diameter. Lay *lefse* side by side on lightly floured waxed paper until all are rolled into circles and ready to fry. Do not cover.
3. *To fry lefse*: Transfer circles with a large metal spatula, one at a time, to a hot, ungreased griddle or 10-inch skillet. Turn several times until lightly browned on both sides. The more you turn, the crisper they will become. For soft *lefse*, turn as little as possible. *Lefse* are tastiest when eaten hot off the griddle. If necessary, wrap in foil and keep in a low (200 degrees) oven until ready to serve.
4. Serve in any of the following ways: Spread with margarine or butter, wrap around thin slices of *gjetost* or cheddar cheese, roll up, and eat out of hand; spread with lingonberry or fruit preserves, roll up, and eat with a fork; spread with yogurt or sour cream, sprinkle with brown sugar, roll up, and eat with a fork.

PEPPARKAKOR
*(Swedish Ginger Snaps)**

YIELD: Approximately 4 dozen

½ pound butter, softened at room
  temperature
1½ cups sugar
1 tablespoon light molasses or Karo
  syrup
2 teaspoons baking soda dissolved
  in a little water

1 egg, well beaten
3¾ cups unbleached white flour
1 tablespoon each: ground
  cinnamon, ginger, and cloves
Juice and rind of 1 orange

*Dough must be made 24 hours in advance.

1. Cream together the butter and sugar. Add the molasses, baking soda, and egg. Mix well. In another bowl, sift together the flour and ground spices. Stir the dry ingredients into the butter-sugar mixture and blend well. Add the orange juice and rind. Shape into a ball, cover, and chill overnight to season.
2. Preheat oven to 375 degrees.
3. Roll out small portions of dough ¹⁄₁₆-inch thick on a lightly floured board. Cut with cookie cutters (traditional shapes are hearts and pigs). Place 1 inch apart on a lightly greased cookie sheet. Bake in a preheated oven 8 to 10 minutes—watch closely to be sure they are just lightly browned. Cool on wire racks. Ice with your favorite frosting, if desired. Store in air-tight containers. These will keep 4 to 5 days at room temperature, or freeze for later use.

PLÄTTAR
(Swedish Pancakes)

YIELD: *Approximately 60 dollar-size pancakes or 6 to 8 servings*

---

1 cup unbleached white flour (may use ½ whole wheat)	3 eggs
¼ teaspoon salt	3 cups milk
1 tablespoon sugar	3 tablespoons melted safflower margarine or butter

1. Sift flour into a bowl. Add the salt and sugar. In another bowl beat the eggs. Add the milk gradually and stir in the 3 tablespoons of melted margarine last. Add the flour all at once and beat until smooth.
2. Brush a griddle or a heavy, cast-iron skillet with melted margarine or vegetable shortening. When skillet is hot, drop batter by tablespoonfuls onto the surface. Cook until the edges brown lightly; turn and brown on the other side until golden. Continue process until all batter is used, brushing skillet as necessary to prevent sticking. If using a Swedish pancake pan with depressions for each pancake, heat it, ungreased, until a drop of water dances on the surface. Brush each cup with melted margarine and add 1 tablespoon batter to each cup. When the surface bubbles and the edges begin to brown, loosen the pancakes with a spatula and turn to brown on the other side until golden.
3. Swedish pancakes taste best when eaten immediately. (If necessary, keep warm in a low (200 degrees) oven until ready to serve). Dust with powdered sugar if desired and serve folded or in stacks. They are irresistible when spread with lingonberry or other fruit preserves and rolled. Serve as a breakfast treat, luncheon or dinner entrée, or a dessert.
Variation: Replace 1 cup of the milk with light cream for a richer pancake.

PULLA
(Finnish Cardamom Coffee Cake)

YIELD: *Two braided coffee cakes, approximately 16 slices each.*

---

2 cups milk
¾ cup safflower margarine or butter, cut into pieces
½ cup warm water (110 degrees)
1 tablespoon sugar
2 packages dry active yeast
2 eggs, well beaten

¾ cup sugar
2 to 3 teaspoons ground cardamom seed
1 teaspoon salt
8 cups unbleached white flour, sifted

1. Scald the milk in a saucepan over medium heat. Remove from heat; add margarine or butter and let it melt in the hot milk. Cool to lukewarm.
2. Combine the warm water with the 1 tablespoon sugar. Sprinkle in yeast, stir to dissolve, and let stand 5 minutes to "foam." Add to lukewarm milk. Transfer to a large mixing bowl. Stir in the eggs, ¾ cup sugar, cardamom, and salt. Beat in flour gradually until dough is firm, but not too stiff. Knead 5 minutes. Place in a greased bowl; turn the dough to grease the top. Cover and let rise in a warm, draft-free spot until doubled in bulk—about 1 to 2 hours. Punch down, and knead again until smooth and satiny—about 10 minutes. Return to bowl, and let rise again until doubled in bulk—about 30 to 60 minutes.
3. Punch down dough and divide in half. Divide each half into 3 equal pieces. Roll each piece into a 16-inch strip. Pinch 3 strips together at one end. Braid fairly tight and pinch the end to seal, tucking it slightly under the braided loaf. Repeat process to make a second loaf. Place loaves lengthwise on an ungreased baking sheet. Let rise again until doubled in bulk—about 45 minutes.
4. Preheat oven to 375 degrees when loaves have almost finished final rising. Bake 20 to 30 minutes or until done. Cool before serving.
Variation: Before baking loaves, combine 1½ teaspoons cinnamon, ½ teaspoon nutmeg, 2 tablespoons sugar, and ¼ cup slivered almonds. Brush tops with milk or a beaten egg and sprinkle with spice-almond mixture.

RIESKA
(Finnish Flat Bread)

YIELD: *8 to 10 servings*

---

2 cups rye flour
¾ teaspoon salt
2 teaspoons sugar
2 teaspoons baking powder

1 cup evaporated milk or light cream
2 tablespoons safflower margarine or butter, melted

1. Preheat oven to 425 degrees.
2. In a large bowl, combine the flour, salt, sugar, and baking powder. Add the milk and melted margarine or butter. Stir with a wooden spoon to form

a smooth dough. Turn dough out onto a lightly floured surface and knead lightly. With floured hands, place dough on a well-greased baking sheet. Pat or roll into a large circle, 12 to 14 inches in diameter and ½ inch thick. Subdivide circle into pull-apart lengths by pressing the handle of a long wooden spoon across the dough to form parallel lines about 1 inch apart. Or, prick the dough well with a fork.

3. Bake in a preheated oven for 15 minutes or until lightly browned.

Variation: Replace 1 cup rye flour with 1 cup whole wheat or barley flour. Or, substitute buttermilk for the evaporated milk and add ½ teaspoon baking soda to the dry ingredients.

SÖT SUPPE
(Norwegian Dried Fruit Soup)   *YIELD: 8 to 10 servings*

½ cup dried pitted prunes
½ cup dried pears
½ cup dried peaches
½ cup dried apricots
¼ cup currants or raisins
1 tart cooking apple, peeled, cored, and sliced
½ cup fruit juice (raspberry is nice)

1 cinnamon stick
½ cup honey or sugar
1 teaspoon cornstarch for thickening if necessary
Lemon slices for garnish
Whipped cream or plain yogurt for garnish—optional

Combine the dried fruits. Place in a bowl and cover with 6 cups cold water. Let stand 30 minutes to puff up. Place in a 6-quart stainless steel or enamel pot. Add the remaining ingredients except the cornstarch and lemon slices. Bring to a boil, cover, and reduce heat to low. Simmer 15 minutes, stirring occasionally with a wooden spoon to prevent fruits from sticking. Taste and adjust sweetening. If mixture is not thick enough, add the cornstarch, dissolved in a little water, and stir until thick. Remove from heat and discard cinnamon stick. Pour into a large bowl and let cool to room temperature. Cover and refrigerate to chill. Serve cold in soup bowls, garnished with lemon slices, as a first course or dessert. If desired, add a dollop of whipped cream or plain yogurt to each serving.

SWEDISH LIMPÁ
                                      YIELD: Two loaves or
                                      approximately 30 slices

1½ cups very warm water
3 tablespoons brown sugar
1 tablespoon dry active yeast
3 tablespoons molasses
2 cups rye flour
½ cup vegetable oil or safflower shortening

2 tablespoons grated orange rind
1 to 2 teaspoons salt
2 teaspoons caraway seed
1 teaspoon anise or fennel seed, crushed
3 cups unbleached white flour

1. Combine the water and sugar. Add the yeast and stir to dissolve. Let stand 5 minutes to "foam." Pour into a large mixing bowl. Add the molasses and rye flour. Beat with a wooden spoon until smooth. Cover with plastic wrap and let rise in a warm spot until doubled in bulk—about 1 to 2 hours.

2. Punch down dough and add the oil, orange rind, salt, caraway seed, and anise seed. Slowly add 2¾ cups white flour. Beat 100 strokes. Cover and let rest 10 minutes. With your hands, work in the remaining ¼ cup flour while dough is still in the bowl or add enough flour to make a stiff dough. Knead 10 minutes or until smooth and elastic. Shape into 2 loaves and place in 2, well-greased 8½- by 4½- by 2½-inch loaf pans. Brush tops with oil. Let rise in pans until doubled—about 45 minutes.

3. Preheat oven to 375 degrees. Bake 40 minutes or until done.

SWEDISH TOSCAS
(Miniature Almond Tarts)   *YIELD: 24 tarts*

Tart Shells:
¾ cup safflower margarine or butter, at room temperature
½ cup sugar
2 cups all-purpose flour (may use half whole wheat), sifted

Filling:
¼ cup safflower margarine or butter
½ cup sugar
1½ tablespoons flour
3 tablespoons cream
⅔ cup very finely chopped blanched almonds

1. Preheat oven to 350 degrees.

2. *To prepare tarts*: Cream the ¾ cup margarine or butter with the ½ cup sugar until smooth and creamy. Add the sifted flour and blend in thoroughly. Gather dough into a ball and pat into a flattened round. With a lightly floured stockinet-covered rolling pin roll out on a lightly floured board into a circle between ¹⁄₁₆- and ⅛-inch thick. Cut into 2-inch circles. Line the bottom and sides of 24, 2-inch tart shells with the circles. Trim away any overhang. Bake 8 to 10 minutes in a preheated oven, watching carefully to prevent burning. Remove tarts from oven and cool slightly before filling. Do not turn off oven.

3. *To prepare filling*: Heat the ¼ cup margarine or butter and ½ cup sugar in a heavy saucepan. Stir in the flour before the margarine melts completely. Add the cream and almonds, stirring constantly until mixture comes to a boil. Remove from heat and pour into tart shells, filling almost to the top. Return to oven for 10 to 12 minutes or until filling is set. Cool before serving.

SCANDINAVIA/RECIPE ANALYSIS CHART

Name of Recipe	Quantity	Calories	CHO gms.	Protein gms.	Total Fat gms.	Saturated Fat gms.	Cholesterol mg.	Dietary Fiber gms.
1. *Kurkkusalaatti* (Finnish Cucumber Salad)	per serving	72	7 (39%)	2 (11%)	4 (50%)	2 (25%)	11	.6
2. *Mrs. Bjorn's Lefse*	per pancake	79	11 (56%)	2 (10%)	3 (34%)	1 (11%)	3	.2
3. *Kauralastut* (Oatmeal Lace Cookies)	per serving	85	8 (38%)	—	6 (62%)	1 (10%)	7	—
4. Farmer's Oatmeal Bread	per slice	97	19 (78%)	3 (12%)	1 (10%)	—	—	—
5. *Pepparkakor* (Swedish Ginger Snaps)	per cookie	100	15 (60%)	1 (4%)	4 (36%)	2 (18%)	17	—
6. *Rieska* (Finnish Flat Bread)	per serving	112	16 (57%)	3 (11%)	4 (32%)	2 (16%)	7	.1
7. *Swedish Toscas*	per serving	157	17 (43%)	2 (5%)	9 (52%)	1 (6%)	18	.1
8. Herring with Sour Cream and Apples	per serving	171	7 (16%)	11 (26%)	11 (58%)	3 (16%)	10	.4
9. *Gravlax* (Swedish Salmon Marinated in Dill)	per serving	184	4 (9%)	15 (33%)	12 (58%)	4 (19%)	—	—
10. Boiled New Potatoes with Whipped Horseradish Sauce	per serving	188	25 (53%)	4 (9%)	8 (38%)	5 (24%)	28	1
11. *Plättar* (Swedish Pancakes)	per serving	190	18 (38%)	7 (15%)	10 (47%)	3 (14%)	128	.1
12. *Swedish Limpá*	per serving	200	28 (56%)	4 (8%)	8 (36%)	1 (5%)	—	—
13. *Söt Suppe* (Norwegian Dried Fruit Soup)	per serving	205	39 (76%)	1 (2%)	5 (22%)	—	—	1.3

Name of Recipe	Quantity	Calories	CHO gms.	Protein gms.	Total Fat gms.	Saturated Fat gms.	Choles- terol mg.	Dietary Fiber gms.
14. *Pulla* (Finnish Cardamom Coffee Cake)	per serving	214	27 (50%)	4 (7%)	10 (43%)	2 (9%)	21	.1
15. *Bruna Boner* (Brown Beans, Swedish Style)	per serving	234	41 (70%)	13 (22%)	2 (8%)	—	—	2.5
16. Braised Red Cabbage	per serving	246	44 (72%)	4 (7%)	6 (21%)	1 (4%)	—	2.0
17. *Lanttalaatikko* (Finnish Rutabaga Casserole)	per serving	256	26 (41%)	7 (11%)	14 (48%)	7 (24%)	118	.9
18. *Aunt June's* Norwegian Apple Cake	per square	345	45 (52%)	3 (3%)	17 (45%)	6 (16%)	39	.4
19. Asparagus with Gjetost Sauce	per serving	358	29 (32%)	11 (12%)	22 (56%)	10 (25%)	34	2.0

Numbers in parentheses (%) indicate percentage of total calories contributed by nutrient.

MENUS

LOW CALORIE SPECIALTIES
(500 to 700 calories per meal)

**KURKKUSALAATTI (FINNISH
CUCUMBER SALAD)**
MRS. BJORN'S LEFSE
Unsweetened Applesauce
BRAISED RED CABBAGE
**KAURALASTUT (OATMEAL LACE
COOKIES)**
Coffee

SWEDISH LIMPÁ
Plain Low-Fat Yogurt
**SOT SUPPE (NORWEGIAN DRIED
FRUIT SOUP)**
Rose Hips Tea

HERRING WITH SOUR CREAM AND APPLES
RIESKA (FINNISH FLAT BREAD)
Boiled Artichoke Hearts
Boiled New Potatoes with Safflower Margarine
Chilled Apple Juice

●

LOW CHOLESTEROL MENUS
(Less than 50 mgs. of cholesterol per meal)

Marinated Beets
Broiled Salmon with Dijon Mustard
**BOILED NEW POTATOES WITH
WHIPPED HORSERADISH SAUCE**
**KAURALASTUT (OATMEAL LACE
COOKIES)**
Cranberry Juice

PLÄTTAR (SWEDISH PANCAKES)
Lingonberry Preserves
Steamed Peas and Carrots
Knob Celery Salad with Vinaigrette
Fresh Raspberries

Aquavit
Tossed Belgium Endive and Grated Beet Salad with Vinaigrette
Baked Cod with Lemon and Dill
ASPARAGUS WITH GJETOST SAUCE
Stewed Rhubarb and Pear Compote

LOW SATURATED FAT SELECTIONS
(Less than 8 grams of saturated fat per meal)

Dill Pickles
MRS. BJORN'S LEFSE
Lingonberry Preserves
Sliced Apples and Apricots
Low-Fat Cottage Cheese
Hot Tea

**GRAVLAX
(SWEDISH SALMON MARINATED
IN DILL)**
FARMER'S OATMEAL BREAD
Tossed Tomato, Mushroom and
Onion Salad
**PEPPARKAKOR (SWEDISH
GINGER SNAPS)**
Coffee

Aquavit
KURKKUSALAATTI (FINNISH CUCUMBER SALAD)
SWEDISH LIMPÁ
Boiled Shrimp with Hot Mustard and Lemon Wedges
SWEDISH TOSCAS

●

HIGH PROTEIN MEALS
(30 or more grams of protein per meal)

**GRAVLAX
(SWEDISH SALMON MARINATED
IN DILL)**
BRAISED RED CABBAGE
**BOILED NEW POTATOES WITH
WHIPPED HORSERADISH SAUCE**
Wedge (2-ounce) of Tybo Cheese
Sliced Apples

**HERRING WITH SOUR CREAM
AND APPLES**
SWEDISH LIMPÁ
**ASPARAGUS WITH GJETOST
SAUCE**
SWEDISH TOSCAS (2)

Wedge (2-ounce) of Danish Havarti Cheese
Hardtack or Flatbrød
LANTTALAATIKKO (FINNISH RUTABAGA CASSEROLE)
BRUNA BONER (BROWN BEANS, SWEDISH STYLE)
PEPPARKAKOR (SWEDISH GINGER SNAPS)
Coffee or Hot Tea

WELL BALANCED LUNCH OR DINNER MENUS
(Selections that conform to recommendations in Dietary Goals for United States*)*

MRS. BJORN'S LEFSE
Plain Yogurt
BRAISED RED CABBAGE
**AUNT JUNE'S NORWEGIAN
APPLE CAKE**
Rose Hips Tea

Sliced Hard-Boiled Eggs
**KURKKUSALAATTI (FINNISH
CUCUMBER SALAD)**
**SÖT SUPPE (NORWEGIAN DRIED
FRUIT SOUP)**
FARMER'S OATMEAL BREAD
**PEPPARKAKOR (SWEDISH
GINGER SNAPS)**
Coffee

**GRAVLAX
(SWEDISH SALMON MARINATED IN DILL)
BRUNA BONER
(BROWN BEANS, SWEDISH STYLE)
BRAISED RED CABBAGE
PULLA (FINNISH CARDAMOM COFFEE CAKE)**
Tea

CHAPTER 15

UNITED STATES
The Melting Pot

Culinary Essentials

From the beginning of her history, the United States has been a "melting pot" of immigrants. They came from the four corners of the earth with feather quilts, straw suitcases, cardboard boxes, and recipes packed in their heads. Their kitchens were spiced with the fragrance of dishes that originated across the seas, and out of their ovens and earthenware pots emerged the American cuisine.

United States cookery is the synthesis of a number of complementary culinary styles. Preparations in the South reflect a strong African influence, embellished with a French accent. Southwestern fare is imbued with American Indian and Spanish overtones, while the dishes of the Midwestern heartland display Eastern European and Scandinavian touches. In the North, Yankee cooks adopted kitchen methods brought by Russian, Italian, and Irish settlers who established themselves along the New England coastline. And finally, the health-minded generation of the 1960s borrowed and popularized culinary concepts—originally introduced by the Indians, Chinese, and Japanese—for their new-fangled creations. The result has been a rich medley of dishes that combine indigenous provisions with the cooking wisdom of many cultures.

Largely due to the resurgence of ethnic cooking as well as economic considerations, foreign foods are appearing on modern-day American menus as frequently as milk and apple pie. Almost anything goes on the contemporary American food front, where East meets West at many a meal. Stir-fried vegetables often share a plate with macaroni and cheese, while crisp bean sprouts have a diplomatic relationship with everything from fresh salads to omelets. Most of these "exotic" victuals—bean sprouts, yogurt, bamboo shoots, and ginger root—are available at your local grocery store, but occasionally, you have to visit an international market for more unusual items.

Tofu is quickly making its way into the American cooking repertoire. This compressed, custardlike soybean cake has received wide acceptance, particularly among those interested in a low-cost, nutritional meat substitute. Borrowed from Oriental cuisines, this protein-rich food may become the "meat and potatoes" of America's future diet. Inexpensive and versatile, *tofu* can be found at Oriental and health food stores.

Chutney, a fiery condiment imported from India, is also working its way into the mainstream of American cooking consciousness. Available at gourmet or international food stores, this chunky mixture can invigorate cheese spreads, fruit salads, and barbeque sauces. Savor chutney and *tofu* in *Almond Tofu with Chutney Sauce*, a lively mingling of American, Chinese, and Indian gastronomy.

Once considered the favored child of food faddists, natural foods now occupy a prominent position in the annals of American cookery. Although most supermarkets have an aisle designated for "health foods," food co-ops and specialty food stores offer a larger assortment of nutrition-oriented items that can add diversity and excitement to your meals. Staples, such as whole wheat flour, brown rice, dried legumes, nuts, and honey, can usually be bought in bulk and at considerable savings at these outlets. Those looking for an alternative to butter or lard will want to investigate safflower shortening, which is not only a fine sautéing and baking medium, but is also low in saturated fat. You might also experiment with some of the cooking oils stocked by these stores. Sunflower and sesame seed oils are among the more common varieties, but you will also find rice bran, avocado, walnut, and almond oil.

Carob powder, also available at co-ops and specialty food stores, is worth considering as a substitute for baking chocolate. Many a chocolate fiend has kicked the habit with this cocoalike powder. Dessert waffles will take on an engaging new flavor if you replace a small amount of flour with carob. The next time you crave a milk shake, whirl cold milk, ripe bananas, honey, and carob in your blender for a unique taste treat. If baking is your forte, you'll enjoy making the *Carob Kahlúa Cake Supreme*, a moist, coffee liqueur-spiked dessert that just might put chocolate cake out of business.

Whether it's carob or chocolate cake, baking is a favorite American pastime. A well-equipped shelf should include two 9- by 5-inch loaf pans for quick breads; two 8-inch round pans, one square pan, and one 9- by 13-inch pan for single or double-layer cakes; pie pans in graduating sizes; a 12-cup muffin tin; a baking sheet for cookies; and a wire rack for cooling. Accurate measuring cups and spoons are essential tools as is an oven thermometer for heat regulation. At least one large mixing bowl and a long-handled spoon are necessary for hand-tossed batters and a rubber spatula is indispensable for scraping every last drop from the bowl. If you don't have an electric mixer (which makes an especially smooth and light cake batter), consider investing in hand beaters.

There are no die-hard traditions when it comes to the number of courses in an American meal. For instance, appetizers are not everyday fare, but rather festive tidbits generally reserved for honored guests. When the occasion arises, you will find *Baked Brie*, a small wheel of almond-garnished cheese warmed until creamy and served like a fondue, a memorable mini-offering. *Chicken Liver Pâté with Cognac*, a smooth, slightly sweet spread mounded on thinly sliced pumpernickel bread, is also well-suited for convivial occasions.

For a conventional American dinner, you might feature *Bluefish with Lemon Pear Stuffing*, a popular East Coast entrée. The appropriate supporting cast for a traditional main course would be rice or baked potato, steamed vegetables or *Vegetables au Gratin*, and a fresh green salad. If you're willing to take a culinary journey off the beaten track, consider a meal of *Stir-Fried Zucchini with Sesame Seeds* and *Chou-Chow Wild Rice*, the latter a crunchy mélange of grains augmented by toasted sunflower seeds and water chestnuts. Accompany these with *Curried Banana Waldorf Salad* and honey-rich *Date Nut Torte*, and you will enjoy a taste of the "new American cuisine."

Seasoning Essentials

American cooks rarely lavish their dishes with a profusion of spices. Instead, they use one or two key seasonings that will improve and blend with the natural savor of selected ingredients. While moderation is the name of the game, American cooks do not hesitate to throw in that extra clove of garlic or teaspoon of cinnamon if it will enhance the quality of a dish. There are no hard and fast rules when it comes to spicing in this cuisine: the finest creations are the products of those who learn to restrain or assert their seasoning prowess as the occasion demands.

Although no one herb plays a dictatorial role in American cooking, thyme, basil, marjoram, and bay leaves are omnipresent in everything from appetizers to side dishes. With the exception of bay leaves, which can easily overpower a dish, you can use these herbs liberally and interchange them in most recipes. Seldom out of place in savory dishes, you can count on them—alone or in combination—to impart a lively aroma and warming flavor to sauces, soups, vegetables, eggs, or seafood preparations. If you are hesitant to throw these amiable seasonings into a dish without specific proportions, remember this rule: you can safely add 1 teaspoon dried thyme, basil, or marjoram (or ⅓ teaspoon each of all three) to a dish that serves four persons; the amount can be increased, a little at a time, until the desired taste is achieved.

Sage, a popular but less ubiquitous American herb, behaves like all strongly-flavored seasonings; a suggestion of it enlivens, while too much will spoil an otherwise superb dish. Best known for contributing the quintessential flavor of a Thanksgiving turkey, sage need not be restricted to holiday menus. You will find its pronounced taste the perfect lift for a cream soup in need of something more. Canapés made with cottage or cream cheese are better for its presence, as are steamed lima beans, peas, and boiled onions. The next time you whip up a batch of herbed biscuits, consider a pinch of sage for an out-of-the-ordinary accent.

Celery seed is also indispensable for adding variety and interest to American creations. A judicious inclusion of this warm and bitter herb will lend character and crunch to stewed vegetables and salads. Celery seed will add intrigue to split pea soup and can be relied upon to perk up French dressing or mayonnaise-based spreads. When a sauce is in need of fresh celery stalks, and you have none on hand, celery seed will supply the missing flavor.

American cooks enjoy all sweet spices, but none is more treasured than cinnamon. Breakfast dishes—pancakes, hot cereal, and toast—are unthinkable without a sprinkling of this highly-scented seasoning. Cinnamon imparts an indefinable zest to fruit pies and can spruce up a bland custard. Winter squash spiced with cinnamon is worth investigating as a departure from the nutmeg-seasoned version; even baked fish or chicken can be enhanced with a hint of this seductively sweet spice. You can also count on ground cinnamon to lend sparkle to a white sauce or chocolate cake.

When you're looking for something that is as warm and fragrant as cinnamon but more penetrating, try the *United States Spice Blend*, a delightful mixture of cinnamon, nutmeg, allspice, ginger, and cardamom. It works beautifully with a variety of foods, especially spice cakes, preserves, pies, and puddings. You can substitute this versatile blend for cinnamon, in equal proportions, in any American recipe.

UNITED STATES SEASONING CHART

BASIL is used freely by American cooks to season vegetables, chicken, fish, and soups. A good pinch of this aromatic herb gives a cheering lift to almost any savory dish made with eggs, rice, tomatoes, or cheese. It blends well with other seasonings and is especially complementary in combination with wine and garlic. For variety, add ½ teaspoon basil to the water when you are cooking peas or artichokes or to the oil when frying mushrooms or eggplants.

BAY LEAVES release their strong, aromatic oils slowly in long-simmering sauces, soups, and vegetable stews. One-half leaf can be added to the cooking water of carrots, cauliflower, rice, or potatoes for a pleasant change of pace. With hearty fish stews, this warm and penetrating herb is welcome. But it has the ability to dominate delicate seafood like red snapper, so use it discreetly. A bay leaf added to a white sauce, cream soup, custard, or rice pudding gives a unique flavor that is loved by some and disliked by others—experiment and see if it works for you. Use the freshest bay leaves possible. When old, brownish, and brittle, they lose their potency and are of little culinary value.

CELERY SEED has a distinct celerylike flavor, although it is not a derivative of the cultivated celery plant. Its nutty-bitter flavor and crunchy texture can add warmth to cottage cheese, cream soups, or split pea soup. When making a mayonnaise-based dressing for a fruit, cabbage, or potato salad, stir ½ teaspoon celery seed into every ½ cup, and you'll be delighted with the results. A small amount of this decisive seasoning will give a boost to bland vegetables such as cold cucumbers, braised lettuce, steamed cabbage, or stewed tomatoes. When fresh celery is not on hand, use celery seed to season vegetable stews, soups, or sauces.

CINNAMON is the American breakfast spice. This warm, sweet, powerful seasoning is omnipresent in waffles, pancakes, and sweet rolls. When combined with sugar (3 parts sugar to 1 part cinnamon), it can be sprinkled over hot cereal, toast, or grapefruit. When not showering early morning fare with its pleasant taste, cinnamon is perking up custards, fruit pies, and coffee cakes. Add a good pinch to your favorite chocolate cake or lavish it over blueberry muffins before baking. Try sprinkling cinnamon-sugar over sliced tomatoes, orange segments, baked bananas, or unsweetened applesauce. Add a dash of this powdered spice to a white sauce or baked chicken for an unusual twist. Buy ground cinnamon in small amounts, and store in a tightly closed bottle away from light. Once exposed to air, its flavor and aroma deteriorate rapidly.

NUTMEG is a spice of countless charms and is welcome in both sweet and savory dishes. Its taste is similar to mace, but more fragrant, nippy, and refined. A pinch of this versatile seasoning will do wonders for eggnog, cream soups, baked mushrooms, lima beans, or cauliflower. Nutmeg is indispensable to spice cakes and fruit syrups and is often used in combination with other sweet spices such as cloves, allspice, and ginger. When freshly grated over sweet potatoes, baked squash, corn kernels, or spinach, nutmeg contributes a brilliant touch. If necessary, mace may be substituted.

PAPRIKA is used generously by American cooks as a colorful red garnish for everything from deviled eggs to cole slaw to cream soups. You can add it liberally to sauces or dressings made of sour cream, yogurt, mayonnaise, butter, or margarine. If available, use Hungarian paprika which has more bite and a fruitier flavor than the common mild American paprika.

MARJORAM is a member of the mint family native to the Mediterranean. Its flavor and aroma fall somewhere between oregano and thyme—you can use these three herbs interchangeably in most recipes. Sweet marjoram, which is mild tasting and highly scented, is the most popular variety in American kitchens. This "stewing" herb is commonly added to long-simmered sauces, soups, and bean dishes. A small amount will give character to eggs, vegetable casseroles, and stuffings. You can use it freely, though not heavy-handedly, to brighten up peas, potatoes, eggplant, or string beans. Pot marjoram, available at many spice shops, is stronger than sweet marjoram and well suited to pungent dishes, such as those with a pronounced onion or garlic flavor, where the gentle nature of sweet marjoram might be overwhelmed. This variety is also superb with tomatoes or mushrooms. Wild marjoram is another name for oregano.

SAGE has a powerful flavor that is enticing to some and repugnant to others. Compared to most herbs, its culinary purposes are limited, although it is indispensable to the bread stuffing of a Thanksgiving turkey. If used in small amounts, sage can add a surprisingly good flavor to herbed biscuits, leek pies, cottage cheese spreads, or cream soups. Toss a good pinch with buttered lima beans, peas, spinach, or zucchini for a delightful fillip.

THYME is used extensively in this cuisine, lending its delicate fragrance to eggs, salad dressings, clam chowder, poultry stuffings, and cream sauces. Thyme butter is a fantastic enhancer for cooked vegetables such as carrots, string beans, turnips, or squash. Proportions vary according to taste preferences, but 4 tablespoons of melted butter or margarine to 1 tablespoon fresh or 1 teaspoon dried thyme is a good guideline; season to taste with salt, pepper, and lemon juice. Thyme blends well with most herbs in this cooking style, but it is especially compatible with marjoram, summer savory, celery leaves, and parsley. A sprig of fresh thyme is equivalent to ½ teaspoon dried thyme.

UNITED STATES SPICE BLEND can be used in place of cinnamon or nutmeg in any recipe when a well-defined spice flavor is desired. Try sprinkling this superb mixture over baked squash or hot fruit compotes. It may also be used exclusively to season pies (especially those made with pumpkin, fruit, or custard), coffee cakes, or sweet cheese desserts. Vanilla, lemon rind, or orange rind can be used as complementary flavors.

Combine and store in an airtight container:

4	tablespoons ground cinnamon
2	tablespoons nutmeg
1¼	teaspoons allspice
1	teaspoon ground ginger
	Pinch of ground cardamom

VANILLA is unrivaled in its ability to heighten the sweetness of fresh fruit and chocolate. It is the quintessential flavor enhancer for baked goods, pies, custards, and puddings. Vanilla beans will produce a superior flavor. Though expensive, you can get a lot of mileage out of one pod; used whole or broken into pieces, it can be washed and reused for several months without lessening its taste or aroma. When its bouquet does diminish, you can grate the pod over hot cereal or into custard and homemade ice cream. Pure vanilla extract is convenient for baked goods such as cakes and cookies.

Other seasonings found in United States cookery: mustard seed, chervil, garlic, tarragon, cloves, ginger, rosemary, parsley, summer savory, mint, allspice, anise, caraway seeds, dill, mace, poppy seeds, and cardamom.

Nutritional Essentials

Not long ago, the American diet was in a state of nutritional chaos. Standard fare meant ham and eggs for breakfast, and it wasn't dinner without a buttered roll, potatoes and gravy, a fat-laden slab of meat, and possibly one lone vegetable course—undoubtedly those pale corn kernels with that awful canned sweetness. In short, American eating preferences encouraged an excessive intake of fat, calories, refined carbohydrates, and cholesterol and ignored the importance of an adequate fiber intake and protein balance.

With the dietary minirevolution of recent years, cooking and eating patterns in these United States have begun to change—albeit incrementally—for the better. These shifts in eating strategy—inspired largely by a myriad of foreign cooking styles—have done much to point the way for adopting healthier methods of food preparation and blending new combinations of unusual ingredients. These changes have been accompanied by the exploration of sensible nutritional philosophies.

The thrust of this culinary-*cum*-nutritional movement can be seen in our everyday lives. Now, a bowl of wheat germ looks strikingly healthful next to the carton of yogurt on the breakfast table. Canned corn has given way to garden-crisp salads topped with avocados and alfalfa sprouts, while chunks of meat have been supplanted by stir-fried vegetables and natural ingredients such as whole grains, sunflower seeds, and soybean curd. Food products which a mere five years ago were either unobtainable or hidden in some little-explored crevice of the grocer's shelf now command a prestigious position in almost every aisle.

Recipes in this chapter reflect this culinary and nutritional metamorphosis. The average calorie content per serving, 220, is quite reasonable by "American standards," and while 49 percent of the total calorie content is fat, only 12 percent is in the saturated form. This means that most people, except those on strict regimes, can partake in the special offerings of the "new" American cuisine.

Now that we have come to appreciate the virtues of unprocessed grains, brown rice has become a basic foodstuff in most health-conscious American kitchens. *Chou-Chow Wild Rice*, enriched with 7 grams of protein, utilizes brown as well as wild rice. Both varieties are preferable to white rice, which usually has been milled until nothing but the starchy endosperm remains. Although brown rice is 9 percent protein, it is low in the essential amino acid lysine and should be served with bean (3 parts rice to 1 part beans), cheese, or chicken dishes to increase the protein value.

Actually, wild rice is not a true rice at all, but rather the seed of a tall aquatic grass native to America and Canada. Because it is harvested with difficulty, this nutty-flavored grain is expensive and considered a gourmet delicacy. This is unfortunate because wild rice—even when compared to brown rice—is a rich source of protein (14 percent), niacin, and fiber. However, you can combine the two varieties together for a dish that is generous on nutrition, light on the pocketbook, and perfectly balanced on the tongue.

Because rice is so widely consumed in our diet, the government has set up standards for replacing some of the nutrients which are removed from white rice during the milling process. Still, enriched white rice is not on a par with brown rice when it comes to protein, fiber, phosphorus, and potassium; this fortification does, however, increase the iron content to above normal levels.

There was a time when the words "whole wheat flour" or "wheat germ" conjured up the image of food faddists preparing strange meals with no redeeming features. Today, they are household words synonymous with good health. All the praise bestowed upon these wholesome grains has not been unfounded. They truly are a wonderful source of many essential nutritional elements and an inexpensive source of protein as well.

Recipes such as *Charlotte Boon Bread*, *Blueberry Muffins*, and *Banana Nut Bread* use whole wheat flour and/or wheat germ, both of which are more nutritious than bleached white flour. Because the bran and germ remain intact, wheat flour supplies substantial amounts of protein, B vitamins, iron, phosphorus, and calcium. Wheat germ, which may be sprinkled over hot cereal or sliced fruit or used in place of bread crumbs, is the most nutritious part of the wheat kernel. Considerably richer in protein (26 grams per 3½-ounce serving) than whole grains, wheat germ is also plentiful in B vitamins, potassium, and iron.

In addition to whole wheat and grains, the dietary fiber movement has also made deep inroads into the American diet. Evidence has accumulated that consuming adequate quantities of dietary fiber—absent from foodstuffs of animal origin—is generally good for our health, possibly protecting us from diseases as diverse as diabetes and cancer (see *Part 2* for a complete discussion of this topic).

One of the richest and most accessible sources of dietary fiber is bran. You can incorporate bran flakes into the following foods: Baked goods or breakfast foods such as muffins, quick breads or pancakes (replace ¼ cup of flour with ¼ cup bran); granola (replace ¼ cup rolled oats with ¼ cup bran); hot cereal (sprinkle 1 teaspoon on top); stuffed vegetables (2 tablespoons of bran per pound of stuffing). Nutritionally speaking, bran goes a long way. One 3½-ounce serving contains a whopping 16 grams of protein and nearly 10 grams of dietary fiber. Other rich sources of fiber include dried red chili peppers, carob powder (see below), guavas, strawberries, sesame seeds, and dried fruit.

Two other items which have found acceptance among nutrition-minded counter-culturists include soybean curd (*tofu*) and bean sprouts. Epicureans familiar with these foods tend to overlook their nutritional assets and downplay their culinary virtues. What a mistake! Borrowed from sophisticated oriental cuisines, soybean curd is a highly nutritious, low-cost, low-calorie food that can be employed in exotic dishes such as *Almond Tofu with Chutney* as well as numerous stir-fried specialties. Available in many varieties, soybean curd is not only rich in protein, but low in fat and cholesterol-free (see *Chinese Nutritional Essentials*).

Bean sprouts, whose first recorded use dates back to 2939 B.C. in China, are not the panacea some people have claimed. However, they do play a vital role in any diet, and it is certainly worthwhile familiarizing yourself with the benefits derived from this highly economical and nutritious food. Bean sprouts are a quick source of energy and are easy to digest. Additionally, they are low in calories and carbohydrates, a plus for weight-watchers. They also contain more vitamin C than oranges or tomatoes and supply most of the nutrients your body needs.

Bean sprouts are developed from seeds; during this maturation process, starch is converted to protein and vitamins are synthesized. Something incredible happens to seeds when they are given warmth and moisture. They release dormant energy, vitamins, and minerals. As the sprout grows, so does their nutritional value. For example, the vitamin C content of soybeans increases 500 percent on the third day of germination. Once fully grown, bean sprouts are easily adapted for use in fresh salads, sandwiches, quiches, and stir-fried vegetables.

American cooks will find carob, derived from the *Ceratonia Siliqua* tree native to the Mediterranean, an ideal substitute for chocolate. Containing about 50 percent natural carbohydrates, carob contains 5 percent protein and contains little fat. This high-fiber, cocoalike powder—delicious in cakes, cookies, pudding, and milk drinks—is a dieter's dream. Try it in the *Carob Kahlúa Cake Supreme* or use it as a replacement for chocolate in other recipes as follows: (1) For cocoa, substitute equal amounts of carob powder, or (2) for one square of baking chocolate, use 3 tablespoons carob powder plus 1 tablespoon water.

Cheese is the major source of protein in the American vegetarian diet. Unfortunately, many of our domestic varieties are quite high in fat and calories (see *Table 7*). You can maximize the protein content of your dishes, and simultaneously reduce saturated fats, cholesterol, salt, and calories by combining smaller amounts of cheese with protein-containing foods from other groups—nuts, seeds, legumes, and grains. For example, bean sprouts and cheddar cheese team up in *Peas Oriental with Mushroom Sauce* and Swiss-like Gruyère cheese is complemented by bread crumbs in *Vegetables au Gratin*.

Nowadays, healthy cooking "American style" requires that you draw upon an expanded repertoire of ingredients and use them creatively in a number of foreign-inspired dishes. This applies especially to the use of cheese, carob powder, wheat flour, whole grains, soybean curd, fresh vegetables, bean sprouts, and legumes. Try the recipes in this chapter and convince yourself that cooking with nutritional, natural foods is consistent with epicurean tastes, and, what's more, it's good for you.

ALMOND TOFU
WITH CHUTNEY SAUCE

YIELD: 6 to 8 servings

5 tablespoons each: soy sauce and
  dry sherry
2 tablespoons chutney
2 garlic cloves, crushed
1 tablespoon cornstarch dissolved
  in 2 tablespoons water
1 pound *tofu*,* cut into 1-inch
  cubes
2 to 4 tablespoons peanut oil
2 teaspoons grated ginger root
2 garlic cloves, minced

½ to 1 cup whole almonds
1 onion, diced
1 green pepper, seeded and diced
1 cup fresh mushrooms, thickly
  sliced
2 green onions, chopped with tops
10 leaves fresh spinach, washed,
  stemmed, and cut into thin strips
2 tablespoons toasted sesame
  seeds—optional

Available at Oriental markets, health food stores, and some supermarkets

1. In a medium-sized bowl, combine the soy sauce, sherry, chutney, crushed garlic, and cornstarch dissolved in water. Add *tofu* and marinate 30 to 60 minutes, stirring occasionally. Drain and reserve marinade.
2. Heat oil in a wok or large skillet until hot. Add the ginger root and minced garlic. Stir-fry 15 seconds. Add the almonds and *tofu*. Sauté until *tofu* is lightly browned, stirring frequently—about 2 minutes. (Don't worry if the tofu breaks into small pieces.) Add the onion, green pepper, and mushrooms. Stir-fry 1 minute. Add the green onions, spinach, and marinade. Stir-fry 1 minute, cover, and simmer until the sauce thickens—about 1 or 2 minutes. Sprinkle with sesame seeds if desired and serve hot over brown rice.

BAKED BRIE

YIELD: Serves 12 to 16.

1 whole Brie (2½ pounds)
3 to 4 ounces sliced or slivered
  almonds

1 loaf French bread

1. Carefully remove the top crust from the Brie, leaving a 1-inch border around the outer edge of the circle. Sprinkle the top with sliced or slivered almonds.
2. Preheat oven to 300 degrees.
3. Place Brie in a round baking dish. Bake, uncovered, until cheese is hot and bubbly. Serve as an appetizer with French bread cut into cubes. Dip cubes of bread in Brie like you would a fondue.

BANANA NUT BREAD
WITH HONEY AND SPICES

YIELD: 16 slices

1 cup whole wheat flour, sifted
¾ cup unbleached white flour, sifted
2 teaspoons double-acting baking powder
¼ teaspoon baking soda
½ teaspoon each: salt, nutmeg, and cinnamon
⅓ cup safflower vegetable shortening or butter, softened to room temperature

1 cup honey, warmed to pouring consistency
2 eggs, well beaten
1 tablespoon vanilla extract
1 teaspoon grated lemon rind
3 small ripe bananas, mashed
½ to 1 cup chopped walnuts

1. Preheat oven to 350 degrees.
2. In a large bowl, combine the flours, baking powder, baking soda, salt, and spices. In another bowl, cream the shortening and honey until creamy and smooth. Beat in the eggs, vanilla, and grated lemon rind. Fold in the dry ingredients, then the mashed bananas and nuts.
3. Place in a well-greased, standard-size loaf pan and bake in a preheated oven for 1 hour or until toothpick inserted in center comes out clean. Cool and cut into slices.
Variation: Replace nuts with chopped dates or raisins.

BEAN SPROUT QUICHE

YIELD: 6 to 8 servings

1 9-inch unbaked pastry shell (p. 380)
½ cup each: grated Swiss and cheddar cheese
1 cup mung or soy bean sprouts
4 green onions, chopped with tops
3 eggs, well beaten

½ cup light cream
½ cup plain yogurt or light cream
½ teaspoon each: salt, dry mustard, and mace
¾ teaspoon grated lemon rind
½ cup slivered almonds

1. Preheat oven to 350 degrees. Adjust rack to middle.
2. Sprinkle cheese evenly over the bottom of the pastry shell. Spread sprouts over the cheese, then sprinkle green onions over the sprouts. Combine the well-beaten eggs, cream, yogurt or cream, and seasonings. Pour evenly into pie shell. Top with slivered almonds.
3. Bake in preheated oven 45 minutes or until toothpick inserted in center comes out clean. Let cool several minutes before cutting into wedges to serve.

BLUEBERRY MUFFINS

YIELD: *14 muffins*

1 cup each: unbleached white flour
and whole wheat flour, sifted
1 tablespoon baking powder
¼ teaspoon salt
½ cup sugar
1 egg

¾ to 1 cup milk
4 tablespoons melted safflower
margarine
1 cup fresh blueberries, washed,
picked over, and patted dry
4 teaspoons sugar

1. Preheat oven to 425 degrees.
2. Sift the flours, baking powder, and salt into a mixing bowl. Stir in the sugar. In another bowl, beat the egg until frothy. Add the milk and melted margarine. Mix well. Make a small well in the center of the flour mixture and pour in the liquid mixture all at once. Stir quickly and lightly, but do not beat. Batter should be just mixed and still lumpy. Quickly stir in the berries. Fill 14 muffin cups or well-greased muffin tins ⅔-full. Fill any empty cups with water. Sprinkle tops of muffins with 4 teaspoons sugar.
3. Bake 25 minutes in a preheated oven or until toothpick inserted in center comes out clean. If using muffin tins, run a spatula around each baked muffin to loosen. Tilt slightly to the side in the pan to keep warm so that they won't steam and soften.

CAROB KAHLÚA CAKE SUPREME

YIELD: *16 servings*

Cake:
1¾ cup each: whole wheat pastry
flour* and brown sugar
¾ cup sifted carob powder*
1½ teaspoons baking soda
1 teaspoon each: salt and cinnamon
⅔ cup safflower margarine or butter,
softened at room temperature
16 ounces plain or coffee-flavored
yogurt
1 ripe banana, mashed
2 eggs, well beaten
2 tablespoons Kahlúa or coffee-
flavored liqueur—optional
½ cup each: sunflower seeds and
walnut pieces

Frosting:
2 tablespoons safflower margarine
or butter
¼ cup honey
½ cup nonfat dry milk powder
⅓ cup sifted carob powder
¼ cup light cream
1½ tablespoons Kahlúa or coffee-
flavored liqueur
1 teaspoon vanilla extract

Available at specialty food stores and many supermarkets.

1. Preheat oven to 350 degrees. Adjust rack to middle. If you are using a glass baking dish, heat oven only to 325 degrees.
2. Sift the flour into a large bowl. Add the brown sugar, sifted carob pow-

der, baking soda, salt, and cinnamon. In the large bowl of an electric mixer combine at low speed the softened margarine, yogurt, mashed banana, eggs, and Kahlúa until smooth and creamy. Add dry ingredients, gradually. Beat 5 minutes at medium speed. Fold in sunflower seeds and walnuts by hand.

3. Pour batter into a well-greased 9- by 13- by 2-inch pan. Bake in a preheated oven for 50 minutes or until toothpick inserted in center comes out clean. Cool completely before frosting.

4. *To prepare frosting*: In a small saucepan, warm over low heat the margarine or butter and honey. Stir in the dry milk and carob powder. Remove from heat, let cool, and stir in the cream, Kahlúa, and vanilla. Cream together to reach a spreading consistency. Spread evenly over the cake and cut into squares to serve.

CHARLOTTE BOON BREAD*

YIELD: Three loaves or 36 slices

1½ cups all-purpose or unbleached white flour
1 cup wheat germ
1 cup finely-crushed honey graham crackers
2 teaspoons baking soda
1 teaspoon salt

½ cup currants or raisins
2 eggs, well beaten
⅓ cup vegetable oil
2 cups buttermilk
¾ cup light molasses
¼ cup maple syrup

1. Preheat oven to 350 degrees.

2. Sift flour before measuring. In a mixing bowl, combine the flour, wheat germ, graham cracker crumbs, baking soda, salt, and currants. With a wire whisk, combine in a separate bowl the eggs, oil, buttermilk, molasses, and syrup. Combine the liquid ingredients gradually with the dry ingredients, beating thoroughly until well blended.

3. Pour into 3, well-greased, 1-pound coffee cans, filling each half full. Bake in a preheated oven 55 minutes. Cool 10 minutes. Turn over onto a cake rack to cool.

*Note: This bread is tastier if baked a day before serving. If you want to freeze the bread, remove from cans and cool thoroughly. Wrap in plastic bags and return to cans. Cover with can lids and freeze.

CHICKEN LIVER PÂTÉ WITH COGNAC

YIELD: Serves 6

½ cup sweet butter
1 large onion, chopped
1¼ pounds chicken livers
1 hard-boiled egg, chopped
1 tablespoon cognac

½ teaspoon salt
Dash pepper
2 green onions with stems, chopped
Pumpernickel or rye bread

1. Place 1 tablespoon of the butter in a large skillet. Sauté chopped onion until tender—about 10 minutes. Remove from skillet and set aside. Heat remaining butter in skillet. Add chicken livers and sauté over medium heat for three to five minutes. Livers should be pink inside.

2. Put onion, livers, egg, and cognac in a blender. Blend at low speed just until smooth. Stir in salt and pepper. Taste and adjust seasonings.

3. Grease and line a loaf pan with wax paper. Fill the pan with the pâté and shape into a loaf. Refrigerate until chilled and firm. When ready to serve, unmold and sprinkle with chopped green onions. Serve with thin slices of pumpernickel or rye bread.

CHICKEN STOCK

YIELD: Approximately 2 quarts stock

3 pounds chicken pieces (necks, backs, wings, and giblets)	3 cloves
4 quarts cold water	2 leeks (white part only)
1 large onion, diced	2 carrots, diced
2 garlic cloves, minced	2 stalks celery, sliced
2 tablespoons safflower oil or rendered chicken fat	3 sprigs parsley
	1 bay leaf
1 large whole onion	1 teaspoon dried thyme
	2 teaspoons salt

Put chicken pieces and water in a large soup pot. Bring to a boil and skim the scum that rises to the surface. Brown the diced onion and garlic in heated oil or chicken fat. Stud the whole onion with the cloves. Add the browned chopped onion, clove-studded onion, leeks, carrots, celery, parsley, bay leaf, and seasonings to the pot. Simmer slowly for 4 hours and continue to remove any scum that forms. When the stock is reduced by one-half of its original volume, remove the vegetables. Strain the stock through a coarse sieve and then through a cheesecloth. Pour into freezer containers and chill in refrigerator. Remove congealed fat from top before storing in freezer.

CHOU-CHOW WILD RICE

YIELD: 8 servings

½ cup wild rice	4 to 6 tablespoons safflower margarine or butter
4 cups vegetable or chicken stock	
½ cup brown rice	1 (5-ounce) can water chestnuts, thinly sliced
1 large onion, finely chopped	
3 ribs celery, diced	½ cup sunflower seeds, toasted
½ pound mushrooms, sliced	4 tablespoons soy sauce
	¼ to ½ teaspoon ground ginger
	½ cup slivered almonds, toasted

1. Thoroughly wash the wild rice in cold water. Place in a bowl and cover with water. Soak at least 2 hours. Drain off remaining water.
2. Bring the stock to a boil in a 3-quart saucepan. Add wild rice and boil for 20 minutes. Add brown rice, continue boiling for 5 minutes. Reduce heat to low, cover tightly with a fitted lid and simmer for 40 minutes. Drain off any remaining liquid.
3. Preheat oven to 350 degrees.
4. Sauté onion, celery, and mushrooms in margarine or butter for 5 minutes. Combine with rice, along with water chestnuts, sunflower seeds, soy sauce, and ginger. Place in a lightly greased, round, 2½-quart casserole (or any other serving dish). Bake uncovered in a preheated oven for 30 minutes. Sprinkle almonds over top and serve immediately.

CURRIED BANANA WALDORF SALAD

YIELD: 6 servings

2 Red Delicious or Cortland apples, diced
2 green-skinned apples, diced
4 ripe bananas, peeled and sliced
Juice of ½ lemon
4 ribs celery, diced
3½ ounces walnuts or pecans, coarsely chopped

½ cup dried currants or raisins
½ cup safflower mayonnaise
½ to 1 teaspoon curry powder (preferably imported Madras Curry Powder)
1 tablespoon honey or brown sugar
1 to 2 tablespoons apple juice
Lettuce leaves

Combine the red and green apples and bananas in a salad bowl. Sprinkle with lemon juice to prevent discoloring. Add the celery, walnuts, and currants. Combine the mayonnaise, curry powder, honey, and apple juice. Toss with salad. Serve on lettuce leaves.

DATE NUT TORTE

YIELD: 9 squares

1 cup chopped pitted dates
1 cup chopped walnuts
1 stick safflower margarine or butter, melted
⅓ cup clover honey
2 large eggs, separated

1 teaspoon vanilla extract
½ cup unbleached white flour
1 teaspoon double-acting baking powder
½ pint whipping cream—optional

1. Preheat oven to 325 degrees.
2. In the large bowl of an electric mixer combine dates and walnuts. Add melted margarine, honey, egg yolks, and vanilla. Combine flour with baking powder and add to mixture. Batter at this point will be very thick. In the small bowl of the mixer beat egg whites until stiff, but not dry, and carefully fold them into batter.
3. Pour mixture into a greased 8- by 8-inch square pan and bake 35 minutes

in a preheated oven. Remove and let cool for at least 30 minutes. Cut into squares.
4. Prechill mixing bowl and electric beaters. Place whipping cream in chilled bowl and beat until thick. Top each square with a dollop of whipped cream.

ETHEL'S ETHEREAL CHEESECAKE
YIELD: 12 slices

Crust:
1 cup graham cracker crumbs
2½ tablespoons safflower margarine, melted
1 tablespoon sugar
1 teaspoon cinnamon

Glaze:
1 quart fresh strawberries (or substitute any berries in season)
9 tablespoons sugar
¼ cup water
Pinch of salt
1⅛ tablespoons cornstarch

Filling:
3, 8-ounce packages Neufchâtel or cream cheese, softened at room temperature
1 cup sugar
2 rounded tablespoons flour
½ teaspoon grated lemon rind
1 teaspoon grated orange rind
1 tablespoon lemon juice
4 eggs, separated, at room temperature
1 cup light cream
1 tablespoon vanilla extract

1. Preheat oven to 300 degrees. Adjust rack to middle.
2. Combine the ingredients for the crust and press evenly over the bottom of a lightly greased, 9-inch, spring-form pan, coming up about 1 to 1½ inches on the sides. Bake 5 minutes in a preheated oven and cool.
3. Beat the cream cheese until fluffy and completely smooth. Add the sugar, flour, grated rinds, and lemon juice. Beat the egg yolks well and add to the mixture, stirring just to mix. Add the cream and vanilla. Beat the egg whites until stiff, but not dry. Slowly and carefully fold in the whites. Turn into the spring-form pan and bake until cake tests done—about 1 to 1½ hours. Turn off the heat and let cake cool in the oven with the door closed for 1 hour.
4. Once cooled, the cake may be glazed at any time. Reserve 1 cup of the berries for the glaze. Remove stems from the remaining strawberries by making a straight cut across the stem end. Arrange over entire top of cake, flat-side-down. (Other kinds of berries should be spread evenly over the top.) Crush reserved cup of berries. Place in a small saucepan with the sugar, water, and salt. Bring to a boil stirring constantly for 2 minutes. Cool slightly. Place in a blender and purée until smooth. If using blackberries or raspberries, press mixture through a fine-mesh strainer to remove any seeds. Return mixture to saucepan. Add the cornstarch and boil for 2 minutes or until liquid is clear and thick. Spoon over berries and let glaze congeal for several hours before serving.
Note: When fresh berries are not in season you can make a glaze with canned berries. Drain the liquid from a 1-pound can of berries and com-

bine in a saucepan with 1 tablespoon cornstarch and 1 tablespoon sugar. Bring to a boil, stirring constantly for 3 minutes. Add berries and remove from stove. When cool, spoon mixture over cheesecake and chill as above.

HERBED SPINACH AND
CHEESE CASSEROLE

YIELD: 9 servings

2 tablespoons safflower margarine or butter
1 onion, finely chopped
6 to 8 large mushrooms, sliced
⅓ cup chopped green onion with tops
2 pounds fresh spinach or 2 packages frozen chopped spinach
2 tablespoons minced fresh parsley
1 teaspoon each: minced garlic cloves and dill weed

½ teaspoon cayenne pepper
Salt and freshly ground pepper to taste
8 ounces Neufchâtel cheese or cream cheese, cut into ½-inch cubes
6 eggs, well beaten
½ cup plain low-fat yogurt or light cream
½ cup walnuts—optional
¼ to ½ cup grated Parmesan or cheddar cheese

1. Heat margarine or butter in a large skillet until hot. Sauté the onion, mushrooms, and green onion. Set aside.
2. Wash fresh spinach well. Trim off stems and discard any blemished leaves. Place in a vegetable steamer with ½ inch of water. Steam until just tender. Cool and chop. (For frozen spinach, cook according to directions on the package.) Squeeze out excess moisture and place spinach in a bowl. Add the sautéed vegetables, parsley, garlic, dill weed, cayenne, salt, and pepper. Taste and adjust seasonings—mixture should be well seasoned.
3. Preheat oven to 350 degrees.
4. Toss the cubes of Neufchâtel or cream cheese with the spinach mixture. Place in a well-greased 9- by 13-inch baking dish. Beat eggs with yogurt or cream. Pour over spinach mixture. Sprinkle walnuts on top and cover with cheese. Bake in a preheated oven until knife inserted in center comes out clean—about 30 minutes. Cut into squares and serve hot.

HOMEMADE CREAM CHEESE

YIELD: Two 8-ounce balls of cream cheese, containing 8 tablespoon servings each.

1 quart light cream*
1½ to 2 tablespoons buttermilk

1 tablespoon sugar or honey
½ teaspoon salt

Do not use cream that contains alginates or monoglycerides as they will prevent the fermenting action of the buttermilk. Check the carton before purchasing.

1. It is essential in making cream cheese to follow strict rules of cleanliness in order to keep out as much bacteria and mold from the air as possible.

Wash your hands thoroughly with hot water and soap before beginning each process. All utensils should be washed before using, and boiling water poured over them. The rest is simple and requires only a few minutes of your time for several days.

2. Heat the cream in a saucepan (preferably a granite saucepan) until lukewarm (90 to 100 degrees). Test temperature by putting a few drops on the inside of your wrist. Remove from heat and stir in the buttermilk (the more buttermilk you use, the more tart the cheese will be). Cover the pot with a clean towel or piece of muslin and let stand at room temperature (70 to 75 degrees is ideal), until a soft curd forms that has the consistency of custard. There should be no flow-like liquid when the pan is tilted. This will take 24 to 48 hours depending on the temperature in the room—the warmer the room, the faster the curd will form.

3. Line a colander with a clean piece of muslin or cheesecloth. Pour the curd into the cloth and let drain 30 minutes. Fold cheesecloth over the top of the curd. Place colander on a wire rack with a 1-inch foot. Place the rack inside a pan to catch the whey. Cover entirely and firmly with clear plastic wrap to make an airtight seal. Refrigerate and let drain 14 to 18 hours.

4. Remove from refrigerator and spoon the curd into a large bowl. Stir in the sugar and salt. Discard the whey that has accumulated in the drip pan.

5. Rewash all utensils. Cut a piece of cheesecloth into 2 pieces, 18 by 24 inches long. Boil for 5 minutes. Wring out cloth and line 2 small, natural (unvarnished and unpainted) wicker baskets or small ceramic molds with drainage holes, allowing the cloth to drape over the sides of the baskets or molds. Fill each with half of the curd and loosely fold the cheesecloth over this. Place them on the rack-over-pan arrangement as before. Cover airtight with clear plastic wrap. Refrigerate again and drain 12 to 24 hours.

6. Remove the cloth from the baskets and cream cheese is now ready to use. Cheese will keep 5 to 7 days wrapped in plastic and refrigerated.

JIM'S BLUEFISH WITH LEMON PEAR STUFFING

YIELD: 4 to 6 servings

1 whole bluefish (3 to 4 pounds), slit and cleaned
1 lemon, thinly sliced
1 pear, cored and thinly sliced
¼ cup fresh chopped parsley

4 green onions, finely chopped with tops
Salt and freshly ground pepper to taste
½ cup dry white wine
Parsley sprigs for garnish

1. Preheat oven to 425 degrees.

2. Layer the lemon slices, pear slices, parsley, and green onions in the cavity of the fish. Place fish in an oiled, oblong baking dish. Sprinkle with salt and pepper, and pour wine over fish. Bake, uncovered, 20 to 25 minutes or until fish flakes easily when tested with a fork. Transfer to a serving platter and surround with sprigs of parsley.

...ER-TAIL PIE CRUST

1½ cups sifted unbleached white or
    all-purpose flour
1½ cups sifted whole wheat flour
    (or use unbleached white or
    all-purpose flour)
½ teaspoon each: salt and sugar

1 cup vegetable shortening
1 beaten egg
1 teaspoon white or apple cider
    vinegar
5 tablespoons cold water

1. Mix the flour, salt, and sugar together in a large bowl. Cut in the shortening with a pastry blender or fork until the mixture resembles coarse meal. Beat egg, vinegar, and water together in a separate bowl and stir into the flour mixture. Blend thoroughly, but do not overmix. Turn out onto a board and quickly press into a ball. Chill one hour or, if in a hurry, chill at least 15 minutes.

2. *To roll out pastry*: Divide dough into 2 equal portions and form each into a ball. Roll out one crust at a time. If you need a double crust, keep the other chilled until ready to roll out. Or, if a single crust is needed, wrap the other in plastic and freeze for a later date. Place dough on a lightly floured sheet of waxed paper; flatten slightly with your palm and lightly dust the top. Cover with a sheet of waxed paper and roll out a circle 3/16-inch thick and 1½ to 2 inches larger than an inverted pie pan.

3. *To line pie shell*: Carefully peel off top piece of waxed paper. Lift dough, still attached to bottom piece of waxed paper, and center it over the pie pan, waxed-paper-side-up. Carefully peel off waxed paper and ease dough gently into the pie pan, pressing lightly with your fingertips. Trim pastry so there is an even 1-inch overhang. To flute the edges: Place your left thumb and index finger on the outside of the pastry rim turning your wrist so fingers are pointing towards you. With your right index finger pull pastry towards you between the left thumb and index finger.

4. *For a partially baked shell*: Preheat oven to 425 degrees. Line crust with a sheet of lightly greased aluminum foil to extend about 1 inch beyond the sides of the pie pan. Fill with dry beans to prevent the crust from rising. Bake on the middle rack for 5 to 6 minutes. Remove from oven, lift out foil, and remove beans (they may be saved and used again for the same purpose). Prick the bottom of the crust and return to oven for 3 to 4 minutes or until slightly browned. If pastry forms large bubbles, reach in and puncture them to let the air escape. Let cool for a few minutes and fill.

5. *For a fully baked shell*: Follow directions for a prebaked pie shell. When pastry is pricked and returned to the oven, bake 12 to 14 minutes (instead of 3 to 4 minutes) or until lightly browned.

PEAS ORIENTAL
WITH MUSHROOM SAUCE

YIELD: 8 to 10 servings

Sauce:
5 tablespoons safflower margarine
  or butter, divided
¼ cup chopped onion
½ cup sliced fresh mushrooms
2 tablespoons all-purpose flour
1 cup hot whole milk
½ cup shredded sharp cheddar
  cheese
1 teaspoon salt
½ teaspoon each: freshly ground
  pepper and dry mustard
¼ teaspoon each: nutmeg and
  marjoram
Pinch of cayenne pepper

Casserole:
3 cups cooked peas
6 ounces sliced water chestnuts
2 cups bean sprouts
½ pound sliced cheddar cheese
2 tablespoons sesame seeds
½ cup sunflower seeds

1. *To prepare sauce*: In a small skillet, melt 3 tablespoons of the margarine or butter. Sauté the onion until transparent. Add mushrooms and sauté until tender. Remove from heat and set aside. Melt remaining margarine or butter in a small saucepan without browning. Add the flour, stirring constantly with a wire whisk to prevent lumps. Cook, without browning, 3 to 5 minutes or until smooth. Slowly add the hot milk, beating constantly. Bring to a slow boil and reduce heat immediately to low. Add shredded cheese and seasonings. Stir until cheese is melted and mixture is thick. Add the onion and mushrooms. Remove from heat.
2. Preheat oven to 350 degrees.
3. *To assemble casserole*: Combine peas, water chestnuts, bean sprouts, and 1½ cups of the mushroom sauce. Place in a 9- by 13-inch pan. Slice the cheddar cheese diagonally into small pieces. Cover the entire top of casserole with cheese. Bake in a preheated oven for 25 minutes. Remove from oven. Sprinkle sesame and sunflower seeds over the cheese. Return to oven for 10 minutes more. Serve immediately. Save remaining sauce for another use.

PINEAPPLE-STUFFED ACORN SQUASH

YIELD: 8 servings

4 medium-sized acorn squash
2 tablespoons safflower margarine
  or butter
4 cups pineapple chunks, fresh or
  canned and packed in natural
  juice

8 tablespoons pineapple or fruit
  juice
½ cup grated coconut, wheat germ,
  or chopped nuts—optional
Cinnamon
Nutmeg

1. Preheat oven to 375 degrees
2. Cut squash in half and remove seeds. Lightly butter the inside of each cavity. If using canned pineapple, drain and reserve the juice. Place ½ cup pineapple chunks plus 1 tablespoon pineapple or fruit juice into each cavity. Sprinkle with coconut, wheat germ, or nuts if desired. Dust tops with cinnamon and nutmeg. Place on a baking sheet and bake in a preheated oven for 1 hour, or until squash is tender. Serve as a main course or side dish.

STIR-FRIED ZUCCHINI WITH SESAME SEEDS   *YIELD: 8 servings*

Peanut, sesame, or vegetable oil
for stir-frying
4 cups zucchini, cut into 2-inch
julienne strips
1 large Bermuda onion, coarsely
chopped
3 teaspoons sesame seeds, divided
Salt and pepper to taste

2 tablespoons soy sauce, divided
1 teaspoon butter
2 cups sliced fresh mushrooms
2 cups fresh bean sprouts (mung or
soybean)

1. Put enough oil in a skillet or in a wok to coat the bottom and prevent sticking.
2. When the oil is hot, add the zucchini and onion. Stir-fry quickly for no more than 2 minutes. Sprinkle 1½ teaspoons of the sesame seeds, salt, pepper, and 1 tablespoon of the soy sauce. Stir to blend. With a slotted spoon, remove vegetables to a bowl.
3. Place the butter in the skillet or wok adding a little more oil if necessary. Add the mushrooms and stir-fry 2 minutes. Add bean sprouts and cook 1 minute. Sprinkle on remaining sesame seeds and soy sauce. Add salt and pepper to taste. Mix together and add to the zucchini-onion mixture. Stir quickly and serve immediately.

VEGETABLES AU GRATIN

YIELD: 8 servings

2 small eggplants, cut into ½-inch
   slices
Salt
3 medium-sized onions, sliced
2 medium-sized zucchini, cut into
   ½-inch rounds
1 pound red potatoes, sliced
2 medium-sized green peppers,
   seeded and cut into strips
4 tablespoons safflower margarine
   or butter
¼ cup chopped parsley

½ cup water
Salt and freshly ground pepper to
   taste
1 bay leaf
2 garlic cloves, minced
⅓ cup grated Grùyere or Parmesan
   cheese
⅓ cup bread crumbs
1 teaspoon mixed dried herbs such
   as thyme, basil, and oregano

1. Salt eggplant slices and set in a colander to drain 30 minutes. Rinse slices and pat dry with paper towels. Cut into cubes.
2. Preheat oven to 400 degrees.
3. Place all the vegetables in a heavy casserole. Dot with the margarine or butter. Add the parsley, water, seasonings, and garlic. Cover and bake in a preheated oven for 40 minutes.
4. Remove the lid. Bake 20 minutes more. Sprinkle with cheese and bread crumbs, mixed with the herbs. Place under broiler to brown, being careful not to burn. Serve immediately as a main course or side dish.

VEGETABLE BROTH

*YIELD: Approximately 2 quarts
or 8, 1-cup servings*

2 to 3 tablespoons safflower
   margarine
2 ribs celery, coarsely chopped
2 carrots, sliced
2 large onions, sliced
1 bunch green onions, chopped
   with tops
2½ quarts water

2 unpeeled red potatoes, quartered
1 small turnip, quartered
6 peppercorns
2 bay leaves
10 sprigs parsley with stems
1 teaspoon thyme

Heat the margarine in the bottom of a soup pot until hot. Sauté the celery, carrots, onions, and green onions until tender. Add the water, potatoes, and turnip. Bring to a boil, skim the surface well, and add the seasonings. Reduce heat and simmer, uncovered, for 2 hours, stirring occasionally. Pour through a large, cheesecloth-lined strainer. Discard the vegetables (or save for another use). Reserve the liquid. Season to taste. Use in any recipe that calls for vegetable stock or broth. Or reheat and serve hot as a clear soup to which a number of items such as noodles or dumplings may be added.

UNITED STATES/RECIPE ANALYSIS CHART

Name of Recipe	Quantity	Calories	CHO gms.	Protein gms.	Total Fat gms.	Saturated Fat gms.	Choles- terol mg.	Dietary Fiber gms.
1. Vegetable Broth	per serving	—	—	—	—	—	—	—
2. Chicken Stock	per serving	—	—	—	—	—	—	—
3. Homemade Cream Cheese	per serving	87	4 (18%)	2 (9%)	7 (73%)	4 (41%)	384	—
4. Stir Fried Zuc-chini with Ses-ame Seeds	per serving	89	8 (36%)	3 (13%)	5 (51%)	1 (10%)	1	.9
5. Charlotte Boon Bread	per serving	95	15 (65%)	2 (8%)	3 (27%)	1 (9%)	17	.2
6. Blueberry Muffins	each	148	25 (68%)	3 (8%)	4 (24%)	1 (6%)	24	.3
7. Vegetables au Gratin	per serving	162	21 (53%)	6 (15%)	6 (32%)	2 (11%)	5	2.5
8. Pineapple-Stuffed Acorn Squash	per serving	175	34 (77%)	3 (7%)	3 (16%)	—	—	4.0
9. *Jim's* Bluefish with Lemon-Pear Stuffing	per serving	180	6 (13%)	30 (67%)	4 (20%)	—	—	1.0
10. Banana Nut Bread with Honey and Spices	per slice	195	30 (62%)	3 (6%)	7 (32%)	1 (5%)	39	.3
11. Herbed Spinach and Cheese Casserole	per serving	198	7 (14%)	11 (22%)	14 (64%)	6 (27%)	204	.8
12. Never-Fail Pie Crust	per slice	246	21 (34%)	4 (7%)	16 (59%)	4 (15%)	26	.4
13. Almond Tofu with Chutney Sauce	per serving	253	15 (24%)	10 (16%)	17 (60%)	2 (7%)	—	1.0
14. Chou-Chow Wild Rice	per serving	278	31 (45%)	7 (10%)	14 (45%)	1 (3%)	—	2.0
15. Peas Oriental with Mushroom Sauce	per serving	288	14 (19%)	13 (18%)	20 (63%)	7 (22%)	31	1.5

Name of Recipe	Quantity	Calories	CHO gms.	Protein gms.	Total Fat gms.	Saturated Fat gms.	Choles- terol mg.	Dietary Fiber gms.
16. *Ethel's* Ethereal Cheesecake	per slice	296	32 (43%)	8 (11%)	15 (46%)	9 (27%)	117	.6
17. Date Nut Torte	per serving	320	32 (40%)	3 (4%)	20 (56%)	1 (3%)	70	.7
18. Chicken Liver Pâté with Cognac	per serving	325	7 (9%)	27 (33%)	21 (58%)	11 (30%)	80	.3
19. Carob Kahlúa Cake Supreme	per serving	345	48 (56%)	7 (8%)	15 (36%)	3 (7%)	40	1.5
20. Baked Brie	per serving	356	17 (19%)	18 (20%)	24 (61%)	—	70	.1
21. Bean Sprout Quiche	per slice	425	27 (24%)	14 (12%)	29 (64%)	8 (17%)	164	.7
22. Curried Banana Waldorf Salad	per serving	450	50 (44%)	4 (4%)	26 (52%)	14 (28%)	9	2.0

Numbers in parentheses (%) indicate percentage of total calories contributed by nutrient.

MENUS

LOW CALORIE SPECIALTIES
(500 to 700 calories per meal)

**JIM'S BLUEFISH WITH LEMON-
PEAR STUFFING
BLUEBERRY MUFFINS
HOMEMADE CREAM CHEESE**
Fresh Strawberries

**PINEAPPLE-STUFFED ACORN
SQUASH
CHARLOTTE BOON BREAD**
Fresh Garden Salad with
Oil and Vinegar Dressing
Sliced Pears and Apples

**STIR-FRIED ZUCCHINI WITH SESAME SEEDS
CHOU-CHOW WILD RICE**
Sliced Tomatoes
BANANA NUT BREAD WITH HONEY AND SPICES

●

LOW CHOLESTEROL MENUS
(Less than 50 mgs. of cholesterol per meal)

Cooked Julienne Carrots with Lemon
**CHOU-CHOW WILD RICE
PEAS ORIENTAL WITH
MUSHROOM SAUCE**
Sliced Fresh Oranges and Papayas

**JIM'S BLUEFISH WITH LEMON-
PEAR STUFFING
VEGETABLES AU GRATIN**
Marinated Cucumbers
**BANANA NUT BREAD WITH
HONEY AND SPICES**

**ALMOND TOFU WITH CHUTNEY SAUCE
STIR-FRIED ZUCCHINI WITH SESAME SEEDS**
Steamed Rice
CAROB KAHLÚA CAKE SUPREME

●

LOW SATURATED FAT SELECTIONS
(Less than 8 grams of saturated fat per meal)

**HERBED SPINACH AND CHEESE
CASSEROLE**
Baked Potato with Chives
Sliced Oranges with Cointreau
DATE NUT TORTE

**ALMOND TOFU WITH CHUTNEY
SAUCE**
Brown Rice
Steamed Pea Pods and Water
Chestnuts
**BANANA NUT BREAD WITH
HONEY AND SPICES**

Tomato Juice
**PEAS ORIENTAL WITH MUSHROOM SAUCE
CHOU-CHOW WILD RICE**
Honeydew Melon

HIGH PROTEIN MEALS
(30 or more grams of protein per meal)

Whole Grain Crackers
CHICKEN LIVER PÂTÉ WITH COGNAC
PINEAPPLE-STUFFED ACORN SQUASH
String Beans with Cashew Nuts
DATE NUT TORTE

BAKED BRIE
HERBED SPINACH AND CHEESE CASSEROLE
CHOU-CHOW WILD RICE
Sliced Cantaloupe

BEAN SPROUT QUICHE
PEAS ORIENTAL WITH MUSHROOM SAUCE
Fresh Fruit Compote
ETHEL'S ETHEREAL CHEESECAKE

●

WELL BALANCED LUNCH OR DINNER MENUS
(Selections that conform to recommendations in Dietary Goals for United States*)*

VEGETABLES AU GRATIN
Herbed Rice
CHARLOTTE BOON BREAD
Fresh Fruit and Cheese Board

Sliced Tomatoes
PINEAPPLE-STUFFED ACORN SQUASH
STIR-FRIED ZUCCHINI WITH SESAME SEEDS
Hot Dinner Rolls
DATE NUT TORTE

JIM'S BLUEFISH WITH LEMON-PEAR STUFFING
CURRIED BANANA WALDORF SALAD
Whole Grain Bread
CAROB KAHLÚA CAKE SUPREME

PART 2

NUTRITION AND HEALTH

Although diseases resulting from a deficient intake of selected nutrients such as iron, folic acid, vitamin B_{12}, and protein are still a problem in the United States, it has become increasingly apparent that the *lack* of dietary nutrients is not our major nutritional problem. Instead, we are now facing the problems associated with *overnutrition*—an excess consumption of calories, meat, and other sources of saturated fat and cholesterol-rich foods, as well as an excess of refined sugar.

To a great extent, these imbalances in our eating behavior have evolved as a side effect of modern food technology and from the impact of affluence on our dietary preferences. It is now felt by many medical scientists and nutrition experts that overconsumption of calories in the form of fatty foods and refined sugar, as well as underconsumption of fiber, are the major dietary factors contributing to the development of our most prevalent diseases—heart attack, high blood pressure, stroke, obesity, and certain cancers.

The adoption of a meatless diet by ten or so million vegetarians in the United States today constitutes a major step towards reversing many of these unhealthy eating patterns. Although the medical profession has traditionally looked somewhat askance at vegetarianism, it now appears as if this kind of diet may be able to exert a profound and beneficial impact upon our health. Given the continuing increase in the world's population and the limited amount of land available for cultivation, the prospect is real that vegetarianism will become a way of life for more and more of us in the future.

There is compelling evidence that a vegetarian diet is associated with lowered incidence of heart disease, several cancers, gallbladder disease, hypertension, multiple sclerosis, and obesity. It is important to realize, however, that we cannot speak of the *typical* vegetarian diet. The content of a meatless diet, like any other diet, depends upon the selection of foods, recipes, and meal plans by the individual. At one end of the vegetarian spectrum are the *vegans*, who consume no meat, fish, eggs, or milk products. They clearly comprise only a small minority of the vegetarian population. Many are *lacto-* or *lacto-ovo-vegetarians*, and include milk or milk and eggs in their diets, respectively. A great majority of the predominantly vegetarian people include fish and poultry in their diets.

Because of the diversity of eating habits and individual preferences among vegetarians, it is somewhat difficult to analyze the quality of a vegetarian diet. But there have been several surveys recently conducted that point to certain trends which have emerged in meatless eaters. First of all, the exclusion of meat and animal products, and the increase in consumption of whole grains, fruits, nuts, seeds, and vegetables leads to a lowered intake of saturated fat and cholesterol, and an increase in polyunsaturated and mono-unsaturated fats. We can infer that the lacto-vegetarian will fall below the lacto-ovo-vegetarian and above the vegan in these measurements—the vegan consuming no cholesterol and little, if any, saturated fat.

As you will learn later, these changes in the level and pattern of fat intake have been implicated as important factors which may be reducing the incidence of many diseases in the vegetarian population. Another aspect of eating behavior often cited is the intake of dietary fiber, which, not surprisingly, is much higher among nonmeat eaters. Considering these dietary practices, it is no wonder that vegetarians, on the average, have lower blood cholesterol levels and weigh ten pounds less than comparably matched meat-eaters.

Many of the diseases which vegetarians seem to be protected from are caused by the interplay of *many* different factors, both dietary and nondietary. But, there is no question that certain nutritional practices which characterize a meatless diet are playing an important role in the prevention of disease. One must realize that just because there is a *tendency* for vegetarian diets to be healthy does not mean that *any* meatless diet is good for you or nutritionally sound. On the contrary, a meatless diet is subject to many of its own nutritional pitfalls, *as well as* those which characterize nonvegetarian diets.

The two objections traditionally raised against vegetarian diets concern the intake of vitamin B$_{12}$ and protein. Both are indeed lower among vegetarians, but with a modicum of planning, the intake of these essential nutrients can meet and generously exceed the minimal daily allowances for all age groups. Perhaps more important for the ovo- and lacto-ovo-vegetarian is learning how to avoid excessive consumption of saturated fat, cholesterol, and refined sugar, while ensuring an adequate intake of both fiber and protein. Attention to these facets of nutrition is key because they are specifically responsible for the improved health effects of a meatless diet. A firm understanding of basic nutrition and the dietary determinants of human disease will also help you maximize the potential health benefits of a vegetarian diet.

The sections which follow will introduce you to the nutritional foundations of a vegetarian diet, so that you will be able to make sensible and educated choices concerning your food intake. Moreover, you will learn the importance of knowing the calorie, fat, protein, fiber, and vitamin composition of the individual foods and recipes which compose your diet. This information is intended to put other parts of this book, especially the *Nutritional Essentials*, *Recipe Analysis Charts*, and *Menu Planning* sections into a more practical and enlightening context.

Our approach to nutrition will emphasize the practical aspects of maintaining a healthful meatless diet. There will be suggestions for how to ensure an adequate intake of essential nutrients as well as for reducing consumption of foods which are thought to give rise to diet-related diseases. The discussions which follow will also help to specify other directions in which your dietary practices might move in order to place you at lower risk for the development of certain serious illnesses and nutrient deficiencies.

In the following sections, our discussions of the *major* dietary nutrients are divided into three parts. First, you will be introduced to the role which each of these plays in the body and how deficiencies (or excesses) can be prevented. Next, you will learn how alterations in your dietary intake of these nutrients are likely to influence your health (or patterns of food consumption which are believed to prevent or promote disease). Finally, the implications of these nutritional concepts for a vegetarian diet are presented. The essential vitamins and minerals will also be discussed, but in less detail.

After the physiological and nutritional roles of the essential nutrients have been considered, we will describe, in sections of their own, the principal food groups contained in a vegetarian diet in terms of these nutrients. These foods are conveniently classified into ten categories: (1) grains and cereals, (2) starches, (3) sugars and sweeteners, (4) legumes, (5) nuts and seeds, (6) vegetables, (7) fruits, (8) eggs, (9) milk and milk products, and (10) fish and poultry. These brief accounts will help you apply important nutritional information directly to your meal table.

A basic knowledge of nutrition and food is absolutely necessary if you want to improve the quality of your health through dietary manipulations. Hopefully, the information contained in the following sections will give you enough insight into your eating practices, so that you can rationally choose foods, recipes, and menu plans that will not only titillate your palate, but provide healthy nourishment for the rest of your body as well.

Essential Nutrients

Recommended Daily Allowances

A good way to begin your nutritional education is to familiarize yourself with those nutrients which are necessary for supporting a normal and healthy life. The Food and Nutrition Board of the National Academy of Sciences publishes formulations of daily nutrient intakes which are considered to be adequate for the maintenance of good nutrition. These formulations are called *Recommended Daily Allowances* (RDA). With the exception of calories, the RDA allows a margin of safety for all essential nutrients in order to account for individual variations. When calculating the RDA, considerations have also been made for sex, height, weight, age, pregnancy, and lactation.

A list of *Essential Dietary Nutrients* is included in *Table 1*. The *Recommended Daily Allowances* for most of these nutrients are presented in *Table 2*. By no means do you need to master all the information in these two charts in order to practice good nutrition. On the other hand, a basic familiarity with the names and allowances of some of the major nutrients (calories, protein, vitamins B$_{12}$ and C, iron, etc.) will not only help you make better-informed decisions when purchasing nutritionally labelled food products, but will also provide a general framework for your dietary planning.

Calories

Food Energy

The human body requires energy to maintain the metabolic processes necessary for life: the movement of skeletal muscles for locomotion, the pumping action of the heart to promote adequate circulation, and the cyclic work of the diaphragm. On the cellular level, food energy is required to ensure tissue biosyntheses, for lactation and thermoregulation. The amount of physiological fuel, expressed in *calories* (kilocalories), that you require depends, to a great extent, upon body size and age, climate, level of physical activity, and basal metabolic rate. It is important to be aware of these determinants of calorie consumption so that you can individualize your intake of food energy.

Calories are derived, in varying degrees, from the protein, fat, carbohydrate and, in some cases, alcohol intake of your diet. Vitamins, micro- and macro-nutrients, and fiber are important or essential parts of the diet, but do not contribute food energy (calories). For this reason, these nutrients are left out of the energy balance equation.

As a rule, the energy needs of the body take priority over other nutritional needs. This means that if you do not provide a sufficient number of calories in your diet, tissue proteins will be broken down and utilized for energy purposes. This can lead to *negative nitrogen balance*, which is an unfavorable nutritional state. For the most part, underconsumption of calories is a much less encountered problem than overconsumption. But, if you are of normal weight, and are engaging in strenuous physical activities, you should be aware of your increased caloric requirements.

In order to have a handle on what your caloric intake is, you should realize that each of the major nutrients (protein, carbohydrate, and fat) and alcohol provide different caloric contributions to your diet; these *food energy values* are expressed as calories (which is the same as kilocalories) per gram of food consumed, or simply, calories/gram (kilocalories/gram). One gram of fat provides about 9 calories/gram, the highest of any nutrient. Ethanol, the main constituent of alcoholic beverages, contributes 7 calories/gram. You can use this information to calculate the caloric content of any food, providing you know the gram weight composition of the major nutrients. For example, a small wedge of cheese may be labelled as having 3 grams of protein, 1 gram of carbohydrate, and 2 grams of fat. The approximate caloric value would be 3 grams protein $\times$ 4 calories/gram = 12 calories, plus 1 gram carbohydrate $\times$ 4 calories/gram = 4 calories, plus 2 grams fat $\times$ 9 calories/gram = 18 calories, for a total of 12 calories + 4 calories + 18 calories = 34 calories.

The *variable* contribution by the major nutrients to your caloric intake plays an important role in determining your total food energy intake. For example, if you are partial to high-fat foods, it is very likely that your calorie intake will be higher than that of an individual who prefers protein- or carbohydrate-containing foods. This is because fat, on a *weight-for-weight* basis, provides more calories than either protein or carbohydrate. Because most foods are composed of varying amounts of all *three* nutrients, you may find it difficult to selectively exclude *fat calories* without eliminating other necessary dietary nutrients. But, if you are careful to choose foods which are *relatively low* in fat content, you will very likely reduce your total calorie intake. The important point is that you can significantly decrease your calorie intake simply by changing your food *preferences* away from fat, and in favor of protein- and carbohydrate-containing foods. A reduction of food energy (i.e. calories) will be accomplished even though your *total* food intake, in terms of *weight*, remains entirely unchanged!

You need to know the desirable weight for a person of your sex, height, and body frame before you can determine the direction in which your calorie intake should be moving. The most practical method for determining this value employs a standard height-weight table (see *Table 3*), which records weights that are associated with the lowest death rates as determined by insurance company data. These data clearly indicate that increasing your weight during adult life will be associated with a shorter life span. You are considered overweight if you exceed the upper range of ideal weight for your sex and body frame. If you are above this upper limit by more than 20 pounds, you are considered to be obese. Most of this excess weight is derived from a combination of *increased* calorie intake and *decreased* physical activity.

Excess consumption of calories in the American diet is the single most important factor in the causation of obesity. Aside from the cosmetic considerations, there are many compelling health reasons for maintaining an ideal body weight. Many serious disorders such as high blood pressure, diabetes, heart disease, lung disease, and strokes are either directly, or indirectly, associated with obesity. The propensity to live a sedentary lifestyle, a progressive fall in the basal metabolic rate, and the failure to decrease caloric intake appropriately are predisposing conditions to body weight gain with age. Only if your calorie intake is reduced, or adjusted for your level of physical activity (see *Table 5*), will you be able to prevent the insidious weight gain that accompanies aging. For these reasons, at least some general feeling for, and preferably more specific knowledge of, the calorie content of your foods, recipes, and menu plans, is necessary to maintain good health.

The recipes in this book have had their calorie content calculated, so that you will be able to apply this information to your nutritional planning. In order to use these calorie determinations, first refer to *Table 3* and determine your ideal body weight. If you fall over these limits, attempt to follow a diet of modest calorie reduction, on the order of 1400 to 1800 calories per day. The *Low Calorie Menus* included with each ethnic cuisine contain 500 to 700 calories each, which is appropriate for a program of weight reduction. If possible, you should try to accompany your reduced caloric intake with increased physical exercise, which can also make a substantial contribution towards weight loss. Finally, you should attempt to satisfy your hunger (and cravings) with low-fat foods because, as previously mentioned, this simple change in your food preferences may help reduce your caloric intake significantly.

Once you have attained your ideal weight, try to follow the recommended caloric intake according to *Table 4*. Remember that you will need to make modifications in your energy intake for your level of physical activity, pregnancy, and lactation (breast feeding). *Table 5* will help you make appropriate adjustments for your exercise program.

Perhaps the most injurious habit in which our society participates is the excess consumption of food eaten after caloric needs have been met. This dietary practice leads to obesity, which is probably the most important disease risk factor over which you can exert control.

Fats

Dietary Fat

Dietary fat (also known as *lipids*) constitutes an important and convenient source of calories in most diets. Fats are an excellent source of food energy and are also required for the absorption of the essential vitamins D, E, A, and K. Within the body, lipids (which is an all-inclusive term for dietary fats) are used as building blocks for cell membranes, nerve coverings, and other brain tissues. In the blood, lipid molecules are complexed with protein to form *lipoproteins*; the blood level of these substances is a very important predictor of heart disease and stroke. Cholesterol, which is a *sterol* lipid, is used as a building block for bile acids, sex hormones, adrenal gland hormones, and vitamin D. It has been implicated as an important factor in the causation of *atherosclerosis*, or hardening of the arteries. A group of lipids, known as polyunsaturated fatty acids, are considered to be essential for our diet. They are used to synthesize a very important group of hormonelike substances called prostaglandins. Your dietary fat intake can play an important role in determining the blood levels of various lipids and, for this reason, can exert a profound impact on your state of health.

Lipids are generally long-chained molecules composed of hydrogen, carbon, and oxygen. For convenience, lipids are usually divided into two major groups, depending upon their structure and primary role in the body's metabolism. The first group of lipids, called *triglycerides*, serve predominantly as a source of energy for your body. Triglyceride is the form in which fats chiefly occur in both food stuffs and in fat depots of most animals. This fat molecule consists of a *glycerol* molecule which is attached to three long-chain *fatty acids* (see *Figure 1*). In other words, one glycerol molecule plus three fatty acids equal a triglyceride lipid. Any one of a number of different fatty acids can be attached to the glycerol molecule in varying combinations. The naturally occurring fatty acids which we consume in our diet include palmitic, oleic, stearic, linoleic, and linolenic. Triglycerides account for about 98 percent of food fats and about 90 percent of the total fat stores in our body.

The fatty acids which comprise your dietary intake can exist in three different forms: as *saturated* fat, *mono-unsaturated* fat, or *polyunsaturated* fat. The distinction between these types of fat is crucial for the purposes of nutritional planning. A fat is said to be *saturated* when there are *single* chemical bonds between all the carbon molecules on the fatty acid skeleton. *Mono-unsaturated* fats contain one double bond on the fatty acid molecule, while *polyunsaturated* fats contain *more than one* double bond on the long-chain skeleton. Stearic and palmitic are the most common fatty acids in saturated fats; palmitoleic and oleic are the most important mono-unsaturated fats; and linoleic and linolenic are the principal polyunsaturates.

Saturated fats are usually of *animal* origin. Their consumption will *raise* your blood cholesterol level. Because foods that are high in protein are also high in saturated fat, lacto- and ovo-lacto-vegetarians may have a tendency to consume large amounts of fat in their diet in order to meet their essential amino acid needs. Saturated fat is present in foods such as butter, cream, lard, whole milk, and cheese made from whole milk or cream. Vegetable fats which are predominantly saturated include coconut oil and palm oil (used in nondairy cream substitutes and some frozen desserts), and cocoa butter (the fat in chocolate). As a rule, the amount of saturation is determined by the degree of hardness. For example, soft tub margarine is usually less saturated than the harder stick margarine.

Polyunsaturated fats, which contain more than one double bond, are primarily from plant sources. If you increase consumption of these fats, you will lower your blood cholesterol level. As mentioned earlier, saturated fats will increase your serum cholesterol. The concept of *polyunsaturated to saturated fat ratio*, abbreviated as P/S ratio, has evolved in order to explain the effect of dietary fat intake on blood cholesterol level. You can use this determination to help you with your nutritional planning. For example, if your P/S fat intake is high, you will stand a good chance of *lowering* your blood cholesterol. Conversely, if this ratio is low, your cholesterol level will very likely rise. *Table 6* contains a listing of the percentages of polyunsaturated and saturated fatty acids found in over fifteen different kinds of vegetable and cooking oils. You can use this information to choose food combinations which will have a high P/S ratio.

The body cannot synthesize the *essential fatty acids* (EFA) linoleic and linolenic acids. As a result, they are considered to be essential for our diet. These polyunsaturated fats are present in large amounts in many vegetable oils (see *Table 6*). Although no strict daily allowance has been established for linoleic and linolenic acids, it appears as if at least 1 to 2 percent of your daily caloric intake should be provided by these polyunsaturated fatty acids. The principal sources of EFA include safflower, corn, and soy oils. Peanuts, walnuts, and other seeds and nuts are also excellent sources of EFA. Fish and poultry products provide only moderate amounts of linoleic acid, but generally more than red meats.

Cholesterol is considered to be a member of the second group of lipids, which, unlike triglycerides, are used primarily for structural, rather than metabolic, purposes in the body. Other members of this *structural* group include sphingolipids, phospholipids, and glycolipids. All of them, including cholesterol, can easily be synthesized by the body, and therefore, are not essential for the diet. Cholesterol is found exclusively in foods of animal origin, including eggs and cheese. A strict vegan diet is virtually cholesterol-free, whereas this nutrient is consumed in varying amounts in other vegetarian diets. To exactly what degree changes in dietary intake of cholesterol can affect *blood levels* of cholesterol is still a matter of debate. Nevertheless, if you want to reduce your blood cholesterol level, a reduction in your intake of this nutrient is strongly recommended.

In general, you can expect that fat will provide a large portion of your total caloric intake. This nutrient also makes an important contribution to the palatability of a diet. Fats provide more food energy (9 calories/gram) than any other nutrient, and for this reason, meals that have a great satiety also tend to be high in calories. Only efforts aimed at making low-fat meals more palatable are likely to succeed in keeping excess calories out of our stomachs. The use of herbs and spices as flavor enhancers may be an important step in shifting our preferences away from high-fat, high-calorie foods.

Role of Dietary Fat in Health and Disease

Death resulting from compromised blood flow to the heart, brain, kidney, and limbs is the single most important determinant of mortality in affluent societies throughout the world. Poor circulation to the heart and other organs results from a process known as *atherosclerosis*, in which hard calcified deposits (called *plaques*) are laid down in the walls of the body's major blood vessels. This process, often beginning soon after adolescence in many men, is what we commonly refer to as "hardening of the arteries." The impact of atherosclerosis on contemporary disease patterns is absolutely staggering. Heart attacks are the leading cause of death in men after the age of thirty-five and in all persons after the age of forty-five. The *prevention* of the disease process which gives rise to heart attacks is one of the leading public health issues in our society today.

The epidemic of atherosclerosis-related disorders, such as heart attack, stroke, peripheral vascular disease, and high blood pressure, may be linked to the changing cultural patterns that have accompanied our evolution into modern, technological societies—machines that have replaced the need for muscle power and physical activity, stress, smoking, and alterations in dietary behavior. Dietary factors that are most often implicated in the genesis of these diseases include the excessive intake of calories, saturated fat, cholesterol, and (refined) sugar. Although atherosclerosis is a disease that has evolved under the influence of *many* factors, the role of *preventative* efforts in the field of human nutrition is an important one. In fact, each of us are in the position to make modifications in our dietary intake of fats and calories that can improve the quality of our general health and, possibly, prevent atherosclerosis.

The evidence incriminating high cholesterol and saturated fat diets is based upon animal experiments, human studies, clinical experience, and world-wide epidemiological studies. The case for moderating your intake of these two nutrients is supported by the following observations:

1. Increasing levels of cholesterol are associated with an increased risk of developing atherosclerotic heart disease.
2. People who have a metabolic disorder characterized by elevated cholesterol levels in the blood develop atherosclerosis at a very young age.
3. Serum levels of cholesterol are higher in people who already have had a heart attack, especially if they had it at an early age.
4. Death rates from heart attack are higher in nations with high average levels of blood cholesterol, and vice versa.
5. People who have high cholesterol levels have diets which are different from those of people who have low values of cholesterol.

6. There is a significant correlation between the intake of saturated fat and the incidence of coronary artery disease in many populations throughout the world.
7. Migrants from "low cholesterol" areas to "high cholesterol" areas are often found to have a higher cholesterol value after changing their dietary pattern.
8. Manipulation of the diet (i.e. lowering of the saturated fat intake, increasing polyunsaturated fat intake, and decreasing cholesterol intake) can significantly alter blood cholesterol levels in humans.
9. In experimental situations, dietary changes in fat composition have caused atherosclerotic deposits in blood vessels to disappear.

The effect of other blood lipids, especially triglycerides, has not been as well studied, but there is considerable data that suggests increased levels of triglycerides *are* also correlated with an increased incidence of atherosclerotic heart disease.

Heart disease is not the only common ailment of industrialized societies that has been connected to excessive fat intake. There are good studies that give some support to the hypothesis that total dietary fat intake may be related to cancer of the breast and colon. Fat derived from *vegetable sources* (polyunsaturated fats such as linoleic), however, did not seem to correlate with an increased risk of tumors in these studies. Although conclusions linking fat intake to cancer are still premature, it is possible that the excessive intake of animal-derived fat plays a greater role in our society's health than has previously been appreciated.

These observations suggest that reducing blood cholesterol triglycerides will probably lead to a lower incidence of heart attacks and other diseases. Though not proven beyond the shadow of a doubt, there is strong evidence that *diet* is the single most important determinant of cholesterol levels in the blood. At least three diseases which are known to predispose to atherosclerosis are also known to be influenced by dietary patterns. These include high blood pressure, diabetes, and obesity. This means that at least half of the factors thought to play a major role in the development of clogged and hardened blood vessels can, in a significant way, be influenced by dietary manipulations. One could not imagine more compelling reasons for altering the fat intake in our diet.

Now that we realize that there is an upward trend in cholesterol and triglyceride levels, exactly what can be done about it? The most obvious cultural factor over which some control can be exerted at the *individual* level is diet. In fact, most doctors working in the field of nutrition-related diseases now feel that a diet which is low in saturated fat and cholesterol and relatively high in polyunsaturates can *prevent* the formation of atherosclerotic deposits. Although there are still some difficulties with *precisely* linking dietary patterns to heart disease, and many of the details are still a bit fuzzy, there is simply too much compelling evidence to brush aside. Despite the controversy surrounding this issue, several major scientific bodies throughout the world, including the American Heart Association, have issued strong recommendations concerning our fat intake. These organizations advocate an eating pattern in which total dietary fat contributes *no more* than 35 percent of daily caloric intake and in which the polyunsaturated to saturated fat ratio (P/S ratio) is equal to one. These recommendations, which also include lowering daily cholesterol intake to less than 300 mg and labeling of fat contents in food, are intended for the general population, not just for individuals who are at a high risk for developing heart disease. Many nutrition experts and physicians are now also surmising that a *well-designed* vegetarian diet may be the perfect framework in which to meet these dietary goals.

The prevention of atherosclerosis is one of the most important tasks facing public health agencies at this time. Whether or not one believes that diet is the *chief* determinant of this disease, the evidence that it plays at least some role is too impressive to ignore. The changes in your food preferences and cooking skills that would result from these recommended dietary modifications are a small price to pay for improving and protecting your health.

Implications for a Vegetarian Diet

A well formulated vegetarian diet appears to be an excellent framework in which to moderate your saturated fat and cholesterol consumption and, at the same time, ensure a more than adequate intake of essential fatty acids (EFA).

As a group, vegetarians appear to have much lower levels of cholesterol and triglycerides in their blood than comparable groups following a nonvegetarian diet. In addition to having lower lipid levels, vegetarians weigh less and are leaner than nonvegetarians. They also appear to have a lower incidence of heart disease and certain cancers than meat-eating groups. Most of these health benefits probably relate to the pattern of dietary fat intake in nonmeat-eaters, and to the reduction in blood lipids which results from these food preferences. Interestingly, the lowering of blood cholesterol levels and triglycerides is most impressive in those vegetarians who have followed a meatless diet for *at least* six months.

While these observations may appear encouraging to those who follow meatless diets, they can be quite misleading. Remember, a vegetarian diet can take all shapes and forms and, when ill-planned, can include tremendous amounts of cholesterol and saturated fat. In fact, many vegetarians have a tendency to become dependent upon high-fat and high-cholesterol foods such as cheese and eggs to meet their protein needs, without realizing that they may be raising their blood cholesterol levels in the process. In order to avoid these pitfalls, you will need to have a feeling for the fat content of foods commonly used in vegetarian cooking.

In a meatless diet, fat intake is derived primarily from vegetable and nut oils, as well as cheese and other dairy products. The former are excellent sources of polyunsaturated fats, while the latter contain primarily saturated fats. In fact, almost all nuts, seeds, and vegetable oils are rich in EFA such as linoleic and linolenic. The exceptions to this include olive oil, coconuts, cashews, and almonds. See *Table 6* for the total fat, polyunsaturated, and mono-unsaturated fat content of commonly used vegetarian foods. Excluding dairy products, the richest sources of saturated fat for vegetarians are coconut, Brazil nuts, and peanut butter, as well as coconut, olive, and cottonseed oils.

Most vegetarians and those who follow "predominantly" vegetarian diets rely heavily upon dairy products to enhance the flavor of food and provide protein for their diet. Because these foods are derived from animals, they tend to have a fat composition which is very similar to meat (i.e., a high saturated fat content). The indiscriminate use of these foods can lead to a saturated fat and cholesterol intake which is undesirable.

In order to avoid these potential pitfalls you should be aware of the fat composition of a wide variety of cheeses. *Table 7* lists the fat content of many domestic and foreign cheeses. Note that many of the *triple-crème* cheeses can be as high as 80 to 90 percent saturated fat. A cheese is said to have a moderate fat content if it is 30 to 40 percent total fat. Low-fat cheeses contain 30 percent or less total fat. Although the polyunsaturated and saturated fat content is not available for many of the exotic cheeses, you can generally assume that most of the fat content will be saturated. Fish and poultry are usually low in total and saturated fat. Seafoods which are somewhat higher in saturated fat include eel, herring, and mackerel. As you probably know, fruits and vegetables contribute very little fat.

Your cooking medium has an important bearing on the composition of your fat intake. Butter is, of course, predominantly saturated fat (80 percent), while margarine is much lower (14 percent). Although margarine is said to be high in polyunsaturates, much of the polyunsaturated fats are converted to mono-unsaturated fat during the processing stage known as *hydrogenation*. Safflower margarine is the most desirable preparation, being 48 percent polyunsaturated. As far as high polyunsaturated fat cooking oils are concerned, the best are safflower, soy, and corn.

Your cholesterol intake will, in great part, be determined by your consumption of egg dishes. A single egg yolk contains 250 mgs which is quite high. Among seafoods, shrimp and tuna have a relatively high content.

The *Nutritional Essentials* and *Recipe Analysis Charts* will make you aware of foods and recipes which are high in total and/or saturated fat. This information is intended to facilitate your nutrition planning. Low saturated fat menu plans are also included for your convenience. In general, you will find that a vegetarian diet will steer you towards a reasonable and healthy fat intake—one that is likely to offer you protection against many of the diseases discussed earlier in this chapter.

Protein

Protein is an essential nutrient for the human diet. Composed of more than twenty amino acids, in varying amounts and sequences, proteins are fundamental to cell function and structure. They act as enzyme catalysts that regulate many of the body's biochemical reactions, as carriers for essential metabolites and minerals, as hormonal regulators, and as structural building blocks for cell membranes, hemoglobin, and muscle fibers. The tremendous number of permutations that are possible among the twenty-two amino acids accounts for both the variability and versatility of proteins found in the body.

An understanding of how proteins are synthesized from amino acids and of the value of different foods in meeting Recommended Daily Allowances for protein is important for planning a healthful diet. With just a modicum of planning, meatless diets can easily provide an adequate protein intake. The key is learning how to formulate *well-balanced* protein; this will give you the freedom to choose among a large variety of grains, legumes, nuts, seeds, and dairy products to satisfy your protein requirements.

When protein is synthesized within a cell, a program or blueprint—determined by genetic information contained in DNA and RNA—designates the specific amino acids that are needed and the sequence of their attachment to one another. The important point is that the manufacture of this long and elaborate molecule (called a *polypeptide*) requires the simultaneous presence of *all* the amino acids destined to become part of the protein macromolecule. There can be no waiting for latecomers; a chain of amino acids is virtually useless if there are any missing links, and if *all* the amino acids are not present in adequate amounts, a biochemically active protein cannot be formed.

If all the amino acids necessary for protein synthesis are available, things usually go according to plan. However, if one is missing, let's say from a dietary deficiency, synthesis comes to a halt. The missing amino acid(s) is(are) called the *limiting* amino acid(s), and must be provided in order to maintain a rate of protein synthesis which can keep pace with tissue turnover. When there is an insufficient nitrogen intake of *essential amino acids* (see *Protein and Health* below), a state of negative nitrogen balance ensues: this is what we call starvation.

The amino acid pool which the body uses for protein synthesis is composed of two major groups: (1) The thirteen *non-essential* amino acids, so-called because the body *is able* to synthesize them providing there is sufficient body nitrogen, and (2) the *essential amino acids*—lysine, threonine, leucine, isoleucine, methionine, tryptophan, valine, phenylalanine, and histidine—which the body is *unable* to manufacture and must be furnished by the diet. For the most part, it is the essential amino acids which are indispensable for maintaining tissue synthesis and nitrogen balance. But, in addition to the need for specific essential amino acids, there is a general requirement for nitrogen; it is provided by dietary protein which provides building blocks that the body uses to synthesize the non-essential amino acids. In general, it is the *quantity* of protein intake which ensures an adequate amount of usable body nitrogen for non-essential amino acids, while the *quality* of protein reflects its essential amino acid content.

As mentioned earlier, if only some of the essential amino acids are available, but others are lacking in the food you eat, your body will not be able to put the amino acids which *are* available to their maximal use. While all nine essential amino acids must be supplied by the diet, three of them— tryptophan, lysine, and methionine—are especially critical when it comes to balancing your overall diet. Empirically, it turns out that if you eat foods that supply these three amino acids in sufficient amounts and proper proportions, you will be getting the necessary quantities of the other essential amino acids as well. Thus, an adequate dietary intake of these three amino acids is a measure of protein completeness, against which you can compare a recipe, a meal, or an entire diet.

Once, it was thought that you had to consume a full complement of essential amino acids at a single sitting in order to provide a pool of usable amino acids. Subsequently, we have learned that the body—by recycling intestinal cells and muscle tissue—is capable of generating a balanced amino acid pool *independently* of short-run nutritional intake; and so, the concept that every meal must contain all the essential amino acids does not strictly hold.

What is important, though, is that you pattern your diet, *as a whole*, to provide the appropriate quantity and quality of essential amino acids. Of course, there are some temporal considerations worth bearing in mind. You cannot maintain a healthy protein balance by following a diet for *long* periods that is lacking in one or more of the essential amino acids; some protein will simply be "wasted" unless there is a steady intake of all the essential amino acids. A good rule of thumb is to plan your diet so that, on a *daily* basis, you combine foods that will guarantee a high-quality protein intake. Because recipes are the building blocks of meals, and meals constitute your dietary pattern, it is extremely helpful to get into the habit of applying protein balance on the recipe level.

Just how much protein does a person need? Estimates of the total daily protein requirements for adults have been determined by nitrogen balance studies, which take into account the quantity and quality of protein required to prevent *negative nitrogen balance* (that is, losing body tissues at a rate faster than they are being made). The protein needs of infants and children are characterized by the amount of protein necessary to support maximal growth.

The Food and Nutrition Board recommends a daily protein allowance of 56 grams for the average man, and 46 grams for the average woman (see

Table 2). How have these determinations been made? The nitrogen losses for a 160-pound (70 kg.) man with an adequate caloric intake amount to about 5.2 grams. The nitrogen content of protein is 16 percent, which means that 33 grams of protein are lost from the body each day to maintain nitrogen balance. This is equivalent to .47 grams of protein per kilogram weight per day. This value has been arbitrarily increased by 30 percent to account for individual variations, resulting in a protein allowance of .6 grams per kilogram of weight each day. Because protein intake is not optimal with respect to distribution of intake and quality, a further correction factor of 75 percent has been introduced to account for inefficiency of protein utilization. This increases the daily allowance to .8 grams per kilogram of weight per day, giving 56 grams for an average 70 kilogram man, and a 46 gram daily allowance for the average 60 kilogram woman.

The protein allowances for infants are based upon human milk as a protein source. As a rule, 2.2 grams of protein per kilogram of body weight is allowed for infants less than six months old, and 2.0 grams per kilogram of weight for the remainder of the first year of life. Children one to ten years of age require increasing amounts of protein for adequate growth, recommended allowances ranging from 26 to 36 grams per day. The pregnant woman is given an additional 30 grams per day allowance (above and beyond the minimum 46 grams needed per day), while it is recommended that an extra 20 grams per day be consumed by the breast-feeding mother.

It should be apparent that the recommended daily allowances for protein have been derived, and that they are not *requirements per se*. Certainly diets which contain less protein cannot necessarily be equated with protein deficiency.

As previously discussed, protein sources, depending upon their composition, have different nutritive values. Two methods have been used to assess the quality of dietary protein. One is a measurement of *biological value*, which is the percent of nitrogen absorbed from a food protein under specific conditions. This determination utilizes the concept of *reference protein*, which is a food capable of producing one gram of new body tissue for every gram consumed. It is assigned a *biological value* of 100. Generally, the *biological value* of a protein takes into account its digestibility, absorption, and the completeness of its essential amino acid composition.

The other method of estimating protein quality relies exclusively upon its essential amino acid content. Egg protein is considered to have the optimal essential amino acid content and is assigned a *chemical score* of 100. Other proteins are evaluated against this "ideal" protein and given a *chemical score* depending upon their total amino acid content and composition. As a rule, foods which lack one or more of the essential acids are given reduced chemical scores.

In this book, we employ the concept of *essential protein* to refer to the nutritive value of protein with respect to its amino acid make-up. If a food, recipe, or cuisine is described as being high in *essential protein*, this means that it has a substantial and well-balanced amino acid composition, and therefore would have a correspondingly high *biological value* or *chemical score*.

Protein and Health

Much has been written about protein deficiency in both vegetarian and nonvegetarian diets. While the body is able to provide a significant degree of protection against amino acid deficiencies, the fact remains that nine amino acids are absolutely essential for the diet. The only way to avoid a protein deficiency state—which ultimately leads to tissue breakdown, weight loss, and susceptibility to disease—is to adopt a well-balanced protein intake, one that ensures adequate quantities of the limiting essential amino acids necessary for synthesis of vital body tissues.

Protein deficiency, manifested by the body's inability to keep pace with the regenerative needs of cells and organs, becomes severe when more than 5 to 10 percent of the body's protein mass has been depleted. Despite the many compensatory physiologic mechanisms that come into play—turnover and recycling of gastrointestinal and muscle cells—eventually the deterioration of bodily functions becomes irreversible. While the manifestations of protein starvation in deficiency states such as *kwashiorkor* and *marasmus* are quite obvious, detecting marginal states of protein deficiency may be extremely difficult.

As a rule, protein deficiency will usually *not* develop in the setting of an *adequate caloric intake*. But when there is simply not enough food to go around—tantamount to outright starvation—there is usually concomitant protein malnutrition. In most cases, people who are consuming enough calories to meet their body's energy requirements are unlikely to develop protein deficiency. But there are important exceptions.

Starchy, monotonous diets consisting of tubers, plantains, cassava, and the like—while high in calories—may be sorely lacking in the essential amino acids. Individuals who are on rigid, self-imposed, calorie-restricted diets (usually for weight-losing purposes) are prone to reduce their protein intake to levels that are not compatible with good health. This is true especially for people who simultaneously are eliminating high-fat foods such as eggs and meat from their diet, since these foods tend to be of high *biological value*. *Vegans*, a subgroup of vegetarians who do not consume eggs or dairy products, are also susceptible to essential amino acid deficiency. Finally, infants and children, who because of rapid tissue synthesis have a tremendous need for protein nourishment, may also suffer from marginal protein deficiency when their diets are not properly planned.

In any case, protein deficiency, as we know it in underdeveloped nations, is uncommon in most industrialized settings. But marginal states of protein malnutrition can occur in the groups already mentioned as well as in pregnant and lactating women, or in any population that is shifting its eating preferences away from meat-centered diets.

The last trend is presently a significant one, characteristic not only of a small group of "counterculturists," but of a significant segment of today's American population. In the future, economic and energy-related pressures may even further encourage the adoption of a diet which relies less and less upon meat and eggs as its primary protein sources. For these reasons, learning how to balance the protein in what you eat is a necessity for any health-conscious cook. Practically speaking, this means developing a sense for how to mix foods and combine ingredients that have different protein compositions.

Implications for a Vegetarian Diet

Any dietary protein of either animal or plant origin is suitable for human nutrition if it provides both a sufficient quantity of nitrogen for non-essential amino acid synthesis and contains an appropriately balanced composition of essential amino acids. Vegetarian diets can easily meet these requirements. In fact, many dairy products—especially eggs, cheeses, and milk—as well as nuts, seeds, and some legumes are very high in essential protein; when these foods are properly combined, meatless meals can supply a nutritious, well-balanced nutrient intake.

The process of combining two or more foods (or meals, or recipes), each of which supplies an essential amino acid which is lacking in one or more of the others, is called *protein complementation*, or, alternatively, *mutual supplementation*. When two or more proteins, each lacking a different essential amino acid, *complement* each other, a higher grade protein is furnished. This combination will supply more *usable* protein. That is, there will be fewer missing links (*limiting* essential amino acids) and protein synthesis in the body will proceed at an acceptable rate.

Who will find these dietary concepts relevant? Vegans (whose intake of high-quality protein is diminished because of the elimination of meat, eggs, and dairy foods from the diet), individuals on strict caloric restriction, pregnant or lactating mothers, infants, children, and anyone who eats a predominantly vegetarian diet should become familiar with these protein-planning strategies.

The easiest and most practical way of conceptualizing protein balance for a meatless diet is to have an idea of the protein composition of the major protein-containing food groups (see *Table 8*). Consulting these tables, you will notice that the average protein content of the four major vegetarian groups—whole grains and cereals, nuts and seeds, legumes, and dairy products—varies considerably. The protein *quality* (that is, completeness with regard to essential amino acids) also differs from group to group.

Some important patterns emerge from this information. Eggs, cheese, milk, chicken, meat, and fish are high in *all* the essential amino acids, but they are especially rich in lysine. Nuts and seeds, as well as grains and cereals, are the only groups generally deficient in the *same* two essential amino acids—isoleucine and lysine. The legume group is the only one characterized by a severe deficiency of tryptophan and methionine (the sulfur-containing essential amino acids).

A few simple "rules of thumb" can be derived from these amino acid patterns. First, each of the four meatless food groups will exhibit *protein complementarity* with any of the others, *with the exception* of the nuts and seed group and the grain and cereal group, which are *not* complementary with each other, since they are both deficient in the same two essential amino acids. Because the dairy group (eggs, milk, milk products, cheeses, yogurt, etc.) is plentiful in all the essential amino acids, it is complementary with *all* the other groups (which are missing at least one essential amino acid). For this reason, you can think of the dairy group as a *universal protein donor*. The legume group, on the other hand, is the only one characterized by a severe lack of tryptophan and methionine, and for this reason can receive supplementation from *any* of the other groups. You can think of it as the *universal protein recipient*. Vegetables, generally, are also deficient in these sulfur-containing amino acids, and consequently can be supplemented by any of the major meatless protein-containing food groups. With only these simple relationships in mind, you will easily be able to formulate complementary protein combinations.

Interestingly, many foreign diets have empirically evolved complementary protein combinations. Corn and beans unite in several Mexican dishes, while wheat and sesame seed combinations are popular in Mideastern cooking. Many other cuisines also employ food combinations that furnish higher quality protein than would otherwise be provided by just a random mixture of foods.

To help familiarize you with the practical aspects of protein balance, the *Nutritional Essentials* that accompany each foreign cuisine in the first part of this book will emphasize cooking methods and food combinations that will augment your intake of essential protein. These protein-planning strategies are illustrated on both the recipe and menu level; meal plans that supply 30 or more grams of high-quality protein are included in each chapter. In general, you can assume that these high-protein menu plans will provide at least one-half of the adult Recommended Daily Allowance.

Finally, a word of caution. While it is apparent that the vegetarian can expect a well-balanced protein intake simply by relying upon dairy products, eggs, and cheeses, this kind of dietary behavior may not be advantageous. True, these foods contain abundant quantities of the essential amino acids, but they are also high in saturated fat, cholesterol, and, frequently, sodium. We know that an excessive intake of these nutrients can worsen heart disease, diabetes, and high blood pressure, so it is not recommended that dairy items be used indiscriminately as a "quick and easy" source of high-grade protein. The alternative is to exploit the complementarity of proteins from the *other* food groups, which, incidentally, are generally lower in calories and richer in dietary fiber than dairy foods.

Carbohydrates

Carbohydrates serve as the chief, readily available energy source in the human body. Typically, this nutrient provides 40 to 50 percent of the total caloric intake in the average American diet. About one-half of these calories are derived from simple sugars (sucrose), and the remainder are provided by *complex carbohydrates* (that is, naturally occurring, unrefined sugars that are found in fruits, vegetables, tubers, and grains). With the exception of ascorbic acid (vitamin C), there are no carbohydrates known to be *essential* for the human diet. For this reason, it is difficult to arrive at an absolute minimum intake requirement for carbohydrates, but it is usually recommended that at least 100 grams (equivalent to 400 calories) be included in the diet to maintain metabolic processes.

Carbohydrates exist as *monosaccharides*, *disaccharides*, and *polysaccharides*; these names classify a carbohydrate as being a simple sugar, a double sugar, or a molecule comprised of many simple sugars, respectively. A simple sugar, or *refined* carbohydrate, is generally not fiber-bound; it has been extracted from its primary food source, and little else remains except sugar molecules. Complex carbohydrates usually refer to naturally occurring sources of mono-, di-, or polysaccharides, such as tubers, grains, vegetables, and fruits. The importance of these distinctions will become apparent later.

Of the many carbohydrates, there are only a few of special importance to human nutrition. The monosaccharide *glucose* is found in sweet fruits such as berries, grapes, and oranges; sweet corn and carrots also contain substantial amounts of glucose. Glucose is the end-product of polysaccharide digestion and is the principal carbohydrate utilized by the cells for energy production.

Fructose, also called "fruit sugar," is another monosaccharide; when linked to glucose they form table sugar or *sucrose* (a disaccharide). Sucrose is derived from cane, beet sugar, molasses, brown sugar, and maple sugar. *Lactose*, a naturally occurring disaccharide contained in milk, is the only carbohydrate of animal origin that is of significance in the diet. After infancy, a relatively high proportion of the nonwhite population is deficient in the enzyme *lactase*, which is necessary for lactose digestion and absorption. This deficiency is characterized by intolerance to foods containing milk and may necessitate elimination of dairy products from the diet.

The three most important dietary polysaccharides are starch, cellulose, and hemicelluloses. Starch is the form in which carbohydrates are stored in the plant. Two types of polysaccharides predominate; (1) *Amylose*, which is a long, unbranched glucose chain, comprising 15 to 20 percent of starchy foods, and (2) *Amylopectin*, a highly branched glucose chain. Both types of polysaccharides can be broken down into their monosaccharide constituents and absorbed by the gastrointestinal tract.

Cellulose, like starch, is composed of a long straight glucose chain, but the linkages between the sugar molecules cannot be broken down by digestive enzymes. Cellulose, along with a number of hemicelluloses, constitutes a large proportion of naturally occurring *dietary fiber*. The other nondigestible carbohydrates that comprise our fiber intake include gums, mucilages, algal polysaccharides, and pectins.

Carbohydrates and Health

Even though carbohydrates are not absolutely essential for the diet, the sources of carbohydrates which you choose may have a significant impact on your health. Sucrose, for example, when consumed in excessive amounts, is known to cause dental caries. It also appears as if many illnesses—heart disease, diabetes, and varicose veins—are more prevalent among people consuming diets which contain large amounts of refined carbohydrates (that is, sugar that has been *extracted* from natural sources such as fruits, vegetables, and grains). Field studies also demonstrate that once refined sugar products are adopted by populations previously on *complex carbohydrate* intakes—who traditionally have had a low prevalence of Western diseases—they too, in time, will begin to show these disease patterns.

You might ask: "If the final product which is absorbed by your gastrointestinal tract is a simple sugar (which it is), why should it matter whether our diet provides the sugar in its *refined* form or in its so-called *complex* form?" Actually, the potential harmful effects of consuming large quantities of refined sugar have nothing to do with the *quality* of the carbohydrate, but with the fact that *consuming refined sugar is usually associated with a large caloric intake*. And it is well known that excessive caloric intakes can cause obesity, which is correlated with the presence of diabetes, heart disease, high blood pressure, as well as a number of other diseases.

Consider sucrose, the ubiquitous disaccharide used as table sugar and found in a large number of baked confections and breads. Because this sugar has been stripped from its natural state, it represents a very *concentrated* source of calories. As table sugar, it is subject to being used indiscriminately in coffee, tea, carbonated beverages, and other foods. This adds so-called "empty calories" to your diet. In fact, you would have to eat four peaches in order to consume the amount of sugar contained in one, 12-ounce soda. Naturally, one becomes satiated after one or two peaches, and this is the point: the high water content, bulk, and fiber content of fresh fruit, vegetables, and grains bring satisfaction to the appetite long before an excessive number of carbohydrate calories have been consumed. This is explained by the fact that food bulk (characteristic of fresh and natural foods) leads to distension of the stomach, which then sends a feedback signal to your hunger center saying, "I'm full." Refined sugar, on the other hand, because it is not fiber-bound, can be concentrated in drinks, confections, toppings, etc., thereby delivering a large number of calories without the "feedback" signals characteristic of natural foods. This is clearly an unwanted state of affairs for most people. Furthermore, many food manufacturers have been found to put sugar in a myriad of products that you would not expect to contain refined carbohydrates. For the most part, this is a method of taste enhancement which delivers unwanted calories to the consumer. The thrust of all this is that by changing your preferences away from refined carbohydrates to complex carbohydrates, you are likely to prevent an excessive intake of calories. In the long run, these changes are likely to prevent obesity and the diseases associated with it.

Of equal importance is the fact that refined carbohydrates are, for the most part, stripped of nutrients such as vitamins and minerals, as well as fiber. This is why refined sugar is referred to as "empty calories." To the contrary, sources of complex carbohydrates—tubers, fruits, whole grains, vegetables, and legumes—are generally excellent sources of essential vitamins, micronutrients, and minerals. The favorable nutritive value of complex carbohydrates becomes especially important for people who need to restrict their food intake for purposes of weight control and for those on tight budgets. Both of these groups would find it hard to meet the Recommended Daily Allowances for certain nutrients if they consumed exclusively carbohydrates of the refined variety. In short, a regular intake of complex carbohydrates, of which natural foods are a good source, is an excellent way to ensure that your diet will be adequate in many of the essential micronutrients and vitamins.

Finally, complex carbohydrates are the single most important source of dietary fiber (see the section *Dietary Fiber*). The protective health benefits of consuming large quantities of fiber are outlined in the next section, but suffice it to say that a shift in dietary preferences away from refined carbohydrates in favor of complex carbohydrates (many of which are not digestible) is probably beneficial to your health.

Implications for a Vegetarian Diet

As a rule, vegetarian diets are ideal for ensuring an adequate intake of complex carbohydrates. Try to make fruits, vegetables, and whole grains a regular part of your dietary intake. They are preferable to refined sugar for the reasons mentioned. While there has been tremendous support for honey as a sugar substitute, many of the disadvantages of refined sugar—lack of vitamins and minerals, highly concentrated calories, lack of fiber—are also characteristic of most honey preparations. Thus, there are no compelling reasons to think honey is any healthier than sugar, and it should certainly not be substituted for natural sources of carbohydrates. Remember, the natural sources of carbohydrates contain bulk and fiber, which by giving a feeling of satiety will at the same time prevent excessive carbohydrate-derived calories, while also providing essential vitamins and nutrients.

Fiber

The fiber revolution is upon us. Long a neglected child, plant fiber has finally become a full-fledged member of the nutrition family. While the daily allowances for vitamins, minerals, fat, carbohydrate, and protein have for the most part been determined, dietary fiber—considered by many to be "nonnutritive"—has not been subjected to this kind of scrutiny. In the last ten years or so, a wave of interest in the effects of fiber on human health has been kindled. Evidence has accumulated that fiber plays an important role in the absorption, digestion, and metabolism of several dietary nutrients; furthermore, it exerts a profound effect upon levels of sugar, fat, and cholesterol circulating in the bloodstream. There is also compelling data that high-fiber regimes may significantly lower the insulin requirements for people with diabetes—an observation of potentially great import. Although the final returns on the issue of dietary fiber and human health are not yet in, suffice it to say that its impact on our well-being is likely to be significant.

The recent enthusiasm about fiber has been generated by provocative evidence that many diseases common to Western society are linked to diets low in fiber. In particular, epidemiologic studies suggest that low-fiber intakes may be responsible for the higher prevalence of cancer of the colon, diverticular disease of the large intestine, and varicose veins which are seen more often in Western people than in rural Africans. Dennis Burkett, who has pioneered much of this exciting work, has recently suggested that fiber-depleted diets may also play a role in heart disease; and even diabetes has been connected to a lack of fiber in the diet.

What is known about the changes in the composition of the Western diet during the last century has done much to support the hypothesis that dietary fiber deficiency is related to disease. Diabetes, colon cancer, and atherosclerotic heart disease have increased over the past one hundred years, during which time the consumption of cereal fibers in the United States decreased by about 90 percent. Unfortunately, because diseases are caused by the interplay of several different factors—diet, drugs, physical activity, environment, and genetic predisposition—field studies alone cannot establish "cause and effect" relationships between fiber in the diet and these common diseases.

What exactly is meant by the term *fiber*? Plant fibers are the edible portions of fruits, vegetables, cereals, seeds, legumes, and grains that are not digested in, or absorbed from, the human intestine. Total dietary fiber contains a variety of substances including cellulose, hemicelluloses, lignins, pectin, gums, mucilages, and storage polysaccharides. The majority of these fibers are not soluble in water, but certain fruits and legumes do contain water-soluble fibers such as pectins, polysaccharides, gums, and some hemicelluloses.

Cellulose, the best known fiber in the plant cell wall, represents about

25 percent of the fiber content of fruit, vegetables, and grains. The hemicelluloses, which include over 250 compounds composed of different types of sugars, comprise about 50 to 75 percent of the insoluble fibers in grains and vegetables. Lignins, extremely resistant to digestion, constitute about 10 percent of total plant fiber. Pectin, of which fruits are the principal source, are completely digested in the human colon and contribute about 40 percent of the plant fibers of various fruits.

Because some dietary fibers are totally insoluble in the intestine and others are completely soluble, it is difficult to generalize about the physiologic effects of fiber-rich foods. For example, it is known that *natural* foods contain a myriad of different fibers, but the effects of each type may be difficult to sort out. Unfortunately, when fiber is extracted from natural food, its effect may be quite different than if it were consumed as part of the intact food. Furthermore, the effects of fiber may be altered by cutting, cooking, and chewing. But despite these limitations of analysis, certain general properties of dietary fiber have been elaborated.

As a rule, foods that contain substantial amounts of insoluble fibers—wheat bran and whole grain products—move much faster (increased *transit time*) through the gastrointestinal tract. This increase in transit time appears to affect the absorption and digestion of several dietary nutrients. Bile salts, the molecular backbone for cholesterol, are excreted at an increased rate by individuals on a high-fiber diet. This fecal wastage may explain the cholesterol lowering effects of high-fiber regimes. There have also been suggestions that diets rich in fiber—because they increase transit time and thereby reduce exposure of the gut lining to potential cancer-forming substances and toxins—may lower the risk for cancer of the colon. Finally, high-carbohydrate, high-fiber diets increase the elimination of fat and nitrogen; the increased excretion of the former results in a fecal loss of food energy, or in other words, calories. While the suggestion has been made that weight loss may accompany high-fiber intakes, all the data is not yet in.

The evidence is impressive that fiber-rich diets have physiologic effects. But exactly how does this relate to health and disease? As mentioned earlier, the principal stimulus for the current enthusiasm about dietary fiber stems from observations made by doctors, nutritionists, and epidemiologists in Africa. Rural populations consuming large quantities of vegetable products, with an average daily fiber content in excess of 50 grams, appear to be free from heart disease, diabetes, and diseases of the colon—maladies that have become so prevalent in modern societies over the past 250 years. What's more, it has been observed over the past twenty years that as these rural groups have migrated to urban environments and adopted Western habits—including the diet—they are beginning to show these same diseases. True, one can explain these observations in ways other than on the basis of this one dietary feature. However, evidence has now been presented that in almost every population studied, the amount of dietary fiber consumed is likely to show correlations with these chronic diseases. Food for thought?

Generally speaking, high-fiber intakes are characteristic of people who follow a vegetarian diet. This is the kind of eating pattern that is apt to include minimally processed foods such as whole grains, legumes, and vegetables. In the Western world, vegetarian subcultures have excellent health records. When compared to the general population, vegetarians are leaner, and on the average, have lower levels of cholesterol and triglycerides in their blood.

The long and short of the fiber controversy is that an increased intake of plant fiber is probably advantageous for most people; very likely, such a diet is especially beneficial for known diabetics, who have been found to require less insulin (by injection) when following high-fiber intakes. While it is unlikely that dietary fiber will come to be regarded as an "essential" nutrient in the classical sense, emerging evidence strongly suggests that an intake on the order of 40 to 50 grams daily may be both practical and "preventive."

Many nutritionists and doctors would agree that our contemporary diets—rich in saturated fat, animal protein, refined carbohydrate, and salt—is not salubrious and is energetically expensive to produce. Its unhealthy features could be easily corrected by decreasing our caloric intake and by increasing consumption of fiber-rich whole grain cereals and bread, potatoes, vegetables, and fruits. (See *Tables 9–13* for listings of the fiber contents of popular foods.) Children should probably be instructed how to follow such a diet. Ultimately, we may all be a bit gassier, but this would be a small price to pay for the possible reduction in the current burden of chronic illnesses that Western habits have bred.

Vitamins

Vitamins are organic substances which the body requires in small amounts to maintain normal metabolic functions. As a rule, they must be supplied by the diet, but some vitamins can be synthesized by normal gastrointestinal bacteria or by the body from precursor molecules. Historically, as the vitamins were discovered, each was assigned a letter, but once its chemical structure was identified, it was given a specific name. For the most part, vitamins are not related chemically and differ considerably in their physiological roles.

Several dietary, as well as nondietary, factors influence the utilization of vitamins. For instance, most of the nicotinic acid (a B-complex vitamin) in cereals is bound in such a way that it cannot be absorbed from the gastrointestinal tract; and the fat-soluble vitamins D, E, A, and K may not be absorbed in sufficient quantities if the digestion of fat is impaired. While most vitamins are essential for the diet, bacteria normally present in the gut (referred to as *normal flora*) are capable of synthesizing significant quantities of certain vitamins, most notably vitamin K, nicotinic acid, riboflavin, vitamin

B_{12}, and folic acid. On the other hand, bacteria may also *extract* vitamins from ingested food, thereby preventing absorption. For these reasons, it may be difficult to define exactly the nutritive value of a diet with respect to a given vitamin by simple reference to its quantitative vitamin content.

Fat-soluble Vitamins

Vitamin A

Vitamin A is a fat-soluble vitamin essential for vision in dim light and also for maintaining the morphologic integrity of body tissues composed of epithelial cells: the skin, cornea, bronchial tree, and small intestine. Preformed vitamin A, called *retinol*, is found exclusively in foods of animal origin. Plants, on the other hand, are rich with naturally occurring pigments called *carotenoids*, which are converted by the intestinal cells into retinol. The most important of the vegetable carotenoids is *B-carotene*, which is split in the gut to yield two molecules of active vitamin A (retinol).

The absorption of B-carotene from the diet is somewhat variable, depending upon the quantity and quality of dietary fat. When vitamin A is lacking in the diet, individuals characteristically develop night blindness as well as profound eye and skin changes. Usually, deficiencies of this nutrient are seen only in people whose diet has been lacking both in dairy produce and vegetables for a substantial period of time.

Retinol is found principally in butter, milk, cheese, egg yolk, liver, and some fatty fish. While the liver oils of halibut and cod are the richest natural sources of vitamin A, these preparations are used primarily as nutritional supplements rather than foods.

Carotenes, from which the body can synthesize vitamin A, are widely distributed among plant foods. B-carotene, in particular, is found in green vegetables such as cabbage and lettuce and is also plentiful in red fruits and vegetables, especially carrots. While all vegetable oils (with the exception of red palm oil) are devoid of vitamin A activity, this vitamin is, in some circumstances, added to margarine in order to provide the same concentration as in butter. Recommended Daily Allowances for adults range from 4000 to 5000 International Units. (See *Tables 14 and 15* for dietary sources of vitamin A activity.)

Vitamin D

Vitamin D is necessary for the normal formation of bone. In addition to its direct action upon bone, vitamin D (also known as cholecalciferol) acts on the small intestine to enhance absorption of calcium and phosphorus and plays a major role in regulating calcium and phosphorus metabolism through direct action on the kidney. Unlike most nutrients (which must be supplied by the diet), a good part of the body's requirements for vitamin D can be obtained from *de novo* synthesis that requires the biochemical integrity of three different organ systems.

In man, cholecalciferol is formed in the skin through the action of ultraviolet light from the sun. Cholecalciferol is not the physiologically active form of vitamin D, so it must undergo further biochemical changes. These conversions involve two hydroxylation steps, first in the liver and finally in the kidney, before cholecalciferol assumes its active form, 1,25, dihydroxycholecalciferol. The specific reactions are not particularly important to remember, but it is useful to know that through the cooperation of the skin, liver, and kidney, the body is able to manufacture large quantities of vitamin D. A dietary supply of this nutrient may not be necessary for individuals living in sun-rich latitudes, where the manufacture of cholecalciferol by the skin is greatly facilitated. In northern latitudes, however, a lack of this vitamin in the diet leads to the deficiency state *rickets*, characterized by abnormal bone deposition and growth.

There are only a few natural sources of vitamin D, chiefly liver oils of fish which obtain the vitamin by ingesting plankton living near the surface of the oceans. Some dairy products, especially milk, are fortified with vitamin D, while cereals, vegetables, and fruit lack this nutrient entirely. Meat and white fish provide insignificant amounts.

Experience has shown that populations in tropical regions exposed to sufficient quantities of sunlight do not require vitamin D in their diets. Most authorities, however, recommend a daily intake of 10 μg for children, which has been shown to protect against rickets, while involving no risk of hypervitaminosis (that is, toxicity resulting from excessive vitamin intake).

Because fat-soluble vitamins are not rapidly excreted or metabolized, they may, if taken in excessive amounts, accumulate in the body tissues causing undesirable side effects. In the case of vitamin D, toxicity usually results when the mother of an infant mistakes her instructions and feeds some concentrated calciferol preparation by the spoonful. Adults who practice vitamin supplementation to extremes may also be susceptible to hypervitaminosis D.

Vitamin E

Fat-soluble vitamin E (a member of the *tocopherols*) is found in all cell membranes. This vitamin has been recognized as a biological antioxidant for over thirty-five years, and recent work supports the concept that this nutrient prevents the destructive oxidation of polyunsaturated fatty acids found in cellular structures. Interestingly, the breakdown products of fats appear in the tissues of both old animals and in those on vitamin E deficient diets. These observations have led to the speculation that this vitamin may have a role in preventing—much like a youth potion—a number of degenerative disorders associated with aging. At present, there is no substantial evidence supporting this view.

Given its wide distribution in foods, dietary deficiency of this vitamin occurs infrequently. The richest sources are vegetable oils, wheat germ, sunflower seed, safflower, and other oils. Consequently, margarine and vegetable shortening are the principal sources of vitamin E in the diet; eggs, butter, and whole grain cereals are moderately good sources.

Vitamin K

Vitamin K is necessary for the formation of blood clotting factors synthesized by the liver. If this vitamin is not supplied in adequate amounts, a bleeding tendency results. Because the body-stores of this nutrient are relatively meager, if intake of vitamin K is stopped, deficiency may develop in a few weeks' time.

The natural sources of vitamin K are the diet and intestinal bacteria. Many species of gastrointestinal bacteria which are part of the normal flora synthesize vitamin K; it is presumably this biosynthesis in the gut which provides much of the body's needs and explains why dietary deficiency of this nutrient is relatively uncommon. Individuals who are taking anticoagulant medications that interfere with the production of clotting factors should maintain a fairly constant intake of vitamin K; excessive fluctuations in vitamin K consumption in these people may effect the action of their medications.

Vitamin K is present in fresh, green leafy vegetables such as cabbage, spinach, broccoli, and lettuce. Beef liver is also a good source, but most other animal foods, cereals, and fruits are poor sources.

Water-soluble Vitamins

Vitamin C (Ascorbic acid)

Vitamin C, otherwise known as ascorbic acid, is a simple sugar that is essential for the human diet. As the most active reducing agent found in human tissues, this vitamin has recently been spurred into the limelight by claims of its efficacy in preventing and treating the "common cold." While its role in this setting remains controversial—with most recent scientific reports suggesting this nutrient plays no role of importance in preventing such ailments—it is well known that ascorbic acid is required for the proper formation of the ground substance or matrix that bind together cells in tissues such as teeth, bone, blood vessels, and collagenous connective tissue.

The deficiency state, *scurvy*, is now seen only occasionally in this country, sometimes in alcoholics and food faddists, but more commonly in the bachelor whose diet is grossly unbalanced and totally devoid of this vitamin. When it does occur, ascorbic acid depletion is characterized by swollen and bleeding gums, poor wound healing, small skin hemorrhages, aching muscles, fatigue, and emotional changes. These manifestations are likely to be present when the body's total ascorbic acid pool of 1.5 grams is depleted, which usually occurs only if the total daily intake falls to less than 45 milligrams. If the dietary intake of vitamin C is adequate, there appears to be little benefit conferred from supplementing this amount with vitamin preparations. In cases where individuals consume more than 3 grams of ascorbic acid per day, much of the excess is excreted unchanged in the urine, suggesting there is little to be gained from high-dose vitamin C therapy.

Ascorbic acid is more limited in its distribution than the other essential water-soluble vitamins. The richest dietary sources include citrus fruits, currants, berries, and fully matured green vegetables. While root vegetables and potatoes contain substantially smaller concentrations, they are nevertheless important sources of this vitamin. In fact, potatoes, because of the large amounts normally eaten by most people, account for a significant portion of the total daily ascorbic acid intakes of populations who cannot afford or do not have access to fruit on a regular basis. Animal foodstuffs contain only small quantities of vitamin C, but the best of such sources are liver and the roe of fishes. Although seeds contain no ascorbic acid, once germinated, their sprouts become a valuable source of this nutrient.

Many plants contain an enzyme that is capable of deactivating vitamin C in the presence of air. This enzyme, which can rapidly oxidize ascorbic acid, appears to have no contact with the vitamin in the intact fruit or vegetable, but is released when leaves or fruits are damaged by drying, bruising, pounding, or cutting. Ascorbic acid is also very soluble in water, and as a result, much may be lost when vegetables are cooked in large quantities of water which is then discarded.

Deciding how much vitamin C is needed for proper bodily function has been beset with some controversy. One school of thought believes the body should be fully *saturated* with the vitamin so that every cell contains as much as it can hold. The other school maintains that as long as the individual appears to be healthy and feels well, he (or she) is probably getting an adequate intake of the vitamin. Both arguments have some justification, with most nutritional experts agreeing that a daily adult intake of 50 to 75 milligrams per day is sufficient to prevent scurvy. As mentioned, a school of thought has recently emerged that claims massive doses on the order of 2 to 8 grams per day can abort or ameliorate symptoms of the common cold. Daily vitamin C doses of this magnitude are, for the most part, excreted by the kidney, and at the present time there is no convincing evidence for the therapeutic efficacy of such mega-doses. (See *Table 16* for dietary sources of ascorbic acid.)

Vitamin B₁₂

Vitamin B_{12} is one of the two essential "anemia-preventing" vitamins (folic acid is the other). Deficiency of this vitamin affects nearly every cell in the body, but its impact is most profound on rapidly dividing cells such as those of the bone marrow and gastrointestinal tract. When this nutrient is severely lacking in the diet, an anemia develops which is frequently accompanied by neurological abnormalities.

Certain individuals have a condition called *pernicious anemia* which results from an acquired deficiency of an *intrinsic factor*, a molecule made by stomach lining cells and required for normal absorption of vitamin B_{12}. Individuals with this disease manifest signs of vitamin B_{12} deficiency even if their dietary intake is adequate. Consequently, injections of vitamin B_{12} are necessary to provide ample amounts for these individuals.

Vitamin B_{12} is unique among the vitamins in that it is not found in any plant foods. As a result of this distribution in nature, the dietary intake of this nutrient is dictated by the consumption of meat and animal-derived products, such as cheeses and dairy foods. This has important implications for *vegans*, a subgroup of vegetarians whose diet is devoid of eggs, milk, and all other foods of animal origin. Individuals who subscribe to such a strict diet are prone to developing vitamin B_{12} deficiency and should—as a precautionary measure—supplement their meals with artificial sources (vitamin tablets) of this nutrient. Interestingly, however, most vegans somehow manage to obtain adequate quantities of this vitamin from their diet. It is speculated they get it from traces in molds which inevitably contaminate many foods.

Lacto-vegetarians (whose diets include milk products but not eggs) and lacto-ovo-vegetarians (who include both milk and eggs) manage to obtain modest but sufficient amounts of vitamin B_{12}. Generally, these groups, unlike the vegans, do not require vitamin supplementation.

As a rule, the dietary intake of this vitamin varies according to the amount of animal products consumed. Fortunately, the normal requirements for an adult to prevent signs of vitamin B_{12} deficiency are probably less than 1 µg per day. While it is impossible to state exactly the desirable intake, a daily intake of 3 to 4 µg is recommended.

Folic Acid

Folic acid is a water-soluble vitamin that plays an important role in the synthesis of building blocks for DNA. When this biochemical pathway is compromised due to a dietary lack of folic acid, an anemia, like that seen in vitamin B_{12} deficiency, results.

Although a severe anemia due to simple dietary deficiency of folic acid is unusual, it is not uncommon in pregnancy, when the need for this vitamin increases substantially. Other conditions can also give rise to folic acid deficiency. Absorption of folic acid from the gastrointestinal tract may be impaired by a number of diseases, while some drugs—oral contraceptives, alcohol, and certain anticonvulsants—interfere with the utilization of folate.

The richest dietary source of folate is liver. Lentils, beans, and orange juice also contain appreciable amounts. With the exception of oranges and grapefruits, fruits are a poor source of folate.

Because food preparation can cause substantial losses of folic acid, this vitamin is best obtained from fresh foods. Canning, prolonged heating, discarded cooking water, and reheating contribute to folic acid losses.

Although it is not possible to give any definite figure for a satisfactory intake of folic acid, 400 μg daily is recommended. In general, a regular intake of fresh, leafy greens and citrus fruit is sufficient to prevent folic acid deficiency in most diets. (See *Table 17* for dietary sources of folic acid.)

Thiamine

In 1890, a Dutch physician working in Java made the observation that domestic fowl fed on "polished rice" developed signs of a disorder known as *beriberi*. Later he demonstrated that something existing in very small amounts in the germ of rice was the nutrient responsible for preventing this deficiency state. Thirty years later, this factor, thiamine (vitamin B_1) was isolated.

Thiamine, an essential vitamin, is concerned with a stage in the breakdown of carbohydrates. Signs of deficiency develop most rapidly in those on a high carbohydrate diet. The nutritional deficiency disorder, beriberi—formerly widespread in rice-eating populations of the East—is characterized by heart failure and neurological impairment. As we know it today, thiamine deficiency is seen primarily in chronic alcoholics and only rarely in individuals with a well-balanced nutrient intake.

The total amount of thiamine in the body is only 25 milligrams, with the highest concentrations being found in the heart, brain, liver, kidneys, and muscles. The body is unable to store any excess of this nutrient, so no benefit is derived from ingesting large doses; any excess is lost in the urine.

Virtually all animals and plants contain thiamine and it is therefore present in all whole natural foods. The only important dietary sources are seeds of plants. Whole grain cereals, nuts, peas, beans, as well as yeast, are the richest sources. Significant quantities of the vitamin are also found in green vegetables, roots, fruit, and dairy foods, but none of these are particularly rich sources. Thiamine content is reduced significantly by extraction due to milling of whole grain flours. Substantial quantities may also be lost when vegetables are cooked in water which is then thrown away. As a rule, approximately 25 percent of the thiamine content is lost in the preparation of an ordinary diet. The Recommended Daily Allowance for an adult is about 1.2 milligrams. (See *Table 19* for dietary sources of thiamine.)

Riboflavin

Riboflavin, an essential water-soluble vitamin, serves as the building block for two *flavoprotein* coenzymes that play a central role in many metabolic processes. Deficiency of this vitamin in the human results in skin eruptions around the lips and seborrheic dermatitis. Late in the course, mild anemia, itching and burning eyes, and neurological problems may occur.

The best sources of riboflavin are liver, milk, eggs, and green vegetables. This vitamin differs from others in the B-complex in that it occurs in good amounts in dairy produce, but is relatively lacking in cereal grains. Usual methods of cooking do not destroy the vitamin, but losses can occur when water in which green vegetables have been boiled is discarded. The Recommended Daily Allowance for riboflavin is about 1.8 milligrams for an average adult. (See *Table 18* for dietary sources of riboflavin.)

Nicotinic Acid (Niacin)

Nicotinic acid, the "pellagra preventing" vitamin, is an important component of the oxidative coenzyme system concerned with energy production within cells. The human body is not entirely dependent on dietary sources of nicotinic acid, as significant amounts can be synthesized in the body from tryptophan, one of the essential amino acids (see the section *Protein*). About 60 milligrams of tryptophan in the diet is required to replace 1 milligram of dietary niacin. Thus, the total niacin intake is equivalent to the nicotinic acid content of the diet *plus* one-sixtieth of the tryptophan intake.

Niacin is widely distributed in plant and animal foods, but in relatively meager amounts. Fish, whole grain cereals, nuts, and some beans are good sources. In maize (corn) and perhaps potatoes, a significant amount of the nicotinic acid exists in a bound, unabsorbable form which can be liberated by treatment with alkalai. Interestingly, in Mexico, tortillas have been made with maize treated with alkaline lime water, a practice which may explain the low incidence of pellagra in that country. (See *Table 20* for dietary sources of nicotinic acid.)

Vitamin B₆—Pyridoxine and Related Compounds

Vitamin B_6 activity is necessary for the enzyme system responsible for the formation of hemoglobin. While there is no distinct clinical syndrome of pyridoxine deficiency, anemia, failure to thrive, peripheral neuropathy, and depression have been associated with a lack of the vitamin B_6 complex.

The vitamin is widely distributed in plant and animal tissues. Good sources are meat, liver, vegetables, and bran. A daily intake of 1 to 2 mg. is sufficient for most adults.

Minerals

Minerals play an important role in a number of bodily processes. The intake of these nutrients depends upon the diet which, from a nutritional point of view, is composed of complex mineral salts containing many different elements.

Of the essential minerals, calcium, magnesium, phosphorus and sulphur are important components of bone and other supporting tissues. Iron, iodine, and fluorine are respectively of major importance for the synthesis of hemoglobin, manufacture of thyroid hormones, and resistance of teeth to caries. In addition to these minerals, a number of trace elements present in extremely small amounts in foods and tissues are also important for the body's metabolic machinery.

Calcium

About 99 percent of the body's calcium resides in the skeleton, which consists chiefly of calcium phosphate salts. All of this calcium must be provided by the diet, and, among common foods, milk products are the richest source. One-half quart of milk contains about .5 grams of calcium, which explains why milk and cheese are especially valuable for growing children.

Calcium needs vary considerably according to age. The bony skeleton of a young child is replaced in its entirety every one to two years, while in adults—whose metabolisms are much slower—turnover occurs over a period of approximately ten to twelve years. This explains why calcium needs are much greater during years of rapid growth.

Bones usually cease to grow in early adulthood. While they may continue to become somewhat more dense for a few years into adult life, by the age of 40 bones begin to atrophy. This process, which occurs most rapidly in postmenopausal women, is known as *osteoporosis*. As a normal and, for the most part, unpreventable part of the normal aging process, osteoporosis predisposes to fractures of the long bones and spine. Treatment with high calcium diets is usually not successful.

It is in the younger age groups that dietary calcium intake is especially important. Starting at the beginning, the fetus, whose calcium needs are supplied by the mother, is generally protected from a deficiency of this nutrient unless the mother is calcium deficient. After birth, the infant becomes entirely dependent on the diet to supply calcium for bone development. Natural sources during this period include the mother's milk, which generally supplies at least 300 mgs. of calcium per day. Although cow's milk contains about four times as much calcium, there is no evidence that this additional amount is either beneficial or harmful.

Except for lactating and pregnant mothers, who require about 1200 mgs. of calcium daily, most adults will meet their calcium needs without special dietary manipulations. Adolescents, whose bony skeletons are continually growing and turning over, also require a substantial calcium content (about 1200 mgs. per day) in their diet.

Table 21 lists the calcium content of commonly used foods. Milk and cheeses are the richest sources, but vegetables, cereal grains, and legumes also provide appreciable amounts.

Iron

Iron is of vital importance to human nutrition. As an important component of hemoglobin molecules in red blood cells, iron is involved in the transfer of oxygen to the body's tissues. Frequently, it is not supplied by the diet in adequate amounts. When the intake of this mineral is not sufficient, a mild to moderate anemia will ensue. If the supply of dietary iron is severely compromised for long periods, a potentially life-threatening anemia can occur. Because the body conserves iron well and maintains large stores of this vital nutrient in the bone, an anemia of this severity is fairly uncommon.

In most adults, iron balance is easily achieved, but during the reproductive period of a woman's life, additional losses inevitably occur: during menstrual periods, in the transfer of iron to the developing fetus, or to the infant from the breast. Roughly speaking, a woman in her reproductive years sustains twice the iron loss of a man or of a woman after menopause. Consequently, the dietary iron intake of menstruating women may not be sufficient to meet the increased demand.

The average adult diet in the United States provides about 10 to 20 mgs. of iron per day, but only 5 to 10 percent of this amount is actually absorbed by the body. When there is an increased need for iron, absorption may become more efficient, approaching 10 to 20 percent.

The amount of iron absorbed by the intestinal tract varies according to whether the dietary source is of plant or animal origin. Iron derived from animal sources is absorbed more completely than iron in vegetable foods. For example, of the total iron content in fish muscle, about 10 to 15 percent is absorbed, whereas only 2 to 5 percent of an equivalent total iron content in spinach would be taken up by the gut. A good rule of thumb is that *ionic iron*, which exists mainly as ferric hydroxide complexes in vegetable foods, is less efficiently absorbed by the body than *heme iron* characteristic of animal-derived foods (see *Table 22*).

Because absorption of iron is so variable, a recommended figure for iron intake may be misleading. Most authorities recommend 10 mg. per day for males and postmenopausal women and 18 mg. per day for women in the reproductive age group. The latter may require iron supplementation in the form of ferrous sulfate tablets. (See *Table 23* for dietary sources of iron.)

Iodine

Before the supplementation of certain foods with iodine, people who lived far from the seacoast often failed to get an adequate supply of this mineral. Now, iodized salt is a reliable source of iodine, and its regular use virtually assures an adequate amount of this nutrient in your diet.

The body contains about 20 to 50 mgs. of iodine; a substantial portion of this total is concentrated by and stored in the thyroid gland. Iodine is unique among the necessary minerals in that it is an essential component of specific hormones. Assuring an adequate intake of this element is a requirement for proper functioning of the thyroid gland. A deficient intake can cause a goiter and a condition known as hypothyroidism, which is manifested by skin thickening, impaired temperature regulation, and sometimes heart failure.

Iodine in food and water is readily absorbed, mostly as inorganic iodide. The iodide content of both animal and plant foods is determined largely by the iodine content of the soil in which these food sources grow. As most soils contain very little iodine, most foodstuffs, plant or animal, are poor sources of this essential element. The only rich source of iodide is seafood, especially haddock, whiting, and herring. As a rule, if fish is eaten once or twice per week, this provides an iodine intake well in excess of 150 μg per day, which is sufficient to prevent goiter (swelling of the thyroid gland) in most cases. Contrary to usual belief, sea water is a poor source of iodide. As mentioned, iodized salt is a reliable source of this mineral, but many individuals who must restrict their intake of salt will have to look to seafood sources for maintaining an adequate iodide intake.

Various figures ranging from 50 to 300 μg per day have been proposed for iodine requirements of an adult. This range is a suitable approximation, but needs are influenced by many dietary factors, hardness of the drinking water, age, sex, exposure to infections, and other stresses.

Copper

Copper is an essential nutrient for animals and is important to such diverse activities as hemoglobin synthesis, bone development, nerve function, and other critical biochemical reactions. Experimental copper deficiency is characterized by anemia and impaired synthesis of white blood cells which are required to fight infection. Although outright deficiency in human beings is rare, it has been seen in severely malnourished infants and adults.

Normal diets provide about 2 mg. of copper per day. Green vegetables, fish, oysters, and liver are good sources, whereas most other foods—milk, meats, bread—are not.

Fluoride

Fluorine is present in trace amounts in many human tissues, most notably the bones, teeth, thyroid gland, and skin. There now is no doubt that small amounts of fluorine in the diet protect against dental caries.

The chief dietary source of fluorine is drinking water, which, if it contains 1 part per million (p.p.m.) of fluoride, then it supplies 1 to 2 mg. daily. Soft waters generally contain very little or no fluorine, whereas extremely hard waters may contain more than 10 p.p.m. In comparison to this source, foodstuffs of the diet are of relatively little importance. In fact, very few foods contain significant amounts with the exception of seafish, which may contain substantial quantities in the range of 5 to 10 p.p.m. Interestingly, another major source of fluoride is Chinese tea, which if drunk on a daily basis, may provide as much as 1 mg. daily.

Studies throughout the world have established that when fluorine is present in the water supply at a concentration of 1 p.p.m. or more, the incidence of dental caries is significantly lower than in areas where water contains only trivial amounts of this element.

This evidence has been the impetus for deliberately adding traces of fluoride to public water supplies presently deficient in this substance.

While it seems reasonable to add small amounts of fluoride to water supplies in order to confer protection against caries, there are still many people who oppose fluoridation of public water.

Sulfur

All living tissues are composed of protein, and all proteins contain sulfur. Most of the body's sulfur is present in the two sulfur-containing amino acids methionine and cysteine. The vitamins thiamin and biton also contain sulfur, while several cellular enzyme systems rely on free sulphydryl groups for their function.

The sulfur-containing amino acids are the principal sources of sulfur in the diet. The importance of an adequate supply of these has already been discussed. In general, a diet containing 40–50 gr. per day of protein will supply a sufficient quantity of sulfur-containing amino acids.

Magnesium

Most of the body's magnesium is present in bone in combination with phosphate. About one-fifth of the total magnesium content is present in soft tissues, and, next to potassium, magnesium is the principal metallic ion inside living cells.

From the nutritional standpoint, most foods, especially vegetables, contain useful amounts of magnesium. Cereals and vegetables combined contribute more than two-thirds of the daily magnesium intake. The recommended intake for adults is 350 mg. per day.

Zinc

The average adult consumes about 10 to 15 mg. of zinc daily. Good dietary sources include meat, unmilled grains, and legumes, whereas fruits and leafy vegetables are poor sources. A deficiency of this trace nutrient, although rare, has been reported in Middle Eastern populations living on unleavened bread.

Nutritionists and physicians have become more attuned to human zinc deficiency, which may develop in alcoholics as well as individuals with tuberculosis, thyroid diseases, cancer, and some malabsorption diseases. The first manifestations of zinc deficiency in man are associated with a change in the smell and taste of foods, which presumably occurs because of the need for zinc in the growth of taste buds. Other features of insufficient dietary zinc include growth retardation or dwarfing, incomplete sexual development, anemia, and learning disabilities. Zinc also appears to be necessary for tissue repair and healing processes.

To prevent zinc deficiency during pregnancy, women should take note of foods rich in this trace element and include them frequently in the diet. The RDA for pregnant and lactating women is about 25 mg., while the average RDA for other adults is 15 mg. and 6 mg. for children.

A diet rich in unrefined, limited-processed foods can provide adequate zinc in the diet without the need for supplementation. A few general guidelines are worth bearing in mind. Whole grain and whole wheat products contain three times as much zinc as white flour. Red meats have a substantially higher zinc content than white meats, so those watching the saturated fat content in their diets need to include rich sources of zinc from vegetable foods.

Cobalt

Cobalt is an important constituent of vitamin B_{12}, an essential dietary nutrient for man. No other physiological role has been found for this trace element, which is provided in the diet in amounts averaging up to 600 mg. per day.

Nickel

Nickel is postulated to play a general role in maintaining cell membrane structure and function, but its exact significance in the human diet has not been clarified.

Chromium

Chromium, present in all organic matter, appears to be required for normal metabolism in several animal species. While marginal chromium deficiency may possibly accompany severe malnutrition, pregnancy, and old age, there is little hard knowledge and no certainty regarding its role in human nutrition.

Manganese

Manganese is an essential nutrient, playing a critical role in a host of cellular enzymes. A human deficiency state has not yet been characterized. Foods rich in manganese include cereals, legumes, leafy vegetables, and tea. Meat, milk, and refined cereals are poor sources.

Selenium

A distinct clinical syndrome in man resulting from selenium deficiency has not yet been characterized. This element, which is about as rare as gold, appears to protect structural proteins from destruction by oxidating enzymes. Recommendations concerning the dietary intake of this nutrient cannot be made at the present time.

Water

Generally speaking, the intake of fluids is largely determined by social customs and habit. The kidney, which is able to excrete or retain salt and water according to the body's needs, is the principal organ regulating fluid balance in the body. Thirst is another important mechanism regulating water balance. Although originally it was thought that thirst was produced by dryness of the throat and mouth, more likely this sensation occurs when the concentration of sodium in the blood rises by as little as 1 to 2 percent, a situation that results from an inadequate intake of water or from other causes of dehydration. Controlled by the hypothalamus, thirst is predominantly associated with water depletion. Heavy exercise, manual labor, high fever, vomiting, and diarrhea can all cause heavy water and salt losses. Usually, these deficiencies can be made up by an adequate oral intake of fluids.

Because the kidney and thirst centers automatically regulate our water fluxes, there is no reason for most adults to plan their diet with this factor in mind. Infants, on the other hand, are susceptible to losing large quantities of fluid from diarrhea and vomiting; an aggressive approach to providing adequate water intake is warranted in this situation.

Salt

Man's need for salt (sodium chloride) has been a subject of controversy for hundreds of years. It is not known exactly when man first began to use salt, although it was certainly available in early civilizations and Homer called it "divine." At one time, salt was the best food preservative available. Even though salted meat and fish were an important part of the diet in early times, a supply of salt, in addition to that normally present in natural foods, is not essential for man.

It is well recognized that people with congestive heart failure, high blood pressure, or severe kidney disease benefit if the salt in their diet is restricted. Whether low salt diets can actually *prevent* high blood pressure is not definitely known at present, although there is convincing evidence that certain individuals, who appear to be exquisitely sensitive to salt intake, will develop hypertension if the amount of sodium chloride in their diet is not regulated.

Most people consume 5 to 20 gr. of sodium chloride per day. Generally speaking, natural foods contain relatively little sodium, but large amounts may be added during cooking. Most processed, canned, and preserved foods have salt added. Bakers, for example, add salt to bread in a concentration of about 1 percent; wheat flours contain less than one-hundredth of this amount in the natural state. Other foods commonly salted during preparation include butter, bacon, and seafood. As a rule, low sodium diets must be prepared utilizing unprocessed vegetables; foods derived from animal sources usually contain more sodium. (See *Tables 24* and *25*.)

Many physicians and nutritionists feel that high-salt diets may predispose otherwise healthy people to hypertension, a potentially lethal disease. Many people, however, find that reducing salt intake is difficult, since sodium chloride enhances the flavor of most foods. Using herbs and spices as seasoning agents will help most people adopt a restricted salt regime.

Potassium

Unlike sodium, most of the potassium content in the body is within cellular tissues. About 80 percent of this amount is in skeletal muscles. The potassium content of foodstuffs is extremely variable, but usually is in the range of 4 to 6 gr. per day. Deficiency or excess of potassium rarely occurs solely as a result of dietary deficiency or excess.

Most foods contain moderate amounts of potassium. Cereals, cheese, eggs, and some fruits contain small amounts of potassium, while orange juice, bananas, and most nuts are rich sources. Generally, one does not need to monitor potassium intake. However, some individuals who are taking potassium-wasting medications (such as diuretics) may want to augment their dietary potassium intake. (See *Table 26* for dietary sources of potassium.)

FOOD

The day is still far off in the future when people will think in terms of preparing a bowl of fiber and complex carbohydrates for breakfast or a dish of high-grade protein without cholesterol for dinner. This is not to say nutritional considerations are not important (they are), but our present cultural patterns dictate that we plan our diet in terms of food products rather than nutrients *per se*. Consequently, it is useful to have a basic feeling for the nutritive values and characteristics of foods used in a wide variety of cooking styles. In the previous chapters, the physiological roles of the essential nutrients—carbohydrates, fats, proteins, fiber, vitamins, and minerals—have been considered. In the following sections, we will describe several foods used in foreign and domestic cooking in terms of these nutrients.

Cereals

The principal cereals used in foreign and domestic cooking are wheat, rice, maize, millet, oats, and rye. Generally speaking, the word "corn" is used in the English-speaking world to mean the most familiar local cereal. For instance, in Scotland, "corn" means oats; in England it signifies wheat; and in our country "corn" connotes maize. All cereals can be pounded into flours to make cakes or porridge, but only wheat and rye flours bake into bread.

In most temperate climates, wheat is presently the cereal of choice. It is grown extensively in parts of South America, the United States, Canada, Europe, Russia, and Northern India. Rice is grown primarily in moist, tropical environments, especially on the deltas of great rivers. Maize, hardy and easily cultivated, is grown extensively in Mexico, the United States, Yugoslavia, Italy, and Egypt. Millet grows in hot climates on poor soil, while oats and barley are grown extensively in temperate regions. Rye, cultivated heavily in Russia and Poland, grows in poor soil and cold climates.

The *whole* grains of all cereals have a similar chemical composition and nutritive value. They provide calories and protein as well as significant amounts of calcium and iron. Whole cereals are lacking ascorbic acid (vitamin C) and are virtually devoid of vitamin A activity. As a rule, whole grains contain appreciable amounts of B-complex vitamins (see *Table 27*).

You should be aware that the distribution of nutrients in cereal grains is not uniform. When a grain is consumed in its entirety, an adequate intake of B vitamins is ensured, but if the grain is first milled, and the outer portions of the seeds discarded, much of this nutrient value will be removed. The extent to which the milling process removes vitamins and fiber is of importance in determining the nutritive value of grain products.

In simple terms, you can envision a cereal grain as a seed consisting of six structures. The two outer coverings, pericarp and testa, are hard and contain much of the indigestible fiber. Beneath them is the aleurone layer which is an envelope of cells rich in protein. These outer layers contain about 12 percent of the grain's total weight. Inside is the endosperm, comprising 85 percent of the grain's total weight. The germ (or embryo)—situated at the lower end of the grain—is attached to the endosperm by a special structure called the scutellum, which is rich in thiamine. The embryo and scutellum constitute about 3 percent of the total grain.

When wheat is milled into flour, the whole grain may be used, but usually, the germ and a portion of the outer layers are separated and discarded as bran. The proportion of the whole grain that *is* used to make flour is known as the *extraction rate*. For example, flour with an 85 percent extraction rate contains 85 percent of the whole grain by weight, 15 percent having been discarded as bran. Thus, a flour of high extraction rate has lost little of the outer layers, which contain high concentrations of fiber, protein, and vitamins. In general, white flour has a low extraction rate, whereas whole wheat flours have considerably higher extraction rates.

Low-extraction flours have several disadvantages. They contain less of the B vitamins and are poorer sources of calcium, iron, protein, and fiber.

Starchy Roots

The potato is the most important food of this class to be found in temperate climates. In tropical regions, *cassava* (also known as manioca, yuca, and tapioca), yams, sweet potatoes, and taro root are all important foods. Arrowroot and a wide variety of other roots are also eaten, but in smaller quantities. As a rule, roots contain large quantities of complex carbohydrates, but are relatively poor in vitamins, protein, and minerals (see *Table 28*).

Potato

In most modern Western civilizations potatoes are a relatively cheap and popular food item. Their reputation for being fattening is largely undeserved; a medium-sized potato contains only about 100 calories. Potatoes contain little protein and, while containing small but not very important amounts of minerals and vitamins, are a rich source of potassium. Although the concentration of ascorbic acid in potatoes is not particularly high, this root can provide significant quantities of this essential vitamin when eaten in large quantities.

Yams

Like potatoes, true yams are rich in carbohydrate and also contain significant amounts of protein. Used in African cooking, the yam is a climbing plant that takes from six to twelve months to develop. The two most important cultivated varieties are the greater yam (*Dioscorea alata*) and the lesser yam (*Dioscorea esculentia*). The former may produce tubers as large as basketballs, while the latter is composed of clusters of smaller tubers.

Sweet Potato

Cultivated extensively in the southern United States and other hot climates, the sweet potato is a popular item in many foreign cuisines. Unlike most tubers, which are vitamin poor, the pigment of red, yellow, or purplish-yellow sweet potatoes contains carotene. It can be a significant source of vitamin A in the diet.

Taro

Widely grown in Africa, Asia, and the Pacific Islands, this herbaceous tuber has the same general nutritive value as potatoes and yams.

Cassava

One of the principal foods of many tropical cuisines, *cassava* root is about 50 to 75 percent water, less than one percent protein, and 25 to 50 percent carbohydrate. A mere 3 percent of its caloric content is derived from protein, which is less than half of the proportion of energy derived from protein in other roots such as potatoes, yams, and taro. Clearly, this lack of protein places *cassava* in a different nutritional class from other roots, and explains why protein malnutrition is common in communities that rely upon this food as a staple.

Tapioca is a derivative of *cassava* from which virtually all protein has been removed. Consequently, it is almost pure carbohydrate and should not be relied upon as an important nutritive food.

Miscellaneous Roots

Tapioca, sago, arrowroot, and ground rice are available as commercial preparations. Provided you realize these foods are almost pure starch, devoid of proteins, minerals, and vitamins, they can be added to certain foreign cuisines for an authentic touch.

Legumes, Nuts, and Seeds

Legumes are the seeds of the *Fabacae* family, which includes peas, beans, and lentils. Members of this food group are also called *pulses*, a word taken from the Latin *puls*, meaning pottage or thick pap. Cultivated in almost all parts of the world, legumes make an important contribution to a wide variety of foreign cuisines.

In many respects, the nutritive properties of legumes resemble those of whole cereal grains, but there are important differences. First, legumes have a higher protein content than most grains. On the average, beans and lentils contain about 20 gr. of protein per 100 gr. of dry weight, compared to 10 gr. for most cereal grains. The biological value of this protein is not especially high, due to the low content of essential sulfur-containing amino acids. Fortunately, legumes are rich in the essential amino acid lysine, which is lacking in most cereals. Consequently, a combination of legume and cereal protein has substantial nutritive value.

As a rule, legumes are rich in most B vitamins except riboflavin. Unlike cereal grains, which lose vitamins and nutrients through milling, the vitamin content present in the seeds of harvested legumes is actually consumed. Although legumes are devoid of vitamin C—as are cereal grains—substantial amounts of ascorbic acid are manufactured on germination. Consequently, sprouted seeds are a good source of vitamin C for those on a predominantly vegetarian diet (see *Table 29*).

Soybeans

The soybean has been a nutritious staple in the Chinese diet for several thousand years. Containing approximately 40 percent protein (twice as much as most other legumes), soy-based foods form the basis for a myriad of unusual sauces and pastes used in the Chinese cuisine. For those who follow a restricted diet or vegetarian regime, soybean curd (*tofu*) can be of immense value in maintaining a low-fat, low-cholesterol diet that is also rich in high-grade protein.

Lentils

Lentils are commonly used in Indian and Egyptian cooking. Containing about 20 percent protein, lentils are the seeds of *Lens esculenta*, of which many varieties are known. The Indian and Egyptian kinds are orange-red in color, while those used in America are green. Nutritious and plentiful in both protein and complex carbohydrates, lentils can readily be made into soups or ground into flour.

Dahl

In addition to lentils, many foreign cuisines rely upon another type of legume called *dahl*. Lentil-like in appearance, *dahls* come in red, orange, and black varieties. These legumes are very popular in Indian cooking and their nutritive value is similar to that of lentils.

Groundnuts

Also known as peanuts and monkey nuts, groundnuts are actually seeds of a leguminous plant; they are therefore properly called legumes (or pulses) and not nuts. Peanuts—while resembling other legumes with respect to certain nutritional features—are much higher in fat content (most of which is polyunsaturated) and virtually devoid of complex carbohydrates. The oil extracted from peanuts is popular in many styles of cooking especially the French and Chinese.

Beans

The lima bean, garden pea, and kidney bean are other pulses important to both Eastern and Western diets. Their nutritive properties compare to those of other legumes. Small quantities of these foods in the diet will (1) significantly increase the quantity and quality of dietary protein, (2) prevent beriberi, and (3) after sprouting, provide appreciable amounts of vitamin C.

Nuts

Most nuts have a high fat and protein content. Because the calorie value and saturated fat content vary considerably among members of this food group, individuals on restricted diets will want to choose nuts according to their nutrient make-up (see *Table 30*).

Seeds

Sunflower, pumpkin, and sesame seeds are commonly used in foreign and domestic cooking. They are an excellent source of protein, essential fatty acids, and fiber.

Vegetables

A myriad of vegetables are employed in cuisines throughout the world. It is somewhat difficult to generalize about their nutritive value, since there is no biological structure that is common to all vegetables. Some, like spinach, lettuce, and cabbages are leaves, while others—onions, radishes, and turnips—are roots. Eggplants and gourds are classified as fruits. Celery is a stalk, while cauliflower and artichokes are flowers. Despite these differences, vegetables are similar with respect to certain nutritive properties (see *Tables 31* and *32*).

Generally speaking, vegetables are not an important source of calories. Considering that most varieties provide about 10 to 50 calories/100 gm., it would be necessary to eat about 4 to 7 kg. (10 to 15 lbs.) of vegetables in one day in order to meet an adult's caloric needs. The considerable fiber content and bulk of vegetables promotes satiety; and this, combined with their meager food energy value (calories), makes them useful in the prevention and treatment of obesity.

Vegetables are not only a poor source of calories, they are also of insignificant value as sources of essential amino acids. While the protein that vegetables do contain is complementary with the amino acids of most other foods, the quantity of this nutrient which can be yielded, even after mutual supplementation, is minimal. This means that at least one of the principal protein-containing food groups must be included in vegetable-based diets if protein needs are to be met.

Although the mineral content of vegetables varies greatly, most green, leafy vegetables contain amounts of calcium that are physiologically significant. The iron content of some vegetables, most notably spinach and lettuce, constitutes an important source for those on vegetarian regimes.

Nearly all vegetables contain small quantities of B vitamins, but their overall contribution in this department is minimal. Leafy vegetables, however, contain enough riboflavin to prevent skin eruptions around the mouth (cheilosis) that result from a deficiency of this vitamin.

Nutritionally, vegetables are valued most for their B-carotene, ascorbic acid, and folic acid content. The last two vitamins are generally lacking in cereals and grains, so vegetables are able to prevent two major deficiencies likely to arise on diets containing excessive amounts of cereals. In this manner, vegetables are able to "balance" a diet.

B-carotene (a precursor of vitamin A) is present in almost all vegetables, but in varying amounts. As a rule, there is a rough correlation between color and B-carotene content. For example, green, leafy vegetables are rich and some, like kale, very rich in this nutrient. Pale vegetables such as cucumber and cauliflower contain very small quantities of carotene.

Vegetables are also touted for their substantial ascorbic acid content. While losses in cooking and preparation may be great, a single helping of vegetables, even if mistreated by the cook, will easily provide enough vitamin C to prevent scurvy.

Seaweed (dulse)

Exotic vegetables are also used as food for man and deserve mention. Seaweed has been used creatively as a food source by the Chinese for thousands of years, and today is eaten widely in Japan. The principal carbohydrates in seaweeds are mannitol and the polysaccharides alginic acid and laminarin. The fat content is extremely low (less than 1 percent), but the mineral and fiber content is appreciable.

Dulse, a red algae of the species *Palmeria palmata*, is an important, commercially available sea vegetable that grows in Canada's Bay of Fundy. A 3½ ounce serving of this decisively flavored vegetable yields enough protein to meet an adult's daily requirement. Also rich in more than twenty minerals and several vitamins, including B_{12} (which it absorbs from its environment), dulse can be added to soups and salads, or toasted and then crushed to decorate hors d'oeuvres.

Mushrooms

Mushrooms are appreciated by those who love good food. Eaten primarily for their delicious flavor, they contain no more than 3 percent protein, less than 2 percent fat, and about 2 percent carbohydrate. In other words, their nutritive value is almost negligible, but as they are good sources of food bulk and low in calories, mushrooms have an important place in low-calorie diets.

Sugar

Easily preserved, cheap, and useful as a flavoring agent, sugar is one of the most popular foods of industrialized urban populations. As a form of readily digested food energy, sugar is without peers, but unfortunately, it lacks every nutrient except refined carbohydrate. Because of its popularity and ease of utilization in cooking, sugar has the tendency to displace more nutritious foodstuffs, which, incidentally, are also frequently lower in calories. The extent to which the consumption of refined sugar has been held responsible for an increase in the incidence of dental caries, heart disease, and diabetes has been discussed earlier.

Crystalline table sugar, one of the purest chemicals produced by the food industry, is 100 percent sucrose and contains no vitamins or minerals. Brown sugar is slightly less refined sucrose, containing small traces of other sugars, some minerals, and coloring agents. Even raw sugar cane, chewed in considerable quantities by children in the tropics, contains only minimal amounts of protein, vitamins, and other nutrients.

Syrup

Syrups, which include molasses and treacles, are highly concentrated solutions in which the sugar has not crystallized out due to the presence of small quantities of other substances. Syrups, especially blackstrap molasses, have some nutritional advantages over table sugar in that they contain significant amounts of calcium and iron, some of which is derived from the vessels in which they have been prepared. Natural syrups, such as maple syrup, contain 20 percent water and carbohydrate.

Honey

With the advent of the American health food movement, honey developed a reputation as a nutritious food. On the whole, this claim is undeserved, as most honeys consist of 20 percent water and about 75 percent carbohydrate, predominantly fructose and glucose with only traces of other nutrients. Despite these rather dismal chemical analyses, honey is still promulgated by many as the "healthy" alternative to table sugar. It is best to view these claims with a jaundiced eye (or a carious tooth as the case may be), and use honey primarily for its attractive and pleasurable qualities.

Fruits

The succulent, pleasant flavors and colorings of fruits have attracted man since the beginning of civilization. Unfortunately, the nutritional virtues of fruits are far less impressive, at least on paper. While ascorbic acid is the only essential nutrient fruits contain in very large amounts, they also contain appreciable quantities of carotene and some B vitamins. Fruits are low in fat and protein, but of course, like vegetables, are a rich source of dietary fiber. Fruits contain substantial quantities of natural sugars (complex carbohydrates) and this, combined with their bulk and moisture content, makes them preferable to concentrated sources of refined carbohydrates such as table sugar and confections (see *Table 33*).

Meat

Although protein of animal origin is not essential for the human diet, the flesh of more than one-hundred species is eaten by man. Meat is of particular value because it contains protein of high biological value. This attribute is offset by the salt, saturated fat, cholesterol, and calorie content which, in some varieties of meat, is excessive. Meats are generally rich in iron and phosphorus, but contain little calcium, vitamin A, or ascorbic acid.

Fowl

Chicken and other fowl contain less fat and cholesterol than beef, yet are equally rich in high-grade protein. Also lower than most animal meats in salt and calorie content, chicken and turkey provide healthy and nutritious alternatives to beef-based diets.

Fish

Fish and other seafoods have a well-merited reputation as being rich and healthy sources of "animal" protein. The energy content ranges from 50 to 80 calories per 100 grams in most varieties. Fish are also distinguished by their low fat content, which is often less than 1 percent in lean varieties such as haddock, whiting, sole, and turbot. Species with intermediate amounts of fat—halibut, mackerel, trout—still contain only 2 to 7 percent fat. High-fat fish, which include salmon, sardines, and eel, may contain up to 15 percent fat, which is still substantially lower than most varieties of beef.

Fish protein has a biological value that is similar to that of land animals. This feature, combined with its low calorie, saturated fat, and salt content, make it nutritionally preferable to beef for individuals on low-calorie, low-fat, or low-salt menu plans.

Except for concentrated fish oils, a rich source of fat-soluble vitamins, fish do not contain appreciable quantities of vitamins or minerals except iodine (see *Table 34*).

Shellfish

This tasty, but expensive, food group includes lobster, shrimp, crab, crayfish, and a host of other crustaceans. On the whole, these items are rich in protein and have a fat content that is appreciably less than beef. However, some shellfish, such as shrimp, are notable for their high cholesterol content. Some people are especially sensitive to shellfish protein and can develop a variety of allergic reactions.

Like the crustaceans, oysters, mussels, and other mollusks contain appreciable amounts of protein, but their fat content is considerably less.

Eggs

Egg protein is considered to have the highest biological value of all the foods eaten by man. As mentioned earlier (see section on *protein*), the amino acid composition of whole hens' eggs is frequently used as a standard against which the chemical score of other proteins is compared.

An average hen's egg weighs about 60 grs. and contains 6 grs. of protein and 6 grs. of fat, mostly of the saturated type. Because of this substantial fat content, and also partly due to its appreciable cholesterol content (300 mgs. per egg), when eaten in large quantities, eggs may raise the blood level of cholesterol.

More than just a valuable source of high-grade protein, eggs are also rich in calcium and iron. Egg yolks are a fair source of vitamins and contain significant quantities of nicotinic acid, riboflavin, and thiamine.

Milk and Milk Products

Milk, and foods derived from it, constitute an important source of protein, calcium, and vitamins for both infants and adults. The fat content of milk varies according to its source and the amount removed in the making of butter or cream. (See *Table 35* for a comparison of the nutrient values of milk from different animals.)

The carbohydrate content in milk is composed of lactose, to which a large proportion of Black and Oriental adult populations may be intolerant.

Cow's milk is a valuable source of calcium, containing about 120 mg. per 100 ml. Milk is a poor source of iron and only a fair source of riboflavin and nicotinic acid.

Sour Milk

Sour milk (yogurt), which is made from milk, is the end-product of lactose being broken down by various bacteria, most commonly *Lactobacillus acidophilus* (which is found in man) or *Lactobacillus bulgaricus* (found in cows). This healthy preparation contains all the protein, calcium, and vitamins of the original milk. Most commercial preparations of yogurt are substantially lower in fat than whole milk (see chart of *Nutrient Analysis of Milk Products*, p. 299).

Kefir, a sour beverage popular in Russia, and more recently in the United States, has an alcohol content of about 1 percent. *Kowmiss* is another popular Russian drink prepared from lactose-rich mare's milk; it may contain up to 3 percent alcohol.

Cheese

The nutritional value of cheeses varies considerably (see *Nutritive Values of Most Popular Natural Cheeses, Table 7*). Most cheeses are 25 to 35 percent protein and range from 10 to 60 percent in fat content. They are also an excellent source of calcium, vitamin A, and riboflavin, but vary considerably in salt content.

Oils and Fats

Oils and fats are treasured by practitioners of both Eastern and Western culinary styles. As a concentrated source of energy and essential fatty acids, this group makes a major contribution to the palatability of food. Fats and oils tend to be expensive, which accounts for the observation that the intake of these nutrients is strongly correlated with affluence. In the United States, fats and oils have traditionally provided 40 to 50 percent of the total food energy, this despite evidence that such a high intake may lead to disturbances in fat metabolism and an elevation in the level of cholesterol in the blood.

Vegetable oils used in cooking include olive, coconut, red palm, soybean, peanut, sesame seed, safflower, and other oils. Their fat composition is given in *Table 6*.

Fats and oils contain very little water and all possess high energy values (800 to 900 Calories per 100 gms). Of course, it is the variations in fatty acid composition that determine the consistency of fat. The ratio of polyunsaturated to saturated fatty acids (P/S) determines whether a fat is hard or liquid at room temperature. Animal fat, which has a low P/S ratio, is generally hard, while oils made from vegetables, seeds, and nuts have a high P/S ratio, and are therefore liquid at room temperature.

Butter and Margarine

Tradition had it that butter (milk fat) was the favored cooking medium in several cuisines. Its use, however, has slackened somewhat, due in great part to the "antisaturated fat" movement promulgated by medical associations and the Senate Subcommittee on Human Nutrition. Containing mostly saturated fat, butter is rich in retinal and contains appreciable amounts of vitamin D.

The use of butter has been supplanted by margarine, which is the end-result of vegetable oils that are hardened by a process known as hydrogenation. While the oils—corn, safflower, soy—from which margarine is made have a high polyunsaturated to saturated fat ratio (P/S), this figure tends to be lowered by the hardening process. Nevertheless, some brands of margarine contain up to 50 percent polyunsaturates predominantly as linoleic acid. The consumption of such margarine, in place of butter, will help lower the plasma cholesterol concentration.

In some cuisines—French, Lebanese, Indian, and Hungarian—butter fats are first clarified by heating, and the resulting product (known as *Ghee*, *Samneh*, or clarified butter) contains almost all the vitamins present in butter. However, losses may be up to 50 percent in some of these clarified preparations.

Herbs and Spices

Civilized men have cultivated herbs and spices for culinary purposes for centuries. Esteemed for their aromatic properties and extraordinary tastes, seasonings are essential to the art of cooking.

Despite their prominence, herbs and spices have little direct nutritional value. However, some, like green chilies, are very rich in ascorbic acid (100mgs./100gms.) and may contribute significant amounts to the diet. Most herbs and spices contain B vitamins as well as iron and calcium in appreciable concentrations, but the amounts consumed are generally too small to make a significant impact.

Perhaps the most important contemporary role of herbs and spices concerns their use as salt substitutes and flavor enhancers. People who need to moderate their salt intake—and they include a significant majority of those with heart disease and high blood pressure—will find herbs and spices invaluable for following restricted diets without compromising the gastronomic appeal of food.

APPENDIX

TABLE 1

Essential Dietary Nutrients

Nitrogenous	Essential Amino Acids	Lysine, threonine, leucine, isoleucine, methionine, tryptophan valine, phenylalanine, histidine
	Nonessential Nitrogen	
Vitamins	Water-soluble	Ascorbic acid, pantothenic acid, cobalamin, biotin, folic acid, nicotinic acid, thiamine, riboflavin, vitamin B_6
	Fat-soluble	Vitamin A (carotene), vitamins D, E, and K
Fats	Polyunsaturated fatty acids	linoleic, arachidonic
Elements	Macro-nutrients	sodium, potassium, calcium, magnesium, phosphorus, chloride, sulfur, carbon
	Micro-nutrients	iron, zinc, copper, manganese, cobalt, iodide

TABLE 2
Recommended daily dietary allowances of Food and Nutrition Board[1]

	Age, years	Weight, kg	Weight, lb	Height, cm	Height, in.	Energy, kcal	Protein, g	Vitamin A activity, RE[2]	Vitamin A activity, IU	Vitamin D, IU	Vitamin E activity,[4] IU
Infants	0.0–0.5	6	14	60	24	kg × 117	kg × 2.2	420[3]	1,400	400	4
	0.5–1.0	9	20	71	28	kg × 108	kg × 2.0	400	2,000	400	5
Children	1–3	13	28	86	34	1,300	23	400	2,000	400	7
	4–6	20	44	110	44	1,800	30	500	2,500	400	9
	7–10	30	66	135	54	2,400	36	700	3,300	400	10
Men	11–14	44	97	158	63	2,800	44	1,000	5,000	400	12
	15–18	61	134	172	69	3,000	54	1,000	5,000	400	15
	19–22	67	147	172	69	3,000	54	1,000	5,000	400	15
	23–50	70	154	172	69	2,700	56	1,000	5,000		15
	51+	70	154	172	69	2,400	56	1,000	5,000		15
Women	11–14	44	97	155	62	2,400	44	800	4,000	400	12
	15–18	54	119	162	65	2,100	48	800	4,000	400	12
	19–22	58	128	162	65	2,100	46	800	4,000	400	12
	23–50	58	128	162	65	2,000	46	800	4,000		12
	51+	58	128	162	65	1,800	46	800	4,000		12
Pregnant						+300	+30	1,000	5,000	400	15
Lactating						+500	+20	1,200	6,000	400	15

Fat-soluble vitamins (Vitamin A, Vitamin D, Vitamin E columns)

[1] Allowances are intended to provide for individual variations among most normal persons in the United States living under usual environmental stresses. Diets should be based on a variety of common foods in order to provide other nutrients for which human requirements have been less well defined.

[2] Retinol equivalents.

[3] Assumed to be all as retinol in milk during the first 6 months of life. All subsequent intakes are assumed to be half as retinol and half as β-carotene when calculated from international units. As retinol equivalents, three-fourths are as retinol and one-fourth as β-carotene.

[4] Total vitamin E activity, estimated to be 80 percent as α-tocopherol and 20 percent as other tocopherols.

TABLE 2, (Continued)

| | Water-soluble vitamins | | | | | | | Minerals | | | | | |
	Ascorbic acid, mg	Folacin,[5] μg	Nicotinic acid,[6] mg	Riboflavin, mg	Thiamine, mg	Vitamin B6, mg	Vitamin B12, μg	Calcium, mg	Phosphorus, mg	Iodine, μg	Iron, mg	Magnesium, mg	Zinc, mg
Infants	35	50	5	0.4	0.3	0.3	0.3	360	240	35	10	60	3
	35	50	8	0.6	0.5	0.4	0.3	540	400	45	15	70	5
Children	40	100	9	0.8	0.7	0.6	1.0	800	800	60	15	150	10
	40	200	12	1.1	0.9	0.9	1.5	800	800	80	10	200	10
	40	300	16	1.2	1.2	1.2	2.0	800	800	110	10	250	10
Men	45	400	18	1.5	1.4	1.6	3.0	1,200	1,200	130	18	350	15
	45	400	20	1.8	1.5	2.0	3.0	1,200	1,200	150	18	400	15
	45	400	20	1.8	1.5	2.0	3.0	800	800	140	10	350	15
	45	400	18	1.6	1.4	2.0	3.0	800	800	130	10	350	15
	45	400	16	1.5	1.2	2.0	3.0	800	800	110	10	350	15
Women	45	400	16	1.3	1.2	1.6	3.0	1,200	1,200	115	18	300	15
	45	400	14	1.4	1.1	2.0	3.0	1,200	1,200	115	18	300	15
	45	400	14	1.4	1.1	2.0	3.0	800	800	100	18	300	15
	45	400	13	1.2	1.0	2.0	3.0	800	800	100	18	300	15
	45	400	12	1.1	1.0	2.0	3.0	800	800	80	10	300	15
Pregnant	60	800	+2	+0.3	+0.3	2.5	4.0	1,200	1,200	125	18+[7]	450	20
Lactating	80	600	+4	+0.5	+0.3	2.5	4.0	1,200	1,200	150	18	450	25

[5] Folacin allowances refer to dietary sources as determined by Lactobacillus casei assay. Pure forms of folacin may be effective in doses less than one-fourth of the recommended dietary allowance.

[6] Although allowances are expressed as nicotinic acid, it is recognized that on the average 1 mg nicotinic acid is derived from each 60 mg dietary tryptophan.

[7] This increased requirement cannot be met by ordinary diets; therefore, the use of supplemental iron is recommended.

Source: Recommended Dietary Allowances, 8th ed., Food and Nutrition Board, National Academy of Sciences—National Research Council, Washington, 1974.

TABLE 3

Ideal Body Weight for Men Over Age 25

HEIGHT (WITH SHOES, 1-INCH HEELS)		WEIGHT IN POUNDS ACCORDING TO FRAME (IN INDOOR CLOTHING)		
		Small Frame	Medium Frame	Large Frame
Feet	Inches			
5	2	112–120	118–129	126–141
5	3	115–123	121–133	129–144
5	4	118–126	124–136	132–148
5	5	121–129	127–139	135–152
5	6	124–133	130–143	138–156
5	7	128–137	134–147	142–161
5	8	132–141	138–152	147–166
5	9	136–145	142–156	151–170
5	10	140–150	146–160	155–174
5	11	144–154	150–165	159–179
6	0	148–158	154–170	164–184
6	1	152–162	158–175	168–189
6	2	156–167	162–180	173–194
6	3	160–171	167–185	178–199
6	4	164–175	172–190	182–204

Courtesy of the Metropolitan Life Insurance Company, New York, N.Y. Derived from data of the 1969 Build and Blood Pressure Study, Society of Actuaries.

Ideal Body Weight for Women Over Age 25

HEIGHT (WITH SHOES, 2-INCH HEELS)		WEIGHT IN POUNDS ACCORDING TO FRAME (IN INDOOR CLOTHING)		
		Small Frame	Medium Frame	Large Frame
Feet	Inches			
4	10	92– 98	96–107	104–119
4	11	94–101	98–110	106–122
5	0	96–104	101–113	109–125
5	1	99–107	104–116	112–128
5	2	102–110	107–119	115–131
5	3	105–113	110–122	118–134
5	4	108–116	113–126	121–138
5	5	111–119	116–130	125–142
5	6	114–123	120–135	129–146
5	7	118–127	124–139	133–150
5	8	122–131	128–143	137–154
5	9	126–135	132–147	141–158
5	10	130–140	136–151	145–163
5	11	134–144	140–155	149–168
6	0	138–148	144–159	153–173

Note: for girls between 18 and 25, subtract 1 pound for each year under 25. Courtesy of the Metropolitan Life Insurance Company, New York, N.Y. Derived from data of the 1959 Build and Blood Pressure Study, Society of Actuaries.

TABLE 4

CALORIC ALLOWANCES FOR MEN AND WOMEN ACCORDING TO AGE AND HEIGHT

| | *Ideal Body Weight* | | | *Caloric Allowance* | |
	kg.	*lb.*	*22 years*	*45 years*	*65 years*
Men	50	110	2,200	2,000	1,850
	55	121	2,350	2,100	1,950
	60	132	2,500	2,300	2,100
	65	143	2,650	2,400	2,200
	70	154	2,800	2,600	2,400
	75	165	2,950	2,700	2,500
	80	176	3,050	2,800	2,600
	85	187	3,200	2,950	2,700
	90	198	3,350	3,100	2,800
	95	209	3,500	3,200	2,900
	100	220	3,700	3,400	3,100
Women	40	88	1,550	1,450	1,300
	45	99	1,700	1,550	1,450
	50	110	1,800	1,650	1,500
	55	121	1,950	1,800	1,650
	58	128	2,000	1,850	1,700
	60	132	2,050	1,900	1,700
	65	143	2,200	2,000	1,850
	70	154	2,300	2,100	1,950

TABLE 5

Calorie Expenditure for Various Kinds of Activity

Type of Activity	Calories per Hour
Sedentary Reading; writing; eating; watching television or movies; listening to the radio; sewing; playing cards; typing; and miscellaneous office work, and other activities done while sitting that require little or no arm movement.	80 to 100
Light Preparing and cooking food; doing dishes; dusting; hand-washing small articles of clothing; ironing; walking slowly; personal care; miscellaneous office work, and other activities done while standing that require some arm movement; and rapid typing and other activities done while sitting that are more strenuous.	110 to 160
Moderate Making beds; mopping and scrubbing; sweeping; light polishing and waxing; laundering by machine; light gardening and carpentry work; walking moderately fast; other activities done while standing that require moderate arm movement; and activities done while sitting that require more vigorous arm movement.	170 to 240
Vigorous Heavy scrubbing and waxing; hand washing large articles of clothing; hanging out clothes; stripping beds; other heavy work; walking fast; bowling; golfing; and gardening.	250 to 350
Strenuous Swimming; playing tennis; running; bicycling; dancing; skiing; and playing football.	350 and more

Reprinted with permission from Normal and Therapeutic Nutrition, *Corinne H. Robinson and Marilyn R. Lawler, Macmillan Publishing Co., Inc., 1977.*

FIGURE 1

Formation of Triglyceride from Fatty Acids and Glycerol

$$
\begin{array}{c}
H \\
| \\
H-C-OH \\
| \\
HO-C-H \\
| \\
H-C-OH \\
| \\
H \\
\text{Glycerol}
\end{array}
\quad + \quad
\begin{array}{c}
R_1-COOH \\
R_2-COOH \\
R_3-COOH \\
\\
\text{3 Fatty Acids}
\end{array}
\quad = \quad
\begin{array}{c}
H \\
| \\
H-C-OOC-R_1 \\
| \\
R_2-COO-C-H \\
| \\
H-C-OOC-R_3 \\
| \\
H \\
\text{Triglyceride}
\end{array}
$$

TABLE 6

Fatty Acid and Cholesterol Content of Fats and Oils

Fat or Oil (per tsp.)	Weight gm	Total Fat gm	Saturated Fat gm	Mono-unsaturated Fatty Acids gm	Poly-unsaturated Fatty Acids gm	Cholesterol mg
Butter	5	3.5	2.3	1.2	—	12
Margarine	5	4.0	1.1	2.5	0.4	—
Special Margarine	5	4.0	0.6	2.3	1.1	—
Cocoa Butter	5	4.0	2.4	1.5	0.1	—
Lard	5	4.0	1.6	1.9	0.5	16
Coconut Oil	5	5.0	4.4	0.5	0.1	—
Corn Oil	5	5.0	0.5	1.8	2.7	—
Cottonseed Oil	5	5.0	1.3	1.2	2.5	—
Olive Oil	5	5.0	0.6	4.0	0.4	—
Palm Oil	5	5.0	2.5	1.6	0.9	—
Peanut Oil	5	4.0	0.9	1.6	1.5	—
Safflower Oil	5	5.0	0.4	1.0	3.6	—
Sesame Oil	5	4.0	0.9	1.0	2.1	—
Soybean Oil	5	5.0	0.8	1.6	2.6	—
Sunflower Oil	5	5.0	0.6	1.1	3.3	—
Vegetable Fat	5	4.0	1.0	2.6	0.4	—

TABLE 7

Nutritive Values of the Most Popular Natural Cheeses

BEER KAESE
See figures for Brick.

BEL PAESE
A one-ounce portion contains 105 calories. Figures for the other nutrients are not available, but would be similar to Brick.

BLUE
A one-ounce portion contains:

Calories: 100
Protein: 6 grams
Fat: 8 grams (5 grams saturated)

Carbohydrate: less than 1 gram
Cholesterol: 21 milligrams
Sodium: 396 milligrams

An excellent source of calcium and phosphorus, and a good source of riboflavin and vitamin A.

BOURSIN
A one-ounce portion would contain approximately 135 calories. Figures for other nutrients are not available, but it would be high in fat and saturated fat as well as cholesterol and low in most other nutrients. Sodium content is unknown.

Brick

A one-ounce portion contains:

Calories: 105

Protein: 7 grams

Fat: 8 grams (5 grams saturated)

Carbohydrate: less than 1 gram

Cholesterol: 27 milligrams

Sodium: 159 milligrams

An excellent source of calcium, phosphorus, and vitamin A, and a good source of riboflavin.

Brie

A one-ounce portion contains:

Calories: 95

Protein: 6 grams

Fat: 8 grams (figures for saturated fat not available, but comparable to Camembert)

Carbohydrate: less than 1 gram

Cholesterol: 28 milligrams

Sodium: 178 milligrams

An excellent source of riboflavin, and a good source of calcium, phosphorus, and vitamin A.

Camembert

A one-ounce portion contains:

Calories: 85

Protein: 6 grams

Fat: 7 grams (4 grams saturated)

Carbohydrate: less than 1 gram

Cholesterol: 20 milligrams

Sodium: 239 milligrams

An excellent source of calcium, phosphorus, vitamin A, and riboflavin.

Cheddar

A one-ounce portion contains:

Calories: 114

Protein: 7 grams

Fat: 9 grams (6 grams saturated)

Carbohydrate: less than 1 gram

Cholesterol: 30 milligrams

Sodium: 176 milligrams

An excellent source of calcium, phosphorus, and vitamin A, and a good source of riboflavin.

Cheshire

A one-ounce portion contains:

Calories: 110

Protein: 7 grams

Fat: 9 grams (figures for saturated fat not available, but would be similar to Cheddar)

Carbohydrate: 1.36 grams

Cholesterol: 29 milligrams

Sodium: 198 milligrams

An excellent source of calcium, phosphorus, and vitamin A, and a good source of riboflavin.

Colby

A one-ounce portion contains:

Calories: 112

Protein: 7 grams

Fat: 9 grams (6 grams saturated)

Carbohydrate: less than 1 gram

Cholesterol: 27 milligrams

Sodium: 171 milligrams

An excellent source of calcium, phosphorus, and vitamin A, and a good source of riboflavin.

COTTAGE, CREAMED
A one-cup (210-gram) portion contains:

Calories: 217	Carbohydrate: 6 grams
Protein: 26 grams	Cholesterol: 31 milligrams
Fat: 9.5 grams (6 grams saturated)	Sodium: 850 milligrams

Also an excellent source of calcium, vitamin A, and riboflavin, and a good source of thiamin when consumed in this large a quantity.

COTTAGE, DRY CURD (unsalted)
A one-cup (145-gram) portion contains:

Calories: 123	Carbohydrate: 2.5 grams
Protein: 25 grams	Cholesterol: 10 milligrams
Fat: less than 1 gram	Sodium: 19 milligrams

Also an excellent source of riboflavin, and a good source of thiamin and calcium when consumed in this quantity.

COTTAGE, LOWFAT (made with 1 percent milk)
A one-cup (226-gram) portion contains:

Calories: 164	Carbohydrate: 6 grams
Protein: 28 grams	Cholesterol: 10 milligrams
Fat: 2 grams (1.5 grams saturated)	Sodium: 918 milligrams

Also an excellent source of calcium and riboflavin, and a good source of vitamin A and thiamin when consumed in this quantity.

CREAM
A one-ounce portion contains:

Calories: 99	Carbohydrate: less than 1 gram
Protein: 2 grams	Cholesterol: 31 milligrams
Fat: 10 grams (6 grams saturated)	Sodium: 84 milligrams

An excellent source of vitamin A, but low in most other nutrients.

DANISH HAVARTI
See figures for Tilsit.

DOUBLE CRÈMES
A one-ounce portion would contain approximately 110 to 120 calories. Figures for the other nutrients are not available, but Double Crèmes are high in fat and saturated fat as well as cholesterol, and low in most other nutrients. Sodium content figures are not available.

DOUBLE GLOUCESTER
Figures not available, but would be similar to Cheddar.

EDAM
A one-ounce portion contains:

Calories: 101	Carbohydrate: less than 1 gram
Protein: 7 grams	Cholesterol: 25 milligrams
Fat: 8 grams (5 grams saturated)	Sodium: 274 milligrams

An excellent source of calcium, phosphorus, and vitamin A, and a good source of riboflavin.

ESROM
Figures not available, but would be similar to Port du Salut.

FETA
A one-ounce portion contains:

Calories: 75
Protein: 4 grams
Fat: 6 grams (4 grams saturated)

Carbohydrate: 1 gram
Cholesterol: 25 milligrams
Sodium: 316 milligrams

An excellent source of calcium and phosphorus. Figures are not available for other nutrients.

FONTINA
A one-ounce portion contains:

Calories: 110
Protein: 7 grams
Fat: 9 grams (5 grams saturated)

Carbohydrate: less than 1 gram
Cholesterol: 33 milligrams
Sodium: Figures not available, but would contain some.

An excellent source of calcium and vitamin A, and a good source of riboflavin.

GJETOST
A one-ounce portion contains:

Calories: 132
Protein: 3 grams
Fat: 8 grams (5 grams saturated)

Carbohydrate: 12 grams
Cholesterol: Figures not available, but would contain some.
Sodium: 170 milligrams

An excellent source of calcium and phosphorus. Figures for other nutrients are not available.

GOLD-N-RICH
Figures not available, but would be similar to Cheddar.

GORGONZOLA
Figures not available, but similar to Roquefort or Blue.

GOUDA
A one-ounce portion contains:

Calories: 101
Protein: 7 grams
Fat: 8 grams (5 grams saturated)

Carbohydrate: less than 1 gram
Cholesterol: 32 milligrams
Sodium: 232 milligrams

An excellent source of calcium and phosphorus, and a good source of riboflavin and vitamin A.

GRUYÈRE
A one-ounce portion contains:

Calories: 117
Protein: 8 grams
Fat: 9 grams (5 grams saturated)

Carbohydrate: less than 1 gram
Cholesterol: 31 milligrams
Sodium: 95 milligrams

An excellent source of calcium, phosphorus, and vitamin A, and a good source of riboflavin.

JARLSBERG

Figures not available, but similar to Swiss. Note that fat and cholesterol content is high.

LIEDERKRANZ

Figures not available, but similar to Limburger.

LIMBURGER

A one-ounce portion contains:

Calories: 93
Protein: 6 grams
Fat: 8 grams (5 grams saturated)

Carbohydrate: less than 1 gram
Cholesterol: 26 milligrams
Sodium: 227 milligrams

An excellent source of calcium, phosphorus, vitamin A, and riboflavin.

MONTEREY (JACK)

A one-ounce portion contains:

Calories: 106
Protein: 7 grams
Fat: 9 grams (figures for saturated fat not available, but would be similar to Cheddar)

Carbohydrate: less than 1 gram
Cholesterol: Figures not available but would be similar to Cheddar.
Sodium: 152 milligrams

An excellent source of calcium, phosphorus, and vitamin A, and a good source of riboflavin.

MOZZARELLA

A one-ounce portion contains:

Calories: 80
Protein: 6 grams
Fat: 6 grams (4 grams saturated)

Carbohydrate: less than 1 gram
Cholesterol: 22 milligrams
Sodium: 106 milligrams

An excellent source of calcium, phosphorus, and a good source of vitamin A and riboflavin.

MOZZARELLA (LOW-MOISTURE)

A one-ounce portion contains:

Calories: 90
Protein: 6 grams
Fat: 7 grams (4 grams saturated)

Carbohydrate: less than 1 gram
Cholesterol: 25 milligrams
Sodium: 118 milligrams

An excellent source of calcium, phosphorus, and vitamin A, and a good source of riboflavin.

MOZZARELLA (PART-SKIM)

A one-ounce portion contains:

Calories: 72
Protein: 7 grams
Fat: 5 grams (3 grams saturated)

Carbohydrate: less than 1 gram
Cholesterol: 16 milligrams
Sodium: 132 milligrams

An excellent source of calcium and phosphorus, and a good source of riboflavin and vitamin A.

MOZZARELLA (LOW-MOISTURE, PART-SKIM)
   A one-ounce portion contains:
 Calories: 79   Carbohydrate: less than 1 gram
 Protein: 8 grams   Cholesterol: 15 milligrams
 Fat: 5 grams (3 grams saturated) Sodium: 150 milligrams
An excellent source of calcium and phosphorus, and a good source of riboflavin and vitamin A.

MUENSTER
   A one-ounce portion contains:
 Calories: 104   Carbohydrate: less than 1 gram
 Protein: 7 grams   Cholesterol: 27 milligrams
 Fat: 9 grams (5 grams saturated) Sodium: 178 milligrams
An excellent source of calcium, phosphorus, and vitamin A, and a good source of riboflavin.

NEUFCHÂTEL
   A one-ounce portion contains:
 Calories: 74   Carbohydrate: less than 1 gram
 Protein: 3 grams   Cholesterol: 22 milligrams
 Fat: 7 grams (4 grams saturated) Sodium: 113 milligrams
An excellent source of vitamin A, but a poor source of most other nutrients.

PARMESAN (GRATED)
   A one-ounce portion contains:
 Calories: 129   Carbohydrate: 1 gram
 Protein: 12 grams   Cholesterol: 22 milligrams
 Fat: 9 grams (5 grams saturated) Sodium: 528 milligrams
An excellent source of calcium and phosphorus, and a good source of riboflavin and vitamin A.

PARMESAN (HARD)
   A one-ounce portion contains:
 Calories: 111   Carbohydrate: 0.91 grams
 Protein: 10 grams   Cholesterol: 19 milligrams
 Fat: 7 grams (5 grams saturated) Sodium: 454 milligrams
An excellent source of calcium and phosphorus, and a good source of riboflavin and vitamin A.

PORT DU SALUT
   A one-ounce portion contains:
 Calories: 100   Carbohydrate: less than 1 gram
 Protein: 7 grams   Cholesterol: 35 milligrams
 Fat: 8 grams (5 grams saturated) Sodium: 151 milligrams
An excellent source of calcium, phosphorus, and vitamin A, and a good source of riboflavin.

PROVOLONE
A one-ounce portion contains:

Calories: 100

Protein: 7 grams

Fat: 8 grams (5 grams saturated)

Carbohydrate: less than 1 gram

Cholesterol: 20 milligrams

Sodium: 248 milligrams

An excellent source of calcium and phosphorus, and a good source of riboflavin and vitamin A.

RICOTTA (PARTLY SKIMMED MILK)
A one-cup (246-gram) portion contains:

Calories: 340

Protein: 28 grams

Fat: 20 grams (12 grams saturated)

Carbohydrate: 13 grams

Cholesterol: 76 milligrams

Sodium: 307 milligrams

An excellent source of calcium, phosphorus, riboflavin, and vitamin A.

RICOTTA (WHOLE MILK)
A one-cup (246-gram) portion contains:

Calories: 428

Protein: 28 grams

Fat: 32 grams (20 grams saturated)

Carbohydrate: 7.5 grams

Cholesterol: 124 milligrams

Sodium: 207 milligrams

An excellent source of calcium, phosphorus, riboflavin, and vitamin A.

ROMANO
A one-ounce portion contains:

Calories: 110

Protein: 9 grams

Fat: 8 grams (figures for saturated fat not available, but would be similar to Parmesan)

Carbohydrate: 1 gram

Cholesterol: 29 milligrams

Sodium: 340 milligrams

An excellent source of calcium and phosphorus, and a good source of riboflavin and vitamin A.

ROQUEFORT
A one-ounce portion contains:

Calories: 105

Protein: 6 grams

Fat: 9 grams (5 grams saturated)

Carbohydrate: less than 1 gram

Cholesterol: 33 milligrams

Sodium: 513 milligrams

An excellent source of calcium, phosphorus, vitamin A, and riboflavin.

STILTON
Figures not available, but similar to Blue.

SWISS
A one-ounce portion contains:

Calories: 107

Protein: 8 grams

Fat: 8 grams (5 grams saturated)

Carbohydrate: 1 gram

Cholesterol: 26 milligrams

Sodium: 74 milligrams

An excellent source of calcium and phosphorus, and a good source of vitamin A and riboflavin.

TILSIT

A one-ounce portion contains:

Calories: 96	Carbohydrate: less than 1 gram
Protein: 7 grams	Cholesterol: 29 milligrams
Fat: 7 grams (5 grams saturated)	Sodium: 213 milligrams

An excellent source of calcium, phosphorus, and vitamin A, and a good source of riboflavin.

TRIPLE CRÈMES

A one-ounce portion would contain approximately 125 to 135 calories. Figures for the other nutrients are not available, but Triple Crèmes are high in fat and saturated fat as well as cholesterol, and low in most other nutrients. Sodium content figures are not available.

WHITE WENSLEYDALE

Figures not available, but similar to Cheddar.

Reprinted with permission from Completely Cheese, *David Kolatch, Editor, Jonathan David Publishers, Inc.*

TABLE 8

Nutritive Value of Major Protein-Containing Food Groups

Average Serving Portion	Total Protein gm	Essential Amino Acid Deficiencies	Essential Amino Acid Strengths
Seafood			
Catfish	18	complete	lysine
Mackerel	22	complete	lysine
Halibut	21	complete	lysine
Red snapper	21	complete	lysine
Shrimp	19	complete	lysine
Dairy Products			
Cottage cheese	17	complete	lysine
Milk	8	complete	lysine
Eggs	11	complete	lysine
Legumes: Beans, Peas, Lentils			
Soybeans	17	sulfur-containing	lysine
Peas	12	tryptophan and sulfur-containing	lysine
Lentils	13	tryptophan and sulfur-containing	lysine
Kidney Beans	12	tryptophan and sulfur-containing	lysine
Nuts and Seeds			
Peanuts	8	isoleucine and lysine	
Sesame seeds	5	isoleucine and lysine	
Walnuts	5	isoleucine and lysine	
Brazil nuts	4	isoleucine and lysine	
Grains and Cereals			
Wheat	8	isoleucine and lysine	
Rye	7	isoleucine and lysine	
Barley	6	isoleucine and lysine	
Oatmeal	4	isoleucine and lysine	
Rice	5	isoleucine and lysine	

TABLE 9

High Fiber Foods

	Fiber Content (gm/100 gm)
Apricots, dried	3.8
Blackberries, boysenberries	4.1
Bran flakes, raw	9.5
Carob powder	7.0
Coconut, fresh	4.0
Figs, dried	4.6
Kumquats, raw	3.7
Olives, salt-cured Greek	3.8
Pears, dried	6.2
Peppers, chili: dried red	26.2
Raspberries, raw black	5.1
Rice bran	11.5
Seaweed, raw kelp	6.8
Sesame seeds, dry whole	6.3
Sunflower seeds	3.8

Source: USDA Handbook No. 8 (1963)

TABLE 10

Dietary Fiber in Vegetables

	Total Dietary Fiber (gm/100 gm)
Leafy Vegetables	
Broccoli tops (boiled)	4.10
Brussels sprouts (boiled)	2.86
Cabbage (boiled)	2.83
Cauliflower (boiled)	1.80
Lettuce	1.53
Onions	2.10
Legumes	
Beans (baked)	7.27
Beans (boiled)	3.35
Peas (canned)	7.85
Root Vegetables	
Carrots (boiled)	3.70
Parsnips (raw)	4.90
Potato (raw)	3.51
Turnips (raw)	2.20

TABLE 11

Dietary Fiber in Fruits

	Total Dietary Fiber (gm/100 gm)
Apples	1.42
Bananas	1.75
Cherries	1.24
Grapefruit	0.44
Guavas	3.64
Mangos	1.00
Peaches	2.28
Pears	2.44
Plums	1.52
Rhubarb	1.78
Strawberries	2.12

TABLE 12

Dietary Fibers in Biscuits

	Total Dietary Fiber (gm/100 gm)
Crispbread, rye	11.73
Crispbread, wheat	4.83
Ginger biscuits	1.99
Matzo	3.85
Oatcakes	4.00
Semisweet	2.31
Wafers (filled)	1.62

TABLE 13

Dietary Fiber in Wheat Flours and Breads

	Total Dietary Fiber (gm/100 gm)
Flours	
White	3.15
Whole wheat	9.51
Bran	44.00
Breads	
White	2.72
Whole wheat	8.50

TABLE 14

Dietary Sources of Vitamin A Activity (preformed retinol)

Food	Range μg retinol equivalents/100 g)	
Halibut-liver oil	600,000–10,000,000	
Cod-liver oil	12,000–	20,000
Herring	27	
Salmon (canned)	24–	75
Sardine (canned)	40–	90
Butter	720–	1,200
Margarine (supplemented)	900	
Eggs	320	
Milk	20–	70
Cheese	300–	520
Beef	0–	15

TABLE 15

Dietary Sources of Vitamin A Activity (carotene)

Food*	Range (μg retinol equivalents/100 g)	
Red Palm Oil (dendê oil)	4,000–10,000	
Carrots	600–	1,500
Leafy Vegetables	8–	1,200
Tomatoes	110–	300
Apricots	70–	280
Bananas	10–	30
Sweet potatoes (red and yellow)	380–	770

*Figures calculated with assumption that 1 μg β-carotene is taken to have same biological value as 0.167 μg retinol.

TABLE 16

Dietary Sources of Vitamin C (Ascorbic Acid)

Food	Range (mg ascorbic acid/ 100 g edible portion)
Black Currants	90–300
Rose Hips	70–460
Fruits (citrus)	25– 60
Apples	5– 10
Pears	5– 10
Plums	5– 10
Strawberries	25– 60
Raspberries	25– 60
Bananas	10– 30
Pineapple	25
Guava	200
Mango	10– 50
Melon	1– 45
Papaya	30–120
Fruit (canned)	1– 25
Cabbages and Lettuce	10– 60
Broccoli and Brussels sprouts	70–100
Potato (raw)	10– 30
Potato (boiled)	10– 15
Sweet Potato	20– 30
Root Vegetables	10– 30
Milk	0– 1
Eggs	trace
Meat	trace

Ordinary cooking of vegetables may cause vitamin C losses of 50 to 75 percent.

TABLE 17

Dietary Sources of Folic Acid

Food	Folic Acid μg/100g
Liver	300
Oysters	250
Spinach	80
White Fish	50
Broccoli	50
Orange Juice	50
Brussels sprouts	30
Beans	30
Cabbage	20
Lettuce	20
Bread	20
Rice	10
Bananas	10
Eggs	8
Chicken	3
Milk	0.3

TABLE 18

Dietary Sources of Riboflavin

Food	Range (mg/100 g edible portion)
Wheat Bran	0.5
Wheat Germ	0.25
Beans	0.15–0.3
Lentils	0.1 –0.3
Peas	0.1 –0.3
Fish	0.2 –0.4
Eggs	0.3 –0.5
Cheese	0.3 –0.5
Milk	0.15
Green Leafy Vegetables	0.05–0.30
Maize	0.1
Nuts	0.2
Fruit (dried)	0.1
Wheat Flour	0.03–0.05
Fruit	0.01–0.10
Vegetables	0.05
Potatoes	0.09

TABLE 19

Dietary Sources of Thiamine

Food	mg/100 g
Yeast (brewer's)	6 –24
Bran (rice or wheat)	2 – 4
Whole Wheat	0.4
Beans	0.4
Lentils	0.4
Millet	0.4
Vegetables	0.02–0.20
Beef	0.07–0.30
Fish	0.01–0.10
Eggs	0.10–0.15

TABLE 20

Dietary Sources of Nicotinic Acid

Food	Range (mg/100 g edible portion)
Wheat Bran (outer portion)	25 –46
Wheat Germ	3.0 – 7.0
Millet	1.3 – 3.2
Rice	2.0 – 4.5
Wheat Flour	4.0 – 5.5
Fish	2.0 – 6.0
Oatmeal	0.9 – 1.3
Beans	1.5 – 3.0
Cashew Nuts	2.0
Fruit (dried)	1.0
Chocolate	1.0
Potato	1.0
Vegetables	0.2 – 1.5
Eggs	0.1
Milk	0.1
Cheese	0.03

TABLE 21

Calcium Content of Common Foods

Food	Range (mg/100 g)
Cheese (hard)	500–1200
Cheese (soft)	80– 725
Milk (cow's)	120
Milk (human)	20– 40
Nuts (shelled)	13– 250
Beans	40– 200
Root Vegetables	20– 100
Leafy Vegetables	25– 250
Eggs	50– 60
Whole Wheat	30– 40
White Flour	13– 20
Millet	20– 50
Fruit	3– 60
Fish	17– 32
Sardines	200– 400
Rice	4– 10
Potatoes	7– 10

TABLE 22

Iron Absorption According to Food Origin

	Range of Iron Content (mg)	Percent of Dose Absorbed
Food of Vegetable Origin		
Rice	2	0.8–1.2
Spinach	2	0.8–1.8
Black Beans	3–4	2.3–3.6
Corn	2–4	3.4–3.9
Lettuce	1–17	3.9–5.8
Wheat	2–4	4.8–6.0
Soybeans	3–4	6.5–7.8
Food of Animal Origin		
Fish Muscle	1–2	11–14
Hemoglobin	3–4	12–14
Veal Liver	3–4	12–18
Veal Muscle	3–4	17–20

TABLE 23

Iron Content of Common Foods

Food	Range (mg/100 g)
Liver	6.0–14.0
Corned Beef	3.0–11.0
Fish	0.5– 1.0
Eggs	2.0– 3.0
Legumes	2.0–14.0
Millet	4.0– 5.5
Oatmeal	4.0– 5.1
Whole Wheat Flour	3.0– 7.0
White Flour	0.7– 1.5
Chocolate	2.8– 4.4
Dried Fruit	9.2–11.3
Leafy Vegetables	0.4–18.0
Root Vegetables	0.3– 2.0
Nuts	1.0– 5.0

TABLE 24

Sodium Content of Common Foods

Food	meq/100 g	
High Content:		
Bread	15	−30
Vegetables (canned)	10	−25
Corned Beef	60	−75
Ham	85	
Bacon	35	−50
Sausage	30	−55
Fish (canned)	15	−45
Cream Cheese	5	−15
Hard Cheese (cheddar, etc.)	20	−65
Butter (salted)	40	−45
Butter (fresh)	10	−15
Margarine	15	
Moderate Content:		
Vegetables (raw)	0.1 − 6.0	
Corn Flour	2.3	
Fruit (dried)	1.4 − 3.4	
White Fish	2.6 − 4.4	
Egg (fresh)	6.0	
Milk	2.2	
Wine and Beer	0.1 − 1.7	
Low Content:		
Wheat Flour	0.04− 0.13	
Rice	0.09− 0.27	
Nuts (without shells)	0.04− 0.22	
Fruits (fresh)	0.04− 0.22	
Fruit Juices	0.02− 0.20	
Butter (unsalted)	0.22	
Prunes (dried)	0.22− 0.53	

Note: *Sodium content of food can be expressed as meq (milliequivalents), grams of sodium (Na,g/100 g), or grams of sodium chloride (NaCl,g/100 g). One meq Na is equivalent to 23 mg Na or 58.5 mg NaCl.*

TABLE 25

Approximate Daily Intake of Sodium According to Dietary Preferences (1 meq Na = 23 mg Na or 58.5 mg NaCl)

	Na (meq)	NaCl (g)
Normal diet	150	9.0
Restricted salt regime	100	6.0
Low sodium diet, moderate	50	3.0
Low sodium diet, strict	25	1.5

TABLE 26

Common Foods Which Are Good Dietary Sources of Potassium

Food	mg/100 g
Dried Fruit	700–1880
Fresh Fruit	120– 370
Fruit Juices	130– 225
Nuts	400– 900
Vegetables	100– 500
Fish	225– 425
Bread	110– 225
Rice	110
Eggs	150
Cheese	100– 200
Milk	150
Treacle	1500
Syrup	225

The following foods are poor sources of potassium: jams, honey, butter, cream, margarine, sugar, oil and tea.

TABLE 27

Nutritive Value of Whole Cereal Grains
(Values per 100g)

	Calories	Protein	Limiting Amino acid	Fat grams	Calcium mg	Iron mg	Thia-mine mg	Nico-tinic mg	Ribo-flavin mg
Wheat	334	12.2	lysine	2.3	30	3.5	0.40	4.0	0.17
Rice	357	7.5	lysine	1.8	15	2.8	0.25	4.0	0.12
Millet	343	10.1	lysine	3.3	30	6.2	0.40	3.5	0.12
Oats	385	13.0	lysine	7.5	60	3.8	0.50	1.3	0.14
Rye	319	11.0	lysine	1.9	50	3.5	0.27	1.2	0.10

Reprinted with permission from Human Nutrition and Dietetics, *Davidson et al., Churchill Livingstone, Edinburgh, London and New York, 1975.*

TABLE 28

Nutritive Value of Starchy Roots
Potato, sweet potato, yams, taro

	Range (per 100 gm)	Selected Value
Moisture, percent	65–85	75
Carbohydrate	210–520	330
Protein	10–25	18
Fat	1.5–2.5	2.0
Calcium	trace	0
Iron	10–30	20
Carotene*	0.5–2.0	0.8
Ascorbic acid	0	0
Thiamine	5–25	15
Riboflavin	0.05–0.10	0.0075
Nicotinic acid	0.03–0.08	0.05
	0.5–1.5	1.0

Reprinted with permission from Human Nutrition and Dietetics, *Davidson et al., Churchill Livingstone, New York, 1975.*
Sweet potato contains 300 μg/100 gm.

TABLE 29

Nutritive Value of Legumes
Peas, beans, and lentils

	Range (per 100 gm)	Selected Value
Moisture, percent	8–15	12
Calories	320–350	340
Carbohydrate*	55–65	60
Protein,* gm	17–25	20
Fat, gm	1–5	2
Calcium, mg	100–200	150
Iron, mg	2–8	6
Carotene, μg	12–120	60
Ascorbic acid, mg†	0	0
Thiamine, mg	0.2–0.6	0.4
Riboflavin, mg	0.1–0.3	0.2
Nicotinic acid, mg	1.5–3.0	2

Reprinted with permission from Human Nutrition and Dietetics, *Davidson et al., Churchill Livingstone, New York, 1975.*
Soybean contains about 20 gm carbohydrate/100 gm and 38 gm protein/100 gm.
†When sprouted 10–15 mg ascorbic acid/100 gm.

TABLE 30

Nutrient Values of Nuts
(per 100 gms)

Nut	Calories	Protein	Fat	Carbohydrate
Almonds, dry	597	18	54	19
Brazil nuts, shelled	646	14	65	11
Cashews, roasted	578	18	48	27
Chestnuts	191	2	1	41
Peanuts	559	26	44	23
Pecans, raw	696	9	73	13
Walnuts, English	654	15	64	15

TABLE 31

Nutritive Value of (a) Green Leafy Vegetables
Cabbage, Brussels sprouts, lettuce,
spinach, parsley, coriander, fenugreek

	Range (per 100 gm)	Selected Value
Moisture, percent	75–80	75
Calories	40–200	80
Carbohydrate, gm	1–12	3
Protein, gm	1–4	2
Fat, gm	Trace	0
Calcium, mg	25–500	100
Iron, mg	1–25	5
Carotene, µg	600–6000	1800
Ascorbic acid, mg	10–200	50
Thiamine, mg	0.03–0.08	0.05
Riboflavin, mg	0.03–0.25	0.08
Nicotinic acid, mg	0.2–1.0	0.05
Folic acid, µg	20–100	50

Reprinted with permission from Human Nutrition and Dietetics, *Davidson et al., Churchill Livingstone, New York, 1975.*

TABLE 32

Nutritive Value of Vegetables (b) Others
Onions, turnips, cauliflower, leeks, eggplant, pumpkins, gourds, etc.

	Range (per 100 gm)	Selected Value
Moisture, percent	70–90	80
Calories	40–200	100
Carbohydrate, gm	10–50	25
Protein, gm	0.5–2.5	1.5
Fat, gm	Trace	0
Calcium, mg	20–100	65
Iron, mg	0.5–4.0	
Carotene, µg	0–180	90
Ascorbic acid, mg	5–100	25
Thiamine, mg	0.05–0.20	0.07
Riboflavin, mg	0.01–0.20	0.05
Nicotinic acid, mg	0.1–1.0	0.05
Folic acid, µg	2–30	10

Reprinted with permission from Human Nutrition and Dietetics, *Davidson et al., Churchill Livingstone, New York, 1975.*

TABLE 33

Nutritive Value of Fruit
Apple, raspberry, orange, peach, mango, tomato, papaya, banana

	Range (per 100 gm)	Selected Value
Moisture, percent	75–90	85
Calories	20–80	50
Carbohydrate, gm	2–20	10
Protein, gm	0.2–2.0	0.5
Fat, gm	0–1	0.5
Calcium, mg	5–40	20
Iron, mg	0.1–1.0	0.3
β-carotene,* µg	0–1800	240
Ascorbic acid	0–300	30
Thiamine, mg	0–0.1	0.04
Riboflavin, mg	0–0.1	0.05
Nicotinic acid, mg	0.2–1.0	0.4

Reprinted with permission from Human Nutrition and Dietetics, *Davidson et al., Churchill Livingstone, New York, 1975.*
*β-carotene content, µg/100 gm: Mango, 600–1500; Tomato, 600–1800; Orange, 90–120.

TABLE 34

Fat and Calorie Content of Fish and Seafood
(per 100 gms)

	Calories	Percent Fat
Bluefish, baked	155	4.2
Clams, raw	81	1.4
Cod, raw	74	.4
Cod, dried	375	2.8
Crabs	104	2.9
Flounder, raw	68	.5
Haddock	158	5.5
Halibut	182	7.8
Herring, raw	191	12.5
Herring, kippered	211	12.9
Lobster	92	1.3
Mackerel	182	11.1
Oysters, raw	84	2.1
Salmon	223	16.5
Sardines	214	11.0
Scallops, raw	78	.1
Shrimp	127	1.4
Tuna fish	198	8.2

TABLE 35

Analyses of Milk from Various Species
(gm/100 ml)

	Carbohydrate	Protein	Fat	Energy (Calories/ 100 ml)
Human	6.8	1.5	4.0	68
Cow	5.0	3.5	3.5	66
Buffalo	4.5	4.3	7.5	103
Goat	4.5	3.7	4.8	76

Reprinted with permission from Human Nutrition and Dietetics, *Davidson et al., Churchill Livingstone; Edinburgh, London and New York, 1975.*

TABLE 36

Diseases of Malnutrition

Principal Disease Conditions	Nutrient Imbalances
Deficiencies	
Underweight	Calorie deficit
Protein-calorie malnutrition	
Kwashiorkor	Principally protein lack
Marasmus	Calorie-protein lack
Dental caries	Calcium, phosphorus, fluorine, vitamins A and D
Anemia, microcytic, hypochromic	Iron
Macrocytic in infancy, pregnancy, malabsorption	Folacin
Pernicious—absorptive defect	Vitamin B_{12}
Goiter, endemic	Iodine
Osteoporosis	Possibly calcium, vitamin D; endocrine factors
Osteomalacia	Vitamin D, calcium, phosphorus
Scurvy; hemorrhagic tendency; inflamed gums; loose teeth	Ascorbic acid
Beriberi; polyneuritis; circulatory failure; emaciation; edema	Thiamin
Pellagra; glossitis; dermatitis; diarrhea; nervous degeneration; dementia	Niacin
Cheilosis; scaling of skin, cracking of lips; light sensitivity; increased vascularization of eyes	Riboflavin
Growth failure, anemia, convulsions in infants	Vitamin B_6
Night blindness; keratomalacia; xerophthalmia; blindness	Vitamin A
Rickets; bone deformities	Vitamin D
Hemorrhagic tendency in infants	Vitamin K
Excesses	
Obesity	Calorie excess
Toxicity; changes in skin, hair, bones, liver	Vitamin A excess
Hypercalcemia, calcification of soft tissues	Vitamin D excess
Dental caries	Sucrose
Atherosclerosis; cardiovascular and cerebrovascular disease*	Too much saturated fat, cholesterol; simple sugars
Hypertension*	Calorie excess; too much salt
Diverticulosis; irritable colon*	Excessively refined diets
Cancer of the colon*	Excessively refined diets; excess of fat leading to excess metabolites of sterols and bile acids

Reprinted with permission from Summary of Diseases of Malnutrition, *Corinne H. Robinson and Marilyn R. Lawler, Macmillan Publishing Co., Inc., 1977 (15th edition).*
In these diseases diet is only one of a number of risk factors that must be considered; more research is needed to fully establish the role of diet.

TABLE 37

Average Nutrient Values Per Dish (by country)							
Name of Country	Calories	CHO gms.	Protein gms.	Total Fat gms.	Saturated Fat gms.	Cholesterol mg.	Dietary Fiber gms.
Poland	134	15 (45%)	5 (15%)	6 (40%)	2 (13%)	74	.5
Russia	151	15 (40%)	7 (19%)	7 (41%)	2 (12%)	43	.5
India	184	22 (48%)	6 (13%)	8 (39%)	2 (9%)	9	.8
Scandinavia	184	23 (50%)	5 (11%)	8 (39%)	3 (15%)	23	.6
Hungary	198	19 (38%)	8 (16%)	10 (46%)	3 (14%)	45	.5
China	206	13 (25%)	7 (14%)	14 (61%)	3 (13%)	34	1.0
United States	220	20 (36%)	8 (15%)	12 (49%)	3 (12%)	55	.9
Lebanon	225	28 (50%)	8 (14%)	9 (36%)	1 (4%)	3	1.3
France	239	16 (27%)	10 (17%)	15 (56%)	(19%)	74	.6
Italy	279	23 (33%)	13 (19%)	15 (48%)	4 (13%)	61	
Brazil	281	23 (33%)	9 (13%)	17 (54%)	6 (19%)	67	1.0
Africa	284	29 (41%)	15 (21%)	12 (38%)	2 (6%)	24	1.4
Mexico	286	27 (38%)	13 (18%)	14 (44%)	4 (13%)	54	1.3
Greece	303	24 (32%)	9 (12%)	19 (56%)	4 (12%)	57	.9
Chile-Peru	326	27 (33%)	14 (17%)	18 (50%)	6 (17%)	66	1.0

SUBSTITUTIONS FOR COMMON FOODS

Food	Amount	Common Substitution
Arrowroot (as thickener)	1 tablespoon	2½ tablespoons all-purpose flour
	2 teaspoons	1 tablespoon cornstarch
Baking powder	1 teaspoon	¼ teaspoon baking soda plus ½ cup yogurt, soured milk or buttermilk
	1 teaspoon	¼ teaspoon baking soda plus ⅝ teaspoon cream of tartar
Baking powder, double acting	¾ teaspoon	1 teaspoon tartrate or phosphate baking powder
Butter	1 cup	14 tablespoons shortening plus ½ teaspoon salt
Buttermilk or sour milk	1 cup	1 cup yogurt
Catsup	½ cup	½ cup tomato sauce plus 2 teaspoons brown sugar or honey plus 1 tablespoon vinegar plus ⅛ teaspoon allspice
Chocolate, semi-sweet	1⅔ ounces	1 ounce unsweetened chocolate plus 4 teaspoons sugar
	4 squares	½ cup chocolate chips
Chocolate, unsweetened	1 ounce	3 tablespoons cocoa plus 1–3 teaspoons fat (use less for Dutch cocoa) or 3 tablespoons carob powder plus 2 tablespoons water
Coffee (for cooking)	1 cup strongly brewed	2 tablespoons instant coffee plus 1 cup boiling water
Cornstarch (as thickener)	1 tablespoon	2 tablespoons all-purpose flour; 1 tablespoon potato starch; or 4 teaspoons quick-cooking oats
Corn syrup	1 cup	1 cup sugar plus ¼ cup liquid called for in recipe
	1 cup (dark syrup)	½ cup honey plus ¼ cup molassses plus ¼ cup maple syrup
	1 cup (light syrup)	1 cup mild-flavored honey
Coconut milk	1 cup	1 cup whole milk
Coconut cream	1 cup	1 cup light cream
Cream, light	1 cup	3 tablespoons butter plus ⅞ cup milk
Cream, heavy (not to be whipped)	1 cup	⅓ cup butter plus ¾ cup milk
Cream, sour (for baking)	1 cup	3 tablespoons butter plus ⅞ cup buttermilk or yogurt
Cream, sour (for dips)	1 cup	1 cup cottage cheese creamed with ¼ cup yogurt or buttermilk

Food	Amount	Common Substitution
Cream sauce (for casseroles only)	1½ cups	1 can condensed cream-style soup plus ¼ cup liquid
Egg yolks (as thickener)	2 yolks	1 whole egg
Flour, all-purpose	1 cup	1⅛ cups cake flour; ½ cup unbleached white flour plus ½ cup whole wheat flour; ⅝ cup potato flour; ⅞ cup cornmeal; 1 cup rye flour; or ¹³⁄₁₆ cup gluten flour
Flour, graham or whole wheat	1 cup (fine)	1 cup all-purpose or unbleached white flour
	1 cup (coarse)	⅞ cup all-purpose or unbleached white flour
Flour, pastry	1 cup	⅞ cup whole wheat pastry flour
Flour, potato (as thickener)	1½ teaspoons	1 tablespoon all-purpose or unbleached white flour
Flour, self-rising	1 cup	1 cup all-purpose or unbleached white flour plus 1¼ teaspoons baking powder plus ⅛ teaspoon salt
Flour, unbleached white	1 cup	1 cup whole wheat pastry flour or ⅞ cup wheat flour. Reduce oil by 1 tablespoon per cup of wheat flour. Increase liquid by 1–2 tablespoons per cup flour. Increase baking powder by ½ teaspoon or, if recipe calls for baking soda, add ½ teaspoon cream of tartar.
Lemon juice	2 teaspoons	1 teaspoon vinegar
Milk (in baking)	1 cup	1 cup fruit juice; ½ cup evaporated milk plus ½ cup water; or 1 cup reconstituted non-fat dry milk plus 2 teaspoons butter
Milk, skim	1 cup	⅓ cup instant non-fat dry milk plus ¾ cup cold water
Milk, whole	1 quart	1 quart skim milk plus 3 tablespoons cream
Mushrooms, fresh	⅓ pound	4 ounces canned and drained button mushrooms
Mushrooms, dried	3 ounces	1 pound fresh mushrooms
Mustard	1 tablespoon prepared	1 teaspoon dried mustard
Shortening, lard or butter	1 cup (solid)	⅞ cup vegetable or nut oil
	1 cup (melted)	1 cup vegetable or nut oil
	1 pound	1 pound safflower shortening
Sugar, castor	1 tablespoon	1 tablespoon superfine sugar

Food	Amount	Common Substitution
Sugar, granulated	1 teaspoon	¼ grain saccharin or ⅛ teaspoon non-caloric sweetener
	1 cup	¾ cup honey (decrease liquid by ¼ cup or, if no liquid in recipe, add ¼ cup flour)
	1 cup	½–¾ cup molasses plus ¼–½ cup raw sugar (decrease liquid by ¼ cup for each cup molasses; omit baking powder and add ½ teaspoon baking soda for each cup)
	1 cup	1 cup brown sugar (packed) or raw turbinado sugar
Sugar, maple	½ cup	1 cup maple syrup
	2 tablespoons (grated and packed)	2 tablespoons white granulated sugar
Tapioca, quick-cooking (as thickener)	1½–2 tablespoons	4 tablespoons pearl tapioca, soaked
	1 teaspoon	1 tablespoon all-purpose flour
Tomato paste	1 tablespoon	1 tablespoon catsup
Tomato puree	1 cup	½ cup tomato paste plus ½ cup water
Tomato sauce	2 cups	¾ cup tomato paste plus 1 cup water plus seasonings
Wine (for marinading)	½ cup	¼ cup vinegar plus ¼ cup water plus 1 tablespoon honey or sugar
Yeast	1 cake (compressed)	1 tablespoon jarred or 1 package active dry yeast

TABLE OF EQUIVALENT WEIGHTS AND MEASURES

Common Baking Ingredients

Food	*Amount*	*Equivalent Measurement*
Baking Soda	1 ounce	2½ tablespoons
Breadcrumbs	⅓ cup fine crumbs	1 slice toast or dried bread
	1 slice fresh bread	⅔ cup lightly packed soft crumbs
	1 cup	3¼ ounces or 90 grams
Chocolate, semi-sweet	1 square	1 ounce
	1 ounce	1 tablespoon melted
	6-ounce package chocolate bits	1 cup chocolate bits
Chocolate, unsweetened	1 square	1 ounce or 4 tablespoons grated
Cocoa	1 pound	4 cups
Cornstarch	1 tablespoon	⅓ ounce or 10 grams
Flour, all-purpose (sifted)	1 tablespoon	¼ ounce or 7½ grams
	4 tablespoons (¼ cup)	1¼ ounces or 35 grams
	5 tablespoons (⅓ cup)	1½ ounces or 50 grams
	½ cup (8 tablespoons)	2½ ounces or 70 grams
	⅔ cup (10½ tablespoons)	3¼ ounces or 100 grams
	¾ cup (12 tablespoons)	3½ ounces or 105 grams
	1 cup	5 ounces or 140 grams
	1 pound (3½ cups)	16 ounces or 454 grams
	2 pounds (7 cups)	1,000 grams
Graham cracker crumbs	1⅓ cups	16 to 18 whole crackers (enough for one 9-inch pie shell)
Honey, Molasses or Corn Syrup	1 cup	12 ounces
	1⅓ cups	1 pound
Salt	1 teaspoon	5 grams
	1 tablespoon	15 grams
Spices (ground)	1 teaspoon	1/12 ounce or ⅔ gram
	2 tablespoons	½ ounce or 15 grams
Sugar, brown	1 tablespoon	⅓ ounce or 10 grams
	½ cup	2⅔ ounces or 80 grams
	1 cup	5⅓ ounces or 160 grams
Sugar, confectioner's	¼ cup	1⅛ ounce or 35 grams
	½ cup	2¼ ounces (scant) or 70 grams
	1 cup	4½ ounces (scant) or 140 grams
	1 pound	3½ cups

	Food	Amount	Equivalent Measurement
Common Baking Ingredients *(continued)*	Sugar, granulated	1 teaspoon	⅙ ounce or 5 grams
		1 tablespoon	½ ounce or 15 grams
		¼ cup	1¾ ounces or 50 grams
		⅓ cup	2¼ ounces or 65 grams
		½ cup	3¼ ounces or 100 grams
		⅔ cup	4½ ounces or 125 grams
		¾ cup	5 ounces or 145 grams
		1 cup	7 ounces or 200 grams
		1 pound	2½ cups or 454 grams
		5 pounds	11¼ cups
	Sugar, powdered (superfine)	2⅓ cups	1 pound
Dairy Products	Cheese, Cheddar	4 ounces (¼ pound)	1 cup grated
		1 pound	4 cups grated
	Cheese, cottage	2 cups	1 pound
	Cheese, cream (or Neufchâtel)	6 ounces	12 tablespoons or ¾ cup
		½ pound	1 cup
	Cheese, hard	1 pound	Approximately 5½ cups when freshly grated
	Cheese, Roquefort	4 ounces	1 cup crumbled
	Cream, light (18–20% fat)	½ pint	1 cup
	Cream, light whipping (30–36% fat)	½ pint	1 cup
	Cream, half & half (10–12% fat)	1 pint	2 cups
	Cream, heavy whipping (36–40% fat)	½ pint	1 cup or 8⅓ ounces
		1 cup	2 cups whipped
	Eggs, large	2 cups	1 pound
		5 whole	1 cup
		8–9 whites	1 cup
		12 yolks	1 cup
	Eggs, medium	1 whole	2 ounces
		9 whole	1 pound
	Milk, condensed	1 (15-ounce) can	1⅓ cups
	Milk, dry non-fat	1 pound	4 cups or 3½–4½ quarts milk
	Milk, evaporated	1 (14-ounce) can	1¾ cups

Food	Amount	Equivalent Measurement
Chicken, breast (whole)	1 large (raw)	2 cups cooked and diced
Chicken, whole	3½ pounds (raw & cleaned)	3 cups cooked and diced
Chicken, Duck or Turkey	1 pound	1 serving
Fish	½ pound	1 serving
Fish fillet	1 pound	3 servings

(left margin: Fish and Fowl)

Food	Amount	Equivalent Measurement
Apples, fresh	1 pound	3 cups pared and diced or sliced
	2 pounds	Enough for one 9-inch pie
Apples, dried	1 pound	4⅓ cups (approximately)
Apricots, fresh	5½ pounds	1 pound dried
Apricots, dried	1 pound	3 cups uncooked or 5 cups cooked
Avocados	1 medium	2 servings when halved
Bananas	1 pound (3–5 medium)	2 cups sliced or 1¾ cups mashed
Berries	1 quart	4 servings
	4 to 5 cups	Enough for one 9-inch pie
Candied fruit	7 ounces	1 cup
Candied peel	5 ounces	1 cup
Cherries	1 pound (pitted)	2 cups or enough for one 9-inch pie
Coconut	3½ ounces (flaked)	1⅓ cups
	¼ pound (dried & grated)	1 cup packed
	1 pound (shredded)	4 cups sweetened or 5 cups unsweetened
Cranberries	1 quart	6–7 cups
	1 pound	3–3½ cups sauce
Currants, dried	5 ounces	1 cup
	1 pound	3¼ cups
Dates	8 ounces (pitted)	1¼ cups chopped or ¼ pound
	1 pound	60 dates (approximately)
Figs	1 pound	2⅔ cups chopped or 4½ cups cooked
Grapefruit	1 medium	1⅓ cups pulp or ⅔ cup juice
Lemons	1 medium	3–4 tablespoons juice plus 2 teaspoons rind
Limes	1 medium	1½ tablespoons juice
	1 pound (8 medium)	1 cup juice

(left margin: Fruit (fresh and dried))

Food	Amount	Equivalent Measurement
Mangoes	4 medium	1 quart pulp
Nectarines	1 pound	4 to 5 average size
Oranges	1 medium	5–6 tablespoons juice plus 2–3 tablespoons rind
	4 medium Valencias	1 cup juice (approximately)
Peaches	1 pound (4 medium)	2 cups sliced
	5 cups sliced	Enough for one 9-inch pie
Pears	1 pound (4 medium)	2 cups sliced
Pineapple	1 medium	2½–3 cups cubed or 4 to 6 servings
Plantains	2 large	4 to 6 servings
Plums	1 pound (10–15 small)	2¼ cups halved and pitted
Prunes	1 pound	2½ cups chopped or 4½ cups pitted and cooked
Raisins	1 pound	3¼ cups seeded raisins or 2¾ unseeded raisins
Strawberries	1 quart (3½–4 cups whole)	2 cups pureed or 4 servings
Quince	1 pound (3 medium)	1½ cups chopped

Fruit (fresh and dried) (continued)

Food	Amount	Equivalent Measurement
Beans, kidney or lima, dry	1 pound	2½ cups uncooked or 6 cups cooked
Beans, navy, dry	1 pound	2 cups uncooked or 5 cups cooked
Cornmeal	1 pound (3 cups)	12 cups cooked
Lentils	1 pound	2¼ cups uncooked or 5 cups cooked
Macaroni	1 pound	4–5 cups uncooked or 10 cups cooked
Noodles (one-inch pieces)	1 cup uncooked	1½ cups cooked (approximately)
Rice, brown	1 cup	1 cup white rice
	1 pound	2 cups
Rice, white	1 pound (uncooked)	8 cups cooked (approximately)
Spaghetti (12-inch pieces)	1 pound (uncooked)	6½ cups cooked (approximately)
Split peas	1 pound (2 cups)	5 cups cooked
Quick cooking oats	1 pound (5 cups uncooked)	10 cups cooked
	1 cup uncooked	1¾ cups cooked

Noodles, Legumes and Grains

Food	Amount	Equivalent Measurement
Almonds	1 oz. (blanched & slivered)	¼ cup
	¾ cup	4 ounces ground and lightly packed
	1 cup	6 ounces whole or ¼ pound shelled
	1 pound (shelled)	¼ pound whole nutmeats or 2⅔ cups ground
Almond paste	1 pound	2⅛ cups
Brazil nuts	2 pounds (in shell)	1 pound shelled or 3 cups (approximately)
Chestnuts	1 pound (in shell)	⅔ cup shelled (30–40 whole) or 2 cups puree
	1 pound (shelled)	2½ cups peeled or 3 servings
Filberts (hazelnuts)	2½ pounds (in shell)	1 pound shelled nuts or 3½ cups nutmeats
Macadamia nuts	6½ ounces	1½ cups chopped (approximately)
Nuts	¼ pound ground	1 cup or 3¾ ounces
Peanuts	1 pound (in shell)	⅔ pound shelled
	1 pound (shelled)	3 cups
Peanut butter	1 pound	1¾ cups
Pecans	3½ ounces	1 cup
	12 halves	3 tablespoons chopped (scant)
	2½ pounds (in shell)	1 pound shelled or 4½ cups (approximately)
Pistachios	1 pound (shelled)	3⅔ cups
Walnuts, black	5½ pounds (in shell)	1 pound shelled or 3 cups (approximately)
Walnuts, English	2–2½ pounds (in shell)	1 pound shelled or 4½ cups
Butter (or Margarine)	1 tablespoon	1 ounce
	1 stick	¼ pound or ½ cup or 8 tablespoons
	½ cup	⅜ cup clarified
	1 cup	¾ cup chicken fat
	2 cups	1 pound
Oil, vegetable or nut	1 cup	7½ ounces
	2 cups	1 pound

Nuts and Nut Butters

Fats and Oils

Vegetables

Food	Amount	Equivalent Measurement
Asparagus	1 pound	2 servings
Bean sprouts	1 pound	4 cups raw or 2 cups cooked
Beets	1 pound (4 medium)	2 cups diced and cooked or 3 to 4 servings
Bok-Choi	1 medium head	4 servings
Broccoli	2 pounds	4 servings
Brussels sprouts	1 pound	3 cups cooked or 4 servings
Cabbage	1 pound 2 small heads (cooked)	4 cups grated 4 to 6 servings
Carrots	½ pound 1 pound (7–8 medium)	1½ cups shredded 2½ cups diced or 3 servings
Cauliflower	1 pound	1½ cups cooked or 3 servings
Celery	1 rib	¾ cup diced (approximately)
Celeriac (celery root)	1½–2 pounds	4 servings
Chard	1 pound (cooked)	2 servings
Corn on cob	2 ears	1 cup kernels (approximately)
Cucumber	2 medium	4 servings
Eggplant	1½ pounds	2½ cups diced and cooked or 4 servings
Endive	2 cups loosely packed 1 Belgian endive	1 serving 2 servings
Fava beans, fresh	5 pounds (in shell)	4 servings when shelled
Fennel, fresh	1 large bunch	4 to 6 servings
Garlic	1 bulb	8–20 cloves
Greens, salad	6–8 cups loosely packed	4 servings
Jerusalem artichokes	1–1½ pounds	4 servings
Kale	1 pound	2 servings
Kohlrabi	1 pound	4 servings
Lima beans, fresh	1 pound (in shell) 3 pounds shelled	1¼ cups shelled 4 servings
Mushrooms	1 pound 1 pound 1 pound	4–5 cups sliced 2 cups cooked or 3 to 4 servings 36–40 small; 25–36 medium-sized; or 15 large
Mustard greens	2 pounds	4 servings

Food	Amount	Equivalent Measurement
Okra	1 pound	4 servings
Onions, yellow	1 pound (4–5 medium)	2½ cups sliced or chopped
	1 medium	½ cup chopped
Parsnips	1½–2 pounds	4 servings
Peas, fresh	1 pound small (in shell)	1 cup shelled or 2 servings
	1 pound large (in shell)	1½ cups shelled
Peas, snow	1 pound	4 servings
Peppers, bell	1 pound (4–7 medium)	4 cups chopped
Potatoes, white or red	1 medium	1 serving
	1 pound (4 medium)	2½ cups diced and cooked or 1½–2 cups mashed
Potatoes, new	2 pounds	4 servings
Pumpkin	1¼ pounds	1 cup cooked and mashed (approximately)
Rhubarb	1 pound (3–4 stalks)	2 cups cut and cooked
	4 cups	Enough to fill one 9-inch pie shell
Shallots	1 (½-ounce size)	1 tablespoon minced
Snap beans	1 pound	3 cups raw or 2½ cups cooked
	1 pound	4 servings
Spinach	1 pound	4 cups raw or 1½ cups cooked
	1 pound	4 servings
Squash, summer	2 pounds	4 cups sliced (raw) or 2 cups cooked and mashed
	2 pounds	4 servings
Squash, spaghetti	3 pounds	4 servings
Squash, winter	2 pounds	2 cups cooked and mashed or 4 servings
Sweet potatoes or yams	1 pound (3 medium)	1½–2 cups cooked and mashed
Tomatoes	1 pound (2–5 medium)	1½ cups peeled and seeded or 1 cup pulp
	1 pound	2 to 4 servings
Turnips	1 pound (3–4 medium)	2 cups cooked or 3 to 4 servings

Vegetables (continued)

STANDARD MEASUREMENTS

A pinch = ⅛ teaspoon or less
1 teaspoon = ⅓ tablespoon
1 tablespoon = 3 teaspoons
2 tablespoons = 1 fluid ounce
1 jigger = 1½ fluid ounces or 3 tablespoons
4 tablespoons = ¼ cup or 2 ounces
5⅓ tablespoons = ⅓ cup or 2⅔ ounces
6 tablespoons = 3 ounces
8 tablespoons = ½ cup or 4 ounces
12 tablespoons = ¾ cup or 6 ounces
16 tablespoons = 1 cup or 8 ounces
⅜ cup = ¼ cup plus 2 tablespoons
⅝ cup = ½ cup plus 2 tablespoons
⅞ cup = ¾ cup plus 2 tablespoons
1 cup = ½ pint or 8 ounces
2 cups = 1 pint or 16 ounces
16 ounces = 1 pound
1 gill, liquid = ½ cup or 4 fluid ounces
1 pint, liquid = 4 gills or 16 fluid ounces
1 quart, liquid = 2 pints or 4 cups
1 gallon, liquid = 4 quarts
8 quarts = 1 peck, such as apples, pears, etc.
4 pecks = 1 bushel

METRIC CONVERSION CHART

U.S. Metric Fluid Volume

	Fluid Drams	Tea-spoons	Table-spoons	Fluid Ounces	¼ Cups	Gills ½ Cups	Cups	Fluid Pints	Fluid Quarts	Gallons	Milli-liters	Liters
1 Fluid Dram	1	¾	¼	⅛ .125	¹⁄₁₆ .0625	.03125	.0156	.0078	.0039	¹⁄₁₀₂₄	3.70	.0037
1 Tea-spoon	1⅓	1	⅓	⅙	¹⁄₁₂	¹⁄₂₄	¹⁄₄₈	¹⁄₉₆	¹⁄₁₉₂	¹⁄₇₆₈	5	.005
1 Table-spoon	4	3	1	½	¼	⅛	¹⁄₁₆	¹⁄₃₂	¹⁄₆₄	¹⁄₂₅₆	15	.015
1 Fluid Ounce	8	6	2	1	½	¼	⅛	¹⁄₁₆	¹⁄₃₂	¹⁄₁₂₈	29.56	.030
¼ Cup	16	12	4	2	1	½	¼	⅛	¹⁄₁₆	¹⁄₆₄	59.125	.059
1 Gill ½ Cup	32	24	8	4	2	1	½	¼	⅛	¹⁄₃₂	118.25	.118
1 Cup	64	48	16	8	4	2	1	½	¼	¹⁄₁₆	236	.236
1 Fluid Pint	128	96	32	16	8	4	2	1	½	⅛	473	.473
1 Fluid Quart	256	192	64	32	16	8	4	2	1	¼	946	.946
1 Gallon	1024	768	256	128	64	32	16	8	4	1	3785.4	3.785
1 Milli-liter	.270	.203 or ⅕	.068	.034	.017	.008	.004	.002	.001	.0003	1	.001 or ¹⁄₁₀₀₀
1 Liter	270.5	203.04	67.68	33.814	16.906	8.453	4.227	2.113	1.057	.264	1000	1

U.S. Metric Mass (Weight)

	Grains	Drams	Ounces	Pounds	Milligrams	Grams	Kilograms
1 Grain	1	.004	.002	¹⁄₇₀₀₀	64.7	.064	.0006
1 Dram	27.34	1	¹⁄₁₆	¹⁄₂₅₆	1770	1.77	.002
1 Ounce	437.5	16	1	¹⁄₁₆	2835	28.35	.028
1 Pound	7000	256	16	1	"Lots"	454	.454
1 Milligram	.015	.0006	1/29,000	1/"Lots"	.1	.001	.000001

SOURCE REFERENCES
FOR NUTRITIONAL ESSENTIALS

Albanese, Anthony, A. *Nutrition for the Elderly*, Current Topics in Nutrition and Disease, Volume 3. Alan R. Liss, New York, 1980.

Cleave, T. L. *The Saccharine Disease*. John Wright and Sons Ltd., Bristol, 1974.

Davidson, Stanley. *Human Nutrition and Dietetics*. Churchill Livingstone, Edinburgh, London, and New York, 1975.

Kolatch, David. *Completely Cheese*. Jonathan David Publishers, Inc., Middle Village, New York, 1979.

Lappe, Francis Moore. *Diet for a Small Planet*. 2nd ed. New York, Ballantine, 1975.

Petersdorf, Robert G. et al. *Harrison's Principles of Internal Medicine*. Ninth edition. McGraw Hill, New York, 1981.

Robertson, Laurel et al., *Laurel's Kitchen*. Bantam, New York, 1978.

Robinson, Corrine H. et al. *Normal and Therapeutic Nutrition*. Macmillan Publishing Co., Inc., New York, 1977.

Rosenthal, Sylvia (ed.). *Fresh Food*. E. P. Dutton, New York, 1978.

Santos, Walter (ed.). *Food and Nutrition Policies and Programs*. Plenum Press, New York, 1980.

Schneider et al. *Nutritional Support of Medical Practice*. Harper and Row Publishers, Inc., New York, 1976.

U.S. Department of Agriculture. *Cheeses of the World*. Dover Publications, Inc., New York, 1972.

Watt, Bernice K. et al. *Composition of foods: Raw, processed, prepared*. U.S. Govt. Printing Office, Washington, D.C., 1964.

SOURCE REFERENCES FOR CULINARY
AND SEASONING ESSENTIALS

Andrade, Margarette de. *Brazilian Cookery: Traditional and Modern.* A Casa Do Livro Eldorado, Rio de Janeiro, Brazil, 1978.

Blue Goose, Inc. *The Buying Guide for Fresh Fruit, Vegetables, Herbs and Nuts.* Blue Goose. 6th ed., 1976.

Chen, Joyce. *The Joyce Chen Cook Book.* J. B. Lippincott Co., New York, 1962.

Child, Julia. *The French Chef.* Alfred A. Knopf, New York, 1968.

Claiborne, Craig. *The New York Times Cook Book.* Harper & Row, New York, 1961.

Culinary Arts Institute. *Polish Cookbook.* Consolidated Book Publishers, Chicago, Illinois, 1976.

David, Elizabeth. *French Provincial Cooking.* Harper & Row, New York, 1962; Penguin Handbooks, Baltimore, 1964.

David, Elizabeth. *Italian Food.* Alfred A. Knopf, New York, 1958; Penguin Handbooks, Baltimore, revised edition, 1969.

Field, Michael. *All Manner of Food.* Alfred A. Knopf, New York, 1970.

Friedlander, Barbara, and Ira Friedlander. *The Vegetable, Fruit & Nut Book.* Today Press/Grosset & Dunlap, New York, 1974.

Goldbeck, Nikki and David Goldbeck. *The Supermarket Handbook: Access to Whole Foods.* Harper & Row, New York, 1973.

Hawkes, Alex C. *Cooking with Vegetables.* Simon & Schuster, New York, 1968.

Hazelton, Nika. *The Art of Scandinavian Cooking.* Macmillan Co., New York, 1965.

Humphry, Sylvia Windle. *Spices, Seasonings and Herbs.* Macmillan Co., New York, 1965.

Jaffrey, Madhur. *An Invitation to Indian Cooking.* Alfred A. Knopf, New York; Random House, New York, 1975.

Jones, Evans. *The World of Cheese*. Alfred A. Knopf, New York, 1976.

Kamman, Madeleine. *The Making Of A Cook*. Weathervane Books, New York, 1971.

Kennedy, Diana. *The Cuisines of Mexico*. Harper & Row, New York, 1972.

Kuo, Irene. *The Key to Chinese Cooking*. Alfred A. Knopf, New York, 1977.

Langseth-Christensen, Lillian and Carol Sturm Smith. *The Complete Kitchen Guide*. Grosset & Dunlap, New York, 1968.

Leonard, Jonathan Norton. *Latin American Cooking*. Time-Life Books, New York, 1968.

McCully, Helen. *Nobody Ever Tells You These Things*. Holt, Reinhart & Winston, New York, 1967.

Nickles, Harry G. and the Editors of Time-Life Books. *Middle East Cooking*. Time-Life Books, New York, 1969.

Nicolaieff, Nina and Nancy Phelan. *The Art of Russian Cookery*. Galahad Books, New York, 1969.

Papashvili, Helen and George Papashvili. *Russian Cooking*. Time-Life Books, New York, 1969.

Pearl, Anita May, Constance Cuttle and Barbara B. Deskins. *Completely Cheese*. Jonathan David Publishers, New York, 1978.

Perl, Lila. *Rice, Spice and Bitter Oranges*. World Publishing Company, Cleveland and New York, 1967.

Price, Vincent and Mary Price. *A Treasury of Great Recipes*. E. P. Dutton, New York, 1964.

Rau, Santha Rana and the Editors of Time-Life Books. *The Cooking of India*. Time-Life Books, New York, 1969.

Roden, Claudia. *A Book of Middle Eastern Food*. Alfred A. Knopf, New York, 1968.

Rombauer, Irma S. and Marion Becker Rombauer. *Joy of Cooking*. Bobbs-Merrill, Indianapolis and New York, 1931, 1943, and 1975.

Rosenthal, Sylvia. *Fresh Food*. Tree Communications, Inc./E. P. Dutton, New York, 1978.

Sacharoff, Shanta Nimbark. *Flavors of India*. 101 Productions, San Francisco, 1972.

Schrecker, Ellen. *Mrs. Chiang's Szechuan Cookbook*. Harper & Row, New York, 1976.

Uvezian, Sonia. *The Best Foods of Russia*. Harcourt, Brace & Jovanovich, New York and London, 1976.

Van der Post, Laurens, and the Editors of Time-Life Books. *African Cooking*. Time-Life Books, New York, 1970.

Wilson, Ellen Gibson. *A West African Cookbook*. M. Evans & Co., New York, 1971.

Wolfert, Paula. *Couscous and Other Good Food from Morocco*. Harper & Row, New York, 1973.

Wolfert, Paula. *Mediterranean Cooking*. Quadrangle Books, New York, 1977.

Women of St. Paul's Greek Orthodox Church. *The Art of Greek Cookery*. Doubleday, New York.

INDEX

achiote, 62

Adeece Howeed (Lentils with Spinach), 245, 247

African cookery, 13–37; menus, 36–37; North, 14–15; nutrition, 18–20; recipe analyses, 34–35; seasoning, 15–18; South, 14; West, 13–14

ají chili, 62

Ají de Gallina (Chicken with Spicy Walnut Sauce), 60, 65, 66

allspice: in Lebanese cookery, 242, 243; in Scandinavian cookery, 340

ALMONDS: Almond Cookies, 21; almond liqueur (Amaretto), 118; Almond Tofu with Chutney Sauce, 362, 369, 371; Crisp Almond Cookies (Sonia's Kamish Bread), 330–31; Miniature Almond Tarts (Swedish Toscas), 354; Sicilian Cream Cake with Chocolate and Almonds (Cassata alla Siciliana), 217, 225

Amaretto (almond liqueur), 118

American cookery. See United States cookery

Anaheim pepper, 63

ANCHOVIES: Tony's Tomato and Anchovy Salad, 232

Andean chili, 62

anise: in Italian cookery, 218; in Mexican cookery, 267

aniseed: in African cookery, 16

annatto oil, 62, 63

Antipasto Supreme, 216, 221, 223

APPLES: Apple Spinach Salad with Sweet and Sour Dressing, 223; Aunt June's Norwegian Apple Cake, 344; Dorka's Apple-Apricot Cake, 295, 303; Herring with Sour Cream and Apples, 338, 343, 348; Red Cabbage and Apple Salad, 308

Apple Spinach Salad with Sweet and Sour Dressing, 223

Aquacates Rellenos (Avocados Stuffed with Vegetables), 67–68

Armenian Fish Plaki Saucier, 321

Armenian Yogurt Soup (Matsunabur), 319, 328

Arroz Brasileiro (Brazilian Rice), 45

Arroz con Leche (Sweet Creamed Rice), 61, 65, 67

ASPARAGUS: Asparagus Frittata, 221, 224; Asparagus Quiche (Quiche Aux Asperges), 115, 133; Asparagus with Gjetost Sauce, 338, 345–46

Aunt June's Norwegian Apple Cake, 339, 344

Authentic Enchilada Sauce, 278

AVOCADOS: in Mexican cookery, 271–72; Avocado Flautas, 270, 271–72, 273; Avocado Cream Dessert (Creme de Abacate), 46; Avocados Stuffed with Vegetables, 67–68

Baked Bananas with Cheese (Bananas Assadas Com Quiejo), 44, 45
Baked Brie, 363, 371
Baked Cheese Triangles (Tyropitta), 144, 161–62
Baked Eggs with Cheese (Huevos Asados con Queso), 281
Baked Green Vegetable Casserole (Lahanika Psita), 155
Baked Red Snapper with Mexican Sauce (Huachinango en Salsa Mexicana), 271, 280–81
Baked Tomatoes Stuffed with Rice (Domates Yemistes me Rizi), 150
Baklajanaya Ikra (Russian Eggplant Caviar), 321
BANANAS: Baked Bananas with Cheese (Bananas Assadas Com Queijo), 44, 45; Banana Milk Liquado 271, 273; Banana Cream Dessert, 46; Banana Nut Bread with Honey and Spices, 368, 372; Banana Omelet (Tortilla de Platanos), 60, 76–77; Banana Raita, 199, 200; Curried Banana Waldorf Salad, 363, 376; Glazed Bananas, 205; Shrimp and Banana Curry, 209
Baqlawa (Layered Nut-Filled Pastry), 247–248
barley, 294
Basic Crêpe Batter, 122
basil: in Chilean cookery, 62; in French cookery, 116; in Italian cookery, 217–18; in Lebanese cookery, 242; in United States cookery, 363, 364
basmati rice, 192
Basmati Rice Pilau Koh-i-noor, 201
Basque Peasant's Soup (Soupe Paysanne), 114, 135
bay leaves: in French cookery, 116–17; in Russian cookery, 317; in United States cookery, 363, 364–65
BEAN CURD: Hot Bean Curd with Ginger-Garlic Sauce, 97; Szechuan Bean Curd in Hot Sauce, 91, 99–100. See also tofu

BEANS, 433; in Mexican cookery, 264; Cabbage and Bean Soup, 171, 172; Essential Bean Burritos, 270, 279; Refried Beans (Frijoles Refritos), 270, 279
BEANS, BLACK: fermented, 84; Black Bean Soup (Sopa de Frijoles Negros), 265, 284–85; Black Beans with Coconut Milk (Feijão de Côco), 43, 47–48
BEANS, BROWN: Brown Beans, Swedish Style (Bruna Boner), 345
BEANS, CRANBERRY: Cranberry Bean Stew with Corn (Porotos Granados), 65, 74–75
BEANS, FAVA, 239; Spicy Fava Bean Spread (Ful Moudammas), 239, 250
BEANS, GARBANZO: Garbanzo Bean and Gorgonzola Cheese Salad, 221, 225; Garbanzo Bean Spread (Hummous B'Tahini), 239, 245, 251
BEANS, STRING: Chilean Marinated String Bean Salad (Ensalades de Porotos Verdes), 70; Dry-Sautéed String Beans (Ganbian Sijidou), 95–96
BEANS, WHITE: White Bean Soup (Soupa Faki), 152
BEAN SPROUTS: in United States cookery, 369; Bean Sprout Quiche, 372
BEETS: in Russian cookery, 319; Beets Igdaloff, 318, 322; Endive and Beet Salad (Salade d'Endives avec Betteraves), 120, 133; Pickled Beet Relish (Cwikla), 294, 302; Ukrainian-Style Beet Soup (Borsch Ukraïnsky), 318, 323
BEVERAGES: Ginger Spice Tea, 204; Moroccan Mint Tea, 28–29; Yerba Maté, 61
Black Bean Soup (Sopa de Frijoles Negros), 265, 284–85
Black Beans with Coconut Milk (Feijão de Côco), 43, 47–48
black mustard seeds, 194–95
Blinchatiye Piroshki s Tvorogom (Cheese Blintzes), 319, 322–23
Blueberry Muffins, 368, 373
Boiled New Potatoes with Whipped Horseradish Sauce, 344–45
Boiled Potato Dumplings (Kartoflane Kluski), 298, 304

Bolillos (Mexican Rolls), 265, 276–77
Borsch, 316
Borsch Ukraïnsky (Ukrainian-Style Beet Soup), 318, 323
bouquet garni, 117
Braised Red Cabbage, 338, 346
Brandy-Cream Sauce, 124
Brazilian cookery, 39–58; menus, 57–58; nutrition, 43–44; recipe analyses, 55–56; seasoning, 40–41
Brazilian Hot Sauce Blend, 41
Brazilian Rice (Arroz Brasileiro), 45
Brazilian Salad, 51
Brazilian Shrimp and Coconut Stew (Vatapá), 40, 41, 54
Brazilian Skillet Dish (Potato and Cheese Frigideira), 44, 50–51
Brazil Nut Chocolate Mousse (Mousse de Castanhas-do-Pará e Chocolate), 49
BREADS: in Scandinavian cookery, 338, 339, 343; Banana Nut Bread with Honey and Spices, 368, 372; Blueberry Muffins, 368, 373; Charlotte Boon Bread, 368, 374; Dark Rye Bread, 294, 302; Farmer's Oatmeal Bread, 338, 343, 346–347; Finnish Cardamom Coffee Cake (Pulla), 339, 352; Finnish Flat Bread (Rieska), 338, 343, 352–353; Greek Holiday Bread, 153; Indian-Style Tortillas (Chapatis), 192, 193, 202; Mealie Bread (Steamed Corn Pudding), 26; Mexican Rolls (Bolillos), 265, 276–77; Mexican Sweet Buns (Pan Dulce), 282–83; Moroccan Bread (L'Hobz), 24–25; Nancy's Poppy Seed Egg Bread, 168, 181; Russian Black Bread, 319, 329; Steamed Corn Pudding (Mealie Bread), 26; Swedish Limpá, 338, 353–54; Toasted Bread Rounds, 265, 285; Whole Wheat Arabic Bread, 240, 256–57
BROCCOLI: Broccoli Pignolia with Raisins, 221, 224; Broccoli with Tangy Sauce, 91, 92
Brown Beans, Swedish Style (Bruna Boner), 345
Bruna Boner (Brown Beans, Swedish Style), 345
Brussels Sprouts Polonaise, 294, 300
BULGUR: in Lebanese cookery, 240; Taboulee Salad, 240, 241, 256

Burritos, Essential Bean, 270, 279
butter, 439
butter, clarified, 243–244; in Indian cookery, 197

CABBAGE: in Hungarian cookery, 171; Braised Red Cabbage, 338, 346; Cabbage and Bean Soup, 171, 172; Londolozi Cabbage Salad, 25; Red Cabbage and Apple Salad, 308; Strudel with Cabbage and Onions, 171, 183; Sweet and Sour Stuffed Cabbage, 316, 318, 331
Caldillo de Congria (Chilean Fish, Tomato and Potato Soup), 60, 68
calories, 394–96, 445–46
Cantaloupe Salad with Poppy Seed Dressing, 172
caraway: in Hungarian cookery, 169; in Polish cookery, 295, 296; in Scandinavian cookery, 340
carbohydrates, 409–11
cardamom: in Indian cookery, 195; in Scandinavian cookery, 340
CAROB: Carob Date Loaf, 245, 248; Carob Kahlúa Cake Supreme, 362, 369, 373–374
carob powder: in Lebanese cookery, 245–46; in United States cookery, 362, 369
Carottes Bourguignonne (Simmered Carrots Burgundy), 120, 122
Carottes Râpées (Shredded Carrot Salad), 123
Carp Roe Pâté (Taramasalata), 144, 161
CARROTS: Shredded Carrot Salad (Carottes Râpées), 123; Simmered Carrots Burgundy (Carottes Bourguignonne), 120, 122; Sweet Carrot Dessert (Gajar Halva), 204
Cashew Vadas (Deep-fried Cashew Balls), 199, 201–02
Cassata alla Siciliana (Sicilian Cream Cake with Chocolate and Almonds), 217, 225
CASSAVA, 431; in African cookery, 14; Fufu Gaitu, 22
cassia, 17
CAULIFLOWER: Cauliflower and Shallot Tart, 115, 120, 123; Cauliflower with Dried Mushroom Sauce, 298, 300; Cauliflower with Tahini Sauce, 245, 249; Rigatoni with Cauliflower, 230; Steamed

Masala Cauliflower (Phulgobi Dam), 198, *207*

cayenne pepper, 62; in African cookery, 16; in Mexican cookery, 267

celery seed, 364, 365

cereals, 429–30

Chapatis (Indian-Style Tortillas), 192, 193, *202*

Charlotte Boon Bread, 368, *374*

CHEESE, 438, 447–54; in French cookery, 114, 120; in Greek cookery, 144, 149; in Italian cookery, 216, 220, 221–22; in Mexican cookery, 264; in Scandinavian cookery, 338, 340; in United States cookery, 369–70; Baked Brie, 363, *371*; Baked Cheese Triangles (Tyropitta), 144, *161–62*; Baked Eggs with Cheese (Huevos Asados con Queso), *281*; Cheese and Chutney Spread, *203*; Cheese-Bean Enchiladas, 264, *270*; Cheese Blintzes (Blinchatiye Piroshki s Tvorogom), 319, *322–23*; Cheese Noodle Soufflé, 319, *324*; Cheese Soufflé, 115, 120, *136–37*; Cream Cheese with Sardines and Red Onions, 319, *325–26*; Farmer's Salad, 171, *175*, *303–04*; Garbanzo Bean and Gorgonzola Cheese Salad, 221, *225*; Greek Cheese Pie, *152*; Herbed Spinach and Cheese Casserole, *378*; Huancayo Potatoes with Cheese and Chili Sauce (Papas a la Huancaina), 60, 65, *72*; Liptoí Cheese Ball, 168, *179*; Miniature Cheese Pies (Empanaditas), *277–78*; Mock Boursin Cheese, 114, 120, *128*; Mousse alla Ricotta *228*; Pepita Pleaser, *283–84*; Potato and Cheese Dumplings (Pierogi), 294, 298, *306–07*; Potato and Cheese Frigideira (Brazilian Skillet Dish), 44, *50–51*; Potatoes with Cheese (Gratin Parmentier), 120, *127*; Spinach-Cheese Pie (Spanakopitta), 149, *159–60*; Tortillas Layered with Cheese and Chili Sauce (Chilequiles Maranze), 264, *275–76*; Vegetables au Gratin, 363, 370, *383*. See also CREAM CHEESE

cheese, types of: Asagio, 216; Bel Paese, 222; Brindza, 316; Caciocavallo, 216; Chihauhau, 264; Crema Dania, 339; Danbo, 338; Danish blue, 338; Danish Camembert, 339; Edam, 338; Esrom, 338; feta, 144, 149; Fontina, 216; Gjetost, 338, 342; Gorgonzola, 216, 222; Havarti, 338; Kasseri, 144, 149; Kefalotyri, 144, 149; Mizithra, 144; Mycella, 338; Parmesan, 216; Pecorino Romano, 216; Queso Añejo, 264; Queso Blanco, 264, 272; Queso Supremo, 264; Samsoe, 338; Taleggio, 222; Tilsiter, 316; Tybo, 338

Cheesecake, Ethel's Ethereal, *377–78*

chervil, 117

Chiao-Tzu (Pot Stickers), 87, 90, *93–94*

CHICKEN: Chicken Crêpes with Brandy-Cream Sauce, *124*; Chicken Fricassee, 171, *173*; Chicken Liver Pâté with Cognac, 363, *374–75*; Chicken on a Bed of Vegetables, *324*; Chicken Paprikas, 171, *173*; Chicken Soup, *301*; Chicken Stock, *375*; Chicken with Spicy Walnut Sauce (Ají de Gallina), 60, 65, *66*; Chicken with Wine and Tomato Sauce (Pollo alla Cacciatora), *229*; Chilean Chicken Empañadas, 60, 65, *68–69*; Chopped Chicken Livers, *301*; Congo Chicken Moambe, *21–22*; Lemon Chicken, *132*; Marinated Chicken with Lemon-Oregano Sauce, *156*; Senegalese Chicken with Peanut Butter Sauce (Maffe), *25–26*; Shredded Chicken with Hot Bean Sauce, 90, *105*. See also poultry.

chicken fat, rendered, *170*

CHICKPEAS: Tunisian Chickpea Soup (Lablabi), 24

Chilean Chicken Empañadas, 60, 65, *68–69*

Chilean cookery, 59–82; menus, 80–82; nutrition, 64–65; recipe analyses, 78–79; seasoning, 61–64

Chilean Fish, Tomato, and Potato Soup (Caldillo de Congria), 60, *68*

Chilean Hot Sauce (Pebre), 60, 64–65, *73*

Chilean Marinated String Bean Salad (Ensalades de Porotos Verdes), *70*

Chilean Seafood Casserole (Chupe de Locos), 65, *69–70*

Chilean Tamales (Humitas), 60, 65, 70–71

Chilequiles Maranze (Tortillas Layered with Cheese and Chili Sauce), 264, 275–76

Chilies Rellenos Rubalcava, 264, 266, 274–75

chili peppers, 268–69; in Chilean and Peruvian cookery, 62–63; in Mexican cookery, 266, 268; preparation of, 61–62; varieties of, 62–63

chili powder, 196

chili sauce, 87

Chinese cookery, 83–112; menus, 110–112, nutrition, 90–91; recipe analyses, 108–09; schools of, 83; seasoning, 86–90

Chinese Vegetable Broth, 94

CHOCOLATE: Brazil Nut Chocolate Mousse (Mousse de Castanhas-do-Pará e Chocolate), 49; Chocolate Butter Cream Molded in Ladyfingers (Pavé au Chocolat), 115, 129; Chocolate Cake (Csokolade Torta), 168, 174; Hungarian Chocolate Frosting, 168, 176; Mexican Chocolate Torte (Torta de Chocolate), 286–87; Sicilian Cream Cake with Chocolate and Almonds (Cassata alla Siciliana), 217, 225

Chopped Chicken Livers, 301

Chopped Eggs with Mushroom "Caviar," 316, 325

Chou-Chow Wild Rice, 363, 368, 375–76

Chunjuan (Spring Rolls), 87, 90, 94–95

Chupe de Locos (Chilean Seafood Casserole), 65, 69–70

CHUTNEY: in United States cookery, 362; Almond Tofu with Chutney Sauce, 362, 369, 371; Cheese and Chutney Spread, 203; Peach and Mango Chutney, 206–07

cilantro: in Chilean and Peruvian cookery, 63; in Mexican cookery, 266

cinnamon, 364, 365; in African cookery, 17; in Greek cookery, 146; in Lebanese cookery, 241, 242; in Scandinavian cookery, 340–41

cloud ears, 84

cloves, 317

Coconut-Honey Ice Cream Balls, 276

COCONUT MILK: in Brazilian cookery, 41, 42; Black Beans with Coconut Milk (Feijão de Côco), 43, 47–48; Brazilian Shrimp and Coconut Stew (Vatapá), 40, 41, 54; Rice Flour Pudding, 50

Cold Sour Cherry Soup (Hidyj-Meggyleves), 176

colór, 61, 63

Congo Chicken Moambe, 13, 20, 21–22

coriander: in Chilean and Peruvian cookery, 63, in Indian cookery, 195; in Mexican cookery, 266, 267; in Russian cookery, 317

CORN: in Mexican cookery, 270; Corn Pudding, 50; Corn-Stuffed Peppers, 270, 271, 274; Cranberry Bean Stew with Corn (Porotos Granados), 65, 74–75; Spicy Corn Custard, 72–73; Steamed Corn Pudding (Mealie Bread), 26

Cranberry Bean Stew with Corn (Porotos Granados), 65, 74–75

CREAM CHEESE: Homemade Cream Cheese, 378–79; Cream Cheese with Sardines and Red Onions, 319, 325–26; Mrs. Siebold's Cream Cheese Dainties, 180

Cream Sauce, 156–57

Creme de Abacate (Avocado Cream Dessert), 46

Crème de Fraises (strawberry liqueur), 118

Crème de Menthe (mint liqueur), 118

Crème Fraîche, 115, 124

CRÊPES: Basic Crêpe Batter, 122; Chicken Crêpes with Brandy-Cream Sauce, 124; Crêpes Stuffed with Eggplant and Zucchini and Topped with Cheese Sauce (Crêpes Ratatouille à la Sauce Mornay), 115, 120, 125–26

Crisp Almond Cookies (Sonia's Kamish Bread), 330–31

croutons, 135

Csokolade Torta (Chocolate Cake), 168, 174

CUCUMBERS: in Hungarian cookery, 171; Finnish Cucumber Salad (Kurkkusalaatti), 349; Marinated Cucumbers Grand Mère, 168, 171, 179; Whipped Yogurt and Cucumber Salad (Cucumber Raita), 193, 203

cumin: in African cookery, 17; in Indian cookery, 196; in Lebanese cookery, 242; in Mexican cookery, 267–68

CURRY POWDER: 193; Curried Banana Waldorf Salad, 363, 376; Pakistani Vegetable Curry, 206; Potato Curry Kashmiri, 198, 208; Quick Curried Tomatoes, 208; Shrimp and Banana Curry, 209

CUSTARD: Custard Baked in Filo (Galatobouryko), 145, 151; South African Custard Pie (Melk Tert), 27–28

Cwikla (Pickled Beet Relish), 294, 302

dahl, 433; in Indian cookery, 192

dairy products, 437–38, 469; in Polish cookery, 298–99; in Russian cookery, 319; in Scandinavian cookery, 342

Dark Rye Bread, 294, 302

DATES: Carob Date Loaf, 245, 248; Date Nut Torte, 363, 376–77; Moroccan Orange-Date Salad, 29; Pistachio Date Crescents, 251–52

Deep-fried Cashew Balls (Cashew Vadas), 199, 201–02

dendê, 39

DESSERTS: in French cookery, 115; in Scandinavian cookery, 339; Almond Cookies, 21; Aunt June's Norwegian Apple Cake, 344; Avocado Cream Dessert (Creme de Abacate), 46; Baked Bananas with Cheese (Bananas Assadas Com Queijo), 44, 45; Banana Cream Dessert, 46; Brazil Nut Chocolate Mousse (Mousse de Castanhas-do-Pará e Chocolate), 49; Carob Date Loaf, 245, 248; Carob Kahlúa Cake Supreme, 362, 369, 373–74; Chocolate Butter Cream Molded in Ladyfingers (Pavé au Chocolat), 115, 129; Chocolate Cake (Csokolade Torta), 168, 174; Coconut-Honey Ice Cream Balls, 276; Crisp Almond Cookies (Sonia's Kamish Bread), 330–31; Date Nut Torte, 363, 376–77; Dorka's Apple-Apricot Cake, 295, 303; Ethel's Ethereal Cheesecake, 377–78; Finnish Cardamom Coffee Cake (Pulla), 339, 352; Fresh Fruit Ambrosia, 48; Glazed Bananas, 205; Honey Spice Cake (Lekakh), 327; Honey-Spiced Pears, 221, 226; Mexican Chocolate Torte (Torta de Chocolate), 286–87; Miniature Almond Tarts (Swedish Toscas), 354; Mousse alla Ricotta, 228; Mrs. Siebold's Cream Cheese Dainties, 180; Oatmeal Lace Cookies (Kauralastut), 348; Pistachio Date Crescents, 251–52; Pound Cake, 230; Rose's Mocha-Walnut Torte, 295, 308–09; Sicilian Cream Cake with Chocolate and Almonds (Cassata alla Siciliana), 217, 225; Swedish Ginger Snaps (Pepparkakor), 339, 350–51; Sweet Carrot Dessert (Gajar Halva), 204; Thousand Leaf Pastry (Mil Hojas), 60–61, 71

Dietary Goals, 9

dill: in Greek cookery, 146; in Hungarian cookery, 169; in Polish cookery, 296; in Russian cookery, 316–17; in Scandinavian cookery, 341

dolmades, 144

Domates Yemistes me Rizi (Baked Tomatoes Stuffed with Rice), 150

Doña Graciela's Bolillos (Mexican Rolls), 265, 276–77

Dorka's Apple-Apricot Cake, 295, 303

DRESSINGS: See SALAD DRESSINGS

Dry-Sautéed String Beans (Ganbian Sijidou), 95–96

EGGPLANT: Eggplant Salad Bulus, 244, 249; Lemon-Eggplant Spread, 327–28; Lover's Eggplant, 98; Meatless Moussaka, 156–57; Russian Eggplant Caviar (Baklajanaya Ikra), 321; Will's Spicy Eggplant with Yogurt, 210

EGGS, 437; Baked Eggs with Cheese (Huevos Asados con Queso), 281; Chopped Eggs with Mushroom "Caviar," 316, 325; Egg and Lemon Soup (Soupa Avgolemono), 144, 159; Egg Barley Casserole, 168; Scrambled Eggs Yucatán Style (Huevos Revueltos Yucatán),

281–82; Stir-fried Eggs and Vegetables with Mandarin Pancakes, 101; Stuffed Eggs from Warsaw, 294, 309
Empadinhas de Camarão (Shrimp Patties), 46–47
Empanaditas (Miniature Cheese Pies), 277–78
Enchilada Casserole, The Great, 285–86
Enchilada Sauce, Authentic, 278
Endive and Beet Salad (Salade d'Endives avec Betteraves), 120, 133
Ensalades de Porotos Verde (Chilean Marinated String Bean Salad), 70
epazote, 266, 268
Essential Bean Burritos, 270, 279
Ethel's Ethereal Cheesecake, 377–378

Faki Yiahni (Lentil Soup), 150
Farfel, 174–75
farina, 44
Farmer's Oatmeal Bread, 338, 343, 346–47
Farmer's Salad, (Hungary) 171, 175, (Poland) 303–04
Farofa (Toasted Manioc Meal), 40, 47
Fatouch (Lebanese Bread Salad), 244, 250
fats, 396–402, 438–39, 446–47
Feijão de Côco (Black Beans with Coconut Milk), 43, 47–48
felafel, 240
fennel: in Italian cookery, 218; in Scandinavian cookery, 341
fenugreek seeds, 196
Feta Cheese Salad Dressing, 144, 151
Fettucine Noodles, Wheat Soy, 220, 233–34
fiber, 368–69, 412–14, 456–57
Filled Noodle Triangles (Kreplach), 178
FILO DOUGH, 143; Baked Cheese Triangles (Tyropitta), 144, 161–62; Custard Baked in Filo (Galatobouryko), 145, 151
fines herbes, 117
Finnish Cardamom Coffee Cake (Pulla), 339, 352
Finnish Cucumber Salad (Kurkkusalaatti), 349
Finnish Flat Bread (Rieska), 338, 343, 352–53

Finnish Rutabaga Casserole (Lanttalaatikko), 339, 349
FISH AND SEAFOOD, 436–37, 469; dried shrimp, 42; Armenian Fish Plaki Saucier, 321; Baked Red Snapper with Mexican Sauce (Huachinango en Salsa Mexicana), 271, 280–81; Brazilian Shrimp and Coconut Stew (Vatapá), 40, 41, 54; Chilean Fish, Tomato, and Potato Soup (Caldillo de Congria), 60, 68; Chilean Seafood Casserole (Chupe de Locos), 65, 69–70; Cream Cheese with Sardines and Red Onions, 319, 325–26; Fish Marinated in Lime and Lemon Juice (Seviche), 60, 64, 76; Fish with Dark Butter Sauce (Poisson au Beurre Noir), 130; Fish with Lemon-Pepper Sauce (Fish Moqueca), 44, 49–50; Ghana Light Soup, 23; Herring with Sour Cream and Apples, 338, 343, 348; Jim's Bluefish with Lemon Pear Stuffing, 363, 379; Poached Fish with Basil Sauce (Poisson Basilique de Dorka Raynor), 131; Kung Pao Shrimp, 90, 97–98; Robin's Shrimp in Tomato-Chili Sauce, 104; Senegalese Fish, 30–31; Shrimp and Scallop Empañadas, 69; Shrimp Patties (Empadinhas de Camarão), 46–47; Spicy Peruvian Shrimp with Tomatoes (Picante de Camarones), 60, 74; Tuna from Gabon, 32. See also SALMON; SHRIMP
flatbrød, 337, 343
Fraises à la Yaourt (Fresh Strawberries with Yogurt), 126
French cookery, 113–42; menus, 141–42; nutrition, 119–21; recipe analyses, 138–40; seasoning, 115–19
Fresh Fruit Ambrosia, 43, 48
Fresh Strawberries with Yogurt (Fraises à la Yaourt), 126
Fried Plantains, 16, 22
Frijoles Refritos (Refried Beans), 270, 279
FRUIT, 436, 468; in Mexican cookery, 265; Brazilian Salad, 51; Fresh Fruit Ambrosia, 48; Fruit Salad with Poppy Seed Dressing, 168; Mexican

Fruit Platter, 271, *282*; Norwegian Dried Fruit Soup (Söt Suppe), *353*. *See also* names of individual fruits

Fufu Gaitu, 14, 19, 22

Ful Moudammas (Spicy Fava Bean Spread), 239, *250*

Gajar Halva (Sweet Carrot Dessert), *204*

Galatobouryko (Custard Baked in Filo), 145, *151*

Ganbian Sijidou (Dry-Sautéed String Beans), *95–96*

garam masala, 193–94, 196–97

Garbanzo Bean and Gorgonzola Cheese Salad, 221, *225*

Garbanzo Bean Spread (Hummous B'Tahini), 239, 245, *251*

gari, 39n.

garlic: in Brazilian cookery, 42–43; in Chinese cookery, 87–88; in French cookery, 117; in Greek cookery, 146–47; in Hungarian cookery, 169; in Italian cookery, 217, 218; in Lebanese cookery, 241, 242

Garlic Sauce (Skordalia), 144, 146, *158*

Gazpacho, 265, *280*

Gerry's Bouillabaisse Bisque, *126–27*

Ghana Light Soup, 14, 19, *23*

ghee, 197

ginger: in African cookery, 15–16, 17; in Chinese cookery, 88; in Indian cookery, 195–96

Ginger-Garlic Sauce, *97*

Ginger Spice Tea, *204*

Gjetost Sauce, *345–46*

Glazed Bananas, 193, *205*

Golden Spiced Rice, 23

Gombaval Tolcott Palacsinta (Mushroom-filled Pancakes), *175*

Graham Cracker Crust, *377*

grains, 465; in United States cookery, 367–68

Gratin Parmentier (Potatoes with Cheese), 120, *127*

Gravlax (Swedish Salmon Marinated in Dill), 338, 343, *347*

Greek Cheese Pie, *152*

Greek cookery, 143–66; menus, 165–66; nutrition, 148–49; recipe analyses, 163–64; seasoning, 145–48

Greek Herb Blend, *147*

Greek Holiday Bread, *153*

Greek Hot Potato Salad (Patato Salata), *157*

Greek Salad Supreme, 149, *154*

green chilies, 195

Green Tomato Sauce (Salsa Verde), *284*

groundnuts, 433

Guacamole Enchiladas, 264,*286*

hearts of palm, 40, 44

Hearts of Palm Salads (Saladas de Palmitos), 44, *51–52*

Herbed Spinach and Cheese Casserole, *378*

herbs: substituting fresh for dried, 6; in French cookery, 115–19. *See also* individual herbs by name

Herring with Sour Cream and Apples, 338, 343, *348*

Hidyj-Meggyleves (Cold Sour Cherry Soup), *176*

hoisin sauce, 83, 89

Homemade Cream Cheese, *378–79*

HONEY, 436; Honey-Orange Syrup, *154–55*; Honey-Spiced Pears, 221, *226*

hontaka chili, 62

HORSERADISH: in Polish cookery, 295, 296; Whipped Horseradish Sauce, *344*

hot and sour flavors, 86

Hot and Sour Mixed Vegetables, 91, *96*

Hot and Sour Soup (Suanla Tang), 91, *106*

Hot Bean Curd with Garlic-Ginger Sauce, 91, *97*

hot bean paste, 88

Hot Bean Sauce, *105*

hot chili oil, 88

How to Clarify Butter, *see* Samneh

Huachinango en Salsa Mexicana (Baked Red Snapper with Mexican Sauce), 271, *280–81*

Huancayo Potatoes with Cheese and Chili Sauce (Papas a la Huancaina), 60, 65, *72*

Huevos Asados con Queso (Baked Eggs with Cheese), *281*

Huevos Revueltos Yucatán (Scrambled Eggs Yucatán Style), *281–82*

Humitas (Chilean Tamales), 60, 65, *70–71*

Hummous B'Tahini (Garbanzo Bean Spread), 239, 245, *251*
Hunan cookery, 83
Hungarian Chocolate Frosting, 168, *176*
Hungarian cookery, 167–89; menus, 187–89; nutrition, 171; recipe analyses, 185–86; seasoning, 168–71
Hungarian paprika, 168, 169, 170–71
Hungarian Sweet Potato Strudel, 167, 168, *177*

Indian cookery, 191–214; menus, 213–14; nutrition, 198–99; recipe analyses, 211–12; seasoning, 193–97
Indian-Style Tortillas (Chapatis), 192, 193, *202*
Italian cookery, 215–38; menus, 237–38; nutrition, 219–22; recipe analyses, 235–36; seasoning, 217–19
Italian Dressing, *226*
Italian Salad Supreme (Salata di Michael Reedy), *231*
Italian Seasoning, 217, *218–19*

jalapeño peppers, 63; in Brazilian cookery, 41, 43; in Mexican cookery, 265
Jim's Bluefish with Lemon Pear Stuffing, 363, *379*
juniper berries, 296

kalamata olives, 144
kale, 44
Kartoflane Kluski (Boiled Potato Dumplings), 298, *304*
kasha, 316, 319
Kasha and Shells, 319, *326*
Kataifi (Shredded Wheat Pastry), 143, 145, *154–55*
Kauralastut (Oatmeal Lace Cookies), *348*
Kotlety z Grzbow (Mushroom Cutlets), 298, *304–05*
Kreplach (Filled Noodle Triangles), *178*
Krupnik (Vegetable Barley Soup), 294, 298, *305*
Kuglis Natasha (Natalie's Potato Kugel), *326*
Kung Pao Shrimp, 90, *97–98*
Kurkkusalaatti (Finnish Cucumber Salad), *349*

Lablabi (Tunisian Chickpea Soup), *24*
Lahanika Psita (Baked Green Vegetable Casserole), *155*
Lanttalaatikko (Finnish Rutabaga Casserole), 339, *349*
Lasagne, Walnut Mushroom, 220, 221, *233*
Lebanese Bread Salad (Fatouch), 243, *250*
Lebanese cookery, 239–61; menus, 260–61; nutrition, 244–46; recipe analyses, 258–59; seasoning, 241–44
Lebanese Herb Blend, *242–43*
Leek and Potato Soup, 120, *127*
Lefse, Mrs. Bjorn's, 343, *350*
legumes, 432, 466
Lekakh (Honey Spice Cake), *327*
LEMONS: in Greek cookery, 145, 147; in Lebanese cookery, 241, 243; Fish Marinated in Lime and Lemon Juice (Seviche), 60, 64, *76*; Lemon Chicken (Poulet au Citron), *132*; Lemon-Eggplant Spread, *327–28*; Lemon Pastry, *128*; Lentil Lemon Soup (Mirielle's Adass bi Hamod), 245, *251*
LENTILS, 432–33; in Indian cookery, 192, 193, 199, 205; Lentil Lemon Soup (Mireille's Adass bi Hamod), 245, *251*; Lentil Soup (Faki Yiahni), *150*; Lentils with Spices (Moong Dahl), 193, 199, *205*; Lentils with Spinach (Adeece Howeed), 245, *247*
L'Hobz (Moroccan Bread), 15, *24–25*
LIMES: in Chilean and Peruvian cookery, 63–64; in Mexican cookery, 267, 269; Fish Marinated in Lime and Lemon Juice (Seviche), 60, 64, *76*
Liptoí Cheese Ball, 168, *179*
liquado, 271
liqueur, 117–18
Liqueur Base, *118*
Londolozi Cabbage Salad, 19, *25*
Lover's Eggplant, *98*

mace, 17–18
Maffe (Senegalese Chicken with Peanut Butter Sauce), 13, 20, *25–26*
mahlepi, 147
Mandarin Pancakes, *99*
MANIOC, 39; Toasted Manioc Meal (Farofa), 40, *47*
Ma-Po Dou-Fu (Szechuan Bean Curd

in Hot Sauce), 91, *99–100*
margarine, 439
marinades, Chinese, 86
Marinara Sauce, *226–27*
Marinated Chicken with Lemon-Oregano Sauce, *156*
Marinated Cucumbers Grand Mère, 168, 171, *179*
Mari's Zucchini with Dill Sauce (Tök Fözelek), *184*
marjoram, 363, 366
Matsunabur (Armenian Yogurt Soup), 319, *328*
Mealie Bread (Steamed Corn Pudding), *26*
meat, 436
Meatless Moussaka, 145, *156–57*
Melk Tert (South African Custard Pie), *27–28*
metric conversion, 483
Mexican chili powder, 269
Mexican Chocolate Torte (Torta de Chocolate), *286–87*
Mexican cookery, 263–92; menus, 290–92; nutrition, 270–72; recipe analyses, 288–89; seasoning, 265–69
Mexican Fruit Platter, 271, *282*
Mexican Rolls (Bolillos), 265, *276–77*
Mexican Sweet Buns (Pan Dulce), *282–83*
Mil Hojas (Thousand Leaf Pastry), 60–61, *71*
minerals, 421–28, 462–65
Minestrone Milanese, 216, 221, *227*
Miniature Almond Tarts (Swedish Toscas), *354*
Miniature Cheese Pies (Empanaditas), *277–78*
mint: in Greek cookery, 145–46, 147; in Lebanese cookery, 241–2, 243
Minted Tomato Salad with Lemon-Pepper Dressing, 15, *28*
mint liqueur (Crème de Menthe), *118*
Mirasol Colorado chili, 63
Mireille's Adass bi Hamod (Lentil Lemon Soup), 245, *251*
miso paste, 88
Mock Boursin Cheese, 114, 120, *128*
Mock Chinese Meatballs, *100*
Mock Lamb Loaf (Potato and Walnut Kibbe), 240, *252–53*
Moong Dahl (Lentils with Spices), 193, 199, *205*

Moo Shu Vegetables (Stir-fried Eggs and Vegetables with Mandarin Pancakes), *101*
Moroccan Almond Cookies, 15, *21*
Moroccan Bread (L'Hobz), *24–25*
Moroccan Carrot Salad with Orange (Shelada Ghezo-maa Alchin), 14, 19, *31*
Moroccan Mint Tea, 15, *28–29*
Moroccan Orange-Date Salad, *29*
Mousse alla Ricotta, *228*
Mousse de Castanhas-do-Pará e Chocolate (Brazil Nut Chocolate Mousse), *49*
Mrs. Bjorn's Lefse (Norwegian Potato Pancakes), 343, *350*
Mrs. Siebold's Cream Cheese Dainties, *180*
MUSHROOMS, 435; dried black, 84; Cauliflower with Dried Mushroom Sauce, 298, *300*; Chopped Eggs with Mushroom "Caviar," 316, *325*; Mushroom Cutlets (Kotlety z Grzbow), 298, *304–05*; Mushroom-filled Pancakes (Gombaval Toltott Palacsinta), *175*; Mushroom Goulash, *180*; Mushroom Pan Pizza, 221, *228–29*; Mushroom Sauce, *381*; Pickled Mushrooms, 316, *328*; Potato and Mushroom Casserole, 294, 298, *307*

Nancy's Poppy Seed Egg Bread, 168, *181*
Natalie's Potato Kugel (Kuglis Natasha), *326*
natural foods: in United States cookery, 362
Never-Fail Pie Crust, *380*
NOODLES: in Italian cookery, 215–16; in Polish cookery, 294; Cheese Noodle Soufflé, 319, *324*; Filled Noodle Triangles (Kreplach), *178*; Kasha and Shells, 319, *326*; Noodle Molds, 294, *305–06*; Noodles with Peking Sauce, *102*; Pasta with Browned Butter Sauce (Spaghetti me Tsigaristo Vootiro), *158*; Poppy Seed Noodles, 168, *182*; Wheat Soy Fettucine Noodles, 220, *233–34*. *See also* PASTA
North African cookery, 14–15
Norwegian Dried Fruit Soup (Söt Suppe), *353*
Norwegian Potato Pancakes (Mrs.

Bjorn's Lefse), 343, *350*
nutmeg: in Italian cookery, 217, 219; in United States cookery, 365
NUTS, 433, 467; in African cookery, 19–20; in Italian cookery, 221; Baqlawa (Layered Nut-filled Pastry), *248–49*; Broccoli Pignolia with Raisins, 221, *224*; Date Nut Torte, 363, *376–77*; Deep-fried Cashew Balls (Cashew Vadas), 199, *201–02*; Pistachio Date Crescents, *251–52*; Pistachio Rice Pilaf, *252*

OATMEAL: Farmer's Oatmeal Bread, 338, 343, *346–47*; Oatmeal Lace Cookies (Kauralastut), *348*
okra, 44
olive oil: in Greek cookery, 145, 147–48; in Italian cookery, 221
ONIONS: in French cookery, 116; Cream Cheese with Sardines and Red Onions, 319, *325–26*; Leek and Potato Soup, 120, *127*; Onion Pie (Torta de Cebolas), 40, *53*; Strudel with Cabbage and Onions, 171, *183*
orange blossom water, 243
ORANGES: Moroccan Carrot Salad with Orange, *31*; Moroccan Orange-Date Salad, *29*; Orange Glaze, *255*
oregano: in Greek cookery, 145, 148; in Italian cookery, 219; in Mexican cookery, 269
oyster sauce, 84

Pakistani Vegetable Curry, *206*
palacsinta, 168, *175*
PANCAKES: Asparagus Frittata, 221, *224*; Mandarin Pancakes, *99*; Norwegian Potato Pancakes (Mrs. Bjorn's Lefse), 343, *350*; Potato Pancakes, 168, *182*; Spinach Frittata *231*; Swedish Pancakes (Plättar), 343, *351*
Pan Dulce (Mexican Sweet Buns), *282–83*
Papas a la Huancaina (Huancayo Potatoes with Cheese and Chili Sauce), 60, 65, *72*
pappadums, 192
paprika: in Hungarian cookery, 168, 169, 170–71; in United States cookery, 365
parsley, 43

PASTA: in Italian cookery, 215–16, 219–20; Pasta with Browned Butter Sauce (Spaghetti me Tsigaristo Vootiro), *158*; Rice with Vermicelli (Riz Bish Shiriyyi), *253*; Rigatoni with Cauliflower, 220, 221, *230*; Walnut Mushroom Lasagne, 220, 221, *233*; Wheat Soy Fettucine Noodles, *233–34*. See also NOODLES
Pastel de Choclo (Spicy Corn Custard), *72–73*
PASTRY: Baked Cheese Triangles (Tyropitta), 144, *161–162*; Baqlawa (Layered Nut-filled Pastry), *247–48*; Custard Baked in Feta (Galatobouryko), 145, *151*; Graham Cracker Crust, *377*; Never-Fail Pie Crust, *380*; Shredded Wheat Pastry (Kataifi), 145, *154–55*; Thousand Leaf Pastry (Mil Hojas), 60–61, *71*
Patato Salata (Greek Hot Potato Salad), *157*
Pavé au Chocolat (Chocolate Butter Cream Molded in Ladyfingers), 115, *129*
Peach and Mango Chutney, 192, 199, *206–07*
PEANUT BUTTER: Congo Chicken Moambe, *21–22*; Senegalese Chicken with Peanut Butter Sauce (Maffe), *25–26*; West African Peanut Soup, *33*
peanut oil, 85
Pears, Honey-Spiced, 221, *226*
PEAS: Peas Marseilles, *130*; Peas Oriental with Mushroom Sauce, 370, *381*
Pebre (Chilean Hot Sauce), 60, 64–65, *73*
Peking cookery, 83
Peking Sauce, *102*
Pepita Pleaser, 271, *283–84*
Pepparkakor (Swedish Ginger Snaps), 339, *350–51*
PEPPERS: in African cookery, 17; in Brazilian cookery, 41, 42, 43; in Mexican cookery, 263; Corn-Stuffed Peppers, 270, 271, *274*; Roasted Pepper Salad, *30*
pequín chili, 62, 63
Peruvian cookery, 59–82; menus, 80–82; nutrition, 64–65; recipe analyses, 78–79; seasoning, 61–64
Peruvian Herb Blend, 62, *64*

Phulgobi Dam (Steamed Masala Cauliflower), 198, 207
Picante de Camarones (Spicy Peruvian Shrimp with Tomatoes), 60, 74
Pickled Beet Relish (Cwikla), 294, 302
Pickled Mushrooms, 316, 328
PIE: Asparagus Quiche (Quiche aux Asperges), 115, 133; Bean Sprout Quiche, 372; Cauliflower and Shallot Tart, 123; Greek Cheese Pie, 152; Miniature Cheese Pie (Empanaditas), 277–78; Onion Pie (Torta de Cebolas), 53; South African Custard Pie (Melk Tert), 27–28; Spinach-Cheese Pie (Spanakopitta), 149, 159–60; Spinach Pies (Sabanikh), 240, 253–54
PIE CRUST, 27, 53; Graham Cracker Crust, 377; Lemon Pastry, 128; Never-Fail Pie Crust, 380
Pierogi (Potato and Cheese Dumplings), 294, 298, 306–07
Pilaf, Pistachio Rice, 252
Pilaf, Spinach and Rice (Spanakórizo), 149, 160
Pineapple-Stuffed Acorn Squash, 381–82
Pine Nut Enchiladas, 264, 270, 286
Pirão de Arroz (Rice-Flour Pudding), 40, 43, 50
Pirão de Milho (Corn Pudding), 50
Pistachio Date Crescents, 251–52
Pistachio Rice Pilaf, 252
Pizza, Mushroom Pan, 228–29
PLAINTAINS: in African cookery, 14, 19; Fried Plantains, 22; Fufu Gaitu, 22
Plättar (Swedish Pancakes), 343, 351
plum sauce, 83, 84
Poached Fish with Basil Sauce (Poisson Basilique de Dorka Raynor), 131
Poached Pears, 217
Poisson au Beurre Noir (Fish with Dark Butter Sauce), 130
Poisson Basilique de Dorka Raynor (Poached Fish with Basil Sauce), 131
Polish cookery, 293–313; menus, 312–13; nutrition, 297–99; recipe analyses, 310–11; seasoning, 295–97
Polish Spice Blend, 295, 297
Pollo alla Cacciatora (Chicken with Wine and Tomato Sauce), 229
Pommes de Terre Aux Fines Herbes (Potatoes with Fine Herbs), 131–32
POPPY SEEDS: in Hungarian cookery, 169, 170; Nancy's Poppy Seed Egg Bread, 168, 181; Poppy Seed Dressing, 172; Poppy Seed Noodles, 168, 182
Porotos Granados (Cranberry Bean Stew with Corn), 65, 74–75
POTATOES, 431; in Chilean and Peruvian cookery, 60; in Polish cookery, 294, 297–98; Boiled New Potatoes with Whipped Horseradish Sauce, 344–45; Boiled Potato Dumplings, 298, 304; Huancayo Potatoes with Cheese and Chili Sauce (Papas a la Huancaina), 60, 65, 72; Leek and Potato Soup, 120, 127; Natalie's Potato Kugel (Kuglis Natasha), 326; Norwegian Potato Pancakes (Mrs. Bjorn's Lefse), 343, 350; Potato and Cheese Dumplings (Pierogi), 294, 298, 306–07; Potato and Cheese Frigideira (Brazilian Skillet Dish), 44, 50–51; Potato and Mushroom Casserole, 294, 298, 307; Potato and Walnut Kibbe (Mock Lamb Loaf), 240, 252–53; Potato Curry Kashmiri, 198, 208; Potatoes with Cheese (Gratin Parmentier), 120, 127; Potatoes with Fine Herbs (Pommes de Terre aux Fines Herbes), 131–32; Potato Pancakes, 168, 182; Tony's Italian Potatoes, 232
Pot Stickers (Chiao-Tzu), 87, 90, 93–94
Poulet au Citron (Lemon Chicken), 132
POULTRY, 20, 436; Stuffed Cornish Hens, 255. See also CHICKEN
Pound Cake, 230
Precious Vegetables with Szechuan Sauce, 103
protein, 403–09, 455
Pulla (Finnish Cardamom Coffee Cake), 339, 352
Pumpkin Puffs, 19, 29

QUICHE: Asparagus Quiche (Quiche aux Asperges), 115, 133; Bean Sprout Quiche, 372. See also PIES
Quick Curried Tomatoes, 208

Raisins, Broccoli Pignolia with, 221, 224

Raita, 193, *203*

Ras El Hanout, 16, *18*

Ratatouille à la Sauce Mornay, 120, *125–26*

Recommended Daily Allowances (RDA), 394, 442–43

Red Cabbage and Apple Salad, *308*

Red Chili Paste, 61, *64*

red peppers: in Chinese cookery, 89, in Indian cookery, 196

Refried Beans (Frijoles Refritos), 270, *279*

RICE: Baked Tomatoes Stuffed with Rice (Domates Yemistes me Rizi), *150*; Basmati Rice Pilau Koh-i-noor, *201*; Brazilian Rice, *45*; Chou-Chow Wild Rice, 363, 368, *375–76*; Golden Spiced Rice, *23*; Pistachio Rice Pilaf, *252*; Rice-Flour Pudding (Pirão de Arroz), 40, 43, *50*; Rice with Vermicelli (Riz Bish Shiriyyi), *253*; South African Rice Salad, *31–32*; Spiced Almond Rice, *200*; Spinach and Rice Pilaf (Spanakórizo), 149, *160*; Steamed Rice, *52*; Sweet Creamed Rice (Arroz con Leche), 61, 65, *67*; West African Lemon Rice, *32*

rice wine, 84

Rieska (Finnish Flat Bread), 338, 343, *352–53*

Rigatoni with Cauliflower, 220, 221, *230*

Riz Bish Shiriyyi (Rice with Vermicelli), *253*

Roasted Pepper Salad, *30*

Robin's Shimp in Tomato-Chili Sauce, *104*

roots, starchy, 430–32, 466

Rose's Mocha-Walnut Torte, 295, *308–09*

Russian Black Bread, 319, *329*

Russian cookery, 315–36; menus, 334–36; nutrition, 318–20; recipe analyses, 332–33; seasoning, 316–18

Russian Eggplant Caviar (Baklajanaya Ikra), *321*

Russian Herb Blend, 317, *318*

RUTABAGAS: Finnish Rutabaga Casserole (Lanttalaatikko), 339, *349*

Sabanikh (Spinach Pies), 240, *253–54*

saffron, 118

sage, 363–64, 366

Salada de Brasileiro (Brazilian Salad), *51*

Saladas de Palmitos (Hearts of Palm Salads), 44, *51–52*

SALAD DRESSINGS, 75; in Greek cookery, 145, *147*; Feta Cheese Salad Dressing, 144, *151*; Italian Dressing, *226*; Lemon-Pepper Dressing, *28*; Poppy Seed Dressing, *172*; Vinaigrette Bulus, *137*; Vinaigrette François, *137*

Salade d'Endives avec Betteraves (Endive and Beet Salad), 120, *133*

Salade Niçoise, *134*

SALADS: Antipasto Supreme, 216, 221, *223*; Apple Spinach Salad with Sweet and Sour Dressing, *223*; Brazilian Salad (Salada de Brasileiro), *51*; Cantaloupe Salad with Poppy Seed Dressing, *172*; Chilean Marinated String Bean Salad (Ensalades de Porotos Verde), *70*; Curried Banana Waldorf Salad, 363, *376*; Eggplant Salad Bulus, 241, *249*; Endive and Beet Salad (Salade d'Endives avec Betteraves), 120, *133*; Farmer's Salad, 171, *175*, *303–04*; Finnish Cucumber Salad (Kurkkusalaatti), *349*; Garbanzo Bean and Gorgonzola Cheese Salad, 221, *225*; Greek Hot Potato Salad (Patato Salata), *157*; Greek Salad Supreme, *154*; Hearts of Palm Salads (Saladas de Palmitos), 44, *51–52*; Italian Salad Supreme (Salata di Michael Reedy), *231*; Lebanese Bread Salad (Fatouch), 244, *250*; Londolozi Cabbage Salad, *25*; Marinated Cucumbers Grand Mère, 168, 171, *179*; Minted Tomato Salad with Lemon-Pepper Dressing, *28*; Moroccan Carrot Salad with Orange (Shelada Ghezo-maa Alchin), *31*; Moroccan Orange-Date Salad, *29*; Red Cabbage and Apple Salad, *308*; Roasted Pepper Salad, *30*; Salade Niçoise, *134*; Salad Salpicon, *75*; South African Rice Salad, *31–32*; Spinach Salad with Homemade Croutons and Vinaigrette, *135*; Taboulee Salad, *256*; Tony's Tomato and Anchovy Salad, *232*; Vegetable Salad (Salat Oliviye), *330*; Villager's

Salad, 149, *162*; Whipped Yogurt and Cucumber Salad (Cucumber Raita), 193, *203*; Yogurt Salad (Salata Lebanee), 254

Salad Salpicon, 75

Salata di Michael Reedy (Italian Salad Supreme), 231

Salata Lebanee (Yogurt Salad), 254

Salat Oliviye (Vegetable Salad), 330

SALMON: Swedish Salmon Marinated in Dill (Gravlax), 338, 343, *347*

Salsa Mexicana, 280

Salsa Piquante, 265, *269*

Salsa Verde (Green Tomato Sauce), 284

salt, 427–28

samneh, 243–44

Sauce Basilique, 116, *131*

Sauce Mornay, *125*

SAUCES: Authentic Enchilada Sauce, 278; Brandy-Cream Sauce, *124*; Brazilian Hot Sauce Blend, *41*; Chilean Hot Sauce (Pebre), 60, *64–65, 73*; Coconut Milk, *42*; Cream Sauce, *156–57*; Garlic Sauce (Skordalia), 144, 146, *158*; Ginger-Garlic Sauce, *97*; Gjetost Sauce, *345–46*; Green Tomato Sauce (Salsa Verde), 284; Honey-Orange Syrup, *154–55*; Hot Bean Sauce, *105*; Marinara Sauce, 226–27; Mushroom Sauce, *381*; Orange Glaze, *255*; Peking Sauce, *102*; Peruvian Herb Blend, 62, *64*; Red Chili Paste, 61, *64*; Salsa Mexicana, 280; Salsa Piquante, 265, *269*; Sauce Basilique, 116, *131*; Sauce Mornay, *125*; Sauce Vanille, *134*; Spicy Walnut Sauce, *66*; Szechuan Sauce, *103*; Tahini Sauce, 239, *256*; Tangy Sauce, *92*; Tomato-Chili Sauce, *104*; Tomato Sauce, *156–57*, 217; Walnut Mushroom Sauce, *233*; Whipped Horseradish Sauce, *344*

Sauce Vanille, *134*

Scandinavian cookery, 337–59; menus, 357–59; nutrition, 341–43; recipe analyses, 355–56; seasoning, 339–41

Scandinavian Spice Blend, 339, *341*

Scrambled Eggs Yucatán Style (Huevos Revueltos Yucatán), 281–82

SEAFOOD: *See* FISH AND SEAFOOD. *See also* individual names of seafood

seasoning, 439

SEASONING BLENDS: Greek Herb Blend, *147*; Italian Seasoning, 217, *218–19*; Lebanese Herb Blend, 242–43; Mexican chili powder, *269*; Polish Spice Blend, 295, *297*; Ras El Hanout, *18*; Russian Herb Blend, 317, *318*; Scandinavian Spice Blend, 339, *341*; Spiced Hungarian Paprika Blend, 168–69, *170*; United States Spice Blend, 364, *366*; West African Spice Blend, *18*

seaweed, 434–35

seeds, 433

Senegalese Chicken with Peanut Butter Sauce (Maffe), 13, 20, *25–26*

Senegalese Fish, 13, *30–31*

serrano pepper, 63

sesame oil, 89

Seviche (Fish Marinated in Lime and Lemon Juice), 60, 64, *76*

SHALLOTS: Cauliflower and Shallot Tart, *123*

Shelada Ghezo-maa Alchin (Moroccan Carrot Salad with Orange), *31*

Shredded Carrot Salad (Carottes Râpées), *123*

Shredded Chicken with Hot Bean Sauce, 91, *105*

Shredded Wheat Pastry (Kataifi), 145, *154–55*

SHRIMP: dried, *42*; Brazilian Shrimp and Coconut Stew (Vatapá), 40, 41, *54*; Kung Pao Shrimp, 90, *97–98*; Robin's Shrimp in Tomato-Chili Sauce, *104*; Shrimp and Banana Curry, *209*; Shrimp and Scallop Empañadas, *69*; Shrimp Patties (Empadinhas de Camarão), *46–47*; Spicy Peruvian Shrimp with Tomatoes (Picante de Camarones), 60, *74*

Sicilian Cream Cake with Chocolate and Almonds (Cassata alla Siciliana, 217, *225*

Simmered Carrots Burgundy (Carottes Bourguignonne), 120, *122*

Skordalia (Garlic Sauce), 144, 146, *158*

solanika peppers, 144

Sonia's Kamish Bread (Crisp Almond Cookies), *330–31*

Sopa de Frijoles Negros (Black Bean Soup), 265, *284–85*

Söt Suppe (Norwegian Dried Fruit Soup), 353
SOUFFLÉS: Cheese Noodle Soufflé, 319, 324; Cheese Soufflé (Soufflé au Fromage), 115, 120, 136–37; Soufflé au Grand Marnier, 136; Spinach Pudding Soufflé (Spenotpudding), 182–83
Soupa Avgolemono (Egg and Lemon Soup), 144, 159
Soupa Faki (White Bean Soup), 152
Soupe Paysanne (Basque Peasant's Soup), 114, 135
SOUPS: in French cookery, 114; in Mexican cookery, 265; Basque Peasant's Soup (Soupe Paysanne), 114, 135; Black Bean Soup (Sopa de Frijoles Negros), 265, 284–85; Cabbage and Bean Soup, 171, 172; Chicken Soup, 301; Chicken Stock, 375; Chilean Fish, Tomato, and Potato Soup (Caldillo de Congria), 60, 68; Chinese Vegetable Broth, 94; Cold Sour Cherry Soup (Hidyj-Meggyleves), 176; Egg and Lemon Soup (Soupa Avgolemono), 144, 159; Gazpacho, 265, 280; Gerry's Bouillabaisse Bisque, 126–27; Ghana Light Soup, 23; Hot and Sour Soup (Suanla Tang), 91, 106; Lablabi (Tunisian Chickpea Soup), 24; Leek and Potato Soup, 120, 127; Lentil Lemon Soup (Mireille's Adass bi Hamod), 245, 251; Lentil Soup (Faki Yiahni), 150; Minestrone Milanese, 216, 221, 227; Norwegian Dried Fruit Soup (Söt Suppe), 353; Tart and Spicy South Indian Soup (Tomato Rasam), 209–10; Tunisian Chickpea Soup (Lablabi), 24; Ukrainian-Style Beet Soup (Borsch Ukraïnsky), 318, 323; Vegetable Barley Soup (Krupnik), 298, 305; Vegetable Broth, 383; West African Peanut Soup, 33; White Bean Soup (Soupa Faki), 152
South African cookery, 14
South African Custard Pie (Melk Tert), 27–28
South African Rice Salad, 31–32
soybean curd, 84, 91. See also tofu
soybeans, 432
soy sauce, 89–90
Spaghetti me Tsigaristo Vootiro (Pasta with Browned Butter Sauce), 158
Spanakopitta (Spinach-Cheese Pies), 149, 159–60
Spanakórizo (Spinach and Rice Pilaf), 149, 160
Spenotpudding (Spinach Pudding Soufflé), 182–83
Spiced Almond Rice, 200
Spiced Hungarian Paprika Blend, 168–69, 170
Spicy Corn Custard, 72–73
Spicy Fava Bean Spread (Ful Moudammas), 239, 250
Spicy Peruvian Shrimp with Tomatoes (Picante de Camarones), 60, 74
SPINACH: in Greek cookery, 149; Apple Spinach Salad with Sweet and Sour Dressing, 223; Herbed Spinach and Cheese Casserole, 378; Lentils with Spinach (Adeece Howeed), 245, 247; Spinach and Rice Pilaf (Spanakórizo), 149, 160; Spinach-Cheese Pies (Spanakopitta), 149, 159–60; Spinach Frittata, 231; Spinach Pies (Sabanikh), 240, 253–54; Spinach Pudding Soufflé (Spenotpudding), 182–83; Spinach Salad with Homemade Croutons and Vinaigrette, 135
Spring Rolls (Chunjuan), 87, 90, 94–95
SQUASH: Pineapple-Stuffed Acorn Squash, 381–82; Stuffed Acorn Squash, 245, 254–55
Steamed Corn Pudding (Mealie Bread), 26
Steamed Masala Cauliflower (Phulgobi Dam), 198, 207
Steamed Rice, 52
Stir-fried Eggs and Vegetables with Mandarin Pancakes (Moo Shu Vegetables), 101
Stir-fried Zucchini with Sesame Seeds, 363, 382
STRAWBERRIES: Fresh Strawberries with Yogurt, 126
strawberry liqueur (Crème de Fraises), 118
STRUDEL: Hungarian Sweet Potato Strudel, 167, 168, 177; Strudel with Cabbage and Onions, 171, 183
Stuffed Acorn Squash, 245, 254–55
Stuffed Cornish Hens, 255

Stuffed Eggs from Warsaw, 294, *309*
Suanla Tang (Hot and Sour Soup), 91, *106*
substitutions: of foods in cooking, 472–74; of herbs, 6
sugar, 435–36
Swedish Ginger Snaps (Pepparkakor), 339, *350–51*
Swedish Limpá, 338, *353–54*
Swedish Pancakes (Plättar), 343, *351*
Swedish Salmon Marinated in Dill (Gravlax), 338, 343, *347*
Swedish Toscas (Miniature Almond Tarts), *354*
Sweet and Sour Stuffed Cabbage, 316, 318, *331*
Sweet Carrot Dessert (Gajar Halva), *204*
Sweet Creamed Rice (Arroz con Leche), 61, 65, *67*
Sweet Hungarian Paprika, 170–71
SWEET POTATOES, 431; Hungarian Sweet Potato Strudel, 167, 168, *177*
syrup, 435
Szechuan Bean Curd in Hot Sauce (Ma-Po Dou-Fu), 91, *99–100*
Szechuan cookery, 83
Szechuan peppercorns, 90
Szechuan Sauce, *103*

Taboulee Salad, 240, 242, *256*
TAHINI, 239–40, 241, 244; Cauliflower with Tahini Sauce, 245, *249*; Tahini Sauce, 239, *256*
Tamales, Chilean (Humitas), 60, 65, *70–71*
tamarind, 196
Tangy Sauce, *92*
tarama, 143–44
Taramasalata (Carp Roe Pâté), 144, *161*
taro, 431
tarragon: in French cookery, 118; in Russian cookery, 318
Tart and Spicy South Indian Soup (Tomato Rasam), *209–10*
TEAS: Ginger Spice Tea, *204*; Moroccan Mint Tea, *28–29*; Yerba Maté, 61
tepín chili, 63
Thousand Leaf Pastry (Mil Hojas), 60–61, *71*
thyme, 363, 366; in French cookery, 118–19; in Greek cookery, 148

tiger lily buds, 84
Toasted Bread Rounds, 265, *285*
Toasted Manioc Meal (Farofa), 40, *47*
tofu: in Chinese cookery, 84, 91; in United States cookery, 362, 369. *See also* soybean curd
Tök Fözelek (Mari's Zucchini with Dill Sauce), *184*
TOMATOES: Baked Tomatoes Stuffed with Rice (Domates Yemistes me Rizi), *150*; Gazpacho, 265, *280*; Minted Tomato Salad with Lemon Pepper Dressing, *28*; Quick Curried Tomatoes, *208*; Spicy Peruvian Shrimp with Tomatoes, *74*; Tart and Spicy South Indian Soup (Tomato Rasam), *209–10*; Tony's Tomato and Anchovy Salad, 232
TOMATOES, GREEN, 263; Green Tomato Sauce (Salsa Verde), *284*
TOMATO SAUCE: in Italian cookery, 217; Tomato-Chili Sauce, *104*; Tomato Sauce, *156–57*
Tony's Italian Potatoes, 232
Tony's Tomato and Anchovy Salad, 232
Torta de Cebolas (Onion Pie), 40, *53*
Torta de Chocolate (Mexican Chocolate Torte), *286–87*
Tortilla de Platanos (Banana Omelet), 60, *76–77*
TORTILLAS, 263–64, 265, 270; Tortillas Layered with Cheese and Chili Sauce (Chilequiles Maranze), 264, *275–76*
tourshi, 144
Tri-Color Vegetables, 91, *106–07*
Tuna from Gabon, 32
Tunisian Chickpea Soup (Lablabi), 24
turmeric, 197
Tyropitta (Baked Cheese Triangles), 144, *161–62*

Ukrainian-Style Beet Soup (Borsch Ukraïnsky), 318, *323*
United States cookery, 361–87; menus, 386–87; nutrition, 367–70; recipe analyses, 384–85; seasoning, 363–67
United States Spice Blend, 364, *366*

VANILLA: in French cookery, 119; in United States cookery, 367; Sauce Vanille, *134*

Vatapá (Brazilian Shrimp and Coconut Stew), 40, 41, *54*
vegetable oil, 85, 86–87
VEGETABLES, 433–35, 467–68; Avocados Stuffed with Vegetables, *67–68*; Baked Green Vegetable Casserole (Lahanika Psita), *155*; Chicken on a Bed of Vegetables, 324; Hot and Sour Mixed Vegetables, *96*; Moo Shu Vegetables, *101*; Pakistani Vegetable Curry, *206*; Precious Vegetables with Szechuan Sauce, *103*; Tri-Color Vegetables, *106–07*; Vegetable Barley Soup (Krupnik), 294, 298, *305*; Vegetable Broth, *383*; Vegetable Salad (Salat Oliviye), *330*; Vegetables Au Gratin, 363, 370, *383*
vegetarianism, xi, xii, 6–7, 391–93; and carbohydrates, 411; and fat, 401–02; and protein, 407–09
Villager's Salad, 149, *162*
Vinaigrette Bulus, *137*
Vinaigrette François, *137*
vinegar, 84
vitamins, 414–21, 458–61

WALNUTS: Potato and Walnut Kibbe (Mock Lamb Loaf), 240, *252–53*; Walnut Mushroom Lasagne, 220, 221, *233*; Walnut Mushroom Sauce, *233*
weights and measures, equivalent, 475–82

West African cookery, 13–14
West African Lemon Rice, *32*
West African Peanut Soup, 20, *33*
West African Spice Blend, 16, *18*
Wheat Soy Fettucine Noodles, 220, *233–34*
White Bean Soup (Soupa Faki), *152*
Whipped Horseradish Sauce, *344*
Whipped Yogurt and Cucumber Salad (Cucumber Raita), 198–99, *203*
Whole Wheat Arabic Bread, 240, *256–57*
WILD RICE: in United States cookery, 368; Chou Chow Wild Rice, 363, 368, *375–76*
Will's Spicy Eggplant with Yogurt, 198, *210*

YAMS, 431; in African cookery, 14, 19; Fufu Gaitu, *22*
Yerba Maté, 61
YOGURT: Armenian Yogurt Soup (Matsunabur), 319, *328*; Whipped Yogurt and Cucumber Salad (Cucumber Raita), 193, *203*; Will's Spicy Eggplant with Yogurt, *210*; Yogurt Salad (Salata Lebanee), *254*

za'atar, 244
ZUCCHINI: Mari's Zucchini with Dill Sauce, *184*; Stir-fried Zucchini with Sesame Seeds, 363, *382*; Zucchini al Limone, *234*; Zucchini Squash with Wine and Shallots, *77*